Contributions to Manag

The series *Contributions to Management Science* contains research publications in all fields of business and management science. These publications are primarily monographs and multiple author works containing new research results, and also feature selected conference-based publications are also considered. The focus of the series lies in presenting the development of latest theoretical and empirical research across different viewpoints.
This book series is indexed in Scopus.

Hemant Merchant
Editor

The New Frontiers of International Business

Development, Evolving Topics, and Implications for Practice

 Springer

Editor
Hemant Merchant
St. Petersburg campus
University of South Florida
St. Petersburg, FL, USA

ISSN 1431-1941   ISSN 2197-716X (electronic)
Contributions to Management Science
ISBN 978-3-031-06005-2   ISBN 978-3-031-06003-8 (eBook)
https://doi.org/10.1007/978-3-031-06003-8

This Springer imprint is published by the registered company Springer Nature Switzerland AG
The registered company address is: Gewerbestrasse 11, 6330 Cham, Switzerland

To our future.
To all who dare to dream it.
And to all who persevere to make it happen.
To Prashanth Mahagaonkar,
For his invaluable editorial nurturing.

Contents

Looking Beyond the Frontiers of Conventional International Business Research: Exploring Opportunities and Making a (Small, But Real) Difference

Hemant Merchant

> *The woods are lovely, dark and deep,*
> *But I have promises to keep,*
> *And miles to go before I sleep,*
> *And miles to go before I sleep.*
> *—Robert Frost*

When Springer first approached me to edit a forward-looking Handbook, my first reaction was a "Thank you, but no." The previous two IB handbooks were edited by luminaries and eminent scholars, both distinguished professors when I was still a doctoral student. Indeed, I was honored to be asked but "No, thank you." Theirs were *very* big shoes to fill and I was unsure I could fill them well, if at all. The passage of time, however, offers a perspective like no other and I relented after Springer's persistence and unshakable faith in what it believed we all could collectively achieve. The world has changed significantly just in the last few years even though our community of scholars has mostly stayed loyal to its conventional research agenda. All upheavals call for strategic and operational disconnects in mindsets and behaviors, so the opportunity this Handbook offered would be a platform from which to incite and invigorate them—of course, with the support of like-minded friends and well-wishers. I was in.

Taking on any momentous assignment is quite challenging. It is never easy to incentivize bold thinkers into lending their cerebral prowess to a project that, even though potentially exciting, would impose a toll on their resources. Fortunately for

H. Merchant (✉)
University of South Florida, St. Petersburg, FL, USA
e-mail: hmerchant@usf.edu

© Springer Nature Switzerland AG 2022
H. Merchant (ed.), *The New Frontiers of International Business*, Contributions to Management Science, https://doi.org/10.1007/978-3-031-06003-8_1

me, nearly everyone I approached almost instantly bought into the challenge that this endeavor presented. A few potential contributors excused themselves late in this project. Only two declined due to ongoing commitments; both offered their good wishes. Indeed, I am grateful—as we all should be—to our contributors who have lent their might to this volume and enthusiastically supported it, both in form and spirit. To me, that is the true essence of any community; it is what makes the reimagined future possible.

To the purists among us, some narratives in this volume will no doubt appear to be primitive for they are—deliberately—broad. There is no compelling reason to constrain the future. Indeed, even the most advanced narratives originate in simple ideas as "raw" as these ideas then seem to be. To those who may, unpardonably, rebuff this volume's forward-looking topics simply as being "fashionable" do so at their own risk. It is much easier to be critical than to be correct. I believe the topics in this volume underscore phenomena that are not only relevant but also urgent for scholars everywhere to consider seriously and tackle quickly. If careful thinking is our currency, then the viewpoints offered in this Handbook surely will add more worth to it.

This 21-chapter compendium is organized in three parts: (1) Enriching IB's research agenda, (2) Inter-disciplinary topics for IB research, and (3) IB's broader societal role. Regardless of where each contribution appears in the Handbook, all chapters directly or indirectly underline four themes. One, several contributions in this volume offer a refreshing twist on topics we are (or should be) studying. As with all well-intended (but not always well-received!) parental rebukes, they criticize our current neglect of the "other side" of the proverbial coin, argue for the need to meaningfully treat this deficit, and offer some starting points for us to consider. Importantly, our contributors hint that introspection and self-reflection will be crucial for our discipline's ongoing advancement. Two, all contributors nudge and encourage us to earnestly revisit our approach to pressing research questions, whether these be conventional questions we have examined (and still do) or challenges now appearing on our radars. Are we framing existing questions in the right way? Are we scanning for the right questions? Indeed, in our ongoing quest to be more relevant as a frontier discipline that can—and must—make a difference to the broader society, it would be prudent to embrace our contributors' keen insights as part of our scholarly/pedagogical agenda. Whether, when, and how we venture beyond our comfort zones are entirely up to us.

Three, to competently execute the suggested reevaluation, several authors urge us to tap into relevant disciplines that are studying these issues with at least as much vigor as we would. These inter-disciplinary undercurrents are rampant throughout this Handbook, and it is sensible to swim with them. By doing so, we can avail of more nuanced, balanced, and holistic perspectives which supplement the "Productivity-Efficiency-Profitability" lenses with which IB scholars have been preoccupied. Finally, several chapters in this Handbook explicitly discuss vanguard "soft" issues which IB scholars have typically shunned—but issues that now occupy the center stage of any serious global discourse. This refocus pertains not only to the soft issues *per se* but also to explicitly recognizing the changing contours of "hard" issues which have dominated previous IB conversations. Our contributors provide us with thought-provoking beginnings to redeploy our collective energy. For sure, the topics in this Handbook are not exhaustive. Many more worthy topics could be added to better serve this volume's soul. But paralysis-by-analysis is for real, and there was no reason to wait when all our contributors were eagerly onboard. The 21 chapters in this Handbook propel us into action and show us a clear way forward. Indeed, I trust you too will appreciate the(se) blessings we currently have than regret not having the manna that will surely follow.

1   Reflections on International Business' Current and Future Agenda

The chapters in Part I, Enriching IB's Research Agenda, present insights into the promising landscape of IB research and offer us useful information to carefully consider. The chapter by Verbeke, Kano, and Johnston is premised on the view that competing successfully in a VUCA world requires MNEs to garner a richer, more nuanced understanding of the opportunities and challenges engendered by relatively recent contextual developments. Their thoughtful piece identifies 10 contemporary modalities that denote ". . .grand challenges in IB research and practice." This chapter carefully motivates us to *jointly* consider the upsides and downsides of these unmistakable trends—something IB scholars have not always done. In suggesting whether a concurrent appraisal of ". . .bright and dark sides" is merely a simple summation of these effects or a time-variant, non-linear outcome, Verbeke et. al expertly highlight important opportunities which lie before us.

The chapter by Gaur and Vashishtha takes a relatively conventional—yet very novel—approach to map the foreseeable domain of IB research. The authors' content analyzes Special Issue calls in *JIBS* and *JWB* to identify research themes which journal editors and seasoned scholars deem to be significant for future research. Gaur and Vashishtha consider the principal research questions posed by Special Issue editors as well as dominant theoretical frameworks used, and the thematic and spatial emphases of these calls. Their contribution identifies seven themes that will shape the topography of (Special Issue-induced) thought leadership in IB research. Gaur and Vashishtha conclude with four more themes that are directly or indirectly showcased elsewhere in this Handbook, and advocate we take a ". . .*bold* stand" (emphasis added) in further advancing our discipline.

The chapter by Wocke and Barnard—both long based in South Africa, and both richly embedded in the African ecosystem of MNEs, governmental agencies, and scholars—offers us fascinating insights into the profound nexus between Sub-Saharan Africa's diversity and recent history and their collective influence on the region's institutions and business environment. These scholars leverage their personal and professional insights to identify four big-picture research themes endemic to Sub-Saharan Africa. Both authors also explicitly acknowledge there are several more interesting topics for researchers to focus on when studying Africa or other world regions with colonial histories. In alerting us to the imperative to

"...*seriously* consider" (emphasis added) Africa as a worthwhile research setting, Wocke and Barnard implicitly warn IB scholars about bypassing the potential rewards of "...theoretical gains" of studying a much-neglected, I think, but also a very promising region of our world.

The next two chapters—also by very well-informed, locally-invested scholars— echo a similar theme. Based in Central Asia, Akemu and Subramanian too call upon IB scholars to consider a broader portfolio of geographies as research settings. Drawing parallels with familiar IB topics, their work underlines the splendor of revisiting them in Central Asia's unique milieu of history and geography and its influence on local (business and non-business) institutions. The authors also candidly discuss the trials of conducting scholarly work in this region. Even though these trials are not endemic to Central Asia, it is worth noting that they seem to arise from a lingering disconnect between the challenges we study and those facing practicing managers. The next chapter by (MENA-based) Stephens also implores us to "...create a more inclusive" scholarly agenda which taps into MENA's extensive contextual diversity and richness. As with previous two chapters, Stephens relies on her rich and diverse experience to deconstruct the region's exoticism. Her work illustrates promising new areas of "...*relevant*" (emphasis added) research not captured in current (read, mainstream) IB publications. Notably, Stephens offers us starting points to meaningfully contribute to current IB discourses—via the MENA pathway that denotes "...an excellent opportunity" for our discipline's continued advancement.

This part's final chapter by Ooesterle and Wolf is a wistful, philosophical reflection on our contributions to IB. These scholars imply our well-intended endeavors often fall short of their mark on the Relevance axis and stress the need for greater vigilance of "...problems that are likely to impair the upgrading of relevance" in IB research. Their essay suggests our general preference for a self-imposed disciplinary quarantine that, effectively, further removes us from interesting work being done elsewhere. Perhaps we are victims of our own "publication" victories, and a slave to all institutions that glorify, amplify, and reward them. Indeed, if this is truly the case, then our scholarship will have completely "...*lost* its close linkage" (emphasis added) to the real challenges facing managers. Fortunately, Ooesterle and Wolf share their insights to help us rethink what we are doing, and how, so that we may deliberately steer ourselves away from an abyss of intellectual irrelevance.

2   Pollinating Inter-disciplinary Thinking in International Business

The chapters in Part II, Inter-disciplinary Topics in IB Research, embellish the preceding part's core theme by demonstrating the power of cross-disciplinary thinking to conventional IB research. Rooted in the "...growing acknowledgement that international business has a larger *transformative* power over societal trends" (emphasis added), Van Assche encourages us to connect mainstream IB research to public policy issues to address pressing societal challenges—some of which are the discussed elsewhere in this volume. A leading proponent of this nexus, Van Assche's contribution starts by formally defining international business policy, and how IB scholarship can mediate the linkage between various government roles and societal challenges. This piece is an insightful narrative, simple in its core ideas but powerful in its ". . .break out [from our] comfort zone" message that we should consciously heed.

Equally thought-provoking, and with futuristic undertones, is the next chapter by Vagadia who competently examines digitization's impact on ". . .(International) Business" and—through it—on the global canvas. Predicting that this impact is ". . .likely to be as dramatic, if not bigger than the previous industrial revolutions," Vagadia unpacks the meaning of digitization and discusses the inevitable impact of 10 current and emerging technologies on organizations, societies, and economies. As with other contributions in this volume, this chapter too promotes a fundamental readjustment that may necessitate ". . .*tearing* up" (emphasis added) incumbent playbooks to fully harness the disruptive power of new technologies for society's greater good.

The chapter by Knight and Khan continues the theme of technology and its disruptive potency but adopts a more scholarship-focused approach. It also identifies several leading technologies, yet differentiates itself by providing an assorted theoretical backdrop against which to continue studying the linkage between technology and IB. These underpinnings are beneficial for they connect the future (i.e., technology development) and past (i.e., established IB frameworks) and serve as an umbilical cord to make sense of what essentially is still evolving. In doing so, Knight and Khan exemplify the essence of careful scholarship. They conclude their work by discussing the practical implications of anticipated technological shifts on organizations worldwide—noting that the ". . .most successful firms will possess an action orientation and technological competency."

The next chapter by Blay and Froese takes a softer, but no less profound, view of how cross-disciplinary thinking can enliven IB research. Their work scrutinizes the notion of Global virtual teams and rests on the view that organizational propensity for such teams ". . .is inevitable." Emphasizing the ongoing inter-play between technology and human resources, Blay and Froese skillfully weave arguments from these distinct domains to increase our understanding of the globally-distributed workplace. Their chapter develops a framework to holistically study this topic and suggests exciting pathways to enrich IB research and practice. Indeed, our current appetite for greater workplace flexibility, combined with an ongoing revisionist view of work, suggests that the tenets in Blay and Froese's dialog will occupy a seat at the head table of global conversations. In that sense, these authors' contribution will serve as a blueprint for future work.

The chapter by Jensen, Manning, and Petersen is equally innovative in demonstrating another adept recombination, here among IB, Operations management, and Strategy. Focusing on "location flexibility" as a basis of sustainable competitive advantage, these authors explore the tradeoffs between efficiency and imitability by splicing arguments from the Supply chain and Resource-based view literatures. Considered separately, one could argue that these two concepts insinuate divergent—even competing—triggers for creating a lasting competitive advantage. Yet, Jensen et. al posit a middle ground that reconciles these seemingly disparate viewpoints. While admittedly a preliminary effort, as these authors declare, their contribution shows the raw power of cross-disciplinary spillovers which supersede the insights generated by solitary perspectives. Indeed, Jensen et al.'s subtle message also delineates certain boundary conditions that *per se* offer additional avenues for continued theoretical development and serious empirical work. Getting fresh perspectives accepted by a community of scholars is, no doubt, still difficult. Yet, Jensen et al.'s work establishes that these ideas are not only imperative for our discipline's advancement but also relevant for tackling the real challenge of crafting a dominant industry position.

The chapter by Oh and Oetzel focuses on four types of non-market risks in IB. Their chapter (rightly) assumes "…growing concerns" about natural and technological disasters and political and social conflicts. It anticipates these risks will "…at least temporarily" change the familiar context in which IB occurs. Among the leading scholars in the "non-market" space, Oh and Oetzel explain the principal characteristics of each of these risks and discuss the main drivers of MNEs' awareness, preparedness, and response to these risks. To advance a topic that is "…still very new to the [IB] discipline," Oh and Oetzel conclude with a 5-point research agenda which many among us will find worthy of pursuit. Indeed, if appropriately channelized, our efforts in these directions could make a critical, and urgently needed, impact.

This part's final chapter, by Birkinshaw, is a short, reflective piece that confronts some of the "…conventional orthodoxies that dominate [IB] literature." It focuses on large, established MNEs domiciled (mostly) in developed markets. Birkinshaw offers a provocative view of the above-noted class of MNEs and argues continuance of their entrenched role—despite certain global commotions that would suggest otherwise. His prediction is bold indeed but, as most of us surely know, it is richly informed by his engagement with MNEs worldwide. Birkinshaw concludes by outlining some thought-provoking implications for MNEs of the future. What trials will these MNEs face and how will they effectively respond to them? Who, fundamentally, will these "…'big beasts' of the corporate world" be? Going forward, what role will they play and be expected to play in an increasingly mindfulness-oriented cosmos? These are fascinating questions, among others, to ponder and discuss—even if they cannot all be tested empirically. In that sense, Birkinshaw inspires us to pause a bit and contemplate the future of MNEs which we may not have thought much about.

3   The Societal Role of International Business and Academia

If the previous part echoed hard IB topics, this part counterbalances it. The chapters in this part mostly focus on soft(er) issues that have *relatively* recently entered mainstream discussions in our discipline. Benito and Fehlner's chapter leads this theme with a discussion of MNE role vis-à-vis the Circular economy, a notion which is similar in spirit to recycling but likely goes beyond it. Drawing on theoretical arguments from the Strategy and IB literatures, these authors map the macro–meso interface to help MNEs shape a more sustainable economic development. Benito and Fehlner conclude their insightful discussion with four promising research themes, noting that more IB research "...is needed" to urgently accelerate transition toward a broader, stronger, and more intense circular ecosystem.

Ghauri and Cooke's chapter similarly emphasizes the sustainability theme (as do the next few chapters). Specifically, it discusses the role of MNEs in achieving United Nations' sustainable development goals whose main purpose is to "...alleviate inequalities, injustice and create a healthy environment for all." Ghauri and Cooke provide an excellent and succinct overview of these 17 intertwined goals and their linkages to MNEs. Clearly, as the chapter suggests, there are many promising and relevant inquiries to mine in this area. Interested IB researchers will surely find that this chapter offers considerable food for thought. However, Ghauri and Cooke also prudently caution us to "...separate the rhetoric from the reality" when conducting research in this domain. Even though CSR is active on corporate radars, it seems that "...greenwashing" is real too. Clearly, Ghauri and Cooke urge careful empiricism. We would do particularly well to consciously heed Ghauri and Cooke's pragmatic thinking.

The chapter by Rao-Nicholson and Liou also discusses the role of MNEs in attaining sustainable development goals, but it does so through the lens of culture. It is an important lens—especially given the fluidity of interpretations in singular contexts—and one that can "...constrain or facilitate" MNEs' responses to societal obligations. Recognizing this tension, Rao-Nicholson and Liou propose a neat conceptual model with three key contingencies. Their work concludes by outlining three fruitful avenues for IB (and non-IB) scholars to consider. In contrast, the next chapter by Rammal takes a downstream view of the sustainability phenomenon to deliberate how MNEs report their sustainability practices to "...engage" with stakeholders worldwide. This is a crucial endeavor for it permits us to isolate "stuff" from fluff. Unless results can be reasonably evaluated (measured?), they can be difficult to improve upon. Rammal's work relies on three well-publicized events to facilitate a better understanding of this fundamental message. Indeed, as Rammal shrewdly concludes, without action "...MNEs will be *merely* identifying the problem without being part of the solution" (emphasis added). Surely, we would not want that schoolish deferment.

The next two chapters change gears while still advocating investigations of important societal issues, albeit from an IB perspective. The chapter by Cervantes, Dang, and Eapen is unique in that it is the only empirical study in this volume. It also stands out for explicitly joining a hard and a soft theme (i.e., FDI and human development). As with some of the previous chapters, the authors recognize inherent duality of phenomena (here, FDI), arguing that there is an optimal level beyond which the net outcomes (here, human development) are negative. This shift from monotonic to non-monotonic thinking is, frankly, quite refreshing. What is the "global optima" (to borrow from Operations Research) beyond which our inputs generate outputs that are *contrary* to those we intended? This is not just a design issue. As many of our contemporaries ponder this dilemma whereas some ignore it and others (especially practitioners) grieve about it, it is sensible to reevaluate what, where, and how we can appreciably contribute to make ourselves more relevant.

The chapter by Muibi and Fitzsimmons also examines a promising area of inquiry: Human migration. It argues that this topic should be important to our discipline but recognizes this may be due to a parochial view of what migration involves and who migrants really are. As such, Muibi and Fitzsimmons offer us a richer, broader metaphor for understanding how we can taxi for an eventual takeoff. Their work derives from a survey of the IB literature. Muibi and Fitzsimmons deserve our compliments for revealing a frontier we have yet to fully appreciate. Their work exposes varied research themes that span disciplines and offer us a large canvas on which to paint attractive murals. Indeed, as these scholars conclude, "...our field's research is *unusually* transactional. Individuals are almost exclusively seen [as] potential resources that may be exploited to facilitate international firm activities. It would be akin to looking at a beautiful river and seeing only the energy-production possibilities of building a dam" (emphasis added).

This volume's final chapter, by Purg and Walravens, is a powerful conclusion to the now well-recognized obligations of academia to the larger society. This recognition transcends any single discipline, including IB. Yet, given its inter-disciplinary foci and global reach, IB can—and must—play a lead role in solidifying this association. Purg and Walravens offer us an inspiring historical narrative about how two Europe-based institutions envisioned and "...put" society at the core of business schools and business enterprises. These scholars document the trials and tribulations of these pioneering efforts and candidly confess to an "... 'innocent naivety': the belief that 'modern' management knowledge and skill would *naturally* offer something 'positive' for society" (emphasis added). Our erudition is a useful starting point, but it is not—and cannot be—an end in itself. Sadly, scholarship does not automatically imply action. Many still seem to suffer from this overly simplistic and lazy approach to fulfilling societal mandates. Fortunately, Purg and Walravens, like other contributors to this volume, offer us a compelling blueprint to leverage the many kernels of actionable wisdom they offer in their short essay.

4   Some Concluding Thoughts

One of the perks of editing a Handbook is the extraordinary privilege to work with thought leaders who not only share their ideas but also infect others with their passion for them. Indeed, I am very fortunate to know and work with our contributors whose contemplations I hope I have fairly summarized in this essay. Another perk is having an early peek into where (and how) these intellectuals think we should channelize our energies. Their profound theses hold a vast repository of ideas and directions that I am honored to present to you. For their participation, enthusiasm, and optimism, I remain deeply grateful. Please join me in sincerely thanking them for the promising pathways they have lit for all of us.

Hemant Merchant is a Professor of Global Business at the University of South Florida and a JIBS Consulting editor. At USF, he received a Global Achievement award for ". . .outstanding contributions to the USF System's mission to ensure student success in a global environment."

Part I

Enriching International Business Research Agenda

The Full Canvas: Exploring the Bright and Dark Sides of International Business Strategy

Alain Verbeke, Liena Kano, and Andrew Kent Johnston

1 Introduction

> [...] there is no consistent, enduring link between the adoption of modern science and technology on the one hand and the progress of reason in human affairs on the other. If anything, new technologies can give a new lease of life to the side of human nature that is not and never will be rational. The Taliban commander directing military operations from his cellular telephone is a familiar late 20th-century figure. Neither the modernization of the economy nor the spread of new technologies leads to the adoption of what we like to think of as a modern, rational worldview. John Gray (1999)

The quote above, written at the close of the last century by (then) Professor of European Thought at the London School of Economics, John Gray, has arguably been confirmed fully by the events of the last two decades. The "modernization of the economy" that Gray alludes to created an integrated worldwide financial system through which the "contagion" of the US subprime mortgage crisis was able to spread, bringing the global economy to its knees in 2008. Less than a decade later, geopolitics returned with a vengeance during the twenty-teens as Trump-era trade wars led to the erection of new tariff barriers between large blocks of the global economy: Europe, Asia, North America, and the emerging economies. Most recently, in 2020, the COVID-19 outbreak saw the interruption of critical global

A. Verbeke (✉)
Haskayne School of Business, University of Calgary, Calgary, AB, Canada

Henley Business School, University of Reading, Henley-on-Thames, UK

Solvay Business School, Brussels, Belgium

University of Calgary, Calgary, AB, Canada
e-mail: alain.verbeke@haskayne.ucalgary.ca

L. Kano · A. K. Johnston
Haskayne School of Business, University of Calgary, Calgary, AB, Canada
e-mail: liena.kano@haskayne.ucalgary.ca; andrew.johnston1@ucalgary.ca

© Springer Nature Switzerland AG 2022   13
H. Merchant (ed.), *The New Frontiers of International Business*, Contributions to
Management Science, https://doi.org/10.1007/978-3-031-06003-8_2

value chains, including those necessary for the production of basic personal protection equipment and pharmaceuticals. For many developed country consumers, the pandemic-induced shortages were the first time they had not been able to easily access once abundant products such as computing components (e.g., graphics processing units, or GPUs), recreational equipment (e.g., bicycles), and—perhaps most distressingly—toilet paper.

These recent trends and events—from the resurgence of economic nationalism in the West to the (likely short-term) disruption of global value chains (GVCs) during the pandemic—have highlighted that the risks and uncertainties that accompany international business (IB) operations have not been "solved" by advances in scientific and technological discovery. If anything, progress in the technological sphere has added layers of complexity, and thus uncertainty, to the decisions faced by managers of multinational enterprises (MNEs). As alluded to by John Gray, bounded rationality and bounded reliability[1] challenges faced by economic actors remain—even in the face of scientific and technological progress.

On the other hand, the doom and gloom predictions regarding the future of IB—i.e., the impending retreat of globalization and the imminent death of GVCs, precipitated by ongoing macro-level trends and sealed by disruptions from the global pandemic—are similarly unrealistic. Essentially, these predictions do not account fully for the indispensable, unique, and positive role of the MNE in restoring global economic order and the MNE's ability to mitigate risks while continuing to create economic value (Contractor, 2022). Only by being aware of new economic developments and technologies, and their associated opportunities and risks (i.e., their "bright" and "dark" sides), can managers be sufficiently equipped to make and adjust decisions capitalizing on the prospects that modern developments present while avoiding potential pitfalls.

In the pages that follow, we will examine ten topics of contemporary relevance to MNE managers and IB scholars:

1. Digital globalization and the MNE
2. Headquarters-subsidiary relationships and the tyranny of the back office
3. Cultural diversity and global teams
4. New forms of nationalism
5. External disruptions and risk mitigation in GVCs
6. The role of boards in firm governance
7. Environmental, social, and governance (ESG) performance and the role of private equity
8. Global innovation ecosystem and institutional fracture

---

[1] Bounded rationality describes economic actors' behavior that is "intendedly rational, but only *limitedly* so" (Simon, 1961: xxiv). Bounded reliability refers to the failure of economic actors to make good on open-ended promises, irrespective of intent (Kano & Verbeke, 2018). Bounded reliability represents an extension of the assumption of opportunism—a central construct in Williamsonian version of transaction cost economics, defined as "self-interest seeking with guile" (Williamson, 1981: 1545)—that also accounts for non-malevolent intentions.

9. Contemporary corporate social responsibility (CSR) expectations and approaches
10. The role of the MNE in climate change mitigation

In analyzing each phenomenon, we start with a position that dominates present scholarly and/or managerial conversation (whether "bright" or "dark"), and follow with the alternative viewpoint, so as to give scope to the "full canvas" of opportunities and challenges of each topic. Our analysis is summarized in Table 1. We then conclude with some reflections on the current state of IB scholarship and how a *full canvas* approach, which explores both the bright and dark sides of IB phenomena, can enhance the quality of IB scholarship and better prepare managers for the decisions they face in an increasingly volatile, uncertain, complex, and ambiguous (VUCA) world.

2 Digital Globalization and the MNE

In a recent *Academy of Management Perspectives* article, Verbeke and Hutzschenreuter (2021a) examine the impacts of digital globalization on MNEs. The authors suggest that, while digital globalization has in many cases allowed firms to increase their digital intensity and extend their global reach (the bright side), it has also given rise to new costs and challenges (the dark side).

Citing the work of Azmeh et al. (2020), Verbeke and Hutzschenreuter (2021a: 3) describe digital globalization as "[. . .] the changes in world trade and foreign direct investment resulting from the deployment of digital assets." The power of digital globalization lies in its ability to offer firms a virtually infinite economy of scale within certain domains. Information, in the form of visual and audio media, financial transactions, and communications, can be replicated and/or transmitted an infinite number of times instantaneously at zero marginal cost.

At the firm level, incorporation of digital assets that can then be mobilized as firm-specific advantages (FSAs) has enabled MNEs to experience increased internationalization and has fueled economic growth and led strategy and IB scholarship to focus on the "bright side" of digital globalization. Digital assets include resources and capabilities such as technologies, data, infrastructure, and business models that support the development and delivery of the firm's products and services.

2.1 The Bright Side Opportunities of Digital Globalization

The extent to which a firm relies upon a digital asset base is referred to as its "digital intensity." Drawing upon the work of Nambisan et al. (2019), Verbeke and Hutzschenreuter (2021a) identify three elements of digital intensity: governance, resources/assets, and customer value focus. Verbeke and Hutzschenreuter (2021a) suggest that increased digital intensity can enhance FSA-infusing properties of the

Table 1 The full canvas approach to contemporary IB issues

Contemporary issue in IB	Bright side: Functional aspects that facilitate value creation and capture	Dark side: Dysfunctional aspects that hinder value creation and capture
1. Digital globalization	• Fast and accurate information sharing • Technological channels enable externalization of activities • Efficient coordination of global operations through advanced predictive analytics • Access to geographically dispersed resources/customers • Positive network externalities	• Risk of unwanted knowledge appropriation • Overestimation of transferability of digital assets/underestimation of the need to recombine home country digital FSAs with LB FSAs in host markets • "Winner-takes-all" or "winner-takes-most" scenarios/reduced consumer choice
2. *HQ-S* relationships	• Subsidiary can be a source of profitable local initiatives due to their access to local knowledge/ability to develop LB FSAs in host markets • Potential to upgrade and transfer subsidiary-specific advantages to the entire MNE network	• Potential dysfunctional motivations on the part of HQ and bounded reliability problems may lead to a tyranny of the back office • Vicious cycles of bounded reliability throughout the organization • Threshold level of knowledge, skills, and experience is required to efficiently orchestrate subsidiary initiatives
3. Cultural diversity and global teams	• Multiple perspectives improve decision-making quality, creativity, and innovation • Broader cognitive base facilitates distance-bridging in host markets • Diverse teams signal equity, diversity, and inclusion (EDI) commitment to employees and external stakeholders	• Bounded rationality problems: Reduced information flows due to different cultural norms related to knowledge sharing; diverging interpretation of information • Bounded reliability problems: Identity-based discordance, enabled biases • Diverging interpretations of and levels of importance attached to aspects of work • Various types of diversity (surface versus deep) yield various types of benefits and challenges for team effectiveness • Diversity affects different intermediate processes (creativity, conflict, communication, satisfaction, social integration) differently, with positive and negative effects canceling each other out; the overall effect of cultural diversity on team performance is zero
4. New forms of nationalism	• Retreat of globalization may not be possible or desirable due to the present level of interconnectedness	• Risks to labor-intensive manufacturing GVCs that rely on efficiencies of offshoring

(continued)

Table 1 (continued)

Contemporary issue in IB	Bright side: Functional aspects that facilitate value creation and capture	Dark side: Dysfunctional aspects that hinder value creation and capture
	of the global economy acting as a structural barrier to nationalism • Deglobalization may prove inefficient at the MNE level as well as too costly at the national level, providing additional barriers • Deglobalization is likely to be marginal rather than fundamental • Globalization of trade is overstated, with most MNEs being regional rather than global • Marginal risks can be addressed at the firm level through changes in strategy • Technology acts as a countervailing force to deglobalization trends	• Barriers to specialized knowledge access • Increased cost of exports and interruption of trade (SMEs are particularly vulnerable) • Forced redistribution of FDI and jobs
5. External disruptions and risk mitigation in GVCs	• Lead firms can mitigate external risks through managerial governance adjustments, making GVCs efficient for the long term • GVCs are designed with a degree of flexibility and severability and are therefore more resilient in the face of external shocks than individual actors that comprise them or vertically integrated firms • Lessons learned from responding to the pandemic will help lead firm managers in building reliable GVCs in the future • The pandemic is a catalyst for productive multi-layer, cross-GVC collaborations	• Predicted structural reshaping of GVCs: Reshoring, vertical (re)integration, reduced geographic footprint • Changes in ownership and control may be difficult to implement/lead to inefficiencies and therefore unlikely to materialize • A large number of spatially dispersed loci of potential disruption make GVCs inherently susceptible to supply and demand shocks • End of GVCs and replacement by regional value chains
6. The role of boards in firm governance	• Effective board oversight prevents value-destroying activities such as executive underperformance, executive overcompensation, overpaying for acquisition, and corruption • Quad-qualification of directors (the simultaneous presence of four traits: independence, expertise, bandwidth, and motivation) significantly increases monitoring effectiveness	• Even quad-qualified directors face severe bounded rationality and bounded reliability challenges when overseeing complex operations • Increasing complexity of international operations further complicates the oversight function • Corporate boards may only be more effective at closing resource gaps and supervising punctuated events
7. ESG and the role of private equity	• Wide-ranging positive externalities of MNE operations	• Unreasonable/unrealistic/ill-informed ESG pressures threaten

(continued)

Table 1 (continued)

Contemporary issue in IB	Bright side: Functional aspects that facilitate value creation and capture	Dark side: Dysfunctional aspects that hinder value creation and capture
	• MNEs are uniquely able to promote international ESG norms and objectives • Positive ESG performance facilitates social contracts in host countries • Helps MNEs overcome host country vulnerabilities • Catalyst for correcting dysfunctional routines/improving governance practices • Catalyst for new LB/NLB FSA development • ESG focuses on reliability toward international stakeholders/facilitates access to host country resources	the MNE's growth and survival • Actions taken in response to unreasonable demands harm local communities • Only private equity provides an efficient antidote to unreasonable ESG demands, but at the expense of public equity markets • Publicly listed firms disappearing from the market, even though—back to the bright side—they can be replaced by private equity firms contributing governance capabilities, improving firm performance, and creating positive spillovers for the global economy
8. Global innovation ecosystem and institutional fracture	• Global enterprise growth, increased FDI, dissemination of advanced technology, and sophisticated management practices • Has increased welfare of much of the world's population	• Increasingly VUCA conditions for MNEs • Misappropriation of IP by "rule of ruler" governments • IP protection requires development of complex dynamic capabilities (knowledge buffering)
9. Contemporary CSR expectations and approaches	• Core CSR approach improves employee engagement, firm reputation, and societal/environmental benefits • Core CSR reduces fragmentation and increases efficiency of CSR efforts • Peripheral CSR leads to better local CSR performance and greater value capture from CSR activities at the firm level • Peripheral CSR facilitates FSA development	• Core CSR does not mitigate the full range of negative externalities • Core CSR requires a globally integrated company/is costly and difficult to implement • Core CSR reduces local responsiveness and may ultimately lead to the tyranny of the back office • Peripheral CSR is only applicable if a number of boundary conditions are met
10. The role of the MNE in climate change mitigation	• Benefits include environmental sustainability, energy security, and energy accessibility • Long-term energy (LTE) transition drives new capability development in MNEs • Consumer demand growth and increased profits • Multi-actor collaborations result in simultaneous reduction of	• Missing link between imposition of LTE transition at the macro-level and enactment at the firm level • Policy does not consider firm-level constraints • Bounded reliability on behalf of both policymakers and affected firms (virtue signaling; political rent-seeking; greenwashing/ceremonial adoption)

(continued)

Table 1 (continued)

Contemporary issue in IB	Bright side: Functional aspects that facilitate value creation and capture	Dark side: Dysfunctional aspects that hinder value creation and capture
	carbon footprint and development of new technologies	• Potential value destruction at the firm level

Source: Compiled by authors

firm's governance, resources/assets, and customer value focus as well. We discuss each below.

FSA-inducing properties of governance refer to the ability of digital technology to disseminate fast and accurate information across all areas of the value chain. The digital integration of MNE headquarters (HQ) with value chain partners has enabled externalization of activities that once needed to be internalized economize on bounded rationality and bounded reliability. Digital technologies such as advanced analytics and artificial intelligence (AI) enable lead firms in a GVC to forecast supply and demand and predict disruptions so as to efficiently map out its global operations (Kano et al., 2021).

FSA-inducing properties of resources and assets are due to the advantage of allowing managers greater discretion over foreign direct investment (FDI) decisions. Because the global spread of digital technologies allows firms more direct access to international markets (for both inputs and outputs), MNE managers can be more selective about where they locate their portfolio of physical (and usually more capital-intensive) assets. Technological tools further aid managers in monitoring and managing physical inventory and communicating with workers, suppliers, intermediaries, and customers across dispersed locations, thus overcoming potential bounded reliability issues (Kano et al., 2021).

FSA-inducing properties of customer value materialize through the creation of positive network externalities that accrue to customers when firms orchestrate their activities through digital networks (e.g., Airbnb, SkipTheDishes, eBay, etc.). The increasing returns to scale created by digital networks on the supply side are mirrored by increasing value to customers on the demand side, as customer value increases through the addition of new customers to networked digital platforms. Verbeke and Hutzschenreuter (2021a) point out that these positive network effects accruing to customers can be further amplified by the use of AI and machine learning that can optimize consumer experiences by, for instance, reducing search costs as well as other transaction costs related to payment and delivery.

2.2   The Dark Side Challenges of Digital Globalization

The bright side advantages of digital globalization described above must be qualified—and tempered—by their dark side counterparts. For each bright side opportunity presented by the three FSA-infusing elements of digital globalization, there is a potential or actual dark side threat that must be accounted for by management scholars and MNE managers.

The dark side of governance. One increasingly recognized dark side threat in the era of digital globalization is the risk of appropriation of FSAs that derive from intellectual property (IP) rights protection (see also Sect. 9). The same features that give digital assets infinite scalability at zero marginal cost (i.e., instant transmission and replication) also make them highly vulnerable to appropriation by other firms and/or political regimes. Thus, while the speed and quality of digital information give MNE managers greater control over value chain activities, the vulnerability of digital information to external appropriation provides a counter-pressure to keep FSA-supporting digital assets (at least partially) under firm ownership (Verbeke & Hutzschenreuter, 2021a).

The dark side of resources/assets. In the same way that traditional brick and mortar firms with international ambitions can be subject to "global illusions" about the redeployability of their FSAs abroad, digital firms can overestimate the extent to which their FSAs can be deployed in a host country market without significant adaption to local conditions. Early unsuccessful attempts by MNEs such as Google, Amazon, and eBay to expand into the Chinese market highlight that digital business models are not always transferable across international borders with little or no modification. Even firms with high levels of digital intensity must often rely upon the availability of local resources with which to recombine their digital assets, so as to compete successfully with local firms. This need for recombination with local assets (whether transacted within or outside of the boundaries of the firm) will often require the deployment of physical assets (including human capital) in the host country (Narula & Verbeke, 2015; Verbeke & Hutzschenreuter, 2021a; Verbeke & Kenworthy, 2008; Wu & Gereffi, 2018).

The dark side of customer value. Although the positive network externalities (economies of scale) that accrue to customers of digital platforms and ecosystems (DPEs) can create significant demand-side value for them, the same forces can also lead to "winner-takes-all" or "winner-takes-most" scenarios where smaller players can no longer compete with dominant MNEs that come to occupy hub positions within the DPE. This reduction in interfirm competition limits consumer choice and creates concomitant negative network externalities in the form of higher switching costs. Furthermore, authoritarian regimes can appropriate local or regional DPEs for political surveillance purposes, though not without unintended consequences that further diminish customer value. For example, it has been suggested that the Chinese Communist Party (CPP) requires domestic firms to have "weak security" that facilitates state access to "email and social media" and as a consequence is also prone to online crime and leaks from domestic and foreign actors (Economist, 2021a).

2.3 Summary

Each of the elements of digital globalization—governance, resources/assets, and customer value—has both a bright and dark side. While digital integration across value chains can help economize on bounded rationality and bounded reliability challenges, it can also add layers of complexity and risk that may counteract these economies. For example, managers may overestimate the extent to which they can deploy digital assets abroad without needing to recombine these with complementary assets (through either direct FDI or contracting). Governance decisions regarding host country selection and the boundaries of the firm must still be assessed soberly by considering local contexts and the recombination requirements necessary to convert home country location-bound FSAs into non-location-bound FSAs or to develop new location-bound FSAs in the host country.

3 Headquarters-Subsidiary Relationships and the Tyranny of the Back Office

One of the most prominent themes within IB research since the field's inception has been the relationship between the MNE's central or regional headquarters (HQ) and its host country subsidiaries. Whereas early studies on headquarters-subsidiary (HQ-S) relationships tended to view subsidiaries as relatively undifferentiated extensions of the firm's home country operations, more recent research sees subsidiaries as potential sources of new, context-specific knowledge which can also benefit the whole MNE network. Here, the corporate HQ plays a central role in orchestrating subsidiary initiatives for the benefit of the MNE. In this section, we examine the bright side opportunities and dark side challenges of HQ-S relationships or, more specifically, of HQ involvement in subsidiary initiative management.

3.1 The Bright Side Opportunities of HQ Involvement in Subsidiary Initiatives

In a survey examining the past and present state of research on *HQ-S* relationships, Kostova et al. (2016) identify five dominant themes that have informed HQ-S research over the past 50 years. The authors group the approaches that IB scholarship has taken to the study of HQ-S relationships into the following, chronologically ordered categories (i.e., historical to most recent dominant approaches): (1) organizational design and control systems; (2) home and host country context; (3) subsidiary roles and regional structures; (4) knowledge creation and transfer; and (5) expatriate management and global human resource management (HRM). The common narrative across these historically dominant categories is a move from an HQ-centric view of HQ-S relationships toward approaches that recognize the knowledge creation potential of subsidiaries. Accordingly, the core unit of analysis in IB research has shifted from the firm to the subsidiary and the subsidiary manager (Rugman et al., 2011). It is increasingly recognized in IB literature that subsidiaries can possess idiosyncratic FSA bundles that can be important sources of knowledge and innovation for the MNE. Their context-specific knowledge of host country markets allows them to react more quickly to local demands. Similarly, their proximity to local knowledge hubs can lead to product and service innovations that may be transferrable within the wider MNE network. In this context, the role of the HQ is to orchestrate and exploit autonomous subsidiary initiatives and to channel knowledge in order to generate maximum value for the MNE network. However, this task comes with challenges, namely, (1) how to successfully assess subsidiary initiatives; (2) how to support initiatives that have the potential to create and capture value; and (3) how to transfer knowledge between HQ and the subsidiary in a way that allows successful initiatives to benefit the entire MNE network. Achieving these objectives entails overcoming significant challenges from bounded rationality (e.g., information gathering, selection, and processing) and bounded reliability (i.e., motivational challenges and competing priorities faced by MNE managers in performing these tasks).

3.2   The Dark Side Challenges of HQ Involvement in Subsidiary Initiatives

Recent IB research acknowledges that managerial analysis of the MNE, especially such complex relational aspects of MNE governance as subsidiary management, should be conducted from a microfoundational perspective, with sufficient attention paid to the behavior of individual managers (Kano & Verbeke, 2019). Accordingly, in a recent conceptual paper, Verbeke and Yuan (2020) explore the microfoundations that inform HQ-S relationships; they suggest that much of the variance among MNEs in their management of HQ-S relationships can be explained by the motivations and abilities of the individual HQ managers. Drawing upon the motivation and ability framework of Mitchell and Daniels (2003), Verbeke and Yuan (2020) propose that the effectiveness of MNE HQ involvement in subsidiary initiatives is determined by a combination of two individual-level attributes of HQ decision-makers: (1) motivation and (2) ability. Insufficient presence or dysfunctional expression of either of the two factors is likely to lead do "dark side" consequences of HQ involvement in subsidiary management.

The dark side of motivation. Verbeke and Yuan (2020) highlight four types of motivation that can inform a HQ manager's approach to subsidiary initiatives: (1) benevolent service of the firm; (2) self-interested service of private objectives; (3) other motivations related to bounded reliability; and (4) controlled responses to MNE stakeholders in line with perceived normative expectations. Of these, only the first—benevolent service of the firm—is likely to promote a positive approach to subsidiary initiatives. The other three (self-interested service of private objectives, other motivations deriving from bounded reliability, and controlled responses to perceived expectations) are all dysfunctional motivations likely to lead to negative impacts on HQ-S relationships and subsidiary initiatives. In cases of strongly dysfunctional motivation, sub-goal pursuit or a desire to exercise authority (either for its own sake or to implement perceptions about how HQ-S relationships should unfold) can lead to a "tyranny of the back office," "i.e., cases whereby individual decision-makers at CHQs choose to intervene for the wrong reasons" (Verbeke & Yuan, 2020: 7). This in turn leads to the demoralizing and demotivation of subsidiary managers and can even result in a vicious cycle of bounded reliability, whereby disgruntled subsidiary managers may pursue sub-goals of their own (Verbeke & Yuan, 2020).

The dark side of ability. Three dimensions of ability that influence the actions of HQ decision-makers in their interactions with subsidiaries are (1) knowledge; (2) skills; and (3) experience.

The ability to collect and process the knowledge needed to properly assess a proposed subsidiary initiative is the most important of the three dimensions. The knowledge that undergirds a new subsidiary initiative is highly context-specific and will often be encumbered with high levels of complexity and ambiguity. Transferring this knowledge from the subsidiary to HQ often involves the traversing of significant cultural, administrative, geographic, and economic (CAGE) distance (Ghemawat, 2001).

While knowledge is the most important dimension of ability, experience and skills also play an important role in determining how a HQ manager will approach subsidiary initiatives. However, the experience HQ managers bring to the table when approaching subsidiary initiatives can be a double-edged sword. While a broad international experience can assist with bridging the CAGE distance required for knowledge transfer from subsidiary to HQ, deeply ingrained patterns of behavior can also lead to identity-based discordance—an expression of bounded reliability whereby managers fail to deliver on commitments due to a personal commitment to a particular identity which may be incongruent with corporate or unit identity. Thus, both the types of experience and skills decision-makers possess *and* their ability to reflexively use and adapt these to the required situation are critical to successfully evaluating and supporting subsidiary initiatives.

3.3   Summary

Subsidiaries may have a strong potential to contribute to the creation of new FSAs within an MNE. However, HQ decision-makers bring a mixed bag of motivations and abilities to the table when assessing and supporting subsidiary initiatives. Individual motivations can be either functional or dysfunctional and of a weak or strong intensity. Only in cases where a strong, functional motivation to serve the firm is paired with a high level of ability is the impact of HQ involvement in a subsidiary initiative likely to contribute to a positive outcome for the firm. Unfortunately, when motivations are dysfunctional, or below threshold levels, the HQ-S relationship will be a negative one, potentially even developing into a "tyranny of the back office." It is crucial that IB scholars and MNE managers alike understand both these bright side opportunities and dark side challenges of HQ-S relationships if they are to reap the benefits of subsidiary knowledge and innovation.

4   Cultural Diversity and Global Teams

A prominent stream within IB and organizational behavior research examines the impact of diversity upon team performance. While these studies have addressed various aspects of diversity (e.g., gender diversity, age diversity, functional diversity, etc.), the most popular theme for scholarly analysis has been the impact of cultural diversity on team performance. In this section, we examine the bright and dark sides of this phenomenon.

4.1   The Bright Side Opportunities of Cultural Diversity

Concomitant with the globalizing trends discussed above has been a growing prevalence of culturally diverse teams within the MNE (at both inter- and intra-national levels). "Diversity is our strength" has become a common political mantra, with both American President Joe Biden and Canadian Prime Minister Justin Trudeau using those words in their own government communications and/or campaigning materials. Top strategic management consulting firms such as McKinsey and Boston Consulting Group have produced reports highlighting the performance-enhancing benefits of diverse teams (Dixon-Fyle et al., 2020; Lorenzo et al., 2018). Culturally diverse teams are argued to benefit from multiple perspectives to bear on problems, and thus make better-quality decisions. Access to various perspectives also facilitates greater creativity in culturally diverse teams, yields broader and more accurate customer insights, and ultimately leads to better innovation outcomes (Grant & Rock, 2016). Specifically in the context of an MNE, diversity of managers' cultural backgrounds broadens the firm's cognitive base and can thus help the MNE bridge various dimensions of distance between home and host countries, particularly if managers have cultural affinity with relevant host markets (Verbeke, 2013). Finally, cultural diversity of teams signals the firm's commitment to equity, diversity, and inclusion (EDI) goals to both employees and external stakeholders and thus increases employee satisfaction and improves the firm's global reputation (Dixon-Fyle et al., 2020).

A quick perusal of the website for any large MNE will almost certainly reveal a statement or even a complete portal devoted to the firm's efforts toward nurturing a diverse working environment. Indeed, in 2021, many of the world's top global firms have dedicated senior executives with the word "diversity" in their title (e.g., Google's "Chief Diversity Officer"). The narrative in the internal and external communications of top global firms, in the business press, and in management consulting reports is clear: diversity has a positive impact on firm performance.

4.2   The Dark Side of Cultural Diversity

Management scholars, however, have not been quite so Panglossian in the reporting of their findings on the impact of cultural diversity on the performance of teams. Indeed, much of the research conducted over the past decade has found that diversity (specifically cultural diversity) can be a double-edged sword when it comes to its impact upon team performance.

In their award-winning meta-analysis examining the impact of cultural diversity on team performance, Stahl et al. (2010) found that the mean effect size of cultural diversity on performance was close to zero (it was in fact slightly negative). This finding mirrors those of the studies encompassed in their meta-analysis, which found the correlation between cultural diversity and performance to be either ambiguous or close to zero. Some studies show a significant, negative relationship between cultural diversity and certain aspects of performance: for example, Gibson and Gibbs (2006) found that national diversity inhibits innovation through differences in norms, expectations, and behavior. Diverging cultural values within a team lead to inconsistent definitions of such core concepts as teamwork and hierarchy, as well as different importance attached to various dimensions of work. Diverging cultural norms around knowledge sharing and communication potentially reduce information flows (Gibson & Gibbs, 2006). Diversity can be responsible for severe bounded rationality problems, whereby managers with different cultural backgrounds select different facets of information as the basis of strategic decisions and/or interpret the same information differently (Verbeke & Yuan, 2005). Differences in cultural values can naturally lead to identity-based discordance (Kano & Verbeke, 2019) and facilitate further bounded reliability challenges by enabling biased behavior (Verbeke et al., 2020).

What explains this gap between the positive diversity narrative that the media and large firms espouse and the empirical findings of management scholars? Reflecting upon this paradox, Stahl et al. point out a rather crude and unidimensional conceptualization of cultural diversity by both practitioners and academics. The authors argue that future research and management practice should move away from the "all or nothing" approach to diversity: ". . .in our own experience with leaders in organizations, the message 'diversity is always good' does not fit with most people's lived experience. . . The [exclusively positive] message itself has the potential to shut down the very dialogue it needs to open up by denying any possibility that diversity can lead to lower performance, and dismissing the importance of contingencies" (Stahl & Maznevski, 2021: 18).

Stahl et al. (2010) propose a model whereby the effects of cultural diversity upon performance are mediated through process gains and losses and moderated by structural contingencies. The authors tease out further nuances in their model by distinguishing between two types of cultural diversity: surface-level versus deep-level cultural diversity.

Stahl et al. (2010: 694) define surface-level diversity as "differences among team members in overt demographic characteristics, such as ... racio-ethnicity and nationality." Deep-level diversity, on the other hand, refers to the "differences among team members' psychological characteristics, including personality, values, and attitudes" (Stahl et al., 2010: 694). The level and type of cultural diversity represent the "input" or independent variables in Stahl et al.'s model.

The intermediate processes specified in Stahl et al.'s model are creativity; conflict; communication effectiveness; team satisfaction; and social integration. They group these processes into convergent and divergent categories and specify the effect on each process in terms of a gain or loss. Creativity and conflict are divergent processes, with creativity producing a gain and conflict producing a loss. Communication, team satisfaction, and social integration are all convergent processes that yield process gains. As diversity is (by definition) a divergent state, the authors predict that diversity will yield gains for creative processes while yielding losses for the others.

While the authors' meta-analysis finds that cultural diversity does indeed yield process gains for creativity and process losses for task conflict and team integration, they find no significant effect of cultural diversity on communication and (counter to expectations) a positive effect on team satisfaction. With the overall effect of cultural diversity on team performance being close to zero, positive and negative effects of cultural diversity on performance appear to be cancelling each other out. As such, managers should consider which aspects of performance are strategically important and subsequently establish desirable levels of cultural diversity required to match relevant performance objectives.

4.3   Summary

Cultural diversity contributes to convergent and divergent processes that can be either beneficial or detrimental to team performance. Reflecting on the findings of Stahl et al.'s (2010) meta-analysis, Minbaeva, Fitzsimmons, and Brewster note that "diversity per se is not necessarily a strategic resource unless it is mobilized and deployed in such a way that differentiates the firm from its competitors" (Minbaeva et al., 2021: 51). Here, Stahl et al.'s (2010) findings provide clear guidance to managers seeking to mobilize cultural diversity as a strategic resource: maximize process gains from creativity (a critical resource for innovation) while mitigating process losses in the areas of conflict, communication, and integration.

5   New Forms of Nationalism

Over the past several years, scholars have been observing signs that the era of (relatively) unfettered global free trade may be waning, in large part due to a corresponding rise in protectionist politics and policies. The earlier optimism of the 1990s suffered ideological setbacks with the 1999 anti-globalization protests in Seattle and the terrorist attacks on the World Trade Centre in 2001. The so-called Washington consensus was proving less than universally popular, contrary to the predictions of some of its more enthusiastic proponents (Stiglitz, 2002). With the benefit of over a decade of hindsight, it now seems that the financial crisis of 2008 and the ensuing Great Recession were, at the very least, a major setback to the economic globalization project. In the intervening years since the "sub-prime mortgage crisis" submerged the global financial system into turmoil, there has been a resurgence of economic nationalism in ways not seen since the Cold War era. In this section, we will examine some of the bright side opportunities and dark side challenges of these emerging trends and their implications for business scholars and managers. Given the generally pessimistic outlook that these trends entail for global business and trade, we will first examine the dark side prognosis before suggesting some possible bright side mitigating factors.

5.1 The Dark Side of New Forms of Nationalism

In a recent publication, Kobrin (2021) reflects on the prevailing sentiments among business scholars at the close of the twentieth century. "Neomedievalist" scholars (among whom Kobrin counted himself) believed that the advent of digital globalization represented a systemic change in the global economic system similar in significance to what the Western world experienced when transitioning from the medieval to the modern era. Fundamental to the proposed epochal scale of this transition was the belief that:

> [...] the digital revolution, the scale and complexity of technology, and the emergence of electronically integrated global networks would render geographic borders, territorial sovereignty, and the entire edifice of the post-Westphalian international state system problematic [...] a new 'transnational' order was emerging comprised of diffuse borders, overlapping authority, and multiple political actors. (Kobrin, 2021: 63–64)

Looking back at these beliefs from the vantage point of 2021, Kobrin argues that the second wave of globalization, which began with the collapse of the Soviet system in the 1980s, in fact, reached a high-water mark in the early 2000s before hitting what is at the very least a significant setback in the recession of 2008/2009. Measures of global financial integration have still not reached their pre-recession peak, and new barriers to trade have sprung up all around the globe, as states implement national economic protectionist policies. Kobrin goes on to highlight the fact that two of the nations which seem to be abandoning the global trade movement with the most enthusiasm, the USA and Great Britain, are the very ones that played the greatest role in establishing the post-war consensus that drove the second wave of economic globalization. Brexit, President Trump's "America first" foreign policies, a reconfiguration of NAFTA, and the US-China trade war are symptomatic of a widespread backlash against globalization and renewed protectionism (Kano et al., 2021).

These recent developments create significant risks for international business, particularly in relation to GVCs, whose very existence is predicated on the liberalization and deregulation of international trade, and the lead firm' ability to seamlessly move knowledge, goods, and people across international borders. Those risks are particularly salient in labor-intensive manufacturing GVCs, where lead firms rely on cost efficiencies from offshoring operations to low-cost countries. Similarly, MNEs that rely on highly specialized knowledge or location-bound assets (e.g., natural resources) in host countries stand to lose significant value due to newly erected trade barriers. The full impact of renewed protectionism on international business will likely take some time to materialize, as the patterns of MNE responses are currently in a state of flux (Kano & Oh, 2020). Yet, preliminary evidence suggests that new nationalism is likely to have winners and losers and that protectionist regimes are unlikely to be the ones to come out on top. Consider, for example, a Brexit-induced boom in investment and jobs in the Netherlands. The Dutch logistics and warehousing industry is growing significantly, with many American and Asian firms shifting operations away from the UK and into the Netherlands, so as to serve European customers seamlessly and efficiently. Meanwhile, thousands of UK firms, particularly SMEs, have been forced to discontinue exports to the EU due to increased shipping costs, logistical bottlenecks, and the sudden addition of duties and tariffs (Partridge, 2021).

5.2   The Bright Side Opportunities of the Interconnected World

Despite the alarming rise of nationalism, it is possible that the global integration of complex value chains may not in fact be reversible without causing severe destruction of value in ways that are not politically palatable to the nations calling for increased national economic isolation (Kobrin, 2021). At the most obvious level, constituents calling for the reshoring of geographically dispersed value chain activities may be unwilling to pay for the increased costs of labor inherent in such a move when these costs are passed along to them in the prices of their favorite consumer goods. Moreover, many of the value chains that produce goods now considered to be staples (the smartphone being a prime example) are so complex and finely sliced at present (Buckley, 2009) that it may not be possible to re-internalize these activities. The knowledge and capabilities required are held, often tacitly, across a disaggregated GVC network. Commenting on the potential impossibility of renationalizing geographically dispersed economic activity without destroying their value creation potential, Kobrin notes that:

> GPNs [global production networks] are relational: the value of any given node flows from the pattern of relationships within the network rather than the attributes of the node itself. That implies mutual dependence: the disaggregation of design and production into relatively narrow 'tasks' increases the dependence of each operation on the system as a whole. The narrower the individual operation, the less likely it will have intrinsic value, and the more likely that its value will depend on integration into the global network. (Kobrin, 2021: 68)

Thus, national governments attempting to reshore disaggregated value chain activities back inside the boundaries of "national champion" firms may find that their levels of mutual dependence upon the economic activity of other nations are simply too high, and thus too costly, for their citizens to stomach.

It should also be noted that, in terms of the actual trade across national borders, the extent of economic globalization is likely exaggerated. Empirical data show that few modern MNEs are truly global in a sense of having a balanced distribution of operations across various regions of the world (Rugman & Verbeke, 2004); in fact, international trade was far more regionalized than globalized even during the height of globalization in the early 2000s. As such, the predicted retreat of trade from global to regional is hardly a radical shift from the status quo.

It follows that changes to the global economy stemming from the new forms of nationalism are quite likely to be marginal, rather than fundamental (Contractor, 2022). The basic efficiency rationale that guides international investment remains, even in the face of renewed protectionism. While economic nationalism certainly creates additional risks for MNEs, these risks can be partially addressed by fine-tuning and adjusting international strategy at the firm level (Contractor, 2022), as we will discuss in the following section. In addition, and as discussed earlier, emerging technologies can serve as a "countervailing force" (Buckley, 2020: 1582) to deglobalization trends.

5.3 Summary

The "second wave" of globalization that began with the collapse of the Soviet system in the 1980s appears to have reached a high-water mark with the onset of the Great Recession of 2008/2009. Since then, the world has seen a resurgence of the types of economic nationalism that characterized the Cold War era, though this time from some of the earlier champions of free markets. The instigation of protectionist and isolationist economic policies in countries which were previously leaders of the global free-trade movement is part of an ideological and political trend that appears to be hostile to many aspects of economic globalization. Many of these countries are now enacting policies aimed at renationalizing production activities that were previously geographically dispersed. However, due to the complexity and mutual interdependence of modern GVCs, it is not yet clear whether these nationalist economic objectives can be achieved without destroying value, and thus national prosperity, at levels that are too high to be politically feasible. The economic rationale for international business remains even in the face of new nationalism, and as such, changes to globalization are likely to be incremental rather than fundamental.

6 External Disruptions and Risk Mitigation in GVCs

Over the past several decades, GVCs have emerged as the dominant form of organizing global economic activity. GVCs have been described as "the world economy's backbone and central nervous system" (Cattaneo et al., 2010: 7) and have been analyzed extensively by scholars, consultants, and practitioners. As discussed in the previous section, slowly unfolding multi-decadal geopolitical changes have sharpened scholars' and other analysts' focus on GVCs. Most recently, the COVID-19 pandemic has delivered a serious and sudden shock to cross-border trade and has amplified this focus, with much popular and academic press predicting significant changes in GVC configurations.

GVC disruption by exogenous events is not a new phenomenon. GVCs have experienced multiple prior shocks, including the 2008 Sichuan earthquake, the 2008–2009 global economic recession, the 2011 Tōhoku tsunami, as well as disruptions associated with government-level economic policies discussed above (Kano & Oh, 2020). However, the COVID-19 pandemic has been described as "an exogenous shock of uncommon magnitude" (Verbeke, 2020: 444), whose intensity, duration, and pervasiveness exceed those of any previous crisis. The pandemic thus shifted scholarly and practitioner attention toward the resilience of GVCs, their susceptibility to disruption, their risk management capacity, and, ultimately, their long-term viability as an international governance form.

Given some of the highly visible disruptions that have occurred during the pandemic, the literature on GVC resilience and risk mitigation may be an area of IB where scholars are currently *overemphasizing* the dark side to the neglect of some broader positive trends and opportunities in GVC governance, as we discuss below.

6.1   The Dark Side Challenges of External Disruptions in GVCs

The profound external shock that COVID-19 represents may be unique in terms of both its global reach and level of impact. No country or economy has been left unscathed by supply-side shocks from outbreaks and lockdowns. Similarly, demand-side shocks due to lockdowns and unemployment have drastically shifted the need for many consumer goods. In parallel, and as discussed in the previous section, macro-institutional factors in the form of geopolitical tensions have seen the re-emergence of trade barriers across some of the world's largest regions and countries. This combination of pandemic-related shocks and the resurgence of economic protectionism have led many popular and scholarly commentators to predict a radical reconfiguration of GVC structures in response to a "new normal" (Verbeke, 2020). It has been argued that COVID-19 illuminated the underlying fragilities of GVCs (Silverthorne, 2020) and is likely to push lead firms to reorchestrate their GVCs by reshoring and by vertically integrating. The GVCs of the future are argued to have a smaller geographic footprint, be regionally focused, and rely less on outsourcing, particularly where strategically important supplies are concerned. Some business reports go so far as to predict an impending end of GVCs (Fortune, 2020; FT, 2020; The Atlantic, 2020).

6.2   The Bright Side Opportunities of Risk Mitigation in GVCs

While acknowledging the profound impact that the COVID-19 pandemic has had on GVCs, some IB scholars have argued that overly pessimistic prognostications on the future of the GVC are premature. To adapt a quote famously attributed to Mark Twain, "rumors of [the GVC's] death are greatly exaggerated."

Some structural changes, such as supplier diversification, reduced Sino-dependence due to trade wars, reduced irreversible commitments abroad, and regionalization of value chains, may indeed occur and are in fact already underway. However, these changes may be marginal and gradual rather than pervasive and urgent (Kano et al., 2021; Verbeke, 2020), because the lead firm's ability to implement these changes hinges on numerous conditions (as noted in Sect. 4). It follows that, in many instances, predicted structural changes may hinder, rather than facilitate, efficiency gains from operating a GVC and as such are unlikely to materialize.

Commenting on the impact of the COVID-19 pandemic on GVCs, Kano et al. (2021) and Verbeke (2020) suggest that lead firm managers in GVCs can respond to such external disruptions by deploying managerial and relational governance tools, particularly when structural reconfigurations are not economically feasible. Specifically, lead firms can mitigate exogenous risks, inter alia, by increasing their investments in predictive analytics, implementing greater contracting safeguards in relationships with suppliers (including greater reliance on equity), increasing their reliance on relational governance, supporting supplier upgrading, engaging in broad-based stakeholder management and corporate diplomacy, and developing advanced resource recombination capabilities (Kano et al., 2021; Verbeke et al., 2021).

Such managerial tools are within the lead firm's proximate control to a greater extent than structural changes in location and ownership and serve long-term strategic considerations (as opposed to reacting to short-term supply and demand disruptions caused by the pandemic). Importantly, lessons learned from responding to the COVID-19 pandemic through changes in governance can help lead firm managers increase GVC resilience in the face of likely future exogenous disruptions.

Finally, the global pandemic may have acted as a catalyst for increased cooperation and innovation across GVCs. Large-scale, multi-layer global R&D collaborations to develop vaccines and therapies exemplify such innovation and represent "happy exceptions" to the isolationist tendencies of firms and governments—as reinforced by the pandemic (Guimón & Narula, 2020). Such multi-stakeholder collaborations increase the long-term efficiency of GVCs by facilitating resource and knowledge sharing (Kano et al., 2021).

6.3   Summary

External disruptions can pose significant dark side challenges to the survival of a GVC. Yet, a GVC's raison d'être, and its ultimate advantage over a vertically integrated firm, is in its ability to orchestrate its evolving network of actors as a response to changing circumstances. As such, it can be argued that a certain degree of resilience is built into the very fabric of a GVC. Admittedly, COVID-19 has disrupted the flow of goods and services across GVCs. However, as lead firm managers recover from the initial shock, they can make governance decisions that target long-term GVC efficiency. By exercising managerial governance mechanisms such as those discussed above, lead firm managers can bolster the resilience of their GVC networks in ways that both substitute and complement (often unfeasible) structural changes. On the bright side, the pandemic has focused managers' attention on strategies to enhance long-term GVC resilience. Responding to the pandemic has forced lead firm managers to broaden their managerial toolkit and has equipped them to build GVCs that are efficient and reliable for the long term.

7 The Role of Boards in Firm Governance

One area of significant interest to business scholars across a range of disciplines (finance, accounting, organizational behavior, and IB) is the role of corporate boards in firm governance. IB scholars have investigated the role of boards in internationalization decisions of MNEs (Sanders & Carpenter, 1998). This line of inquiry is particularly developed in family firm internationalization research, where independent board members are often seen as contributing relevant internationalization knowledge, strategic planning competencies, and objective outside scrutiny of international governance decisions (Arregle et al., 2012; Calabrò & Mussolino, 2013).

Theoretically, the two perspectives which have dominated much of the scholarly discussion about the role of boards are agency theory (Fama & Jensen, 1983) and resource dependence theory, or RDT (Pfeffer & Salancik, 1978). Correspondingly, the dominant conceptions of the role of boards are monitoring and resource provisioning, with the former being the subject of the most scholarly research (Hillman et al., 2009). Board monitoring is argued to prevent such value-destroying activities as executive team underperformance, CEO overcompensation, overpaying for acquisitions, and fraudulent behavior. However, the near-daily news coverage of corporate failures and scandals calls into serious question the ability of boards to perform this monitoring function effectively, and recent scholarship echoes this skepticism (Boivie et al., 2016). In this section, we will examine the role of the board in terms of its monitoring and resource provision functions.

7.1 The Bright Side Opportunities of Board Monitoring

In their review of the literature on board monitoring, Hambrick et al. (2015) note that the bulk of the scholarship in this area adopts a structural approach to the analysis of boards and their ability to carry out the monitoring function. The key structural variables commonly identified are (1) the size of the board; (2) the relative composition of the board (the ratio of independent board members versus members of the top management team); and (3) the existence of various board sub-committees, e.g., audit, nomination, compensation, etc. However, Hambrick et al.'s (2015) analysis of extant empirical studies yields no compelling evidence that board structure affects its ability to perform its oversight function. Similarly, a meta-analysis by Dalton et al.

(1998) finds no significant relationship between firm performance and structural features of boards.

Hambrick et al. (2015) propose an alternative framework. They draw upon the organizational psychology literature to identify the *individual* variables which may increase a board's effectiveness in monitoring. They propose a model consisting of four traits (the "quad model") which they argue will significantly increase the likelihood that a board will be effective in its monitoring function: (1) independence; (2) expertise; (3) bandwidth; and (4) motivation. Crucially, Hambrick et al. argue that all four quad model factors must be present in a single director—that is, it is not enough for these four factors to be distributed in aggregate across the directors which comprise the board.

Perhaps the most interesting implication of this proposition is that the presence of even one board member with all four attributes will supposedly greatly increase a board's ability to monitor effectively monitor the firm's operations. The quad model has found some recent empirical support. In a study published in the *Journal of Corporate Finance*, Gorshunov et al. (2021) show that the presence of at least one quad-qualified audit committee director decreased the probability of financial corruption in a public firm by 72%. This has led Hambrick et al. (2015) to conclude their paper with optimism about the potential for quad-qualified directors to improve the oversight capability of boards.

7.2 The Dark Side Challenges of Board Monitoring and the Case for Alternative Board Functions

At the dark side end of the spectrum, Boivie et al. (2016) are more skeptical. They point to the regular and high-profile failures of boards to prevent executive underperformance or misconduct and argue that business journalists, academics, and shareholders alike may be expecting too much from boards and their directors. Like Hambrick et al. (2015), Boivie et al. (2016) also conclude that the extant research on the impact of board characteristics on monitoring performance has failed to produce any significant findings.

Boivie et al. (2016) concede that the lack of significant findings *may* be due to the focus on structural variables rather than individual characteristics. However, they suggest that the more likely reason for a lack of convincing evidence is that, in most situations, it simply is not possible for a board to effectively monitor a large and complex organization in the way its role is conceived by agency theory. Boivie et al. (2016) argue that boards face insurmountable barriers to effective monitoring which arise at multiple levels: individual, group, and firm. These barriers exist due to compounded information processing challenges (i.e., bounded rationality). To succeed in their monitoring role, boards must be able to obtain, process, and share information effectively. Standing between the board and the effective execution of these information-based activities are barriers that include individual capabilities and external commitments (i.e., bounded rationality and bounded reliability challenges); group structure and dynamics (e.g., independence of the board, frequency of meetings, diversity challenges, etc.); and the complexity deriving from the firm's size and scope of operations. Boivie et al. (2016) argue that the barriers to effective information processing at each level compound to make the execution of effective monitoring a highly unlikely event, hence the paucity of empirical findings supporting the effectiveness of boards in monitoring. Although Boivie et al. (2016) do not comment specifically on the impact of the level of firm internationalization on successful board oversight, it seems reasonable to assume that the informational barriers to effective monitoring would increase in firms with internationally dispersed operations. Internationalization adds significant complexity to the firm's operations, whereby geographic dispersion of units, cross-country differences, and specialized knowledge requirements introduce additional dimensions of bounded rationality, namely, multifacetedness of information and divergence in judgement on identical information (Verbeke & Yuan, 2005). International dispersion also amplifies bounded reliability challenges faced by corporate boards, by increasing the likelihood of preference reversal and identity discordance (Kano & Verbeke, 2019). As such, barriers to effective monitoring identified by Boivie et al. (2016) are likely to be particularly pronounced in MNE boards. This contention is partially supported empirically: Sanders and Carpenter (1998) argue that the increased complexity arising from international operations may be responsible for the positive relationship they find between board size and firm internationalization.

Given their pessimism regarding the ability of boards to effectively perform their monitoring role, Boivie et al. (2016) argue that scholars and practitioners should turn their attention to the two other functions that boards can fulfil: resource provision and the supervision of "punctuated events." Resource provision includes, inter alia, the provision of network connections beneficial to the firm, knowledge and advice deriving from directors' domains of expertise, and the legitimacy which can be conferred by the appointment of highly regarded directors. The supervision of punctuated events refers to the board's role in, for instance, audit committees, executive appointments, and financial restatements. Because punctuated events are, by definition, of an occasional and limited nature, they impose less of a cognitive burden upon directors and are more likely to have successful outcomes. This approach is consistent with IB scholarship, where boards (especially those of family firms and international new ventures) are often seen as the origin of important resources required for successful internationalization, such as international knowledge, sophisticated managerial capabilities, reputation, and host country network connections (Arregle et al., 2021).

7.3 Summary

The extant literature on board governance has focused primarily on two functions that boards can fulfil: monitoring and resource provision. In both the academic and popular business press, the focus has generally been on the monitoring function of boards. However, research has not discovered any significant connections between structural variables of board composition and the effectiveness of board monitoring.

Whereas board monitoring effectiveness can be improved by the targeted recruiting of quad-qualified directors, it appears that even quad-qualified boards face insurmountable bounded rationality and bounded reliability challenges in overseeing complex operations. These challenges are amplified in an MNE, where cross-border distance and increased operational complexity further hinder the board's monitoring function. Rather than focusing exclusively on the board's monitoring role, practitioners and researchers should consider other functions of corporate boards: resource provision and supervision of punctuated events. MNE board members can contribute important internationalization resources, including international knowledge, access to local networks, reputational resources, and management capabilities.

8   ESG Expectations and the Role of Private Equity

MNEs are unique in their ability to create economic value for immediate stakeholder groups (**i.e.,** owners, employees, suppliers, and customers) while also developing and disseminating innovative products and practices which produce positive externalities for society. Often, these positive benefits fall under one or all of the following categories: environmental, social, and governance (ESG). While ESG initiatives by MNEs can often be Pareto-improving (i.e., provide net benefits to all parties), they can also, when driven by irrational ideology rather than facts, threaten the very survival of the firm. In this section, we examine the bright and dark sides of ESG initiatives undertaken by MNEs and the role that private equity can play as an antidote to irrational ESG requests by activist media and other pressure groups.

8.1   The Bright Side Opportunities of ESG Pressures on the MNE

Verbeke and Lee (2021) refer to the unique ability of MNEs to create "win-win" scenarios for the firm and its societal stakeholders as "benevolent resource recombination." The capability to perform benevolent resource recombination, they argue, derives from the unique governance abilities of MNEs. Successful large MNEs are able to facilitate resource recombination across product and geographic space while reconciling international and local pressures and priorities, increasing the world's economic welfare as a result. According to Verbeke and Lee:

> MNE governance models could therefore, subject to necessary qualification, serve as best practices for the future, public institutions of international and global governance that will become increasingly important, as pressure mounts from the type of problems described by the 'tragedy of the commons'. (Verbeke & Lee, 2021: 433)

At the same time, MNEs (even the large, globally successful ones) are inherently vulnerable when crossing international borders into host country locations. Verbeke and Lee highlight five types of such vulnerability: (1) vulnerability to competition from existing or new international rivals; (2) vulnerability deriving from the bounded rationality and bounded reliability challenges of running dispersed internal affiliate networks; (3) vulnerability to actors supplying required complementary resources; (4) vulnerability to the decisions of sovereign governments and other host country stakeholders; and (5) vulnerability to the scrutiny of international media and pressure groups. These vulnerabilities force even the most successful MNEs and their managers to enter (either implicitly or explicitly) into social contracts in host countries, seeking a so-called "social license to operate" from local stakeholders. The pressures of competition, media and NGO scrutiny, and compliance to local and international rules and norms require that MNEs respond to criticisms and correct dysfunctional routines and behaviors if they are to grow and survive. Paying attention to ESG expectations in host countries facilitates development of important, location-bound FSAs in these areas. These FSAs can potentially be upgraded and transferred to other units, thus helping the MNE overcome its host country vulnerabilities across different locations. In turn, a global reputation for ESG leadership signals reliability to the MNE's stakeholders and thus facilitates access to a range of resources and capabilities in host locations.

8.2 The Dark Side Challenges of ESG Pressures on MNE and the Case for Private Equity

While MNEs are uniquely able to respond to international pressures and promote ESG norms and objectives through resource recombination, the benefits of an ESG focus are subject to qualification. Stakeholder pressures to achieve ESG objectives can become detached from reality, leading to unreasonable expectations and pressure on MNE managers. Large institutional investors such as public sector pension plans and sovereign wealth funds, as well as foreign-owned MNEs, seem to be particularly vulnerable to these types of unreasonable ESG demands by activist media and other pressure groups. This pressure is often applied to public firms through their shareholders and through equity markets, further amplified through social media. Ultimately, unrealistic, unreasonable, and ideology-driven ESG demands may threaten the firm's growth and survival. Moreover, MNEs' response to ill-informed ESG pressures may in fact harm, rather than improve, community welfare. For example, Narula (2019) convincingly demonstrates that MNEs' efforts to enforce strict labor standards in emerging economies in response to stakeholder demands may limit local enterprise growth and reduce employment prospects among the most vulnerable local population.

When MNEs are faced with unreasonable demands that are detrimental to both the firm's survival and the community's welfare, private equity can provide an effective alternative. Verbeke and Lee (2021: 436) suggest that "private equity can be a powerful antidote against the tyranny of unreasonable demands for ever stronger ESG-performance that can threaten growth and survival." The move to private equity supports shifting the focus (and resources) from externally imposed ESG performance parameters to economic value creation and capture through efficiency. In the future, MNEs' global activities are likely to be increasingly financed by private equity firms such as The Blackstone Group, The Carlyle Group, Kohlberg Kravis Roberts (KKR), and CVC Capital Partners. Verbeke and Lee (2021) suggest that private governance is likely to prove stakeholder-centric: private equity firms can contribute superior governance capabilities that facilitate global competitiveness and thus better performance and, consequently, greater positive externalities of MNE activities. Extant research has already shown evidence to the positive spillovers of private equity (Levinson, 2006).

8.3 Summary

MNEs possess unique governance capabilities and resource bundles that allow them to create value for stakeholders (owners, employees, suppliers, and customers) while also creating positive externalities which promote global ESG objectives. However, pressure by activist media and stakeholder groups to achieve unrealistic levels of ESG performance can threaten MNE growth and even survival. When this happens, MNE owners and managers may resort to a private equity purchase as an antidote to irrational and ideologically driven ESG pressures. Paradoxically, a change to private ownership may, in fact, promote better social outcomes by saving (rather than killing) the "goose that lays the golden egg," thereby allowing the firm to continue providing value to its societal stakeholders through ESG initiatives grounded in facts rather than misinformation or irrational ideology.

9   Global Innovation Ecosystem and Institutional Fracture

"I think it's well documented that the Chinese government steals technology from American companies." Facebook Founder and CEO Mark Zuckerberg answering to questioning by Congressman Greg Steube during a congressional antitrust hearing on big tech in 2020 (Wall Street Journal, 2020)

One of the most significant features of economic globalization has been the growth of the once peripheral economies outside of North America, Europe, and Japan. Among these developing economies, the meteoric rise of China stands out above the rest. One of the assumptions of neoliberal economists and political scientists, writing in the 1990s following the collapse of the Soviet system, was that the global triumph of the free-market capitalist economic system would inevitably lead to the global triumph of the liberal democratic political system (Fukuyama, 1989). With 30-plus years of hindsight, it seems safe to say that this global flourishing of political liberalism has not materialized. While the CCP has embraced aspects of private enterprise (or, at least, a version of it), China's political institutions show no sign of moving toward a liberal democratic system of government. If anything, recent years have seen an increase in political oppression internally (e.g., increased surveillance and police presence in Hong Kong; state-sponsored internment and mistreatment of Uyghur Muslims; repression of Christians) and military aggression externally (e.g., in the South China Sea) (Economist, 2021b; Guardian, 2021; Lendon, 2021; Mead, 2020).

One of the hallmarks of China's unique "variety of capitalism" (VoC) (Jackson & Deeg, 2008) is the subordination of all aspects of economic policy to the objectives of the CCP. This includes strict regulation of both inbound and outbound FDI: inbound FDI is subject to restrictions that ensure high levels of local partnership/ownership, while outbound FDI is often directed through state-owned enterprises (SOEs) for the achievement of national/strategic (rather than purely economic) objectives. While the mobilization of tariffs and trade policy for the pursuit of national political objectives is certainly not unique to China, scholars have voiced concerns about the CCP's willingness to violate IP norms and laws in order to appropriate proprietary technologies and innovations. Petricevic and Teece (2019) argue that the CCP's approach is creating a bifurcated global economic system characterized by IP protection challenges that threaten global open innovation.

9.1   The Bright Side Opportunities of the Global Innovation Ecosystem

Commenting on the character of global economic development during the second half of the twentieth century, Petricevic and Teece (2019) note that the post-World War II period has been the time of peace and prosperity, characterized by enterprise growth, increased global investment, and transfer of advanced technology to different parts of the world. As a result, the welfare of much of the world's population has been lifted. Petricevic and Teece (2019: 1487) credit the MNE for the creation of this global innovation ecosystem: "At the micro-level, the transfer of managerial best practices in a variety of functional areas, and in overall firm-level governance, may well have been the greatest contribution of the post-WWII system—in a downward cascading motion—to the functioning of the world economy, and it was brought about by multinational enterprise (MNE) investment and capability transfers."

They further note that micro-level best practices and capabilities also cascaded upward to macro-level political institutions, promoting beneficial practices in the areas of, for example, governance, accounting, and transparency. This apparently virtuous circle, whereby unfettered global trade disseminated managerial best practices to developing countries, while simultaneously lifting those countries out of poverty and spreading the values of the European enlightenment, led to optimistic declarations of "the end of history" (Fukuyama, 1989) and that "the world is flat" (Friedman, 1953). The central belief expressed in these statements is that national borders and, increasingly, national differences were diminishing in importance.

The driving force behind these changes was the MNE. It is therefore unsurprising that contemporary management scholarship in the decades following World War II assumed the continuation of liberal trade policies and the expansion of the role of the MNE and its class of international managers. This is not to imply that management scholars naively assumed that national differences had vanished. Indeed, many influential papers have highlighted the continuing importance of institutional differences when crossing national borders. These differences were conceptualized variously as, inter alia, "distance" (Ghemawat, 2001), "varieties of capitalism" (Jackson & Deeg, 2008), "core and periphery" (Benito & Narula, 2007), etc. What these scholars did not necessarily foresee at the time, however, was the possibility that the wealth-generating power of global free trade and open innovation could be mobilized by an autocratic regime like the CCP in open defiance of the rules and norms which supposedly governed the global economic system. Petricevic and Teece (2019) argue that opportunistic economic policies such as those pursued by the CCP are creating a bifurcated global system characterized by "rule of law" countries on the one side and "rule of ruler" countries on the other.

9.2   The Dark Side Challenges of a Bifurcated Global System

Petricevic and Teece (2019: 1491) define a rule of law country as one in which "government decisions require applying legal and moral principles in a non-discriminatory way." Concerning economic activity, a key aspect of rule of law government is the protection of IP rights. Historically, IP rights have been deemed a foundational element of free societies which allows entrepreneurs to profit from innovations and encourages innovators to pursue risky ideas. In contrast, the economic policies of rule of ruler governments such as the CCP subordinate rule of law principles to strategic political objectives, including the acquisition of proprietary innovations and technology. While this acquisition often happens through legal market mechanisms such as international merger and acquisition activity and the upgrading of value chain activities located in China (e.g., Haier, HTC, and many others), the CCP also used non-market means to acquire technologies. These means often entail either asymmetric enforcement or violations of IP rules and norms. Specifically, Petricevic and Teece (2019) point to the use of cyber-enabled industrial surveillance, the requirement that foreign firms transfer sensitive IP rights to Chinese joint venture partners, and the active involvement of CCP members in the workplaces of foreign subsidiaries. China's use of industrial espionage in order to access technology is now well-documented (Blumenthal & Zhang, 2021; Canadian Press Staff, 2021; Guardian, 2020; Reuters, 2021; United States Department of Justice, 2021). Such systematic and competitive linking of cross-border technological exchanges to a nation-state's geopolitical objectives (typically at the expense of other countries' technological capabilities) has been termed the "new techno-nationalism" (Luo, 2021) and has arguably compromised and destabilized the open global innovation ecosystem.

Leaving aside the geopolitical considerations caused by the rise of the new techno-nationalism, the bifurcation of the global economic system into rule of law and rule of ruler countries creates significant challenges for managers governing international business activities, with a key consideration being how to prevent the misappropriation of sensitive IP. Petricevic and Teece argue that navigating the changed global innovation ecosystem successfully will require the careful nurturing of new dynamic capabilities (DCs) aimed at both adapting to and shaping these changes. Key among these new DCs is a capability for "knowledge buffering" (Petricevic & Teece, 2019: 1500), which entails the dispersion of knowledge across the MNE value chain while protecting sensitive IP.

Developing these capabilities is challenging given that large MNEs operate in complex ecosystems with multiple and multi-layer linkages. Some MNEs have been able to successfully buffer knowledge by increasing social complexity of their internal networks (Yan et al., 2021), dispersing sensitive knowledge across multiple foreign units (Gooris & Peeters, 2016), or explicitly structuring intangible resources so as to obscure the sources of innovation to external parties (McGaughey et al., 2000). Successful implementation of such strategies requires significant entrepreneurial acumen and relational competency on behalf of MNE managers.

9.3   Summary

The global economic norms and institutions that informed the liberalizing trade policies of the late twentieth and early twentieth century are showing signs of fracture. The international economic system is becoming bifurcated into "rule of law" and "rule of ruler" countries. The violations of international trade rules and norms by rule of ruler countries are amplifying VUCA conditions for MNEs. Of particular concern is the misappropriation of sensitive IP by political actors such as the CCP operating under the principles of new techno-nationalism. Firms wishing to profit from innovation and costly IP investments must cultivate dynamic capabilities (DCs) that allow them to implement *knowledge buffering* practices within their value chains. Only by cultivating such DCs can firms both adapt to and shape the new, bifurcated, global system.

10   Contemporary CSR Expectations and Approaches

In recent decades, both managers and scholars have increasingly focused on what has come to be known as corporate social responsibility (CSR). The increased visibility of the consequences of MNE activities in previously distant corners of the globe (e.g., the Rana Plaza disaster in Bangladesh) has made the management of reputational risks across all value chain activities a top priority of MNE managers. However, this increased commitment toward reducing the negative externalities of MNE activities raises additional questions about how firms should strategically approach their CSR initiatives.

Van Balen, Haezendonck, and Verbeke (2021: 2) identify two dominant approaches to CSR activity within both business practice and theory: (1) core CSR strategies and (2) peripheral CSR strategies. The core CSR approach focuses on initiatives that build upon a firm's extant capabilities and are linked firmly to the firm's core business model. Peripheral CSR strategies, on the other hand, view CSR activities as deliberately divorced from the firm's core business objectives.

Historically, much of the management scholarship has argued in favor of the core CSR approach and disparaged the peripheral CSR approach. In the following sections, however, we argue that the core CSR approach can be unnecessarily limiting and result in sub-optimal outcomes for both the firm and its societal stakeholders.

10.1   The Bright Side Opportunities of the Core CSR Approach

The core CSR approach has many advocates in the management scholarship (see, e.g., Aguinis & Glavas, 2013; Burke & Logsdon, 1996; Kytle & Ruggie, 2005; Laszlo & Zhexembayeva, 2011; Porter & Kramer, 2007). These scholars argue for a view of CSR that is bound up in the core capabilities and business model of the firm.

In their paper arguing in favor of the core CSR approach, Aguinis and Glavas (2013) contend that a core approach builds upon sound psychological foundations such as enhanced employee pride in their work and increased meaningfulness. These benefits arise, they argue, because staff engaging with core CSR initiatives are able to "present more of their whole selves" (Aguinis & Glavas, 2013: 319). The beneficial outcomes of a core CSR approach include improved employee engagement, improved firm reputation, improved societal and environmental benefits, and increased consumer purchase intention. From a global coordination perspective, a core CSR strategy is more efficient in that it avoids complexity and fragmentation of geographically dispersed, local CSR efforts, amplifies global benefits of CSR, and shields the MNE from potentially unsuccessful or unproductive subsidiary-level/peripheral CSR initiatives.

In contrast to these purported benefits of the core CSR approach, Porter and Kramer (2007: 7) (quoted in van Balen et al., 2021: 3) describe the peripheral CSR approach as a "hodgepodge of uncoordinated CSR and philanthropic activities disconnected from the company's strategy that neither make any meaningful social impact nor strengthen the firm's long-term competitiveness."

10.2   The Dark Side Challenges of the Core CSR Approach and the Case for Peripheral CSR

In their article examining core and peripheral CSR approaches toward plant closures, Van Balen et al. (2021) challenge the purported dominance of a core CSR strategy. The authors review several studies on core versus peripheral CSR approaches and find that "there is no conclusive evidence that the core CSR initiatives are intrinsically more valuable than initiatives more peripheral to the firm's main business operations" (van Balen et al., 2021: 3). On the societal stakeholder side of the value equation, there is no reason to expect a core CSR approach to be sufficient to mitigate the full range of negative externalities caused by the firm's activities: for example, an automobile manufacturer is unlikely to have the core competences necessary to mitigate the negative psychological impact a plant closure may have on a local community.

Further, implementing successfully a core CSR approach requires an internally integrated firm, with tight linkages across units. Without such integration, a core CSR system could be incredibly difficult and costly to operate in an international environment. Most importantly, a centralized CSR system does not account for host country context: that is, core CSR approach limits the extent to which host country stakeholders can be consulted, discourages subsidiary initiative in addressing local CSR needs (Muller, 2006), and ignores subsidiary-specific CSR competencies. In extreme cases, top-down implementation of core CSR can cause negative consequences discussed in the preceding sections of this chapters, such as the tyranny of the back office and/or significant, negative externalities in host communities.

As such, peripheral CSR approach is likely to provide superior value to a firm's local stakeholders in most situations. This contention is supported by empirical evidence: for example, Muller (2006) finds that decentralized CSR practices result in higher local CSR performance. The question then remains whether a peripheral CSR approach provides superior value to firms versus a core CSR approach. Drawing conclusions from an in-depth case study analyzing the closure of a large Belgian industrial plant, van Balen et al. (2021) find that a peripheral approach can provide superior value to the firm in the form of reputational benefits, new unique competences, and superior financial performance. However, the superiority of a peripheral CSR approach depends upon four necessary conditions: (1) the presence of institutional penalties and rewards which incentivize firms to take on CSR projects; (2) the presence of external knowledge networks which can be tapped into for the development of competences required for the CSR initiative in question; (3) the presence of favorable market conditions; and (4) a long-term CSR investment horizon.

10.3   Summary

Mainstream management scholarship has tended to make the normative argument that firms can adequately fulfill their CSR commitments through a core approach, which only pursues centralized initiatives that align with the core business model. However, this approach fails to respond to a diverse range of international stakeholders, inhibits local initiatives, and can ultimately leave many negative societal externalities unaddressed. Unmitigated social externalities can accumulate and eventually harm the firm's stakeholders and damage its reputation. Firms with a long-term investment horizon should therefore also take a long-term view of CSR activities and cultivate peripheral competences which address the full range of negative externalities cause by their activities and establish a better fit with diverse stakeholder needs. Doing so will not only provide superior value to societal stakeholders but will shore up a firm's reputation-based FSAs and lead to new capability development.

11   International Business and the Fight Against Climate Change

In a highly cited *JIBS* article, Buckley et al. (2017) call for a "renaissance" in IB scholarship. The authors argue that, in order to maintain its position as a relevant and exciting area of the social sciences, IB must seek to address the "grand challenges" confronting business leaders and policymakers in our present age. One such challenge is the global fight against climate change.

The primary vehicle through which individuals, businesses, and governments are seeking to combat climate change is through a shift away from hydrocarbon fuel sources (i.e., coal, oil and gas, and their derivatives) toward renewables such as wind, solar, and hydro. Over the past 20 years, the role of the MNE in tackling the long-term energy (LTE) transition has become a vibrant area of IB research.

In their review of the IB scholarship on the LTE transition, Bass and Grøgaard (2021) highlight two dominant approaches in the way IB scholars view MNEs with respect to the LTE transition. In the first approach, MNEs are seen as producers of renewable energy. Research taking this first view focuses on the innovation processes through which MNEs develop new products and routines that advance both the capacity and accessibility of renewable energy generation. In the second approach, MNEs are viewed as consumers of energy that may or may not be attempting to shift the balance of their energy consumption from high-carbon toward low-carbon and/or renewable sources. Here again, however, we find that there is a focus on the bright side narrative (or, perhaps, a "naïve" side narrative) and a somewhat neglected dark side.

11.1   The Bright Side Opportunities of the Long-Term Energy Transition

The long-term benefits of LTE extend beyond environmental sustainability and include such desirable outcome as energy security (i.e., safeguarding against attacks, instabilities, and energy supply manipulations, Finley, 2019) and energy accessibility (i.e., assuring reliable sources of energy outside of resource-rich countries). Worldwide recognition of these benefits has translated into rapid growth of renewable energy markets and, consequently, entrepreneurial opportunities for MNEs (Bass & Grøgaard, 2021).

The changing global energy landscape has served as an impetus for new capability development. In an empirical paper examining the imposition of carbon capture and storage (CCS) technology requirements on Canadian energy producers, Verbeke et al. (2017) introduced the concept of "imposed innovation." Verbeke et al. define imposed innovations as those which are undertaken by profit-seeking firms under the coercion by non-market actors (e.g., governments, NGOs, social activists, etc.). Interestingly, the coercion by non-market actors through imposed innovation can sometimes lead to the creation of new FSAs. In these cases, new CCS technologies and processes resulting from imposed innovations created new consumer demand

and allowed the innovating firms to capture Schumpeterian rents (i.e., higher-than-normal returns deriving from successful innovation projects). Similarly, Bass and Grøgaard (2021) suggest that energy industry incumbents can upgrade their existing FSAs to exploit opportunities in low-carbon and renewable energy sectors. Examples of MNEs that have applied their extant capabilities to re-focus on renewables include Denmark-based Ørsted, UK-based BP, and many others.

LTE transition has driven a focus on reduced carbon footprint and has given rise to creative collaborations between large energy consumers and suppliers of alternative energy sources. For example, Facebook has invested into a solar project as part of its commitment to switch to renewable energy; Microsoft is collaborating with oil and gas MNEs to develop a new CCS system (Bass & Grøgaard, 2021). These examples show how a variety of actors, including large MNEs from both within and outside the energy industry, technology start-ups, and non-market actors, can collaborate to achieve a joint objective of reducing energy consumption while developing alternative energy solutions.

11.2 The Dark Side Challenges of the Long-Term Energy Transition

Unfortunately, the linkage between LTE transition intention (typically imposed at the macro-level) and firm-level action does not always materialize as hoped for (Verbeke & Hutzschenreuter, 2021b). MNEs are assumed to engage in innovation as a result of externally imposed LTE transition commitments, but in reality, imposed innovations are not necessarily enacted at the firm level. Moreover, enacting commitments mandated by powerful non-market actors may destroy both shareholder and stakeholder value (Verbeke et al., 2017). Both policymakers and affected firms face severe bounded rationality and bounded reliability challenges when attempting to impose and enact LTE commitments. Policymakers do not understand firm-level transition processes nor the level of capital investment required on behalf of the firm to enact an imposed commitment. MNEs, in turn, are expected to enact regulations that are designed without firm-level considerations in mind and are therefore ambiguous and potentially unrealistic. Further, both sides assume bounded reliability on behalf of the other party. For example, MNEs suspect "virtue signaling" on behalf of regulators, while regulators (as well as the general public) frequently accuse MNEs seeking to enact (or rather circumvent) imposed commitments by greenwashing and political rent seeking (Swanson, 2020).

As a result, there is a strong possibility of a disconnect between the objectives of the macro-level forces imposing the transition and the actual enactment of LTE transitions by the affected firms (Verbeke & Hutzschenreuter, 2021b). When firms resist unrealistic or ill-informed commitments, no tangible innovation outcome is likely to result.

Addressing this disconnect is an important direction for future research in IB. Some preliminary evidence suggests that effective LTE transition programs should take into account firm-level features when establishing the timing and scope of imposed commitments (Andreou & Kellard, 2021) and that affected firms should be given greater latitude in enactment approaches: specifically, decisions about innovation processes and investment should be left in the hands of managers who have the necessary competences in the relevant knowledge areas (Verbeke et al., 2017).

11.3 Summary

The global LTE transition represents a "grand challenge" of contemporary IB research. Firms undergoing energy transition face a number of opportunities and challenges, including entering new markets, developing new capabilities, forming new partnerships, and, importantly, addressing expectations of powerful macro-level actors who drive LTE objectives. A direct link between imposed macro-level commitments and firm-level enactment is often assumed, yet poorly formulated policy is likely to meet resistance or marginal compliance (rather than valuable innovation) at the firm level. In this case, LTE transition benefits for either the firm or the society/environment will not materialize. Firms facing imposed innovation requirements from non-market actors must consider their strategies carefully if they are to avoid destroying value. Likewise, policymakers seeking to promote the LTE transition should leverage realistic policies that are most likely to illicit responses of active engagement from firms.

12   Conclusion

In this chapter, we have attempted to present a full canvas approach to contemporary IB phenomena by exploring both the bright and the dark sides of each issue. We posit that to compete successfully in the increasingly VUCA world, MNE managers need to achieve a more comprehensive and dynamic understanding of both the opportunities and challenges presented by new developments in their operational environments. Such intelligence is required to maximize economic value from the potential positive contributions of each development while safeguarding against negative consequences. Doing so will not only facilitate the MNE's survival and longevity, but it will also support its unique and constructive role in society and the broader environment.

The full canvas approach advocated here requires that IB scholars fully embrace the complexity of the MNE and its environment (Eden & Nielsen, 2020). Fortunately, IB theory is versatile and sophisticated, with a unique ability to simplify complex problems (Verbeke et al., 2021). Armed with the powerful tool that is IB theory, academia and management should be able to address complex, real-world phenomena in a more comprehensive way, to advance IB scholarship and improve managerial practice in internationally operating firms.

References

Aguinis, H., & Glavas, A. (2013). Embedded versus peripheral corporate social responsibility: Psychological foundations. *Industrial and Organizational Psychology, 6*(4), 314–332.

Andreou, P. C., & Kellard, N. M. (2021). Corporate environmental proactivity: Evidence from the European Union's emission trading system. *British Journal of Management, 32*(3), 630–647.

Arregle, J. L., Chirico, F., Kano, L., Kundu, S. K., Majocchi, A., & Schulze, W. S. (2021). Family firm internationalization: Past research and an agenda for the future. *Journal of International Business Studies.* https://doi.org/10.1057/s41267-021-00425-2

Arregle, J.-L., Naldi, L., Nordqvist, M., & Hitt, M. A. (2012). Internationalization of family-controlled firms: A study of the effects of external involvement in governance. *Entrepreneurship Theory and Practice, 36*(6), 1115–1143.

Azmeh, S., Foster, C., & Echavarri, J. (2020). The international trade regime and the quest for free digital trade. *International Studies Review, 22*(3), 671–692.

van Balen, M., Haezendonck, E., & Verbeke, A. (2021). Mitigating the environmental and social footprint of brownfields: The case for a peripheral CSR approach. *European Management Journal.* https://doi.org/10.1016/j.emj.2021.04.006

Bass, E., & Grøgaard, B. (2021). The long-term energy transition: Drivers, outcomes, and the role of the multinational enterprise. *Journal of International Business Studies, 52*(5), 807–823.

Benito, G. R., & Narula, R. (2007). States and firms on the periphery: The challenges of a globalizing world. In *Multinationals on the periphery* (pp. 1–24). Springer.

Blumenthal, D., & Zhang, L. (2021). China is stealing our technology and intellectual property. Congress must stop it. *National Review.* Retrieved August 4, 2021, from https://www.nationalreview.com/2021/06/china-is-stealing-our-technology-and-intellectual-property-congress-must-stop-it/

Boivie, S., Bednar, M. K., Aguilera, R. V., & Andrus, J. L. (2016). Are boards designed to fail? The implausibility of effective board monitoring. *Academy of Management Annals, 10*(1), 319–407.

Buckley, P. J. (2009). The impact of the global factory on economic development. *Journal of World Business, 44*(2), 131–143.

Buckley, P. J. (2020). The theory and empirics of the structural reshaping of globalization. *Journal of International Business Studies, 51*(2020), 1580–1592.

Buckley, P. J., Doh, J. P., & Benischke, M. H. (2017). Towards a renaissance in international business research? Big questions, grand challenges, and the future of IB scholarship. *Journal of International Business Studies, 48*(9), 1045–1064.

Burke, L., & Logsdon, J. M. (1996). How corporate social responsibility pays off. *Long Range Planning, 29*(4), 495–502.

Calabrò, A., & Mussolino, D. (2013). How do boards of directors contribute to family SME export intensity? The role of formal and informal governance mechanisms. *Journal of Management & Governance, 17*(2), 363–403.

Canadian Press Staff. (2021). Spy chief says China is bent on stealing Canadian secrets, silencing critics. *CTVNews.* Retrieved August 4, 2021, from https://www.ctvnews.ca/canada/spy-chief-says-china-is-bent-on-stealing-canadian-secrets-silencing-critics-1.5301971

Cattaneo, O., Gereffi, G., & Staritz, C. (2010). *Global value chains in a postcrisis world: A development perspective.* World Bank.

Contractor, F. J. (2022). The world economy will need even more globalization in the post-pandemic 2021 decade. *Journal of International Business Studies, 53*(1), 156–171. https://doi.org/10.1057/s41267-020-00394-y

Dalton, D. R., Daily, C. M., Ellstrand, A. E., & Johnson, J. L. (1998). Meta-analytic reviews of board composition, leadership structure, and financial performance. *Strategic Management Journal, 19*(3), 269–290.

Dixon-Fyle, S., Dolan, K., Hunt, V., & Prince, S. (2020). *Diversity wins: How inclusion matters.* McKinsey & Company. https://www.mckinsey.com/featured-insights/diversity-and-inclusion/diversity-wins-how-inclusion-matters

Economist. (2021a). China's domestic surveillance programmes benefit foreign spies. *The Economist.* Retrieved August 28, 2021, from https://www.economist.com/china/2021/04/22/chinas-domestic-surveillance-programmes-benefit-foreign-spies

Economist. (2021b). What is happening to the Uyghurs in Xinjiang? *The Economist.* Retrieved August 3, 2021, from https://www.economist.com/the-economist-explains/2021/07/12/what-is-happening-to-the-uyghurs-in-xinjiang

Eden, L., & Nielsen, B. B. (2020). Research methods in international business: The challenge of complexity. *Journal of International Business Studies, 51*(9), 1609–1620.

Fama, E. F., & Jensen, M. C. (1983). Separation of ownership and control. *The Journal of Law & Economics, 26*(2), 301–325.

Finley, M. (2019). *Energy security and the energy transition: A classic framework for a new challenge. Baker institute report no. 11.25.19.* Rice University's Baker Institute for Public Policy. https://doi.org/10.25613/DWEP-Y289

Fortune. (2020). The Coronavirus is already disrupting the global supply chain, starting with these commodities. Retrieved from https://fortune.com/2020/01/31/coronavirus-global-supply-chain-commodities/

Friedman, M. (1953). *Essays in positive economics.* University of Chicago Press.

FT. (2020). Will Coronavirus pandemic finally kill off global supply chains? Retrieved from https://www.ft.com/content/4ee0817a-809f-11ea-b0fb-13524ae1056b

Fukuyama, F. (1989). The end of history? *The National Interest, 16,* 3–18.

Ghemawat, P. (2001). Distance still matters. *Harvard Business Review, 79*(8), 137–147.

Gibson, C. B., & Gibbs, J. L. (2006). Unpacking the concept of virtuality: The effects of geographic dispersion, electronic dependence, dynamic structure, and national diversity on team innovation. *Administrative Science Quarterly, 51,* 451–495.

Gooris, J., & Peeters, C. (2016). Fragmenting global business processes: A protection for proprietary information. *Journal of International Business Studies, 47*(5), 535–562.

Gorshunov, M. A., Armenakis, A. A., Harris, S. G., & Walker, H. J. (2021). Quad-qualified audit committee director: Implications for monitoring and reducing financial corruption. *Journal of Corporate Finance, 66,* 101854.

Grant, H., & Rock, D. (2016). Why diverse teams are smarter. *Harvard Business Review, 4*(4), 2–5.

Gray, J. (1999). The new statesman essay - The myth of progress. *New Statesman.* Retrieved July 2, 2021, from https://www.newstatesman.com/node/148940

Guardian. (2020). China theft of technology is biggest law enforcement threat to US, FBI says. *the Guardian.* Retrieved August 4, 2021, from http://www.theguardian.com/world/2020/feb/06/china-technology-theft-fbi-biggest-threat

Guardian. (2021). Hong Kong: G7 calls on China to end "oppression" of democratic values. *The Guardian.* Retrieved August 3, 2021, from http://www.theguardian.com/world/2021/mar/13/hong-kong-g7-calls-on-china-to-end-oppression-of-democratic-values

Guimón, J., & Narula, R. (2020). A happy exception: The pandemic is driving global scientific collaboration. *Issues in Science and Technology.* Retrieved from https://issues.org/pandemic-global-scientific-collaboration/

Hambrick, D. C., Misangyi, V. F., & Park, C. A. (2015). The quad model for identifying a corporate director's potential for effective monitoring: Toward a new theory of board sufficiency. *Academy of Management Review, 40*(3), 323–344.

Hillman, A. J., Withers, M. C., & Collins, B. J. (2009). Resource dependence theory: A review. *Journal of Management, 35*(6), 1404–1427.

Jackson, G., & Deeg, R. (2008). Comparing capitalisms: Understanding institutional diversity and its implications for international business. *Journal of International Business Studies, 39*(4), 540–561.

Kano, L., & Verbeke, A. (2018). Family firm internationalization: Heritage assets and the impact of bifurcation bias. *Global Strategy Journal, 8*(1), 158–183. https://doi.org/10.1002/gsj.1186

Kano, L., Narula, R., & Surdu, I. (2021). Global value chain (re)configuration: Understanding the long-term structural and managerial impacts of Covid-19. *California Management Review*, advance online publication.

Kano, L., & Oh, C. H. (2020). Global value chains in the post-COVID world: Governance for reliability. *Journal of Management Studies, 57*(8), 1773–1777.

Kano, L., & Verbeke, A. (2019). Theories of the multinational firm: A microfoundational perspective. *Global Strategy Journal, 9*(1), 117–147.

Kobrin, S. J. (2021). Is a networked world economy sustainable? In A. Verbeke, R. van Tulder, E. L. Rose, & Y. Wei (Eds.), *The multiple dimensions of institutional complexity in international business research* (pp. 63–70). Emerald Publishing Limited.

Kostova, T., Marano, V., & Tallman, S. (2016). Headquarters–subsidiary relationships in MNCs: Fifty years of evolving research. *The World of Global Business 1965–2015, 51*(1), 176–184.

Kytle, B., & Ruggie, J. G. (2005). *Corporate social responsibility as risk management: A model for multinationals*. Harvard University.

Laszlo, C., & Zhexembayeva, N. (2011). Embedded sustainability: The next big competitive advantage, advance online publication 1 January.

Lendon, B. (2021). India to deploy naval task force into South China Sea and beyond. *CNN*. Retrieved August 3, 2021, from https://www.cnn.com/2021/08/03/asia/india-warships-south-china-sea-intl-hnk-ml/index.html

Levinson, M. (2006). *The box: How the shipping container made the world smaller and the world economy bigger*. Princeton University Press.

Lorenzo, R., Voigt, N., Tsusaka, M., & Abouzahr, K. (2018). How diverse leadership teams boost innovation. *BCG.com*. Retrieved from https://www.bcg.com/en-us/publications/2018/how-diverse-leadership-teams-boost-innovation

Luo, Y. (2021). A general framework of digitization risks in international business. *Journal of International Business Studies*. Retrieved from https://doi-org.ezproxy.lib.ucalgary.ca/10.1057/s41267-021-00448-9

McGaughey, S. L., Liesch, P. W., & Poulson, D. (2000). An unconventional approach to intellectual property protection: The case of an Australian firm transferring shipbuilding technologies to China. *Journal of World Business, 35*(1), 1–20.

Mead, W. R. (2020). Opinion. Beijing's collision with Christians. *Wall Street Journal*. Retrieved August 3, 2021, from https://www.wsj.com/articles/beijings-collision-with-christians-11608593160

Minbaeva, D., Fitzsimmons, S., & Brewster, C. (2021). Beyond the double-edged sword of cultural diversity in teams: Progress, critique, and next steps. *Journal of International Business Studies, 52*(1), 45–55.

Mitchell, T. R., & Daniels, D. (2003). Motivation. In W. C. Borman, D. R. Ilgen, R. J. Klimoski, & I. B. Weiner (Eds.), *Handbook of psychology, volume 12: Industrial and organizational psychology* (pp. 225–254). Wiley.

Muller, A. (2006). Global versus local CSR strategies. *European Management Journal, 24*(2–3), 189–198.

Nambisan, S., Wright, M., & Feldman, M. (2019). The digital transformation of innovation and entrepreneurship: Progress, challenges and key themes. *Research Policy, 48*, 103773.

Narula, R. (2019). Enforcing higher labor standards within developing country value chains: Consequences for MNEs and informal actors in a dual economy. *Journal of International Business Studies, 50*(9), 1622–1635.

Narula, R., & Verbeke, A. (2015). Making internalization theory good for practice: The essence of Alan Rugman's contributions to international business. *Journal of World Business, 50*(4), 612–622.

Partridge, J. (2021). Brexit: Dutch warehouse boom as UK firms forced to invest abroad. *The Guardian*. Retrieved from https://www.theguardian.com/world/2021/jan/26/brexit-dutch-warehouse-boom-as-uk-firms-forced-to-invest-abroad?fbclid=IwAR3dMH-D2G96kzpQseTofgzMOPY87gTpPrABSGbhs999Jg82hskdDXDGq60

Petricevic, O., & Teece, D. J. (2019). The structural reshaping of globalization: Implications for strategic sectors, profiting from innovation, and the multinational enterprise. *Journal of International Business Studies, 50*(9), 1487–1512.

Pfeffer, J., & Salancik, G. (1978). *The external control of organizations: A resource dependence perspective.* Harper & Row.

Porter, M., & Kramer, M. (2007). Strategy and society: The link between competitive advantage and corporate social responsibility. *Harvard Business Review, 84*(78–92), 163.

Reuters. (2021). U.S. trade war pushing China to steal tech, talent, Taiwan says. *Reuters.* Retrieved August 4, 2021, from https://www.reuters.com/article/us-taiwan-china-tech-idUSKBN2BN0II

Rugman, A. M., & Verbeke, A. (2004). A perspective on regional and global strategies of multinational enterprises. *Journal of International Business Studies, 35*(1), 3–18.

Rugman, A. M., Verbeke, A., & Nguyen, Q. T. K. (2011). Fifty years of international business theory and beyond. *Management International Review, 51*(6), 755–786.

Sanders, W. G., & Carpenter, M. A. (1998). Internationalization and firm governance: The roles of CEO compensation, top team composition, and board structure. *Academy of Management Journal, 41*(2), 158.

Silverthorne, S. (2020). *Has COVID-19 broken the global value chain?* Harvard Business School. Available at https://hbswk.hbs.edu/item/has-covid-19-broken-the-global-value-chain. Accessed 27 May 2020.

Simon, H. (1961). *Administrative behavior.* Macmillan.

Stahl, G. K., & Maznevski, M. L. (2021). Unraveling the effects of cultural diversity in teams: A retrospective of research on multicultural work groups and an agenda for future research. *Journal of International Business Studies, 52*(1), 4–22.

Stahl, G. K., Maznevski, M. L., Voigt, A., & Jonsen, K. (2010). Unraveling the effects of cultural diversity in teams: A meta-analysis of research on multicultural work groups. *Journal of International Business Studies, 41*(4), 690–709.

Stiglitz, J. E. (2002). *Globalization and its discontents.* W. W. Norton.

Swanson, A. (November 29, 2020). Nike and Coca-Cola lobby against Xinjiang forced labor bill. *New York Times.*

The Atlantic. (2020). *The modern supply chain is snapping.* Retrieved from https://www.theatlantic.com/ideas/archive/2020/03/supply-chains-and-coronavirus/608329/

United States Department of Justice. (2021). *Four Chinese nationals working with the Ministry of State Security charged with global computer intrusion campaign targeting intellectual property and confidential business information, including infectious disease research.* Retrieved August 4, 2021, from https://www.justice.gov/opa/pr/four-chinese-nationals-working-ministry-state-security-charged-global-computer-intrusion

Verbeke, A. (2013). *International business strategy.* Cambridge University Press.

Verbeke, A. (2020). Will the COVID-19 pandemic really change the governance of global value chains? *British Journal of Management, 31*(3), 444–446.

Verbeke, A., & Hutzschenreuter, T. (2021a). The dark side of digital globalization. *Academy of Management Perspectives.* https://doi.org/10.5465/amp.2020.0015

Verbeke, A., & Hutzschenreuter, T. (2021b). Imposing versus enacting commitments for the long-term energy transition: Perspectives from the firm. *British Journal of Management, 32*(3), 569–578.

Verbeke, A., Hutzschenreuter, T., & Pyasi, N. (2021). The dark side of B2B relationships in GVCs - Micro-foundational influences and strategic governance tools. *Journal of Business Research, 135*, 816–828.

Verbeke, A., & Kenworthy, T. P. (2008). Multidivisional vs metanational governance of the multinational enterprise. *Journal of International Business Studies, 39*(6), 940–956.

Verbeke, A., & Lee, I. H. I. (2021). *International business strategy* (3rd ed.). Cambridge University Press.

Verbeke, A., Osiyevskyy, O., & Backman, C. A. (2017). Strategic responses to imposed innovation projects: The case of carbon capture and storage in the Alberta oil sands industry. *Long Range Planning, 50*(5), 684–698.

Verbeke, A., van Tulder, R., Rose, E. L., & Wei, Y. (Eds.). (2021). *The multiple dimensions of institutional complexity in international business research: Progress in international business research* (Vol. 15). Edward Elgar.

Verbeke, A., & Yuan, W. (2005). Subsidiary autonomous activities in multinational enterprises: A transaction cost perspective. *Management International Review, 45*(2), 31–52.

Verbeke, A., & Yuan, W. (2020). The tyranny of the head office? Revisiting corporate headquarters' (CHQs) role in MNE subsidiary initiatives. *Journal of Organization Design, 9*(1), 2.

Verbeke, A., Yuan, W., & Kano, L. (2020). A values-based analysis of bifurcation bias and its impact on family firm internationalization. *Asia Pacific Journal of Management, 37*(2), 449–477.

Wall Street Journal. (2020). Question for CEOs: Does China steal from U.S. tech companies? *WSJ. com*. Retrieved August 2, 2021, from https://www.wsj.com/livecoverage/https-www-wsj-com-livecoverage-tech-ceos-hearing-2020/card/O39WKSXwbDcIIpTt0ECY

Williamson, O. E. (1981). The modern corporation: Origins, evolution, attributes. *Journal of Economic Literature, 19*(4), 1537–1568. http://www.jstor.org/stable/2724566

Wu, X., & Gereffi, G. (2018). Amazon and Alibaba: Internet governance, business models, and internationalization strategies. In R. van Tulder, A. Verbeke, & L. Piscitello (Eds.), *International business in the information and digital age* (pp. 327–356). Emerald Publishing Limited. https://doi.org/10.1108/S1745-886220180000013014

Yan, Y., Li, J., & Zhang, J. (2021). Protecting intellectual property in foreign subsidiaries: An internal network defense perspective. *Journal of International Business Studies*. https://doi.org/10.1057/s41267-021-00430-5

Alain Verbeke holds the McCaig Chair in Management at the University of Calgary. He is also the Inaugural Alan M. Rugman Memorial Fellow at the Henley Business School, University of Reading, and an Adjunct Professor at the Solvay Business School, Vrije Universiteit Brussel. He is the Editor-in-Chief of the *Journal of International Business Studies*. He has crafted over 40 books and over 40 substantive contributions published in AJG 4/4*journals.

Liena Kano is an Associate Professor of Strategy and Global Management and a McCaig Family Future Fund Professor in International Family Business at the Haskayne School of Business, University of Calgary, Canada. Her research interests intersect international business, strategic management, and entrepreneurship, with a particular focus on novel applications of internalization theory and on microfoundations that underlie complex international governance decisions.

Andrew Kent Johnston is a PhD student and researcher in Strategy and Global Management at the Haskayne School of Business, University of Calgary. His research interests include the impact of home and host country national institutions on the strategies of international firms and environmental negotiations between large firms, national governments, and Indigenous groups.

Emerging Research Themes in International Business

Ajai S. Gaur and Aishwarya Vashishtha

1   Introduction

International business (IB) scholarship has evolved in significant ways over the past half a century. The roots of modern IB scholarship can be traced back to the early works in understanding the rationale behind foreign direct investment (FDI) by the US multinational enterprises (MNEs) into Europe. Scholars examined the paradox of the success of US MNEs in Europe, despite the local indigenous firms having a better understanding of the local markets. The answer to this question lay in US MNEs possessing certain ownership-specific advantages that helped them overcome the locational disadvantages in host nations (Hymer, 1960; Kindleberger, 1969; McManus, 1973). The analysis of the success of US MNEs in Europe and other host nations leads to the emergence of internalization theory (Buckley & Casson, 1976) as a dominant theoretical paradigm in the IB field. Later, Dunning (1980) proposed an eclectic framework arguing that ownership-based, locational-based, and internalization advantages as necessary and sufficient conditions for FDI.

Building on this early work, scholars have examined a variety of research questions. Some recent reviews have documented these research questions for specific journals. For example, Buckley and Casson (2021) analyzed 30 years of research published in the *International Business Review* and identified six major research fields: FDI; existence, strategies, and organizational structures of MNEs; new forms of IB; emerging market multinationals; offshoring and the disaggregation of global value chains; and MNEs responses to pressures for social responsibility and sustainability. Likewise, Mukherjee, Kumar, et al. (2021) conducted a bibliometric analysis of articles published in *Management International Review* from 2006 to 2020 and identified six major clusters of research: culture; emerging

A. S. Gaur (✉) · A. Vashishtha
Department of Management and Global Business, Rutgers Business School - Newark and New Brunswick, Newark, NJ, USA
e-mail: ajai@business.rutgers.edu; av726@scarletmail.rutgers.edu

© Springer Nature Switzerland AG 2022
H. Merchant (ed.), *The New Frontiers of International Business*, Contributions to Management Science, https://doi.org/10.1007/978-3-031-06003-8_3

economies; innovation and knowledge transfer; firm internationalization; entry modes; and internationalization-performance relationship. Gaur and Kumar (2018) summarize several other review studies (e.g., Griffith et al., 2008; Seno-Alday, 2010) that have summarized the published work in the IB field. While these studies attempt to provide an agenda for future scholarship, there are inherent limitations in proposing such an agenda based on the work that has been published in the past.

In this chapter, we analyze the special issue calls that were given out by two leading IB journals—*Journal of International Business Studies (JIBS)* and *Journal of World Business (JWB)*—to identify the themes that journal editors and thought leaders consider as important areas for future scholarship. Both JIBS and JWB invite special issue proposals through an open call, encouraging scholars to submit proposals on research themes that are important and relevant but have not received enough scholarly attention. The guest editors for these special issues are often senior scholars who are thought leaders in the specific sub-field with an excellent publishing record. Typically, these journals receive 20–30 proposals every year, from which only 3–4 are selected. The main consideration in the selection of special issue proposals is if the proposed theme has the scope to generate scholarly debate in the coming years. Thus, special issue proposals reflect research themes that have the potential for future scholarship. We focus on recent calls issued between 2015 and mid-2021 to ensure that the analysis yields themes that are timely and are likely to remain important in the near future. Some of these special issues are still in process and will be completed in the next 2–3 years, which further ensures that our analysis identifies timely and relevant research themes.

We acknowledge that the focus on only two journals, JIBS and JWB, limits the scope of topics that have emerged as important ones in recent years. While the leading journals in a field reflect the cutting-edge scholarship, we hope to expand this analysis by including other important IB journals to present a more comprehensive analysis of emerging research themes in future work. In our analysis, we look into the main research questions posed by the SI editors, the premise of proposing these questions, the main theoretical frameworks used, and the thematic and geographic focus in these special issues.

2   Method: Content Analysis of Special Issue Calls

We obtained information on special issues from the website of JIBS and JWB. For some of the older special issues, we could not obtain the special issue calls. In such cases, we downloaded the guest editorials that were published at the conclusion of the special issue. The guest editorial reflects not only the content of the special issue call but also the articles that are published in a given special issue. We followed Gaur and Kumar (2018) to analyze the special issues along with a few coding categories— year of SI completion, guest editors, topic, theme, theoretical focus, and geographic focus. We identified a total of 14 special issues for JIBS and 23 for JWB. Seven JIBS special issues and ten JWB special issues were in process at the time of data coding, which was done in July 2021. Interestingly, all of the special issues involved at least one senior scholar who has served in the editorial capacity in a leading IB journal[1]. Table 1 summarizes this information.

3   Emerging Research Themes

3.1   Internationalization

Internationalization remains a dominant theme in multiple special issues. While the focus of earlier work on internalization was to examine the costs and benefits of international expansion and its linkage with firm performance, more recent work in this domain examines the internationalization of specific types of firms such as entrepreneurial ventures (Bahl et al., 2021), business groups (Singh & Delios, 2017), emerging economy firms (Singh, 2009, 2012), the role of home market context (Pattnaik et al., 2021), and exogenous shocks on firm internationalization. Some of the more recent SIs in this domain examine how firms respond to the changing geopolitical environment by either scaling up or scaling back from their international commitments. For example, Kafouros et al. (2021)'s SI in JWB underlines the dearth of content on de-internationalization and subsequent re-internationalization processes and their consequences for MNEs. A closer examination of the special issues on the theme of internationalization suggests a shift from the prior focus on the Uppsala model (Johanson & Vahlne, 1977) to gaining a more nuanced understanding of the contextual factors and the process of international expansion of different types of firms.

The continued focus on internationalization in special issues is not surprising, given that international expansion is a key theme in IB research. Buckley (2002) argued that the IB research agenda was running out of steam with no new distinctive topics around which scholars could build definitive research agendas. In response to Buckley (2002), Peng (2004) argued that firm internationalization (and its consequences) remains a key theme for future IB scholarship, and the same is reflected even after 15 years since this debate appeared in JIBS.

3.2   Innovation

Knowledge and innovation-based competitive advantages have been a key factor in the international expansion of MNEs from developed countries and remain so today (Andersson et al., 2015; Pérez-Nordtvedt et al., 2015). Several special issues focus on knowledge creation and knowledge transfer from the perspective of MNEs from developed as well as emerging economies. In the last couple of decades, MNEs' investment in emerging economies has focused on knowledge-seeking from purely

---

[1] This is true after excluding the supervising editor affiliated with the respective journals.

Table 1 Summary of special issues in JIBS and JWB (2014–2021)

Completion date	Topic	Guest editors	Theme	Geographic focus	Theoretical focus
Journal of International Business Studies					
2017	The role of financial and legal institutions in international corporate governance	Cumming et al., (2017)	Corporate legislation and governance	Global	Corporate governance
2017	International business responses to institutional voids	Doh et al., (2017)	Institutions	Emerging economies	Institutional voids
2018	The creation and capture of entrepreneurial opportunities across national borders	Knight et al., (2018)	Entrepreneurship	Global	Entrepreneurship
2018	Zoom in, zoom out, and beyond: Locational boundaries in international business	Mudambi et al., (2018)	Strategy	Global	Regionalization
2019	Making dynamic capabilities actionable for international business	Zahra et al., (2017)	Strategy	Global	Dynamic capabilities theory
2019	Applying and advancing internalization theory: Explaining the experience of the multinational enterprise in the twenty-first century	Narula et al., (2019)	Strategy (internalization)	Global	Internalization theory
2020	Making connections: Social networks in international business	Cuypers et al., (2020)	Networks	Global	Networks and social capital
In process	Business model innovations in a disruptive global environment: An international marketing perspective	Kumar et al., (2021)	Marketing	Emerging economies	Business models and marketing theories
In process	Studying intellectual property rights in international business through multiple levels of analysis	Cui et al., (2019)	Intellectual property rights	Global	OLI framework
In process	Informal institutions and international business	Dau et al., (2018)	Institutions	Global	Institutional theory
In process	Innovation in and from emerging economies	Anand et al., (2021)	Strategy (innovation)	Emerging economies	Innovation, knowledge-based view

			Focus on the context of study		
In process	Global mobility of people: Challenges and opportunities for international business	Fitzsimmons et al., (2021)	Migration	Global	Global HR theories
In process	The global scope of corporate sustainability: Multinational firms, supply chains, and the private governance of social and environmental issues	Beugelsdijk et al., (2021)	Sustainability	Global	Sustainable business models
In process	International marketing	Hult et al., (2019)	Marketing	Global	Cross-cultural consumer behavior
Journal of World Business					
2017	Emerging market multinationals: Perspectives from Latin America	Aguilera et al., (2017)	Internationalization	Latin America	Comparative and competitive advantages
2018	Business group affiliation and internationalization of emerging market firms	Gaur et al., (2015)	Internationalization	Emerging economies	Institutional theory
2018	Natural resources, multinational enterprises, and sustainable development	Shapiro et al., (2018)	Sustainability	Global	Sustainability
2018	Impact of the home country on internationalization	Cuervo-Cazurra et al., (2018)	Internationalization	Global	Internationalization theories
2018	Contextualizing international business research: Enhancing rigor and relevance	Teagarden et al., (2018)	Focus on the context of study	Global	Institutional and cultural environment
2019	National corporate governance and the multinational enterprise	Bhaumik et al., (2019)	Corporate governance	Emerging economies	Corporate governance
2020	Internationalization of social enterprises	Alon et al., (2020)	Internationalization	Global	Social entrepreneurship
2020	Interplay between intercultural communications and IB research	Szkudlarek et al., (2020)	Culture	Global	Culture and IB
2020	State capitalism in the international context	Wright et al., (2020)	State capitalism	Global	State ownership
2020	Risk mitigation and management strategies of multinational enterprises	Cavusgil et al., (2020)	Risk management	Global	MNE organization

(continued)

Table 1 (continued)

Completion date	Topic	Guest editors	Theme	Geographic focus	Theoretical focus
2021	The nature of innovation in global value chains	Ambos et al., (2021)	Global value chains	Global	Innovation and knowledge management
2021	Exploring the next generation of international entrepreneurship	Chakravarty et al., (2021)	Entrepreneurship	Global	International entrepreneurship theories
2021	Global migrants: Understanding the implications for international business and management	Hajro et al., (2019)	Migration	Global	Global HRM and migration
In process	Cycles and waves of internationalization: Determinants and consequences of de-internationalization and re-internationalization	Kafouros et al., (2021)	Internationalization	Global	Internationalization theories
In process	From "bring in" to "go global": Learning and innovation of Chinese firms along the path of inward and outward internationalization	Lyles et al., (2021)	Knowledge transfer, innovation	Emerging economies (China)	Knowledge-based view
In process	MNEs and exogenous shocks: Learning from pandemics and other major disruptions	Ahlstrom et al., (2021)	Strategy	Global	Strategic adaptation
In process	Scale-ups and scaling in an international business context	Tippmann et al., (2021)	Internationalization	Global	Internationalization
In process	Family business and international business: Breaking silos and establishing a rigorous way forward	Arregle et al., (2021)	Family firm internationalization	Global	International entrepreneurship
In process	Market and nonmarket approaches to strategic agility	Tarba et al., (2019)	Strategic agility	Global	Strategic agility
In process	Lateral collaborations across multinational enterprise structures	Schotter et al., (2019)	Lateral collaborations	Global	MNE organization
In process	Time matters: Rethinking the role of time in international business research	Plakoyiannaki et al., (2020)	Time in IB	Global	Methods focus

| In process | Reconsidering, reconceptualizing, and refashioning empirical methodology in IB research | Delios et al., (2020) | Methods in IB | Global | Methods focus |
| In process | Challenging the orthodoxy in international business research | Delios et al., (2020) | New emerging themes | Global | New themes |

Source: Table compiled by authors

resource-seeking or market-seeking type. This is reflected in the special issues commissioned by both JIBS and JWB.

For example, JWB issued a call in 2020 on the learning process of Chinese firms along the path of inward and outward internationalization. This SI poses questions such as what innovation mechanisms Chinese firms undertake along the path of internationalization, what have been their learning outcomes, and what factors are conducive or impediments to the innovation process. Another JIBS SI call by Anand, McDermott, Mudambi, and Narula (2021) encourages scholars to investigate what promotes or hinders innovation in developing countries and what factors facilitate knowledge transfer into and out of a developing economy. JIBS issued another call in a related area, focusing on how internalization theory can be advanced and applied to explain the existence of an MNC in the twenty-first century. This call highlights how the advancements in technology, particularly in the ICT field, have given firms an opportunity to internalize and reduce their costs through innovations.

3.3 Entrepreneurship

Firms are facing an overwhelming level of uncertainty in present times. The uncertainty is particularly challenging for entrepreneurs as managers need to rely on their subjective interpretation to chalk out a strategy for their international ventures. While MNCs can take the risk of entering an unexplored market with some basic information on the support of their resources and formulating the full strategy later, entrepreneurs have to do more comprehensive research and analysis before embarking on the international journey (Zahra et al., 2005).

Several probable areas for researches have been highlighted in the SI calls related to entrepreneurship. Editors have especially stressed asymmetric information leading to adverse selection and underlined the emergence of modern technologies like social media that can play a pivotal role in narrowing the gap in information asymmetry by building informational capabilities. The former relates to the category of institutionalism, where it was suggested by Cantwell et al. (2010) that the presence of institutional voids (Khanna & Palepu, 1997) in emerging economies, in particular, is likely to offer opportunities for institutional entrepreneurship (DiMaggio, 1998) and co-evolution.

Both JIBS and JWB issued calls that had direct or indirect linkages to the theme of international entrepreneurship. The JWB call on the next generation of international entrepreneurship (Chakravarty et al., 2021) focuses on how information asymmetry across national borders leads to the problem of adverse selection and how the adoption of emerging digital technologies, including social media, helps in reducing the asymmetric information for new ventures. In another open call, Arregle et al. (2021) highlight several research questions related to the international expansion of family firms. JWB had another call related to social entrepreneurship, which focused on the internationalization of social enterprises (Alon et al., 2020). Previously, JIBS issued a call that encouraged scholars to study the creation and capture of entrepreneurial opportunities across national borders (Knight et al., 2018). JIBS had a few other calls that examined the evolution of new business models in the context of both entrepreneurial and large firms (Kumar et al., 2020) and the study of social networks (Cuypers et al., 2020).

As these calls demonstrate, there are several dimensions of international entrepreneurship that are open for examination. The COVID-19 pandemic has disrupted the global business environments in ways that firms need to rethink their business models for the post-COVID era. Zahra (2021) argues that the re-shaping of global value chains, disruption of business networks, and the damage to institutions that support international business activities open up several opportunities for entrepreneurial firms. These include examination of the nature of international entrepreneurial activities by large and small firms; the strategic choices that firms make to cope up in the post-pandemic environment such as scaling down of business operations, retrenchment, or diversification; integration of social mission into the business mission; and the role of businesses in shaping the external environment in which they are embedded.

3.4   Emerging Economies and Firms

Emerging economies as contexts for theory development, testing, and analysis of new phenomena remain important. There have been several SIs focusing on emerging economies, which is consistent with the general trend of greater scholarly attention to this context (Govindarajan & Ramamurti, 2011; Lee et al., 2017; Narula, 2012). Three of the JIBS SIs and four of the JWB SIs focused on emerging markets, with two JWB SI focusing specifically on Latin America and China.

With the increasing integration between developing and developed economies in the context of value chains and innovation, new opportunities and challenges are emerging. EMNCs' innovation activities have pushed researchers to reconsider the factors that facilitate knowledge transfer (Andersson et al., 2015; Gaur et al., 2019; Nuruzzaman et al., 2018; Nuruzzaman & Singh, 2019). The shift in the direction of transfer of knowledge has mainly been attributed to the knowledge brought back to the home country from a developing country which is used by a developed economy to form new products (Brandt & Thun, 2010; Govindarajan & Ramamurti, 2011; Herrigel et al., 2013). Understanding these changes and their impact on firms requires new studies examining how advanced economy MNCs change their strategies to learn from and compete with emerging economy MNCs, what strategies EMNEs follow to capture new markets, and what promotes and hinders those strategies. There is some evidence suggesting that the strategies and organizational mechanisms required in EMNEs are somewhat different from the traditional models of MNC behavior (Aulakh & Kotabe, 2008; Contractor et al., 2007; Hoskisson et al., 2013; Luo & Tung, 2007; Meyer et al., 2009). However, there is a dearth of research on the learning mechanisms and management of MNCs as they operate in emerging economies (Mukherjee, Makarius, & Stevens, 2021). The JWB special issue call for September 2016 edition raises these questions, besides asking what role does distance (institutional, organizational, geographical) (Berry et al., 2010) play in the LKM (Learning and Knowledge Management) strategies of DMNCs and EMNCs.

The SIs on China focus on the international expansion of Chinese firms and the operations of MNEs in China. While most countries clearly lay down policies to attract inward foreign investment, very few have made similar efforts in formulating strategies aimed at promoting outward foreign investment (UNCTAD, 2018). China is one of the few nations that give equal weightage to inward and outward investments (Zhang, 2006). Chinese firms' aggressive outward foreign investments are part of the state capitalism and come under their "Go Global" agenda (Buckley et al., 2018). Some scholars have argued that emerging economy firms expand internationally to escape from the stifling domestic environment (Gaur et al., 2018) or to springboard in search of advantages that they can use in their home markets (Kumar et al., 2020; Luo & Tung, 2007; Scalera et al., 2020). The 2020 call by JWB invited papers on Chinese MNEs' learning trajectory during the course of inward and outward internationalization and the factors that support or impede the learning process.

The focus on context is also reflected in some other SIs that do not have a specific geographic focus. For example, JWB published a special issue on contextualizing IB research. This SI encouraged scholars to gain a deeper understanding of the context that they study and make use of the context to enhance the theoretical depth and empirical rigor.

3.5   Digital Technologies and New Business Models

The Third Industrial Revolution has triggered locational, organizational, and institutional changes (Makarius et al., 2020). This has led to accelerated knowledge creation, diffusion, and complexity (Foss & Pedersen, 2004), inter-organizational collaboration and openness (Chesbrough, 2003), and co-evolution of institutions with technological innovation (North, 1990). Alcácer et al. (2016) in their SI call for an analysis of how the OLI advantages of the firms have changed with the emergence of ICT. While, intuitively, IT revolution allows firms to outsource some of their production stages or operate from cheaper locations, thus dispersing the supply chain (Chen & Kamal, 2016), it may also result in the narrowing of supply chain due to some of the computer-based technologies. For example, 3D printing technique might render the global value chain of some of the MNCs rather redundant (Laplume et al., 2016). Moreover, the internet has not replaced the physical presence element in some of the firms where face-to-face interaction may be required for competence creation.

In recent years, IB scholars have written extensively on born-digital firms (firms that primarily offer ICT-based services) and born-global firms (firms that are international right from the beginning) (Banalieva & Dhanaraj, 2019; Brouthers et al., 2016; Chen et al., 2019; Coviello et al., 2017; Li et al., 2019; Nambisan et al., 2019; Shaheer & Li, 2020). For traditional firms, the implementation of technology for advantage creation should be accompanied by corresponding organizational changes

(Kapoor & Lee, 2013). This raises questions about the strategies that traditional firms can adopt to leverage data competence and what structural changes do MNEs need to bring for cross-border transfer of digital business models (Strange et al., 2020).

JIBS has commissioned a SI in 2021 on business model innovations (BMIs) in a disruptive global environment with a focus on international marketing. Here, the editors pose several important questions, including how do BMIs improve the marketing strategy of a firm and how disruptions in the value chain influence business model innovations. JWB's special issues on scale-ups and scaling in an IB context (Tippmann et al., 2021) and challenging the orthodoxy in IB research (Delios, Li, et al., 2020) also encourage investigation of the role of digital technologies and new business models in the IB context.

3.6   Institutions, Culture, and IB

Cross-national differences as reflected in the national institutions and culture continue to dominate the IB scholarship. Several publications and special issues have focused on understanding how cross-national differences impact different IB-related activities (Singh & Gaur, 2012). While the past research focused on different aspects of cross-national differences measured in terms of cultural and institutional distances and their impact on MNC strategies and performance, more recent work has moved toward developing a nuanced understanding of specific aspects of institutions and culture.

For example, Dau et al. (2018) in their JIBS SI argued that while formal institutions have been extensively covered in the IB literature, informal institutions have not received adequate attention. This SI encouraged scholars to come up with novel ways of measuring informal institutions and examine the interactions between formal and informal institutions and the impact of informal institutions on MNE strategy. An earlier SI of JIBS focused on comparing the nature of institutional voids in emerging and advanced economies and differences in MNEs' strategies in responding to them (Doh et al., 2017). Other calls looked at more specific aspects of institutions such as financial and legal institutions (Cumming et al., 2017) and intellectual property protection (Cui et al., 2019) and their impact on MNEs.

Compared to institutions, culture has received relatively less attention in special issues in leading journals, despite the continued dominance of different aspects of culture in specific research papers. This suggests that the novelty of culture as a construct for IB scholarship may be on a decline. The only SI call on culture during the time period of this study was issued by JWB (Szkudlarek et al., 2020). This call examined the interplay between intercultural communications and IB research and argued that we need to shift our focus from a cross-cultural perspective to an intercultural perspective and from a static perspective to a processual perspective. Some of the recent research has started to examine culture in a more nuanced way moving beyond the construct of cultural distance (Singh et al., 2019).

3.7   Other Emerging Themes

Some other important research themes emerged from the analysis of the SIs, even though only one or two SIs were devoted to such themes. For example, corporate sustainability has emerged as an important topic of research in the IB domain even though only two SIs (one each in JIBS and JWB) were specifically devoted to this topic (Holtbrügge & Dögl, 2012; Kolk et al., 2017). The SIs on sustainability gave a call to study the differences between developed and developing countries on sustainable businesses and how developing countries and MNEs affect each other with regard to sustainability. Sustainability is being viewed in broader terms as something that is about not just environmental protection but also economic prosperity and social equity (Bansal, 2005; Bansal & Song, 2017).

In the 2021 JIBS SI (Beugelsdijk et al., 2021), guest editors ask some basic questions such as how we define a sustainable business for an MNE and how the practice of sustainability is different from corporate social responsibility. Relatedly, the SI asks if sustainable global value chains are even possible. Many countries have implemented strict regulations to ensure that business and human rights violations do not take place in supply chains of businesses. Beugelsdijk et al. (2021) in their JIBS SI invite scholars to examine how MNCs respond to the increasing pressure of being environmentally and socially responsible and how they ensure this responsibility among their global suppliers. JWB issued a special issue call that was to be handled by the JWB editors on the role of MNCs in UN sustainable development goals (SDGs). This call focused on specific ways by which multinational organizations contribute to or impede progress toward UN SDGs and what importance do sustainable development goals hold in multinational organizations' decisions.

There have also been calls on the impact of the COVID-19 pandemic and other such disruptions on IB activities (Fainshmidt et al., 2021). The 2021 call from JWB invited papers on how MNEs respond to different types of exogenous shocks (Ahlstrom et al., 2021). JWB issued a few other calls that indirectly examined the impact of the COVID-19 pandemic on issues pertaining to MNEs such as scaling in IB context (Tippmann et al., 2021) and determinants and consequences of de-internationalization and re-internationalization. COVID-19 pandemic also significantly impacted the global movement of labor force and forced MNCs to reconfigure their global value chains. JIBS issued a SI call to examine how global mobility of people impacts IB activities (Fitzsimmons et al., 2021). The 2021 call of JWB on "challenging the orthodoxy in IB research" presents several themes for future scholarly work. In this call, the guest editors (Delios, Welch, et al., 2020) present three thematic areas for future scholarly work—social and societal aspects of IB, the digital world and theories of IB, and globalization, global value chains, and IB.

4   Conclusion

Our analysis of the SIs published in JIBS and JWB between 2015 and mid-2021 reveals some interesting insights. First, there has been a visible shift in the importance of different topics as reflected by the recent special issues. While topics such as internationalization and entry mode received significant scholarly attention, the recent trends suggest a shift toward topics such as sustainability, global value chains, migration, digitization, and innovation. Second, recent special issues demonstrate a greater focus on phenomena such as sustainability and migration that are socially relevant and practically important. Third, there is increased focus on multidisciplinarity in both the theoretical and empirical approaches to address a given set of problems. While multidisciplinarity in theoretical approaches has been often discussed in conferences and other academic discourse, recent calls have made an explicit note of the need to borrow from and integrate with other disciplines while developing the theoretical explanations for a given empirical question. JWB has issued calls on methodological advances, encouraging scholars to utilize novel methods such as big data analytics, historical accounts, ethnographies, narratives, and photography, borrowing from different disciplines.

It should be noted that the SI calls lacked a focus on specific theories, even though internalization theory; OLI framework; institutional perspective, from both the sociological tradition and the economics tradition; resource-based view; dynamic capability perspective; and knowledge-based view were evoked upon in several SI calls. Only JIBS had SI calls that had a clear theoretical focus on internalization theory, dynamic capabilities, and institutional perspective. This is not surprising given that IB topics tend to be more phenomena-driven. In fact, JWB has made it an explicit part of its positioning to focus on phenomena-based research (Doh, 2015), and this is reflected in the type of SI calls that have been put forth by JWB.

Acedo and Cassillas (2005) argue that integration of the field by theory is necessary and stresses the importance of OLI. However, even though Dunning's OLI framework and internalization theory have been the main theoretical frameworks in a large number of IB studies, there is no single unifying framework for all of IB research. We posit that the complexity of IB research arising due to the focus on phenomena, interdisciplinary, and several layers of analysis makes it difficult to identify a narrow set of theoretical foundations. Such a lack of a unified theoretical framework is not a weakness of the field but a reflection of its relative maturity.

However, this maturity is unequally developed. While some of the "classic" topics have strong theoretical foundations, many others lack any specific framework and often rely on too much eclecticism. For example, research on internationalization is strongly routed in the OLI framework, but studies on sustainability rely on multiple theories depending on the specific research question. This provides an opportunity for further theory development. For example, even though there are several IB studies and some SI calls focused on network relationships, network theory and methods are relatively underused in the IB literature. Furthermore, as many topics address a phenomenon on either country, firm, or individual levels, they reflect the different starting points of IB research on the macro and micro level (Cantwell & Brannen, 2016) with different theoretical perspectives. Some of the topics deal with multiple levels, and they can play a leading role in developing a multi-level theory to explain IB phenomena.

The multi-level nature of the IB phenomena could be better explained if scholars utilize novel methodological approaches, including multi-level research methods and big data analytics, to make use of large swaths of data that are increasingly accessible for scholarly work. For example, the importance of language is well recognized within IB, but the analysis of text is relatively rare. With the analytic tools in text and visual analysis (Duriau et al., 2007), content analysis is a maturing method to develop new constructs that can more accurately represent the variables of interest. In addition, translation tools into English allow the use of raw data in different languages which is particularly important for IB studies. As many methods are based on word counts, the results are relatively insensitive to translation issues. Text analysis is not limited to content, but extends to sentiment and discourse analysis. Sentiment analysis, which is the assessment of positive or negative moods, can provide new avenues for a nuanced analysis of the micro-foundations of decision-making in global organizations.

Finally, there are a few important themes that deserve attention by IB scholars but are not reflected in any recent SIs. For example, there is scope to do further work on the topic of risk management (Singh & Gaur, 2021) with research on climate change and terrorism. Other topics such as globalization and regionalization probably need a revival. Given the dynamic nature of the IB field and recent events and sentiments against globalization, time is ripe for IB scholars to revisit some of these topics and study them in a theoretically rigorous manner. Recent years have not only sharpened the global awareness of terrorism but also brought growing nationalism in many economies around the world. The emergence of right-wing nationalists is likely to result in greater internal focus in many economies. As IB scholars, we often take growing openness for international business as granted—we may need to reconsider this premise. Several scholars have argued that the fear of losing due to globalization is driving individuals to prefer right-wing and populist parties (Casson, 2021; Cuervo-Cazurra et al., 2020). As IB scholars, we need to take these fears seriously; research on the impact of globalization on individuals and how to mitigate its potential detrimental effects seems to be an overdue topic. While the existing work largely focuses on the MNE, its subsidiaries, the individuals within the MNE, and the relationship with its stakeholders, there is a need to give more attention to the impact of firms on a broader set of stakeholders. For example, the research on expatriates need to move beyond individual employees in large organizations and include the role of migrants for local entrepreneurship and innovation. We hope our review encourages scholars to find relevant research questions and take a bold stand in advancing the IB field.

References

Acedo, F. J., & Cassillas, J. C. (2005). Internationalization of Spanish family SMEs: An analysis of family involvement. *International Journal of Globalisation and Small Business, 1*(2). https://doi.org/10.1504/IJGSB.2005.008010

Aguilera, R. V., Ciravegna, L., Cuervo-Cazurra, A., & Gonzalez-Perez, M. A. (2017). Emerging market multinationals: Perspectives from Latin America. *Journal of World Business, 52*(4), 447–460.

Ahlstrom, D., Ciravegna, L., Michailova, S., Gaur, A., & Oh, C. H. (2021). MNEs and exogenous shocks: Learning from pandemics and other major disruptions. *Journal of World Business*, call for papers. Retrieved from the AIB email archives.

Alcácer, J., Cantwell, J. & Piscitello, L. (2016). Internationalization in the information age: A new era for places, firms, and international business networks?. Journal of International Business Studies, 47, 499–512.

Alon, I., Mersland, R., Musteen, M., & Randøy, T. (2020). The research frontier on internationalization of social enterprises. *Journal of World Business, 55*(5), 101091.

Ambos, B., Brandl, K., Perri, A., Scalera, V. G., & Assche, A. V. (2021). The nature of innovation in global value chains. *Journal of World Business, 56*(4), 101221.

Anand, J., McDermott, G., Mudambi, R., & Narula, R. (2021). Innovation in and from emerging economies. *Journal of International Business Studies, 52*, 545–559.

Andersson, U., Gaur, A. S., Mudambi, R., & Persson, M. (2015). Inter-unit knowledge transfer in multinational enterprises. *Global Strategy Journal, 5*(3), 241–255.

Arregle, J., Calabrò, A., Hitt, M. A., Kano, L., & Schwens, C. (2021). Family business and international business: Breaking silos and establishing a rigorous way forward. *Journal of World Business*, call for papers. Retrieved from the AIB email archives.

Aulakh, P. S., & Kotabe, M. (2008). Institutional changes and organizational transformation in developing economies. *Journal of International Management, 14*(3), 209–216.

Bahl, M., Lahiri, S., & Mukherjee, D. (2021). Managing internationalization and innovation tradeoffs in entrepreneurial firms: Evidence from transition economies. *Journal of World Business, 56*(1), 101150.

Banalieva, E. R., & Dhanaraj, C. (2019). Internalization theory for the digital economy. *Journal of International Business Studies, 50*(8), 1372–1387.

Bansal, P. (2005). Evolving sustainably: A longitudinal study of corporate sustainable development. *Strategic Management Journal, 26*(3), 197–218.

Bansal, T., & Song, H. (2017). Similar but not the same: Differentiating corporate sustainability from corporate responsibility. *The Academy of Management Annals, 11*(1), 105–149.

Berry, H., Guillén, M., & Zhou, N. (2010). An institutional approach to cross-national distance. *Journal of International Business Studies, 41*(9), 1460–1480.

Beugelsdijk, S., Doh, J., Kostova, T., Marano, V., & Wilhelm, M. (2021). The global scope of corporate sustainability: Multinational firms, supply chains, and the private governance of social and environmental issues. *Journal of International Business Studies*, call for papers. Retrieved from the AIB email archives.

Bhaumik, S., Driffield, N., Gaur, A., Mickiewicz, T., & Vaaler, P. (2019). National corporate governance and the multinational enterprise. *Journal of World Business, 54*(4), 234–243.

Brandt, L., & Thun, E. (2010). The fight for the middle: Upgrading, competition, and industrial development in China. *World Development, 38*(11), 1555–1574.

Brouthers, K. D., Geisser, K. D., & Rothlauf, F. (2016). Explaining the internationalization of i-business firms. *Journal of International Business Studies, 47*(5), 513–534.

Buckley, P. J. (2002). Is the international business research agenda running out of steam. *Journal of International Business Studies, 33*(2), 365–373.

Buckley, P. J., & Casson, M. C. (1976). *The future of the multinational enterprise*. Homes and Meier Press.

Buckley, P. J., & Casson, M. C. (2021). Thirty years of international business review and international business research. *International Business Review, 30*(2). https://doi.org/10.1016/j.ibusrev.2021.101795

Buckley, P. J., Clegg, L. J., Voss, H., Cross, A. R., Liu, X., & Zheng, P. (2018). A retrospective and agenda for future research on Chinese outward foreign direct investment. *Journal of International Business Studies, 49*(1), 4–23.

Cantwell, J., & Brannen, M. Y. (2016). The changing nature of the international business field, and the progress of JIBS. *Journal of International Business Studies, 47*(9), 1023–1031.

Cantwell, J., Dunning, J. H., & Lundan, S. M. (2010). An evolutionary approach to understanding international business activity: The co-evolution of MNEs and the institutional environment. *Journal of International Business Studies, 41*(4), 567–586.

Casson, M. (2021). International business policy in an age of political turbulence. *Journal of World Business, 56*(6), 101263.

Cavusgil, S. T., Deligonul, S., Ghauri, P., Bamiatzi, V., Mellahi, K., & Park, B. (2020). Risk mitigation and management strategies of multinational enterprises. *Journal of World Business, 55*(2).

Chakravarty, S., Cumming, D. J., Murtinu, S., Scalera, V. G., & Schwens, C. (2021). Exploring the next generation of international entrepreneurship. *Journal of World Business, 56*(5), 101229.

Chen, L., Shaheer, N., Yi, J., & Li, S. (2019). The international penetration of ibusiness firms: Network effects, liabilities of outsidership and country clout. *Journal of International Business Studies, 50*(2), 172–192.

Chen, W., & Kamal, F. (2016). The impact of information and communication technology adoption on multinational firm boundary decisions. *Journal of International Business Studies, 47*(5), 563–576.

Chesbrough, H. W. (2003). *Open innovation: The new imperative for creating and profiting from technology*. Harvard Business Press.

Contractor, F. J., Kumar, V., & Kundu, S. K. (2007). Nature of the relationship between international expansion and performance: The case of emerging market firms. *Journal of World Business, 42*(4), 401–417.

Coviello, N., Kano, L., & Liesch, P. W. (2017). Adapting the Uppsala model to a modern world: Macro-context and microfoundations. *Journal of International Business Studies, 48*(9), 1151–1164.

Cuervo-Cazurra, A., Doz, Y., & Gaur, A. (2020). Skepticism of globalization and global strategy: Increasing regulations and countervailing strategies. *Global Strategy Journal, 10*(1), 3–31.

Cuervo-Cazurra, A., Luo, Y., Ramamurti, R., & Ang, S. H. (2018). Impact of the home country on internationalization. *Journal of World Business, 53*(5), 593–604.

Cui, V., Minbaeva, D., Narula, R., & Vertinsky, I. (2019). Studying intellectual property rights in international business through multiple levels of analysis. *Journal of International Business Studies,* call for papers. Retrieved from the AIB email archives.

Cumming, D., Filatotchev, I., Knill, A., Senbet, L., & Reeb, D. (2017). The role of financial and legal institutions in international corporate governance. *Journal of International Business Studies, 48*(2), 123–147.

Cuypers, I. R. P., Ertug, G., Cantwell, J., Zaheer, A., & Kilduff, M. (2020). Making connections: Social networks in international business. *Journal of International Business Studies, 51*(5), 714–736.

Dau, L. A., Chacar, A., Lyles, M., & Li, J. (2018). Informal institutions and international business. *Journal of International Business Studies,* call for papers. Retrieved from the AIB email archives.

Delios, A., Li, J., Schotter, A. P. J., Vrontis, D., & Gaur, A. (2020). Challenging the orthodoxy in international business research. *Journal of World Business,* call for papers.

Delios, A., Welch, C., Nielsen, B., Brewster C., Tippmann, E., & Aguinis, H. (2020). Reconsidering, reconceptualizing and refashioning empirical methodology in IB research. *Journal of World Business,* Retrieved from the AIB email archives.

DiMaggio, P. (1998). The new institutionalism: Avenues of collaboration. *Journal of Institutional and Theoretical Economics, 154*(4), 696–705.

Doh, J. (2015). From the Editor: Why we need phenomenon-based research in international business. *Journal of World Business, 50*(4), 609–611.

Doh, J., Rodrigues, S., Saka-Helmhout, A., & Makhija, M. (2017). International business responses to institutional voids. *Journal of International Business Studies, 48*(3), 293–307.

Dunning, J. (1980). Toward an eclectic theory of international production: Some empirical tests. *Journal of International Business Studies, 11*, 9–31.

Duriau, V. J., Reger, R. K., & Pfarrer, M. D. (2007). A content analysis of the content analysis literature in organization studies: Research themes, data sources, and methodological refinements. *Organizational Research Methods, 10*(1), 5–34.

Fainshmidt, S., Andrews, D., Gaur, A. S., & Schotter, A. (2021). Recalibrating management research for the post-COVID scientific enterprise. *Journal of Management Studies, 58*(5), 1416–1420.

Fitzsimmons, S., Minbaeva, D., Phene, A., & Narula, R. (2021). Global mobility of people: Challenges and opportunities for international business. *Journal of International Business Studies*, call for papers. Retrieved from the AIB email archives.

Foss, N. J., & Pedersen, T. (2004). Organizing knowledge processes in the multinational corporation: An introduction. *Journal of International Business Studies, 35*(5), 340–349.

Gaur, A., & Kumar, M. (2018). A systematic approach to conducting review studies: An assessment of content analysis in 25 years of IB research. *Journal of World Business, 53*(2), 280–289.

Gaur, A., Lu, J., Kumar, V., & Hoskisson, R. (2015). Business group affiliation and internationalization of emerging market firms. *Journal of World Business*, call for papers. Retrieved from the AIB email archives.

Gaur, A., Ma, X., & Ding, Z. (2018). Home country supportiveness/unfavorableness and outward foreign direct investment from China. *Journal of International Business Studies, 49*(3), 324–345.

Gaur, A. S., Ma, H., & Ge, B. (2019). MNC strategy, knowledge transfer context, and knowledge flow in MNCs. *Journal of Knowledge Management, 23*(9), 1885–1900.

Govindarajan, V., & Ramamurti, R. (2011). Reverse innovation, emerging markets, and global strategy. *Global Strategy Journal, 1*(3–4), 191–205.

Griffith, D. A., Cavusgil, S. T., & Xu, S. (2008). Emerging themes in international business research. *Journal of International Business Studies, 39*, 1220–1235.

Hajro, A., Caprar, D. V., Zikic, J., & Stahl, G. K. (2019). Global migrants: Understanding the implications for international business and management. *Journal of World Business, 56*(2), 101192.

Herrigel, G., Wittke, V., & Voskamp, U. (2013). The process of Chinese manufacturing upgrading: Transitioning from unilateral to recursive mutual learning relations. *Global Strategy Journal, 3*(1), 109–125.

Holtbrügge, D., & Dögl, C. (2012). How international is corporate environmental responsibility? A literature review. *Journal of International Management, 18*(2), 180–195.

Hoskisson, R. E., Wright, M., Filatotchev, I., & Peng, M. W. (2013). Emerging multinationals from mid-range economies: The influence of institutions and factor markets. *Journal of Management Studies, 50*(7), 1295–1321.

Hult, G. T. M., Katsikeas, C. S., & Samiee, S. (2019). International marketing. *Journal of International Business Studies*, call for papers. Retrieved from the AIB email archives.

Hymer, S. (1960). *The international operations of national firms: A study of direct foreign investment*. The MIT Press.

Johanson, J., & Vahlne, J. (1977). The internationalization process of the firm – A model of knowledge development and increasing foreign market commitments. *Journal of International Business Studies, 8*, 23–32.

Kafouros, M., Cavusgil, S. T., Devinney, T. M., Ganotakis, P., & Fainshmidt, S. (2021). Cycles of de-internationalization and re-internationalization: Towards an integrative framework. *Journal of World Business*. https://doi.org/10.1016/j.jwb.2021.101257

Kapoor, R., & Lee, J. M. (2013). Coordinating and competing in ecosystems: How organizational forms shape new technology investments. *Strategic Management Journal, 34*(3), 274–296.

Khanna, T., & Palepu, K. G. (1997). Why focused strategies may be wrong for emerging markets. *Harvard Business Review, 75*(4), 41–51.

Kindleberger, C. P. (1969). The theory of direct investment. In C. Kindleberger (Ed.), *American business abroad*. Yale University Press.

Knight, G. A., Reuber, A. R., Liesch, P. W., & Zhou, L. (2018). The creation and capture of entrepreneurial opportunities across national borders. *Journal of International Business Studies, 49*(4), 395–406.

Kolk, A., Kourula, A., & Pisani, N. (2017). Multinational enterprises and the sustainable development goals: What do we know and how to proceed? *Transnational Corporations, 24*(3), 9–32.

Kumar, V., Samiee, S., Cornwell, B., & Katsikeas, C. (2021). Business model innovations in a disruptive global environment: An international marketing perspective. *Journal of International Business Studies,* call for papers. Retrieved from the AIB email archives.

Kumar, V., Singh, D., Purkayastha, A., Popli, M., & Gaur, A. (2020). Springboard internationalization by emerging market firms: Speed of first cross-border acquisition. *Journal of International Business Studies, 51*(2), 172–193.

Laplume, A. O., Petersen, B., & Pearce, J. M. (2016). Global value chains from a 3D printing perspective. *Journal of International Business Studies, 47*(5), 595–609.

Lee, C. Y., Lee, J. H., & Gaur, A. S. (2017). Are large business groups conducive to industry innovation? The moderating role of technological appropriability. *Asia Pacific Journal of Management, 34*(2), 313–337.

Li, J., Chen, L., Yi, J., Mao, J., & Liao, J. (2019). Ecosystem-specific advantages in international digital commerce. *Journal of International Business Studies, 50*(9), 1448–1463.

Luo, Y., & Tung, R. L. (2007). International expansion of emerging market enterprises: A springboard perspective. *Journal of International Business Studies, 38*(4), 481–498.

Lyles, M. A., Tsang, E. W. K., Li, S., Hong, J. F. L., Cooke, F. L, & Lu, J. (2021). From "bring in" to "go global": Learning and innovation of Chinese firms along the path of inward and outward internationalization. *Journal of World Business,* call for papers.

Makarius, E. E., Mukherjee, D., Fox, J., & Fox, A. K. (2020). Rising with the machines: A sociotechnical framework for bringing artificial intelligence into the organization. *Journal of Business Research, 120*, 262–273.

McManus, J. C. (1973). *The theory of the international firm*. SAGE.

Meyer, K. E., Estrin, S., Bhaumik, S. K., & Peng, M. W. (2009). Institutions, resources, and entry strategies in emerging economies. *Strategic Management Journal, 30*(1), 61–80.

Mudambi, R., Li, L., Ma, X., Makino, S., Qian, G., & Boschma, R. (2018). Zoom in, zoom out, and beyond: Locational boundaries in international business. *Journal of International Business Studies, 49*(8), 929–941.

Mukherjee, D., Kumar, S., Donthu, N., & Pandey, N. (2021). Research published in management international review from 2006 to 2020: A bibliometric analysis and future directions. *Management International Review*. https://doi.org/10.1007/s11575-021-00454-x

Mukherjee, D., Makarius, E., & Stevens, C. E. (2021). A reputation transfer perspective on the internationalization of emerging market firms. *Journal of Business Research, 123*(C), 568–579.

Nambisan, S., Zahra, S. A., & Luo, Y. (2019). Global platforms and ecosystems: Implications for international business theories. *Journal of International Business Studies, 50*(9), 1464–1486.

Narula, R. (2012). Do we need different frameworks to explain infant MNEs from developing countries? *Global Strategy Journal, 2*(3), 188–204.

Narula, R., Asmussen, C. G., Chi, T., & Kundu, S. K. (2019). Applying and advancing internalization theory: Explaining the experience of the multinational enterprise in the 21st century. *Journal of International Business Studies, 50*(8), 1231–1252.

North, D. (1990). *Institutions, institutional change, and economic performance*. Cambridge University Press.

Nuruzzaman, N., & Singh, D. (2019). Exchange characteristics, capability upgrading, and innovation performance: Evidence from Latin America. *Journal of Knowledge Management, 23*(9), 1747–1763.

Nuruzzaman, N., Singh, D., & Pattnaik, C. (2018). Competing to be innovative: Foreign competition and imitative innovation of emerging economy firms. *International Business Review, 28*(5), 101490.

Pattnaik, C., Singh, D., & Gaur, A. S. (2021). Home country learning and international expansion of emerging market multinationals. *Journal of International Management, 27*(3), 100781.

Peng, M. (2004). Identifying the big question in international business research. 35 (2): 99–108.

Pérez-Nordtvedt, L., Mukherjee, D., & Kedia, B. L. (2015). Cross-border learning, technological turbulence and firm performance. *Management International Review, 55*, 23–51.

Plakoyiannaki, E., Paavilainen-Mäntymäki, E., Hassett, M. E., Rose, E. L., Liesch, P. W., & Andersson, U. (2020). Time matters: Rethinking the role of time in international business research. *Journal of World Business*, call for papers. Retrieved from the AIB email archives.

Scalera, V. G., Mukherjee, D., & Piscitello, L. (2020). Ownership strategies in knowledge-intensive cross-border acquisitions: Comparing Chinese and Indian MNEs. *Asia Pacific Journal of Management, 37*(1), 155–185.

Schotter, A. P. J., Maznevski, M., Doz, Y., & Stahl, G. K. (2019). Lateral collaborations across multinational enterprise structures. *Journal of World Business*, call for papers. Retrieved from the AIB email archives.

Seno-Alday, S. (2010). International business thought: A 50-year footprint. *Journal of International Management, 16*(1), 16–31.

Shaheer, N. A., & Li, S. (2020). The CAGE around cyberspace? How digital innovations internationalize in a virtual world. *Journal of Business Venturing, 35*(1). https://doi.org/10.1016/j.jbusvent.2018.08.002

Shapiro, D., Hobdari, B., Peng, M. W., & Oh, C. H. (2018). Natural resources, multinational enterprises and sustainable development. *Journal of World Business, 53*(1), 1–14.

Singh, D. (2009). Export performance of emerging market firms. *International Business Review, 18*(4), 321–330.

Singh, D. (2012). Emerging economies and multinational corporations: An institutional approach to subsidiary management. *International Journal of Emerging Markets, 7*(4), 397–410.

Singh, D., & Delios, A. (2017). Corporate governance, board networks and growth strategies. *Journal of World Business, 52*(5), 615–627.

Singh, D., & Gaur, A. (2012). Institutional distance and international strategy. In A. Verbeke & H. Merchant (Eds.), *Handbook of research on international strategic management* (pp. 328–341). Edward Elgar Publishing.

Singh, D., & Gaur, A. S. (2021). Risk mitigation in international B2B relationships: Role of institutions and governance. *Journal of Business Research, 136*, 1–9.

Singh, D., Pattnaik, C., Lee, J. Y., & Gaur, A. S. (2019). Subsidiary staffing, cultural friction, and subsidiary performance: Evidence from Korean subsidiaries in 63 countries. *Human Resource Management, 58*(2), 219–234.

Strange, R., Fleury, M. T. L., & Chen, L. (2020). The impact of digital technologies on firms' international strategies. *Journal of International Management*, call for papers. Retrieved from the AIB email archives.

Szkudlarek, B., Zander, L., Nardon, L., & Osland, J. (2020). Interplay between intercultural communications and IB research. *Journal of World Business, 55*(6), 101126.

Tarba, S. Y., Frynas, J. G., Liu, Y., Wood, G., Sarala, R. M., & Fainshmidt, S. (2019). Market and nonmarket approaches to strategic agility. *Journal of World Business*, call for papers. Retrieved from the AIB email archives.

Teagarden, M. B., Glinow, M. A. V., & Mellahi, K. (2018). Contextualizing international business research: Enhancing rigor and relevance. *Journal of World Business, 53*(3), 303–306.

Tippmann, E., Ambos, T., Giudice, M.D., Monaghan, S., & Ringov, D. (2021). Scale-ups and scaling in an international business context. *Journal of World Business*, call for papers. Retrieved from the AIB email archives.

United Nations Conference on Trade and Development (UNCTAD). (2018). *World investment report*. United Nations.

Wright, M., Wood, G., Musacchio, A., Okhmatovskiy, I., Grosman, A., & Doh, J. P. (2020). State capitalism in international context: Varieties and variations. *Journal of World Business, 56*(2), 101160.

Zahra, S. A. (2021). International entrepreneurship in the post Covid world. *Journal of World Business, 56*(1), 101–143.

Zahra, S. A., George, G., & Wiklund, J. (2005). Ownership and the internationalization of small firms. *Journal of Management, 31*(2), 210–233.

Zahra, S. A., Petricevic, O., Luo, Y., & Zollo, M. (2017). Making dynamic capabilities actionable for international business. *Journal of International Business Studies*, call for papers. Retrieved from the AIB email archives.

Zhang, K. H. (2006). *Foreign direct investment and economic growth in China: A panel data study for 1992-2004*. Conference of WTO, China and the Asian Economies, IV: Economic integration and economic development, University of International Business and Economics, Beijing, China.

Ajai S. Gaur is a Professor of Strategic Management and International Business at Rutgers Business School. He is a Fellow of the Academy of International Business and currently serves as the Editor-in-Chief of the *Journal of World Business* and a Consulting Editor at the *Journal of International Business Studies*. He served as the President of the Asia Academy of Management from 2015 to 2019.

Aishwarya Vashishtha is a Ph.D. student in International Business at Rutgers Business School. He did his MBA and MS in Data Analytics at Clarkson University, New York. His research interests are in emerging economies and emerging technologies, though he is also exploring other areas as a doctoral student.

The Lingering Effect of Slavery and Colonial History on International Business: The Case of Sub-Saharan Africa

Albert Wöcke and Helena Barnard

1   Introduction

In the first decade of 2000, Africa grew at a faster rate than Asia. *The Economist* led with an article in December 2011 that projected that Africa could replace Asia as the fastest growing region in the next few decades. The cover was entitled "Africa Rising"[1] and highlighted various reasons why the continent was growing at a quicker pace than Asia. These reasons included the commodities boom, the investment in infrastructure by non-Western countries such as China and Brazil, and the rapid expansion of the African middle class, as well as the expansion of telecommunications, infrastructure, mobile banking, and retail across SSA. But at the same time, *The Economist* warned that it was still difficult to do business in many Sub-Saharan Africa (SSA) countries, many governments were outrageously corrupt, and politicians stubbornly stayed in power for longer than they should. This context leads to our suggested themes for scholars interested in International Business in SSA (Table 1).

These themes have been repeated in scholarly work. Although the African continent, and, in particular, SSA[2], is seen as a region of great opportunities, various scholars have also pointed out the challenges of doing business in Africa (Asongu & Odhiambo, 2019; Barnard et al., 2017). These tensions suggest that SSA offers a rich context for IB research. In this chapter, we suggest that both slavery and the quite recent and lingering colonial history of Africa are important but understudied

---

[1] https://www.economist.com/leaders/2011/12/03/africa-rising
[2] North Africa in many ways is closer to the Middle East than to sub-Saharan Africa. In this chapter, we refer to SSA and Africa interchangeably.

A. Wöcke (✉) · H. Barnard
Gordon Institute of Business Science, University of Pretoria, Johannesburg, South Africa
e-mail: wockea@gibs.co.za; barnardh@gibs.co.za

© Springer Nature Switzerland AG 2022   73
H. Merchant (ed.), *The New Frontiers of International Business*, Contributions to Management Science, https://doi.org/10.1007/978-3-031-06003-8_4

Table 1 Suggested research themes for Sub-Saharan Africa

Research theme	Suggested research areas/questions
Research Theme 1: The interplay of historical, colonial, and emerging institutions	Explanation for (lack of) FDI in SSA through comparison with global trends Isolating the role of colonialism on institutions and continuing effects of colonialism on international trade The effects of institutional change on FDI and IB in SSA (including the regionalization and formation of economic blocs across Africa) Ranking the importance of institutions and evaluating how important these are for IB
Research Theme 2: The search for redress	How social processes, such as dehumanization, explain the FDI and IB patterns in SSA The impact (and classification) of indigenization policies and conditions on FDI in SSA Relations/tensions between MNEs and local partners from redress policies The success of redress policies, such as indigenization policies, on FDI and/or social outcomes
Research Theme 3: Managing local relationships	Explaining the complexity of stakeholders and their relations in SSA Local stakeholders and MNE impact on communities and governments Network modes of entry and spillovers in SSA The role of economic elites in sustaining or replacing political elites in SSA MNEs and economic elites in SSA
Research Theme 4: Remittances as key in international business	"Non-traditional" sources of funding in SSA (foreign aid and remittances) The role and extent of diaspora remittances and the effects of such to countries of origin Remittances as an unexplained category of international business

Source: Authors

explanations for how international business in Africa takes place and suggest areas for research currently and into the foreseeable future.

We are not the first scholars to suggest the importance of Africa's difficult past on business today: Pierce and Snyder (2020) suggest that firms in Africa are more likely to have concentrated ownership structures where the tragedy of slavery was greatest, because its weakening effects on institutions and social capital persist to this day. Meouloud et al. (2019) showed the effect of the French metropole on the internationalization of Francophone colonies, while Glaister, Driffield, and Lin found that colonial history influenced foreign direct investment (FDI) into previous colonies, although they pointed out the relationship was "more nuanced and complex than previously considered" (Glaister et al., 2020: 315).

It is with this complexity that we are concerned. We believe the painful historical legacy of Africa continues to shape business on the continent, requiring much more scholarly attention than the topic has received in the past. In the remainder of the chapter, we provide a short review of the slave trade and colonial history of Africa and identify four ways in which Africa's history continues to shape international business on the continent, namely, institutions, redress, local relationships, and remittances. We suggest opportunities for future research in those areas.

2   Historical Context of SSA

The historical context of SSA is important to understand the nature of the institutions and the complexities of doing business there.

Even before colonialization, Africa was subjected to at least four waves of slave trade between 1400 and 1900 (Nunn, 2008). The slave trades were the largest human migration in history, and more than 18 million people are recorded as sold into slavery across the four waves. In fact, it is estimated that Africa's population was only half of what it should have been by 1850 (Manning, 1990). The slave trade left lasting legacies that went beyond institutions and included social and ethnic fragmentation, political instability, and the destruction of pre-colonial institutions. Nunn (2008) showed that the slave trade played a major role in the ethnic fractionalization and distrust between SSA societies today. Nunn (2008) further empirically showed a relationship between the number of slaves taken from a country and its modern economic development; this was due to slavery impeding the formation of ethnic groups and slave trades undermining political structures. Scholars (e.g., Luiz, 2015) have started examining the consequences of ethno-linguistic diversity for established concepts like cultural distance, but much more needs to be done to understand what that and other forms of diversity mean for IB.

Prior to colonialism, SSA had a mix of empires, tribal and village-based societies, such as the Shongai in West Africa, the Buganda empire in Eastern Africa, and chiefdoms and loose tribal alliances in other parts of Africa (Michalopoulos & Papaioannou, 2013). These political structures varied in their degree of industrialization and institutions. There were various types of institutions to deal with property rights; legal disputes; the performance of chiefs and kings, including methods of recall; and varying degrees of bureaucracy and sophistication. Ethnic groups that formed large states created bureaucracy to provide policing and other public goods and services (Acemoglu & Robinson, 2012).

A correlation has been found between countries with centralized, complex pre-colonial institutions and their current economic performance (Michalopoulos & Papaioannou, 2013). The historical structures that endure in modern SSA nations involve a hybrid of colonial and pre-colonial institutions. In most SSA countries, traditional chiefs and tribal leaders cooperate in assigning property rights and resolving legal disputes. This requires a complex approach to legal contracts that include stakeholder management and community engagement.

In 1950, with the exception of Liberia, Ethiopia, and Egypt, the entire African continent was ruled by four European countries, namely, Britain, France, Portugal, and Belgium. By 1980, all of SSA was independent[3].

The development of African institutions and the continent's relations with the rest of the world are a direct result of SSA's recent colonial history, followed by its often-challenging struggles for independence.

In 1884, Otto von Bismarck convened a conference in Berlin that would regulate European colonialization of the African continent. This conference led to what is known as "the scramble for Africa" where the continent was effectively partitioned up the continent into protectorates, colonies, and free-trade areas. The intention of the conference was to limit potential conflict among the European powers in case they ran up against each other as they claimed the borders of their control. The scramble for Africa lasted until 1913 and was characterized by the establishment of borders that the European powers drew up without actually having visited many of the areas that they claimed.

The randomly drawn up borders by the colonizers crossed through many of these societies and divided some and included others together where smaller societies now dominated a section of a larger society. This led to the collapse of pre-colonial institutions where territories had fragmented societies, although it has been found that in territories where pre-colonial institutions were more centralized and complex, there were an engagement with colonizers and a greater adoption of Western institutions (Michalopoulos & Papaioannou, 2013).

The result was a large number of landlocked countries and very heterogeneous populations with resultant ethno-linguistic fractionalization (Luiz, 2015) as ancestral lands straddled national borders. When these countries gained independence some 50 years later, the borders became national borders, and new governments have to deal with the challenges of ethnic partitioning and the division of ancestral land across national borders; countries without harbors and therefore restricted trade; and heterogeneous populations that were engaged in ethnic conflict, which limited governments' ability to rule (Michalopoulos & Papaioannou, 2016).

Given this challenging historical background, it seems intuitive that difficulties can also be expected in institutions and beyond, in how business in Africa is conducted. Ironically, however, the little international business scholarship that does exist about the effect of colonialism on firms in SSA has tended to highlight the more "positive" outcomes of the colonial history. For example, Meouloud et al. (2019) describe how firms from Francophone African countries internationalize to

---

[3]The case of South Africa and its territory South-West Africa (now Namibia) is more ambiguous. Although South Africa gained formal independence from Britain in 1910, and Germany relinquished South-West Africa as a territory to South Africa in 1919, both were governed by a white minority regime under the Apartheid system. Namibia gained independence in 1990; South Africa had its first democratic elections in 1994 when, after a long struggle, the government of Nelson Mandela was elected.

France first in order to gain legitimacy, while Glaister et al. (2020) study how FDI is facilitated by prior colonial ties.

How the colonial legacy has shaped some of the difficulties faced by businesses in Africa has yet to be systematically examined. It is undisputable that the colonial history has created difficulties in doing business in Africa that remain present to the current day. Yet there is also substantial economic growth in contemporary SSA (George et al., 2016). This creates opportunities for IB scholars to do research that blends multi-lens perspectives, e.g., from history, institutional economics, and economic development.

This background provides our first research theme: Legacies of Slavery and Colonialism on International Business in SSA. This research theme may include the following questions about the evolution of institutions in SSA, the relationships between SSA countries and the former colonial powers and how this impacts on IB and FDI, and FDI and redress/social justice.

3   Overview of Contemporary SSA

Sub-Saharan Africa consists of 48 different countries (see map, Fig. 1, and Table 2) and consists of more than 1 billion people, and half the population will still be below 25 by 2050 (World Bank, 2021). The African continent is more diverse than any other continent with thousands of ethnic groups with their own languages (or dialects) and cultures (Green, 2012). Estimates of different languages vary between 1200 and 3000 different languages on the continent. Nigeria, for example, has more than 470 languages, the Democratic Republic of Congo has more than 240 languages, and Ethiopia has almost 90 different languages (United Nations Economic Commission for Africa, 2010). It is largely uncertain how many languages there are due to a lack of infrastructure to measure the extent of the languages. Although local languages are used more frequently outside the cities, the business languages in SSA are mainly the languages of the colonizers, namely, English, French, and Portuguese.

Over the past decade, SSA has generally attracted <5% of global FDI. All of its economies are developing or emergent, despite the fact that the SSA region grew as quickly or sometimes quicker than Asia relative to the sizes of the respective economies. In addition, the economic impact of the COVID-19 pandemic on SSA has been worse than most other regions with the IMF predicting the region to have the slowest post-pandemic growth in the world. Moreover, the economic slowdown of 2020 to 2021 increased social tensions and political instability (IMF, 2021). Predictions for FDI growth for the region were only 3.8% in 2022 (IMF, 2021).

Nonetheless, SSA also has several advantages that other geographies have to a lesser extent (see Table 3 comparing SSA to other regions). These include a young population with a potential youth dividend, rapid urbanization and growing markets, some of the fastest growing economies on the planet, and the rapid adoption of technologies in certain sectors, e.g., financial services. The trend over the last decade has been for FDI in SSA to be dominated by resources and infrastructure sectors,

Fig. 1 Map of Sub-Saharan Africa (Source: https://www.librarything.com/topic/183039)

followed by financial services, IT, and, more recently, FMCG and retail businesses taking advantage of the emerging urban middle class that previous was too small to be of interest. However, the disadvantages for SSA countries continue to be dominated by poor development, lack of infrastructure, and a reliance on foreign aid in the region. This is however not universal across the region, and some countries fare much better than others.

4   Legacies of Slavery and Colonialism in Sub-Saharan Africa

The legacies of slavery and colonialism are apparent across SSA in factors like ongoing ethnic tensions, the borders drawn up by the colonial powers, the business and administrative languages of the countries, and their institutions. We discuss four ways in which these legacies shape contemporary business in Africa, namely,

Table 2 Selected sub-Saharan country indicators

Country name	GDP US$ bn, 2020	GDP growth annual %, 2020	FDI, net inflows BoP, current US$, 2019	Population total 2020	Population growth annual %, 2020	Life expectancy at birth, total years, 2019	Mobile cellular subscriptions per 100 people, 2020	Net official development assistance and official aid received current US$, 2019	Personal remittances received, current US$, 2020	Days required to start a business, 2019
Angola	62.3	−4.0%	−4098 m	32,866,268	3.2%	61	45	49 m	8 m	36,00
Benin	15.6	3.8%	218 m	12,123,198	2.7%	62	92	602 m	206 m	8,50
Botswana	15.8	−7.9%	260 m	2,351,625	2.1%	70	162	68 m	46 m	48,00
Burkina Faso	17.3	2.0%	162 m	20,903,278	2.8%	62	106	1148 m	464 m	13,00
Burundi	3.3	0.3	1 m	11,890,781	3.1%	62	56	588 m	45 m	5,00
Cabo Verde	1.7	−14.8%	107 m	555,988	1.1%	73	98	152 m	243 m	9,00
Cameroon	39.8	0.7%	1024 m	26,545,864	2.6%	59	95	1335 m	339 m	13,50
Central African Republic	2.3	0.0%	25 m	4,829,764	1.8%	53	..	753 m	0	22,00
Chad	10.1	−0.9%	566 m	16,425,859	3%	54	53	707 m	0	58,00
Comoros	1.2	4.9%	3 m	869,595	2.2%	64	54	78 m	161 m	16,00
Congo, Dem. Rep.	49.8	0.8%	1350 m	89,561,404	3.1%	61	46	3025 m	1109 m	7,00
Congo, Rep.	10.9	−7.9%	3366 m	5,518,092	2.5%	65	..	187 m	..	49,50
Cote d'Ivoire	61.3	1.8%	848 m	26,378,275	2.5%	58	152	1201 m	323 m	6,00
Equatorial Guinea	10.1	−4.9%	452 m	1,402,985	3.4%	59	..	64 m	..	33,00
Eritrea	2	8.7%	67 m	3,213,969	1.4%	66	..	276 m	..	84,00
Eswatini	4	−1.6%	127 m	1,160,164	1%	60	..	73 m	112 m	21,50

(continued)

Table 2 (continued)

Country name	GDP US$ bn, 2020	GDP growth annual %, 2020	FDI, net inflows BoP, current US$, 2019	Population total 2020	Population growth annual %, 2020	Life expectancy at birth, total years, 2019	Mobile cellular subscriptions per 100 people, 2020	Net official development assistance and official aid received current US$, 2019	Personal remittances received, current US$, 2020	Days required to start a business, 2019
Ethiopia	107.6	6.1%	2516 m	114,963,583	2.5%	67	..	4809 m	504 m	32
Gabon	15.6	−1.3%	1553 m	2,225,728	2.4%	66	139	116 m	17 m	10
Gambia, The	1.9	0.0%	32 m	2,416,664	2.9%	62	111	194 m	297 m	8
Ghana	72.4	0.4%	3879 m	31,072,945	2.1%	64	130	936 m	3564 m	13
Guinea	15.7	7.0%	44 m	13,132,792	2.8%	62	..	580 m	151 m	15
Guinea-Bissau	1.4	−2.4%	71 m	1,967,998	2.4%	58	97	120 m	122 m	8,5
Kenya	98.9	−0.3%	1332 m	53,771,300	2.3%	67	114	3250 m	3100 m	23
Lesotho	1.8	−11.1%	117 m	2,142,252	0.8	54	73	145 m	426 m	15
Liberia	2.9	−2.9%	86 m	5,057,677	241%	64	..	597 m	333 m	18
Madagascar	13.7	−4.2%	474 m	27,691,019	2.6%	67	..	756 m	391 m	8
Malawi	12	0.8%	98 m	19,129,955	2.7%	64	52	1206 m	189 m	37
Mauritius	11	−14.9%	472 m	1,265,740	0%	74	150	22 m	271 m	4,5
Mozambique	14	−1.3%	2180 m	31,255,435	2.9%	61	..	1907 m	348 m	17
Namibia	10.7	−8.0%	−176 m	2,540,916	1.8%	64	102	148 m	55 m	54
Niger	13.7	1.5%	717 m	24,206,636	3.8%	62	..	1490 m	300 m	10
Nigeria	432.3	−1.8%	2305 m	206,139,587	2.5%	55	99	3517 m	17,207 m	7,2
Rwanda	10.3	−3.4%	384 m	12,952,209	2.5%	69	82	1191 m	241 m	4
São Tomé and Príncipe	0.5	3.1%	24 m	219,161	1.9%	70	79	51 m	8 m	7
Senegal	25	0.9	983 m	16,743,930	2.7%	68	114	1443 m	2561 m	6

Sierra Leone	1.1	−2.2%	342 m	7,976,985	2.1%	55	86	594 m	59 m	8
South Africa	301.9	−7.0%	5116 m	59,308,690	1.3%	64	162	971 m	810 m	40
South Sudan	12	−10.8%	231 m	11,193,729	1.2%	58	..	1885 m	1200 m	13
Tanzania	62.4	2.0%	990 m	59,734,213	2.9%	65	86	2153 m	409 m	29,5
Togo	7.5	1.8%	345 m	8,278,737	2.4%	61	79	411 m	440 m	2,5
Uganda	37.4	2.9%	1266 m	45,741,000	3.3%	63	61	2100 m	1051 m	24
Zambia	19	−3.0%	547 m	18,383,956	2.9%	64	104	976 m	134 m	8,5
Zimbabwe	16.7	−8.0%	280 m	14,862,927	1.5%	61	89	974 m	1209 m	27

Source: Authors compiled from World Bank data

Table 3 Sub-Saharan Africa comparison to selected regions

	SSA	East Asia and Pacific	Latin America and Caribbean	Middle East and North Africa
Surface area (sq. km)	24,287,427	24,868,162	20,425,979	11,385,551
GDP US$ millions in 2020	1,687,597	27,037,637	4,698,073	3,036,299
GDP growth in 2020	−2%	−0.4%	−6.6%	−3.1%
GDP per capita US$ in 2020	1485	11,495	7202	6733
Population total (thousands)	1,136,046	2,352,037	652,276	464,554
Population growth	2.6%	0.5%	0.9%	1.7%
Population 0–14 years % of total population	42%	20%	24%	31%
Population 15–65% of total population	55%	69%	67%	58%
Labor force total (thousands)	428,466	1,251,825	292,097	149,109
Unemployment (% of total labor force unemployed)	6.6%	4.3%	10.3%	10.6%
Urban population (thousands)	468,643	1,427,569	529,082	306,458
Electric power consumption (kwh per capita)	487	3678	2158	2869

East Asia and Pacific include Australia, China, India, Japan and Korea, and New Zealand and Singapore, which are either large economies or developed economies
Source: Authors compiled from World Bank data
SSA generally excludes the North African (Arab) countries. Those countries are grayed out in the map below
Source: https://www.librarything.com/topic/183039

(1) institutions, (2) the ongoing need for redress and what that means for multinationals, (3) the management of local relationships, and (4) remittances as a key form of international business. We specifically outline why there is value in further studying them in international business research.

4.1 Research Theme 1: The Interplay of Historical, Colonial, and Emerging Institutions

In spite of repeated calls (e.g., Buckley, 2009; Jones & Khanna, 2006), history remains at the margins of international business research. Yet in the context of Africa, it is clear that the past is still very much present and that scholars need to examine the interplay of historical, colonial, and emerging institutions to make sense of business on the continent.

Thus, business in Africa is confronted with not only institutional weakness but also institutional uncertainty, where players do not know what will be the shape or interpretation of institutional elements. Since most of the countries on the continent gained independence, SSA has been plagued by institutional uncertainty and the lack of institutional development. Institutional uncertainty has been accompanied by political upheavals, lack of democracy, and non-democratic regime changes. There is progress toward democracy, but it seems slow (Lynch & Crawford, 2011). As late as 2021, Mozambique faced a terrorist insurgency in the north, and in Eswatini (formerly known as Swaziland), the royal family was facing its greatest challenge in more than a century.

Such events are likely to lead to changes in institutions and ease of doing business in the region. Although scholars have started examining institutions in Africa (e.g., Luiz et al., 2017; Saka-Helmhout et al., 2019), the complexity of institutions in Africa requires much more attention. Thus, the foundations of institutions need to be sought among pre-colonial, colonial, and post-colonial influences. In this endeavor, history cannot be omitted. Indeed, in a historical assessment, Austin et al. (2017) argue that the turbulence associated with Africa is in fact typical of markets emerging from colonialism.

Although the historical focus on how countries attract FDI has been on market size, labor costs, infrastructure, and other economic factors (e.g., Dunning, 1980; Grosse & Trevino, 1996), since the seminal work by North (1990) in the 1990s, a greater focus has been on institutions. The focus on institutions made it possible to link democratic institutions, political stability, and the rule of law to FDI attractiveness (e.g., Loree & Guisinger, 1995). Soon thereafter, studies were extended to include institutions that deterred FDI, such as high tax rates, corruption, and cultural distance (e.g., Globerman & Shapiro, 2003). However, the results of these studies were largely inconclusive. In his meta-analysis, Bailey (2018) argued that there was a need for describing mediating and moderating factors that influence the attractiveness or otherwise of institutions for FDI. Comparing the institutional environments of North America, Europe, and Asia, Bailey (2018) concluded that there was a modestly positive relationship between FDI attractiveness and democratic institutions, political stability, and the rule of law, although the study also showed the strength of tax regimes and region in attracting FDI.

Unfortunately, the meta-analysis does not include Africa—an oversight that should be corrected by future scholars to establish whether or not global trends hold in the African context. Moreover, the evidence does not seem to adequately explain observed FDI in the African context. The bulk of recent FDI was directed at Nigeria, Angola, Egypt, Ethiopia, and South Africa. These are very heterogeneous countries with very different approaches to rule of law and democracy and also different degrees of stability. A country like Ghana that not only scores highly on these dimensions but also has one of the biggest economies on the continent does not attract as much FDI.

It would be incorrect to assume that the current institutions of countries in SSA are directly attributable to their colonial experience. In modern post-colonial countries in SSA, while there is a clear orientation toward business language and high-level legal system, e.g., common law in former British colonies and civil law elements in former French colonies, there are very different institutions around the rule of law, property rights, and resolution of legal disputes. Future research needs to unpack this diversity of effects.

Another factor shaping international business and institutions in Africa relate to Pan-Africanism and regional integration. The post-colonial era in Africa, wherein much of Africa was caught up in the Cold War tensions, created a strong drive for Pan-Africanism, which, in turn, created continental bodies such as the African Union (AU). The African Union was formed in 1999 as a successor of the Organization of African Unity, which was established in 1963 at a time when most African states were gaining their independence from the colonial powers. The AU (and OAU before it) was established with the vision of a united Pan-Africa that transcended ethnic and national differences.

OAU reflected the sentiment of newly independent countries during the Cold War and was concerned with socialism (described as African socialism) and African unity. The OAU activities were mainly focussed on fighting remnants of colonialism and apartheid. The OAU's successor, the AU was still concerned with a Pan African vision, but now had an economic vision to drive African growth and economic development through increased cooperation and integration of African states (AU, 2021). In March 2018 members of the African Union signed an agreement to establish ACFTA, the African Continental Free Trade Area (AU, 2018). The ACFTA is intended to lead to a continental free-trade area that integrates Africa's markets and boosting intra-African trade. The agreement is intended to deepen economic integration of the continent with eventual free movement of people, goods and services, and capital. The success of the ACFTA is dependent on the signatory countries allowing oversight of their institutions and the largest economies (Nigeria, South Africa, and Egypt mainly) not dominating smaller countries.

While the diverse institutions in SSA will certainly be challenging, the main benefits of the ACFTA will be to simplify the overlapping regional structures across the continent. The African Union recognizes eight regional economic communities, with some countries belonging to multiple communities. The evolution of the ACFTA and greater integration will provide a fascinating opportunity for IB scholars to engage in comparative studies of the evolution of institutions and their impact on business. The integration of economies will lead to migration and the rapid expansion of the African middle class and African MNEs that dominate the region and compete with developed market MNEs more directly. The nature of spillovers on the continent may also change, and African firms have the opportunity to become regional champions with the support of their governments. This is an important area for research for scholars interested in SSA or the evolution of institutions.

Contractor et al. (2020) argue that MNEs are willing to trade off a country's poor institutions for stronger institutions in the future and that they take a long-term view of their investment. The authors found that contract enforcement was the most important institution for FDI. However, what happens when the government and underlying institutions change? Given that institutions are contested, dramatic political and social turmoil are often the norm rather than the exception in Africa. Some foreign firms have shown themselves adept at managing under such conditions, for example, Shell in Nigeria, MTN in the Sudan, and Standard Chartered Bank in Zimbabwe. All of these foreign firms have managed to operate through political tumult and regime changes.

These firms are not free from controversy: Hennchen (2015) discusses the ongoing controversy around Shell in Nigeria, while Wöcke and Beamish (2017) discuss the US$5.2bn fined issued MTN by Nigerian regulators in 2015. Shortly after a change of government in Nigeria, MTN was accused of not complying with regulations about the registration of mobile network subscribers. MTN managed to reduce the fine significantly after it fundamentally changed its approach to managing government and regulator relations and now measures subsidiaries on stakeholder engagement metrics (Wöcke & Beamish, 2017). But both when and how they succeed and their failures are in need of further research.

Finally, given evidence of the importance of non-typical institutions like religion (Barnard & Mamabolo, 2022), further questions need to be asked about which institutions matter in Africa and how they function. Religion is an important institution in business because it provides normative and cultural-cognitive guidelines to executives. There may well be other institutions that are not captured in traditional databases that help shape African business, but scholars need to investigate the practices in management in Africa to be able to identify if such cases exist.

4.2 Research Theme 2: The Search for Redress

There is increasingly recognition of the importance of non-market (Rodgers et al., 2019) and corporate social responsibility (Dartey-Baah & Amoako, 2021) strategies of MNEs. One particular form that this can take is in offering redress for the trauma of the past. The slave trade and colonialism have shaped life and business in Africa for more than 500 years. Moreover, colonialism ended only about a half-century ago. An important consideration has to be what the experience of slavery and colonization has done to Africans. In terms of research opportunities, understanding how MNEs respond to that legacy is crucial.

A necessary prerequisite for the slave trade and colonialism was to dehumanize people, to regard their societies as inferior, and to delegitimize their institutions. Dehumanization is the process by which full humanity is denied to others, a process that is accompanied by cruelty and suffering (Haslam, 2006). Moreover, every-day social cognitive processes are affected by perceptions of being non-human (Haslam, 2006).

If a long history of international contact has left Africans feeling that they are not seen as fully human, an important question has to be whether (and, if so, to what extent and through which mechanisms) such a sense persists, as well as how it can be overcome. Another important question for scholars has to be how the painful past and the search for redress play out when Africans engage in international business. One important strategy used is to "indigenize" local economies.

The stated intent of such indigenization policies is typically to strengthen the African economy and to provide greater economic control to locals. An awareness of the colonial relations of the past, together with the low level of economic development, explains why indigenization polices are imposed on foreign partners in many SSA countries. Such indigenization policies range from nationalization to compulsory partnerships with locals and have been found across Africa, e.g., Ghana, Nigeria, and Zambia.

More recently, indigenization has been taking place in Zimbabwe (not only through the controversial "land grabs" in 2000 but also through the "Indigenisation and Economic Empowerment Act" of 2008). After the discovery of gas reserves in Mozambique attracted the attention of multinational enterprises (MNEs) from the USA, Brazil, and South Africa, the Mozambique government has steadily increased indigenization requirements for foreign firms. This was generally due to pressure from locals who were not satisfied with the spillovers from the FDI and used network connections to change regulations for foreign firms. Most host countries in SSA have regulations to maximize positive spillover effects from FDI, but this can create tensions as the regulations can be as fluid as the institutions in the host country.

Conditions for indigenization differ; in the case of the Zimbabwe, at least 51 percent of the equity in foreign firms had to be paid over to indigenous Zimbabweans. Often, MNEs are expected to form joint ventures with local partners and invest in local businesses as a condition for operating in the country. It is hardly surprising that the process is fraught.

An example is the evolution of the South African Mining Charter. In 2004, the democratic government together with industry stakeholders signed the first Mining Charter. One of the key elements of the charter was to change the ownership of mines. Mining companies were required to transfer 15% equity in their South African operations to Black South African within 5 years and 26% within 10 years. There were not many Black South Africans who could afford to buy these shares, so the regulations required mining companies to establish a fund to pay for the equity stakes for the new shareholders. Because the fund was too small to pay for this large shift in equity, mining companies had to create share-funded schemes to pay for the equity stakes of their new partners.

Mining companies responded to these regulations by restructuring their operations and ring-fencing their South African operations, thereby keeping their international operations independent of the South African regulations. The benefits of these new funding schemes are not unequivocal; they sometimes put Black shareholders in debt, and communities and trade unions did not experience much benefit from the Mining Charter. Moreover, in response to pressure from Black business and the unions, the South African government proposed new targets for Black equity and suggested that mining companies had to maintain the level of Black South African shareholding at 26% for the duration of the life of the mine.

Much as this timeline may appear very long to contemporary managers and scholars of MNEs, such a requirement must be understood in light of the fact that Africans still experience the negative consequences of various forms of colonial oppression. But practically, this meant that the mines were expected to dilute existing shareholders again and fund stakes for new shareholders whenever Black shareholders sold their shares to international or White South Africans. Such policies increase the costs of doing business in those countries or entrench rent-seeking business practices by local elites, and MNE managers in these countries have to manage complex relationships which does not reflect in panel data.

The roles of the local partners of an MNE in Africa are another important area for research. The selection of a local partner goes beyond that of selecting a joint venture partner, and the motives for selecting a local partner would range from compliance with local FDI regulations, access to markets, reducing risk through gaining access to the political elite, and actually changing institutions to the benefit of the MNE (Higley & Burton, 2006). We suggest that tensions between MNEs and their local partners will increase when the local partner is less capable and not able to create much value beyond network access, but the empirical work for such a suggestion has yet to be undertaken. There is a need for more case studies and studies that examine how the various redress activities, like indigenization, are understood and attempted. Understanding why such strategies succeed or fail is also critical, not only for international business scholars but also for practitioners.

4.3   Research Theme 3: Managing Local Relationships

A final consideration is around local relationships. Africa resembles most emerging markets in that personal relationships are important (Meyer & Peng, 2005), but we want to highlight two sets of relationships where the colonial experience has had an important effect on how those relationships play out. The first is with communities and local stakeholders, who are often impoverished, with little education, and suspicious about MNEs. The second set of relationships is with local elites.

Stakeholder management in SSA is complex. Simply identifying who are stakeholders and how they relate to each other, not to mention the MNE, is hard. Stakeholders are tightly interconnected and relationships and rivalries are often historical, long predating the entry of the MNE. They reflect in terms of ethnicities, government, and tribal groupings and even economic interests. In practice, this means that managing local communities and partners can lead to tensions that are more intense in Africa than in many other regions and such tensions can sometimes lead to violent conflict. Whether because of indigenization requirements or because of MNEs' internationalization strategies (Chipp et al., 2019), MNEs have to engage with local communities. MNEs and communities work with different institutional logics (Newenham-Kahindi & Stevens, 2018), and it is therefore to be expected that the host country government will occasionally have to intervene when differences cannot be resolved. This is an important area for further research from an IB perspective.

It is important to note that MNEs' entry can be destructive in these communities (Brandl et al., 2021) or at least to fall short of the high expectations of communities (Eweje, 2006). It is perhaps relevant that Hymer (1970) developed his argument about the centrality and dangers of power as a key organizing mechanism for MNEs after having served as a Peace Corps volunteer in Ghana: The relationship between the MNE and its communities in Ghana was characterized by a stark imbalance of power between the MNE and its host country communities. This insight about the role of power from more than half a century ago needs further research: How an MNE manages or mismanages the powerful position in which it finds itself—and how communities respond—is a research theme that resonates across the continent and also in other contexts characterized by inequality.

There are also relatively few constraints on government when institutions are underdeveloped, when the middle class is small, and where the government dominates the formal economy. This makes it less predictable what actions will transpire, leaving MNEs in the challenging position of having to engage with locals without much clarity about what to expect if locals do not find their efforts acceptable.

Another important set of relationships is with local elites. As is typical of post-colonial countries (Wegner et al., 2013), the political systems in Africa consist almost entirely of Limited Access Order countries (North et al., 2009). Limited Access Order countries are characterized by restrictions on access to political and/or economic institutions in a society. Political elites try to maintain those restrictions but will amend them under pressure from members of a society (normally a group competing with the elite). Economic elites have an interest in maintaining the stability of the institutions, but when the stability of the institutions is threatened, they will form pacts with other groups in society, and the institutions are changed to accommodate these new pacts.

SSA is characterized by political elites either that have a long tenure compared to Western standards or that are removed in non-democratic ways or through political changes that are generally accompanied by significant institutional changes. Past research has focused on political risk, the political elite, and their impact on national institution. But the interests of MNEs may be more aligned to that of the economic elite in many of these countries where the economic elites are more concerned with maintaining economic stability or, when this is not possible, expanding power networks and influence.

While political elites shuffle their inner circle to survive, economic elites utilize other non-market strategies and may form foreign alliances to pressure the political elites. These actions include mobilizing through the media and funding political activity and may even include replacing a political role player (Gallego & Pitchik, 2004; Vanderhill, 2022). In countries such as South Africa, the economic elite foresaw the collapse of the apartheid system and acted as change agents to convert the existing political order to a democratic order and entrench a liberal economic system (Albertus & Menaldo, 2014). Moreover, in developing economies, the differences between political and economic elites are often blurred, and economic elites are able to directly influence national institutions (Acemoglu & Robinson, 2012). An interesting phenomenon in SSA countries is the regular non-democratic changes of government, yet the economic elites remain relatively stable. This has important implications for MNEs that operate in the region and could provide data on effective non-market strategies and political relationship between business and government. There is also a need to study the role of the economic elites in regime change and development of institutions.

Partnering with local firms allow MNEs to access networks that include government agencies and politically connected individuals. Understanding the local power relations and maintaining relationships is an important component of operating in these markets, and elites are important gatekeepers in this process. Where localization and indigenization policies are a requirement and MNEs have to choose local partners, MNEs tend to select members of the elite as partners. Engagement with government often takes place through elites.

The role of political connections in emerging markets is not new, but although there is a sizable body of literature on elites in political science, there are very few studies on political and economic elites and institutions in international business. Such studies will make an important contribution to our understanding of risk and non-market activities of MNEs. Some of the questions that we consider important include how elites build and maintain alliances between competing political elites, the strategies that elites use to maintain their influence on societies that have undergone radical (sometimes violent) political change, and the role of MNEs in sustaining or competing with economic elites in SSA.

4.4   Research Theme 4: Remittances as Key in International Business

Businesses operating in Africa have to deal with institutional problems such as endemic corruption, foreign exchange challenges, and difficulties with the repatriation of profits. As Omobowale (2015: 108) puts it, "The 'stories' of Africa in modern times have remained that of despair and underdevelopment leading to emigration and the deployment of international aid." We want to argue that these "stories" are in opportunities to research international business and Africa through very different theoretical lenses.

Foreign aid is also an important source of funding to the economies of many countries in SSA, although its benefits are less clear. Although foreign aid may assist individuals and groupings in the country, there is no conclusive evidence that such aid leads to improved institutions or economic growth (Babalola & Shittu, 2020). In fact, the link between foreign aid and growth is contested, with studies typically reporting mixed findings. Babalola and Shittu (2020) found that foreign aid actually reduced economic growth unless it was accompanied by trade openness. Foreign aid has been found to contribute positively to growth for low- rather than middle-income countries (Alemu & Lee, 2015), especially when focused on the development of human or physical infrastructure (Selaya & Sunesen, 2012). Countries that are dependent of foreign aid generally have poor institutions, are often dictatorships, lack property rights or rule of law, and experience high degrees of violence (Asongu, 2015).

The large diaspora sending back to remittances and the persistent need for foreign aid are linked. Diasporans are people who have left their home to seek a better future elsewhere (Barnard et al., 2019), and the countries they have left are often also the main recipients of foreign aid. At the same time, countries that are frequently in need of aid rarely make for attractive FDI destinations. In Africa, countries do not receive much FDI, but remittances from diasporans are an important but understudied dimension of international business.

Indeed, cross-border business in Africa is often facilitated not through the better-understood FDI, but rather by remittances (Chitambara, 2019) or foreign aid (Asongu, 2015). Remittances are small-sum, individual-to-individual, or household-to-household transfers (Barnard et al., 2019). They take place outside of organizations, and the small sums involved resulted in IB scholars overlooking them as a potential enabler of (per defining international) business. But although remittances were initially assumed to be for household expenditure only (a function they still perform), they are increasingly recognized as sources not only of venture funding (Pitelis et al., 2021; Vaaler, 2011).

Moreover, the cumulative amount remittances represent is substantial: By 2018, remittances represented US$500 billion (out of a total of US$ 600 billion annual remittances) of the foreign inflows going to low- and middle-income countries (World Bank, 2019). Indeed, they are increasingly recognized as sources not only of venture funding but also of industrialization and technological upgrading (Asongu & Odhiambo, 2020; Efobi et al., 2019).

These positive consequences were previously associated mainly with FDI. In a world with strong competition for "good" FDI (Narula & Dunning, 2000, 2010), where Africa may often not emerge the winner, are remittances taking on (some part of) that developmental role? And if so, how? The importance of remittances raises multiple possible research themes.

5   Future Trends and Prospects

In this chapter, we have argued that the legacy of slavery and of colonialism is key to understanding how international business in Africa plays out today. However, this important area has received very little attention. We highlighted four broad areas of research and some of the numerous topics that can be covered under those areas. These areas alone—there are of course more—should give ample reason for IB scholars to seriously consider Africa as a research setting rich with opportunity.

We first focused on institutions. The dynamic overlay of pre-colonial, colonial, and newly emerging institutions makes for a complex institutional environment, but the institutions in SSA are not yet as well understood as they could be.

Second, we discussed indigenization polices, and how new policies are still being introduced, even though colonialism ended half a century ago. These attempts at redress are deemed needed because African countries have not yet recovered from the damage wrought by colonialism, but they introduce multiple challenges to MNEs. Scholarship is needed to untangle expectations and actions from the side of both governments and MNEs.

We then highlighted two types of important local relationships. Because of the extractive colonial relationships, many Africans are poor, and they have high expectations of the developmental role of MNEs (Eweje, 2006). Relationships with communities are complex and they carry high stakes. But there are also relationships with political and economic elites. Explicitly investigating how these powerful individuals shape economies in their less developed home countries is an important area for future research.

Finally, we explained how remittances are an important international enabler of business in Africa. Understanding not only the micro-ventures supported by remittances but also their macro consequences is not yet well understood and requires additional research.

it is important to remember that Africa is not the only part of the world with a colonial past. Insights from Africa can therefore be of value beyond its borders. But much more needs to be done to systematically unpack the legacy of slavery and colonialism in Africa. Practically speaking, amid concerns that China is (re-) colonizing Africa, it is important to understand more about Africa's original colonial past. In this chapter, we have also shown the theoretical gains from taking seriously Africa's history. In addition to the suggestions we made, it is likely that other theories can be deepened by looking at how painful history lingers. The suggestions here are therefore only a first step toward realizing the scholarly potential of studying the African continent.

References

Acemoglu, D., & Robinson, J. A. (2012). *Why nations fail: The origins of power, prosperity and poverty (1st)* (1st ed., p. 529). Crown.

African Union. (2018). *Agreement establishing the African continental free trade area*. Retrieved from https://au.int/sites/default/files/treaties/36437-treaty-consolidated_text_on_cfta_-_en.pdf

African Union. (2021). *About the African Union*. Retrieved from https://au.int/en/overview

Albertus, M., & Menaldo, V. (2014). Gaming democracy: Elite dominance during transition and the prospects for redistribution. *British Journal of Political Science, 44*(3), 575–603.

Alemu, A. M., & Lee, J. S. (2015). Foreign aid on economic growth in Africa: A comparison of low and middle-income countries. *South African Journal of Economic and Management Sciences, 18*(4), 449–462.

Asongu, S. (2015). On the dynamic effects of foreign aid on corruption, No 15/015, Working Papers of the African Governance and Development Institute, African Governance and Development Institute.

Asongu, S. A., & Odhiambo, N. M. (2019). Challenges of doing business in Africa: A systematic review. *Journal of African Business, 20*(2), 259–268.

Asongu, S. A., & Odhiambo, N. M. (2020). Remittances, the diffusion of information and industrialization in Africa. *Contemporary Social Science, 15*(1), 98–117.

Austin, G., Dávila, C., & Jones, G. (2017). The alternative business history: Business in emerging markets. *Business History Review, 91*(3), 537–569.

Babalola, S., & Shittu, W. (2020). Foreign aid and economic growth in West Africa: Examining the roles of institutions. *International Economic Journal, 34*(3), 534–552. https://doi.org/10.1080/10168737.2020.1780292

Bailey, N. (2018). Exploring the relationship between institutional factors and FDI attractiveness: A meta-analytic review. *International Business Review, 27*, 139–148.

Barnard, H., Cuervo-Cazurra, A., & Manning, S. (2017). Africa business research as a laboratory for theory-building: Extreme conditions, new phenomena, and alternative paradigms of social relationships. *Management and Organization Review, 13*(3), 467–495.

Barnard, H., Deeds, D., Mudambi, R., & Vaaler, P. M. (2019). Migrants, migration policies, and international business research: Current trends and new directions. *Journal of International Business Policy, 2*(1), 275–288.

Barnard, H., & Mamabolo, A. (2022). On religion as an institution in international business: Executives' lived experience in four African countries. *Journal of World Business, 57*(1). https://doi.org/10.1016/j.jwb.2021.101262

Brandl, K., Moore, E., Meyer, C., & Doh, J. (2021). The impact of multinational enterprises on community informal institutions and rural poverty. *Journal of International Business Studies.* https://doi.org/10.1057/s41267-020-00400-3

Buckley, P. J. (2009). Business history and international business. *Business History, 51*(3), 307–333.

Chipp, K., Wöcke, A., Strandberg, C., & Chiba, M. (2019). Overcoming African institutional voids: Market entry with networks. *European Business Review, 31*(3), 304–316.

Chitambara, P. (2019). Remittances, institutions and growth in Africa. *International Migration, 57*(5), 56–70.

Contractor, F., Dangol, R., Nuruzzaman, N., & Raghunath, S. (2020). How do country regulations and business environment impact foreign direct investment (FDI) inflows? *International Business Review, 29*(2), 101640.

Dartey-Baah, K., & Amoako, G. K. (2021). Global CSR, drivers and consequences: A systematic review. *Journal of Global Responsibility.* https://doi.org/10.1108/jgr-12-2020-0103

Dunning, J. (1980). Toward an eclectic theory of international production: Some empirical tests. *Journal of International Business Studies, 11*, 9–31. https://doi.org/10.1057/palgrave.jibs. 8490593

Efobi, U., Asongu, S., Okafor, C., Tchamyou, V., & Tanankem, B. (2019). Remittances, finance and industrialization in Africa. *Journal of Multinational Financial Management, 49*, 54–66.

Eweje, G. (2006). The role of MNEs in community development initiatives in developing countries: Corporate social responsibility at work in Nigeria and South Africa. *Business & Society, 45*(2), 93–129.

Gallego, M., & Pitchik, C. (2004). An economic theory of leadership turnover. *Journal of Public Economics, 88*(12), 2361–2382.

George, G., Corbishley, C., Khayesi, J. N., Haas, M. R., & Tihanyi, L. (2016). Bringing Africa in: Promising directions for management. *Academy of Management Journal, 59*(2), 377–393.

Glaister, K. W., Driffield, N., & Lin, Y. (2020). Foreign direct investment to Africa: Is there a colonial legacy? *Management International Review, 60*(3), 315–349.

Globerman, S., & Shapiro, D. (2003). Governance infrastructure and U.S. foreign direct investment. *Journal of International Business Studies, 3*, 19–39.

Green, E. (2012). Explaining African ethnic diversity. *International Political Science Review, 34*(3), 235–253.

Grosse, R., & Trevino, L. J. (1996). Foreign direct investment in the United States: An analysis by country of origin. *Journal of International Business Studies, 27*(1), 139–155.

Haslam, N. (2006). Dehumanization: An integrative review. *Personality and Social Psychology Review, 10*(3), 252–264.

Hennchen, E. (2015). Royal Dutch shell in Nigeria: Where do responsibilities end? *Journal of Business Ethics, 129*(1), 1–25.

Higley, J., & Burton, M. G. (2006). *Elite foundations of liberal democracy.* Rowman and Littlefield.

Hymer, S. (1970). *The efficiency (contradictions) of multinational corporations.* American Economic Review, American Economic Association, Vol. 60(2), pp. 441–448, May.

IMF. (2021). Sub-Saharan Africa: One planet, two worlds, three stories. Press release no. 21/306. Retrieved from https://www.imf.org/en/News/Articles/2021/10/20/pr21306-sub-saharan-africa-one-planet-two-worlds-three-stories

Jones, G., & Khanna, T. (2006). Bringing history (back) into international business. *Journal of International Business Studies, 37*(4), 453–468.

Loree, D., & Guisinger, S. (1995). Policy and non-policy determinants of U.S. equity foreign direct investment. *Journal of International Business Studies, 26*, 281–299. https://doi.org/10.1057/palgrave.jibs.8490174

Luiz, J., Stringfellow, D., & Jefthas, A. (2017). Institutional complementarity and substitution as an internationalization strategy: The emergence of an African multinational giant. *Global Strategy Journal, 7*(1), 83–103.

Luiz, J. M. (2015). The impact of ethno-linguistic fractionalization on cultural measures: Dynamics, endogeneity and modernization. *Journal of International Business Studies, 46*(9), 1080–1098.

Lynch, G., & Crawford, G. (2011). Democratization in Africa 1990–2010: An assessment. *Democratization, 18*(2), 275–310.

Manning, P. (1990). *Slavery and African life.* Cambridge University Press.

Meouloud, T. A., Mudambi, R., & Hill, T. L. (2019). The metropolitan effect: Colonial influence on the internationalization of francophone African firms. *Management and Organization Review, 15*(1), 31–53.

Meyer, K. E., & Peng, M. W. (2005). Probing theoretically into central and Eastern Europe: Transactions, resources, and institutions. *Journal of International Business Studies, 36*(6), 600–621.

Michalopoulos, S., & Papaioannou, E. (2013). Pre-colonial ethnic institutions and contemporary African development. *Econometrica, 81*(1), 113–152.

Michalopoulos, S., & Papaioannou, E. (2016). The scramble for Africa and its legacy. In *The new Palgrave dictionary of economics.* Palgrave Macmillan. https://doi.org/10.1057/978-1-349-95121-5_3041-1

Narula, R., & Dunning, J. H. (2000). Industrial development, globalization and multinational enterprises: New realities for developing countries. *Oxford Development Studies, 28*(2), 141–167.

Narula, R., & Dunning, J. H. (2010). Multinational enterprises, development and globalization: Some clarifications and a research agenda. *Oxford Development Studies, 38*(3), 263–287.

Newenham-Kahindi, A., & Stevens, C. E. (2018). An institutional logics approach to liability of foreignness: The case of mining MNEs in Sub-Saharan Africa. *Journal of International Business Studies, 49*(7), 881–901.

North, C., Wallis, J., & Weingast, B. (2009). *Violence and social orders: A conceptual framework for interpreting recorded human history.* Cambridge University Press. https://doi.org/10.1017/CBO9780511575839

Omobowale, A. O. (2015). Stories of the 'dark' continent: Crude constructions, diasporic identity, and international aid to Africa. *International Sociology, 30*(2), 108–118.

Pierce, L., & Snyder, J. A. (2020). Historical origins of firm ownership structure: The persistent effects of the African slave trade. *Academy of Management Journal, 63*(6), 1687–1713.

Nunn, N. (2008). The long term effects of Africa's slave trades. *Quarterly Journal of Economics, 123*(1), 139–176.

Pitelis, E. E., Kafouros, M., & Pitelis, C. N. (2021). Follow the people and the money: Effects of inward FDI on migrant remittances and the contingent role of new firm creation and institutional infrastructure in emerging economies. *Journal of World Business, 56*(2), 101178.

Rodgers, P., Stokes, P., Tarba, S., & Khan, Z. (2019). The role of non-market strategies in establishing legitimacy: The case of service MNEs in emerging economies. *Management International Review, 59*(4), 515–540.

Saka-Helmhout, A., Chappin, M., & Vermeulen, P. (2019). Multiple paths to firm innovation in Sub-Saharan Africa: How informal institutions matter. *Organization Studies, 41*(11), 1551–1575.

Selaya, P., & Sunesen, E. R. (2012). Does foreign aid increase foreign direct investment? *World Development, 40*(11), 2155–2176.

United Nations Economic Commission for Africa. (2010). Diversity management in Africa: Findings from the African peer review mechanism and a framework for analysis and policymaking. http://citeseerx.ist.psu.edu/viewdoc/download?doi=10.1.1.233.869&rep=rep1&type=pdf

Vaaler, P. M. (2011). Immigrant remittances and the venture investment environment of developing countries. *Journal of International Business Studies, 42*(9), 1121–1149.

Vanderhill, R. (2022). *Promoting authoritarianism abroad.* Lynne Rienner Publishers. https://doi.org/10.1515/9781626370104

Wegner, G., Heinrich-Mechergui, M. L., & Mechergui, T. (2013). Limited access order in Tunisia: Elements of a political economy of autocratic regimes. *International Journal of Public Administration, 36*(11), 743–753.

Wöcke, A., & Beamish, P. (2017). *MTN and the Nigerian fine.* Ivey Case Publishing W17084-PDF-ENG

World Bank. (2019). *Record high remittances sent globally in 2018.* World Bank. https://www.worldbank.org/en/news/press-release/2019/04/08/record-high-remittancessent-globally-in-2018

World Bank Group. (2021). *Global economic prospects, January 2021.* International Bank for Reconstruction and Development/The World Bank.

Albert Wöcke is a former trade unionist turned academic. He is interested in international HR and business in emerging markets, with particular interest in Africa. His work has been published in the *International Journal of Human Resource Management, Journal of International Management* and *The International Business Review* he consults widely to Multinationals in Africa. He has produced several case studies that are taught internationally on several continents. He is currently working on institutions and their impact on firms in Africa. He obtained his PhD from the University of the Witwatersrand in South Africa.

Helena Barnard is the director of doctoral programmes at the University of Pretoria's Gordon Institute of Business Science (GIBS), South Africa, having received her PhD in Management from Rutgers University. Her research interests are in how knowledge (and with it, technology, organizational practices, and innovation) moves between more and less developed countries, particularly in Africa.

IB Research Opportunities in Central Asia

Onajomo Akemu and Venkat Subramanian

1   Introduction

The countries of Central Asia—Kazakhstan, Uzbekistan, Kyrgyzstan, Tajikistan, and Turkmenistan—share a common geography and history.[1] Located in an arid region in the heart of the Eurasian landmass, Central Asia encompasses the Silk Road, the historic overland route between Europe and Asia (Fig. 1). The region has been inhabited since antiquity by various Turkic and Mongol tribes who developed sophisticated civilizations in the riverine south as well as nomadic pastoralism in the northern and central steppes (Collins, 2006: 1–4; Pomfret, 1995: 1–5).

The five Central Asian countries are predominantly Muslim. The majority populations of Kazakhstan (Kazakhs), Kyrgyzstan (Kyrgyz), Uzbekistan (Uzbeks), and Turkmenistan (Turkmen) speak close-related Turkic languages, while Tajikistan's Tajiks and more recent Slavic, German, and Korean immigrants are the main non-Turkic groups in the region (Pomfret, 1995: 3–6). All five countries came under Russian imperial rule in the nineteenth century and became titular republics under the Soviet Union after the 1917 Russian Revolution (Cooley, 2012: 17–18). After the collapse of the USSR in the early 1990s, the Central Asian republics became independent countries and suffered some of the most sustained economic contractions among the former Soviet Union countries.[2] However, over the next two decades, these economies recovered, while nation states of varying stabilities have emerged (Collins, 2006: 1–6). Table 1 presents a snapshot of

---

[1] Officially, Kyrgyzstan is called the Kyrgyz Republic.

[2] We use the terms USSR and Soviet Union interchangeably. Former USSR countries are Armenia, Azerbaijan, Belarus, Estonia, Georgia, Kazakhstan, Kyrgyzstan, Latvia, Lithuania, Moldova, Russia, Tajikistan, Turkmenistan, Ukraine, and Uzbekistan.

O. Akemu (✉) · V. Subramanian
Graduate School of Business (GSB), Nazarbayev University, Nur-Sultan, Kazakhstan
e-mail: onajomo.akemu@nu.edu.kz; subban.venkat@nu.edu.kz

© Springer Nature Switzerland AG 2022   95
H. Merchant (ed.), *The New Frontiers of International Business*, Contributions to
Management Science, https://doi.org/10.1007/978-3-031-06003-8_5

Fig. 1 Maps of Central Asia and Kazakhstan (detail): (**a**) Central Asia and (**b**) Kazakhstan. Source: United Nations

Table 1 Central Asian countries' basic economic data 2019–2020

	Population, (millions)	Area (thousands sq. km)	GDP per capita ($)	Urbanization rate (%)	Life expectancy, (years)
Kazakhstan	18.8	2725	9056	57.7	73
Kyrgyzstan	6.6	200	1174	36.9	72
Tajikistan	9.5	141	859	27.5	71
Turkmenistan	6.0	488	7612	52.5	68
Uzbekistan	34.2	449	1686	50.4	72

Source: The World Bank

the population, gross domestic product (GDP) per capita, and life expectancy of the Central Asian countries.

Despite the historical, economic, and political similarities, the Central Asian countries differ in significant respects: Kazakhstan and Turkmenistan, endowed with abundant mining and petroleum resources, are the richest countries in the region and have the highest urbanization rates as Table 1 shows; Uzbekistan and Tajikistan, less endowed with natural resources, are predominantly rural and poorer.

Even though Central Asia has risen in economic and geopolitical significance in the last two decades (cf. Collins, 2006; Cooley, 2012; Nordin & Weissmann, 2018), international business (IB) scholars have largely ignored the region. Using the Web of Science database, we searched past issues of the six premier IB journals—*Journal of International Business* (JIBS), *Global Strategy Journal, Journal of World Business, Management International Review, International Business Review*, and *Journal of International Management*—but found only two articles in which at least one of the Central Asian countries was the main empirical setting. We are not sure why scholars have ignored Central Asia, given the recent rise in strategy and IB research in emerging countries (e.g., Cuervo-Cazurra & Genc, 2008; Hoskisson et al., 2000; Luo & Tung, 2007; Meyer & Peng, 2016). We speculate that scholarly neglect of Central Asian countries may be due to the relatively small economic footprint of the region (compared to emerging markets such as Russia, China, and Turkey) and its perceived isolation from the global economy.

In this chapter, we show that the Central Asian context holds promise for advancing IB research. Using Kazakhstan, the most developed country in Central Asia, as a lens into the region, we argue that Central Asia presents at least four opportunities to advance IB research. First, due to its geographical proximity and economic links to regional powers Russia, China, and Turkey, Central Asia is susceptible to exogenous shocks involving its powerful neighbors. Since MNEs in the region are not isolated from these events, the region offers IB scholars ways to study the influence of geopolitical discontinuities such as inter-state conflict and sanctions on the policies of MNEs, an undeveloped area of IB scholarship (Sun et al., 2021).

Second, Central Asia offers opportunities to understand the nonmarket strategies (NMS) that foreign MNEs adopt to navigate the host country environment at the *host country-MNE* and *home country-MNE* interaction levels. As Post-Soviet Central

Asia emerges as an important arena for great power competition involving Russia (the former imperial power), China (with the need for energy and security on its Western border), and the United States (with the need to secure adjacent regions such as Afghanistan) (Cooley, 2012; Nordin & Weissmann, 2018), it is likely that the economic concerns of foreign MNEs coincide with the security interests of their home country (great power) governments (Phan, 2019). Yet, the IB literature largely ignores the links between international politics and MNE policy, especially in contexts of heightened national security interests. Central Asia offers the opportunity to study this link.

Third, as Central Asian firms start to internationalize their operations, the region offers opportunities to further understand the dynamics of internationalization of state-owned enterprises (SOEs), an emerging area of inquiry in IB scholarship (Cuervo-Cazurra et al., 2014; Kalasin et al., 2020; Wang et al., 2012). Much of that research, focused on emerging countries such as Brazil, China, and Russia, assumes the existence of a unitary state. However, Central Asian governments, who control their internationalizing SOEs, operate not only on formal affiliation within the modern state but also on informal clan networks (Collins, 2006). Central Asia may enable scholars obtain a disaggregated understanding of the impact of formal versus informal affiliation of SOEs' decision-makers on firms' FDI location choices, level, and type of FDI.

Lastly, Central Asia could be fertile ground for investigating whether developed country MNEs (DMNEs)—with superior brands and technology—are more likely than emerging market MNEs (EMNEs) to compete successfully in smaller emerging markets. Research so far has highlighted the firm-specific advantages that EMNEs enjoy because of their ability to negotiate weak institutional environments (Celly et al., 2016; Cuervo-Cazurra & Genc, 2008; Holburn & Zelner, 2010). Central Asia offers an additional explanation: EMNEs may compete successfully in other emerging countries not simply because they have developed capabilities to build cooperative relationships in weak institutional contexts, but also because of the peculiarities of industry structure and the cognitive maps of that individual managers use to navigate their host country environments.

This chapter is organized as follows: first, we present a brief historical and economic overview of Kazakhstan, the most developed country in the region. Thereafter, we present three cases of internationalization of Kazakh firms and then follow up with a discussion of the key themes from the cases. We conclude by reflecting on the challenges in doing organizational research in the region, and opportunities that Central Asia holds for advancing IB research.

2   Kazakhstan: Brief Historical and Macroeconomic Overview

2.1   State-Led Modernization, Resource Booms, and a New Capital City

Kazakhstan's demography and economic development, like that of the other Central Asian countries, were indelibly transformed by the USSR's policies (Collins, 2006; Cooley, 2012; Pomfret, 1995). During the premiership of Joseph Stalin (1922–1952), the Soviet regime built a vast network of labor camps in northern Kazakhstan where political prisoners from across the USSR were detained, becoming involuntary migrants to Kazakhstan (Bissenova, 2012). After Stalin's death, Nikita Khrushchev's government encouraged one to two million ethnic Russians, Belarusians, Ukrainians, and Volga Germans to settle Kazakhstan's "virgin" steppe lands. These waves of forced and voluntary migration altered Kazakhstan's ethnic composition so that by 1979, the population was 36% ethnic Kazakh and 41% Russian (Svanberg, 2014: 1–16). In effect, by the end of the twentieth century, ethnic Kazakhs were a minority in their titular republic.

Under Soviet central planning, Kazakhstan suffered far-reaching ecological damage. The Aral Sea, once the fourth largest lake in the world shrunk to 10% of its original size due to intentive state-directed irrigation (Pomfret, 1995: 28–32). Furthermore, extensive nuclear tests conducted by the Soviet regime between 1949 and 1989 in Semipalatinsk eventually took a devastating human toll in the form of cancers and birth defects among the local population (Nazarbayev, 2012; Pomfret, 1995: 28–32).

The impact of the Soviet system on Kazakhstan's economy was more favorable. While a part of the USSR, Kazakhstan became a significant grain exporter, heavy industries, related to processing of coal and iron ore and manufacture of military equipment, were well-developed (Olcott, 1995: 271–298; Pomfret, 1995: 32–35, 75–97); physical infrastructure such as roads, railroads, and air routes were developed; and universal literacy was achieved. After the Soviet Union collapsed in 1991, Kazakhstan became an independent republic under the leadership of Nursultan Nazarbayev.

At independence, Kazakhstan was a lower middle-income country. However, its significant but decaying industrial infrastructure was designed to serve Russia. As Pomfret put it, "all [Kazakh] roads, railways and air routes led to Moscow" (Pomfret, 1995: 134). Thus, when the Soviet Union disintegrated, Kazakhstan suffered severe economic dislocation. Between 1991 and 1995, Kazakhstan's GDP fell by 40% and inflation hit 2200% (Alam et al., 2000). Since reaching a nadir in the immediate post-independence era, standards of living in Kazakhstan have improved remarkably. This is largely due to proceeds in the last 25 years from export of the country's significant natural resources, such as iron ore, copper, uranium, and hydrocarbons.

In 1997, Kazakhstan's government moved the country's capital from Almaty in the south to Astana in the north of the country (Fig. 1). Since becoming the country's capital, Astana has emerged as a showcase of futuristic architecture (Fig. 2), colorfully described as "brash and grandiose—and wildly attractive" by *National*

© With kind permission of copyright owner, Dr. Marek Jochec.

Source: SAM_0046 by Alex J. Butler is licensed under CC BY 2.0

Fig. 2 Nur-Sultan, a modern metropolis in the steppes. (Top) Skyline showing Baiterek Tower; (Bottom) Khan Shatyr, the largest "tent" in the world

Geographic Magazine (Lancaster, 2012). The city hosted the 2017 World Expo and was renamed Nur-Sultan in 2019 in honor of President Nursultan Nazarbayev.[3]

Kazakhstan is currently considered an upper middle-income country (The World Bank, 2019). Its population of 19 million people remains ethnically diverse. About

---

[3] We use the historically correct name of the city throughout this chapter.

58% of the population live in major cities, the largest of which are Almaty (population 1.9 million), Nur-Sultan (1.1 million) and Shymkent (1.0 million), Aqtöbe (500,000), and Qaraghandy (500,000) (Bureau of National Statistics Republic of Kazakhstan, 2021). Kazakh and Russian are official languages while English has become popular particularly among younger Kazakhs living in the major urban centers.

2.2 Macroeconomic Overview

Being an integral part of the USSR, Kazakhstan inherited a highly planned economy at independence: private property was non-existent; and prices were controlled by government bureaucrats (Alam et al., 2000). Over the past three decades, as price liberalization and privatization took root, the economy has grown to be the largest economy in Central Asia and second largest (after Russia) among the former USSR countries.

Starting from a relatively low base in the 1990s, Kazakhstan's GDP grew steadily in the 2000s. In 1999, Kazakhstan's GDP was $17 billion and GDP per capita $1132; by 2013, GDP had increased to $237 billion, while GDP per capita reached approximately $14,000 (International Monetary Fund, 2021). GDP growth, fueled by the global boom in commodity prices in the 2000s, was accompanied by declines in the poverty rate from 47% to 2.5%. Figure 3 compares the trends in GDP per capita of Kazakhstan, the other four Central Asian countries, and Russia.

Kazakhstan's GDP per capita has since dropped from the 2013 peak due to various factors: decline in oil prices; Western-led sanctions on Kazakhstan's largest trading partner, Russia, which led to devaluation of the national currency (the tenge); and the 2020 COVID-19 pandemic which led to 2.6% decline in GDP. Nevertheless, with a GDP per capita of $9056 in 2020, Kazakhstan is still the most prosperous country in Central Asia.

Over half (54%) of GDP growth in the period 2000–2019 was concentrated in wholesale and retail trade, manufacturing, taxes on products and transportation, and storage sectors (Fig. 4). As of 2019, services accounted for 52% of Kazakhstan's GDP; primary industries, such as agriculture, mining, quarrying, forestry, and fishing, 21% of GDP; manufacturing 11%; taxes on imports and products 9%; and construction 4% (Statistics Committee of Kazakhstan, 2021).

Kazakhstan's export sector is dominated by merchandise exports. In the period 2008–2018, 91% of Kazakhstan's exports were merchandise and 9% services (National Bank of Kazakhstan, 2021a). Figure 5 and Fig. 6 show a breakdown of the country's merchandise and service exports, respectively. Fuel and mining products (the dark blue trend in Fig. 5) were the predominant form of exports in the period 2008–2019. In 2019, for instance, Kazakhstan's fuels and mining products comprised $46 billion (81%), while chemicals, iron and steel, agricultural products, and manufactured goods generated $11 billion (19%) of merchandise exports. Transportation and travel are the principal forms of service export in the period 2008–2018, accounting for almost $6.3 billion (86%) of service exports in 2018.

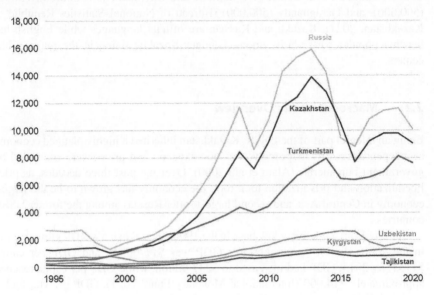

Fig. 3 Comparison GDP per capita of Central Asian countries and Russia 2010–2019. Source: World Bank

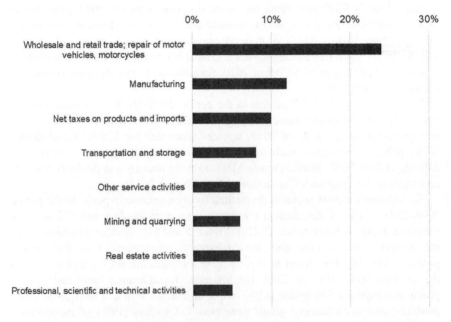

Fig. 4 Sector share of change in Kazakhstan's real GDP, 2010–2019. 100% = KZT 12,647 billion. Source: Bureau of National Statistics Republic of Kazakhstan

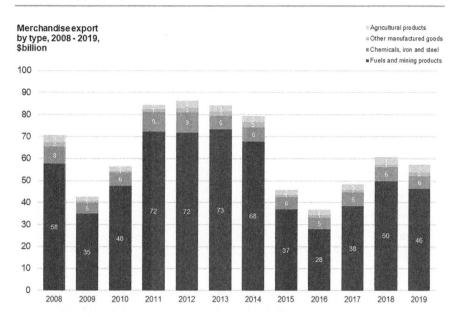

Fig. 5 Kazakhstan's export merchandise mix, 2004–2019. Source: World Trade Organization. Data labels represent dollar amounts

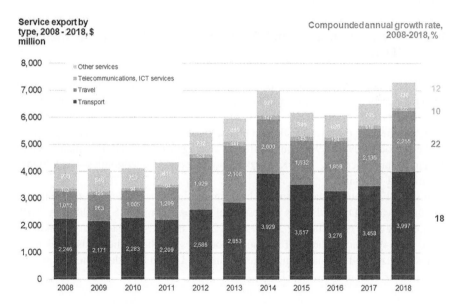

Fig. 6 Kazakhstan's service export mix, 2008–2018. Source: National Bank of Kazakhstan. Data labels represent dollar amounts

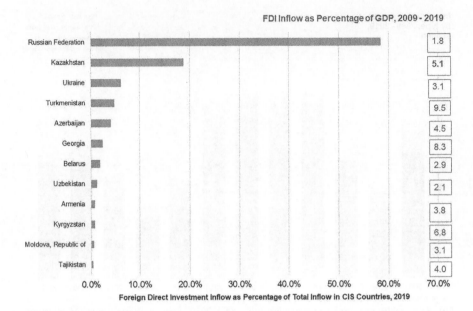

Fig. 7 Share of IFDI stock of countries in the CIS region, 2019. Source: United Nations Conference on Trade and Development

2.3   Trends in Inward and Outward Foreign Direct Investment (FDI)

Kazakhstan is an attractive destination for FDI. In 2019, for instance, Kazakhstan attracted nearly 20% of all inward FDI (IFDI) among the CIS countries.[4] See Fig. 7. (Russia attracted almost 60% of IFDI in the same period.) Kazakhstan's inward FDI intensity, the ratio of inward FDI to GDP in a given year, is also relatively high: IFDI in the period 2009–2019 accounted for an average of 5.1% GDP annually. Only Turkmenistan, Georgia, and Kyrgyzstan—with smaller economies—had higher inward FDI intensity.

Inward FDI into Kazakhstan has been increasing since independence (Fig. 8). Annual inward FDI reached its highest level of approximately $14 billion in 2018, but tapered off at $3 billion in 2019. As of 2019, inward FDI stock in Kazakhstan stood at $149 billion. The top FDI source countries are the Netherlands, the United States, Switzerland, China, France, Russia, and the United Kingdom; they contribute 70% of Kazakhstan's inward FDI (Fig. 9).

---

[4]The Commonwealth of Independent States (CIS) consists of 12 former USSR republics: Armenia, Azerbaijan, Belarus, Georgia, Kazakhstan, Kyrgyzstan, Moldova, Russia, Tajikistan, Turkmenistan, Ukraine, and Uzbekistan. Latvia, Lithuania, and Estonia, though former USSR republics, are not part of the CIS.

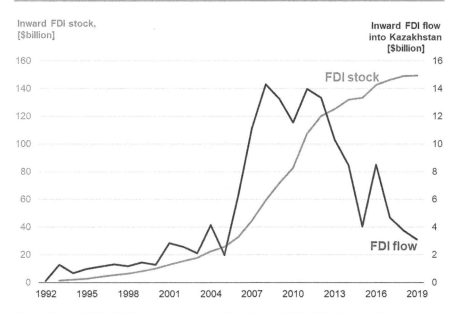

Fig. 8 Inward FDI (IFDI) stock and flow in Kazakhstan, 1993–2019. Source: United Nations Conference on Trade and Development

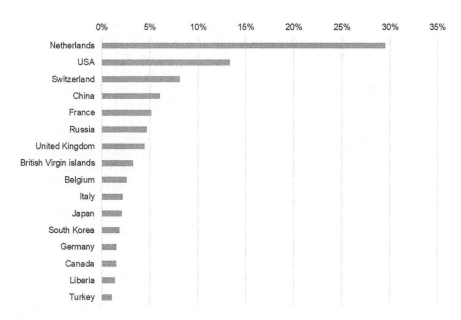

Fig. 9 Top Sources of IFDI stock into Kazakhstan, 2019. 100% = $149 billion. Source: National Bank of Kazakhstan

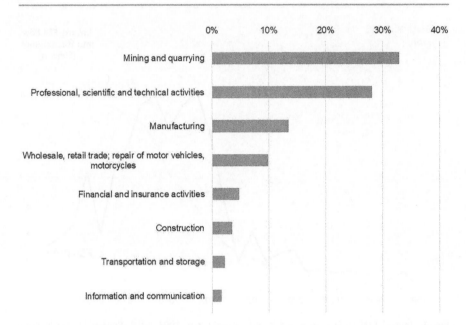

Fig. 10 Sectoral breakdown of IFDI stock in Kazakhstan per sector, 2019.100% = $149 billion. Source: National Bank of Kazakhstan

Given Kazakhstan's abundant natural resources, it is unsurprising that the mining and quarrying sector receives the largest share of inward FDI—33% (Fig. 10); 30% of FDI is channeled to service sectors such as professional and technical services; manufacturing accounts for 13% of FDI, while trade attracts about 10%.

Kazakh firms are not only recipients of FDI; increasingly, they also invest abroad. Figure 11 shows the outward FDI (OFDI) trends of Kazakh firms since the country gained independence from the Soviet Union. The OFDI stock of Kazakh firms rose from virtually zero in 1995 and peaked at $27 billion in 2015. Since 2015, OFDI stock has decreased from the peak to about $16 billion. The top five destinations for outward FDI by Kazakh firms in the period 2005–2020 were the Netherlands (59%), the United Kingdom (9%), the Russian Federation (6%), the Cayman Islands (3%), and Ireland (3%) (National Bank of Kazakhstan, 2021b).

Interestingly, The Netherlands is the top destination and source of OFDI and IFDI respectively. This pattern may indicate round tripping, whereby Kazakh firms invest in Kazakhstan using special investment vehicles domiciled in The Netherlands that take advantage of The Netherlands's tax laws. Though the data is inconclusive, round tripping is consistent with another piece of evidence: the most attractive sector for Kazakh firms investing abroad is "professional, scientific and technical services." This sector comprising firms whose main activities is "head offices, management and consultancy services" accounted for $2.2billion average annual OFDI from Kazakhstan between 2010 and 2020 (See Fig. 12).

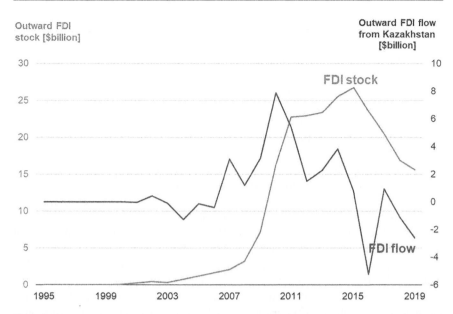

Fig. 11 Outward FDI (OFDI) stock and flow from Kazakhstan, 1995–2019. Source: United Nations Conference on Trade and Development

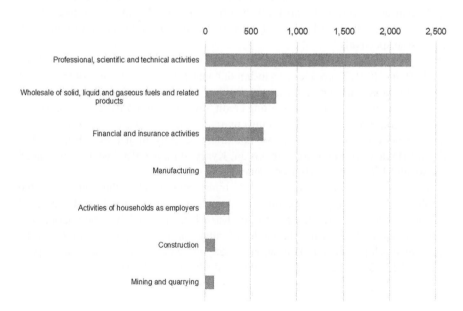

Fig. 12 Average gross annual OFDI per sector from Kazakhstan, 2010–2020, $million. Source: National Bank of Kazakhstan

Kazakhstan has also benefited from its proximity to large emerging markets—China, Russia, and Turkey. As an indication of Kazakhstan's importance to China's global objectives, President Xi Jinping of China announced the Belt and Road Initiative (BRI), an ambitious infrastructure project linking China with Europe, while on a state visit to Kazakhstan in 2013 (Ministry of Foreign Affairs of the People's Republic of China, 2013). Since the announcement, Kazakhstan has received significant Chinese investments in road and rail infrastructure connecting China to Russia and Europe (Shepard, 2016).

2.4 The Business Environment in Kazakhstan

Kazakhstan's business environment is ranked highest among the Central Asian countries. The World Economic Forum (WEF) competitive index, a measure of the "set of institutions, policies and factors that determine the level of productivity" (Schwab, 2019: xiii), compares the business environments of 141 countries. The index (scaled 0–100) is computed from a country's score on (1) the quality of the enabling environment for productivity, institutions, infrastructure, ICT adoption, and macroeconomic stability; (2) human capital, the health and skills of the workforce; (3) size and sophistication of labor markets, product markets, the financial system, and economy; and (4) the quality of the innovation ecosystem reflected in the dynamism and innovation capability of firms. Overall, Kazakhstan ranked 55 in 2019 (Schwab, 2019: 314–317), while Kyrgyzstan and Tajikistan were ranked 96 and 104, respectively.[5]

Another index, the World Bank's annual Ease of Doing Business survey (The World Bank, 2021a), provides a snapshot of countries on ten measures of the ease of doing business: starting a business, dealing with construction permits, getting electricity, registering property, getting credit, protecting minority investors, paying taxes, trading across borders, enforcing contracts, and resolving insolvency. In 2020, Kazakhstan was ranked 25 (of 190 countries), slightly higher than Russia (28), China (31), and Turkey (33). Uzbekistan, Kyrgyzstan, and Tajikistan were ranked 69, 80, and 106, respectively (see Table 2).

So far, we have traced Kazakhstan's transformation after the collapse of the USSR into a relatively prosperous and attractive economy for FDI. In the next section, we present case studies of three Kazakh firms that have internationalized their operations. We discuss the modes of entry that the companies employed, the firms' ownership structure, their target market, and their internationalization experience to date. Thereafter, we discuss the implications for IB research.

---

[5]Turkmenistan and Uzbekistan were not featured in 2019 WEF report.

Table 2 Ease of doing business in Central Asian countries compared with selected countries

Economy	United States	Kazakhstan	Russian Federation	China	Turkey	Uzbekistan	Kyrgyz Republic	Tajikistan
Overall ranking	6	25	28	31	33	69	80	106
Starting a business	55	22	40	27	77	8	42	36
Dealing with construction permits	24	37	26	33	53	132	90	137
Getting electricity	64	67	7	12	41	36	143	163
Registering property	39	24	12	28	27	72	7	77
Getting credit	4	25	25	80	37	67	15	11
Protecting minority investors	36	7	72	28	21	37	128	128
Paying taxes	25	64	58	105	26	69	117	139
Trading across borders	39	105	99	56	44	152	89	141
Enforcing contracts	17	4	21	5	24	22	134	76
Resolving insolvency	2	42	57	51	120	100	78	153

Source: The World Bank

3   Air Astana

Air Astana is Kazakhstan's flagship carrier. The airline, founded in 2001, is owned by the Air Astana Company, a joint venture between the government of Kazakhstan represented by Samruk-Kazyna, the country's national wealth fund, and BAE Systems PLC of the United Kingdom (Air Astana, 2021). Air Astana operates from two hubs: Almaty, Kazakhstan's industrial capital in the south of the country, and Nur-Sultan, the administrative capital in the north. (See Fig. 1b for the location of both cities.) In 2019, Air Astana generated revenues of $899 million and operating profit of $79 million (Air Astana, 2020: 36). In 2020, due to the COVID pandemic, revenue dropped to $400 million, and the company suffered an operating loss of $69 million. As of early 2020, the company employed about 4800 people (Air Astana, 2021). Air Astana's current Board of Directors consists of representatives of Samruk-Kazyna, BAE Systems, independent directors, and the President and CEO Peter Foster (Air Astana, 2021: 9).

3.1   Scope of Operations: To Make or Buy Maintenance Services

Air Astana is widely regarded as the leading airline in Central Asia (Air Astana, 2018). In the 2010s, as the airline developed an network of routes primarily to destinations in the former Soviet Union, Europe, and Asia, senior managers began considering entering the market for aircraft maintenance. At the time, Air Astana's 450-staff engineering and maintenance department provided in-house maintenance service on the company's fleet of aircraft. These services included routine engine changes, landing gear changes, and inspections known in the airline industry as A-checks.

In 2012, with the engineering staff gaining experience in these routine checks, senior managers became more confident that they could perform more complicated maintenance known as C-checks. At the time, Air Astana outsourced C-checks on its fleet, consisting of Boeing B757 and B767; Airbus A319, A320, and A321; and Embraer E190 aircrafts, to maintenance, repair, and overhaul (MRO) facilities in China, Russia, and Portugal (Harbison, 2019). The principal rationale for doing the complex maintenance in-house was to reduce engineering and maintenance costs, which amounted to nearly 15% of Air Astana's operating expenses (Air Astana, 2015: 184–186).[6]

The engineering team at Air Astana proposed to open an MRO facility to perform C-checks if the airline's fleet size reached 20 aircraft. Economic analysis, however, indicated that an in-house MRO operation could not break even at that fleet strength since MRO facilities tend to be asset specific, i.e., they are tailored to a specific

---

[6] As we write this chapter (November 2021), Air Astana operates a fleet of 34 aircraft consisting of Boeing 767, Airbus A320, Airbus A320neo, Airbus A321, Airbus A321neo, A321neo LR, and Embraer E190-E2 aircrafts (Air Astana, 2021).

aircraft type and are subject to scale economies with inventory and equipment. By 2013–2014, however, Air Astana's fleet had expanded to 30 aircraft. As the company adopted an ambitious strategy to double its fleet size within a decade (Air Astana, 2015: 10), the economics of upgrading the company's MRO capabilities became more attractive.

Air Astana's management decided to center the company's MRO capabilities on the Airbus A320 aircraft because they expected the number of Airbus A320 aircraft within the fleet to grow (Air Astana, 2015). Focusing MRO capability on the Airbus A320 model not only allowed Air Astana's engineering and maintenance staff service the company's growing fleet in-house, but it also enabled Air Astana to target airlines in the region with Airbus planes in their fleet. At the time, there were about 2000 Airbus aircraft in the region (1300 were in China and 500 in Russia and Turkey). Air Astana management hoped that the MRO facilities would attract clients from neighboring countries such as Russia, Tajikistan, and Kyrgyzstan.

Air Astana also had to decide the location of the MRO operation within Kazakhstan. The choice boiled down to Nur-Sultan (Astana) in the north, which is close to Russia, and Almaty in the south, close to China (see Fig. 1). Air Astana maintenance operations in both these cities' airports presented different challenges to an MRO. On one hand, Almaty remained a key hub for Air Astana as 70% of its fleet was stationed in Almaty. Yet, Air Astana's facilities in Almaty, leased from the airport operator, were considered too small for an MRO operation. The airport territory was already congested; it was virtually impossible to build an essential spare part warehouse within the airport. This meant that the warehouse had to be located outside the airport, creating additional customs clearance and security hurdles.

Nur-Sultan's newer airport, on the other hand, offered more flexibility. Air Astana owned the facility at Nur-Sultan airport. Furthermore, the airport's commodious hangar could host two A320 planes or three Embraers or one wide-body Boeing 787 Dreamliner. Thus, Air Astana management decided to establish the MRO at Nur-Sultan in 2015. The MRO facility at Nur-Sultan airport was eventually completed and commissioned in 2018 (Air Astana, 2018; Khaidar, 2018).

3.2   Internationalization: Local Value Addition in Global Value Chain

Air Astana management assumed that the company has two sources of competitive advantage in the MRO business. First, managers hoped to leverage Kazakhstan's location, close to China and Russia, important markets for Airbus, to gain a foothold in those markets. Second, low wage rates in Kazakhstan also reduced the cost of providing MRO services. Engineering staff at Air Astana regularly traveled to China and Europe to learn about maintenance work; in the process, they had learned how to perform those operations themselves. Air Astana's management thus thought the company had a pool of relatively low-wage qualified engineering staff and had no need to hire expensive expatriate personnel to staff its MRO operation.

The company also enjoyed additional advantages that enabled it to develop an internationalization strategy: support from the Kazakh government and international managerial expertise. Senior management comprised expatriate managers who brought managerial capability from the global airline industry to Air Astana. Peter Foster, for instance, the President/CEO since 2005, had 35 years' experience at Cathay Pacific Airways and Royal Brunei Airlines. Unlike in other state-owned enterprises (SOEs) in transition countries, where political patronage plays a major role in strategic decisions (Musacchio et al., 2015), Air Astana management was given the leeway to lead the airline based on commercial rather than political considerations. In addition, the government invested in infrastructure that benefited the airline. Nur-Sultan's airport, for instance, was modernized in preparation for the 2017 Expo. The larger airport and the global exhibition allowed the airline to leverage increased passenger traffic to further build its brand and network.

Nevertheless, Air Astana faced several challenges as it established the MRO operation. These challenges can be classified at the firm, industry, and institutional levels. We elaborate on these.

3.2.1   Firm Level: Capability Gaps

Regardless of support from the Kazakh government and an internationally reputable management team, Air Astana was a relatively new entrant in an industry that prizes operational excellence, safety, and reliability. The principal challenge facing Air Astana was how to gain international credibility and certification for its third-party MRO services. Managers soon discovered that MRO operations required more skilled engineering and technical staff than they had initially thought. There was a paucity in supply of well-trained engineers from the country's only civil aviation academy located in Almaty. Moreover, these engineers were not instructed in the EU's standard of aviation; hence, the few students who graduated from the academy were not qualified to work in MRO operations.

Air Astana managers responded by creating internship and certification programs for engineering students. These, however, ended in failure. The student interns did not like the career prospects in the engineering departments of the airline. As the chief engineer at Air Astana observed, "we had students from top engineering schools interning with us. We took them in the hope that they would want to work with us after graduating; however, they did not want to work with us, they wanted to go directly to offices, become directors, and we understand that."

3.2.2   Industry Dynamics, Competition, and Location Challenges

It is expensive to keep inventories of aircraft spare parts. Thus, most airlines use just-in-time (JIT) purchasing systems to acquire spare parts needed for aircraft maintenance and repair. MROs located in European industrial clusters benefit from being co-located with other MROs in a single market; in case of emergency repairs, parts can be easily transported without custom controls and at low logisitics costs. Doing just-in-time delivery for an MRO operation in Kazakhstan, located far from the major aerospace hubs in Europe and America, involved more complicated logistics. To address this logistical challenge, Air Astana negotiated with its main supplier to establish a "hot shelf" of parts located in Nur-Sultan, but owned by the supplier (Air Astana was billed when parts are by the airline.)

Air Astana relied principally on European suppliers instead of on Russian suppliers because even though Russia and Kazakhstan belong to a single customs union, European suppliers were able to guarantee speed of delivery, high quality, and competitive prices.

Other challenges for Air Astana's third-party MRO business included competition within the major airline hubs in the region—in Russia, Turkey, and China. All three major aerospace markets had MRO operators that serviced local carriers. Air Astana management could only hope to cater to residual demand from those markets. As the chief engineer at Air Astana remarked, "There are some MROs in Russia, but they are not enough for the demand, and we certainly expect that some of the airlines will fly in and repair their planes in Kazakhstan."

3.2.3   Institutional Friction

The nearest MROs outside Kazakhstan, where Air Astana could secure spare parts at short notice, were located in China and Turkey. However, this meant crew and aircraft had to pass through customs control and pay additional transportation and customs clearance fees, resulting in delayed repairs which, in turn, made the MRO operation uncompetitive. Cumbersome customs legislation in Kazakhstan further complicated managing the supply chain. Air Astana manager complained that spare parts were often stuck with customs agents as the company tried to reach an agreement with the government authorities for speedy processing in Almaty. Since the Nur-Sultan MRO center was completed, Air Astana reported conducting maintenance services for Qatar Airways, Turkish Airlines, and LOT Polish Airlines (Air Astana, 2020: 33) and claimed its MRO facilities service more than 20 third-party airlines (Pozzi, 2021).

In sum, Air Astana, Kazakhstan's flagship carrier, has emerged as an important regional airline. The company has attempted to incorporate itself more fully into global supply chains by entering the market in MRO services. However, the company has struggled to hone the capabilities to serve discerning foreign clients while facing down competition from providers in more established aerospace markets such as China, Russia, and Turkey. Despite enjoying the support of its home country government, Air Astana still suffers from the disadvantages of its location: institutional friction in the form of complex custom clearance procedures and remoteness from global supply chains conspire to reduce the efficiency of the firm's supply chain and increase its transaction costs.

4   BI Holding

Privately held BI Holding is the largest construction company in Kazakhstan (BI Group, 2021). In 2019, the company ranked as the 186th largest construction company by revenue in the world (ENR: Engineering News Record, 2019). In that year, BI had 5800 employees; it generated 412 billion tenge ($1.1 billion) in revenue with operating profit of 57 billion tenge ($150 million).

BI was founded in 1995 by Aidyn Rakhimbayev, Askhat Omarov, and Bauyrzhan Issabayev shortly before Kazakhstan's government moved the capital to Astana. Sustained by soaring commodity prices in the 2000s, the government financed a construction boom in Astana as buildings and civil infrastructure were erected to befit the capital city. BI began constructing residential apartments for the city's growing population as the capital attracted people seeking employment and social mobility. BI's founders, at the helm of the company, retain executive control: Rakhimbayev is the Chairman of the Board of BI Holding, while Omarov and Issabayev are directors.

4.1   Scope of Operations: Dominating the Domestic Market

BI companies operate across most segments of Kazakhstan's construction industry. BI Development, the largest BI company by revenue (see Table 3), constructs residential and commercial real estate principally in Nur-Sultan, Atyrau, and Almaty (see Fig. 1 for location of those cities). BI Construction & Engineering focuses on the construction of assets in the civil and industrial segments for municipal governments, oil and gas companies, and manufacturing companies. See Table 3 and Fig. 13.

BI Infra Construction operates in the civil segment, constructing roads and bridges for Kazakhstan's state-owned companies and national infrastructure bodies. In 2013, BI Infra Construction completed roads in northwest Kazakhstan (Fig. 1) that form part of the Western Europe-Western China Transit Corridor, a key link in China's Belt and Road Initiative (Shepard, 2016). BI Property and BI Clients operate residential and commercial real estate, respectively, providing maintenance, repair, and plumbing services to customers in business centers, apartment complexes, and single-family units in Nur-Sultan, Atyrau, and Almaty.

Table 3 Overview of BI companies

	Share of revenue, % (2019)[a]	Profit margin, %	Market share, %
BI Construction & Engineering	33	8	Civil: 13 Industrial: 5
BI Development	51	12	Nur-Sultan: 50 Almaty: 12 Atyrau: 42
BI Infra Construction	14	- 4	9
BI Property	3	2	N/A
BI Clients	–	0	16

Source: Table compiled by authors
[a]Percentages do not add up to 100 due to rounding

© With kind permission of copyright owner, Dr. Marek Jochec.

Source: BI Group (https://images.app.goo.gl/jwcriaBmri7mjdcf9)

Fig. 13 Civil infrastructure projects constructed by BI in Nur-Sultan (Astana). (Top) Botanical Garden; (Bottom) Peace Wall

4.2   Internationalization: Home Advantages Do Not Transfer Easily

As the company dominated the building segment in Kazakhstan's capital city, it enjoyed at least three advantages. First, BI had significant bargaining power with suppliers. A BI manager we interviewed put it succinctly, "we [BI] get the best price [in Kazakhstan] from suppliers and subcontractors." Such privileged relationships with suppliers translate into operational efficiency advantage for the company.

Second, through years of experience in the sector in Kazakhstan, BI developed internal project management processes which—coupled with the company's cost advantage with suppliers—allowed it to reliably build structures on time and within budget. This translated to reputational advantage in commercial tender applications where clients highly prized reliability, assurance of quality, and on-time delivery.

Lastly, the company developed relationships with municipal authorities that allowed it to navigate the formidable bureaucratic process required to acquire construction inputs, such as prime land in Nur-Sultan and municipal services, such as electricity and heating, required to develop real estate.

Realizing that BI enjoyed a commanding share of the home market, Rakhimbayev and his leadership team decided to pursue projects in foreign markets in 2016. "We were now getting too big for one country. So, we decided to go out of Kazakhstan," one manager recalled. We summarize BI's internationalization experience to date: in Georgia, Russia, Saudi Arabia, and Uzbekistan.

4.2.1 Georgia

In 2017, the government of Georgia announced an open tender for construction of highways in the country. Georgia, with a population of 3.7 million, was considered an attractive market because it has a shared history with Kazakhstan as part of the USSR and a relatively transparent business and political culture. Said one BI manager involved in the tender process, "Georgia is a very open country—they have European Union flags everywhere and so on; they feel like they are a part of Europe." BI's leaders reasoned that if the company could compete in Georgia, then it had a shot at the European Union's large, mature infrastructure markets.

The tender attracted bids from European, Indian, Chinese, and Turkish construction companies. When the results of the bid were announced in late 2017, the top seven bids were from Chinese companies. BI could not compete with large Chinese infrastructure companies. "So, you have this open country, but you have this Chinese competition...we realized this [price competition in a foreign market] was not for us."

4.2.2 Russia

Entering Russia's construction market seemed like a "natural" choice for BI in 2019 due to strong historical and economic ties between Kazakhstan and Russia. BI's leaders discovered quickly, however, that BI faced several disadvantages in Russia. First, unlike in Kazakhstan, BI enjoyed little leverage with suppliers in Russia. Local subcontractors tended to offer high prices to foreign contractors. A manager familiar with BI's efforts in Russia commented: "If you are very active on the [Russian] market they give you a discount. If not...they charge a higher price meaning your price will be higher than that of your competitors."

Second, the importance that Russian public sector clients placed on relationships set insurmountable barriers to new entrants. Another manager recalled BI's experience bidding for a road construction project in West Russia, "The personal relations [with government clients] are very important. If you go to government projects you need references...they will ask you, 'Have you completed three projects like this in Russia?'...you may be a perfect road constructor in Kazakhstan but what are you going to do when you come to Russia?"

Third, payment terms in construction contracts put onerous obligations on contractors, but awarded Russian clients many rights. This increased the risks for BI, with lower institutional knowledge and local networks. "If you are foreigner, you cannot sign this contract...the contractual terms are not acceptable." BI leaders eventually pulled out the company of the Russian market.

4.2.3   Saudi Arabia

In 2019, BI was invited to bid for a lucrative infrastructure project in Saudi Arabia. BI's leaders saw the tender as an opportunity to win a major project (>$100 million value) that would set BI on a course to operating in major construction markets. As BI's engineers prepared the tender document, however, they encountered the limitations of their home country's banking system. In order to submit tenders, bidding contractors in Saudi Arabia were required to pay a hefty bid bond. The bond is essentially a financial guarantee that the bidding company will construct the asset if they win the tender. If the company cannot construct the asset after winning the tender, then they forfeit the bond. No Kazakh bank could offer the guarantee to the Saudi client; there were no official relations between Saudi and Kazakh banks. BI Group had to borrow the money to pay the bid bond. Given the high cost of capital in Kazakhstan (The Business Year, 2017), it was unlikely that the Saudi project would generate the anticipated margins to support such a high interest loan.

There were ways to reduce the bid cost and improve margins. BI's leaders could have, for instance, hired engineers in Saudi Arabia instead of bringing them from Kazakhstan. However, cost reduction was not Rakhimbayev's only concern: it was not clear to BI's leaders what value they would have added to the client by simply reducing cost:

[I]f you bring a Kazakh engineer to Saudi Arabia it is very expensive...The Kazakh engineer is 3–4 times more expensive than an Egyptian engineer...You may hire Egyptian engineers in Saudi Arabia, but what then your contribution to this project? Is it just the name BI Group with the same structure as a local company? (Manager #1, BI)

Like they did in Russia, Rakhimbayev and his leadership team pulled the plug on the Saudi Arabian internationalization effort.

4.2.4   Uzbekistan

Bordering Kazakhstan in the south (Fig. 1), Uzbekistan is more populous, but considerably poorer than Kazakhstan (see Table 1). Though Uzbekistan and Kazakhstan share similar cultures, languages and history, Uzbekistan—under its first President Islam Karimov—was relatively closed to foreign investment. Since Karimov's death in 2016, however, the country has become more open to foreign investment (Nishanov, 2017).

In 2017, BI created a joint venture with an Uzbek company to construct commercial and residential real estate in the country's capital, Tashkent. Though projects in Uzbekistan were lower value than construction projects in Russia and Saudi Arabia, BI's leaders concluded that Tashkent had an underserved residential real estate market; they hoped to draw on BI capabilities in building residential apartments in Kazakhstan to provide housing to customers in Tashkent, a city with a population of nearly three million people:

> We understand that people [in Tashkent] need and look for apartments that give value for money...When I have been to Uzbekistan—my first time was maybe two years ago—I think it [Tashkent] really reminds me of Astana [Nur-Sultan] ten years ago. We think it is a great opportunity for us to expand our market and our brand. (Manager #2, BI)

These efforts appear to be more successful. In early 2020, BI's joint venture (JV) in Uzbekistan won a tender for the construction of Tashkent's International School. Also, in March 2020, BI's joint venture in Uzbekistan invested $33 million in an 850-unit business segment residential property in Tashkent. Of the 850 units, 60 had been pre-sold at the time of writing (UZ Daily, 2020).

In sum then, BI is a privately owned mid-size construction firm dominant in its home market in Kazakhstan. It enjoys cost advantages, reputation advantages, and local institutional knowledge. In order to seek new markets, BI has in recent years tried expanding operations to countries in the former Soviet Union, but has met with limited success in those ventures.

5 KazMunayGas (KMG)

KazMunayGas (KMG) is Kazakhstan's national oil and gas company. The company, formed in February 2002, is currently owned by two state-controlled entities: Kazakhstan's sovereign wealth fund, Samruk-Kazyna (90.42% equity stake), and the central bank, the National Bank of Kazakhstan (9.58%). KMG was formed to control the Kazakh government's interests in the country's oil and gas sector (Kaiser & Pulsipher, 2007). After independence from the Soviet Union, Kazakhstan's government had offered generous contractual terms to foreign oil and gas companies in order to attract new sources of expertise and investment into the country's declining oil industry. KMG's 2002 formation was widely seen as a way for the government to renegotiate its unfavorable position in previously signed agreements (Kaiser & Pulsipher, 2007).

5.1 Scope of Operations

KMG operates in Kazakhstan and Romania. In 2019, KMG generated approximately revenue $18 billion and EBITDA $5 billion and had about 71,000 employees (KazMunayGas, 2019: 74–77). As we write this chapter, the company's CEO and head of the management board is Aidarbayev Serikovich, an oil industry veteran and former mayor of Mangistau, west Kazakhstan (see Fig. 1). KMG's Board of Directors consists of three foreign directors (American, Australian, and British), three representatives of Samruk-Kazyna, and the CEO. The Chairman of the Board is Chris Walton, an Australian (KazMunayGas, 2021a).

KMG plays a pervasive role in Kazakhstan's oil and gas sector (Kaiser & Pulsipher, 2007). The company is a vertically integrated oil and gas company, operating in every stage of the industry value chain—upstream, midstream, and downstream.

The upstream segment of the industry consists of firms involved in the exploration and production of crude hydrocarbons. In this segment, KMG's footprint includes joint ventures—with foreign oil and gas majors—in companies that operate Kazakhstan's three giant oilfields, Tengiz, Karachaganak, and Kashagan, located in western and northwest of the country. KMG also operates through wholly owned subsidiaries or joint ventures smaller assets within Kazakhstan (KazMunayGas, 2019: 44–45). Table 4 shows KMG's assets in Kazakhstan's upstream oil and gas industry.

In the midstream segment of the value chain, i.e., firms that transport and distribute hydrocarbons, KMG is the monopoly operator within Kazakhstan.

Table 4 KMG assets in Kazakhstan's upstream oil and gas industry

Field	Operating company	Shareholders (country of origin)	Equity stake, %
Tengiz	Tengizchevroil (TCO)	KMG (Kazakhstan)	20
		Chevron (USA)	50
		ExxonMobil	25
		LukArco	5
Karachaganak	Karachaganak Petroleum Operating	KMG (Kazakhstan)	10
		Royal Dutch Shell (Netherlands)	29.5
		ENI (Italy)	29.5
		Lukoil (Russia)	18
		Chevron (USA)	13.5
Kashagan	North Caspian Operating Company (NCOC)	KMG (Kazakhstan)	16.88
		ENI (Italy)	16.81
		ExxonMobil (USA)	16.81
		Total (France)	16.81
		Royal Dutch Shell (Netherlands)	16.81
		China National Petroleum Company (China)	8.33
		Inpex (Japan)	7.56

Sources: North Caspian Operating Company (NCOC), KazMunayGas Annual Report 2019

KMG's pipelines transport crude hydrocarbons from oilfields in Kazakhstan to Russia and to western China (see Fig. 1). The company also owns a 20.75% stake in the multinational Caspian Pipeline Consortium, which operates a 1500 km pipeline transporting crude oil from the giant oilfields in northwest Kazakhstan (Fig. 1) to the Black Sea for onward export to Europe (KazMunayGas, 2019).

In the downstream segment, wherein crude oil is refined and converted into products such as gasoline, diesel, and petrochemicals, KMG operates through wholly owned subsidiaries and joint ventures three refineries across Kazakhstan. KMG, through its subsidiary KMG International, owns and operates two refineries in Romania.

5.2   Internationalization: Acquisition of Rompetrol Group

In August 2007, KMG acquired in a private auction 75% stake in The Rompetrol Group (TRG), a Romanian former state-owned oil and gas company, for $2.7 billion (KazMunayGas International, 2007). TRG had been privatized in 1993 during the wave of market reforms that were introduced at the end of communism in Romania. At the time of KMG's acquisition, TRG was active in refining, marketing, and trading of oil as well as in providing engineering services to the oil industry (KazMunayGas, 2008; Kroes, 2007). KMG subsequently acquired the remaining 25% of TRG's shares for an undisclosed sum in 2009 (Reuters, 2009). As a result of the acquisition, KMG obtained controlling interest in TRG's key assets: the Petromidia Refinery, the largest refinery in Romania located on the Black Sea coast; the Vega Refinery, the only naphtha-producing refinery in Central and Eastern Europe; and 902 retail stations across Romania, France, Spain, Ukraine, Albania, Georgia, and Moldova (KazMunayGas, 2008: 26–27, 2019).

KMG's acquisition of TRG appears to be a case of market-seeking FDI wherein a corporation "may consider it necessary, as part of its global production and marketing strategy, to have a physical presence in the leading markets served by its competitors" (Dunning & Lundan, 2008: 71). In the mid-2000s, as oil prices soared and the giant Kashagan oilfield was expected onstream, KMG needed to transport oil to European and Chinese markets without relying on Russian pipelines. The company built in 2005 the Kazakhstan-China pipeline, and the Petromidia Refinery was central to the diversification strategy: KMG exports its crude oil to Europe and the Petromidia Refinery through the Black Sea ports.

Furthermore, KMG wanted enter the downstream segment of the industry. A foothold in Romania, a high-growth emerging economy, which joined the European Union (EU) in January 2007, enabled KMG to access the EU's large single market, particularly countries in Central and Eastern Europe. Following the acquisition, KMG's erstwhile CEO stated, "The acquisition of a majority stake in TRG provides us with a footprint in important downstream markets in Europe, including France, Romania, Moldova and Bulgaria, as well as the ability to utilize TRG as a platform for future expansion...in the high-growth markets of the Black Sea, Balkans and Mediterranean regions" (KazMunayGas International, 2007). KMG later justified the acquisition as way to become a "vertically integrated company of the international level, implementing both exploration, and oil refining, relying on TRG's experience on the European market of oil products" (KazMunayGas, 2008: 27).

After KMG acquired 100% of TRG shares in 2009, TRG was renamed KMG International. However, KMG did not change the brand: all filling stations were still operated under the Rompetrol brand (Rompetrol, 2021). KMG International operates 284 filling stations, and 779 other points of sale across Romania operate in the retail sector in Bulgaria (58 fuel stations, 1 fuel depot), Moldova (95 stations with 73 affiliated shops and 2 fuel depots), and Georgia (85 filling stations, 2 fuel depots) (KazMunayGas, 2021b: 75). According to KMG's consolidated financial statements, KMG's Romanian subsidiary contributed 4.2% of the company's EBITDA (KazMunayGas, 2021b: 76).

KMG's Board of Directors manages KMG International. The Board approves TRG's business plans and budgets and decides on acquisitions and divestitures. At the operational level, senior staff from KMG in Kazakhstan are deputized to work at the Romanian subsidiary. About 50% of the senior management is from KMG Kazakhstan, while at the lower technical levels, that percentage is around 1%. There is indication of knowledge transfer between the Romanian subsidiary and KMG's subsidiaries in Kazakhstan. Rompetrol subsidiary's refineries are considered to be the best performing among KMG's refineries. As such, other KMG refineries benefit from the sharing of operational knowledge.

KMG's market-seeking acquisition of TRG's has faced political scrutiny within Romania. In April 2016, the Prosecutor's Office of Romania opened an investigation of organized crime involving 14 KMG employees. Shortly thereafter, the Romanian government froze KMG's Petromidia Refinery asset alleging irregularities in how Rompetrol had been privatized in the 1990s. According to the Romanian government, TRG's previous owners had a tax liability of $170 million which the government wanted to claim from KMG. KMG executives in Romania, however, believed that the move presaged an intention to nationalize TRG's refineries. They wanted to pay the debt through a combination of cash and shares, whereas Romania's government wanted it in cash. After protracted negotiations, both parties agreed to a payment arrangement, approved by Romania's parliament: in 2018, a Kazakhstan-Romanian investment fund was founded to channel up to $1 billion investment into Romania over a 7-year period (KazMunayGas, 2018). Charges were eventually dismissed in 2019 (KazMunayGas, 2019, 2021b).

6   Discussion

6.1   Internationalization of Kazakh Firms: Motives, Location Choice, and Entry Modes

The three internationalizing Kazakh firms we presented vary in ownership from private to state-owned and in the scale of internationalization from being fully domestic to having international operations.

6.1.1   Motives for Internationalization

Kazakh firms are newcomers to outward internationalization. However, their motives for internationalization are in line with established literature (Dunning & Lundan, 2008: 67–74): market-seeking and strategic asset-seeking. In seeking markets abroad, Kazakh firms such as BI Holding used FDI as a "springboard" to escape a significant domestic market constraint, the small size of their home market (Luo & Tung, 2007).

Yet, these motives are not mutually exclusive; capability development, as well as market-seeking motives, feature prominently in the internationalization decisions of the firms. For instance, as KMG sought access to the downstream sector of the oil industry in Central and Eastern Europe, it learned how to compete in a sophisticated industry sector. Similarly, BI's leaders hoped that by operating in more developed markets, the company would develop capabilities to operate in more sophisticated, lucrative segments of the construction industry outside Kazakhstan. In Air Astana's case, the company's internationalization efforts centered on attracting international clients (from Turkey, China, and Russia) incorporating airline infrastructure into a global value chain by setting up in Kazakhstan value-added activities (airplane maintenance and repair), previously performed in more developed countries.

6.1.2   Location Choice

The Netherlands accounts for the majority (59%) of OFDI from Kazakhstan. Kazakh firms may be taking advantage of the Netherlands' tax laws to set up investment vehicles through which FDI is redirected to other countries. Russia accounts for 6% of OFDI from Kazakhstan. It is fair to assume that unlike FDI directed to the Netherlands, OFDI from Kazakhstan to Russia is intended to take substantive control of firms which add value in Russia itself. If so, then Kazakh firms tend to substantively invest in markets like Russia with similar cultural and institutional environments (Peng et al., 2009) where they may have enjoy the advantage of being able to navigate the institutional settings better than firms from dissimilar institutional backgrounds (Cuervo-Cazurra & Genc, 2008).

6.1.3   Entry Modes of Kazakh Firms

We observe two entry modes among the cases: wholly owned acquisitions (KMG) and joint ventures (BI Holding, Air Astana). KMG's reliance on wholly owned subsidiaries suggests an emphasis on control, while BI and Air Astana's entry modes suggest risk aversion (Peng & Meyer, 2016: 346–352).[7] These entry modes may reflect the Kazakh firms' advantages and their industry peculiarities.

KMG is a state-owned cash-rich firm with access to a valuable resources (crude hydrocarbons); it primarily emphasized equity control and organic growth in its market-seeking acquisitions. Furthermore, despite the complexity of the oil and gas industry, the downstream oil and gas industry involves essentially the production

---

[7]During interviews, BI managers clearly expressed preference for joint ventures because it enabled BI to understand the "rules of the game" in the local market by learning from a local partner.

and marketing of standardized products, such as fuels and petrochemicals. The industry supply chain is global: refining companies sell these standardized products on global markets ultimately to downstream oil and gas marketing firms. Firms compete in this segment of the industry chain by "building cost advantages through the realization of economies of scale" (Bartlett & Ghoshal, 1998: 18). As in the retail sector, purchasing decisions are made by heterogeneous, dispersed customers; however, regulatory approval for refineries, for instance, tends to be concentrated at the national level in host countries. KMG could leverage access to its high-value resource in running its Romanian refineries and sell standardized refined products, but had only to deal with national regulators in Romania following their acquisition of TRG. Hence, the company could afford a non-collaborative entry mode, which allowed control without sacrificing learning about the host countries' market.

BI Holding, on the other hand, is a mid-size firm that operates in an industry notorious for endemic corruption and rent-seeking (Chan & Owusu, 2017). Approvals for permits and purchasing decisions are typically opaque; they are made at the discretion of varied local government and institutional stakeholders. Moreover, supply chains in the construction industry, especially in the civil and building segments, are decidedly local: constructio companies depend on preferential relationships with key local suppliers. Put simply, competing in this industry implies that a foreign firm be locally embedded. Unsurprisingly, then BI Group emphasized acquisitive growth instead of equity control in its international forays.

6.2   Central Asia: Opportunities for Advancing IB Research

Drawing on the case studies and the IB literature, we argue that Central Asia presents at least four broad opportunities for advancing IB research. The first concerns the impact of geopolitical risk on how MNEs navigate their business environment. The five Central Asian countries—Kazakhstan, Kyrgyzstan, Tajikistan, Turkmenistan, and Uzbekistan—are sandwiched between two regional powers, Russia and China, and are culturally proximate to another emerging regional power, Turkey.[8] (Kazakhstan shares a border with Russia and China, the region's main trading partners. See Fig. 1.) Exogenous political shocks involving Central Asia's powerful neighbors may reverberate across the region's business environment since, a foreign MNEs operating in such situations are not "hermetically sealed from the realpolitik of international relations" (Phan, 2019: 1). For instance, in 2014, when the United States and the European Union (EU) imposed sanctions on Russia following the Crimean crisis (Åslund & Snegovaya, 2021), Kazakhstan's currency, the tenge, depreciated significantly following the depreciation of the Russian ruble. For Kazakhstan, a country dependent on oil and gas exports to fund government

---

[8]The official languages of Kazakhstan (Kazakh), Kyrgyzstan (Kyrgyz), Uzbekistan (Uzbek), and Turkmenistan (Turkmen) are mutually intelligible and belong to the same family of languages (Turkic) as Turkish. Tajik, the official language of Tajikistan, is a Persian language.

expenditure, such geopolitical risk threatens inward FDI into that sector. More recently, Western-led sanctions on Russia following Russia's February 2022 invasion of Ukraine significantly impacted the operations of MNEs subsidiaries in Kazakhstan by disrupting supply chains and MNE's ability to raise funds. For instance, managers at a subsidiary of a Western MNE in Kazakhstan have prepared detailed plans for evacuating their Kazakh operations; one manager of a Kazakh MNE that issues bonds on the London Stock Exchange (LSE) complained to us that the sanctions on Russia have increased his company's cost of capital: "No one [in London] even wants to touch us because they are afraid that we're connected to Russia." Yet, the IB literature lacks supranational-level studies evaluating the impact of geopolitical discontinuities on MNE behaviors and policies (Sun et al., 2021). Central Asia, due to its geographical location and susceptibility to exogenous shocks involving its powerful neighbors, is fertile ground for studying how MNEs evaluate and address geopolitical risk affecting their host country business environment and their business operations.

The second opportunity for advancing IB research, closely related to the first, is the importance of nonmarket strategies (NMS) to an MNE's overall business policy. Post-Soviet Central Asia has emerged as an important arena for great power politics (Cooley, 2012: 1–13; Pomfret, 1995: 7–8). China's Belt and Road Initiative, an ambitious geopolitical and economic project consisting of networks of overland transportation, pipeline, and power grids across Eurasia, is backed by "substantial [Chinese] financial as well as political firepower" (Nordin & Weissmann, 2018: 231); it envisions Central Asia, especially Kazakhstan, as critical to its achievement. Furthermore, China maintains an interest in Kazakhstan due to the need to maintain security on its Western border (Cooley, 2012: 6–7); Russia, the former imperial power in Central Asia, keen to maintain regional primacy, sponsors the Eurasian Economic Union (EEU) bloc to promote trade with Central Asian countries (Cooley, 2012: 59–61); and the United States, a power from further afield, maintains an interest in the region due to its need to stabilize adjacent regions, such as Afghanistan (Cooley, 2012: 6–7).

Competition between regional powers, Russia and China, and the United States, as well as interest from other powers such as the EU and Turkey, means that local Central Asian elites often struggle to protect national sovereignty without becoming client states to the great powers (Rachel et al., 2020). Nevertheless, as Alexander Cooley, a noted political scientist, observes, "Central Asian states are not passive pawns in the strategic maneuverings of the great powers, but important actors in their own right" (Cooley, 2012: 8). Since independence from the Soviet Union in the 1990s, Central Asian governments have played a complex balancing act to secure FDI from Western, Russian, and Chinese firms into strategic industries, such as oil and gas, while navigating the diverging interests of the great powers. The Kazakh government, for instance, seeking to reduce the country's dependence on Russian oil export pipelines (Pomfret, 1995: 134), exploited China's growing desire for energy security in the last two decades (Cooley, 2012: 90–93). Working through KazMunayGas, and China National Oil and Gas Exploration and Development Corporation (CNODC), the Kazakh government commissioned, in 2005, pipelines carrying oil from the Caspian Sea in Western Kazakhstan directly to China, bypassing Russia.

In the same vein, the Kazakh government has sought to maintain interest from Russia, China, as well as Western countries (Rachel et al., 2020), by balancing the equity stake of MNEs from those countries in its three giant oilfields (see Table 4). The implication then is that in Central Asia, MNEs' nonmarket strategies (NMS), defined as the pattern of actions taken by the MNE to "improve its performance by managing the institutional or societal context of economic competition" (Mellahi et al., 2016: 144), are likely to dominate their market-based strategies, especially in politically salient industries.

Bargaining models are an important research stream within the IB literature that examines MNE's nonmarket strategies (Ramamurti, 2001; Sun et al., 2021). Ramamurti's (2001) influential two-tier bargaining model, rooted in the experiences of developed country MNEs (DMNEs) as they channeled FDI into developing countries in the 1990s, depicts MNE-host country relations as the outcome of bargaining processes that play out at two levels: first, bargaining between host and home country governments either bilaterally or through multilateral institutions and then, bargaining between the DMNE and the developing country host government, the outcome of which depended on the respective strengths and weaknesses of the parties. However, the model downplays the interactions between DMNEs and their home country governments (Li et al., 2013). Central Asia offers an opportunity to empirically test those interactions ignored in the two-tier model.

Given the region's intrinsic economic significance (large deposits of minerals, oil, and gas in Kazakhstan and Turkmenistan) and the security objectives of the great powers, what role do MNEs' respective home country governments play in facilitating FDI from their countries to the region? How does the salience of the MNEs' industry sector impact the role of respective home country governments? How is the two-tier model, originally proposed by Ramamurti (2001) and extended by Li et al. (2013) to explain Chinese FDI into Africa's natural resource sectors, modified in a region where there is open geopolitical competition between MNEs' home countries?

MNEs' nonmarket strategies in a particular host country are influenced not only by the national objectives of their home (great power) country governments (Phan, 2019) but also by the exigencies of navigating interests of local Central Asian elite who control access to profitable market opportunities. These business elites, with close ties to the state, control traditionally important industries, such as telecommunications, electricity, banking, and mining, as well as less obviously strategic industries such as retail. For instance, Samruk-Kazyna, Kazakhstan's national wealth fund, is a holding company wholly owned by the Kazakh government; it controls various state-owned subsidiaries—including Air Astana and KazMunayGas—whose assets amounted to 57% of the country's GDP in 2010 (Organization for Economic Cooperation and Development, 2013: 66). A foreign MNE operating in Kazakhstan is likely to encounter Samruk-Kazyna's commercial and non-commercial interests. Thus, to compete successfully in Central Asia, foreign MNEs need to understand the local political/power equations and adjust their nonmarket strategies accordingly.

IB research suggests that the ability of an MNE subsidiary to successfully build cooperative relationships with pivotal political actors in places such as Central Asia characterized by heightened rent-seeking rests on firm-specific nonmarket routines (Doh et al., 2012; Frynas et al., 2006; Sun et al., 2010) honed in the home country (Holburn & Zelner, 2010). Central Asia offers the opportunity to advance understanding of NMS by examining not only the firm- and institutional-level antecedents of NMS but also the individual (cognitive) and network (relational) antecedents of an NMS' nonmarket strategies, a relatively unexamined approach to nonmarket strategy within MNEs (Sun et al., 2021). It may be, for instance, that regardless of the prior internationalization experience of the MNE, Western subsidiary managers—with ultimate decision-making authority in the host country—have different cognitive maps of their business environments and the role of the firm than Russian or Chinese managers; this, in turn, may influence their ability to craft cooperative relationships with influential local political actors. It may also be that diversity of the top management team (TMT) of the subsidiary influences the firm's attention and choice of political alliances in its nonmarket strategy.

Nonmarket strategies (NMS) are vital to the success not only of foreign MNEs operating in Central Asian host countries but also of privately held Central Asian firms internationalizing abroad. Theory suggests that firms internationalize to exploit firm-specific advantages in foreign markets (Cuervo-Cazurra & Genc, 2008), to escape home country institutional and market constraints (Dunning & Lundan, 2008), or to acquire more sophisticated capabilities that they can deploy in their home markets (Cuervo-Cazurra et al., 2018; Luo & Tung, 2007). Unlike firms from larger emerging economies such as China, Brazil, Russia, and Turkey, which enjoy market advantages, such as cost competitiveness, or possess intangible assets such as brands and operational expertise, it is not clear what firm-specific advantages Kazakh firms, for instance, have to exploit in international markets. The OFDI activities of Kazakh firms may thus present an opportunity to study the role of nonmarket or political action in firms' internationalization strategies as leading Kazakh firms depend—formally and informally—on state support. Managers, for instance, whom we interviewed hoped that their firms would get official government support in guaranteeing loans to help their internationalization efforts. Yet, the Kazakh state, unlike the Chinese state (Shepard, 2016) or the Korean state, does not have a clear market-driven (or geopolitical) internationalization agenda. Though many state-owned firms dominate sectors such as banking, we are not aware of designated national champions that are expected to internationalize in line with Kazakhstan's industrial policy. How then do state actors decide which firms' internationalization efforts will receive support? How do private firms become incorporated ab initio into global value chains such China's BRI as part of their OFDI efforts?

Third, Central Asia offers opportunities to study the dynamics of internationalization of state-owned enterprises (SOEs). Large Kazakh firms, such as Air Astana and KMG, are state-owned. The burgeoning stream of research examining the internationalization of SOEs suggests that state ownership in firms influences the location, type, and levels of FDI of SOEs (Cuervo-Cazurra et al., 2014; Kalasin et al., 2020; Wang et al., 2012). This body of work, which focuses on large emerging economies such as China (Buckley et al., 2007; Cuervo-Cazurra et al., 2014; Kalasin et al., 2020), usually assumes that SOEs are clients of or respond to the actions of a unitary state. However, state actors in many emerging countries are not unitary; they may exist at various levels such as central and local governments and pursue distinct internationalization agendas (Wang et al., 2012).

In Central Asian countries, state actors can be distinguished not only across formal government affiliation levels—central versus local—but also across informal ethnic or clan affiliation, which pre-date and exist simultaneously with the modern state (Collins, 2006; Minbaeva et al., 2022). Central Asia thus offers the opportunity to examine the influence of informal ethnic networks, independent of formal government affiliation, on the internationalization strategies of SOEs. In the process, Central Asia may enable scholars to obtain a disaggregated understanding of the impact of formal versus informal affiliation of SOEs' key decision-makers on the firms' FDI location, level, and type of FDI.

Lastly, Central Asia could be fertile ground for research examining conditions under which developed country MNEs (DMNEs) are more likely than emerging market MNEs (EMNEs) to compete successfully in smaller emerging markets. Cuervo-Cazurra and Genc (2008) and Celly et al. (2016) argue that EMNEs possess firm-specific advantages in emerging markets that are similar to their home countries. Russian and Chinese MNEs, in particular, bring different competitive advantages to Central Asian markets compared to western MNEs (Subramanian & Abilova, 2020). It may be that the ability of an EMNE to compete successfully in another emerging country depends not only on institutional distance between home and host country but also on the nature of the industry.

In Kazakhstan, DMNEs with capital endowments and superior technology dominate in capital-intensive sectors such as oil and gas. However, in sectors such as retail, banking, and telecommunications, EMNEs appear to outcompete Western MNEs—and local Kazakh firms—by being better able to navigate the institutional environment and possessing superior marketing and distribution capabilities. In 2018, Telia, a Swedish-Finnish telecom operator with subsidiaries in Central Asia, divested its operations in Kazakhstan after it was hit by a series of bribery scandals in its Uzbekistan subsidiary (BBC, 2021; Patterson & Gauthier-Villars, 2015). Telia sold its holding in Kcell, its subsidiary in Kazakhstan, to Kazakhtelecom, a company wholly owned by Samruk-Kazyna (Telia company, 2018). Shortly thereafter, in 2019, Swedish telecom operator Tele2 AB also sold its stake in its Kazakhstan subsidiary to Kazakhtelecom. These divestments effectively gave Kazakhtelecom control of three of Kazakhstan's four mobile telecom operators (Reuters, 2019). The only telecom operator controlled by a foreign privately held MNE in Kazakhstan (38% market share) is Beeline, a subsidiary of Russia's Veon.[9]

---

[9] https://www.veon.com/our-brands/beeline-kazakhstan/

Similarly, Western MNEs do not figure prominently in Kazakhstan's highly concentrated commercial banking sector in which the largest 5 (of the 27) commercial banks in Kazakhstan control 67% of client deposits, 66% of the commercial loan portfolio, and 64% of total assets (National Bank of Kazakhstan, 2021c: 14). Of the top five, Russia's Sberbank (the third largest) is the largest controlled by a foreign MNE; the only large bank subsidiary controlled by a Western MNE is Citibank (#10). Another Western MNE, HSBC (United Kingdom), sold its Kazakhstan subsidiary to Kazakhstan's Halyk Bank in 2014 (Reuters, 2014), which subsequently sold controlling interests in the subsidiary to Chinese investors, China CITIC Bank and China Shuangwei Investment Corporation (Reuters, 2018).

6.3 Doing Organizational Research in Central Asia: Tales from the Field in Kazakhstan

Though the Central Asian context has unique features that enable advancement of IB scholarship, the region presents challenges and opportunities for conducting organizational research. Here, we draw on our experience doing research in Kazakhstan to highlight these challenges and opportunities. They relate to the nascent organizational research culture and difficulty in accessing broad-based firm-level data.

Academic institutions in Kazakhstan, and in Central Asian more broadly, remain at the periphery of the global organizational research landscape. We speculate that the reasons for relative inattention to organizational research stems partly from the countries' low investment in research and development (R&D). Central Asian countries—Kazakhstan, Kyrgyzstan, Tajikistan, and Uzbekistan—spend about 0.1% of GDP on research and development (R&D) (The World Bank, 2021b), much lower than the investment levels of Turkey and Russia, which devote approximately 1% of GDP to R&D.

Low levels of R&D spending at the national level are reflected in the raison d'être of local universities. Kazakh universities, especially those that offer social science programs, are set up principally to teach. Faculty are not incentivized to publish in top academic journals; as such, few local academics tend to be active members of professional bodies such as the Academy of Management (AOM) and the Academy of International Business (AIB). As of November 2021, there were only five registered AOM members at Central Asian academic institutions (two in Kazakhstan, two in Kyrgyzstan, and one in Uzbekistan). Similarly, the Academy of International Business (AIB) has only two registered members within institutions in the region and has no regional chapter in Central Asia. Unsurprisingly, the country's universities do not offer globally accredited graduate training programs in management and organizational research.

That does not mean, however, that there are no talented Kazakh students interested in doing graduate work in organization studies. On the contrary, we have observed keen interest in organizational research among students. For our research projects, we have successfully recruited talented young Kazakh researchers as research assistants (RAs). These young researchers, trained in Kazakhstan's impressive mathematics and science academies and in reputable Western universities, have subsequently gone on to pursue graduate studies at top US and European business schools.

The government of Kazakhstan, a relatively rich country, has recognized the need to develop world-class research capacity in the country as part of its long-term development agenda. It established in 2010 Nazarbayev University as an autonomous, US-style, research university. Generously funded by the government, Nazarbayev University, our home institution, has since its inception attracted well-published research faculty trained at top US and European research universities across the medical, social, and physical sciences—as well as the most talented Kazakh students from its top-tier high schools and from outside Kazakhstan.

Related to the nascent research culture at Kazakhstan's universities is the attitude of local business leaders to primary data collection. It is not unusual for organizational scholars based in Western universities to send survey requests to Fortune 500 companies and expect to achieve a response rate suitable for publication in top journals such as the *Journal of International Business Studies* (JIBS), *Strategic Management Journal* (SMJ), and the *Academy of Management Journal* (AMJ). There is often an unstated assumption that firms in Europe and the United States are in principle open to being studied by academics. In our experience, however, managers in large Kazakh companies are reluctant to share data about their companies.

We assume that managers of large Kazakh firms, like many managers of firms in Western countries, are often skeptical about academic research because they do not see the value of academic research to their business. We suspect that Kazakh managers' reluctance to share data may additionally stem from fear of being reprimanded by their superiors for doing so. For instance, as we wrote this chapter, we contacted a senior manager within a Kazakh company to confirm the company's 2020 market share. The company had published its 2017 market share on its website; we wanted to know whether market share had changed since 2017. To our surprise, our contact was reluctant to share this information. Even after we pointed out to her that the 2017 information was publicly available on her company's website, she said she had to confirm with her boss before releasing the information to us. In a 2021 executive MBA class, one of us asked a senior manager of the local subsidiary of a German MNE what her company's operating profit was. Even though the information was publicly available in the company's annual report, the manager refused to tell the class because it was supposedly a company secret. We have found that accessing firm data, especially in large Kazakh firms, involves navigating the skepticism of managers; in our experience, access usually occurs only with the express approval of a firm's top leaders. (The primary data on which this chapter is based were obtained with the support from the firms' top managers or from mid-level managers on the condition of anonymity.)

While obtaining primary data about large firms is a complicated affair that involves balancing the interests of the company's senior leaders against the researcher's interest, secondary firm-level data is relatively abundant. The government collects firm-level data on revenue, profit, number of employees, hierarchical levels, board memberships, and number of foreign subsidiaries. In theory, the data should be accessible to the public; in practice, access is restricted to those with the requisite personal networks referred to locally as *agaschki*. (There is abundant aggregated regional-level and national-level data at Kazakhstan's national statistics office.) One of us needed firm-level data on employment for a research project he was working on. He knew, from his contacts within Kazakhstan's statistical agency, that the data is systematically collected and reported to the country's statistical agency. However, he could only access the data after working through approvals and with the assistance of an influential government official.

Despite these limitations, secondary firm-level data is becoming publicly available in Kazakhstan. Sources include multilateral institutions such as the World Bank and the Asian Development Bank (ADB) who regularly collect firm-level data on financial performance and business practices, private database firms such as PitchBook[10] that increasingly track cross-border mergers and acquisitions (M&As) used for academic research, and private equity (PE) and venture capital (VC) companies based within and outside the region[11] that are actively investing in non-resource sectors in Central Asia.

IB scholars interested in studying cross-border MNE practices, policies, and patterns in Central Asia using primary data would do well to invest in building relationships with key decision-makers within large companies or with policymakers involved in FDI. Our research projects have been enhanced by cultivating relationships with these decision-makers. Furthermore, researchers should be prepared to mentor younger researchers in the region during a research collaboration.

7   Conclusion

It is unsurprising that the Central Asian region, comprising Kazakhstan, Uzbekistan, Kyrgyzstan, Tajikistan, and Turkmenistan, has been ignored by international business (IB) scholarship. Compared to emerging countries, such as China, Russia, Brazil, and Turkey, which have commanded much scholarly attention, Central Asian economies are small. Nevertheless, Central Asia, located at the crossroads between the large markets of Asia and Europe, and an important arena for great power competition among Russia, China, and the United States, has witnessed significant inward FDI and economic growth. Kazakhstan, the most prosperous country in Central Asia, has emerged as a stable upper middle-income country, attracting nearly $150 billion of inward FDI. Kazakh firms, like many other emerging country firms (EMFs), have also invested abroad to the tune of about $16 billion.

---

[10] https://pitchbook.com/

[11] Prominent firms include Falconry Venture Capital (https://falconryfund.kz/); Highland Capital (https://highland.kg/#section6), and Sturgeon Capital (https://www.sturgeoncapital.com/).

Using Kazakhstan as a lens into the region, we present three cases of Kazakh firms—Air Astana, BI Group, and KazMunayGas—that have attempted to internationalize their operations. We find that classical motives for internationalization (e. g., market-seeking, strategic asset-seeking) apply to the internationalization patterns of these firms. Furthermore, these firms use internationalization as a springboard to escape their small domestic markets.

Central Asia presents unique contextual features to address several questions that have potential to advance IB scholarship. Being susceptible to exogenous shocks involving its powerful neighbors, Central Asia is fertile ground for supranational studies on how MNEs evaluate, anticipate, and respond to geopolitical risk affecting their business operations, a key gap in the IB literature. Second, due to its importance to the security, economic, and geopolitical interests of the great powers—Russia, China, and the United States—Central Asia offers the opportunity to examine the nonmarket strategies (NMS), specifically bargaining strategies, that MNEs employ to interact with their home country (great power) governments. Doing so will refine scholarly understanding of MNE bargaining models, which tend to downplay MNE-home country interactions. Third, as IB interest in the internationalization of state-owned enterprises (SOEs) grows, the Central Asian context may challenge the dominant assumption that SOEs respond to unitary domestic state actors. Informal fragmentary ethnic alliances, which pre-date and co-exist with formal state apparatus, may be a potent influence on the direction, level, and location of FDI. If so, what role then does the formal state play in promoting internationalization where there is no clear industrial policy to do so? Finally, Central Asia could fruitfully allow scholars examine better whether developed country MNEs (DMNEs) outperform emerging market MNEs (EMNEs) when competing in a third (smaller) emerging market.

We hope to stimulate IB researchers' interest in interpreting the Central Asian context using insights from the IB as well as international relations (IR) literature in order to advance our long-established theories of firm internationalization.

Acknowledgment   The research in this chapter was made possible by the support of Nazarbayev University Faculty Development Research Grants 090118FD5301 and GSB2020001.

References

Air Astana. (2015). *Air Astana: Annual report 2014*. Retrieved August 9, 2021, from https://airastana.com/Portals/2/About-Us/Corporate-Governance/Annual-Reports/Annual-Reports-en/Annual_Report_2014_EN.pdf

Air Astana. (2018). *Air Astana: Annual report 2017*. Retrieved August 9, 2021, from https://airastana.com/Portals/2/About-Us/Corporate-Governance/Annual-Reports/Annual-Reports-en/Annual_Report_2017_EN.pdf

Air Astana. (2020). *Air Astana: Annual report 2019*. Retrieved July 29, 2021, from https://airastana.com/Portals/2/About-Us/Corporate-Governance/Annual-Reports/Annual-Reports-en/Air%20Astana_AR19_ENGLISH%20Web.pdf?ver=2020-10-05-021526-370

Air Astana. (2021). *Air Astana: Annual report 2020*. Retrieved July 29, 2021, from https://airastana.com/Portals/2/About-Us/Corporate-Governance/Annual-Reports/2020%20year/Air_Astana_AR20_ENGLISH_Web.pdf?ver=2021-06-11-044002-297

Alam, A., Banerji, A., Mitra, P., Aksoy, M. A., & Freinkman, L. (2000). *Uzbekistan and Kazakhstan: A tale of two transition paths. World Bank Policy Research Working Paper*. Retrieved November 2, 2021, from https://openknowledge.worldbank.org/handle/10986/19763

Åslund, A., & Snegovaya, M. (2021). *The impact of Western sanctions on Russia and how they can be made even more effective*. Retrieved October 3, 2021, from https://www.atlanticcouncil.org/wp-content/uploads/2021/05/The-impact-of-Western-sanctions-on-Russia-and-how-they-can-be-made-even-more-effective-5.2.pdf

Bartlett, C. A., & Ghoshal, S. (1998). *Managing across borders: The transnational solution*. Harvard Business School Press.

BBC. (2021). *Pandora papers: Tory donor Mohamed Amersi involved in telecoms corruption scandal*. Retrieved November 15, 2021, from https://www.bbc.com/news/uk-politics-58783460

Bissenova, A. (2012). *Post-socialist dreamworlds: Housing boom and urban development in Kazakhstan*. https://ecommons.cornell.edu/bitstream/handle/1813/29225/azb3thesisPDF.pdf?sequence=1&isAllowed=y

Buckley, P. J., Clegg, L. J., Cross, A. R., Liu, X., Voss, H., & Zheng, P. (2007). The determinants of Chinese outward foreign direct investment. *Journal of International Business Studies, 38*(4).

Bureau of National Statistics Republic of Kazakhstan. (2021). *Main socio-economic indicators*. Retrieved September 4, 2021, from https://stat.gov.kz/

Celly, N., Kathuria, A., & Subramanian, V. (2016). Overview of Indian multinationals. In M. Thite, A. Wilkinson, & P. Budhwar (Eds.), *Emerging Indian multinationals: Strategic players in a multipolar world*. Oxford University Press.

Chan, A. P. C., & Owusu, E. K. (2017). Corruption forms in the construction industry: Literature review. *Journal of Construction Engineering and Management, 143*(8), 1–12.

Collins, K. (2006). *Clan politics and regime transition in central Asia*. Cambridge University Press.

Cooley, A. (2012). *Great games, local rules: The new great power contest in central Asia. Great games, local rules: The new great power contest in central Asia*. Oxford University Press.

Cuervo-Cazurra, A., & Genc, M. (2008). Transforming disadvantages into advantages: developing-country MNEs in the least developed countries. *Journal of International Business Studies, 39*(6), 957–979.

Cuervo-Cazurra, A., Inkpen, A., Musacchio, A., & Ramaswamy, K. (2014). Governments as owners: State-owned multinational companies. *Journal of International Business Studies, 45*(8), 919–942.

Cuervo-Cazurra, A., Luo, Y., Ramamurti, R., & Ang, S. H. (2018). The Impact of the home country on internationalization. *Journal of World Business, 53*(5), 593–604.

Doh, J. P., Lawton, T. C., & Rajwani, T. (2012). Advancing nonmarket strategy research: Institutional perspectives in a changing world. *Academy of Management Perspectives, 26*(3), 22–39.

Dunning, J. H., & Lundan, S. M. (2008). *Multinational enterprises and the global economy*. Edward Elgar Publishing.

ENR: Engineering News Record. (2019). ENR 2019 top 250 global contractors 101–200. *Engineering News Record*. Retrieved July 3, 2021, from https://www.enr.com/toplists/2019-Top-250-Global-Contractors-2

Frynas, J. G., Mellahi, K., & Pigman, G. A. (2006). First mover advantages in international business and firm-specific political resources. *Strategic Management Journal, 27*(4), 321–345.

Harbison, I. (2019). *Air Astana develops MRO capabilities for new aircraft types*. Retrieved July 30, 2021, from https://www.aviationbusinessnews.com/mro/air-astana-mro-capabilities-new-aircraft/

Holburn, G. L. F., & Zelner, B. A. (2010). Political capabilities, policy risk, and international investment strategy: Evidence from the global electric power generation industry. *Strategic Management Journal, 31*(12), 1290–1315.

Hoskisson, R. E., Eden, L., Lau, C. M., & Wright, M. (2000). Strategy in emerging economies. *Academy of Management Journal, 43*(3), 249–267.

International Monetary Fund. (2021). *World economic outlook database*. Retrieved July 6, 2021, from https://www.imf.org/en/Publications/WEO/weo-database/2021/April

Kaiser, M. J., & Pulsipher, A. G. (2007). A review of the oil and gas sector in Kazakhstan. *Energy Policy, 35*(2), 1300–1314.

Kalasin, K., Cuervo-Cazurra, A., & Ramamurti, R. (2020). State ownership and international expansion: The S-curve relationship. *Global Strategy Journal, 10*(2), 386–418.

KazMunayGas. (2008). *Annual report of JSC NC "KazMunayGas" for 2008*. Retrieved July 5, 2021, from https://www.kmg.kz/uploads/reporting-and-financial-result/67b9bff90acf476b/God_othcet_2008_EN.pdf

KazMunayGas. (2018). *Annual report*. Retrieved July 20, 2021, from https://www.kmg.kz/uploads/reporting-and-financial-result/272ede75d8454f06/KMG_ANNUAL_REPORT_2018_ENG.pdf

KazMunayGas. (2019). *Annual report*. http://ir.kmg.kz/storage/files/efba6caf32a34f5c/KMG_AR_2019_ENG_30.04_1451.pdf

KazMunayGas. (2021a). *KazMunayGas: The board of directors*. Retrieved July 5, 2021, from https://www.kmg.kz/eng/kompaniya/korporativnoe_upravlenie/sovet_direktorov/

KazMunayGas. (2021b). *Annual report 2020: Fostering sustainability through growth*. Retrieved July 5, 2021, from https://www.kmg.kz/uploads/reports/KMG_AR2020_ENG.pdf

KazMunayGas International. (2007). *KazMunayGas and rompetrol holding SA announce the acquisition by KazMunayGas of a 75% interest in Th*. Retrieved July 20, 2021, from https://kmginternational.com/mediaroom/press-releases//kazmunaygas-and-rompetrol-holding-sa-announce-the-acquisition-by-kazmunaygas-of-a-75-interest-in-th-id-571-cmsid-471

Khaidar, A. (2018). New Air Astana operations facility expected to cut maintenance costs. *The Astana Times*. Retrieved August 11, 2021, from https://astanatimes.com/2018/05/new-air-astana-operations-facility-expected-to-cut-maintenance-costs/

Kroes, N. (2007). *Case No comp/M.4934 - KazMunaiGaz/Rompetrol*. Retrieved July 5, 2021, from https://ec.europa.eu/competition/mergers/cases/decisions/m4934_20071119_20310_en.pdf

Lancaster, J. (2012). Tomorrowland. *National Geographic Magazine, 2*.

Li, J., Newenham-Kahindi, A., Shapiro, D. M., & Chen, V. Z. (2013). The two-tier bargaining model revisited: Theory and evidence from China's natural resource investments in Africa. *Global Strategy Journal, 3*(4), 300–321.

Luo, Y., & Tung, R. L. (2007). International expansion of emerging market enterprises: A springboard perspective. *Journal of International Business Studies, 38*(4), 481–498.

Mellahi, K., Frynas, J. G., Sun, P., & Siegel, D. (2016). A review of the nonmarket strategy literature: Toward a multi-theoretical integration. *Journal of Management, 42*(1), 143–173.

Meyer, K. E., & Peng, M. W. (2016). Theoretical foundations of emerging economy business research. *Journal of International Business Studies, 47*(1), 3–22.

Minbaeva, D. B., Ledeneva, A., Muratbekova-Touron, M., & Horak, S. (2022). Explaining the persistence of informal institutions: The role of informal networks. *Academy of Management Review*. https://doi.org/10.5465/amr.2020.0224

Ministry of Foreign Affairs of the People's Republic of China. (2013). *President Xi Jinping delivers important speech and proposes to build a silk road economic belt with central Asian countries*. Retrieved October 2, 2021, from https://www.fmprc.gov.cn/mfa_eng/topics_665678/xjpfwzysiesgjtfhshzzfh_665686/t1076334.shtml

Musacchio, A., Lazzarini, S. G., & Aguilera, R. V. (2015). New varieties of state capitalism: Strategic and governance implications. *Academy of Management Perspectives, 29*(1), 115–131.

National Bank of Kazakhstan. (2021a). *Balance of payments*. Retrieved September 16, 2021, from https://nationalbank.kz/en/news/platezhnyy-balans-vn-sektora/7528

National Bank of Kazakhstan. (2021b). *Gross outflow of direct investment abroad from Kazakhstan's direct investors: Breakdown by residents' types of economic activities/countries*.

Retrieved September 20, 2021, from https://nationalbank.kz/en/news/pryamye-investicii-po-napravleniyu-vlozheniya

National Bank of Kazakhstan. (2021c). *Current state of the banking sector of Kazakhstan.* Retrieved November 15, 2021, from https://finreg.kz

Nazarbayev, N. (2012). What Iran can learn from Kazakhstan. *New York Times.* Retrieved June 22, 2020, from https://www.nytimes.com/2012/03/26/opinion/what-iran-can-learn-from-kazakhstan.html

Nishanov, B. (2017). Uzbekistan: The year after. *Freedom House.* Retrieved October 3, 2021, from https://freedomhouse.org/report/analytical-brief/2017/uzbekistan-year-after

Nordin, A. H. M., & Weissmann, M. (2018). Will Trump make China great again? The belt and road initiative and international order. *International Affairs, 94*(2), 231–249.

Olcott, M. B. (1995). *The Kazakhs* (2nd ed.). Hoover Institution Press.

Organization for Economic Cooperation and Development. (2013). *OECD review of agricultural policies: Kazakhstan 2013.* Paris.

Patterson, S., & Gauthier-Villars, D. (2015). U.S. seeks to seize $1 billion in telecom probe. *The Wall Street Journal.* Retrieved November 15, 2021, from https://www.wsj.com/articles/u-s-seeks-to-seize-1-billion-in-telecom-probe-1439497898

Peng, M. W., & Meyer, K. (2016). *International Business* (2nd ed.). Cengage Learning.

Peng, M. W., Sun, S. L., Pinkham, B., & Chen, H. (2009). The institution-based view as a third leg for a strategy tripod. *Academy of Management Perspectives, 23*(3), 63–81.

Phan, P. H. (2019). International politics and management research: A glaring white space calling out to be filled. *Academy of Management Perspectives, 33*(1), 1–2.

Pomfret, R. (1995). *The economies of central Asia.* Princeton University Press.

Pozzi, J. (2021). Inside Air Astana's maintenance division. *Aviation Week.* Retrieved July 30, 2021, from https://aviationweek.com/mro/safety-ops-regulation/inside-air-astanas-maintenance-division

Rachel, V., Sandra, F. J., & Roza, T. (2020). Between the bear and the dragon: Multivectorism in Kazakhstan as a model strategy for secondary powers. *International Affairs, 96*(4), 975–993.

Ramamurti, R. (2001). The obsolescing "Bargaining Model"? MNC-host developing country relations revisited. *Journal of International Business Studies, 32*, 23–39.

Reuters. (2009). KazMunayGas acquires remaining 25 pct of Rompetrol. *Reuters.* Retrieved July 5, 2021, from https://www.reuters.com/article/romania-kazmunaygas-rompetrol-idUKLQ9174220090626

Reuters. (2014). *HSBC extends global retreat with $176 million sale of Kazakh bank.* Retrieved November 15, 2021, from https://www.reuters.com/article/uk-hsbc-kazakhstan-idUKBREA1P0KC20140226

Reuters. (2018). China CITIC Bank outlines big ambitions for new Kazakh unit. *Reuters.*

Reuters. (2019). Update 1-Sweden's Tele2 agrees deal to exit Kazakhstan. *Reuters.* Retrieved November 15, 2021, from https://www.reuters.com/article/tele2-kazakhstan-idUSL5N22Z1FX

Rompetrol. (2021). *Retail: The energizing center, place where we meet the customers.* Retrieved July 20, 2021, from https://www.rompetrol.com/what-we-do/operations/retail

Schwab, K. (2019). *The global competitiveness report.* Retrieved May 16, 2021, from http://www3.weforum.org/docs/WEF_TheGlobalCompetitivenessReport2019.pdf

Shepard, W. (2016). The Western Europe-Western China expressway to connect the Yellow Sea with The Baltic. *Forbes.* Retrieved September 8, 2020, from https://www.forbes.com/sites/wadeshepard/2016/07/10/the-western-europe-western-china-expressway-to-connect-the-yellow-sea-with-the-baltic/#4d61d33a6c95

Statistics Committee of Kazakhstan. (2021). *Kazakhstan economic indicators.* Retrieved September 16, 2021, from https://old.stat.gov.kz/faces/wcnav_externalId/homeNationalAccountIntegrated?_adf.ctrl-state=10n2seh0g9_64&_afrLoop=13721536875476656#%40%3F_afrLoop%3D13721536875476656%26_adf.ctrl-state%3Degu73g0xp_4

Subramanian, V., & Abilova, A. (2020). Emerging market multinationals: The case of Kazakhstan. In A. Cuervo-Cazurra, W. Newburry, & S. Ho Park (Eds.), *Building strategic capabilities in emerging markets* (pp. 186–206). Cambridge University Press.

Sun, P., Doh, J. P., Rajwani, T., & Siegel, D. (2021). Navigating cross-border institutional complexity: A review and assessment of multinational nonmarket strategy research. *Journal of International Business Studies, 52,* 1818–1853.

Sun, P., Mellahi, K., & Thun, E. (2010). The dynamic value of MNE political embeddedness: The case of the Chinese automobile industry. *Journal of International Business Studies, 41*(7), 1161–1182.

Svanberg, I. (2014). The Kazak Nation. In I. Svanberg (Ed.), *Contemporary Kazaks: Cultural and social perspectives.* Routledge.

Telia Company. (2018). *Divestment of KCell complete.* Retrieved November 15, 2021, from https://www.teliacompany.com/en/news/news-articles/2018/kcell-closing/

The Business Year. (2017). Highly involved. *Kazakhstan: Construction and real estate review.* Retrieved September 1, 2020, from https://www.thebusinessyear.com/kazakhstan-2017/highly-involved/interview

The World Bank. (2019). *The World Bank in Kazakhstan: Country snapshot.* Retrieved June 5, 2020, from http://pubdocs.worldbank.org/en/278551571374560680/Kazakhstan-Snapshot-Oct2019.pdf

The World Bank. (2021a). *Doing business: Measuring business regulations.* Retrieved September 22, 2021, from https://www.doingbusiness.org/en/custom-query

The World Bank. (2021b). *Research and development expenditure (% of GDP).* Retrieved November 16, 2021, from https://data.worldbank.org/indicator/GB.XPD.RSDV.GD.ZS?end=2018&locations=KZ-UZ-TJ-TM-KG&start=2009

UZ Daily. (2020). *Murad Buildings and BI Group are investing US$33 million in the project and plan to commission nearly 60 thousand square meters. m of housing.* Retrieved September 28, 2020, from http://www.uzdaily.com/en/post/55090

Wang, C., Hong, J., Kafouros, M., & Wright, M. (2012). Exploring the role of government involvement in outward FDI from emerging economies. *Journal of International Business Studies, 43*(7), 655–676.

Dr. Onajomo Akemu is an Assistant Professor of Management and Entrepreneurship at Nazarbayev University Graduate School of Business (NUGSB). He obtained his PhD from Rotterdam School of Management (RSM), Erasmus University. His research focuses on strategy formation within rapidly-growing ventures and on the improvement of qualitative methods, especially ethnography. His work has appeared in the *Journal of Management Studies, Organizational Research Methods* and *Journal of Organizational Behavior.* Prior to academia, he worked as an engineer in the international oil industry and has advised start-ups in The Netherlands and in Kazakhstan.

Venkat Subramanian is Venkat Subramanian is an Associate Dean and Associate Professor of Strategy at Nazarbayev University Graduate School of Business and Visiting Researcher at Vives, KU Leuven. He was a Research Fellow in Strategy and International Management at Catholic University of Leuven, Belgium, a Research Associate in Strategy and Finance at INSEAD, France, before going on to complete a PhD in Management at the Solvay Business School, Universite Libre de Bruxelles, Belgium. He has published in leading academic and practitioner journals, and in the business press, on topics of strategy and international business. He has advised start-ups in Europe and Asia.

IB Research Opportunities in the Middle East and North Africa

Melodena Stephens

1 Middle East North Africa Region

The Middle East North Africa region (MENA) is approximately 21 countries across the Middle East (or West Asia) and North Africa. The classification of countries is fluid; for example, the World Bank's (2021) list of countries differs from the USA Trade list of MENA countries. The region's geopolitics have a vital role in deciding the classification, and hence, Israel is often excluded in many of the lists. Sometimes Turkey is added to the list, and this classification is referred to as MENAT. The region is bound by some similarities (religion, culture, weather) but has stark differences looking at labor resources, climate, or even security. Though the dominant religion is Islam, there are two major sects: Sunnis (Wahhabism falls here, and it is estimated that 90% of the Muslims are Sunnis) and Shias. Wahhabism (which has a more strict interpretation of Islam) has a strong influence in KSA. The tensions between both sects have resulted in unrest in the region.

Despite the heterogeneity, the research on this region collectively or from each country is low (see Table 1). On average, the ranking for the number of full-time equivalent researchers per Mn population is inadequate for MENA (see Table 1). These numbers translate to lower research output, lower collaborations, and citations. Some of the reasons are systemic—IB is seen as a part of business studies; hence the research being published may fall in other domains; second, the region is so diverse and data-scarce that qualitative studies predominate but are harder to publish as they are very contextual; and last but not least, the nascency of research culture also has challenges in funding and for publishing in top tier journals (see Stephens Balakrishnan, 2013a).

The narrative currently dominating international business is very western-centric, and if other emerging markets are being published, it is being dominated by China

M. Stephens (✉)
Mohammed Bin Rashid School of Government, Dubai, United Arab Emirates
e-mail: melodena.stephensb@mbrsg.ac.ae

© Springer Nature Switzerland AG 2022   137
H. Merchant (ed.), *The New Frontiers of International Business*, Contributions to Management Science, https://doi.org/10.1007/978-3-031-06003-8_6

Table 1 MENA research—some compiled facts

| | | | | | | | | | Business and international management (SCIMAGOJR) 2021 | | Global innovation index 2021 rank out 123 countries | | | | | |
Rank	Country	Region	Documents	Citable documents	Citations	Self-citations	Citations per document	H index	Researchers FTE/mn pop	R&D % GDP	QS University Score	University/ industry research collaboration	Knowledge-intensive employment	Scientific & technical articles/bn PPP$ GDP	Citable documents H-index
30	Turkey	Middle East	2687	2463	37,003	3987	13,77	81	46	39	45	70	73	54	35
35	Iran	Middle East	2305	2210	13,673	3405	5,93	47	44	44	44	117	77	21	40
39	Israel	Middle East	1509	1450	43,101	3605	28,56	97	1	1	29	1	8	16	16
40	United Arab Emirates	Middle East	1498	1466	11,787	1411	7,87	43	36	29	36	22	41	97	61
46	Saudi Arabia	Middle East	1211	1183	9532	902	7,87	43	n/a	46	31	35	53	62	39
51	Tunisia	Africa	1081	1058	4003	662	3,7	26	43	56	77	95	75	13	69
54	Egypt	Africa/ Middle East	842	832	8638	661	10,26	34	61	49	48	79	45	59	47
56	Jordan	Middle East	685	675	3490	495	5,09	25	63	51	54	55	n/a	33	78
66	Lebanon	Middle East	344	334	5634	464	16,38	34	n/a	n/a	43	58	n/a	43	61
67	Morocco	Africa	320	311	1557	147	4,87	15	51	50	77	113	110	63	66
68	Oman	Middle East	318	313	1847	160	5,81	18	79	89	64	38	81	99	88

70	Kuwait	Middle East	297	294	3965	171	13,35	26	67	111	72	54	68	106	82
74	Qatar	Middle East	275	271	2914	252	10,6	22	64	65	62	16	83	88	81
78	Bahrain	Middle East	202	199	918	78	4,54	15	74	106	70	90	70	116	115
86	Algeria	Africa	113	113	312	74	2,76	9	55	61	77	88	86	86	77
88	Iraq	Middle East	109	106	425	59	3,9	11	n/a	n/a	n/a	n/a	n/a	n/a	n/a
101	Palestine	Middle East	65	63	492	37	7,57	11	n/a	n/a	n/a	n/a	n/a	n/a	n/a
108	Yemen	Middle East	42	42	214	14	5,1	7	n/a	n/a	77	126	101	96	121
121	Libya	Africa	25	25	136	12	5,44	5	n/a	n/a	n/a	n/a	n/a	n/a	n/a
126	Syrian Arab Republic	Middle East	18	18	91	3	5,06	5	n/a	n/a	n/a	n/a	n/a	n/a	n/a
176	Djibouti	Africa	1	1	2	0	2	1	n/a	n/a	n/a	n/a	n/a	n/a	n/a

Source: Compiled by Author

Table 2 Heterogeneity in MENA

Factor	Range
Classifications	MENA: Bahrain, Egypt, Iran, Iraq, Israel, Jordan, Kuwait, Lebanon, Libya, Morocco, Oman, Palestine, Qatar, Kingdom of Saudi Arabia (KSA), Syria, Algeria, Tunisia, Djibouti, United Arab Emirates (UAE), Yemen ME: Normally, this varies based on perspective. Includes MENA and may include the predominantly Islamic regions of North Africa, Western Asia, and Central Asia GCC: Bahrain, Kuwait, Oman, Qatar, KSA, and UAE Mashreq: Egypt, Lebanon, Israel, Palestine, Jordan, and Syria Levant: Syria, Lebanon, Palestine, Israel and Jordan, Iraq, and GCC MENAT: MENA and Turkey Maghreb: Morocco, Algeria, Tunisia, Libya, and Mauritania MENASA: Middle East, North Africa, and South Asia AMEA: Africa, Middle East, and Asia
Religion	Sunni (90%), Shia (10%)
Income	1/5 live on less than US$2 per day; MENA average is US$6536 with $43,103 (UAE) at one extreme to US$824+ (Yemen)
Resource-poor, labor abundant countries	Djibouti, Egypt, Jordan, Lebanon, Morocco, Tunisia, and Palestine
Resource-rich, labor poor	GCC, The GCC countries, and Libya are heavily dependent on expatriate labor OPEC MENA Countries: GCC, Algeria, Iran, Iraq, and Libya. Syria also produces oil
Strategic chokepoints for global trade	Egypt, UAE, Djibouti (for GCC it is Straits of Hormuz and of Bab al-Mandab)
Strategic points for food security (export supply) in the region	Iran, Turkey, Egypt (GCC has low food security)
Aid dependent countries	Jordan, Lebanon, Egypt, Syria, Yemen, Palestine, Iraq
Aid donors	UAE, KSA, Kuwait and Qatar
Refugee source counters	Syria, Iraq, Palestine, Libya
Refugee host countries	Lebanon, Turkey, Jordan
Average age	28% of the population of the Middle East and 60% of the Arab population are aged between 15 and 29
Currency tied to the USD	GCC (except Kuwait), Jordan, Lebanon, Iraq

Compiled by Author (some of the sources: Chantham House, 2017; EIA, 2017; World Bank, 2021b; O'Sullivan et al., 2011; McKee et al., 2017; YouthPolicy.Org, 2021)

and India studies. The Middle East North Africa region is heterogenous when looking at country groupings, oil resources, workforce, aid and aid dependency, logistics, refugee hosts, displaced people, and economy (see Table 2). Country data is not readily available due to systems, conflict, or corruption, adding to researchers' challenges (Buttorff et al., 2020; Lages et al., 2015; Stephens Balakrishnan, 2013a). The lack of data for research (see Stephens Balakrishnan, 2013a) and the growing need to understand it better provide a rich backdrop for future studies. This chapter aims to introduce researchers to new areas of study that conventional IB researchers have missed.

2   MENA as a Heterogeneous Region of Study

The MENA region is heterogeneous, as illustrated in Table 3 and hence needs to be understood in greater depth from each country's perspective. In terms of economy, the GCC countries (Bahrain, Kuwait, Oman, Qatar, Kingdom of Saudi Arabia, and the United Arab Emirates) have oil resources and a high per capita GDP that has equaled or, in some cases, exceeded the levels of the G10 nations. The GCC countries represent 0.8% of the global population yet contribute 2.4 times or 1.9% to the global GDP (The First Abu Dhabi Bank, 2020). However, MENA as a region has 43% of its population living on less than US$5.50 per day—the largest percentage in the world (World Bank, 2021a). So this disparity rather than homogeneity is crucial to understanding this region, especially if international businesses need to embed sustainable development goals and achieve things like zero poverty, health, education, peace, and climate change through partnerships with the governments in the region.

I have chosen four topics that are not frequently addressed by IB scholars but are of significant importance for businesses operating in the region (for other research themes, look at the papers Griffith et al., 2008 and Calma & Suder, 2020 put together). The topics for discussion below are nonmarket studies, business and crisis management, sustainable development studies, and halal markets. While IB studies tangentially touch on some areas like nonmarket studies and sustainable development, there are additional areas that are highlighted below. These four topics are not exhaustive but represent areas not often emphasized or fragmented in IB literature.

The first reason is context. Without a deep understanding of context, some of the results may have no relevance in a region that does not have the same culture, institutional context, and mindset as the west. Some of the reasons are geographic, historical, or political.[1] I remember one example when I was teaching in a class. It was the last class of the semester, and at the end, the male student put up his hand and said—I resigned from my job. Another female student said the same thing. I jokingly asked them whether it was my lecture. Then began one of the most profound moments of my life. Both of them were from Syria, which was in the early days of the Syrian Civil War. He said, that at the beginning of the year, he would call his father every day, and if he was late to pick up the phone, he would panic, thinking something awful had happened. "Sometimes I could hear the airstrike behind in the background. Now I am numb, I call, and if he is late picking up—I think he is dead."

---

[1] Henry Kissinger writes an interesting perspective of western diplomacy in his book "Diplomacy" that pushed country power via trade internationally.

Table 3 Strategic MENA points of trade (logistics)

Chokepoint	Location	Global trade	Issues
Hormuz	Access to Arab Gulf and oil-producing countries (Iraq, Kuwait, Kingdom of Saudi Arabia, United Arab Emirates) Only KSA and UAE can circumvent via pipeline. At narrowest is 20 km	30% of crude, 30% of LNG	2011 Iran threatened to close the chokepoint due to economic sanctions
Bab-el-Mandeb Strait	Horn of Africa and the Middle East. At narrowest, 18 km	70% of wheat imports for Algeria, Tunisia, Libya, and Egypt. 32% of the global potassium chloride (most heavily traded fertilizer). Can disrupt direct flows between European and North African to Asian markets, for tankers leaving Arab gulf and reaching the Suez Canal or the Sumed Pipeline	Conflict with Yemen, piracy
The Suez Canal	Connects Egypt and connects the Red Sea to the Mediterranean Sea	Food trade, petroleum, and LNG also accounted for 17% and 6% of Suez cargo. Fifty ships per day in 2021 travel through the canal (~12% of total global trade)	2020 Ever Given disaster, which got stuck in the Suez canal and blocked traffic for 6 days, resulted in ~300 vessels on both sides being blocked (~US $9.6 billion in trade). In 1956 shut down due to Israeli forces invading the Sinai peninsula (which was a response to Egypt's nationalization of the canal)
Turkish Straits	Europe and Asia, Bosporus connect the Black Sea with the Sea of Marmara. The Dardanelles is a 40-mile waterway that links the Sea of Marmara with the Aegean and Mediterranean Seas. 800 m wide at its narrowest point	Russia's primary route to access European markets	

Compiled by Author

When she had last contacted her family, the female student said that they were celebrating a wedding, and she asked them how they could do that with so much death and destruction. But the family explained it was a celebration of life, and they had so few moments to celebrate. She said—for years, I had never understood why my Lebanese colleague party so hard—for the first time, she can empathize. They both resigned because they felt helpless about the situation from home, and by leaving their secure jobs, they were hoping to exert some control over their life. Context matters. Do HR policies in such regions include mental healthcare and wellbeing? Family assistance?

How would you design leave policies in a region fraught with conflict? For example, how do you create workplace cultures where expats outnumber local populations (like in the UAE)? Or the issue of managing business operations, when does it become corruption, when you barter with the trade office (since your currency may have devalued like in Lebanon), when you accept gifts (this culture is common in the region - when is a gift a bribe?). While I do not go into depth into these issues, in my experience across the world—these are real challenges leading to perspectives that may incorrectly label the MENA region, its people, and its businesses practices.

2.1 Nonmarket Studies

Firms use nonmarket strategies to gain a foothold in new markets. As a topic, this is not new and has been around since the 1980s (Akbar & Kisilowski, 2020). Nonmarket strategies are defined as actions that include bargaining and alignment strategies to influence the host and home nation governments to change the legal, regulatory, or societal context of the way of doing business (Boddewyn, 2015, 2016; Boddewyn & Brewer, 1994; Bach & Allen, 2010; Hillman & Hitt, 1999). The available options are captured in Fig. 1 (adapted from Akbar & Kisilowski, 2020), which are strategies that firms use to balance societal and economic impacts based on regulatory pressure. Clegg (2019: 111) identifies these future research areas as "analyses of policy antecedents, firm influence upon policy, policy implementation, policy uptake, and impact."

Quadrant A focuses on firms adopting passive compliance regarding government mandates or proactively using corporate social responsibility (CSR) to slightly exceed governmental regulations. In quadrant B, the default strategy is compliance through bargaining on the final shape of the measure with execution through conciliatory partnerships. In quadrant C, the dominant nonmarket strategy is also non-bargaining, but with selective avoidance. This response gives the impression that the firm is in compliance, but perhaps they do not enforce regulations with the highest level of scrutiny. Finally, in the last quadrant D, there is a substantial economic impact but a low societal impact. In this case, the firm has the upper hand and hence can resort to conflictual bargaining with political actors, to drive a hard bargain (also see Boddewyn & Brewer, 1994).

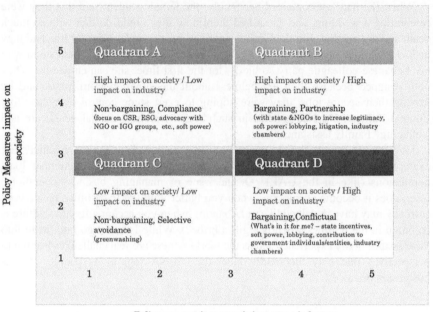

Policy measure's economic impact on industry

Fig. 1 Nonmarket strategies. Source: Authors (adapted from Akbar & Kisilowski, 2020)

Though some studies exist in the region, for example, aviation in the context of the pandemic (see Akbar & Kisilowski, 2020), it is an area for future researchers to dive in. The MNEs operating in the MENA region have often operated through local representation. The most significant oil and gas players are present in the Middle East, but there is tremendous state control. Oil drilling rights or concessions are given to interested parties, typically International Oil Companies ("IOCs"), and profits are shared with National Oil Companies ("NOCs"), since before the formation of many of these countries (The World Today, 1958). For example, a concessions agreement for 75 years with Petroleum Concession Limited (a British-based company) and the Sultan of Muscat and Oman was entered into on June 24, 1937 (Powell, 2021).

Many MNEs like BP, Exxon Mobil, Occidental Petroleum, Sumitomo Chemical Co, Total S. A., Royal Dutch Shell PLC operate via joint ventures. Several state-owned enterprises (SOEs) also exist in this arena, like China National Offshore Oil Corporation, known as CNOOC, China National Petroleum Corporation, known as CNPC (from China); Petroliam Nasional Berhad, known as Petronas (Malaysia); and Gazprom Neft OAO (Russia). This industry is filled with multiple state players lobbying for host country attention to operate a profitable business. This type of study is rare in IB research.

Part of the challenge is the complexity of managing in this space, which overlaps with international relations, home country security and soft power, and business opportunity, which is often not addressed by IB researchers. For example, when

Emirates started flying into Europe, it did not want to be known as a Middle Eastern airline (especially after 9–11, 2001). So they began to sponsor football in Europe in 2004. Fans saw the "Fly Emirates" tagline on jerseys in TV advertisements and placements on the football fields. Emirates successfully used the campaign "We all speak the same language – football" in 2006 when they became the main sponsor of the FIFA 2006 Cup. This allowed them to find a common language and distance themselves from the negative connotation of the conflict in the Middle East. Dubai now has the most international passenger traffic in the world. These insights need in-depth cases with longitudinal data to understand the context and actions. MENA has several such issues—for example, refugees, price of oil, or sustainability (how can you use sustainability metrics when there is water and food scarcity?).

When MENA was yet to be discovered as a key geographic area for trade in the globalization map, franchisee agreements were given to prominent trading families. For example, the M.H. Alshaya Co. (Kuwait) was founded in 1890 as a shipping company. It has since acquired franchise rights for UK brands: in 1983, Mothercare (initially for Kuwait and in 2005 for Russia) and H&M (initially for Kuwait and in 2006 for the Middle East); Top Shop (for Turkey in 2002): and USA brands like Payless ShoeSource (in 2009); American Eagle Outfitters (2010); Victoria Secret (2010) and Starbucks (partnership in 1999). The group has approximately 90 brands and 4000 stores across the GCC!

For the retail brands, if the franchising contracts were given in perpetuity or as master franchisees (Justis & Judd, 1986) and the country had "Agency Laws," which protect local franchisees and sales agents, the contracts would not be easily termina-ble. In these cases, the challenge of managing the brand would fall in the nonmarket strategy. A case study of KFC's operations in Mecca (Stephens Balakrishnan, 2013b) is one such example where the parent company worked with the master franchisee to find ways to operate in the city. During the Hajj, an annual event, 2.5 million Muslims participated. In this holy city, only Muslims are allowed. They pray five times a day, and all work must stop by law. This fact, the high volume demand, and other cultural nuances resulted in a change in strategy for staffing, branding, and operations. These types of studies that are rich in context are absent from IB literature, and though they may feature as teaching cases, they do not capture the theory shifts required to do business in international markets.

KFC (part of Yum! Restaurants International) is held by Master Franchise Americana (Kuwait). Adeptio (UAE) bought a majority stake in Americana for US $2.4 billion in 2016 (67% of share). The negotiations have taken 2 years, and the acquisition was one of the largest M&As at that time in the region (Reuters, 2016). The impact of Americana is vast as it is listed on the Kuwait Stock Exchange, has 60,000 employees, and operates 1200 food and beverage outlets across the MENA. While the IB community does document subsidiary-parent relationships, these types of firm relationships are under-explored. Later in the year, KSA's SWF—the Saudi Public Investment Fund, bought a 50% stake into Adepito (MEED, 2016). These organizations (host or home) are private flagship companies for governments (much like Google, Apple, BASF, Shell) for their respective governments and states step in to safeguard business and political interests. The inter-relationships between firms, countries, and governments are complex and worth diving into in greater detail, as illustrated above.

With the constantly changing context, MNEs that want to keep their legitimacy[2] in the shifting political situations will find nonmarket strategies like investment in relationships with key stakeholders becoming more critical (see Darendeli & Hill, 2016; Vivoda, 2009). During the pandemic, innovation was a big opportunity for SMEs and MNEs to contribute to the local economies with regulatory changes—whether it was perfume manufacturers scaling up or pivoting to hand sanitizers (Mejren, 2020; Scatena, 2020) or industries pivoting to mask manufacturing (The National, 2021; Khaleej Times, 2020). Since so little is known about the context and the way of operating a business, there is an opportunity to test existing theories and explore new concepts.

For example, instruments developed in a western context may no longer be applicable in MENA. Theories adopted in a western context[3] may need to be redefined and tested across countries in a MENA context. Methodologies need to suit the context. If there is a predisposition to answer on the higher end of the Likert scale for sensitive matters (Stephens Balakrishnan, 2013a)—would surveys be the best methodology, and what does it do for cross-country comparisons? Last but certainly not least. Start with the research question and its relevance and contribution to the region and IB studies (not just is it publishable).

Possible research questions could be

1. How do firms use reverse country of origin (product toward country image) to their advantage?
2. How do firms bargain with governments to further their international reach?
3. How is bartering used to manage the flow of goods?
4. How do firms keep their legitimacy in the host country when their home country image is tarnished?
5. What is the role of IP in international franchise agreements, and how do firms manage the brand when they have little control?
6. How much can a global brand be adapted without losing its "globalness"?

2.2   MENA and Conflict

This region has high geopolitical tension, being home to proxy wars due to the so-called "balance of terror" involving local countries and others like Russia and the USA (Hiltermann, 2020). Many existing conflicts build on previous events, and other conflicts were due to shifting borders and decolonization. It is estimated that

---

[2]For more on franchising in MENA see: https://www.americanbar.org/content/dam/aba/events/franchising/2009/w2.pdf.

[3]To be fair there is huge number of papers emerging from China and India and but again these are not representative of all other countries left out.

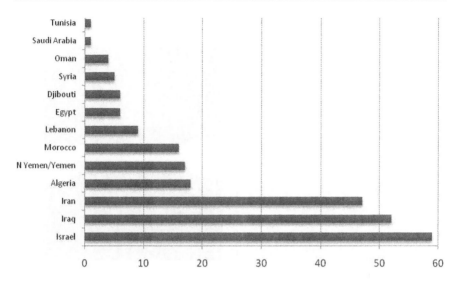

Fig. 2 Year of Conflict (MENA) from 1960 to 2009. Source: Ross et al. (2011)

90% of the conflicts existing in the first 10 years of the 21st Century were in places where a civil war had taken place, and though the number went down in the 1960s (43%) and 1970s (57%), it still is very high (World Bank, 2011b). This constant unrest raises great questions on whether an international business can exist using the best practices of the west alone. In many developed countries, when the safety of employees is threatened, offices close. How do you operate in adverse conditions when these cannot be met?

This is one of the questions I asked the Aramex co-founder, Fadi Ghandour, a recent recipient of the 2017 AIB Fellows International Executive of the Year Award. The company operated through the civil wars in Lebanon, in the Gulf War in 1989 when Kuwait was invaded by Iraq, the Bahrain riots of 2011, the 2nd Intifada (2000–2005), and the Egyptian revolution, for example (for more read Stephens Balakrishnan, 2013a). Fadi would say that it was not possible to close the operations as many families depended on the salaries for survival. They would take the highest level of precautions and use any information from the ground to reroute deliveries, but they could not close an office for a year. This area of study—HR safe practices would be one area for more research.

The World Bank (2011a, 2011b, vii) states, *"Accounting for 15 percent of the world's conflicts while only housing 5.5 percent of the population, the MENA region has seen a disproportionate level of conflict, particularly civil wars, since the end of the Second World War. . . .While some countries in the region experience significant economic hardship due to conflict, economic indicators in the region as a whole tends to recover more quickly than in other parts of the world."* How to operate is an essential question for international firms as places like Israel, Iran, and Iraq have close to 50 years of conflict, with Morocco, Yemen, and Algeria having 15 years—see Fig. 2 (Ross et al., 2011).

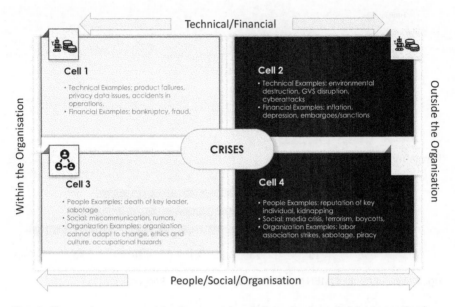

Fig. 3 Types of corporate crisis. Source: Adapted from Stephens Balakrishnan (Stephens Balakrishnan, 2016b)

In a case I documented on a company called Souktel (Stephens Balakrishnan, 2016a), the founder began with the assumption that there were few jobs available for Palestinians. More profound research showed that there were jobs, but crossing the checkpoints raised by the Israelis in the West Bank was lengthy, mentally disturbing, and sometimes dangerous. It was estimated in 2011 that there were 522 roadblocks and checkpoints limiting Palestinian movement in the West Bank and an additional 495 "flying checkpoints" at that time.[4] The solution was to use SMS as a text for job matching. It was funded through a Harvard Business School grant and later the World Bank. The firm was initially registered in the USA though it operated in Palestine. It raises interesting questions for the theory we use to define born globals. While profitable, it is not a traditional for-profit international business. More research may be needed on social enterprises and how they internationalize in terms of funding (versus sales).

One area of study is crisis management. In the Journal of International Business Studies, Czinkota et al. (Czinkota et al., 2010, p. 826) voiced the need for IB scholars *"to offer useful perspectives and effective solutions that shed needed light on terrorism and help reduce its destructive effects for IB and multinational firms."* MENA region often faces crises in Cells 2 and 4 (see Fig. 3). The ability to manage a crisis may also overlap with foresight studies (something not embraced by IB scholars). MENA faces cumulative crises (Hwang & Lichentahal, 2000), which, if

---

[4]Embassy of Palestine: https://www.ambasciatapalestina.com/en/political/checkpoint/ [Accessed 2 December, 2021].

ignored, can erupt into a problem that spills over geographic boundaries, like the Arab Spring or the Intifada movement (Cali, 2015; Gal & Rock, 2018; Stephens Balakrishnan, 2016b). The latter impacted trade via boycotts of American brands (Knudsen et al., 2008; The Economist, 2000; Benstead & Reif, 2017). IB scholars could see if crisis management, risk identification or, contingency approaches in MENA differ from other geographic areas. For example, a case I documented of how the UAE handled the Eyjafjallajokull Iceland volcano crisis found that when 20% of the global aviation (or 1.2 million passengers a day) were impacted by European airspace closure, Etihad used that opportunity to bring people to the country while they waited for a flight back "home" (Stephens Balakrishnan, 2012). This strategy was not a one off as recently UAE did something similar during the pandemic using the World Expo 2020.

The defense industry is valued at US$2 trillion (Deloitte, 2021). Defense is heavily dependent on policy (Steinbock, 2014). As more subcontracting occurs, it becomes a key area of study, especially as offshore companies are created for winning defense contracts. In the global defense sector, there is a poignant need for more cases of firm lobbying and political behavior and the (lack of) alignment with state interests (see Kim, 2019). Boddewyn and Brewer (1994), in their conceptual article, highlighted the importance of understanding the "space," which is the crossing of borders of political and economic space.

In terms of managing the politics of running a business during conflict (and many MNEs operate in the MENA region in industries like oil, defense, aviation, logistics, etc.), few scholars have ventured into this field. One interesting model is Banfield et al. (2003)—see Fig. 4. It looks at the space corporations occupy in areas fraught with conflict and politics (home and host). The highest level corporations can aspire to is peace-building, but this is not easy as political agendas, emotions of people, and perceptions of truth may vary. This concept also overlaps with firm ethics and values of business (Stephens, 2020). However, it is critical to understand this space because firms can influence politics and societies.

Further, firms need to operate by ensuring to agreed business values in a region prone to high tension and conflict. In one example, a German multinational, GEA Group, found that when contracts were being negotiated in the MENA region, every time there was a revision, the HQ in Germany would react very negatively, assuming corruption. A senior manager found that the way to manage this situation was to relocate people from the legal department to the MENA office, so they understood what the culture was. They then began to realize that a contract was only considered final when it was signed, and till that time was considered flexible and open to negotiation (unlike the Germans who thought it was once final once a verbal or written pre-agreement was in place) (Michael et al., 2015).

Another area of interest in trade and logistics is the rich topic of international business resilience, adaptability, and policy on managing chokepoints and their challenges. MENA is home to four strategic choke points for global trade—the Turkish Straits, Bab-el-Mandeb Strait, the Suez Canal, and Hormuz (see Table 3). Surprisingly there is little research on this area though it is vital to address it from a logistics and trade point of view. Dubai (UAE) hosts the world's largest

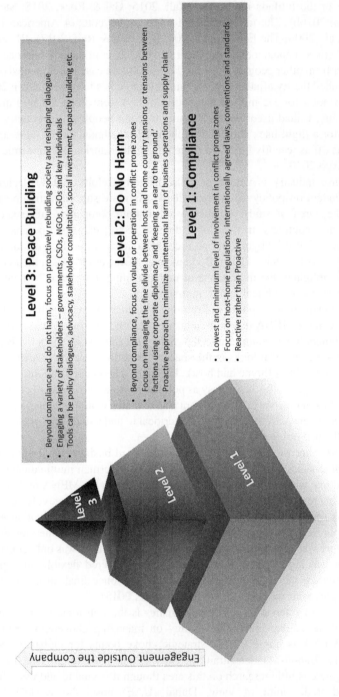

Level 3: Peace Building

- Beyond compliance and do not harm, focus on proactively rebuilding society and reshaping dialogue
- Engaging a variety of stakeholders – governments, CSOs, NGOs, IGOs and key individuals
- Tools can be policy dialogues, advocacy, stakeholder consultation, social investment, capacity building etc.

Level 2: Do No Harm

- Beyond compliance, focus on values or operation in conflict prone zones
- Focus on managing the fine divide between host and home country tensions or tensions between factions using corporate diplomacy and 'keeping an ear to the ground.'
- Proactive approach to minimize unintentional harm of busines operations and supply chain

Level 1: Compliance

- Lowest and minimum level of involvement in conflict prone zones
- Focus on host-home regulations, internationally agreed laws, conventions and standards
- Reactive rather than Proactive

Level 3

Level 2

Level 1

Engagement Outside the Company

Fig. 4 Strategies for managing corporate–conflict dynamics. Adapted from Banfield et al. (2003)

humanitarian logistics center. The International Humanitarian City (IHC) hosts 87 UN organizations, non-profits, non-governmental organizations, and private sector companies, reaching 126 countries during the pandemic (IHC, 2021). UAE airlines and location also played a critical part in Covid vaccine supply chain delivery, pivoting from passenger traffic to cargo traffic. In addition, the Hope consortium built a "freezer farm" in the UAE with a capacity to store more than 11 million COVID-19 vaccine doses (UAE, 2021). The way humanitarian logistics are managed versus conventional trade is also a new area of research.

Some research questions could be:

1. How would firms manage political unrest and conflict from a human capacity and business perspective?
2. How do firms safeguard IP from growing nationalization and protectionism?
3. How do international firms contribute to peacekeeping and humanitarianism?
4. How can firms safeguard from logistical hiatus that hurt production?
5. How does the defense business differ from other MNC businesses?

2.3   Sustainable Development Studies

The 17 Sustainable Development Goals (SDG) goals were ambitious targets adopted by 193 countries in 2015, to be achieved by 2030. While there is a strong perception that adopting SDGs in business values or operations also increases the bottom line (Muhmad & Muhamad, 2020), the context of MENA provides additional areas for strategic input, as explained further below. Many SDGs are wicked problems, and one of the challenges is evidence-based policymaking (Eden & Wagstaff, 2021). Van Zanten and Van Tulder (2018) highlight that international business research, in general, did not keep track of the role of companies in the context of SDGs. Much of the terminology today revolves around corporate social responsibility (CSR), corporate citizenship, corporate sustainability, or business ethics, but the MENA context may also be relevant.

In the MENA region, one of the challenges associated with monitoring the impact of the contribution to SDGs is the culture. In Islam, zakat is one of the five pillars of the religion. It is considered a religious duty of each Muslim and is a charitable donation of 2.5% of physical and financial assets (Ahmad et al., 2013). Businesses are a significant contributor of zakat (Umar et al., 2021). There are eight types of zakat: for the poor or low-income, the needy or who is in difficulty, zakat administrators, those whose hearts are to be reconciled, those in bondage or captives/slaves, the debt-ridden, in the cause of God, and those who are stranded or traveling with few resources (Abdullah & Suhaib, 2011). Zakat substantially impacts poverty reduction (Aziz et al., 2020 documents a few studies); however, record-keeping is challenging. It is estimated that the zakat collected from the Muslim world is approximately US$10 billion (Al-mubarak, 2016). In addition to this, there is waqf (an endowment to a cause that is religious, charitable, or educational), sadaqah, a voluntary donation, and awqah, an estate fund. These cannot be neatly labeled as CSR initiatives. Hence understanding the region and the context is critical for researchers who assume CSR is a separate budget item correlated to financial performance. Previous studies show the need to understand the context (Jamali et al., 2020) and cultural differences (Munro, 2013).

From an overall view, most of the population is young (less than 35 years), and the greatest fear is the rising unemployment which will become another source of destabilization. Employment is becoming a method of signaling and getting external legitimacy through local talent recruitment (Forstenlechner & Mellahi, 2011; Mellahi & Forstenlechner, 2011). For example, Saudisation, Emiratisation, or Omanisation have strong government support but many challenges when implemented in the private sector. The reason often is cultural and the fact that the state benefits are more attractive than the private sector. This could be a topic of research for IB scholars. For example, Careem (which was acquired by Uber) used a local employment initiative in Saudi to get legitimacy in KSA (Stephens, 2019). Gender balance is another area of focus. Many scholars assume that woman empowerment is higher in the west than in the MENA region, yet, in UAE, women are empowered by law and culture, holding key posts in the government and private sector.[5]

The pressing issues of this region are refugees and unemployment. IB scholars are attracted by the topic of global mobility yet focus on expatriate, global entrepreneurs, or economic migrants as opposed to refugees, a societal issue that firms can positively contribute to (Lee et al., 2020; Szkudlarek et al., 2019; Van Assche, 2019). MENA is one of the largest contributors to refugees, and each unrest or conflict displaces previous refugees (see Stephens Balakrishnan, 2016b, Al Nahayan & Stephens, 2019). Some countries are refugee sources like Syria (6.6 million) and Yemen (UNHCR, 2021). Syria is the world's largest refugee contributor, facing civil war since 2011. Other countries in the region are refugee hosts—like Lebanon (hosts 134 refugees per 1000 inhabitants), Jordan (69 per 1000), and Turkey (43 per 1000) (Amnesty International, 2021). For decades, Jordan has been taking in Palestinians and giving them passports (so the numbers are not reflected in the refugee statistics). Iraq and Libya were also refugee hosts countries till the "War of Terror" began. Many of their refugees originated from Iran, Palestine, and Africa but fled to neighboring countries during the War on Terror, along with the newly formed Iraqi and Libyan refugees. Syria also hosted refugees till the Civil War began. While there has been some exciting work on entrepreneurship in refugee camps (Al Nahayan & Stephens, 2019), and there exist differences in policies between countries for work opportunities for refugees, this is an area most IB scholars have not ventured into. For work rights for refugees, the Jordan compact focused on Syrian refugees (in Lebanon, for example, refugees do not live in camps and hence can work). This strategy of contributing to employment opportunities for local populations or refugees overlaps with corporate diplomacy and soft power (see

---

[5]More available in the UAE Embassy in Washington: https://www.uae-embassy.org/about-uae/women-uae.

Stephens et al., 2020). This is still a relatively unexplored area of research in the IB community. Some MNEs like UPS focus on contributing to the humanitarian relief and refugee situation, but more research in this field is needed (Reade et al., 2019; Christensen et al., 2019; Stephens et al., 2020).

Some research questions could be:

1. How can we encourage firms to hire refugees and add to the global talent pool?
2. What are the governance and ethical responsibilities for the firms?
3. How do different cultures embrace CSR, and what are the IB policies that must change?

2.4   Products Conforming to Islam

There are more than 1.6 billion Muslims in the world. Once in their lifetime, if able, they should make a pilgrimage to Mecca, in the Kingdom of Saudi Arabia. This gives KSA tremendous soft power. In this region, there is also a huge market for halal products. Halal products are defined as products "lawful" or "permitted" by Islam. Izberk-Bilgin and Nakata (2016) state, *"Halal is more encompassing; it emphasizes purity in substance and prescribes consumption of products closest to their natural state. This can mean seeking goods free of pesticides, preservatives, antibiotics, and GMOs for consumers. Halal also refers to purity in conscience and conduct, requiring believers to engage in good deeds and make ethical choices. Thus, halal is closely tied to fair trade, organic agriculture, animal welfare, food safety, and ecological economics. Holistically understood, halal is consistent with and reflects sustainability and corporate social responsibility (CSR) values."* There is a strong association of halal with food—and the IB community has underexplored the issue of global value chains and how countries like Brazil and Australia have embedded themselves into the halal market. The halal market is estimated to be US $1.9 trillion (ResearchandMarkets, 2021).

It now includes other foods (besides meat), cosmetics, pharmaceuticals, and Islamic Finance. The area has been ignored by IB researchers. Future certifications, financing or trade, and greater transparency of the supply chain with blockchain may change the way MNEs operate. For example, pharma products and vaccines often contain gelatin derived from pork which is forbidden for consumption. This spurs innovation to capture white spots (Eckelt et al., 2016) in the IP value chain. Most production of halal gelatin is from non-Islamic countries (over 78% from the USA and Europe). Though 57 nations belong to the Organisation of the Islamic Cooperation, there is no standard halal certification, which makes global supply challenging. Brands that reflect the religious heritage (as opposed to the country of origin (COO) effect) are under-researched areas by IB scholars. For example, Mecca-Cola began in France and now is in Africa and Asia. Countries like Australia and Brazil battle for halal meat exports. More studies on brand origin confusion and brand authenticity can be done when looking at the country of origin studies.

Table 4 Halal business: examples

Nations (top five exporters to organisation of islamic cooperation (OIC) countries)	Top MNC halal vendors (not in order)	Top islamic finance
1. Brazil at US$16.2 billion	1. BRF (Brazil)—Estimated US$ 11 Billion Revenue	1. Al Rajhi Bak (KSA)
2. India at US$14.4 billion	2. Nestle (Switzerland)—Nestlé Malaysia is the company's largest producer of halal products (300 products). These halal-certified products are sourced, produced, and distributed according to Islamic laws and resulted in US$1.29 billion in sales in 2018	2. Dubai Islamic Bank (UAE)
3. USA at US$13.8 billion	3. Examples of Local players: Al Islami Foods (Dubai, UAE)—complex supply chain: beef and poultry from Brazil, vegetables from the Netherlands and Belgium, fruit from Egypt, and seafood from the UAE and Vietnam—Estimated US$14 Million (revenue -) Examples like this will let IB scholars realize the complexity of supply chain based on factors not limited to price	Kuwait Finance House (Kuwait)
4. Russia at US$11.9 billion		Maybank Islamic (Malaysia)
5. Argentina at US$10.2 billion		Qatar Islamic (Qatar)

Source: Compiled from various sources (For the various source see: http://tradearabia.com/news/IND_376964.html; https://www.businesswire.com/news/home/20170524006206/en/Top-5-Vendors-in-the-Halal-Food-Market-from-2017-to-2021-Technavio; https://www.theasianbanker.com/ab500/2018-2019/largest-islamic-banks)

The rise of the Islamic index and the importance of Islamic finance should not be ignored as it is valued at US$2 Trillion (DIFC, 2021). Islamic stocks perform better than conventional stocks (Sayani & Balakrishnan, 2013; Ludwig (2005). Hakim and Rashidian (2002) conclude that the factors impacting Islamic stocks' market are different from regular stocks. This concept of "value-based financing" has also been an ignored area of IB scholarly work. For example, Gavi, the Vaccine Alliance, used sukuks as vehicles to finance its vaccine program, considering most of its recipient countries (pre-covid) were Muslim countries (Stephens Balakrishnan, 2016c) (Table 4).

Some research questions could be:

1. How does the international halal business differ from regular business in terms of trade?
2. How does halal branding affect global brands?
3. What is the fine line between commercialization and religion in the international arena?
4. How does a country of origin affect the authenticity of religion-based brands?

5. How does business risk get impacted with international Sharia financing (which depends on profit and loss sharing principles)?

3 Conclusion

In short, MENA is an excellent area for IB scholars to study outliers (Aharoni, 2011; Gerring, 2008) and find stress points in commonly adopted and taught IB theory. As Aharoni highlights, a theory is context-dependent (p. 49). By highlighting the phenomena under study, cases can bring rich data to how firms operate in various contexts (Fletcher et al., 2018). There is an excellent opportunity to contribute to the dialogue on global trade, especially as the world's economic center moves toward the east. It is estimated that this movement accelerated during the pandemic, and between 2020 and 2021, the shift is 1.8× the average of 2015–2019 (Euler Hermes, 2021). New initiatives like the Regional Comprehensive Economic Partnership (RCEP) may grow in power, creating a bloc equivalent to the EU. The push back to globalization to ensure minimum critical supply (USA's CHIPS for America Act) and the need for large firms to pay a minimum of 15% corporate tax in the country from which they get profits (Thomas, 2021) are significant signals that highlight firms need nonmarket strategies. The DHL Global Connectedness (2020) report highlights we still have some ways to go to be genuinely globalized.

Here are a few strategies to increase research output in the region, considering the difficulty in getting qualitative research published in topic journals.

1. Increase International Collaborations: A study looking at 4.2 million papers published between 1975 to 2005 finds that the fastest-growing authorship combination was from multi-university studies, and these often (if they are top tier universities) produce high-impact papers (Jones et al., 2008). Out of 429 ranked Universities, MENA's highest-ranked university was ranked 244—KSA's King Abdulla University of Science and Technology (Sciamago, 2021). Hence MENA authors should look outside the region for co-authors. Looking at scientific publications for the MENA between 1981 and 2013 in 17 countries (9.8 million publication records), it was found that international collaborations led to an increase in publication activity (Siddiqi et al., 2016). There is no reason why this cannot hold for IB studies. As seen in Table 1, publication numbers are low for MENA, and there is also a need to increase partnerships with the industry. Research culture needs to change, but so does the institutional context that encourages research (Stephens Balakrishnan, 2013a). Work done by organizations like the Academy of International Business—MENA is in the right direction. Scholars need to take advantage of opportunities like these.
2. Focus on instrument relevance: If we assume the context is vital for research, then the current methodological tools being used may need to be adapted for the region. It may be important to look at face validity and content validity (Taherdoost, 2016; Lakshmi & Mohideen, 2013). Another challenge is data equivalence, *'the extent to which the elements of a research design have the*

same meaning, and can be applied in the same way, in different cultural contexts' (Hult et al., 2008: 1027). In the same paper, a study of 167 papers from 1995 to 2005 found that most IB researchers report insufficient information with respect to data equivalence (construct equivalence, measurement equivalence, and data collection equivalence) which would make cross-cultural study findings less robust. This is an area that MENA researchers should advocate and contribute to.

3. Qualitative Studies: Literature reviews sum up the state of research, and this is an area that MENA scholars can contribute to. There are various methodologies— systematic reviews, meta-analysis, or comprehensive reviews- all of which need to be rigorous (Kunisch et al., 2018). The sample and method must be carefully planned (Hiebl, 2021). Further, there are emerging opportunities to contribute to IB policy. Birkinshaw, Brannen, and Tung (Birkinshaw et al., 2011: 573) state: *"In order to understand the complexities of emergent and evolving phenomena scattered over distance, and the differentiated contexts typical to many topics under investigation in IB, it is often inappropriate to engage in large-scale, cross-sectional studies or reductionist methods in the absence of well-developed theory. Rather, thick description, exploratory research and comparative case analysis that focus on inductive theory building and hypotheses generation may be more suitable."*

4. Interdisciplinary Research: IB cannot exist without other disciplines (some of the topics like soft power and nonmarket strategies discussed above overlap with international relations). Cheng et al. (Cheng et al., 2009) explain that single researchers often conduct interdisciplinary studies exploring complex problems relevant to IB. International business policy or how governments instigate change that affects firms operating in the international arena is another area worth investigating (Lundan, 2018). These are some ways for MENA scholars to begin adding to the body of research. This sentiment was echoed by Dunning (Dunning, 1989) to *"read and study well outside our own area of training."* Cheng et al. (2009) further reinforce the fact that *"Thus, moving forward is not about reformulating novel dependent or independent variables; it is about addressing a phenomenon that can only be unpacked by combining theories, concepts, data and methods from multiple disciplines to explore the scope or boundary conditions of multiple disciplinary perspectives and the benefits of their integration."*

This short chapter just highlights a few areas for future study, but there are many more areas for research like HR practices (adoption from global standards), expatriate management (when expats live in the region); finance or product pricing (when looking at currency fluctuation); logistics responses with shifts in regulatory policies (green or halal logistics); reverse country of origin (similar to soft power), IP and innovation, and global brand management. I encourage our existing IB community to look beyond their borders and work with MENA scholars to add to the scholarly debates. The knowledge about the region will ensure that the theory we teach is robust, help the practitioners and our students prepare for the new world and new ways of operating.

References

Abdullah, M., & Suhaib, A. Q. (2011). The impact of zakat on social life of Muslim society introduction: Zakat: Meaning, definition and significance of zakat. *Pakistan Journal of Islamic Research, 8*, 85–91.

Aharoni, Y. (2011). Fifty years of case research in international business: The power of outliers and black swans. In *Rethinking the case study in international business and management research.* Edward Elgar Publishing.

Ahmad, C. Y., Safiah, M., Azizah, D., Normah, I., & Mohd Ali, M. D. (2013). Zakat disbursement via capital assistance: A case study of Majlis Agama Islam Johor. *Journal of Emerging Economies and Islamic Research, 1*(2), 1–19. https://doi.org/10.1088/1751-8113/44/8/085201

Akbar, Y. H., & Kisilowski, M. (2020). To bargain or not to bargain: Airlines, legitimacy and nonmarket strategy in a COVID-19 world. *Journal of Air Transport Management, 88*, 101867. https://doi.org/10.1016/j.jairtraman.2020.101867

Al Nahyan, S. S., & Stephens, M. (2019). Reforming policies on refugees. In M. Stephens, M. M. El Sholkamy, I. A. Moonesar, & R. Awamleh (Eds.), *Actions and insights: Middle East North Africa (vol 7): Future Governments* (pp. 119–134). Emerald Group Publishing. Translated into Arabic in 2020 and published by Qindeel Publishing, UAE.

Al-mubarak, T. (2016). The Maqasid of Zakah and Awqaf and their roles in inclusive finance. *Islam and Civilisational Renewal, 7*(2), 217–230. https://doi.org/10.12816/0035198

Amnesty International. (2021). The world's refugees in numbers. Available: https://www.amnesty.org/en/what-we-do/refugees-asylum-seekers-and-migrants/global-refugee-crisis-statistics-and-facts/. Accessed 1 Oct 2021.

Aziz, Y., Mansor, F., Waqar, S., & Haji Abdullah, L. (2020). The nexus between zakat and poverty reduction, is the effective utilization of zakat necessary for achieving SDGs: A multidimensional poverty index approach. *Asian Social Work and Policy Review, 14*(3), 235–247.

Bach, D., & Allen, D. (2010). What every CEO needs to know about nonmarket strategy. *MIT Sloan Management Review, 51*(3), 41.

Banfield, J., Haufler, V., & Lilly, D. (2003). In conflict prone zones: Public policy responses and a framework for action. http://www.conflictsensitivity.org/sites/default/files/transnational_Corporations_Conflict_prone.pdf. Accessed 11 Dec 2014.

Benstead, L. J., & Reif, M. (2017). Coke, Pepsi or Mecca Cola? Why product characteristics affect the likelihood of collective action problems and boycott success. *Politics, Groups, and Identities, 5*(2), 220–241.

Birkinshaw, J., Brannen, M. Y., & Tung, R. L. (2011). From a distance and generalizable to up close and grounded: Reclaiming a place for qualitative methods in international business research. *Journal of International Business Studies, 42*, 573–581.

Boddewyn, J. J. (2015). Political aspects of MNE theory. In *The eclectic paradigm* (pp. 85–110). Palgrave Macmillan.

Boddewyn, J. J. (2016). International business–government relations research 1945–2015: Concepts, typologies, theories and methodologies. *Journal of World Business, 51*(1), 10–22.

Boddewyn, J. J., & Brewer, T. L. (1994). International-business political behavior: New theoretical directions. *Academy of Management Review, 19*(1), 119–143.

Buttorff, G., Shalaby, M. & Allam, N. (2020). A survey reveals how the pandemic has hurt MENA research. Al-Fanar Media, dated September 23. Available: https://www.al-fanarmedia.org/2020/09/a-survey-reveals-how-the-pandemic-has-hurt-mena-research/

Cali, M. (2015). Trade, employment and conflict: Evidence from the Second Intifada. ODI. Available: https://odi.org/en/publications/trade-employment-and-conflict-evidence-from-the-second-intifada/. Accessed 2 Oct 2021.

Calma, A., & Suder, G. (2020). Mapping international business and international business policy research: Intellectual structure and research trends. *International Business Review, 29*(3), 101691.

Chantham House. (2017). Chokepoints and vulnerabilities in global food trade. https://www. chathamhouse.org/2017/06/chokepoints-and-vulnerabilities-global-food-trade. Accessed 21 Oct 2021.

Cheng, J. L., Henisz, W. J., Roth, K., & Swaminathan, A. (2009). From the editors: Advancing interdisciplinary research in the field of international business. *Prospects, Issues and Challenges, 40*, 1070–1074.

Christensen, L., Newman, A., Herrick, H., & Godfrey, P. (2019). Separate but not equal: Toward a nomological net for migrants and migrant entrepreneurship. *Journal of International Business Policy.* https://doi.org/10.1057/s42214-019-00041-w

Clegg, J. (2019). From the editor: International business policy: What it is, and what it is not. *Journal of International Business Policy, 2*(2), 111–118.

Czinkota, M. R., Knight, G., Liesch, P. W., & Steen, J. (2010). Terrorism and international business: A research agenda. *Journal of International Business Studies, 41*(5), 826–843.

Darendeli, I. S., & Hill, T. L. (2016). Uncovering the complex relationships between political risk and MNE firm legitimacy: Insights from Libya. *Journal of International Business Studies, 47*(1), 68–92.

Deloitte. (2021). 2021 aerospace and defense industry outlook. https://www2.deloitte.com/us/en/ pages/manufacturing/articles/global-aerospace-and-defense-industry-outlook.html. Accessed 7 Oct 2021.

DHL. (2020). Global connectedness index.

DIFC. (2021). Islamic finance. https://www.difc.ae/business/areas-business/islamic-finance/. Accessed 1 Oct 2021.

Dunning, J. H. (1989). The study of international business: A plea for a more interdisciplinary approach. *Journal of International Business Studies, 20*(3), 411–436.

Eckelt, D., Dülme, C., Gausemeier, J., & Hemel, S. (2016). Detecting white spots in innovation-driven intellectual property management. *Technology Innovation Management Review, 6*(7), 34–47.

Eden, L., & Wagstaff, M. F. (2021). Evidence-based policymaking and the wicked problem of SDG 5 gender equality. *Journal of International Business Policy, 4*(1), 28–57.

EIA. (2017). Three important oil chokepoints. Available: https://www.eia.gov/todayinenergy/ detail.php?id=32352 Accessed 1 Nov 2021.

Fletcher, M., Zhao, Y., Plakoyiannaki, E., & Buck, T. (2018). Three pathways to case selection in international business: A twenty-year review, analysis and synthesis. *International Business Review, 27*(4), 755–766.

Forstenlechner, I., & Mellahi, K. (2011). Gaining legitimacy through hiring local workforce at a premium: The case of MNEs in the United Arab Emirates. *Journal of World Business, 46*(4), 455–461.

Gal, Y. & Rock, B. (2018). Israeli-Palestinian trade: In-Depth analysis. Tony Blair Institute for Global Change. https://institute.global/advisory/israeli-palestinian-trade-depth-analysis. Accessed 14 Sept 2021.

Gerring, J. (2008). Case selection for case-study analysis: Qualitative and quantitative techniques. In *The Oxford handbook of political methodology.*

Griffith, D. A., Cavusgil, S. T., & Xu, S. (2008). Emerging themes in international business research. *Journal of International Business Studies, 39*(7), 1220–1235.

Hakim, S. & Rashidian, M. (2002). Risk and return of Islamic stock market indexes. paper presented at the Economic Research Forum Annual Meetings, Sharjah, UAE.

Hermes, E. (2021). The world is moving east, fast. Available: https://www.eulerhermes.com/ content/dam/onemarketing/ehndbx/eulerhermes_com/en_gl/erd/publications/pdf/2021_01_18_ AsiaPostCovid19.pdf. Accessed 20 Oct 2021.

Hiebl, M. R. (2021). Sample selection in systematic literature reviews of management research. *Organizational Research Methods.* 1094428120986851.

Hillman, A. J., & Hitt, M. A. (1999). Corporate political strategy formulation: A model of approach, participation, and strategy decisions. *Academy of Management Review, 24*(4), 825–842.

Hiltermann, J. (2020). Tackling intersecting conflicts in the MENA region. *International Crisis Group*. dated January 15. https://www.crisisgroup.org/middle-east-north-africa/tackling-intersecting-conflicts-mena-region. Accessed 12 Sept 2021

Hult, G. T. M., Ketchen, D. J., Griffith, D. A., Finnegan, C. A., Gonzalez-Padron, T., Harmancioglu, N., Huang, Y., Berk Talay, M., & Cavusgil, S. T. (2008). Data equivalence in cross-cultural international business research: Assessment and guidelines. *Journal of International Business Studies, 39*(6), 1027–1044.

Hwang, P., & Lichtenthal, J. D. (2000). Anatomy of organizational crises. *Journal of Contingencies and Crisis Management, 8*(3), 129–140.

IHC. (2021). 2020 annual report. https://www.ihc.ae/wp-content/uploads/2021/05/IHC-Annual-Report-2020-english.pdf. Accessed 20 Oct 2021.

Izberk-Bilgin, E., & Nakata, C. C. (2016). A new look at faith-based marketing: The global halal market. *Business Horizons, 59*(3), 285–292.

Jamali, D., Jain, T., Samara, G., & Zoghbi, E. (2020). How institutions affect CSR practices in the Middle East and North Africa: A critical review. *Journal of World Business, 55*(5), 101127.

Jones, B. F., Wuchty, S., & Uzzi, B. (2008). Multi-university research teams: Shifting impact, geography, and stratification in science. *Science, 322*(5905), 1259–1262.

Justis, R. T., & Judd, R. (1986). Master franchising: A new look. *Journal of Small Business Management, 24*(3), 16–21.

Khaleej Times. (2020). Fine hygienic holding: 'Don't worry: It's fine'. https://www.khaleejtimes.com/business-and-technology-review/fine-hygienic-holding-dont-worry-its-fine. Accessed 22 Sept 2021.

Kim, J. H. (2019). Is your playing field unleveled? US defense contracts and foreign firm lobbying. *Strategic Management Journal, 40*(12), 1911–1937.

Knudsen, K., Aggarwal, P., & Maamoun, A. (2008). The burden of identity: Responding to product boycotts in the Middle East. *Journal of Business & Economics Research, 6*(11), 17–26.

Kunisch, S., Menz, M., Bartunek, J. M., Cardinal, L. B., & Denyer, D. (2018). Feature topic at organizational research methods: How to conduct rigorous and impactful literature reviews? *Organizational Research Methods, 21*(3), 519–523.

Lages, C., Pfajfar, G., & Shoham, A. (2015). Challenges in conducting and publishing research on the Middle East and Africa in leading journals. *International Marketing Review, 32*(1), 52–77.

Lakshmi, S., & Mohideen, M. A. (2013). Issues in reliability and validity of research. *International Journal of Management Research and Reviews, 3*(4), 2752.

Lee, E., Szkudlarek, B., Nguyen, D., & Nardon, L. (2020). Unveiling the canvas ceiling: A multidisciplinary literature review of refugee employment and workforce integration. *International Journal of Management Reviews, 22*, 193–216.

Ludwig, M. (2005). Kaiser's Amana income fund beats S&P500 by following Islamic law. *Bloomberg News*. dated July 7.

Lundan, S. M. (2018). From the editor: Engaging international business scholars with public policy issues. *Journal of International Business Policy, 1*(1–2), 1–11.

McKee, M., Keulertz, M., Habibi, N., Mulligan, M., & Woertz, E. (2017). Middle East and North Africa regional architecture: Mapping geopolitical shifts, regional order and domestic transformations. Working Paper. https://www.iai.it/sites/default/files/menara_wp_3.pdf

MEED. (2016). https://www.meed.com/saudi-arabias-pif-gets-26-6bn-funds-injection/

Mejren, R. (2020). Watch: How this UAE factory makes hand sanitizer. Gulf News. https://gulfnews.com/uae/health/watch-how-this-uae-factory-makes-hand-sanitiser-1.70690742. Accessed 15 June 2021.

Mellahi, K., & Forstenlechner, I. (2011). Employment relations in oil-rich Gulf countries. In *Research handbook of comparative employment relations*. Edward Elgar Publishing.

Michael, I., Stephens, M., & Khan, Z. (2015). GEA Group—doing business in the Middle East. *Emerald Emerging Markets Case Studies, 5*(3). https://doi.org/10.1108/EEMCS-03-2015-0038

Muhmad, S. N., & Muhamad, R. (2020). Sustainable business practices and financial performance during pre-and post-SDG adoption periods: A systematic review. *Journal of Sustainable Finance & Investment*, 1–19.

Munro, V. (2013). Stakeholder understanding of corporate social responsibility (CSR) in emerging markets with a focus on Middle East, Africa (MEA) and Asia. *Journal of Global Policy and Governance*, 2(1), 59–77.

O'Sullivan, A., Rey, M.-E., & Mendez, J. G. (2011). *Opportunities and challenges in the MENA region*. OECD.

Powell, A. (2021). Understanding petroleum regimes in the MENA region. *Al Tamimi*. https://www.tamimi.com/law-update-articles/understanding-petroleum-regimes-mena-region/. Accessed 12 July 2021

Reade, C., Oetzel, J., & McKenna, M. (2019). Unmanaged migration and the role of MNEs in reducing push factors and promoting peace: A strategic HRM perspective. *Journal of International Business Policy*. https://doi.org/10.1057/s42214-019-00043-8

ResearchandMarkets. (2021). Halal food market global industry trends. https://www.researchandmarkets.com/reports/5311860/halal-food-market-global-industry-trends-share. Accessed 12 July 2021.

Reuters. (2016). Dubai group pays $2.4 billion for control of Kuwait's Americana. https://www.reuters.com/article/us-americana-m-a-idUSKCN0Z40OW

Ross, M., Mazeheri, N., & Kaiser, K. (2011). The "Resource Curse" in MENA? Political transitions, resource wealth, economic shocks, and conflict risk. *World Bank*. https://doi.org/10.1596/1813-9450-5742

Sayani, H., & Balakrishnan, M. S. (2013). Marketing an Islamic index: Perceived value of KMI30 index. *Management Research Review*, 326–358.

Scatena, J. (2020). Turkey's unique hand-sanitising method. https://www.etsy.com/listing/746516034/50x-blank-toothpicks-mini-flag-paper?ga_order=most_relevant&ga_search_type=all&ga_view_type=gallery&ga_search_query=toothpick+flags+blank&ref=sr_gallery-1-2&organic_search_click=1. Accessed 5 July 2021.

Sciamago. (2021). Institutions rankings Middle East. Available: https://www.scimagoir.com/rankings.php?sector=Higher+educ.&country=Middle%20East . Accessed 1 Dec 2021.

Siddiqi, A., Stoppani, J., Anadon, L. D., & Narayanamurti, V. (2016). Scientific wealth in Middle East and North Africa: Productivity, indigeneity, and specialty in 1981–2013. *PLoS One, 11*(11), e0164500. https://doi.org/10.1371/journal.pone.0164500

Steinbock, D. (2014). The erosion of America's defense innovation. *American Foreign Policy Interests, 36*(6), 366–374.

Stephens Balakrishnan, M. (2012). *Etihad airways: Reputation management: An example of Eyjafjallajokull Iceland volcano', Actions and Insights—Middle East North Africa: Managing in uncertain times* (p. 143). Emerald Group Publishing.

Stephens Balakrishnan, M. (2013a). Methods to increase research output: Some tips looking at the MENA region. *International Journal of Emerging Markets*, 8(3), 215–239.

Stephens Balakrishnan, M. (2013b). Americana Group: KFC in Mecca (or Makkah). In M. S. Balakrishnan, I. Michael, & I. A. Moonesar (Eds.), *Actions and insights: Middle East North Africa* (East Meets West) (Vol. 3, pp. 123–137). Emerald Group Publishing.

Stephens Balakrishnan, M. (2016a). Soutkel: Using m-technology to impact emerging markets. In M. S. Balakrishnan & V. Lindsay (Eds.), *Actions and insights: Middle East North Africa* (Social entrepreneurs) (Vol. 5, pp. 271–287). Emerald Group Publishing.

Stephens Balakrishnan, M. (2016b). Managing at the edge of chaos: Middle East North Africa–perspectives for international management. In H. Merchant (Ed.), *Handbook of contemporary research on emerging markets* (pp. 317–354). Edward Elgar Publishing.

Stephens Balakrishnan, M. (2016c). Gavi: The Vaccine Alliance: Saving lives one vaccine at a time. In M. S. Balakrishnan & V. Lindsay (Eds.), *Actions and Insights: Middle East North Africa* (Social entrepreneurship) (Vol. 5, pp. 135–191). Emerald Group Publishing.

Stephens, M. (2019). Careem: Taking a local problem-solving approach to the sharing economy. In M. Stephens, M. M. El Sholkamy, I. M., Moonesar, & R. Awamleh (Eds.), Actions and insights: Middle East North Africa (Vol. 7): Future Governments (pp. 347–366).

Stephens, M. (2020). *Business with purpose: Advancing social enterprise*. World Scientific Publishing Company.

Stephens, M., Al Nahyan, S.S., Mouwiya, A., Bodolica, V., & Spraggon, M. (2020). Country soft power using international brands—the humanitarian context. 62nd Academy of International Business Annual Conference, Virtual.

Szkudlarek, B., Nardon, L., Osland, J., Adler, N., & Lee, E. S. (2019). When context matters: What happens to international theory when researchers study refugees. *Academy of Management Perspectives, 35*(3), 461–484.

Taherdoost, H. (2016). Validity and reliability of the research instrument; how to test the validation of a questionnaire/survey in a research. How to test the validation of a questionnaire/survey in a research (August 10, 2016).

The Economist. (2000). Cairene shoppers' Intifada. https://www.economist.com/international/2000/11/02/cairene-shoppers-intifada. Accessed 3 July 2021.

The First Abu Dhabi Bank. (2020). The GCC facts and figures 2020. Available: https://www.bankfab.com/-/media/fabgroup/home/cib/market-insights/macro-strategy-and-economic-update/pdf/20200824ms.pdf?view=1. Accessed 7 May 2021

The National. (2021). Coronavirus: UAE mask manufacturer to go global to limit spread of pandemic, dated October 16. https://www.thenationalnews.com/uae/health/coronavirus-uae-mask-manufacturer-to-go-global-to-limit-spread-of-pandemic-1.1047418. Accessed 22 July 2021.

The World Today. (1958). New oil agreements in the Middle East. *The World Today, 14*(4), 135–143. http://www.jstor.org/stable/40393842. Accessed 10 Oct 2021

Thomas, L. (2021). 130 countries back global minimum corporate tax of 15%. *Reuters*. dated July 2, https://www.reuters.com/business/countries-backs-global-minimum-corporate-tax-least-15-2021-07-01/. Accessed 16 Oct 2021

UAE. (2021). Distributing COVID-19 vaccines globally. Available: https://u.ae/en/information-and-services/justice-safety-and-the-law/handling-the-covid-19-outbreak/distributing-covid-19-vaccines-globally . Accessed 22 Oct 2021.

Umar, U. H., Abubakar, M., & Sharifai, I. I. (2021). Why does business zakat contribute insignificantly to achieving "SDG-1: Ending Poverty" in Nigeria? Evidence from recordkeeping practices. Islamic Wealth and the SDGs: Global strategies for socio-economic Impact, p. 219.

UNHCR. (2021). Figure at a glance. https://www.unhcr.org/figures-at-a-glance.html. Accessed 8 May 2021.

US Trade. (2021). Middle East North Africa. https://ustr.gov/countries-regions/europe-middle-east/middle-east/north-africa. Accessed 7 May 2021.

Van Assche, A. (2019). From the editor: Steering a policy turn in international business— Opportunities and challenges. *Journal of International Business Policy, 1*, 117–127.

Van Zanten, J. A., & Van Tulder, R. (2018). Multinational enterprises and the sustainable development goals: An institutional approach to corporate engagement. *Journal of International Business Policy, 1*(3), 208–233.

Vivoda, V. (2009). Resource nationalism, bargaining and international oil companies: Challenges and change in the new millennium. *New Political Economy, 14*(4), 517–534.

World Bank. (2011a). Reducing conflict risk conflict, fragility and development in the Middle East and North Africa. https://www.worldbank.org/content/dam/Worldbank/document/MNA/WDR2011-Conflict-MENA.pdf. Accessed 10 Oct 2021.

World Bank. (2011b). *World development report 2011* (pp. 81–82).
World Bank. (2021a). March 2021 global poverty update from the World Bank. https://blogs.
    worldbank.org/opendata/march-2021-global-poverty-update-world-bank.   Accessed
    21 Sept 2021.
World Bank. (2021b). MENA https://www.worldbank.org/en/region/mena https://data.worldbank.
    org/country/ZQ. Accessed 7 May 2021.
YouthPolicy.Org. (2021). MENA: Youth facts. Available: https://www.youthpolicy.org/mappings/
    regionalyouthscenes/mena/facts/

Melodena Stephens is Professor of Innovation Management,
Mohammed Bin Rashid School of Government (MBRSG) in
Dubai, UAE. Three decades of experience in various leadership
roles across several countries. Winner of several teaching and
research awards. On the board of three IEEE SA Ethics
Committees. Prolific author, most recent books: *Agile Government, AI Smart Kit* and *Business With Purpose*. She consults and
trains in strategy, innovation (policy and market development),
agile government and crisis reputation management.

The Relevance Problem of International Business Research

Michael-Jörg Oesterle and Joachim Wolf

1 Relevance as a Matter of Perspective

The discussion on relevant research seems to be a constant phenomenon of self-reflection within the academic field of International Business (IB). Already in 1991, the Academy of International Business organized its annual meeting as conference dedicated to the topic "Relevance in International Business Research." In his speech as outgoing AIB President John D. Daniels shared his thoughts on the topic leading to the plea that relevance needs more linkages. Whereas nowadays relevance is mostly viewed as being equal to applied research (that can be [directly] transferred to and implemented by the business practice; see the ongoing debate on rigor vs. relevance), John D. Daniels showed that relevance can be interpreted by taking also the opposite perspective—relevance via theory building: "During the past few months I have heard enough comments to realize that AIB members have divergent views on relevance, ranging from 'only theory building is relevant' to equating relevance with applied research" (1991: 177).

As so far the topic "relevance" should be approached by clarifying first the question to whom IB research could be relevant. Figuring research simply as a value creating chain of units and their activities with scholars as producers, journals as outlets of research results, the real business world as source and object of research, and consumers of research like other scholars, students, and practitioners shows that the respective process consists of different elements with most likely also different interests. This means that not all participants of the process might be guided by the same understanding of relevance.

M.-J. Oesterle (✉)
University of Stuttgart, Stuttgart, Germany
e-mail: michael-joerg.oesterle@bwi.uni-stuttgart.de

J. Wolf
University of Kiel, Kiel, Germany
e-mail: wolf@bwl.uni-kiel.de

© Springer Nature Switzerland AG 2022
H. Merchant (ed.), *The New Frontiers of International Business*, Contributions to Management Science, https://doi.org/10.1007/978-3-031-06003-8_7

According to Popper (1995: 4) "our aim as scientists is objective truth; more truth, more interesting truth, more intelligible truth." Especially the dimension "interesting truth" makes clear that the results of research should attract attention or should be relevant. However, in an academic discipline like IB that is dealing with real phenomena attention articulated only by other scholars is not enough. If no research outcomes are produced that attract the attention of practitioners the discipline would uncouple itself from its object endangering, e.g., the willingness of practitioners to fill out questionnaires, to be interview partners, to deliver material for case studies or to fund research projects: In the words of John Dunning ". . . the effectiveness of our scholastic efforts to study and teach international business is entirely dependent on our capability to marshal and organise the necessary human and other assets so as to supply a range of end products which are acceptable to the academic community of which we are part, our paymasters and the main purchasers of our products, viz. the business community" (1989: 411). So the question is not about rigor vs. relevance but how to produce true relevant results fostering the progress of theory and the real business world.

On the other side, younger scholars struggling for a tenured position (job) in the academic sphere might be guided also by the interest to use their research to promote their own careers. Relevance is in this case not automatically the same as in the ideal first case but dominated by that what high-ranked journals expect. To be attractive to the job market (junior) scholars have to follow the rules of the game, i.e. to run that kind of research in terms of topics, concepts, methodology, and outcome that meets the (standardized) expectations of the journals or better—the respective scientific community as occupants of the ivory tower. The journals themselves are under competitive pressure seeking to become more relevant in terms of getting higher impact factors. Relevant are therefore those papers that will be cited by members of the scientific community. Higher numbers of citations receive most likely those papers that follow as outcome of the perceived dominating dimension "rigor" the generally accepted principles of producing research results. This means, one has to deal with a topic being in fashion (new trends are normally set by prominent and leading scholars, not the young ones) and has to treat it with the established instruments—application of sophisticated, preferably new theories (Tourish, 2020), ambitious conceptual thoughts and/or ambitious empirical analyses, mostly quantitative ones.

However, that kind of research is not (always) very attractive to those that are both objects (input) and potential customers of the scientific production process— the real business world and its decision-makers. They expect research results that help them to make their business more efficient and effective or—in a more general sense—to get along better with the challenges business has to face. According to several studies (e.g., Gopinath & Hoffman, 1995; Oesterle & Laudien, 2007) and our own impression IB scholars do not always know or care for (e.g., Lewin, 2004) what problems international firms see and have to solve.

The following discussion of the question, what could be done to make research in the IB field (more) relevant will try to incorporate critically those perspectives showed above that are specific to the IB field. Some of the already described perspectives are focussing on problems that are typical of today's business administration as academic discipline in general, e.g., rigor-orientation, methodological narrowness in terms of emphasizing quantitative empirical analyses, and large distance to practitioners at least in their (potential) function as customers of research output. As so far the following sections are guided by the idea of a problem-centered discussion, taking such problems as starting point that are content-wise typical of the discipline IB. By doing so the presented thoughts will of course not be able to reflect a one-best-way solution. Their basic motivation and goal are rather to help producing a higher degree of awareness toward the problems that are likely to impair the up-grading of relevance in the IB research process. In this context relevance will be first discussed as problem within IB research; a further subsection will focus on IB research as a system that is—according to our impression—not intensively interacting with other disciplines of business administration and beyond, thereby likely to overlook already existing knowledge and not fully realizing the chance to broaden and deepen the own knowledge bases: The consequence of paradigmatically sticking to an own perspective is favoring a limited ability to explain the real world of IB, because already existing approaches of other disciplines to describe and to explain phenomena of IB are not sufficiently employed or exploited. And finally, the last section will focus on common misunderstandings of authors when it comes to submitting their research papers to relevant journals in the field of IB.

2 Some Examples of IB's Loss of Practical Relevance

In the introduction section of this essay, we have discussed the relevance question more generally as it is valid for all subfields of business administration. We argued that answering this question will always require a specification of the respective target group. It has to be defined out of which perspective the relevance problem is viewed. If the relevance question will be discussed out of a researcher's perspective, this will lead to a different answer than if it will be discussed out of the perspective of business practice. While we fully understand that non-tenured faculty members have to conduct research activities in a way so that they can help them to get tenure, we think that it is highly problematic if most business administration research and therefore also IB research is oriented toward this direction. If business administration research *as such*—and thus IB research also—will go this way then it will ignore the need to deliver research output being helpful for the decision-makers in business practice.

Furthermore, in the introduction section, we argued that this causes the need to deliver research output that practitioners perceive to be interesting. If IB researchers will provide knowledge practitioners consider to be uninteresting then IB research will not have any impact on MNCs' actions. Of course, not all IB research has to be practice-oriented. But if (nearly) none of it is practice-oriented, the IB community has a severe problem.

In the following, we will present examples showing that during the last decades IB research has lost its close linkage to the business practice.

Example 1: Research on the Management of MNCs

Until the mid of the 1990s most research on the management of MNCs was focused on MNCs' strategy and organization issues. In the strategy area, quite many studies explored MNCs' *strategic orientations* (e.g., Doz, 1980; Porter, 1986). These studies tried to specify under which firm-external and -internal conditions which type of strategic orientation (international, multi-domestic, global, blocked global/transnational) fits best. *By doing so, this strand of research corresponded heavily with decisions MNC managers were responsible for.* It helped them to formulate MNCs' strategies solidly. These days, a main aspect of the research on MNCs' *organizational issues* were coordination instruments MNCs' headquarters and subsidiaries inserted to ensure and improve the alignment between MNCs' subunits (headquarters vs. subsidiaries; subsidiaries among themselves). This research analyzed both formal and informal coordination mechanisms. On the one hand, there was a substantial and growing body of knowledge being focused on formal coordination mechanisms. Here the research on MNCs' organizational structures (e.g., Daniels et al., 1984; Egelhoff, 1982; Stopford & Wells Jr., 1972) was most prominent. This so-called international strategy-structure research clarified under which MNC strategy which organizational structure tended to fit well. *Again, by doing so, this stream of research corresponded tremendously with decision and choice questions MNC managers had to deal with.* In this period, studies on informal coordination mechanisms were also focused on approaches that could be used by MNC managers. For instance, there were quite many studies questioning in which contextual situation informal coordination instruments like manager transfers, visits, or corporate culture should be inserted. *Again, this research had a close linkage to MNC managers' decision situation*: They had to decide how intense their MNC shall use these subtle coordination instruments. Even Bartlett and Ghoshal's (1989) work on the transnational solution followed this idea since it argued that in blocked global industries, which became more and more typical at these days, an organizational form called "transnational solution" would fit best. *A commonality of all these topics of research was that the studies were focused on instruments MNC managers were able to insert.*

But then, in line with Kogut and Zander's (1992, 1993) seminal publications, this "instrument-oriented" research started to get replaced by studies having a more social-scientific, non-design-oriented nature. Some of these studies shall be mentioned here as examples for this new research epoch: Gupta and Govindarajan (1991) analyzed differences in subsidiary contexts along two dimensions: (a) the extent to which the subsidiary is a user of knowledge from the rest of the corporation and (b) the extent to which the subsidiary is a provider of such knowledge to the rest of the corporation. Based on this, subsidiary archetypes were described. A few years later, Zander and Kogut focused narrowly on selected facets of intra-MNC knowledge transfer, e.g., tacitness of know-how (Zander & Kogut, 1995). In 2000, again Gupta and Govindarajan investigated both theoretically and empirically the determinants of intra-MNC knowledge flow patterns. They conceptualized and tested hypotheses like the following: "ceteris paribus, the higher the level of the host country's economic development relative to the home country, the greater will be the knowledge outflows from that subsidiary to the parent corporation" (Gupta & Govindarajan, 2000: 478). Minbaeva et al. (2003) mainly referred on the concept of absorptive capacity as a key factor explaining the success of MNCs' knowledge flows. These authors suggested that absorptive capacity should be conceptualized as being comprised of both ability and motivation. *In comparison to the older instrument-oriented studies, the newer knowledge-transfer-oriented studies are more descriptive and academic, and they deal with more abstract constructs. By doing so, the results of these studies are more difficult to transfer to the business practice.* For instance, for MNC managers it is hard to assess the tacitness of knowledge, to estimate the volume of knowledge flowing in and out of their subsidiaries, or to identify promising ways to increase a subunit's level of absorptive capacity. *As a consequence, this type of research has a more indirect practical relevance, if any.*

Example 2: Research on Distance as a Central Explanatory Variable
During the last 25 years, many IB studies have taken "distance" as a key variable of inquiry. As a consequence, distance became a key concept in IB research. Most studies focused on the distance between MNCs' home country and the respective foreign country where the MNC is doing business. Without any question, the Kogut and Singh (1988) article on the influence of national culture on the choice of foreign entry mode was a cornerstone of the "distance research" since it suggested a frequently used method to measure cultural distance (Konara & Mohr, 2019). While over the years the conceptual focus of distance has changed and widened significantly (e.g., psychic distance, geographical distance, political distance, institutional distance), the general logic of this research stream tended to remain stable, since distance was constantly seen as a key predictor of the behavior of MNCs and their managers, and of the success of MNCs'/managers' actions. For instance, Morosini et al. (1998) rejected the standard assumption that national cultural distance hinders cross-border acquisition performance. Instead, they found a positive association between national cultural distance and cross-border acquisition performance. Brouthers and Brouthers (2001) took the inconsistent results on the relationship between national cultural distance and foreign entry mode choice (some scholars found high cultural distance associated with choosing wholly owned modes while others found high cultural distance linked to a preference for joint ventures) as a starting point for their own research. They found cultural distance to be related to both types of foreign entry modes. Given this, they theorized and tested that the level of investment risk in the target country can help to explain the choice between these entry modes. Consistent with this finding, Tihanyi et al. (2005) meta-analysis showed that cultural distance itself is not a significant predictor of entry mode choice. Instead, moderator effects were able to lead to significant results. Dow and Karunaratna (2006) focused on psychic distance measures as predictors of trade flows. They found that the most common psychic distance surrogate—a composite measure of Hofstede's cultural dimensions—is not a significant predictor of trade flows. Berry et al. (2010) disaggregated the construct of distance by proposing a set of multidimensional measures, including economic, financial, political,

administrative, cultural, demographic, knowledge, and global connectedness as well as geographic distance. Further, they suggested to use the Mahalanobis measure instead of the Euclidian distance measure. They provided evidence that the suggested distance measurement method is more powerful to explain MNCs' foreign expansion choices. Shenkar (2012) identified several conceptual illusions (illusion of symmetry, illusion of stability, illusion of causality, and illusion of discordance) and problematic methodological assumptions (assumption of corporate homogeneity, assumption of spatial homogeneity, and assumption of equivalence) in IB's research on cultural distance. Harzing and Pudelko (2016) scrutinized the explanatory power of the concept of (cultural) distance. Based on a review of 92 prior studies on entry mode choice and an own empirical investigation they concluded that the explanatory power of distance is highly limited.

Given this heterogeneity of findings and the fact that the results vary heavily by the measurement of distance, out of the current hindsight perspective it is really interesting to see how long and resistantly IB research has considered distance as a key predictor of MNCs' foreign business activities. We are pretty confident that a key cause for this is the quite easy access to distance-related data. This means that many scholars have modelled their research activity based on the availability of data and not on a careful musing on the decision process MNC managers typically go through. Or in other words: Do we really think that an MNC manager, if s(he) has to make a decision which foreign market to enter and which foreign market entry mode to use, above all analyzes types of distance existing between the home country and the host country?—No. Instead, managers being responsible for foreign market entry (decisions) mainly think in categories like market size, market potential, purchasing power, necessary investment intensity, degree of rivalry in the foreign market, or other factors characterizing the host country market as such and not the distance existing between the home and the host country.

There is a further reason why the extreme focusing of current IB research on quantitative distance measures is problematic: The more IB research has concentrated on quantitative distance measures, the less it has studied qualitative characteristics of the respective foreign country where MNCs want to do business. Unlike the current way of IB research, MNC managers, if they consider to start a business activity in a foreign country, have to perform a detailed analysis of different kinds of characteristics of the respective country. They have to analyze the country in depth. Do IB researchers, if they work with quantitative distance data (e.g., a calculation of the political distance between the home country and the foreign country with "4", the geographical distance with "2" and the social distance with "3," etc.), provide a picture of the host country, which is sufficiently multifaceted and informationally rich enough, so that this can be used as an information basis for managers to start business activities in this foreign country?—No. We think that the reductionist information provided by most of the contemporary IB research is of quite little help for business practice. By working with such highly integrated distance-oriented data, current researchers have gone away from a key strength of traditional IB research which was to deliver detailed insights into the peculiarities of foreign markets and foreign countries.

All in all, we think that the IB community has overheated the intensity of studying the distance variable. By doing so, it has created a further gap between its own research activities and the decision problems MNC managers have to deal with.

Example 3: Dominance of Non-Replicable and Weak Relationships in IB Research

Before we will start to focus on our third example, let us recap which kind of research results managers want to receive from business administration research. As mentioned in the first section of this essay, managers want to receive interesting and reliable research results which provide information what to do so that their firm's long-term success will be supported. These results shall refer to levers that have a substantial impact on the firm's success.

If we compare this kind of demand with the kind of research output contemporary IB research is providing, a noticeable gap seems to get obvious.

(a) First, without any doubt, during the last decades IB research (like other fields in business administration research), has made a development toward narrower, more focused conceptual frameworks. As a consequence, if a contemporary empirical IB researcher refrains from conceptualizing and testing moderated relationships, (s)he will receive substantial critique by journals' reviewers. As a further consequence, (s)he tends to have no chance to get her(his) work published in a decent IB journal. Of course, there are cases where a specification of moderated relationships seems to be necessary (e.g., if previous results have led to inconsistent findings), but it is quite clear that current IB research is not limiting the conceptualization and testing of moderated relationships to such special cases. Instead, the specification of moderated relationships became a fashionable trend, i.e., factual requirements have not initiated them. They are frequently used although, in the relevant field of study, no inconsistent findings are reported. Further, a large portion of moderated relationships seems to be developed in a data-driven manner and they are "made plausible" by contrived logics. Many of these relationships seem to be complemented by post-hoc logics. This fashionable trend toward the use of moderated relationships is highly problematic, since they are typically supported in the studies in which they are introduced, but they are rarely confirmed in subsequent studies. Since most moderated relationships are not well confirmed, they derogate the robustness of IB's research's body of knowledge and this, in turn, will lead to research findings MNC managers cannot trust (for further aspects of science's reproducibility and replicability crisis see Aguinis et al., 2017).

(b) A further reason for the existing gap is that empirical IB research, unlike other fields of management research, has continued to sharpen its attention to quantification (Delios, 2017). While other fields of the academic world started to question "the value of kowtowing to the 0.05 deity" (Delios, 2017: 392), the IB community has not done so yet. In the era of big data this is especially problematic since, because of huge numbers of observations, even extremely weak relationships between variables will master to skip over such threshold values. Again: Do we really think that MNC managers are interested in levers having a *minimal* influence on the efficiency and effectiveness variables they want to steer?

3   IB Research as a Closed System? A Plea for a More Intensive Look Beyond the Borderlines

Already a first, only superficial look on sources used by papers that have been published in high-ranked IB journals (JIBS, JWB, GSJ, IBR, JIM, but also in our "own" journal MIR) leads us to the impression that the majority of those sources is originated in the field itself; furthermore and to a (much) lower extent sources stemming from a closely related discipline, i.e., (international) economics seem to be used.

However, the conclusion out of this impression that there are likely only few other scientific disciplines that are interested in problems international firms have to face and solve would be wrong. This is because there is a) indeed a number of other sub-disciplines of business administration and management that are also interested in research on problems and challenges international firms are facing; and b) beyond business administration and management further scientific disciplines can easily be identified that are also—at least partially—dedicated to the research on international firms. As so far John Dunning's already in 1989 formulated plea for a more interdisciplinary approach of studying IB has still not reached the full extent of realization (Dunning, 1989: 411 et seq., especially 430).

In the following, we would like to discuss IB-specific problems originating from a too strong discipline-focused sourcing of research outcomes. In this context, we also provide examples of other scientific disciplines that are interested in research on international firms, too. Thus, they should be viewed as further sources of knowledge on the object of research, i.e. the international firm.

Research on FDI and respective location choices can be labeled as one of the core fields of IB research (Blonigen, 2005; Paul & Feliciano-Cestero, 2021; Paul & Singh, 2017; Werner, 2002). Therefore we take this field as starting point of the following thoughts. As we know from the real business world international location choices are not only guided by the availability of resources, market size, or production cost advantages, but also by taxation differences. However, taxation issues and according location choices seem to be still a not very well researched phenomenon in IB. As so far research published in journals dedicated to international taxation could be exploited and employed in a much stronger way.

However, the focus on research results stemming from the own field, i.e., IB, is as so far expectable as business administration and management are scientific disciplines that show after much more than 100 years of existence in the USA and Europe (Engwall & Zamagni, 1998; Wren & Van Fleet, 1983) a high degree of specialization. Yet, when specialization leads to a concentration of sourcing knowledge only from the knowledge pool of the own sub-discipline scientific progress can be slowed down. This is because "foreign knowledge" that has value for the problem under research in the field of IB has lower chances to be discovered and to be employed. As so far it is not surprising that core problems of IB, e.g., FDI, HQ-subsidiary-relationships, implementation of Regional HQs, or internationalization as process are approached/encountered only by a rather narrow set of theories (for internationalization see especially Surdu et al., 2021: 1047) established in the IB field and thereby not taking into account that also taxation, financing, or management accounting issues can influence the decisions of managers and the aforementioned outcomes.

The phenomenon of overlooking "foreign" knowledge seems to be even more existing when we focus our discussion on knowledge that could be sourced by IB scholars from more distant disciplines like international economic geography, international (political) relations, or sociology. Those disciplines are also treating problems of the international firm; however, they are approaching the problems most likely via perspectives being not (exactly) those of IB.

As so far problems of the complex real business world are viewed by different disciplinary perspectives (Cheng et al., 2009: 1070 et seq.), but IB up to now does not show very strong interest in employing such different perspectives. By doing so the chance to describe and explain existing IB problem in an integrative way will not be used fully, making our identification of research questions, the work for respective answers, and finally our solution-oriented offers to practitioners not that powerful as they could be. Given this our plea is to look more intensively beyond the discipline-oriented borderlines in order to scan and to employ knowledge of other disciplines to elaborate stronger and thereby for practitioners more attractive and relevant descriptions, explanations, and practice-oriented solutions of real business world problems.

4   The Basic Relevance Problem of Journals (and Potential Authors) in the Context of Submissions

All major IB journals publish well-defined Aims and Scope statements. Scholars being interested in submitting their research papers to one of these journals should know the rules of the game, i.e., they should be able to assess if their paper fits the Editorial Policy (Aims and Scope) of the respective journals. In other words: They should be able to judge if their research is relevant to the respective journal. But obviously, this is not the case. Because we have no respective data of other journals we feel free to describe in general the situation of MIR. During the last years we received not only more and more submissions (not only due to the fact, that scholars of more nations (e.g., PRC or Brazil) are now interested in the IB field). We also receive a growing number of submissions that are not relevant to MIR, since they do not meet the journal's Editorial Policy. As an IB journal, MIR is only interested in research dealing with IB problems, but not in research dedicated to other topics like the effectiveness and efficiency of quality management systems in country A.

Some years ago there was an interesting debate initiated by Jean J. Boddewyn (2016a, 2016b). This debate followed a tradition established by Nehrt, Truitt, and

Wright already in 1970 (Nehrt et al., 1970). It tried to specify which requirements should be met that research is truly IB research. But this interesting debate and its outcomes seem to have not reached many of those being interested in publishing in IB journals. This is, because beside submissions dealing definitely not with questions of IB we receive submissions that are based on international data but do not analyze for an international dependent or independent variable. Such submissions do also not fit the Editorial Policy of MIR (and most likely that of other IB journals).

As so far we would like to motivate researchers being interested in problems of IB to assure themselves first if they have a perspective on IB that is in line with the field's broadly accepted definition of (content-wise) objects of research. And second they should develop a closer, more precise look at the Aims and Scope statements of journals to ensure that a potential submission is—in a basic way—relevant to the respective journal.

5 Summary: What To Do?

In the current contribution, we have discussed the state of IB research. We have analyzed scholars' research behavior and especially IB's relevance issues being a consequence of this behavior. In the contribution's first section we saw that relevance is not an absolute concept. Instead, its meaning depends on the perspective the respective person involved actively or passively in the research process is taking. Further, we have learned that especially with respect to the research process itself a field's social structure and its social processes heavily influence the predominant meaning of relevance. In the second section, we have presented some examples indicating that IB research's practical relevance has abated over the years. While earlier IB studies were heavily focused on decisions practitioners had to make, more recent IB research has a stronger social-scientific nature. Design-oriented issues are not that important in contemporary IB research. If we wanted to be more pronounced or even provocative, we could say that recent IB research tends to be rather sociology or economics of the international firm than part of business administration as it was understood over decades. Of course, IB scholars themselves have to decide if they want to make their research more practically useful in the future. If they do so, they could consider hints as they were suggested in the literature already quite long ago (e.g., Wolf & Rosenberg, 2012). Especially, we have to intensify our contact to practitioners being responsible for international firms. Otherwise many IB scholars will continue to study phenomena being not very important to the business world and they will run the risk of conceptualizing the phenomena under study wrongly.

Yet, what is questionable and disturbing is the fact that in the IB field there are many studies that conceptualize and test relationships that never got confirmed in subsequent studies. This is in sharp conflict with science's goal to provide not only interesting but also reliable knowledge. And we also have to lament that the field's strong tendency toward quantitative analyses has led to a state where qualitative aspects of IB got underemphasized. This is problematic since, for an international manager, it always had been central to consider and to deal with qualitative peculiarities of the foreign environments. In the contribution's third section we diagnosed that the community of IB scholars is still quite closed. This is disadvantageous since in both the studied phenomenon itself as well as in adjacent academic disciplines there are quite many issues, topics, and concepts that can and should be considered more by IB scholars in the future. The fourth section provides strong hints that in IB's scientific community there seem to be quite many scholars who obviously have never carefully thought about general aspects and the boundaries of the IB field. Many seem to start IB research activities without having ever thought about such fundamental questions relating to the IB field. Otherwise, journals like MIR would not get so many submissions being clearly outside of the journal's scope. That said, we want to encourage our colleagues to solidly muse on the content of the field they are belonging to or they wish to belong to. This seems pretty easy to do, since the established literature (see our references) has delivered many contributions dealing with this question.

References

Aguinis, H., Cascio, W. F., & Ramani, R. S. (2017). Science's reproducibility and replicability crisis: International business is not immune. *Journal of International Business Studies, 48*(6), 653–663.

Bartlett, C. A., & Ghoshal, S. (1989). *Managing across borders: The transnational solution.* Harvard Business School Press.

Berry, H., Guillén, M. F., & Zhou, N. (2010). An institutional approach to cross-national distance. *Journal of International Business Studies, 41*(9), 1460–1480.

Blonigen, B. A. (2005). A review of the empirical determinants of FDI. *Atlantic Economic Journal, 33*(1), 383–403.

Boddewyn, J. J. (2016a). Is your "IB" research truly "international"? *AIB Insights, 16*(2), 3–5.

Boddewyn, J. J. (2016b). What you, readers of AIB insights, said: Responses to the article "Is Your 'IB' Research Truly 'International'?". *AIB Insights, 16*(4), 18–19.

Brouthers, K. D., & Brouthers, L. (2001). Explaining the national cultural distance paradox. *Journal of International Business Studies, 32*(1), 177–189.

Cheng, J., Henisz, W., Roth, K., & Swaminathan, A. (2009). From the editors: Advancing interdisciplinary research in the field of international business: Prospects, issues and challenges. *Journal of International Business Studies, 40*(7), 1070–1074.

Daniels, J. D. (1991). Relevance in international business research: A need for more linkages. *Journal of International Business Studies, 22*(2), 177–186.

Daniels, J. D., Pitts, R. A., & Tretter, M. J. (1984). Strategy and structure of U.S. multinationals: An exploratory study. *Academy of Management Journal, 27*(2), 292–307.

Delios, A. (2017). The death and rebirth (?) of international business research. *Journal of Management Studies, 54*(3), 391–397.

Dow, D., & Karunaratna, A. (2006). Developing a multidimensional instrument to measure psychic distance stimuli. *Journal of International Business Studies, 37*(5), 578–602.

Doz, Y. L. (1980). Multinational strategy and structure in government controlled business. *Columbia Journal of World Business, 15*(3), 14–25.

Dunning, J. (1989). The study of international business: A plea for a more interdisciplinary approach. *Journal for International Business Studies, 20*(3), 411–436.

Egelhoff, W. G. (1982). Strategy and structure in multinational corporations: An information processing approach. *Administrative Science Quarterly, 27*(3), 435–458.

Engwall, L., & Zamagni, V. (1998). *Management education in historical perspective*. Manchester University Press.

Gopinath, C., & Hoffman, R. C. (1995). The relevance of strategy research: Practitioners and academic viewpoints. *Journal of Management Studies, 32*(5), 575–594.

Gupta, A. K., & Govindarajan, V. (1991). Knowledge flows and the structure of control in multinational corporations. *Academy of Management Review, 16*(4), 768–792.

Gupta, A. K., & Govindarajan, V. (2000). Knowledge flows within multinational corporations. *Strategic Management Journal, 21*(4), 473–496.

Harzing, A.-W., & Pudelko, M. (2016). Do we need to distance ourselves from the distance concept? Why home and host country context might Matter more than (cultural) distance. *Management International Review, 56*(1), 1–34.

Kogut, B., & Singh, H. (1988). The effect of national culture on the choice of entry mode. *Journal of International Business Studies, 19*(3), 411–432.

Kogut, B., & Zander, U. (1992). Knowledge of the firm, combinative capabilities, and the replication of technology. *Organization Science, 3*(3), 383–397.

Kogut, B., & Zander, U. (1993). Knowledge of the firm and the evolutionary theory of the multinational corporation. *Journal of International Business Studies, 24*(4), 625–645.

Konara, P., & Mohr, A. (2019). Why we should stop using the Kogut and Singh index. *Management International Review, 59*(3), 335–354.

Lewin, A. Y. (2004). Letter from the editor. *Journal of International Business Studies, 35*(1), 79–80.

Minbaeva, D. B., Pedersen, T., Björkman, I., & Fey, C. F. (2003). MNC knowledge transfer, subsidiary absorptive capacity, and HRM. *Journal of International Business Studies, 34*(6), 586–599.

Morosini, P., Shane, S., & Singh, H. (1998). National cultural distance and cross-border acquisition performance. *Journal of International Business Studies, 29*(1), 137–158.

Nehrt, L., Truitt, J. F., & Wright, R. (1970). *International business research: Past, present, and future*. Indiana University Graduate School of Business.

Oesterle, M.-J., & Laudien, S. (2007). The future of international business research and the relevance gap: A German perspective. *European Journal of International Management, 1*(1/2), 39–55.

Paul, J., & Feliciano-Cestero, M. M. (2021). Five decades of research on foreign direct investment by MNEs: An overview and research agenda. *Journal of Business Research, 124*, 800–812.

Paul, J., & Singh, G. (2017). The 45 years of foreign direct investment research: Approaches, advances, and analytical areas. *The World Economy, 40*(11), 2512–2527.

Popper, K. R. (1995). *Search of a better world: Lectures and essays from thirty years*. Routledge.

Porter, M. E. (1986). Changing patterns of international competition. *California Management Review, 28*(2), 9–40.

Shenkar, O. (2012). Cultural distance revisited: Towards a more rigorous conceptualization and measurement of cultural differences. *Journal of International Business Studies, 43*(1), 1–11.

Stopford, J. M., & Wells, L. T., Jr. (1972). *Managing the multinational enterprise*. Basic Books.

Surdu, I., Greve, H. R., & Benito, G. R. G. (2021). Back to basics: Behavioral theory and internationalization. *Journal of International Business Studies, 52*(6), 1047–1068.

Tihanyi, L., Griffith, D. A., & Russell, C. J. (2005). The effect of cultural distance on entry mode choice, international diversification, and MNE performance: A meta-analysis. *Journal of International Business Studies, 36*(3), 270–283.

Tourish, D. (2020). The triumph of nonsense in management studies. *Academy of Management Learning and Education, 19*(1), 99–109.

Werner, S. (2002). Recent developments in international management research: A review of 20 top management journals. *Journal of Management, 28*(3), 277–305.

Wolf, J., & Rosenberg, T. (2012). How individual scholars can reduce the rigor-relevance gap in management research. *Business Research, 5*(2), 178–196.

Wren, D. A., & Van Fleet, D. D. (1983). History in schools of business. *Business and Economic History, 12*(1), 29–35.

Zander, U., & Kogut, B. (1995). Knowledge and the speed of the transfer and imitation of organizational capabilities: An empirical test. *Organization Science, 6*(1), 76–92.

Michael-Jörg Oesterle is Full Professor of International and Strategic Management at the University of Stuttgart, Germany. Before he joined the University of Stuttgart in 2011 he was Full Professor at the Universities of Bremen and Mainz, Germany. Since 2006 he is Co-Editor-in-Chief of Management International Review (MIR).

Joachim Wolf is Full Professor of Organization Theory and Design at the University of Kiel (Germany). From 1994 to 2005, he served as an Associate Editor for Management International Review (MIR). Since 2006, he is Co-Editor-in-Chief of this journal. Joachim's research is focused on MNCs' strategies and organizational forms.

Part II

Inter-Disciplinary Topics for International Business Research

International Business Policy: A Primer

Ari Van Assche

1 Introduction

After a period of lowered interest, international business policy has recently roared back onto the academic scene (Lundan, 2018; Van Assche & Lundan, 2020). A variety of trends have contributed to the renewed attention to the policy side of international business. First, populism has erupted across the globe in the wake of the Great Recession of 2008–2009, which has fed a wave of antitrade sentiment (Rodrik, 2018), and has challenged long-standing views on international business policy (Kobrin, 2020). Several national leaders jumped on the populist bandwagon by throwing their support behind export mercantilism (Evenett, 2019), renegotiating or leaving trade agreements (Casadei & Iammarino, 2021), or embarking on trade wars (Bown & Irwin, 2019). Academics have responded by analyzing the rationales behind the reversals in international business policies (Van Assche & Gangnes, 2019a; Kobrin, 2020) and how these policy shifts impact international business flows (Van Assche & Gangnes, 2019b; Gereffi et al., 2021).

Second, technological changes have altered the ways how firms conduct international business, raising the question of what this means for the effectiveness of traditional policies. One new international business trend that has received lots of attention is the emergence of global value chains. Another is the widespread adoption of new digital technologies by manufacturing firms including robotics-enabled automation, AI-enhanced systems, and supply chain digitalization (e.g., Internet of Things, blockchain, and additive manufacturing). Both are dramatically transforming the global trade and investment landscape (Zhan, 2021), and are pushing scholars to ask how public policies should be redesigned to reflect these new global realities (Gereffi, 2019; Pietrobelli et al., 2021).

A. Van Assche (✉)
HEC Montréal, Montreal, QC, Canada
e-mail: ari.van-assche@hec.ca

© Springer Nature Switzerland AG 2022
H. Merchant (ed.), *The New Frontiers of International Business*, Contributions to Management Science, https://doi.org/10.1007/978-3-031-06003-8_8

Third, there is a growing acknowledgment that international business has a larger transformative power over societal trends than was previously thought. Many pundits connote international business with labor market turbulence (Autor et al., 2016), rising income inequality (Grossman & Helpman, 2018), environmental degradation (Singhania & Saini, 2021), and weakening economic resilience (Gereffi, 2020). Others point out that this same transformative power of international business can be used to attain the United Nations' Sustainable Development Goals if they are properly harnessed (Van Zanten & Van Tulder, 2018). International business scholars have contributed to these discussions by developing new research on the relation between international business and grand societal challenges (Buckley et al., 2017), by analyzing the complex link of international business with poverty (Kolk et al., 2018), human rights (Wettstein et al., 2019) and income inequality (Zhao et al., 2021), and by evaluating the implications for international business policy (Van Tulder et al., 2021).

The Academy of International Business (AIB) has recognized the importance of these trends and has responded by creating the new *Journal of International Business Policy* in 2018. In the past 3 years, this journal has published a wide variety of papers on public policy related to international business. AIB has also rekindled its relations with UNCTAD to strengthen the nexus of complementarity between international business research and the policy practitioner community (Lundan & Assche, 2021).

Yet, despite the huge academic enthusiasm about the topic in international business circles, there remains substantial ambiguity about what international business policy really is. Despite several recent editorials in the *Journal of International Business Policy* and other journals on the topic, extant scholarship has failed to pin down a formal definition of international business policy or delineated what topics the research field encompasses. Scholars have rather taken an "I know it when I will see it" approach, which has been a natural step in the progression of the emerging research field, but which needs to be overcome for the research field to mature and to distinguish itself from other areas of international business.

The goal of this chapter is to address this gap in the literature. We start off with the development of a formal definition of international business policy. Next, we use it to delineate the types of research questions that are at the center of the research field. Finally, we discuss a roadmap for research on international business policy.

2   Defining International Business Policy

A logical place to begin is to determine what scholars mean with international business policy. This sounds simple enough, but it is actually quite hard to determine since researchers seldom provide a definition. A rare exception is Lundan (2018) who, in her inaugural editorial of the *Journal of International Business Policy,* describes international business policy as the area of public policy that relates to international business. Similarly, Clegg (2019) defines international business policy as a "change [in public policy] intentionally instigated by a government to have an action upon the decision making and behavior of firms within the international business domain." Such definitions are accurate in the sense that they encompass pretty much anything that can be considered international business policy. But they are at the same time so broad that they do little to convey what the field of international business policy studies and how this differs from traditional international business research or scholarship in other related fields.

A common feature of both definitions is that they treat international business policy as a subcategory of public policy, and so an important stepping stone for developing a more actionable definition of international business policy is to dissect the concept of "public policy." Political scientists commonly describe public policy as a course of action that a public entity takes to address a particular societal challenge (Smith & Larimer, 2018; Knill & Tosun, 2020). This definition is instructive for our purposes since it highlights a series of defining characteristics of public policy. First, it refers to actions that are taken by decision-makers in public entities, that is, by policymakers. Second, it focuses on tackling challenges at the societal level that require collective engagement. The study of public policy is thus about (1) identifying important societal challenges that require government action to be effectively addressed, (2) formulating government-directed solutions to these societal problems, and (3) assessing the impact of the proposed solutions on the target problem (DeLeon, 2006; Smith & Larimer, 2018).

A second steppingstone is to identify what area of public policy is covered by international business policy. Political scientists generally classify public policies into different subcategories according to the domain that policymakers try to shape to address a societal problem. That is, subcategories of public policy describe the means used to tackle societal goals and not the ends themselves. Foreign policy, for example, refers to those public policies that shape the activities and relationships of one state in its interactions with other states to reach certain societal goals. Industrial policy describes the actions that governments take to shape the development of specific industries with the aim to address certain societal problems. Agricultural policy are government-directed actions that shape the agriculture sector to reach certain goals. We can follow this same approach to develop a formal definition of international business policy:

International business policy is a mix of actions that a public authority takes to shape international business with the goal of addressing a societal challenge.

This definition has the advantage that it provides a clear picture what the field of international business policy studies (see Fig. 1). It analyzes the *policy process* by asking what societal challenges public authorities at different levels decide to or should prioritize by shaping international business through their actions. It conducts *policy analysis* by studying the optimal international-business-shaping actions that policymakers should adopt to address these societal challenges. And it performs *policy evaluation* by analyzing the effectiveness of these actions in addressing societal challenges.

Fig. 1 Field of international business policy research. Source: author's own figure

---

3   Addressing Societal Challenges

Public policy is a statement by a government of what it intends to do about a societal challenge. But what is a societal challenge precisely? And which political processes do governments use to determine which societal challenges to prioritize?

A societal challenge describes any real-life problem that has a large and often heterogeneous impact on different groups of society and that require coordinated and sustained efforts from multiple stakeholders to get resolved (DeTombe, 2002). Many of these challenges are "wicked" in the sense that they are complex, systemic, interconnected, requiring insights from many perspectives (Eden & Wagstaff, 2021).

Societal challenges occur across a wide variety of dimensions, all of which may be addressed in the field of international business policy. To just name a few, they comprise of economic problems such as slowing economic growth, the rise of precarious work, or the negative employment effects of automation on at least some types of workers; they include social problems such as entrenched racism, gender or other types of inequality, or police brutality; they cover health problems such as vaccine hesitancy, drug addiction or rising healthcare costs; they include environmental problems such as climate change, water shortage or air pollution.

It is important to recognize that societal challenges occur across different levels of government, even though priorities may differ substantially. Cities, for example, face urbanized societal challenges such as homelessness and cluster performance that are of less concern for national policymakers. Policymakers in international organizations prioritize challenges related to global public goods and beggar-thy-neighbor problems which are not spotlighted by state or provincial governments.

The priorities in terms of societal challenges also vary across countries. Least developed countries face challenges of informality and poverty that are more muted in developed countries. Oil-exporting countries are more concerned about economic diversification than countries that have a highly differentiated economy. Water-scarce countries have an existential urge to find solutions against chronic water shortages.

There are a set of urgent societal challenges that transcend geographic, economic, and societal borders and are therefore universally shared. Sometimes referred to as "grand challenges" (George et al., 2016; Buckley et al., 2017), these include environmental threats like climate change, demographic, health and well-being concerns, and the difficulties of generating sustainable and inclusive growth. Policy-wise, one of the most authoritative current frameworks addressing grand challenges is undoubtedly the United Nations Sustainable Development Goals (SDGs) agenda, a plan of action to promote sustainable development by tackling a range of issues from gender equality to peace and justice (Van Tulder et al., 2021; Van Zanten & Van Tulder, 2018).

Finally, government priorities in terms of societal challenges are influenced by ideology and politics. Governments rank societal challenges through a complex negotiation between the state and societal actors. Political ideology, special interests, the mass media, and public opinion all play a role in the identification and line-up of societal challenges that governments feel need to be addressed. In Canada, for example, ideology explains why the Canadian government decided to adopt a "progressive trade agenda" that seeks to ensure that the benefits and opportunities that flow from trade and investment are more likely shared among Canadians after the Liberal Party's rise to power in 2015. What this means is that international business policy not only considers the normative question of how the shaping of international business can address societal challenges but also the positive question of how political processes affect governments' choices which societal challenges to tackle through international business policy.

All these types of societal challenges and the processes behind their prioritization can fall under the purview of international business policy—as long as they can be effectively addressed through the government-directed shaping of international business. In other words, international business policy scholarship is not confined to societal challenges that are international of nature (e.g., pandemic) nor is it limited to societal challenges that are prioritized by international organizations (e.g., SDGs). Rather, the boundaries of the field are delineated by the presumed or real ability of international business to help effectively address a societal challenge that has been prioritized by a public entity.

4   Shaping International Business

International business policy is limited to those public policies that can address a societal challenge through the shaping of international business. This puts two important conditions on the scope of the research field. First, international business needs to have the presumed or real transformative power to influence a societal challenge. Second, public authorities need to have the ability to shape international business through their actions.

4.1   Transformative Power of International Business

It is easy to show that the first condition is met in many situations. It is well known that international business exacerbates or alleviates many societal challenges that are of first-order importance for policymakers (Zhan, 2021). Evidence abounds, for example, that international business matters for one of the societal challenges of highest public priority: the creation of economic growth (Didier & Pinat, 2017). International trade and foreign direct investment can boost an economy's efficiency by allowing countries or regions to specialize in those sectors in which they have a latent comparative advantage, thus allowing domestic resources to flow to their most productive use. It can also spur local growth by increasing domestic actors' access to foreign knowledge pockets through global knowledge connectedness (Cano-Kollmann et al., 2016), boosting local innovation performance (Turkina & Van Assche, 2018).

New international business trends influence this nexus between international business and economic growth. The emergence of global value chains, for example, gives rise to a finer-grained international division of labor where countries or regions functionally specialize in value chain stages instead of entire industries (Timmer et al., 2019) and gain access to foreign knowledge through their global value chain linkages (Ambos et al., 2021). This is critical for developing countries that can embark on fast-track industrialization by focusing on simpler production stages that suit their existing capabilities and by developing upgrading opportunities through their links with lead firms (Gereffi et al., 2005). And it also benefits developed countries that can specialize in high-value-added intangible tasks such as R&D and marketing while de-specializing in manufacturing (Ambos et al., 2021; Van Assche, 2020; Jaax & Miroudot, 2021). Understanding the impact of these new trends on a societal challenge is important since it may affect the urgency of developing an international business policy but may also require a redesign of policy thinking on the topic (Gereffi, 2019; Pietrobelli et al., 2021).

The transformative power of international business, however, is not always for the good. Even if international business creates significant economic progress, the benefits leave many behind. Economists have long recognized that international trade creates both winners and losers and that current institutions do not ensure that the winners sufficiently compensate the losers so that everyone gains. Several recent studies nonetheless show that the extent of negative societal challenges that trade and international business can generate is broader than traditionally thought. Import competition from China not only led to massive job losses among U.S. blue-collar workers (Autor et al., 2013). These workers ended up with lower lifetime income, were less likely to marry, were more likely to end up on disability, and were more likely to die at an earlier age (Autor et al., 2014); and the districts exposed to larger imports from China disproportionately removed moderate representatives from office in the 2000s (Autor et al., 2016). Global connectedness spurs growth in many global cities, but it also generates local disconnectedness with its neighboring regions whose livelihood traditionally depends on their links with cities (Lorenzen et al., 2020). These findings have led to vibrant new research on the link between international business and rising income inequalities within countries (Buchholz et al., 2020; Zhao et al., 2021) as well as the relation between international business and populism (Rodrik, 2018).

Other scholars have turned their attention to the link between international business and environmental sustainability. The relation here is ambiguous. On the dark side, companies may use international business to move pollution-intensive activities to countries with lower environmental policy stringency—the so-called pollution haven hypothesis—thus undermining governments' efforts to combat global environmental degradation (Bu & Wagner, 2016). On the bright side, international business improves access to new technologies that can be used to make local production processes more efficient by diminishing the use of inputs such as energy, water, and other environmentally harmful substances (Patala et al., 2021). The question of how to properly harness international business for environmental sustainability thus remains high on the agenda for international business policy research.

The COVID-19 pandemic has put a new societal challenge on the spotlight: how does international business affect a country's ability to provide essential goods? The instigator was the shortages of personal protective equipment (PPE) at the beginning of the pandemic and the difficulties of many countries to obtain vaccines once they became available. Several pundits were quick to point fingers at countries' overreliance on imports for their supply of essential goods (Evenett, 2020). Across government, academic, and consultancy circles, calls were made to make supply chains more resilient by forcing manufacturing and supply networks to diversify and localize. Here again, academics played an important role in nuancing these views by showing that international business was not at the origin of essential good shortages during the pandemic (Gereffi, 2020) and that the link between international business and resilience is more complicated than generally thought (Miroudot, 2020).

Here again, one needs to keep in mind that a government's decision to engage in an international business policy is often based on the perceived transformative power of international business which may well differ substantially from its real power. Many populist leaders, for example, are more than happy to connote key societal ills with globalization-related factors such as immigration and trade liberalization even if empirical evidence of these links remains scant (Rodrik, 2018). A key task for international business policy research is thus to validate the accuracy of government narratives related to the transformative power of international business.

4.2   Power of Public Authorities to Shape International Business

A link between international business and a societal challenge is not sufficient for it to be relevant for the field of international business policy. Public authorities also need to have the capability to shape international business through strategic actions. This is an important condition since the scope of authority that falls under the purview of governments and the effectiveness of their actions faces important limitations.

Clegg (2019) points out the importance of governance capability in his editorial for the *Journal of International Business Policy* that explains why studies on institutions do not necessarily pass the relevance-to-policy test. According to him, "Institutions shape behavior, but it is policy that changes behavior." He continues: "[i]nstitutions are not relevant to international business policy simply by virtue of shaping behavior. However, if they are amenable to government control or, more generally official control, and they have either (or both) a theoretical or empirical effect upon international business, then public action to change them falls within the scope of international business policy." In other words, an important stress test for international business policy research is that it focuses on phenomena that can be altered through public actions.

The condition of governance capability is particularly relevant since international business itself influences public power. A highly influential literature in international business has modeled foreign direct investment as the outcome of a bargaining game between multinational firms, home countries and host countries (Kobrin, 1987; Ramamurti, 2001; Vernon, 1971). Other scholars have pointed out that governments have been losing regulatory powers precisely because many social and economic interactions are expanding beyond the reach of territorially bound national jurisdictions (Doh, 2005). Multinational firms' international tax avoidance practices, for example, have reduced the capabilities of governments to earn tax income on locally generated value added (Ting & Gray, 2019). International production fragmentation has made it easier for multinational firms to shirk tariffs or quotas by relocating production facilities to third countries (Van Assche & Gangnes, 2019b).

The decline in governance capability of countries is partly compensated by the emergence of new forms of global governance. The World Health Organization has the mandate to establish, monitor, and enforce international norms and standards that ensure that all countries around the world invest sufficiently to develop the ability to rapidly detect, assess, report and respond to new outbreaks (Ruger & Yach, 2009). The World Trade Organization has the triple task of providing a negotiation platform for its members to draw up new trade rules; of conducting the day-to-day work of monitoring members' compliance with existing rules; and of providing a formal dispute settlement mechanism when disagreements arise between members (Rodrik, 2020). International business policy has the duty to evaluate governance capabilities and their shifts at the sub-national, national and international levels.

New international business trends may at the same increase governance capabilities in some instances. For example, there is a growing acknowledgment that harnessing lead firms of global value chains can go far in promoting social standards and environmental stewardship across the globe. Lead firms have the corporate power to define the terms and conditions that global suppliers need to abide to for them to participate in a global value chain. The ability of lead firms to dictate the terms under which lower-level actors operate in a global value chain has led to a vibrant academic debate about the role of private governance in filling gaps in global regulation. Many MNEs have implemented corporate social responsibility

(CSR) initiatives in their supply chains as a way of independently regulating labor issues, including the establishment of codes of conduct and the implementation of third-party monitoring of working and environmental conditions. While several scholars have pointed out the positive role that private governance can play in addressing market failures that public governance has difficulties tackling (Scherer & Palazzo, 2011), others have warned that it is relatively ineffective (Locke et al., 2009), depends on the institutional environment (Goerzen et al., 2021), and may weaken state regulation and create parallel regulatory systems (Rossi, 2019).

5   Government-Directed Actions

The final dimension of international business policy is the instruments and actions that public authorities have at their disposal to address societal challenges through the shaping of international business. Focusing on global value chains, Horner (2017) suggests that policymakers have four types of actions at their disposal: (a) the government can act as a *facilitator* of international business by using directives and regulations that stimulate international business transactions; (b) it can act as a *regulator* of international business by restricting private market transactions; (c) it can act as a *producer* by directly engaging in international business through state-owned production activities; and finally (d) it can act as a *buyer* that procures products and services, which may comprise distinct economic, social, and environmental requirements. International business scholars generally acknowledge the former two roles of the state while downplaying or ignoring the latter.

5.1   Facilitator

International business growth has the potential to alleviate many societal challenges—most notably the generation of economic growth—and governments, therefore, adopt a variety of policies and initiatives that aim to directly or indirectly facilitate or boost international business.

Policymakers can facilitate international business directly by unequivocally incentivizing exports and outward foreign direct investment or by reducing barriers on imports and inward foreign direct investment. Most countries, for example, run active export promotion programs to facilitate national firms' exports into foreign markets. These programs often involve the provision of export support services, export credit insurance and subsidies associated with export requirements to help national firms overcome challenges related to operating in an international environment (Moons & van Bergeijk, 2017). Similarly, countries often use inward FDI policies such as tax breaks, duty exemptions and loans to attract inward foreign direct investment (Tavares-Lehmann et al., 2016).

Governments can also spur international business indirectly by implementing market-friendly policy interventions that eliminate those market distortions that inhibit countries from specializing in their latent comparative advantages or prevent their firms and people from developing global knowledge connectedness. Among others, this involves maintaining a stable business environment in which it is easy for companies to establish and operate business; creating high-quality institutions; developing an efficient and robust infrastructure; and fostering a healthy innovation environment. It also means the elimination of market distortions that provoke a suboptimal allocation of resources by sending the private sector wrong signals. For example, restrictions in factor markets and constricting regulations can prevent the competitive pricing of production factors and thus stifle international business. What this of course implies is that domestic policies (e.g., labor market policy) may well fall within the realm of international business policy if it helps shape international business to shape a societal challenge.

5.2   Regulator

The many dark sides of international business means that policymakers often need to develop policies and directives that harness global business transactions to tackle societal challenges. Evidence abounds that policymakers often put limitations on inward FDI from state-owned enterprises (SOEs) originating from emerging markets due to worries about their non-business motives (Cuervo-Cazurra, 2018; Li et al., 2021). Other scholars argue that sustainable development can be enhanced by giving priority to "Recognized Sustainable Investors" (Sauvant, 2021).

Government can also put restrictions on the international business activities of their own firms for national security or other purposes. During the U.S.-China trade war, the U.S. implemented a series of export controls to attempt to cut off Huawei's access to semiconductors (Bown, 2020). During the COVID-19 pandemic, both the European Union and the United States threatened to put export controls on locally produced vaccines (Evenett et al., 2021). Several countries have recently adopted modern slavery laws that prohibits firms from importing goods that have been produced in whole or in part by forced or compulsory labor.

5.3   Producer

Besides shaping international business externally through the facilitation and regulation of the business environment, public authorities can also influence international business by directly inserting themselves in the market. Almost all countries act as producers by operating their own state-owned companies (SOEs). They may do so to take control of productive capacity in key strategic sectors (e.g., security and natural resources) or to boost production in industries where externalities make it less likely for the private sector to invest (Cuervo-Cazurra et al., 2014; Horner, 2017). Analyzing SOEs from an international business policy perspective is an understudied research area that has gained relevance in today's world with rising geopolitical turbulence (Li et al., 2021).

5.4   Buyer

Finally, an instrument that has been almost completely ignored in the field of international business policy is public authorities' ability to insert themselves in the market as powerful buyers through public procurement. Just like lead firms in GVCs, the "state as a buyer" has the power to shape international business by imposing technical or other conditions that firms need to meet for them to be considered for public procurement (Dallas et al., 2021). This is a potent tool since it can be used to force lead firms to promote social standards and environmental stewardship more actively throughout their global value chain or to require them to develop a more resilient supply chain.

6   A Roadmap for International Business Policy

The definition and delineation of the field of international business policy that this chapter provides illustrates both the distinctive nature of the research area as well as the central role that traditional international business scholarship can play in the development of international business policy.

Traditional international business research has lots to offer to our understanding of international business policy. Extant scholarship's deep knowledge of how the international environment (including policy) influences the activities, strategies, structures, and decision-making processes of firms is critical for determining (1) the link between government-directed actions and international business and (2) the relation between international business and societal challenges. In other words, traditional international business scholarship is a key building block for understanding policy process, policy analysis, and policy evaluation. Understanding how international business influences aggregate phenomena is critical for under-standing why governments prioritize certain societal challenges (policy process). Assessing how different policy tools affect international business is important to determine the optimal international-business-shaping actions that policymakers should adopt to address these societal challenges (policy analysis). And evaluating the effectiveness of international business policy relies on a deep understanding of international business mechanisms (policy evaluation).

A policy turn in international business research is nonetheless needed for the field of international business policy to realize its full potential (Van Assche, 2018). Scholars need to break out their comfort zone and select research topics based on their relevance for policymakers and societies and not for managers. Instead of analyzing how a new business trend matters for firm performance, scholars need to reflect on its importance for societal challenges (Buckley et al., 2017). In addition to asking how firms reconfigure their strategies and structures in reaction to a policy action, researchers need to in the same breath ask how these reconfigurations affect societal outcomes and which combination of actors is central to achieving a specific outcome. Finally, scholars need to concentrate on the actions that governments can take to better harness international business for grand societal challenges.

Embarking on this policy turn may well develop a breath of fresh air that not only boosts research in the field of international business policy but also permeates throughout the entire field of international business. In today's world with rising geopolitical turbulence, the competitiveness of multinational firms may well depend on its dynamic capabilities to deal with changes in the international business policy environment. Just like multinational firms may develop geopolitical jockeying strategies that can boost their international competitiveness (Li et al., 2021), they may similarly strengthen the sustainability and resilience of their operations by internalizing the implications of their actions on societal challenges. We see this as a fruitful future research agenda.

References

Ambos, B., Brandl, K., Perri, A., Scalera, V. G., & Van Assche, A. (2021). The nature of innovation in global value chains. *Journal of World Business, 56*(4), 101221.

Autor, D. H., Dorn, D., & Hanson, G. H. (2013). The China syndrome: Local labor market effects of import competition in the United States. *American Economic Review, 103*(6), 2121–2168.

Autor, D. H., Dorn, D., Hanson, G. H., & Song, J. (2014). Trade adjustment: Worker-level evidence. *The Quarterly Journal of Economics, 129*(4), 1799–1860.

Autor, D. H., Dorn, D., & Hanson, G. H. (2016). The China shock: Learning from labor-market adjustment to large changes in trade. *Annual Review of Economics, 8*, 205–240.

Bown, C. P. (2020). How the United States marched the semiconductor industry into its trade war with China. *East Asian Economic Review, 24*(4), 349–388.

Bown, C. P., & Irwin, D. A. (2019). Trump's assault on the global trading system: And why decoupling from China will change everything. *Foreign Affairs, 98*, 125.

Bu, M., & Wagner, M. (2016). Racing to the bottom and racing to the top: The crucial role of firm characteristics in foreign direct investment choices. *Journal of International Business Studies, 47*(9), 1032–1057.

Buchholz, M., Bathelt, H., & Cantwell, J. A. (2020). Income divergence and global connectivity of US urban regions. *Journal of International Business Policy, 3*(3), 229–248.

Buckley, P. J., Doh, J. P., & Benischke, M. H. (2017). Towards a renaissance in international business research? Big questions, grand challenges, and the future of IB scholarship. *Journal of International Business Studies, 48*(9), 1045–1064.

Cano-Kollmann, M., Cantwell, J., Hannigan, T. J., Mudambi, R., & Song, J. (2016). Knowledge connectivity: An agenda for innovation research in international business. *Journal of International Business Studies, 47*(3), 255–262.

Casadei, P., & Iammarino, S. (2021). Trade policy shocks in the UK textile and apparel value chain: Firm perceptions of Brexit uncertainty. *Journal of International Business Policy, 4*(2), 262–285.

Clegg, J. (2019). From the editor: International business policy: What it is, and what it is not. *Journal of International Business Policy, 2*(2), 111–118.

Cuervo-Cazurra, A. (2018). Thanks but no thanks: State-owned multinationals from emerging markets and host-country policies. *Journal of International Business Policy, 1*(3), 128–156.

Cuervo-Cazurra, A., Inkpen, A., Musacchio, A., & Ramaswamy, K. (2014). Governments as owners: State-owned multinational companies. *Journal of International Business Studies, 45*(8), 919–942.

Dallas, M. P., Horner, R., & Li, L. (2021). The mutual constraints of states and global value chains during COVID-19: The case of personal protective equipment. *World Development, 139*, 105324.

DeLeon, P. (2006). The historical roots of the field. In *The Oxford handbook of public policy*.

DeTombe, D. J. (2002). Complex societal problems in operational research. *European Journal of Operational Research, 140*(2), 232–240.

Didier, T., & Pinat, M. (2017). The nature of trade and growth linkages. World Bank Policy Research Working Paper, (8168).

Doh, J. P. (2005). Offshore outsourcing: Implications for international business and strategic management theory and practice. *Journal of Management Studies, 42*(3), 695–704.

Eden, L., & Wagstaff, M. F. (2021). Evidence-based policymaking and the wicked problem of SDG 5 gender equality. *Journal of International Business Policy, 4*(1), 28–57.

Evenett, S., Hoekman, B, Rocha, N., & Ruta, M. (2021). The Covid-19 vaccine production Club: Will value chains temper nationalism? World Bank Policy Research Working Paper No. 9565.

Evenett, S. J. (2019). Protectionism, state discrimination, and international business since the onset of the global financial crisis. *Journal of International Business Policy, 2*(1), 9–36.

Evenett, S. J. (2020). Chinese whispers: COVID-19, global supply chains in essential goods, and public policy. *Journal of International Business Policy, 3*(4), 408–429.

George, G., Howard-Grenville, J., Joshi, A., & Tihanyi, L. (2016). Understanding and tackling societal grand challenges through management research. *Academy of Management Journal, 59*(6), 1880–1895.

Gereffi, G. (2019). Global value chains and international development policy: Bringing firms, networks and policy-engaged scholarship back in. *Journal of International Business Policy, 2*(3), 195–210.

Gereffi, G. (2020). What does the COVID-19 pandemic teach us about global value chains? The case of medical supplies. *Journal of International Business Policy, 3*(3), 287–301.

Gereffi, G., Humphrey, J., & Sturgeon, T. (2005). The governance of global value chains. *Review of International Political Economy, 12*(1), 78–104.

Gereffi, G., Lim, H. C., & Lee, J. (2021). Trade policies, firm strategies, and adaptive reconfigurations of global value chains. *Journal of International Business Policy*, 1–17.

Goerzen, A., Iskander, S. P., & Hofstetter, J. (2021). The effect of institutional pressures on business-led interventions to improve social compliance among emerging market suppliers in global value chains. *Journal of International Business Policy, 4*(3), 347–367.

Grossman, G. M., & Helpman, E. (2018). Growth, trade, and inequality. *Econometrica, 86*(1), 37–83.

Horner, R. (2017). Beyond facilitator? State roles in global value chains and global production networks. *Geography Compass, 11*(2), e12307.

Jaax, A., & Miroudot, S. (2021). Capturing value in GVCs through intangible assets: The role of the trade–investment–intellectual property nexus. *Journal of International Business Policy*, 1–20.

Knill, C., & Tosun, J. (2020). *Public policy: A new introduction.* Red Globe Press.

Kobrin, S. J. (1987). Testing the bargaining hypothesis in the manufacturing sector in developing countries. *International Organization, 41*(4), 609–638.

Kobrin, S. J. (2020). How globalization became a thing that goes bump in the night. *Journal of International Business Policy, 3*(3), 280–286.

Kolk, A., Rivera-Santos, M., & Rufín, C. (2018). Multinationals, international business, and poverty: A cross-disciplinary research overview and conceptual framework. *Journal of International Business Policy, 1*(1), 92–115.

Li, J., Van Assche, A., Li, L., & Qian, G. (2021). Foreign direct investment along the belt and road: A political economy perspective. *Journal of International Business Studies*, 1–18.

Locke, R., Amengual, M., & Mangla, A. (2009). Virtue out of necessity? Compliance, commitment, and the improvement of labor conditions in global supply chains. *Politics and Society, 37*(3), 319–351.

Lorenzen, M., Mudambi, R., & Schotter, A. (2020). International connectedness and local disconnectedness: MNE strategy, city-regions and disruption. *Journal of International Business Studies, 51*(8), 1199–1222.

Lundan, S., & Assche, A. (2021). From the editors: Reflections on the nexus of complementarity between international business research and the policy practitioner community. *Journal of International Business Policy, 4*(2), 201–205.

Lundan, S. M. (2018). From the editor: Engaging international business scholars with public policy issues.

Miroudot, S. (2020). Reshaping the policy debate on the implications of COVID-19 for global supply chains. *Journal of International Business Policy, 3*(4), 430–442.

Moons, S. J., & van Bergeijk, P. A. (2017). Does economic diplomacy work? A meta-analysis of its impact on trade and investment. *The World Economy, 40*(2), 336–368.

Patala, S., Juntunen, J. K., Lundan, S., & Ritvala, T. (2021). Multinational energy utilities in the energy transition: A configurational study of the drivers of FDI in renewables. *Journal of International Business Studies, 52*(5), 930–950.

Pietrobelli, C., Rabellotti, R., & Van Assche, A. (2021). Making sense of global value chain-oriented policies: The trifecta of tasks, linkages, and firms. *Journal of International Business Policy., 4*(3).

Ramamurti, R. (2001). The obsolescing 'bargaining model'? MNC-host developing country relations revisited. *Journal of International Business Studies, 32*(1), 23–39.

Rodrik, D. (2018). Populism and the economics of globalization. *Journal of international business policy, 1*(1), 12–33.

Rodrik, D. (2020). Putting global governance in its place. *The World Bank Research Observer, 35*(1), 1–18.

Rossi, A. (2019). Applying the GVC framework to policy: The ILO experience. *Journal of International Business Policy, 2*(3), 211–216.

Ruger, J. P., & Yach, D. (2009). The global role of the World Health Organization. *Global Health Governance, 2*(2), 1–11.

Sauvant, K. P. (2021). Improving the distribution of FDI benefits: The need for policy-oriented research, advice, and advocacy. *Journal of International Business Policy, 4*(2), 244–261.

Scherer, A. G., & Palazzo, G. (2011). The new political role of business in a globalized world: A review of a new perspective on CSR and its implications for the firm, governance, and democracy. *Journal of Management Studies, 48*(4), 899–931.

Singhania, M., & Saini, N. (2021). Demystifying pollution haven hypothesis: Role of FDI. *Journal of Business Research, 123*, 516–528.

Smith, K. B., & Larimer, C. W. (2018). *The public policy theory primer*. Routledge.

Tavares-Lehmann, A. T., Toledano, P., Johnson, L., & Sachs, L. (Eds.). (2016). *Rethinking investment incentives: Trends and policy options*. Columbia University Press.

Timmer, M. P., Miroudot, S., & de Vries, G. J. (2019). Functional specialisation in trade. *Journal of Economic Geography, 19*(1), 1–30.

Ting, A., & Gray, S. J. (2019). The rise of the digital economy: Rethinking the taxation of multinational enterprises. *Journal of International Business Studies, 50*(9), 1656–1667.

Turkina, E., & Van Assche, A. (2018). Global connectedness and local innovation in industrial clusters. *Journal of International Business Studies, 49*(6), 706–728.

Van Assche, A. (2018). From the editor: Steering a policy turn in international business–opportunities and challenges.

Van Assche, A. (2020). *Trade, investment and intangibles: The ABCs of global value chain-oriented policies (No. 242)*. OECD Publishing.

Van Assche, A., & Gangnes, B. (2019a). Global value chains and the fragmentation of trade policy coalitions. *Transnational Corporations Journal, 26*(1).

Van Assche, A., & Gangnes, B. (2019b). Production switching and vulnerability to protectionism. In *International business in a VUCA world: The changing role of states and firms*. Emerald Publishing Limited.

Van Assche, A., & Lundan, S. (2020). From the editor: COVID-19 and international business policy. *Journal of International Business Policy, 3*(3), 273–279.

Van Tulder, R., Rodrigues, S. B., Mirza, H., & Sexsmith, K. (2021). The UN's sustainable development goals: Can multinational enterprises lead the decade of action?

Van Zanten, J. A., & Van Tulder, R. (2018). Multinational enterprises and the sustainable development goals: An institutional approach to corporate engagement. *Journal of International Business Policy, 1*(3), 208–233.

Vernon, R. (1971). *Sovereignty at bay* (pp. 44–59). Pelican.

Wettstein, F., Giuliani, E., Santangelo, G. D., & Stahl, G. K. (2019). International business and human rights: A research agenda. *Journal of World Business, 54*(1), 54–65.

Zhan, J. X. (2021). GVC transformation and a new investment landscape in the 2020s: Driving forces, directions, and a forward-looking research and policy agenda. *Journal of International Business Policy, 4*(2), 206–220.

Zhao, S., Gooderham, P., Papanastassiou, M., & Harzing, A. W. (2021). Guest editorial [Special Issue: Do multinational enterprise contribute to, or reduce global inequality?]. *Critical Perspectives on International Business, 17*(1), 1–7.

Ari Van Assche is Professor of International Business at HEC Montréal and deputy editor of the *Journal of International Business Policy*. His research focuses on the organization of global value chains and their implications for international trade, sustainability, industrial clusters, and public policy.

Digitization and Implications for (International) Business

Bharat Vagadia

1   Introduction

The digital revolution that we see evolve in front of our eyes has applications and systems that are collecting, distributing, and making available massive amounts of data to almost any situation, which can be reproduced infinitely at virtually zero cost and used for significant productivity gains. The impact this digital revolution will have on society and economies is likely to be as dramatic, if not bigger, than the previous industrial revolutions.

The World Economic Forum estimates point to more than US$10 trillion of value from digitization in five key global industries over the next decade.[1] In 2018, McKinsey Global Institute estimated that an additional $13 trillion could be added to global GDP by 2030 through digitization, automation, and Artificial Intelligence (AI).[2]

1.1   Digitalization: What Does It Mean?

Digitization of businesses is not new, although it is taking on a new dimension as we see the convergence of emerging technologies and innovative business and operating models emerge. The Internet (a key enabler) has already diffused into virtually all

---

[1] World Economic Forum (2017). Digital transformation initiative telecommunications industry. The five key global industries are: E-commerce (US$3.1 trillion), Automotive (US$2.6 trillion), Logistics (US$2.1 trillion), Electricity (US$1.5 trillion), and Media and Entertainment (US$0.7 trillion).

[2] Assessing the economic impact of artificial intelligence. ITU Trends. Issue Paper No. 1. September 2018.

B. Vagadia (✉)
Global Telecommunications and Digital Executive, London, UK
e-mail: BV@DigitalDisruption.xyz

© Springer Nature Switzerland AG 2022
H. Merchant (ed.), *The New Frontiers of International Business*, Contributions to
Management Science, https://doi.org/10.1007/978-3-031-06003-8_9

aspects of our lives and all industry sectors. It is already reshaping how we socially interact with each other, how we consume entertainment, and how we buy and pay for goods and services. The digital economy is benefiting consumers by either creating entirely new categories of products and services or new means for their consumption, through entirely new business models and players.

For businesses, digitalization is creating opportunities as well as threats. When digitally capable firms collide with traditional businesses, they do not simply replace them with something cheaper, or more differentiated for higher quality. They do not just create a new value proposition to serve customers—they can potentially enable the emergence of a new and increasingly powerful breed of firms—ones that leverage a different kind of operating model and which compete in different ways. The use of digital technologies also presents new opportunities for SMEs to expand and succeed in foreign markets and for start-ups to enter and disrupt existing markets (so-called digital natives). Digitalization is also enabling some multinationals to reduce their cost base and monetize the massive data they have to hand.

Some of these new business models take the form of what are sometimes called "platform businesses." Many of the products and services delivered through these platforms are of high quality, with low prices, and in many cases a monetary price of zero (e.g., Facebook). Seven out of the ten most valuable public companies in the world by market capitalization were digital platforms, as of April 2020; these were Apple, Microsoft, Amazon, Alphabet, Facebook, Tencent Holdings, and Alibaba Group.[3]

These new forms of business themselves have only been possible through the substantially lower cost of starting a business and ability to scale, through things like cloud computing, their access to global markets through the Internet, and a consumer base that is now always digitally connected, with the ability to securely transact.

So why are digitally enabled businesses growing so rapidly and being valued at such rates? Traditional corporate leaders typically face a set of challenges to grow and expand usually as a result of constraints placed by their operating model. Digital businesses dissolve these intrinsic limits of scalability and scope. Their operating models are designed to scale at rates that traditional firms just cannot fathom.

Digital Masters, as the authors have labeled them in their book "Leading Digital," are 26% more profitable than their industry competitors and generate 9% more revenues. These firms use technology as an enabler to reconfigure their organizational structures, processes, and potentially their entire business model.[4] Reinventing the business model does not have to be about changing the rules of an industry, replacing products or services, or creating new digital business, but about reconfiguring the value created and captured using new digital technologies.

Nevertheless, you simply cannot start from the perspective of what technology to adopt—but from a mindset of how you can deliver greater value to customers and

---

[3] https://www.statista.com/statistics/263264/top-companies-in-the-world-by-market-capitalization/

[4] Westerman, G., Bonnet, D., and McAfee, A. (2014). Leading Digital. Harvard Business Review Press. October 2014.

how that can be delivered operationally and better enabled through digital technologies.

1.2 Impact on Policymaking

While the adoption of digital technologies has the potential to have profound changes to the competitor landscape and on consumers, it equally has the potential for a profound impact on societies and economies, some of which we may not necessarily desire.

To turn these disruptive technologies into a force for good may require us to tear up existing government policies and regulatory approaches that have served us reasonably well to date. However, the very nature of these digital technologies means that jurisdictional national boundaries are dissolving, their reach is global, their adoption pervasive, and the way they work is not always transparent or predictable.

Digitalization holds the promise of improving productivity performance through innovation and by reductions in the costs of a range of business processes. But at the same time, many economies have experienced a slowdown in productivity growth that has sparked a lively debate about whether and how digital technologies boost productivity. While digital technologies can replicate valuable ideas, insights, and innovations at a very low cost, potentially creating bounty for society and wealth for innovators, it can diminish the demand for previously important types of labor, having a correspondingly adverse impact on people's wages.

Not all countries will follow the same trajectory, however. Over time, the impact of automation is likely to be felt more heavily on developing countries than in developed countries. If you take most of the costs of labor out of the equation by installing robots and other types of automation, then the competitive advantage of low wages largely disappears. The distribution of wealth created by digital technologies will be skewed to those individuals, those companies, those communities, and those countries that are digitally savvy. On the other hand, by enhancing connectivity, financial inclusion, and access to trade and public services, technology has the potential to be a great equalizer.[5]

Each country's policymakers and regulators will need to orchestrate an ecosystem and regulatory environment that magnifies the positive externalities associated with such disruptive technologies while minimizing potential negative externalities. To date, there is no overall regulatory authority covering the entire digital sphere. Regulation is fragmented with overlaps and gaps. This will need to change.

---

[5]The Impact of Digital Technologies, UN. See: https://www.un.org/en/un75/impact-digital-technologies

2   The Digital Revolution

Digitizing the firm can drive significant productivity improvements through mechanisms that are many and varied.[6] Some of these include: speed and strength by being faster, stronger, more precise, and consistent than workers; productivity enhancements by combining sensors, actuators, big data analytics, and cloud computing; and predictability enhancements enabled by new sensors, artificial intelligence, and machine to machine (M2M) communications, which can reduce disruptions to production.

Digital technologies also allow connectivity and communication across nations. Its nature means that businesses can scale quickly and with relative ease. All dimensions of digital are global: digital activities can take place internationally, and digital business models can globally span sectors and countries to offer digital goods and services.

Whether we like it or not, digital technologies are transforming business and society.

For businesses, it has already started reshaping how they market to and interact with their customers, as well as how they deliver customer service. The first wave of the Internet-enabled innovations that started in the early century with the emergence of Web 2.0 technologies was followed by advances in ubiquitous connectivity, smartphones, and cloud infrastructure. Thanks to these new technologies, today's consumers are no longer constrained to buying from stores in their immediate community, city, or even in their own country.

The COVID-19 pandemic has only accelerated the adoption of digital technologies by both consumers as well as businesses. Amazon, the digital retail giant, saw unprecedented growth in its retail sales; consumers, young and old, become accustomed to buying their goods and services online. Almost all businesses explored how they can reach customers through online channels—many even developing their own mobile apps. Different sectors and countries faired differently of course, depending on how digitally savvy they were in the first place and the effort, resources, and speed required for them to digitize.

This digital revolution has also profoundly transformed international trade, in terms of what we trade, how we trade, and who is trading. The rapid expansion of access to trusted digital payments has made it possible for consumers to conveniently make purchases for goods and services from merchants around the world.

While there has been much change and in a short period of time, this is only the beginning. This so-called fourth machine age is just emerging with further advances in digital technologies/computing and, more importantly, their convergence, driven by the Internet of Things (IOT), Artificial Intelligence (AI), and high-speed ubiquitous connectivity (5G). It would be wrong to assume that this new revolution is only driven by data. While data is a fundamental enabler for this fourth revolution, it is

---

[6]OECD. (2016). Enabling the next production revolution: the future of manufacturing and services. Interim Report. Meeting of the OECD Council at Ministerial Level, 1–2 June 2016.

disruption through engineering and physics such as miniaturization, nanotechnologies, energy storage, etc., which cannot be overlooked. The most significant advancements are happening where these two disruptive forces intersect.

Many of these new digital technologies can be classified as general-purpose technologies, where their impact has the potential to deliver significant boosts to output due to large productivity gains. These digital technologies not only create new markets, new forms of trade, and new products, but they also lower trade costs and change trade patterns—making it possible for firms in remote areas to sell digital products around the whole world or by making it profitable for firms in high-income countries to re-shore certain activities.

The service sector is leading the charge in terms of the adoption of digital technologies—roughly 50% of traded services are digitally enabled compared with 15% of traded goods.[7] While traditional Internet-enabled disruption mainly focused on the service sector, new advances in IOT, AI, digital twins, and 3D printing will now have an equally dramatic impact on the manufacturing sector. However, it may take another 30 years for full, worldwide diffusion of emerging smart automation and AI technologies.[8]

2.1   Characteristics of Being Digital

We have discussed the impact digitalization and digital technologies have already had on businesses, but what does being digital actually mean?

There are probably five fundamental characteristics of the digital-enabled firm that are useful to look at; these are: a) the role of data to the firm; b) the significant returns to scale that are enabled by the use of digital; c) the network externalities enjoyed; d) the inability for customers to switch easily or for new entrants to come into the space; and e) the global nature of the firm. These characteristics help explain why you simply cannot ignore digitalization:[9]

1. The role of data is a critical ingredient for gathering insight and driving algorithms. The ability to use data to develop new, innovative services and products is a competitive driver for data-enabled firms.
2. The cost of production of digital services is much less proportional to the number of customers served, driving significant returns to scale through economies of scale and scope. While this aspect is not novel as such (bigger factories or retailers are often more efficient than smaller ones), the digital world pushes it to the

---

[7]Digital Globalization: The New Era of Global Flows. (2016). McKinsey Global Institute. February 2016.

[8]Twenty-five years of digitization: Ten insights into how to play it right. (2019). McKinsey Global Institute. May 2019.

[9]See also: Competition Policy for the digital era. (2019). EU Report.

extreme and this can result in a significant competitive advantage for the digitally enabled firm.

3. Network externalities are strengthened by firms exploiting two and multisided markets that characterize platform ecosystems. Initial work on two-sided markets by Jean Tirole, Nobel laureate in economics, goes back to the pre-digital platform era where he discussed cross-subsidies in the credit card companies such as Visa. In many ways, subsidizing one business activity with another one is nothing new. Many businesses do it to build complementarities, which can be monetized (take the examples of printers or razors). However, the platform ecosystem strengthens this logic further as the ecosystem operates on modularity, where different complementary goods can be combined for the benefit of the platform operator.

4. The lack of data mobility and interoperability means it is difficult for competitors to enter easily or for consumers to switch to alternative competitors. The inability to multi-home means customers are effectively tied to the digital-enabled firm.

5. Digital goods and services can be delivered globally cutting across national jurisdictions and regulations. Most of the digital businesses that sell globally do not have a physical presence, company registration, or licenses to operate within the countries they serve—meaning they can access global customers without the bureaucracy or costs of setting up operations in these countries.

While each of these is important, the most important characteristic of being digital that has been exploited by high-growth digital firms is the network externality effect. Digital natives talk about creating ecosystems rather than simply replicating existing products or services. This ecosystem approach allows these firms to exploit the network effects, to expand their business reach through bringing onboard more partners through modularity, and building an ecosystem that becomes costly for consumers and suppliers to leave.

The digitalization of an ecosystem also allows for use of long-tail market strategies where it is easy for digital firms to expand into different market niches which would normally be cost-prohibitive. This approach allows companies to tap into previously unserved markets and realize significant profits by selling low volumes of hard-to-find items to many customers. A business model based on the long tail works for a company based on digital distribution, where the cost of stocking extra inventory is near zero.

3 Digital Technologies and Their Implications for Businesses

3.1 Current Technologies

There are a number of digital technologies that many firms already use. Many of these are used to address a particular problem, whether it is to improve marketing reach to potential customers, to align sales with production orders, or just to keep a record of customer interactions. While it is not the intent to explain these technologies here—it is worth mentioning some of the more important ones.

Firms use these digital technologies but are not digital firms. The technologies they deploy do not have a transformative impact on the firm.

3.1.1   ERM and CRM

The working horse of almost every large firm is the Enterprise Resource Planning (ERM) software, used to standardize, streamline, and integrate most of the business processes across finance, human resources, procurement, warehouse storage, and distribution. Their focus is inward. Customer Relationship Management (CRM) software, likewise a stable technology in almost all large firms, is designed to record and store every piece of information regarding customer interactions. In both of these cases, the technology is not used to rethink how to increase customer value or how the firm can capture such value, only how to incrementally improve the existing operating model.

3.1.2   RPA

Another technology that has gained momentum is Robotic Process Automation (RPA), typically used to replace humans performing menial and repetitive tasks on the assembly line, in the warehouse, or in financial management. Again, firms use the technology to drive down costs (of the order of about 20–25% of FTE savings).[10] The same comments as apply to ERM and CRM also apply to RPA—in that it is not a transformative technology.

3.1.3   Big Data/Business Intelligence and Cloud Computing

Two more interesting technologies that are starting to make firms think more broadly about how they can transform their operating models through the use of technology are big data/business intelligence and cloud computing. If used and integrated appropriately, they can help transform the operating model of the firm. Big data captures, stores, and makes sense of the huge amounts of data that may be gathered by the firm. Given the data sets can increase exponentially as day-to-day operational data is captured and stored, most firms need to utilize cloud computing to implement big data technologies.

The fundamental raison d'être for utilizing cloud computing (a bridge between the old and new digital technologies) is that they are elastic, that is they dynamically determine the amount of resources an application requires and then automatically provision and de-provision the computing infrastructure to support the application. Effectively, cloud computing gives firms the right, but not the obligation, to scale up if and when demand increases. The mass emergence of digital-native companies today would not be possible without easy, immediate, and affordable access to the scalable computing resources available through the elastic cloud infrastructure.

---

[10]Digital Directions: A perspective on the impact of digital technologies (2020). EY Report. April 2020. The report notes that up to 40% of RPA projects fail however.

3.1.4   E-commerce and Digital Payments

One final technology that I want to mention, which is not new, but where there have been incremental improvements, is digital payments and broader E-commerce. These technologies and the underlying infrastructure is allowing firms to scale globally and access geographic markets that would have been impossible a decade ago. These have served to help build consumer trust and enable seamless, secure transactions. Whether it is sending a text to pay for a bus ticket in Prague, using a QR code to pay for groceries in China, or tapping a sales terminal with a mobile phone in the Doha, even before COVID-19, these ways of paying for goods and services were evidence of a steady shift to digital payments.[11]

Unfortunately, the change in the business-to-business (B2B) payments area has been slower. A vast amount of B2B payments are still heavily reliant on paper checks and invoices.[12] This is an area ripe for transformation. It would be hard to find a single digital business to make use of this antiquated process. It would seem strange to aspire to be an agile fast-moving business when you rely on payment mechanisms that take days to clear and require significant paper-based processes. International business operations and a non-digital payment platform would appear to be an oxymoron.

3.2   Emerging Technologies

There are a number of, what some label, emerging technologies. These technologies are being used by some leading-edge firms and are proving to have a disruptive effect on their business and operating models. While each of these emerging technologies is being developed independently and used for different purposes, the fundamental question is how these technologies are interconnected and what disruptive impact they can have on business and operating models. Figure 1 shows the interconnectedness of some of these key emerging technologies.

To make sense of this order of complexity, we need a simple framework to understand how these technologies relate to each other and what impact they might have not only individually but also collectively. Such a framework needs to start from a perspective of how data moves along the value chain from data capture to the applications that make use of data. In the end, digital is after all about the use of data to create value. Figure 2 illustrates a framework I have developed for looking at the data ecosystem and the key technologies that sit at each layer of this ecosystem.

---

[11] Payments 2025 & beyond: Navigating the payments matrix - Charting a course amid evolution and revolution. See: https://www.pwc.com/gx/en/industries/financial-services/publications/finan cial-services-in-2025/payments-in-2025.html

[12] https://www.statista.com/statistics/291321/share-of-businesses-using-checks-in-the-united-king dom-uk-by-purpose/. 49% of UK businesses used checks to pay a supplier in 2019.

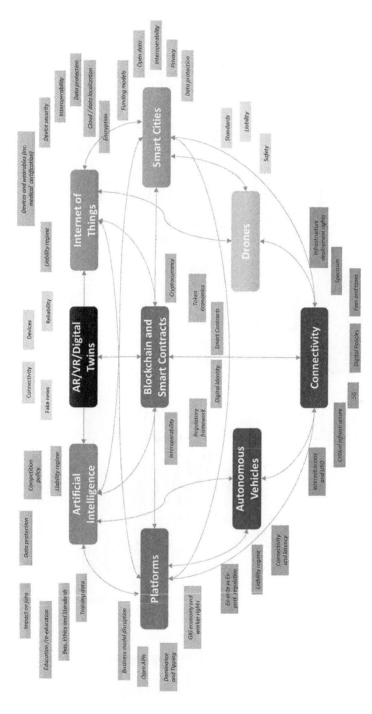

Fig. 1 Interconnectedness of emerging technologies. Figure compiled by author

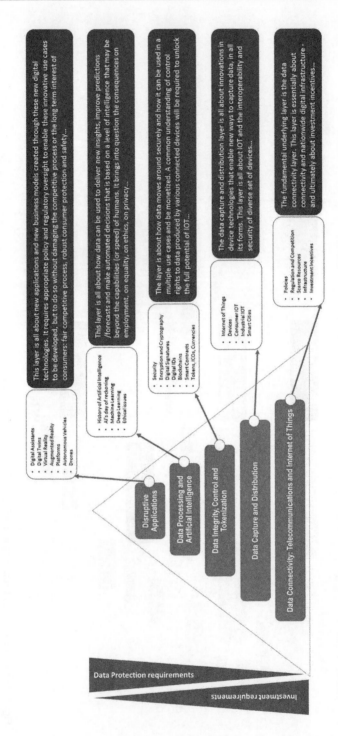

Fig. 2 The data ecosystem. Figure compiled by author

It would be impossible to look at all of these layers and technologies in detail within this chapter—something I have done so in my book Digital Disruption.[13] Nevertheless, it is worth examining some of the more transformative technologies here.

3.2.1   IoT

Internet of Things (IOT) is an umbrella term for technologies that allow objects to communicate. It includes a range of technologies, such as passive radio-frequency identification (RFID) and near-field communication (NFC); and technologies that cover large distances such as machine-to-machine (M2M) communication. While IOT enabling automation is per se, not new, it is the amorphous, pervasive connected, ad-hoc, distributed, easy-to-design, easy-to-deploy, easy-to-"mash up," and massively commoditized nature of the sensing, computing, and actuators enabled by IOT that makes it a new and explosive capability. IOT will enable, and in some cases force, new business models. Firms will move away from selling products to selling a service enabled through IOT. When businesses move toward an "as-as-service" model through the use of IOT, it will open up additional value creation opportunities for customers, which can also open up opportunities to extract value by digital firms.

3.2.2   Blockchain and Smart Contracts

Blockchain at its core is a form of distributed ledger, which its advocates claim has the promise to reshape industries by enabling trust, providing transparency, and reducing friction across business ecosystems, potentially lowering costs, reducing transaction settlement times, and improving cash flow. The Blockchain database is not stored in any single location, meaning the records it keeps are truly public (well in some cases) and easily verifiable. The digital nature of the ledger enables the implementation of smart contracts. Users can set up algorithms and rules that automatically trigger transactions. A firm could signal via the Blockchain that a particular good has been received or the product could have GPS functionality embedded, which would automatically log a location update, which in turn triggers a payment, eliminating inefficiencies, unnecessary intermediary costs, and reduce the potential for fraud or errors—something that could be invaluable for facilitating international trade.

3.2.3   Artificial Intelligence

As the world stands at the cusp of this transformative technology, much is at stake. Deployed wisely, Artificial Intelligence (AI) holds the promise of addressing some of the world's most intractable challenges, from climate change and poverty, to disease eradication. Used in bad faith, it can lead the world on a downward spiral of totalitarianism and war, endangering—according to Hawking—the very survival of

---

[13] Digital Disruption: Implications and opportunities for Economies, Society, Policy Makers and Business Leaders. (2020). Vagadia, B. See: https://www.springer.com/gp/book/9783030544935

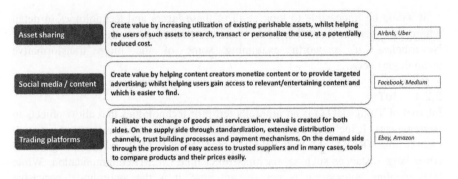

Fig. 3 Platform types. Figure compiled by author

humankind itself. In 2017, PwC forecast that GDP worldwide could be as much as 14% higher in 2030 because of AI technologies, which it valued as potentially contributing some US$15.7 trillion to the global economy. The majority of the gains would, in its assessment, come from retail, financial services, and healthcare in terms of greater productivity, enhanced products, and higher demand.[14]

3.2.4   Platforms

Platforms are typically intermediaries; they connect two or more distinct groups, for instance, buyers and sellers, or content providers and individuals, where the platform owner may not actually own the assets or services being transacted. These platforms are enabled through a combination of web and mobile apps, cloud computing, big data, AI, digital payments, and increasingly virtual and augmented reality—all made possible through ubiquitous smartphone connectivity. Figure 3 illustrates the three types of platform models observed today.

The significance of platforms in the economy can be observed when we compare their valuations compared to traditional firms. In 1990, the top three automakers in the USA had among them nominal revenues of approximately US$250 billion and a market capitalization of US$36 billion, employing over one million employees. In 2014, the top three companies in Silicon Valley had nominal revenues of US$247 billion, but a market capitalization of over US$1 trillion and only 137,000 employees. Seven of the top 12 largest companies by market capitalization, Alibaba, Alphabet, Amazon, Apple, Facebook, Microsoft, and Tencent are all effectively platform or ecosystem players.

3.2.5   Virtual, Augmented, and Mixed Reality

Many firms, primarily in entertainment and gaming, are today utilizing Virtual Reality (VR), Augmented Reality (AR), and Mixed Reality (MR), allowing brick

---

[14]PwC. (2017). Sizing the prize: what's the real value of AI for your business and how can you capitalise? See: https://www.pwc.com/gx/en/issues/data-and-analytics/publications/artificial-intelligence-study.html

and mortar retailers to take their showroom experiences to another level, creating unique experiences that blend digital and physical shopping—and extending the appeal of the showrooms globally. According to recent estimates by Goldman Sachs, VR and AR are expected to grow into a US$95 billion market by 2025.[15] The strongest demand for these technologies currently comes from industries in the creative economy; however, over time, many applications of VR and AR applications will find their way into a number of sectors, including the healthcare and education sectors.

3.2.6 3D Printing

Invented three decades ago, 3D printing has only recently become a viable technology. The industry was worth just over US$4 billion in 2014 with some estimating an average growth rate of 25% per annum, and if that continues, it could be worth just over US$50 billion by 2025.[16] The real societal impact of 3D maybe even more profound over the long term. The very design of towns and cities and populations over time have been largely determined by the industrial revolution. If 3D printing really does become a substitute for mass manufacturing, large clusters of labor around large plants will no longer be necessary.

4 Digitally Driven Business and Operating Models

4.1 Business Model Redesign: Creating Value

The new breed of digital firms is all about innovation in the business model, experimenting, and recombining various aspects of value creation and value capture. Digital companies take traditional business models and stand them on their head. They start with a customer's pain point and mobilize resources to solve it. They use data and insight to understand customer needs, to connect with their supply chain partners, their employees, and ultimately to build a competitive advantage.

In traditional firms, value creation and capture is typically created and captured from the same source, that is, through sales of goods and services through the price mechanisms. In digital businesses, the sources and options for value creation and capture are broader because value creation and capture can be separated more easily and often come from different stakeholders. The Nest thermostat creates value by digitizing the entire home temperature control process, from fuel purchase to temperature setting to powering the heating, ventilation, and air-conditioning system and connecting it to Nest's cloud data services. The thermostat aggregates its data on

---

[15] Immersive Virtual Reality Supporting Content For Evaluating Interface Using Oculus Rift and Leap Motion. Kento Yasui, K., Kawai, R., and Arakawa, T. (2019). International Journal of Innovative Computing, Information and Control. Volume 15, Number 2, April 2019.

[16] UNCTAD. (2018). Technology and Innovation Report 2018, Harnessing Frontier Technologies for Sustainable Development.

real-time energy consumption and shares that data with utilities, which helps improve their energy consumption forecasts and thus achieve greater operating efficiency. Nest can push cost savings back to customers by reducing their energy bills. Nest captures value by charging two or three times the price of conventional thermostats and it makes money from electric utilities on the basis of outcomes. Thus Nest will not only play in the US$3 billion global thermostat industry; it will help shape the US$6 trillion energy sector. It can also jump into other sectors by opening up its digital cloud platform to devices and services from other providers. Another example of a change to business model and correspondingly its operating model is Philips. In 2015, Philips signed a deal to sell lighting to Amsterdam Schiphol Airport. Schiphol Group pays only for the light it uses, and Philips retains ownership of the bulbs and their maintenance. Instead of investing in all the equipment, the customer only pays for the light it actually uses. For Philips, this new business model requires it to reconfigure its operating model and make use of new emerging technologies such as IOT and AI. Instead of being incentivized to sell more bulbs, Philips is motivated to create bulbs that last longer and are more efficient, aligning with its wider sustainable development goals.[17]

Many firms are doing digital versus being digital, that is, they use technology to fix isolated problems rather than as part of an overall business strategy. Instead of starting with a piece of technology and figuring out ways to apply it to their business, digital leaders think of outcomes their customers most value and how to deliver them using digital technologies.

Simply investing in digital technologies to digitalize existing functions and processes is not enough. Firms need to start from a blank sheet and look at how they can deliver greater value to customers, examine what customers will demand in the near future, who their real competitors are, and how they can maintain their competitive advantage either by being smarter, cheaper, or faster, or indeed all three.

Digital firms think differently in another critical way. They realize that the concept of the vertically integrated enterprise going it alone is antiquated. The world is moving too fast. They need to build an ecosystem and digital foundations to create unique value that benefits all participants and this approach cannot be accomplished alone—they instead, attempt to create an ecosystem. In many ways, while most firms are not platforms, they need to start thinking like platform players—and move beyond looking at sectors and to the wider ecosystem.[18] They need to examine how they can utilize digital technologies so they can replicate the operating models of platform businesses—that is, becoming agile at developing and scaling the business.

This is certainly not an easy task. Digitizing products or channels to market may well cannibalize existing revenues as customers may expect digitally available products to be cheaper than traditionally sourced goods. A careful approach is

---

[17] https://www.lighting.philips.com/main/cases/cases/airports/schiphol-airport
[18] Winning in digital ecosystems. (2018). Digital McKinsey, January 2018; and Competing in a world without borders. McKinsey Quarterly, July 2017.

required to balance the risks of cannibalization of some of the revenue stream in the short-term versus the longer-term risks of the business becoming wholly uncompetitive or irrelevant to customers.

4.2   Operating Model Redesign: Capturing Value

Operating models deliver the value promised to customers. Ultimately the goal of an operating model is to deliver value at scale, to achieve sufficient scope, and to respond to changes. In traditional firms, the intrinsic scalability and economies of scope that could be derived from technology are limited by the operating architecture of the firm that it was deployed in. But digitally enabled firms are designed and architected to release the full potential of digital networks, data algorithms, and AI. The more a firm is designed for scale and scope in its operating model, the more value it can create and capture.

A digitally enabled firm must go from siloes, un-connected IT into a true software/algorithm enabled data-driven operating architecture. This is done in order to remove human interaction from the critical path in the operating model. The marginal cost of serving an additional customer using digital agents transforms the process of increasing capacity and makes it easier to scale. The problem of increasing complexity is managed through software and analytics, rather than hiring more layers of managers.[19]

Alipay started life in 2004 as a simple payment solution for the goods transacted on Alibaba's marketplace.[20] It then expanded its payment solution to a wider audience outside of simple transactions on Alibaba. It has since rapidly expanded its business model built on a new kind of digital operating system. One of its expanded product ranges is providing loans to millions of customers in China. The loan approval and issuance processes rely solely on credit scores and are entirely digital and AI driven, where each loan application is run through 3000 risk control strategies. It can process loans at a cost of RMB 2 compared with RMB 2000 at a traditional bank. With the digital systems in place, it does not need physical bank locations or a large workforce; it can scale on mass.[21]

As digital business models advance, location, distance, and real estate become less relevant. Beyond removing human bottlenecks, digital technologies are intrinsically modular and can easily enable business connections usually through the use of APIs to external communities of partners or potential customers; just as Alipay did by extending its offering to a wider audience outside of its existing domain.

---

[19] Westerman, G., Bonnet, D., and McAfee, A. (2014). Leading Digital. Harvard Business Review Press. October 2014.

[20] Alipay is a third-party mobile and online payment platform, established China in February 2004 by Alibaba Group.

[21] Competing in the age of AI: Iansiti, M and Lakhani, K. Harvard Business Review Press.

Successful firms do not just deliver a product or service but have a relentless focus on delivering a great customer experience. In traditional firms, this experience is delivered through your front office employees or your customer service staff. The problem is that as firms scale, the challenges of continually delivering a great customer experience become more difficult. You need to hire more staff, you need to train them, you need to start standardizing some of your processes, thereby losing that individual personalized experience and customers start to feel they are just another dollar sign rather than individuals.

Digitally savvy firms attempt to utilize digital technologies and data to be able to scale without the need for more staff or losing that individual personalized customer experience. When you login into your Netflix page, what you see is individualized to you, based on historic data on what you like, what you do not like; even changing the icons of the movies that are displayed to your taste. The same goes with Amazon; while they serve millions of customers with the same technology platform, as customers, we get to see a personalized experience. These digitally savvy firms also extend this relentless focus on great customer service to their ecosystem partners—suppliers and partners.

4.3   Digital Transformation Strategies

A key challenge in driving digital transformation is that the whole organization is optimized for the current business model. Fundamentally, the organization itself prohibits breakout from the old model. To transform the organization requires a break out from the old model, old people, old metrics, and old investment profiles.

The operating model is one of the biggest challenges of digital transformation. Successful operating models in the digital era enable speed of both action and decision-making and collaboration across internal functions and with external partners with an appropriate level of risk-taking. Put another way, successful operating models bring about a step-change in the firm's agility. Information Technology (IT) systems have helped improve the performance of many traditional firms, but these IT systems generally mirror the firm's silos and specialized architecture. Although improving efficiency and internal responsiveness—they drive only incremental improvements to economies of scale and scope across operating units. Traditional technologies do not change the structure of the firm per se.

Digital transformation is not just about bringing cross-functional teams and IT systems together, but also about bringing cross-functional data together. In traditional firms, software applications and data are still embedded in individual, largely autonomous, and siloed organizational units. IT and data are most often gathered in a distributed and inconsistent fashion, separated and isolated by existing organizational subdivisions and by generations of highly specialized and often incompatible legacy technology. Large firms often have thousands of enterprise applications and IT systems, working with a variety of scattered databases and supporting diverse data models and structures.

The seven 'A's of high performing organizations	Broad elements
Accountability	Boards, teams and individuals in terms of control, risk and performance
Awareness	Listening to signals which suggest the need to adjust
Agility	Strategy, implementation plans, workforce, delegation
Adaptability	Pliable structures, including command and control and planning
Alignment	To vision and strategy and across departments, across functions and stakeholders
Action	Concrete visible action and tracking
Achievement	Collecting the right dots and connecting them – objective and benefit realization

Fig. 4 The seven As of high-performance organizations. Table compiled by author

A more strategic and integrated approach to organizational design is needed to transform the firm, one that integrates the vision and mission with strategic objectives, with policies, processes, controls, decisions, issues, and risks, and these ultimately to actions and tasks that are carried out by stakeholders across the enterprise. Well-developed structures and systems can lead to better decision-making and better and faster decisions. The importance of these structures and systems becomes even more important as firm's attempt to "invert" and seek value from outside of the organization and develop an array of partnerships. Figure 4 details the seven As of high-performance organizations.[22]

Delivering on the seven 7As starts and ends with having the right people in the organization. Nothing will be more important than recruiting, training, and retaining the right workers to operate and lead the digital enterprise. Employees with new perspectives and capabilities are needed to execute digital strategies. This new wave of workers think fast on their feet, are continually learning, play well in teams, and can expect to be in a new job, maybe a new career, every few years. These employees need to be provided the ground rules of how they are expected to behave. They need a digital culture. The culture and organizational design must support, reward, and encourage the appropriate behaviors behind the strategy. Trying to transform an old bureaucratic firm by instilling digital technologies without changing the organizational design from a hierarchy to a flatter firm, from centralized to decentralized decision-making, from a meticulously planned to an agile structure, and from a culture supportive of a risk-averse—job for life—to a learning and adapting culture—is bound to fail.

---

[22] Adopted from by earlier book: Enterprise Governance - Driving Enterprise Performance Through Strategic Alignment. (2014). Vagadia, B. see: https://www.springer.com/gp/book/9783642385889

5 The Data Ecosystem and Impact on Society and Policymakers

The rapid scale of change that is enabled by digitization is already impacting large swathes of society. The way people interact with their friends and colleagues, the way people get their news, or the way society buys goods and services has profoundly changed in the last decade. As a society we are giving access to our personal data—what we like, who we like, where we go, and what we watch online—some without us even noticing. The very fabric of trade is changing—we are sometimes transacting not with fiat money but through the intrinsic value of our personal data. The nature of competition is changing primarily through greater automation and new ecosystems. This is already starting to impact employment patterns and the wages people earn.

These are just some of the societal impacts of digitization. This is however just the start—the impact of digitization is going to be much wider and deeper. It will require major policy responses—some of which may need us to have a wholesale rethink about what we value as a society—some of which will need to be coordinated globally.

5.1 Consumer Implications

5.1.1 Privacy and Freedom

In a world where data is becoming the new oil, the incentives to steal, pilfer, illegally sell, or otherwise abuse data increase dramatically. It, therefore, becomes natural for individuals to guard against access to their personal data. On the other hand, significant economic and social value can be accrued when data is being used more intelligently and combined. It is therefore vital that a happy balance is found between these two extremes. Many countries, recognizing this, have sought to introduce data protection laws. The most stringent of these was the introduction of the General Data Protection Regulation (GDPR) within the EU which enhanced upon the previous data protection directive. The GDPR was designed with the data economy in mind and was primarily a response to the power of large data processors such as Google having access to and processing the personal details of European residents while potentially being outside the jurisdiction of the EU. Many other countries, including the USA and China, have taken a less aggressive approach to data protection. While Europe's practice of data minimization and high data privacy standards can be seen as economically disadvantageous against the likes of China, where personal data flows more freely, in the long run, digital "prosperity" will inevitably have to go hand in hand with citizens' well-being.

5.1.2 Loss of Employment

There is no doubt the widespread usage of digital technologies will have a profound impact on employment. The changes to employment are already evident. Jobs involving significant amounts of repetition have already been affected by technology and remain at a high risk of automation. The Bank of England put potential job losses at around half the British workforce.[23] A study by PwC estimated that some 30% of British jobs are vulnerable to automation from AI and robotics by the early 2030s; the comparable estimates for the USA and Germany are 38% and 35%, respectively, while Japan is somewhat lower at 21%.[24] However, forecasts of mass unemployment arising from AI are open to criticism. Jobs are comprised of tasks, which themselves vary in the degree to which they can be automated.[25]

5.1.3 Pressure on Wages

While not all jobs will be displaced, a more worrying development is that as some jobs do get automated, the competition for the remaining jobs will increase. Such supply increases will put downward pressure on wages for those remaining jobs. At the same time, when returns on capital are greater than the returns on labor, firms will invest in AI and machines to perform tasks rather than hire staff. The only way people can remain competitive will be to work for less.

5.1.4 Loss of Security

The platform economy ("gig," "sharing," or "on-demand" economies), though small today, is growing quickly across many sectors. The adoption of such a model lowers transaction costs of firms accessing a larger pool of potential workers and suppliers, with workers increasingly engaged as independent contract workers. This has benefits for some workers (greater flexibility, additional income, and access to work), but at the same time, these jobs rely mostly on non-standard work arrangements that may limit access to regular jobs, offer less promising employment careers, and reduce access to social protection as employees effectively become self-employed.

5.2   Economic and Societal Implications

5.2.1 Competition Policy

Digital transformation will have a significant impact on the way firms enter and compete in the market, particularly as processes become replicable at near-zero cost margin. This digital disruption creates new entrepreneurial activities and may lower the barrier to entry for some. However, it may also widen the gap between those firms who can gain market share and those who cannot. At the heart of this disparity

---

[23] Haldane, A. (2015). Labour's share: speech given at Trades Union Congress, Bank of England, London, 12 November 2015.

[24] PwC. (2017). Up to 30% of existing UK jobs could be impacted by automation by early 2030s, but this should be offset by job gains elsewhere in economy. PwC Blog, 24 March 2017. See: https://pwc.blogs.com/press_room/2017/03/up-to-30-of-existing-uk-jobs-could-be-impacted-byautomation-by-early-2030s-but-this-should-be-offse.html

[25] R. and Susskind, D. (2016). The future of the professions: how technology will transform the work of human experts. OUP Oxford; Reprint edition (22 October 2015).

will be who controls the data. In markets where network externalities and returns to scale are strong, and especially in the absence of multi-homing, protocol, and data interoperability, or strong differentiation, there may be room in the market for only a limited number of large competitors—who will push smaller competitors out of the market. Competition policy will need to be redesigned to be relevant for a digital era.

5.2.2   International Trade Policy
Digital transformation is fundamentally changing what and how we trade, including reductions in cost of delivery, trade facilitation, trade in data, and corresponding de Minimis rules. Digitalization is blurring traditional distinctions between goods and services and the borders these cross, making it more difficult to identify the specific rules that apply to specific transactions. Given that data underpins trade, whether directly or indirectly, measures that restrict its flow can have trade consequences. Many of the new trade agreements have specific clauses for cross-border data flows—however, concerns over sovereignty, state security, and consumer data protection remain.

5.2.3   Taxation and Social Security
Digitalization, the way in which it is changing business models and how digital firms set up their corporate entities in global low tax jurisdictions, is having a major impact on national taxation. Given the lack of international consensus on how to address these challenges and the tremendous political pressure in some countries to take action, some countries have already implemented or have proposed short-term unilateral tax measures. In recent years, several countries around the world have implemented a tax on many digital services, ranging from online advertising and digital platforms to search engines and the trading of data. The tax is commonly called Digital Services Tax (DST). Italy, Austria, Spain, France, and the UK all apply a tax rate varying between just a few percentages up to 5% on digital services. Others have proposed a similar tax or are still considering it. Either way, as digital businesses grow and transcend national boundaries, their impact on the tax take will demand action from policymakers.

5.2.4   Inequality
It is clear that digital disruption has not positively touched everyone to date and that may only get worse over time. The lack of reliable and affordable connectivity infrastructure remains a critical challenge. Globally, some 4 billion people do not have access to appropriate or affordable broadband. Even where people have access to broadband, many lack digital identities limiting their ability to access many online services. The longer those countries and their citizens remain excluded from the online world, the greater their missed development opportunities. Policymakers may need to invest in digital infrastructure to reduce such inequalities paid for by additional taxes.

5.2.5   Data Monoliths and Potential for Social Biases

AI has the potential to help us make better, more rational decisions based on data rather than instinct or gut feeling. However, AI can amplify existing biases, where these human biases are built into the data. These biases are often a function of imperfect training data used to train the AI. It is not that AI itself that is biased, but rather that AI makes visible the biases in society or derives the bias from the imperfect data used to train the AI.[26] The problem is that much of the valuable training data for AI is held by a few large data monoliths. In the absence of policy and regulation, a few large global firms will dominate the AI world and the applications that are enabled through AI.

5.2.6   Loss of Control and Manipulation

Online platforms such as Facebook have come to play a quasi-public role, essentially regulating what individuals read, see, hear, or say, while harvesting data to refine their understanding of people's behavior, preferences and potentially undermining the democratic process itself. Sophisticated AI systems might allow groups to target precisely the right message at precisely the right time to maximum persuasive potential. Such a technology is sinister when applied to voting intention, but pernicious when applied to recruitment for terrorist acts, for example. There is much discussion in the policy field around how these platforms should be regulated and held to account.

Dr. Bharat Vagadia is a global telecommunications and digital executive with deep experience in public policy, regulation, strategy, enterprise governance, strategic alliances, and data ecosystems. He is the author of four books: (1) Digital Disruption, (2) Enterprise Governance, (3) Strategic Outsourcing, and (4) A Legal Handbook on Outsourcing.

---

[26]Take, for example, the recent case where an image classification algorithm on Google classified images of African-American individuals as gorillas. Google apologized for the incident - see: BBC News (1 July 2015).

Effects of Emerging Technologies on International Business

Gary Knight and Zaheer Khan

Various emergent technologies are increasing the efficiency and effectiveness of international business. In this chapter, we address key emerging technologies including big data, analytics, blockchain, 5G, the Internet of Things (IoT), artificial intelligence (AI), robotics, additive manufacturing (AM), and digital platforms and their impact on decoupling and reconfiguration of value chain activities (e.g., Yamin & Sinkovics, 2010). The current period of technological advancement is sometimes called the "Fourth Industrial Revolution," or Industry 4.0. Organizations are employing Industry 4.0 technologies to maximize effectiveness and efficiency in their global activities.

History has been marked by key intersections between phases of technological development and globalization. In the nineteenth century, developments in water and steam power led to key advances in manufacturing and productivity. In the late 1800s and early 1900s, commercialization of electricity enabled the development of mass production. Rapid industrialization combined with advances in transportation and communications technologies coincided with the rise of international trade and investment. Since the 1980s, the rise of information technologies has supported massive growth in international business (Chase-Dunn et al., 2000; Schwab, 2016).

Technologies are driving the interconnectedness of the world economy and creating significant opportunities for firms based in developed and developing

G. Knight (✉)
Helen S. Jackson Chair in Global Management, Atkinson Graduate School of Management, Willamette University, Salem, OR, USA

Global Entrepreneurship and International Business, Business School, University of Aberdeen, Aberdeen, Scotland, UK
e-mail: gknight@willamette.edu

Z. Khan
Strategy & International Business, Business School, University of Aberdeen, Aberdeen, Scotland, UK
e-mail: zaheer.khan@abdn.ac.uk

© Springer Nature Switzerland AG 2022   217
H. Merchant (ed.), *The New Frontiers of International Business*, Contributions to Management Science, https://doi.org/10.1007/978-3-031-06003-8_10

economies to disperse and restructure their value chain activities, and potentially organize production at a global scale. Increasingly, digital technologies are the connective networks of the global economy. Cross-border data flows have increased dramatically and are expected to experience further magnitudes of growth in the 2020s. By 2021, the Internet had penetrated about two-thirds of the world population, a growth rate of more than 1000% during the prior two decades. North America and Europe have led the way in Internet usage, with an average penetration rate of about 90%. Simultaneously, the largest gains in Internet adoption have occurred in the Middle East, Latin America, and Asia (Internet World Stats, 2021). The number of cellular subscriptions worldwide is now greater than the planet's population (Lund et al., 2019). The rapid expansion of communications and content along global digital pathways is reflected in large part by companies interacting with subsidiaries, suppliers, and customers. Low-cost and instant digital communications have greatly lowered the transaction costs historically associated with international trade.

In this chapter, we first provide a theoretical background on technology and international business. We then summarize the key technologies that are driving changes in international business. Finally, we conclude by discussing the implications of such trends for organizational activities and operations around the world.

1   Background

Theory on foreign direct investment (FDI) explains how multinational enterprises (MNEs) undertake value chain activities via the production and management of networks around the world (e.g., Dunning, 1981). Historically, firms have internationalized production to profit from factor of production advantages available in other countries. The eclectic paradigm and the monopolistic advantage perspective revealed how MNEs overcome the challenges of internationalization by acquiring ownership-specific and monopolistic advantages (Dunning, 1981; Hymer, 1976; Rugman, 1980). The integration-responsiveness framework stresses the tension between pressures to globalize and to respond to customers in local markets (Roth & Morrison, 1990). Firms develop specific capabilities to manage international production, sourcing, and related management challenges (Buckley, 2009b; Rugman, 1980), and to maximize competitive advantages in these areas (e.g., Tallman & Fladmoe-Lindquist, 2002; Teece, 2014). The "global factory" refers to the international industrial ecosystem in which the production of goods and services is undertaken by producers both internal and external to individual firms (Buckley, 2009a, 2009b). Over time, a global ecosystem has emerged comprising suppliers, partners, distributors, and alliances. Partly responding to global competition, MNEs have "fine sliced" and distributed value-chain activities among distinct subsidiaries and affiliates in order to minimize costs at every stage of production (Buckley, 2009a, 2009b; Mudambi, 2008).

Various recent developments are reflected by the concept of "disruptive technology" (Christensen, 1997)—the emergence of new technologies that foster industrial growth by creating new industries through the introduction of methods, products, and services that are substantially cheaper, better, or more convenient than those available previously (Kostoff et al., 2004). For example, the rise of information and communications technologies (ICTs), especially the Internet, triggered the emergence of new industries and redefined existing industries (Kostoff et al., 2004). ICTs have facilitated the development of new organizational forms that replaced more traditional organizational forms in the realm of the MNE (e.g., Buckley, 2009b). In this way, ICTs and successor technologies have contributed enormously to optimizing the management of complex and turbulent international environments.

The technology acceptance model (TAM; Davis, 1986, 1989) describes how technological, societal, and human-level factors—including ease-of-use and perceived usefulness—influence the acceptance of new technologies. Scholars have used the TAM to predict acceptance of the Internet (Singh et al., 2006), information systems (Almutairi, 2007), software platforms (Venkatesh & Davis, 2000), and adoption of internet banking (cf. Lai & Li, 2005). The TAM is a useful framework when examining technology in the international context because such factors as knowledge, experience, and resources affect awareness on the utility and comfort of adopting and using advanced technologies (Davis, 1989). The perceived utility of new technologies also has been linked to awareness of existing alternatives or lack thereof. In numerous countries in Africa, for example, growing knowledge of and rising comfort with FIN-tech applications facilitated widespread adoption and use of banking services (Arner et al., 2016). Adoption of the Internet was relatively slow in countries characterized by limited income and education levels (McCoy et al., 2007). In various ways, the rise of new technologies will hold substantial implications for productive activities around the world.

2   The Emerging Technologies

In the following pages, we define and summarize the nature of emergent technologies that are driving shifts in international business.

2.1   Big Data

'"Big data" refers to very large and variable datasets that require highly sophisticated computer programming for efficient storage, manipulation, and analysis. The data can arise from various sources, including social media and machines. For example, smartphones, sensors, point-of-sale terminals, and organizational databases are all potential sources. Data are generated at an ever-increasing pace—for example, Google receives several million queries every minute. The great majority of big data has little or no utility. A key challenge facing firms is to collect, process, and analyze data efficiently and effectively (Cai & Zhu, 2015; Chen et al., 2012).

Another challenge is the availability of skilled workers who can process and utilize big data to create value. Most data-related skills are concentrated in developed economies (e.g., Tambe, 2014), which has far-reaching implications for developing economies where appropriate skills are in short supply.

Big data can be structured (typically numeric and easily formatted) or unstructured (relatively free form and qualitative). The data can be used across the firm to learn, improve, and achieve various goals. For example, big data are used extensively in R&D, market research, sourcing, production, marketing, and customer support. The data typically are stored in databases and analyzed with software specifically designed to handle large, complex datasets. Data analysts examine relationships among different types of data, such as demographic data and purchase history, to identify actionable relationships and other intelligence (Chen et al., 2012; George et al., 2016). The goal of big data typically is to increase the efficiency and effectiveness of various organizational operations. Analysts may use descriptive statistics and applied mathematical tools to measure phenomena, detect trends, and forecast future events (e.g., Sheng et al., 2020). The data can be used to infer new guidance and practical findings arising from revealed relationships and dependencies, or to perform predictions of outcomes and behaviors. Organizations can leverage big data analytics to enhance their performance and develop a sustainable competitive advantage (Gupta & George, 2016; Sheng et al., 2020).

2.2   Analytics

Analytics refers to the systematic, computational analysis of data and statistics. While technologies and methods for analyzing data have improved greatly, today most companies lag behind in this area and are capturing only a small portion of the enormous value available from skillful data analysis (Mulligan et al., 2021). Analytics have grown in importance due to abundant data, the ability to tap value by integrating data from multiple sources, ongoing needs for more sophisticated decision-making, as well as limitations on decision-making associated with bounded rationality and other human constraints (Chen et al., 2012; Gupta & George, 2016).

Sophisticated analytics has the potential to disrupt industries by providing radically new insights and models. For example, digital platform firms can use analytics to match buyers and sellers in real time. Skillfully managed data can personalize products and services. New analytical techniques can fuel innovative products, services, and processes. Data and analytics enable faster and more accurate decision-making. Enormous advances stand to be gained in the areas of manufacturing, retail, and government, in addition to a wide range of industries such as healthcare and finance. Smart analytics can contribute enormously to the efficiency of digital platform businesses, such as ride- and car-sharing, which account for a fast-growing proportion of total vehicle usage. Matching car users and owners is greatly enhanced through smart analytics (Chen et al., 2012; Gupta & George, 2016).

However, various barriers impede progress in capturing value from data and analytics. These include limited availability of appropriate technology, the presence of intra-corporate silos that inhibit data sharing, skeptical or unenlightened corporate leadership, and perhaps most importantly, the lack of is the lack of talent—data scientists and other data managers equipped to perform research, analysis, and management tasks are in short supply. Machine learning is an outgrowth of smart analytics and is associated with various capabilities that can greatly expand the volume, scope, and applications for automation. Such advances can greatly increase productivity in manufacturing processes worldwide (Chen et al., 2012; Gupta & George, 2016; Mulligan et al., 2021).

2.3   Blockchain

Blockchain is a type of decentralized digital ledger, a way of recording transactions in which records are spread across various widely distributed authorities. Each authority operates independently while copying and saving each change to the ledger identically. "Blocks" are the records of transactions that blockchain compiles and are secured cryptographically, with each containing a digital fingerprint of past and present records. When a given block is completed, it is added to the previous block, resulting in a chain of blocks. Blockchain transactions exist simultaneously in widely distributed databases that store the data and execute the transactions. Security of the data and recordkeeping is optimized—hacking, fraud, data loss, and other types of failure are effectively eliminated because the entire system is decentralized and verified through broad-based consensus (Dinh et al., 2018; Loop, 2017; Yli-Huumo et al., 2016). All blocks are recorded digitally, removing the need for reconciliation or paper trails, resulting in greater efficiency, cost savings, and more accurate record-keeping. It eliminates the traditional need for input—identification, authentication, record-keeping, clearing, and settling—from accountants, auditors, banks, lawyers, government entities, legal authorities, and other intermediaries. In total, blockchain constitutes a decentralized, consensus-based, continuously appended, immutable, and fully secure digital ledger (Dinh et al., 2018; Loop, 2017; Yli-Huumo et al., 2016).

Blockchain enables the use of "smart contracts," which establish conditions necessary to complete a transaction. When the conditions are met, the contract is executed automatically and is time-stamped on the blockchain. Eliminating intermediaries results in great savings of time, energy, and cost. Blockchain holds great potential to revolutionize international contracting, transactions, accounting, supply chain management, and financial services. By maximizing trust, traceability, and security by eliminating potentially harmful intermediary manipulation, blockchain is well suited to international transactions (Dinh et al., 2018; Loop, 2017; Yli-Huumo et al., 2016).

Currently, various functional areas of global commerce—including banking, finance, supply chain, marketing and sales, distribution, and legal—are gradually adopting blockchain and all the potential it holds. Healthcare providers are recording medical data on blockchain to optimize patient care. International remittances can be realized much faster, cheaper, and safer. In international retailing, the removal of third parties between buyers and sellers results in cost- and time-savings and increased security. The transparency that blockchain provides to global supply chains provides for more accurate forecasting, thus optimizing inventory and reducing holding costs. Blockchain provides near real-time data from global supply chains, which enhances service, creates value, and cuts costs. Blockchain can reduce counterfeit goods trade by increasing the transparency, authenticity, and traceability of transactions (Dinh et al., 2018; Loop, 2017; Yli-Huumo et al., 2016).

2.4   5G

The fifth generation of wireless technology (5G) refers to the next phase of broadband cellular networks for smartphones and other devices that use mobile technology. Cellular telephone companies began launching 5G technology in 2019, with adoption by about two billion people by the mid-2020s (Barakabitze et al., 2020; Shafique et al., 2020). The technology holds important implications for IoT, through its connectivity to the Internet. When combined with IoT, 5G is greatly increasing the speed and efficiency of smart devices and equipment, such as home appliances, security systems, and infrastructure in energy and transportation. The 5G technology is propelling usage of the Internet and Internet-dependent systems such as intranets, extranets, social media, and email to unprecedented levels of speed. More than 20 billion "things" are expected to join the IoT in the 2020s, thanks in largest part to 5G technology. In the current decade, 5G bandwidth is expected to become 100 to 1000 times greater than 4G technology, transmitting data at 10 to potentially 1000 gigabytes per second. Such developments are revolutionizing technology worldwide. Essentially, all industries and sectors that currently benefit from cellular technology and IoT will experience an enormous boost in operational efficiency and effectiveness (Barakabitze et al., 2020; Shafique et al., 2020). Simultaneously, 5G is increasing access to the global marketplace by residents of developing economies and by SMEs and other firms that historically lacked sufficient resources to do substantial international business.

2.5   Internet of Things (IoT)

IoT refers to connecting machines and devices to each other online. It reflects the global network of smartphones, tablets, and industrial devices that assemble and share information electronically, and access the Internet. Multiple trends have converged to support progress in IoT, including advances in analytics, machine learning, computing, and sensors. Recent explosive growth of devices that connect to the Internet has been a huge, facilitating trend. Worldwide, mobile telephony and app development are growing enormously (Boston Consulting Group, 2015;Sanou, 2018 ; Shafique et al., 2020). IoT has applications for consumers, including home automation, wearable technology, and appliances with remoting monitoring capabilities. For example, IoT is a major growing factor in healthcare, where it is used to monitor health conditions, provide emergency notifications, and assist the elderly or those with disabilities. IoT technology supports manufacturing by connecting various devices equipped with sensing, processing, communications, and networking capabilities. IoT is facilitating rapid development, manufacturing, and optimization of new products and services. The technology has applications in infrastructure related to communications, transportation, and energy (Boston Consulting Group, 2015; Li et al., 2018; Shafique et al., 2020).

The number of smartphone users now exceeds 50% of world population, a dramatic rise in the past decade. The number of connected devices per person has increased from nearly none in the early 2000s to a half-dozen by 2020 (Sanou, 2018; Shafique et al., 2020). Consumers and managers alike connect to a wide range of apps and information sources. Mobile telephones are especially transformative in developing economies, where many people access the Internet by phone. The number of smartphone users is more than four billion, and growing. Some 90% of people worldwide now live in range of cellular networks. Many countries, including numerous emerging markets, have made key investments in Internet technology. These include Belgium, Singapore, South Korea, and Sweden, as well as China, Qatar, Romania, and Thailand (Boston Consulting Group, 2015; Li et al., 2018; Sanou, 2018).

2.6   Artificial Intelligence (AI)

AI facilitates the simulation of human intelligence so that machinery and equipment operate and function much like humans, including the ability to learn and solve problems, all aimed at taking needed actions and achieving specific goals. A higher level of AI involves "machine learning," which refers to computer programs that automatically learn from and take action on new data, without human assistance. AI and machine learning have grown in sophistication due to advances in storage systems, processing speeds, problem analysis, and decision-making. AI functionality ranges from performing simple activities that are single-task oriented to complex activities that entail multiple, complex tasks. Firms may develop algorithms within AI programs that can complete a wide range of tasks (Finlay, 2018; McKinsey & Company., 2020; Morikawa, 2017).

Examples of machines that employ AI include computers that manage supply chains, organize various tasks in a manufacturing process, and undertake complex decision-making in areas like finance, healthcare, and management. AI can substitute for humans in the performance of many functions all along the value chain, along the range of R&D, market research, procurement, manufacturing, marketing and customer interaction, distribution, and technical support. In various ways, AI can support company value chain activities in operations worldwide, particularly in situations where human labor is scarce, costly, or not sufficiently able to undertake needed tasks. When combined with big data, AI provides the means to rationalize operations and analyze consumer characteristics and trends (Finlay, 2018; McKinsey & Company., 2020).

2.7   Robotics

Closely related to AI is robotics, which reflects the design, creation, and use of machines to perform tasks historically done by humans. Robots are widely used in industry to perform repetitive or hazardous tasks. Robotics is increasingly integrated with AI. Many robots incorporate human-like senses, including vision, touch, and the ability to sense temperature, and many can undertake simple decision-making. The most sophisticated robots assimilate data and respond to new information so that they improve their operations continuously (International Federation of Robotics, 2018; Smids et al., 2020). Top areas that are benefiting from robotics include healthcare, defense, public safety, mining, and automotive, as well as various other manufacturing industries. South Korea, Singapore, Germany, Japan, Sweden, and the United States are leading the way in the installation of robots to perform manufacturing and other productive activities (International Federation of Robotics, 2018; Zinser et al., 2015).

New-generation robots collaborate with humans to perform non-routine and cognitive tasks. The potential application and use of robots is broadening, and managers increasingly will work with robots. Robots generate substantial cost savings, increased efficiency, superior outcomes, and productivity in regions or fields characterized by insufficient workers (Autor, 2015). Robots can work without interruption, including 24 hours per day if needed. They do not require lighting, heating, or other ambient conditions needed for humans, which reduces energy usage. Robots perform highly precise and repeatable movements, which improves quality and reduces the need to correct errors. Many firms install robots to perform tasks that otherwise would be outsourced to countries with lower labor costs (International Federation of Robotics, 2018; Morikawa, 2017; Zinser et al., 2015). This tendency facilitates the ability to maintain manufacturing in developed economies like Europe, Japan, and North America with higher labor costs and helps companies remain sustainable and competitive (Zinser et al., 2015). Robots tend to replace lower-skills workers, but create jobs for managers and higher-skills workers. Robots enhance competitive advantages for large companies and SMEs alike (Autor, 2015; BBC, 2018).

2.8   Additive Manufacturing (AM)

AM, more commonly called "3D printing," refers to the use of digital designs in a printer in which liquid or powdered raw material is deposited in thin layers and fused together to create physical objects (Hannibal & Knight, 2018). Manufacturing via AM is relatively slow compared to traditional mass production, but in other ways, the technology provides numerous advantages. For instance, firms can decouple their downstream activities from upstream activities, thus leading to cost savings and better coordination of activities across value chains. AM is expected to increase mass customization and affect the structure of manufacturing around the world, with a growing ability to produce goods more locally, as well as enabling firms to vertically organize their value chain activities (Ben-Ner & Siemsen, 2017; Berman, 2012; D'Aveni, 2013). With the growing availability of appropriate materials, AM now has applications in nearly every industry that produces or benefits from physical products.

AM is facilitating the localization of production (Hannibal & Knight, 2018; Laplume et al., 2016). For example, by using household 3D printers, individuals could produce their own basic home appliances and other tools, spare parts for household needs, certain types of apparel, or other products characterized by relatively high transportation costs, time sensitivity, and demand. City- or region-based print facilities could supply larger and more complex items, replacing the need to import such goods from abroad (D'Aveni, 2013; Hannibal & Knight, 2018).

The aggregate effect of AM likely will be to increase the efficiency or effectiveness of goods production, by producing goods more effectively and in a more customized or desirable form, using a more efficient supply chain of design, raw materials, and final production (Laplume et al., 2016). The full potential of AM can be realized by combining it with other industry 4.0 technologies. Widespread adoption of AM likely will provide substantial economic and competitive advantages in a wide range of fields (Hannibal & Knight, 2018).

2.9   Digital Platforms

Digital platforms refer to app- or software-based online infrastructure that enables transactions among users. Some digital platforms help users manage and navigate large amounts of information (e.g., Google, Yahoo, LinkedIn). Other platforms function as "matchmakers," facilitating transactions among users (e.g., Amazon, Alibaba, Yandex) (Matzler et al., 2015; Sutherland & Jarrahi, 2018).

Emerging technologies have played an important role in the development of the platform economy. Advancements in digital technologies facilitate the connection of sellers and buyers via multi-sided platforms that are spread across the globe (Matzler et al., 2015; McKinsey Global Institute, 2016). Many digital platforms combine various features, such as when social media enable both information search and matchmaking between users. Digital platforms can be relatively decentralized, and not tied to any particular country (Sutherland & Jarrahi, 2018). The effect of digital technologies on business has been revolutionary. The cost of computer and digital processing has fallen by more than 30% annually in recent decades and continues to fall (McKinsey Global Institute, 2016). Digital platforms facilitate multisided markets and generate direct and indirect network economies by connecting diverse actors to central platforms (Evans & Gawer, 2016; Evans & Schmalensee, 2016; Zeng et al., 2019). Digital platforms have created a winner-take-all phenomenon (Galbraith, 1995), where a platform with a large number of participants tip the market in its favor (Eisenmann et al., 2006). Digital platforms also perform regulatory functions by setting entry rules and transaction mechanisms for network members (e.g., Boudreau & Hagiu, 2009).

Digital platforms create competitive advantages by giving companies new ways to outperform rivals (Sutherland & Jarrahi, 2018). The platforms provide disproportionate benefits to smaller firms, allowing them to market their products and services across the world (cf. Zeng et al., 2021). Internally-used digital platforms enable firms to interact with foreign partners and value-chain members efficiently and effectively, giving rise to important productivity gains. Digital flows of information and commerce are connecting the world in unprecedented ways. The platforms and related applications facilitate international buying and selling of goods and services (Evans & Gawer, 2016). For example, sharing-economy firms such as Uber and Airbnb use specialized apps and the Internet to facilitate the joint creation of value and services between asset owners and asset users. Worldwide, Uber allows people who need temporary transportation to hire drivers and vehicles owned by others. Airbnb allows travelers to rent other people's homes. Such sharing economy platforms allow a large number of complementors to participate and create value within the ecosystem and are emerging on a global scale as a new form of organization (Matzler et al., 2015; McKinsey Global Institute, 2016). By providing complementary products and services, the complementors are essentially shifting the innovation and production processes outside the firm's boundaries to the level of network partners. A vast amount of data is also created and shared on buyers and sellers connected through platforms, which enable firms to drive significant value by leveraging big data (Eisenmann et al., 2011; Evans & Gawer, 2016; Zeng et al., 2021).

3   Discussion and Implications

In various ways, the technologies examined in this chapter hold important implications for both theory and practice.

3.1   Theoretical Implications

Emergent technologies will enhance the broader performance of MNEs. They are improving coordination and knowledge-sharing across network partners and reducing traditional costs and barriers associated with manufacturing, distribution, logistics, and other such activities. Emergent technologies will substantially affect the value chain activities of MNEs. For instance, analytics, blockchain, 5G, IoT, AI, robotics, and digital platforms will increase productivity and the efficiency of manufacturing. In various ways, the technologies can reduce the benefits long associated with locating productive activities in countries that feature lower labor costs, superior productivity, and other advantages. Efficiencies and falling production costs will justify locating manufacturing in more developed economies. For example, the use of robots has reduced the costs of manufacturing and invigorated industrial production in Germany and Japan (e.g., Ranasinghe, 2015; Zinser et al., 2015). AM is shifting the nature and pattern of production in almost every industry (Ben-Ner & Siemsen, 2017; Hannibal & Knight, 2018).

In these and other ways, current technological trends hold implications for traditional views on the global production ecosystem. Shifts underway may necessitate enhancements to extant views on the "global factory" (e.g., Buckley, 2009b) and related explanations on international production (e.g., Dunning, 1981). Firms that embrace emergent technologies are obtaining increased monopolistic and firm-specific advantages, while simultaneously, some traditional location-specific advantages are declining (cf. Dunning, 1981; Hymer). MNEs that embrace the new technologies will need to acquire specific capabilities that facilitate performance-enhancing management of production, sourcing, and related activities.

In various ways, recent developments highlight the emergence of "disruptive technologies" (Christensen, 1997)—technical advances that promote industrial growth through the introduction of methods, products, and services that are cheaper, better, or more expedient than those available previously (Kostoff et al., 2004). For example, the rise of digital platforms is triggering the emergence of new industries and redefining existing industries. Amazon, Spotify, and similar firms reflect the rise of new business models that are challenging the extant paradigm in retailing.

The emergence of revolutionary technologies can be examined within the technology acceptance model (TAM; Davis, 1986, 1989), which explains how nation-level technological sophistication, as well as societal and human-level factors, affect the acceptance of new technologies. Available knowledge, experience, and resources in individual countries will affect the capacity to adopt and exploit new era technologies (Davis, 1989). While developed economies are likely to perform well in new technology acceptance, developing economies may experience lower average levels of connectedness and technological development, and also lack critical skills in creating value through emerging technologies. In the public policy realm, action will be needed to reduce the "digital divide," to help developing economies adopt and utilize the latest technologies. Alongside the usual advantages that technology brings, countries that adopt leading technologies will be better positioned to integrate more efficiently into international flows of information and trade.

3.2   Practical Implications

In large part due to emergent technologies described in this chapter, the nature of international business, country-based business models, and indeed national borders themselves are evolving rapidly. The cost of transmitting and handling data and information globally has fallen to essentially zero. Companies now enjoy a much greater ability to interact, collaborate, obtain, and utilize information worldwide than ever before. Technologies are facilitating the codification and sharing of knowledge on a global scale. Companies are profiting from substantially lower costs of international interactions and transactions. Digital tools are improving the effectiveness of value chains worldwide. Technologies are reducing the costs of logistics and transportation. The Internet facilitates the ability to find new opportunities worldwide, and e-commerce is driving global buying and selling.

New technologies are increasing the productivity of local manufacturing. This tendency reduces firms' cost of domestic operations and increases the attractiveness of homegrown, local manufacturing (UNCTAD, 2019). Technological breakthroughs in IoT, artificial intelligence, robotics, and AM are blurring the lines between the physical and digital spheres. Novel technologies signal a new era in global production because they portend the digitalization of many physical goods. AM technology is altering the pattern of global production. Thanks to AM and technologies that facilitate automation, much manufacturing is "de-globalizing" and shifting away from China, Mexico, Eastern Europe, and other historically popular locations characterized by low-cost labor. Digital distribution and increasingly localized manufacturing of physical goods are bringing production closer to the end-user. AM technology is likely to engender smaller-scale production organized at the level of individual countries, municipalities, and even individual households. The rise of AM will push firms to rethink planning and strategy on the configuration and coordination of value chains (Hannibal & Knight, 2018; Strange & Zucchella, 2017), and necessitate novel thinking and new business models on the development, organization, and management of company value chains. Such shifts likely will engender a revolution in production and consumption, perhaps similar to transformations that ensued from the industrial revolution.

Digital technologies are boosting the efficiency and growth of international trade in services, which is growing faster than that of trade in merchandise. Blockchain, 5G, IoT, and digital platforms have been especially instrumental in this trend. For example, 5G wireless networks are accelerating the delivery of services as well as the repair and maintenance of machinery from remote locations. One interesting outcome is the free movement, at zero cost, of various digital services, such as email and social media. Wikipedia is a widely used information source worldwide and provides such services for free. Every day, worldwide millions of consumers access songs and playlists on Spotify. Facebook provides free services to billions of users. Historically, most services had to be delivered in person by local suppliers. That trend is shifting where various services—including insurance, banking and finance, media, and professional services—are now provided globally on a massive scale. India and several other countries provide medical transcription, healthcare, technical support, accounting, engineering, and various back-office services via the Internet. Digital platforms and 5G are playing a key role.

The intersection of digital technologies with international business is shifting the structure of global trade. From Africa to Asia to Latin America, as people become digitally connected, they consume more international services. Retailing has been revolutionized by giant digital platform firms that sell their offerings worldwide through online sites and drive enormous value through direct and indirect network effects. Retailing is increasingly dominated by digital platform companies. The national origin of major players—Alibaba, Amazon, eBay, Jingdong, Rakuten, and Suning—holds less relevance today than that of earlier, large brick-and-mortar retailers.

New technologies are also affecting logistics and transportation. For example, IoT increases the efficiency of goods delivery through advanced shipment tracking and inventory management. AI improves transportation efficiency by optimizing trucking, rail, and even ocean shipments. Automated document processing accelerates the passage of goods through customs. Blockchain is reducing transit times and accelerating international payments. Relatedly, robotics, AM, IoT, AI, blockchain, and digital platforms are reducing barriers of complexity and distance in supply chains worldwide. The collective effect of various technologies on logistics and transportation could increase overall merchandise trade in the coming decade.

Some technologies—especially big data, analytics, and blockchain—are facilitating greater transparency in value chain activities. For example, companies like RiskWatch International and Red Canary leverage such technologies to provide services to analyze and alert firms about emergent or potential risks in supply chains, distribution channels, and other value-chain functions. Blockchain can resolve challenges facing firms that engage in exporting related to information asymmetry between buyers and suppliers. Information asymmetries present in typical international buyer–seller transactions increase risk and arise in the areas of payment, accounting, and logistics, among others. Buyers and sellers typically reside in different legal jurisdictions, which complicates the resolution of contractual conflicts. Blockchain can address such issues by reducing information asymmetries while eliminating redundant intermediaries in the exporting process.

Other technologies, such as AI, robotics, and AM, are lowering the cost of manufacturing in ways that are shifting the locus and pattern of global production. Such technologies make manufacturing in developed economies like Japan, Europe, and North America viable again. For example, by allowing many goods to be produced on site, additive manufacturing is reducing the need to import various products. Various goods, such as music and books, that were formerly produced in physical form, can now be streamed around the world using digital platforms. As automation and additive manufacturing reduce the costs of local production, manufacturing increasingly will be relocated near key consumer markets worldwide. Such technologies are likely to shift the location of manufacturing for some goods and eliminate the need to manufacture others.

Many digital platform firms operate in highly dynamic industries that are undergoing massive change and technological disruption. Such firms gain substantial value through their base of users and complementors and are expanding operations across multiple industries and geographies (Eisenmann et al., 2011). These firms are changing the dynamics of competition and value creation—they are shifting the rules of the game. Such trends represent a new era in international business in which commerce is conducted on a global scale with lower cost and better coordination, while leveraging the assets and capabilities of complementors and other participants. Much can be learned from the global operations of digital platforms and their mechanisms for value capture and creation.

A key challenge relates to how firms will respond to all the emergent changes. Technological advances are occurring faster than firms can comprehend, manage, or profit from. Organizations that adopt and master the latest technology gain competitive advantages over rivals—firms need to develop and implement planning aimed at maximizing their uptake and utilization of the most relevant technologies.

Most of the technologies highlighted in this chapter relate to the management and use of information. Big data, smart analytics, blockchain, IoT, AI, and digital platforms all refer to the management and leveraging of information and knowledge. Firms need to incorporate analytics and data-driven insights into their day-to-day processes and activities. All along the value chain—R&D, product design, supply chain, manufacturing, marketing and sales, distribution, finance, and general decision-making—enormous gains can be won from developing advanced analytical capabilities. Skillful management of information translates into various competitive advantages arising from enhanced innovation, market targeting, capacity to customize products and services, added-value of offerings, supply chain management, and productivity, as well as increased transparency of governance and operations. Superior capabilities in the latest technologies foretell countless opportunities to market products and services around the world, targeting consumers, firms, and governments.

3.3   Implementing Strategy

Initially, implementing an appropriate strategy for embracing and exploiting the new technologies requires a strategic vision. Senior management must take steps to create a digital culture across the organization, through such initiatives as investing in the latest technologies, recruiting digital talent, and embedding Industry 4.0 in organizational processes. The most successful firms will possess an action orientation and technological competency. They will co-opt solutions with partners and customers. The path forward will come with challenges. Various factors will impede the adoption of key technologies on a global scale. Initially, infrastructure and capabilities vary substantially by country. For example, a lack of skills impedes Internet access, especially in developing economies. Few countries possess a substantial cadre of workers skilled in smart analytics. Experience, knowledge, and other human factors affect acceptance and facility with new technologies. MNEs may struggle to implant the latest systems in countries characterized by inadequate skills and lower technological development.

Many technologies are tinged with controversy. Adopting the latest systems will provoke resistance. In manufacturing and other productive activities, automation, robotics, and AI are associated with job loss. For example, McDonald's is installing digital kiosks to take food orders, leading to job loss in the restaurant industry. The auto industry has embraced robots to perform many productive tasks. Just as occurred in earlier technological revolutions, there will be significant shifts in the nature and location of jobs. In most cases, however, the adoption of automation, AI, robotics, and related technologies mainly affects lower-skill jobs and less-educated workers. Historical experience reveals that such technologies will not make humans redundant. Earlier industrial revolutions were disruptive too but resulted in countless new, higher-quality jobs. Consistent with the "creative destruction" view (Schumpeter, 1975), new industries will be created, leading to new and better jobs. For example, the invention of the automobile eliminated the carriage industry; the rise of personal computers wiped out the typewriter industry; video streaming technology terminated the DVD player, which itself had eliminated the VCR.

Education holds perhaps the greatest potential to provide a path forward. Many schools are developing new curricula to educate the workers of tomorrow. The jobs least vulnerable to automation and digitalization include creative or technical positions or jobs that require interpersonal skills and emotional intelligence. Education, especially in key fields, can insulate workers from threat of job loss.

In terms of manufacturing strategy, managers may need to re-evaluate and revise established models of international production. De-globalization of production arising from AM and increased automation, for example, suggests how much production can be re-located to more developed economies characterized by higher, human-based production costs. Firms are achieving better control over supply chains. Labor productivity is rising. In some ways, the technologies are making developed economies (characterized by relatively costly labor) viable again as production platforms. The technologies are also helping to mitigate rising average age and demographic trends in which the proportion of productive workers in some countries is falling.

Firms need to leverage the new technologies to enhance innovativeness and innovation capabilities. Managers need to make key technologies central to organizational architecture, strategy development, and processes. AI, robotics, and IoT in particular serve to improve the efficiency of processes and routine activities, and help make firms become more agile and flexible. Management needs to leverage the new technologies to increase the benefits of the firm's offerings and enhance the organizational value proposition. Firms need to be proactive and entrepreneurial to embrace Industry 4.0 and manage rapid technological change.

The rise of new technologies heralds a new, exciting era in strategy and management related to global value chains. Identifying, understanding, and seizing the opportunities associated with such shifts will be key to organizational performance, especially among MNEs. Managers need to undertake planning and develop appropriate strategies to leverage revolutionary technological developments. Skillful adoption and use of the latest technologies, alongside associated firm-level innovations, should provide important competitive advantages. Advanced preparation is needed by conducting appropriate research to decide which technologies to adopt, and how best to integrate them in company operations. Technology acquisition is beneficial when the firm invests through its value chain to improve various organizational activities.

3.4   Conclusion

Technological advances are increasing the pace of globalization. International trade has become more efficient. Emergent technologies can reduce country risk by increasing transparency, access to information, and the ability to coordinate, control, and monitor global operations. The technologies are reducing the transaction costs of international business and making internationalization easier for all firms. Companies are enjoying greater control and flexibility of international operations by connecting with the digital ecosystem. Emergent technologies and the rapid pace of change are disrupting business models. Innovation is transforming lifestyles, organizations, and nature of competition. The rise of the connected ecosystem presents enormous new opportunities. The implications of the new technologies are as significant as the invention of electricity or development of the modern containerized shipping. In both cases, globalization and international business experienced major structural shifts, leading to the emergence of huge opportunities that propelled early adopters to leadership positions in their respective fields. Such major technology can shift the trajectory of the world economy, by driving new business models and positive societal evolution.

References

Almutairi, H. (2007). Is the 'technology acceptance model' universally applicable? The case of the Kuwaiti ministries. *Journal of Global Information Technology Management, 10*, 57–80.

Arner, D., Barberis, J., & Buckley, R. (2016). 150 years of Fintech: An evolutionary analysis. *Jassa: The Finsia Journal of Applied Finance, 3*, 22–29.

Autor, D. (2015). Why are there still so many jobs? The history and future of workplace automation. *Journal of Economic Perspectives, 29*(3), 3–30.

Barakabitze, A., Ahmad, A., Mijumbi, R., & Hines, A. (2020). 5G network slicing using SDN and NFV: A survey of taxonomy, architectures and future challenges. *Computer Networks, 167*, 106984–107024.

BBC. (2018, September 17). WEF: Robots 'will create more jobs than they displace'. *BBC*. https://www.bbc.com/news/business-45545228.

Ben-Ner, A., & Siemsen, E. (2017). Decentralization and localization of production: The organizational and economic consequences of additive manufacturing (3D printing). *California Management Review, 59*, 5–23.

Berman, B. (2012). 3-D printing: The new industrial revolution. *Business Horizons, 55*, 155–162.

Boston Consulting Group. (2015, March 20). The mobile internet takes off everywhere. *BCG Perspectives*. www.bcgperspectives.com.

Boudreau, K., & Hagiu, A. (2009). *Platform rules: Regulation of an ecosystem by a private actor. Platforms, markets and innovation.* Edward Elgar Publishing.

Buckley, P. (2009a). The impact of the global factory on economic development. *Journal of World Business, 44*(2), 131–143.

Buckley, P. (2009b). Internalisation thinking: From the multinational enterprise to the global factory. *International Business Review, 18*(3), 224–235.

Cai, L., & Zhu, Y. (2015). The challenges of data quality and data quality assessment in the big data era. *Data Science Journal, 14*(2), 1–10.

Chase-Dunn, C., Kawano, Y., & Brewer, B. (2000). World globalization since 1795: Waves of integration in the world-system. *American Sociological Review, 65*(1), 77–95.

Chen, H., Chiang, R., & Storey, V. (2012). Business intelligence and analytics: From big data to big impact. *MIS Quarterly, 36*(4), 1165–1188.

Christensen, C. (1997). *The innovator's dilemma: When new technologies cause great firms to fail.* Harvard Business Review Press.

D'Aveni, R. (2013). 3D printing will change the world. *Harvard Business Review, 91*, 22–22.

Davis, F. (1986). *A technology acceptance model for empirically testing new end-user information systems: Theory and results.* Massachusetts Institute of Technology.

Davis, F. (1989). Perceived usefulness, perceived ease of use, and user acceptance of information technology. *MIS Quarterly, 13*, 319–340.

Dinh, T., Liu, R., Zhang, M., Chen, G., Ooi, B., & Wang, J. (2018). Untangling blockchain: A data processing view of blockchain systems. *IEEE Transactions on Knowledge and Data Engineering, 30*(7), 1366–1385.

Dunning, J. (1981). *International production and the multinational enterprise.* Allen & Unwin.

Eisenmann, T., Geoffrey, P., & Van Alstyne, M. (2011). Platform envelopment. *Strategic Management Journal, 32*(12), 1270–1285.

Eisenmann, T., Parker, G., & Van Alstyne, M. W. (2006). Strategies for two-sided markets. *Harvard Business Review, 84*(10), 92–101.

Evans, P., & Gawer, A. (2016). *The rise of the platform enterprise: A global survey.* The Center for Global Enterprise.

Evans, D. S., & Schmalensee, R. (2016). *Matchmakers: The new economics of multisided platforms.* Harvard Business Review Press.

Finlay, S. (2018). *Artificial intelligence and machine learning for business.* Relativistic.

Galbraith, J. K. (1995). The winner takes all. . . sometimes. *Harvard Business Review, 73*(6), 44–45.

George, G., Osinga, E., Lavie, D., & Scott, B. (2016). Big data and data science methods for management research. *Academy of Management Journal, 59*(5), 1493–1507.

Gupta, M., & George, J. F. (2016). Toward the development of a big data analytics capability. *Information and Management, 53*(8), 1049–1064.

Hannibal, M., & Knight, G. (2018). Additive manufacturing and the global factory: Disruptive technologies and the location of international business. *International Business Review, 27*(6), 116–127.

Hymer, S. (1976). *The international operations of National Firms.* MIT Press.

International Federation of Robotics. (2018, October 18). Welcome to the IFR press conference, 2018, Tokyo. www.ifr.org.

Internet World Stats. (2021). *World internet usage and population statistics.* Accessed July 28, 2021, from www.internetworldstats.com/stats.htm

Kostoff, R., Boylan, R., & Simons, G. (2004). Disruptive technology roadmaps. *Technological Forecasting and Social Change, 71*, 141–159.

Lai, V. S., & Li, H. (2005). Technology acceptance model for internet banking: An invariance analysis. *Information & Management, 42*(2), 373–386.

Laplume, A. O., Petersen, B., & Pearce, J. (2016). Global value chains from a 3D printing perspective. *Journal of International Business Studies, 47*, 595–609.

Li, S., Xu, L., & Zhao, S. (2018). 5G internet of things: A survey. *Journal of Industrial Information Integration, 10*, 1–9.

Loop, P. (2017, January 13). Blockchain: The next evolution of supply chains. *Industry Week.* www.industryweek.com/supply-chain/blockchain-next-evolution-supply-chains.

Lund, S., Manyika, J., Woetzel, J., Bughin, J., Krishnan, M., Seong, J., & Muir, M. (2019). *Globalization in transition: The future of trade and value chains.* McKinsey & Company: McKinsey Global Institute. www.mckinsey.com/mgi

Matzler, K., Veider, V., & Kathan, W. (2015). Adapting to the sharing economy. *MIT Sloan Management Review, 56*(2), 71–82.

McCoy, S., Galletta, D., & King, W. (2007). Applying TAM across cultures: The need for caution. *European Journal of Information Systems, 16*, 81–90.

McKinsey & Company. (2020, November 17). *The state of AI in 2020.* www.mckinsey.com.

McKinsey Global Institute. (2016). *Digital globalization: The new era of global flows.* www. mckinsey.com.

Morikawa, M. (2017). Firms' expectations about the impact of AI and robotics: Evidence from a survey. *Economic Inquiry, 55*(2), 1054–1063.

Mudambi, R. (2008). Location, control and innovation in knowledge-intensive industries. *Journal of Economic Geography, 8*(5), 699–725.

Mulligan, C., Northcote, N., Röder, T., & Vesuvala, S. (2021, April 26). The strategy-analytics revolution. *McKinsey & Company.* www.mckinsey.com.

Ranasinghe, D. (2015, April 14). Robots: The new low-cost worker. *CNBC.* www.cnbc.com.

Roth, K., & Morrison, A. (1990). An empirical analysis of the integration-responsiveness framework in global industries. *Journal of International Business Studies, 21,* 541–564.

Rugman, A. (1980). Internalization as a general theory of foreign direct investment: A re-appraisal of the literature. *Review of World Economics, 116,* 365–379.

Sanou, B. (2018). *Measuring the information society report 2018.* International Telecommunication Union.

Schumpeter, J. (1975). *Capitalism, socialism and democracy.* Harper.

Schwab, K. (2016. The fourth industrial revolution: What it means, how to respond. *World Economic Forum.* www.weforum.org.

Shafique, K., Khawaja, B., Sabir, F., Qazi, S., & Mustaqim, M. (2020). Internet of things (IoT) for next-generation smart systems: A review of current challenges, future trends and prospects for emerging 5G-IoT scenarios. *IEEEAccess, 8,* 23022–23040.

Sheng, J., Amankwah-Amoah, J., Khan, Z., & Wang, X. (2020). COVID-19 pandemic in the new era of big data analytics: Methodological innovations and future research directions. *British Journal of Management.* in press.

Singh, N., Fassott, G., Chao, M., & Hoffmann, J. (2006). Understanding international web site usage: A cross-national study of German, Brazilian, and Taiwanese online consumers. *International Marketing Review, 23,* 83–97.

Smids, J., Nyholm, S., & Berkers, H. (2020). Robots in the workplace: A threat to—Or opportunity for—Meaningful work? *Philosophy & Technology, 33,* 503–522.

Strange, R., & Zucchella, A. (2017). Industry 4.0, global value chains and international business. *Multinational Business Review, 25*(3), 174–184.

Sutherland, W., & Jarrahi, M. (2018). The sharing economy and digital platforms: A review and research agenda. *International Journal of Information Management, 43,* 328–341.

Tallman, S., & Fladmoe-Lindquist, K. (2002). Internationalization, globalization, and capability-based strategy. *California Management Review, 45*(1), 116–135.

Tambe, P. (2014). Big data investment, skills, and firm value. *Management Science, 60*(6), 1452–1469.

Teece, D. (2014). A dynamic capabilities-based entrepreneurial theory of the multinational enterprise. *Journal of International Business Studies, 45,* 8–37.

UNCTAD. (2019). *World investment report 2019.* United Nations Conference on Trade and Development. www.unctad.org

Venkatesh, V., & Davis, F. (2000). A theoretical extension of the technology acceptance model: Four longitudinal field studies. *Management Science, 46,* 186–204.

Yamin, M., & Sinkovics, R. (2010). ICT deployment and resource-based power in multinational enterprise futures. *The Futures of International Business, 42*(9), 952–959.

Yli-Huumo, J., Ko, D., Choi, S., Park, S., & Smolander, K. (2016). Where is current research on blockchain technology?—A systematic review. *PLoS One, 11*(10), e0163477.

Zeng, J., Khan, Z., & De Silva, M. (2019). The emergence of multi-sided platform MNEs: Internalization theory and networks. *International Business Review, 28*(6), 101598.

Zeng, J., Tavalaei, M. M., & Khan, Z. (2021). Sharing economy platform firms and their resource orchestration approaches. *Journal of Business Research, 136,* 451–465.

Zinser, M., Rose, J., & Sirkin, H. (2015, September 23). The robotics revolution: The next great leap in manufacturing. *Boston Consulting Group.* www.bcg.com.

Gary Knight is Professor and Helen Jackson Chair of International Management in the Atkinson Graduate School of Management, Willamette University, Salem and Portland, Oregon, USA. He is a Fellow of the Academy of International Business, in which he also served as Vice President during 2019–2022.

Zaheer Khan is a Professor in Strategy & International Business and Founding Director of Africa-Asia Centre for Sustainability Research at the University of Aberdeen, UK. He is an elected Fellow of the Academy of Social Sciences. His research focuses on global technology management, international alliances, and emerging markets' firms. His works have appeared in the Journal of International Business Studies, Journal of World Business, Global Strategy Journal, Management International Review, Human Relations, and Journal of Corporate Finance, among others.

The Future of Global Work: Challenges and Recommendations for Global Virtual Teamwork

Tobias Blay and Fabian Jintae Froese

1 Introduction

In the past few decades, organizations have expanded their operations overseas, including establishing foreign subsidiaries. To manage their foreign subsidiaries, multinational enterprises (MNEs) have increasingly used expatriates (Bebenroth & Froese, 2020). In response to this trend, the importance of expatriation has increased accordingly within international business research (e.g., Bhaskar-Shrinivas et al., 2005; Froese et al., 2021; Stoermer et al., 2021). Prior research has often explored the reasons behind expatriate success (for a review, see: Bhaskar-Shrinivas et al., 2005), and established that it is important to consider the expatriation cycle's different stages; from pre-assignment preparation, the actual international assignment, and their repatriation (Bonache et al., 2020). For instance, careful selection and training is of particular importance in the preparation stage (Kim & Froese, 2012), while organizational support is especially relevant during and after the expatriation (e.g. Froese et al., 2021).

Globalization has demanded various types of global work during the past few decades outside of the aforementioned expatriation within MNEs. Shaffer et al. (2012) have developed a sophisticated taxonomy of global work. The matrix describes five different types of global work experience and their relationship according to the dimensions of physical mobility (e.g., physical cross-border mobility), cognitive flexibility (adaption to, e.g., foreign cultures), and non-work disruption (disruption or interference of work role requirements with employee's outside of work activities). First, self-initiated or corporate expatriates relocate to a foreign country to work and live there permanently or at least for an extended period of time (usually with their family members) (Froese & Peltokorpi, 2013; Stoermer et al., 2020). They have high cognitive flexibility, high physical mobility, and moderate

T. Blay · F. J. Froese (✉)
University of Goettingen, Goettingen, Germany
e-mail: tobiasludwiggerhard.blay@uni-goettingen.de; ffroese@uni-goettingen.de

© Springer Nature Switzerland AG 2022
H. Merchant (ed.), *The New Frontiers of International Business*, Contributions to Management Science, https://doi.org/10.1007/978-3-031-06003-8_11

non-work disruption. Second, short-term assignees maintain a temporary residence abroad, as their assignment is often project-specific or limited in time (Brewster et al., 2020). Their adaption to the foreign culture is less pronounced and their families do not normally relocate with them (i.e., low cognitive flexibility, high physical mobility, and non-work disruption). Third, international business travelers and flexpatriates spend few weeks or months in the foreign country and are characterized by a high level of physical mobility (Brewster et al., 2020). Both require a relatively high level of cognitive flexibility and a high degree of non-work disruption (due to a high adaption to foreign cultures because of a second residence and a greater separation from their family) but it should be noted that there exists a nuanced difference between the two types. Fourth, global domestics rarely travel overseas and often use technologies to interact with various stakeholders (low physical mobility). Hence, their cognitive flexibility as well as their non-work disruption are developed at a lower level. The fifth form of global work is characterized as global virtual teams (GVT) (Shaffer et al., 2012; Taras et al., 2019). Its members communicate exclusively through electronic information and collaboration tools, are geographically distributed (often across countries or continents) and work on (inter)dependent organizational tasks to achieve a common goal (Maznevski et al., 2006). As stated by Shaffer et al. (2012), they do not travel to foreign countries (therefore no physical mobility) but have to be cognitively flexible due to a high level of interactions with foreign cultures. Due to time differences, GVT attend conference calls outside of working hours, which increases their non-work disruption. GVT are therefore challenged by multiple indicators (Shaffer et al., 2012) that can affect the performance.

Work processes' increasing globalization and decentralization, along with a dynamic environment and exponential growth of digital interaction and collaboration technologies have reduced the necessity of physical relocation as well as the first three types of global work. However, global work remains important, irrespective of the increasing deployment of collaboration technologies within organizations. Additionally, environmental changes, such as the COVID-19 pandemic, have even accelerated the trend toward "going digital" within fully virtual teams instead of meeting face to face (Culture Wizard, 2020). According to a Deloitte Study, 70% of the executives surveyed expect an increased usage of online collaboration platforms in the future, as physical meetings lose out to many forms of purely digital cooperation (Agarwal et al., 2018), and 89% of executives working for MNEs stated that they work in at least one (global) virtual team. Also, nearly 90% of the respondents confirmed, that GVT work is critical to their respective productivity (Culture Wizard, 2018).

Examined together, the trend toward increased global work in the form of GVT is inevitable. Curiously, however, while abundant research has been devoted to expatriation (e.g. Bhaskar-Shrinivas et al., 2005; Bonache et al., 2020), i.e., the first three types of global work, GVT remains an underexplored research area. This chapter will seek to increase our collective understanding of GVT and provide thought-provoking ideas for future GVT research and practice. To that end, we will provide an overview of GVT and discuss typical challenges GVT workers face in the following section, followed by key topics for future research and practice. We will end this chapter with a summary of key findings and implications.

2   The Main Dimensions of Global Virtual Teamwork

In this section, we will provide a comparative review for understanding GVT's main dimensions within the broader context of international business. We (1) identify key aspects of global virtual teamwork, (2) review their importance for international business, (3) and discuss challenges.

GVT can be classified by several main dimensions. Many researchers emphasize the importance of virtuality in this special form of team collaboration (de Guinea et al., 2012). The two most frequently used dimensions in this context are (geographical) dispersion and the utilization of technology (Cohen & Gibson, 2003). While the latter emphasizes the technological context and technology dependence (e.g., value and type) of virtual team members, (geographical) dispersion focuses on the existence of subgroups in the virtual team environment. Subgroups can arise from different factors, such as temporality (time-zone differences), diversity of the team members' characteristics (e.g., cultural, demographics) or a team member's residential location (Jarman, 2005). In the remainder of this chapter, we would seek to give a brief introduction to these two main dimensions of global teamwork virtuality and to highlight their most relevant characteristics in the context of international business. Figure 1 summarizes and combines the dimensions of virtuality and their characteristics.

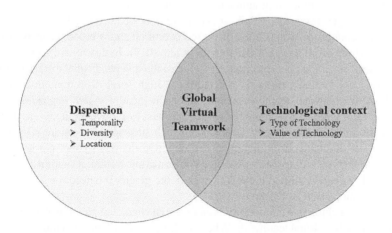

Fig. 1 Dimensions of Global Virtual Teamwork. Source: Authors' own figure derived from de Guinea et al. (2012), Cohen and Gibson (2003), Jarman (2005), Raghuram et al. (2019)

2.1   Dispersion

Dispersion calls attention to different types of distances between the virtual work arrangement and the team members. One characteristic of dispersion is the temporal distribution of virtual team workers (e.g., O'Leary & Cummings, 2007). Therefore, we highlight Temporality as the first characteristic of dispersion in the context of global virtual teamwork followed by Diversity and Location.

2.2   Temporality

Temporality or temporal dispersion in GVT occurs when there is no overlap of the regular working hours of team members. This normally occurs when virtual teams are distributed across different time zones. Since dealing with different time zones is common in an international business environment, it also occurs frequently in global teamwork scenarios. There is a consensus in virtual team literature that time dispersion increases conflicts, hinders intrateam collaborations, undermines the trust and commitment of virtual team members, and precludes team decision-making. One possible reason is that time zone differences cause communication delays and decelerate team coordination due to issues with information sharing (Raghuram et al., 2019) which may affect performance. It is a challenge for global virtual team members to develop and maintain social bonds within the team that connect tasks to individuals (Cramton & Webber, 2005). In summary, time zone differences are a major challenge when working globally in teams.

Since time zone differences represent a major boundary for the simultaneous processing of tasks, communication in GVT often occurs in a time-delayed manner. Team members, therefore, often rely on synchronous and asynchronous communication tools. While for synchronous communication media (e.g., telephone, video-conferencing) real-time communication is essential, asynchronous correspondence (e.g., messenger services, e-mail, social media) is characterized by a time lag. Therefore, communication is often dispersed over time and is based on an asynchronous exchange of information (Raghuram et al., 2019). In this regard, communication channel selection (asynchronous vs. synchronous) depends on the complexity of the task. Less complex tasks do not require a high level of communication and collaboration between team members. Since the need for interdependence and reciprocal communication cannot be reduced for tasks of low complexity, asynchronous communication is usually sufficient. In such situations, it is more effective to rely on non-simultaneous communication tools. On the other hand, the higher the level of collaborative decision-making or information exchange within the group (e.g., challenging, complex or dynamic tasks), the greater the need for synchronous communication (Bell & Kozlowski, 2002).

We can conclude that temporality is an essential characteristic of dispersion in the context of global virtual teamwork. When working in GVT, attention must be paid to time zone differences and the temporality of communication (asynchronous or synchronous). However, there are several other factors that characterize global virtual teamwork. One of these aforementioned characteristics is Diversity.

2.3   Diversity

A second dimension of dispersion in global virtual work teams is Diversity. It refers to the amount of distribution among the characteristics of team members. Diversity can be differentiated between personal and contextual Diversity. Personal Diversity refers to the personal perceptions or characteristics of global virtual team members (e.g., gender, age, personal values and cultural intelligence, etc.). Contextual Diversity describes the environmental characteristics and context in which the team members are embedded (e.g., economic and human situation/development, income equality, importance of religion, etc.) (Taras et al., 2019). In the international business context, personal Diversity is particularly relevant. The workforce of MNEs is often composed of a variety of cultural subgroups classified by religion, ethnicity, or other characteristics. It is therefore common that their (virtual) teams often consist of multicultural team members (Johnson et al., 2006). In particular, team members' norms and cultural values can therefore affect the relationships and interactions of team members (Raghuram et al., 2019). The majority of relevant literature is conflicted regarding whether Diversity has a positive or negative impact on the effectiveness of virtual teamwork. It is a complex construct that can be seen not just as a single factor, but in the context with other team constructs. Diversity, therefore, varies in terms of magnitude and direction in its relationship to team effectiveness (Taras et al., 2019). Irrespective, Diversity is a central characteristic of Dispersion in the context of global virtual teamwork.

2.4   Location

A third dimension of dispersion in the context of GVT is the team members' Location. It can be conceptualized as a configuration of team members (physical) locations or as their spatial separation. The locational dispersion and distribution of GVT members can be due to isolates and geographic subgroups. The latter describes teams in which their team members work in different locations. The location-based subgroups have no physical contact with one another. Isolates denotes individuals who work alone and are separated from their team members within a GVT (Raghuram et al., 2019). Although Location describes the physical presence in a particular environment, it also represents the context in which global virtual team members are embedded. The context of GVT can differ in terms of their administrative frameworks, their organizational affiliation, their social networks and norms or the cultural environment. Since team members of GVT often have little insights or a limited understanding of the locational context of their peers (Jimenez et al., 2017), it is challenging to execute complex tasks or to find a common denominator. This challenge becomes more pronounced when the social context of the Location (e.g. relocation, change of political context, etc.) of the team members changes (Jimenez et al., 2017).

In summary, the (physical) Location is a main characteristic in global virtual teamwork that has to be considered when working both globally and virtually. Despite the importance of factors related to Dispersion in GVT, Technology is another central dimension to consider when working in global virtual teams.

2.5   Technological Context

When working in global dispersed teams, team members must be connected via virtual tools to ensure communication and information exchange. GVT rely on communication technologies that meet the requirements and purpose of the task. Since virtual teamwork is technology-dependent, GVT need to figure out (1) what type of technology they should use when interacting and (2) identify the value of the communication tool chosen (Raghuram et al., 2019). In this regard, we break down technological context into two sections: Type of technology and its respective value. For this reason, we first identify the main types of technology that GVT use and then assess their value for effective global virtual teamwork.

2.6   Type of Technology

GVT use a wide range of communication types to interact with their team members. Research separates computer-mediated communication (CMC) tools into two types: Asynchronous communication technologies and synchronous communication technologies. Team members do not respond directly with asynchronous technologies. Communication, therefore, does not take place in real-time, but with a delay. Such communication channels can be e-mails, discussion forums, groupware (e.g., intranet, newsgroups, document sharing services) or websites (Bell & Kozlowski, 2002; Duranti & de Almeida, 2012). Groupware in particular is often used by team members to share documents or exchange information. Examples of those tools are Dropbox, Trello, Google Docs, Slack, Basecamp (Jimenez et al., 2017) or services provided by the employer.

Conversations with synchronous communication technologies occur in real time. Team members can instantly reply to their team members during live meetings. There are several categories of synchronous communication technologies where real-time conversation can occur. Tools that fulfill this purpose are messaging services (e.g. chats), teleconferences (with video and/or audio), or internet-based virtual meeting rooms (Bell & Kozlowski, 2002; Duranti & de Almeida, 2012) such as Zoom, Skype, or Google Hangouts. When thinking about the best type of communication technology, a mix of different types of communication technologies (asynchronous and synchronous) generates the highest team output. It helps to keep track of things while staying connected with team members without losing too much information about the work's progress (Accenture, 2020). We, therefore, conclude that the selection of the appropriate types of technology can be an asset when working in global virtual teams.

2.7 Value of Technology

When working virtually in a global team, knowing the different types of technologies is critical to team success. Since GVT have a high technology dependency (Raghuram et al., 2019), it is also important to know the value of the technology used during task work.

Task complexity is the main selection criterion to assess the value of the type of technology. Different communication tools add differing levels of value based upon their respective scope and purpose with regard to decision-making and information sharing (Duranti & de Almeida, 2012). Therefore, a high task-technology fit is associated with the selection of suitable communication tools in order to carry out organizational tasks virtually (Raghuram et al., 2019). Individual preferences and experiences are second criteria associated with the value of the communication tool. Having good experiences with the technology, individuals tend to rate a certain type of tool higher, which again increases the chance of use. Thus, the perceived value of the technology can depend on individual taste (Hollingshead et al., 1993). Another criterion for assessing the value of technology in global virtual teamwork is the media richness of a communication tool. The media richness theory (Daft et al., 1987) helps to understand how individuals can evaluate the value of technology in the context of GVT. There are three indicators to evaluate the functionality of a tool: Richness, interactivity, and social presence. Richness refers to the ability to communicate a particular stimulus (e.g., verbal and non-verbal) to provide an area of communication that enables fast shared understanding. Interactivity means the pace at which feedback can be exchanged. Social presence describes the perceived degree of proximity between the participants. Therefore, the higher all three indicators are, the better a virtual conversation can depict personal (e.g., face-to-face) communication (Daft et al., 1987).

In summary, identifying different types of technologies and their respective value for the team members is an important dimension and challenge for working globally in teams. In this section of the chapter, we wanted to provide an overview of the most important dimensions of global virtual teamwork (e.g., dispersion and technology context) and the challenges individuals face while working virtually. In order to understand future decisive implications for the aforementioned GVT dimensions, we will provide an outlook into the future of global virtual teamwork.

3 The Future of GVT Research and Practice

Having provided an overview of key characteristics and challenges of GVT, we will now provide an outlook of key topics for the future of GVT research and practice. We understand this chapter as an agenda for the "future of global (virtual)

Fig. 2 Dimensions of the
Future of Global Virtual Team
Research and Practice.
Source: Authors' own figure
derived from Johnson et al.
(2006), Makarius and Larson
(2017), Gilson et al. (2015),
Hill et al. (1998)

teamwork." Based on our review of the GVT and related literature, we identified three key topics for the future of GVT: (1) Developing Cultural and Virtual Intelligence, (2) New and Emerging Technologies, and (3) the Well-Being and Work–Life Balance of global virtual team members. We have summarized the key trends in Fig. 2 and describe them in the following sections.

3.1 Developing Global Virtual Teamwork Specific Forms of Intelligence

To succeed in the challenging work environment of GVT, workers need to possess and/or develop certain characteristics. Since this new form of work collaboration consists of two key elements, "globality" (e.g., cross-border and intercultural exchanges), and "virtuality" (e.g., no physical contact with team members) it is therefore important that the team members develop Cultural Intelligence (Johnson et al., 2006) as well as Virtual Intelligence (Makarius & Larson, 2017). We first introduce each concept and then describe how to develop Cultural Intelligence (CI) and Virtual Intelligence (VI) relevant in virtual international business contexts.

3.2 Developing Cultural Intelligence

Cultural Intelligence and Competence, defined as "an individual's effectiveness in drawing upon a set of knowledge, skills and personal attributes in order to work successfully with people from different national cultural backgrounds at home or abroad" (Johnson et al., 2006: 530), is particularly important when working globally (Froese et al., 2016; Stoermer et al., 2021). As the number of global teamwork interactions increases due to easier and faster access to cross-border meeting situations (e.g., virtual instead of face-to-face meetings) (Agarwal et al., 2018), a higher quantity of cross-cultural interactions is the result. GVT often meet with many people around the world. In order to work effectively with (team) members from different cultures, it is therefore critical to develop Cultural Intelligence and Competence (Johnson et al., 2006).

Thus, CI is a behavioral modification for effective (virtual) interactions with individuals from different cultures, regardless of whether the person interacts in their home or in a foreign culture (which is more the case in the context of international business). To demonstrate CI, the person must actively use the inter-cultural skills, attributes, and knowledge that they possess and apply them to the given circumstances (situation), which can sometimes be challenging (Johnson et al., 2006). However, when there is a high level of CI, individuals are more likely to perform better. Cultural Intelligence and Competence can be developed based on the three dimensions of knowledge, skills, personal attributes in international business (Johnson et al., 2006) in order to increase the quality of interactions in a global virtual teamwork environment.

The first dimension in developing CI is to gain cultural knowledge (Johnson et al., 2006). According to Hofstede (2001), cultural knowledge can be divided into culture-general knowledge and culture-specific knowledge. To develop CI in a virtual setting, both forms of knowledge should be considered. Cultural-general knowledge focuses on the knowledge and the awareness of cultural differences. It relates to the key components of culture, such as learning of cultural values and the complex environment of IB (e.g., political, legal, economic systems) or gaining an intercultural understanding (Johnson et al., 2006). To develop CI, individuals should be able to recognize environmental differences in their virtual team members are embedded during project work. Cultural-specific knowledge refers to the specific recognition/understanding of different cultures (e.g., information about laws, history, hygiene, politics, etc.). Cultural-specific training helps to learn cultural-specific knowledge (Johnson et al., 2006). A higher level of cultural-specific knowledge goes hand in hand with an increase in a culture-based memory system (Taylor, 1981). Therefore, it is important that individuals gain an adequate level of knowledge about the cultural characteristics of the virtual team members to reduce interpersonal tensions.

The second dimension to developing CI and cultural competences is the development of cultural skills. This behavioral component includes the acquisition of aptitudes and abilities (Johnson et al., 2006). Perceptual skills (e.g., learning from social experiences), relational skills (e.g. empathy, flexibility, sociability) and adaptive skills (e.g., ability to display a well- or quickly-developed behavior set) are types of skills (Thomas et al., 2008) that help to adapt to a different cultural environment. Since the cultural diversity can be much higher in virtual team meetings compared to cross-border face-to-face meetings, it is crucial for global virtual team worker to possess cultural skills.

The third dimension in developing cultural competences (e.g., CI) is to focus on the personal attributes (Johnson et al., 2006) of GVT members. Personal attributes include internalized values, beliefs, and norms, as well as personality traits such as loyalty, tolerance, or perseverance. Depending on whether they are present in the right amount, they can either hinder or support the development of CI. Nevertheless, they are the most important factor for individuals who work in a cross-cultural context (Johnson et al., 2006) as personality traits are often responsible for a change in team functioning (Molleman, 2005). We find that in order to gain/develop high CI, it is major to foster the growth of "cross-cultural-friendly" personal attributes among the virtual team members. They help to improve team functioning and interindividual understanding.

3.3   Developing Virtual Intelligence

As work settings (in global enterprises) will become increasingly virtual in the future (Culture Wizard, 2020), skills to deal with "online" settings will be a critical success factor. In this regard, Virtual Intelligence helps individuals to better handle "virtual worlds".

Virtual Intelligence is a special form of contextualized intelligence. It helps to increase the adaption processes of the individual to a virtual work context. It also addresses the new situational conditions and complexity of contexts that virtual work environments require (Makarius & Larson, 2017). Similar to other forms of intelligence, it enables individuals to act effectively and purposefully and to think rationally (Wechsler, 1944) while working virtually. Through the key components of recognizing, directing, and maintaining cognitive resources, individuals are able to develop VI to work effectively in a fully virtual work setting (Makarius & Larson, 2017). In the following paragraphs, we introduce the three main components of VI and delve into how VI can be developed through the components.

The first component of Virtual Intelligence includes recognizing that the context of a virtual work situation differs from a conventional situation. Since virtual work settings have a high potential for distraction (e.g. from technological or other distractions), it is important to recognize where attention should be paid to and which information is irrelevant and should be therefore filtered out. As the context in GVT can change rapidly from virtual to non-virtual work setting, cognitive flexibility helps to adapt behavior and to recognize the (non)virtuality of the context that people are exposed to while working (Makarius & Larson, 2017). A high level of cognitive flexibility in recognizing a changing context has been shown to contribute to faster adaption to virtual work settings (Reyt & Wiesenfeld, 2015). Hence, we believe that the recognition of heterogeneities should be developed while working in GVT. It increases the ability to identify essential differences between virtual and non-virtual work situations and helps to adapt behavior to virtual work settings more quickly.

Directing cognitive resources through reasoning and planning to influence virtual work behavior is the second component of Virtual Intelligence (Makarius & Larson, 2017). Reasoning is the ability to solve problems and shape concepts using new procedures or information (Flanagan et al., 2007). Planning includes the ability to organize and identify steps prior to task processing (Jurado & Rosselli, 2007). Both cognitive resources are important to adapt to a virtual environment as they help to build trust, coordinate information, establish norms, and select the most well-suited collaboration tools. With a high level of directing, virtual team workers are better equipped to mobilize their cognitive resources and to act appropriately in accordance with their respective virtual settings (Makarius & Larson, 2017). For these reasons, reasoning and planning, by directing cognitive resources, helps to improve the match between behavior and the virtual work context. We recommend keeping this in mind when developing VI for individuals working in a global virtual team setting.

After individuals have recognized the virtual setting and directed their cognitive resources through planning and reasoning, the final component for developing Virtual Intelligence includes the need to maintain cognitive resources (for managing information in the virtual work context). Individuals monitor and update their knowledge gained while working in a virtual environment. The maintenance of knowledge helps to increase success and reduce malfunctioning adaption processes when changing the virtual context (Makarius & Larson, 2017). It is therefore of importance for individuals who work in GVT to establish processes for maintaining virtually acquired knowledge.

3.4   New and Emerging Technologies in the Virtual Team Context

As the number of individuals who work in a fully virtual team environment increases (Culture Wizard, 2020), GVT need interaction tools that resemble face-to-face collaborations (Jimenez et al., 2017). Hence, we propose how new and emerging technologies should be designed in the virtual team context to meet these needs and introduce a technological trend that may be "fashionable" in the near future.

As companies started to begin using GVT to perform tasks, Townsend et al. (1998) found that there are three basic categories of technology to consider, when working in GVT: Desktop Videoconferencing Systems (DVCS) are the central system during work in GVT. They are necessary to simulate face-to-face meetings and to ensure complex communication channels. Collaborative Software Systems (CSS) ensure that team members can collaborate interactively and independently. CSS offer a comprehensive environment for teamwork. Internet and Intranet connect team members and software systems and help to work together quickly in a targeted manner.

The combination of all three technology categories increases the success of GVT work. It is therefore crucial for high team performance to link video, voice, interactivity, independence, and the collaboration tool of team members to create more opportunities for participation in a virtual environment (Murray, 2020). In particular, improving the similarity between virtual meetings and face-to-face interactions is an important technological element for the future success of GVT (Kaiser et al., 2020). In this regard, immersive environments (e.g. 3D virtual environments) are an emerging technology that is receiving a great deal of organizational attention. Although physically dispersed in different locations, GVT members can share a digital 3D room. They work through avatars to interact, manipulate, and navigate common tasks (Gilson et al., 2015). This type of technology simulates a "real-life" scenario using virtual or augmented reality technologies and gives the impression of physical contact with team members. It provides the greatest value to a virtual team when the GVT members use it for interactive meetings or collaborative creations. By seeing the whole person (including mouth and hand movements), immerse environments convey the feeling of a physical contact with team members. Since this emerging technology is accessible via mobile devices (e.g., laptop or smartphone), GVT can easily use it (Kaiser et al., 2020). Therefore, 3D technology is useful for global virtual teamwork situations, as it ensures a high level of Media Richness, thereby, increasing the social presence of the members.

Since immersive environments are a new form of virtual collaboration, there are a few issues to be aware of when working with such tools: A high level of hardware and thus technological expertise is required for the use of 3D technologies. For a comprehensive experience of immersive environments, GVT members need an Augmented-Reality/Virtual-Reality headset with a complicated operation system (Kaiser et al., 2020). This limits the number of individuals willing to use such a technology.

3.5   Well-Being at Work

A GVT is highly technology-dependent and characterized by dispersion (e.g., temporality or location). In GVT, individuals often work independently on common tasks, are physically dispersed, and do not have a strong relationship with their teammates. Thus, the well-being of team members is seen as an important factor in shaping the performance and affectation among the team participants (Gilson et al., 2015). The concern for the well-being of GVT is an asset and success factor for the acceptance of global virtual teamwork. To date, research on well-being in a virtual environment has been limited. For some individuals, global virtual teamwork leads to greater autonomy and independence, while others fell into isolation, loneliness, and depression (Gilson et al., 2015) without any physical contact. In order to still achieve a high level of acceptance among completely virtual and global teams, organizations can implement a variety of measures in the future to combine virtuality and well-being in the fields of team functionality and the design of the work environment:

Team functionality: Organizations should form teams based on the individual characteristics of the team members. Forming teams based on work preferences, styles, and personal needs (Volini & Fisher, 2021) supports interindividual sympathy. The implementation of comfort criteria (e.g. evaluations, recognition programs) can lead to individuals talking about their personal (well-being) situation. In addition, the initialization of non-work meetings (Volini & Fisher, 2021) supports the exchange of non-work information between teammates and allows flock together on a more private level.

Design of work environments: While team functionality focuses on interindividual processes to increase the well-being of team members, the design of work environments emphasizes the virtual context. Therefore, the working environment of (global) virtual team members should be designed in such a manner that it supports mental, emotional, and physical needs. This includes modeling well-being behavior (e.g. taking micro-breaks, decrease number of video-based meetings). Finally, the integration of new technologies such as virtual reality (Volini & Fisher, 2021) supports interindividual interactions and can protect against loneliness.

Virtual technologies also offer the opportunity for employees to work during non-work hours (e.g., weekends or during vacations). In addition, time zone differences increase the likelihood of working in the evening or at night (Raghuram et al., 2019). Consequently, there is a high potential to blur boundaries between private and work life (Hill et al., 1998) which can affect performance and health (Gilson et al., 2015). As global virtual teamwork collaboration increases, MNEs should take steps to support the work–life balance in GVT. Creating strict non-work hour slots is one solution to improve the work–life balance. Additionally, organizations may emphasize a restriction on early/late work calls (Dahik et al., 2020). Both approaches can be implemented to ensure work–life balance.

4   Conclusion

Globalization, environmental changes, e.g., COVID-19, changing demography, and technology have had a significant impact on the nature of global work. While the past was dominated by physical relocation of expatriates across borders, MNEs increasingly embrace global virtual work, often via GVT. This chapter reviewed the extant literature and provided an outlook of the future of global work. We provided an overview of the key dimensions and challenges of GVT. GVT can be distinguished by dispersion (temporality, diversity, location), and technology context (type and value of technology).

GVT creates new challenges and opportunities for MNEs. We have discussed key topics for the future of global work relevant both for research and practice. While GVT can reduce the cost of expatriation and increase efficiency, such work arrangements can be challenging for employees. Thus, careful selection and training of GVT workers is key. Given the complexity of the GVT work, GVT workers need to possess cultural and virtual intelligence. MNEs can use such criteria in their selection processes and develop such traits among their incumbent employees. To facilitate collaboration and the reduction of boundaries in GVT, MNEs could look to leverage latest technologies such as collaborative software systems and/or 3D technology. Given rapid external changes and preferences of younger generation, i.e., millennials and generation Z, organizations should support the well-being and work–life balance of their employees (Volini & Fisher, 2021). In the context of global virtual teamwork, MNEs should emphasize team member well-being (e.g., team functionality and the design of the work environment) and work–life balance to ensure the success of this new form of global teamwork in the future.

References

Accenture. (2020). *Virtual ways of working*. Accessed June 23, 2021, from https://www.accenture.com/_acnmedia/PDF-127/Accenture-Virtual-Ways-Working.pdf#zoom=40

Agarwal, D., Bersin, J., Lahiri, G., Schwartz, J., & Volini, E. (2018). *Deloitte global human capital trends. The hyper-connected workplace*. Accessed June 18, 2021, from https://www2.deloitte.com/content/dam/insights/us/articles/HCTrends2018/2018-HCtrends_Rise-of-the-social-enterprise.pdf

Bebenroth, R., & Froese, F. J. (2020). Consequences of expatriate top manager replacement on foreign subsidiary performance. *Journal of International Management, 26*(2), 100730.

Bell, B. S., & Kozlowski, S. W. J. (2002). A typology of virtual teams: Implications for effective leadership. *Group & Organization Management, 27*(1), 14–49.

Bhaskar-Shrinivas, P., Harrison, D., Shaffer, M. A., & Luk, D. M. (2005). Input-based and time-based models of international adjustment: Meta-analytic evidence and theoretical extension. *Academy of Management Journal, 48*(2), 257–280.

Bonache, J., Brewster, C., & Froese, F. J. (2020). Global mobility – Reasons, trends, and strategies. In J. Bonache, C. Brewster, & F. J. Froese (Eds.), *Global mobility and the management of expatriates* (pp. 1–28). Cambridge University Press.

Brewster, C., Dickmann, M., & Suutari, V. (2020). Short-term assignees, international business travelers, and international commuters. In J. Bonache, C. Brewster, & F. J. Froese (Eds.), *Global mobility and the management of expatriates* (pp. 153–180). Cambridge University Press.

Cohen, S. G., & Gibson, C. B. (2003). In the beginning: Introduction and framework. In S. G. Cohen & C. B. Gibson (Eds.), *Virtual teams that work: Creating conditions for virtual team effectiveness* (pp. 1–13). Jossey-Bass.

Cramton, C. D., & Webber, S. S. (2005). Relationships among geographic dispersion, team processes, and effectiveness in software development work teams. *Journal of Business Research, 58*(6), 758–765.

Culture Wizard. (2018). *Trends in high-performing global virtual teams*. Accessed June 18, 2021, from https://content.ebulletins.com/hubfs/C1/Culture%20Wizard/LL-2018%20Trends%20in%20Global%20VTs%20Draft%2012%20and%20a%20half.pdf

Culture Wizard. (2020). *Trends in global virtual work. Metamorphosis of the global workforce*. Accessed June 18, 2021, from https://cdn2.hubspot.net/hubfs/466336/VTS-ExecutiveBrief-2020-FInal.pdf?_ga=2.192853610.1556005674.1601920431-1783803064.1601920431

Daft, R., Lengel, R., & Trevino, L. K. (1987). Message equivocality, media selection, and manager performance: Implications for information support systems. *Management Information Systems Quarterly, 11*, 355–366.

Dahik, A., Lovich, D., Kreafle, C., Bailey, A., Kilmann, J., Kennedy, D., Roongta, P., Schuler, F., Tomlin, L., & Wenstrup, J. (2020). *What 12,000 employees have to say about the future of remote work*. Accessed June 28, 2021, from https://www.bcg.com/de-de/publications/2020/valuable-productivity-gains-covid-19

De Guinea, A., Webster, J., & Staples, D. (2012). A meta-analysis of the consequences of virtualness on team functioning. *Information & Management, 49*, 301–308.

Duranti, C. M., & de Almeida, F. C. (2012). Is more technology better for communication in international virtual teams? *International Journal of E-Collaboration, 8*(1), 36–52.

Flanagan, D. P., Ortiz, S. O., & Alfonso, V. C. (2007). *Essentials of cross-battery assessment* (2nd ed.). John Wiley & Sons.

Froese, F. J., Kim, K., & Eng, A. (2016). Language, cultural intelligence, and inpatriate turnover intentions: Leveraging values in multinational corporations through inpatriates. *Management International Review, 56*, 283–301.

Froese, F. J., & Peltokorpi, V. (2013). Organizational expatriates and self-initiated expatriates: Differences in cross-cultural adjustment and job satisfaction. *International Journal of Human Resource Management, 24*, 1953–1967.

Froese, F. J., Stoermer, S., Reiche, S., & Klar, S. (2021). Best of both worlds: How embeddedness fit in the host unit and the headquarters improve repatriate knowledge transfer. *Journal of International Business Studies, 52*, 1331–1349.

Gilson, L. L., Maynard, M. T., Jones Young, N. C., Vartiainen, M., & Hakonen, M. (2015). Virtual teams research: 10 years, 10 themes, and 10 opportunities. *Journal of Management, 41*(5), 1313–1337.

Hill, E. J., Miller, B. C., Weiner, S. P., & Colihan, J. (1998). Influences of the virtual office on aspects of work and work/life balance. *Personnel Psychology, 51*(3), 667–683.

Hofstede, G. (2001). *Culture's consequences: Comparing values, behaviors, institutions, and organizations across nations.* Sage Publications.

Hollingshead, A., McGrath, J., & O'Connor, K. (1993). Group task performance and communication technology: A longitudinal study of computer-mediated versus face-to-face work groups. *Small Group Research, 24*, 307–333.

Jarman, R. (2005). When success isn't everything – case studies of two virtual teams. *Group Decision and Negotiation, 14*(4), 333–354.

Jimenez, A., Boehe, D., Taras, V., & Caprar, D. (2017). Working across boundaries: Current and future perspectives on global virtual teams. *Journal of International Management, 23*(4), 341–349.

Johnson, J. P., Lenartowicz, T., & Apud, S. (2006). Cross-cultural competence in international business: Toward a definition and a model. *Journal of International Business Studies, 37*(4), 525–543.

Jurado, M. B., & Rosselli, M. (2007). The elusive nature of executive functions: A review of our current understanding. *Neuropsychology Review, 17*(3), 213–233.

Kaiser, R., Schatsky, D., & Jones, R. (2020). *Collaboration at a distance. Technology for remote, high-touch scenarios.* Accessed June 28, 2021, from https://www2.deloitte.com/za/en/insights/focus/signals-for-strategists/virtual-team-collaboration.html

Kim, J., & Froese, F. J. (2012). Expatriation willingness in Asia: The importance of host-country characteristics and employees' role commitments. *International Journal of Human Resource Management, 23*(16), 3414–3433.

Makarius, E., & Larson, B. (2017). Changing the perspective of virtual work: Building virtual intelligence at the individual level. *The Academy of Management Perspectives, 31*, 159–178.

Maznevski, M., Davison, S. C., & Jonsen, K. (2006). Global virtual team dynamics and effectiveness. In G. K. Stahl & I. Björkman (Eds.), *Handbook of research in international human resource management* (pp. 364–384). Edward Elgar.

Molleman, E. (2005). Diversity in demographic characteristics, abilities and personality traits: Do Faultlines affect team functioning? *Group Decision and Negotiation, 14*(3), 173–193.

Murray, E. (2020). *The next generation of office communication tech.* Accessed June 28, 2021, from https://hbr.org/2020/10/the-next-generation-of-office-communication-tech

O'Leary, M., & Cummings, J. (2007). The spatial, temporal, and configurational characteristics of geographic dispersion in teams. *MIS Quarterly, 31*, 433–452.

Raghuram, S., Sharon Hill, N., Gibbs, J. L., & Maruping, L. M. (2019). Virtual work: Bridging research clusters. *The Academy of Management Annals, 13*(1), 308–341.

Reyt, J.-N., & Wiesenfeld, B. M. (2015). Seeing the forest for the trees: Exploratory learning, mobile technology, and knowledge workers' role integration behaviors. *Academy of Management Journal, 58*(3), 739–762.

Shaffer, M. A., Kraimer, M. L., Chen, Y.-P., & Bolino, M. C. (2012). Choices, challenges, and career consequences of global work experiences. *Journal of Management, 38*(4), 1282–1327.

Stoermer, S., Davies, S., & Froese, F. J. (2021). The influence of expatriates' cultural intelligence on embeddedness and knowledge sharing: The moderating effects of host country context. *Journal of International Business Studies, 52*(3), 432–453.

Stoermer, S., Froese, F. J., & Peltokorpi, V. (2020). Self-initiated expatriates. In J. Bonache, C. Brewster, & F. J. Froese (Eds.), *Global mobility and the management of expatriates* (pp. 181–203). Cambridge University Press.

Taras, V., Baak, D., Caprar, D., Dow, D., Froese, F. J., Jimenez, A., & Magnusson, P. (2019). Diverse effects of diversity: Disaggregating effects of diversity in global virtual team. *Journal of International Management, 25*(4), 100689.

Taylor, S. (1981). A categorization approach to stereotyping. In D. L. Hamilton (Ed.), *Cognitive processes in stereotyping and intergroup behavior* (pp. 83–114). Taylor & Francis.

Thomas, D. C., Elron, E., Stahl, G., Ekelund, B. Z., Ravlin, E. C., Cerdin, J.-L., Poelmans, S., Brislin, R., Pekerti, A., Aycan, Z., Maznevski, M., Au, K., & Lazarova, M. B. (2008). Cultural intelligence: Domain and assessment. *International Journal of Cross Cultural Management, 8*(2), 123–143.

Townsend, A. M., DeMarie, S. M., & Hendrickson, A. R. (1998). Virtual teams: Technology and the workplace of the future. *Academy of Management Perspectives, 12*(3), 17–29.

Volini, E., & Fisher, J. (2021). *How to integrate well-being into work so employees perform and feel their best.* Accessed June 28, 2021, from https://www.forbes.com/sites/deloitte/2021/03/08/how-to-integrate-well-being-into-work-so-employees-perform-and-feel-their-best/?sh=3 6cfdaccb87b

Wechsler, D. (1944). *The measurement of adult intelligence.* Williams & Wilkins.

Tobias Blay is a research associate and doctoral student at the Chair of HR-Management and Asian Business at the University of Goettingen, Germany. His research focuses on global virtual work collaborations and virtual teams. He holds a Master's degree in Sociology, majoring in work organization and HR management.

Fabian Jintae Froese is Chair Professor of HR-Management and Asian Business at the University of Goettingen, Germany, and Joint Appointment Professor of International Business at Yonsei University, South Korea. In addition, he is Editor-in-Chief of Asian Business & Management and Associate Editor of the International Journal of Human Resource Management.

Location Flexibility in Global Supply Chains: The Efficiency-Imitability Tradeoff and Sustained Competitive Advantage

Peter D. Ørberg Jensen, Stephan Manning, and Bent Petersen

Increased volatility is the new normal for globalized and interconnected supply chains. Supply chain risk management approaches configured for more stable times now need to be updated. World Economic Forum (2013: 7)

Many firms today are dependent on supply chain networks that were designed when the business environment was more certain, and under the assumption that the future would be more like the past. Now that those organisations are confronted with significantly changed circumstances, it may be the case conventional supply chain structures and practices are no longer fit for purpose. Christopher and Holweg (2017: 3)

1   Introduction

In March 2011, Toyota's operations were severely affected by an earthquake off the east coast of Japan and the resulting tsunami. The company had to close 12 factories in Japan. Other parts of its supply chain, including suppliers and car dealers, were also affected. Toyota's estimated daily loss was USD 62 million, and 6 months passed before its supply chain was back to full capacity. In the face of similar

P. D. Ø. Jensen (✉)
Department of Strategy and Innovation, Copenhagen Business School, Frederiksberg, Denmark
e-mail: poe.si@cbs.dk

S. Manning
School of Business, Management and Economics, University of Sussex, Sussex House, Falmer, Brighton, UK
e-mail: S.D.Manning@sussex.ac.uk

B. Petersen
Department of International Economics, Government and Business, Copenhagen Business School, Frederiksberg, Denmark
e-mail: bp.egb@cbs.dk

© Springer Nature Switzerland AG 2022   253
H. Merchant (ed.), *The New Frontiers of International Business*, Contributions to
Management Science, https://doi.org/10.1007/978-3-031-06003-8_12

disasters, the company has since worked to improve its contingency plans to 2 weeks with the aim of reducing its recovery period. A major reason why Toyota's recovery from the disaster was so lengthy and costly was the company's inability to reconfigure its supply chain in a flexible way across the various production locations.

The Toyota example illustrates that as firms increasingly concentrate functions across multiple locations in order to benefit from location advantages related to costs, time zones, and access to talent, they also become more exposed to a variety of unanticipated risks in the external environment (Porter, 1986). In addition to the instant impact of natural disasters (Knemeyer et al., 2009), challenges in the firm's external environment may relate to political instability (Hahn et al., 2009) or a lack of adequate infrastructure (Doh et al., 2009). Moreover, firms may encounter unforeseen opportunities, such as shifting talent pools, pockets of expertise, and new provider capabilities (Ethiraj et al., 2005; Lewin et al., 2009).

While the impact of volatility and risk in the external environment on the firm has been a long-standing topic in the globalization debate, ample evidence indicates that the world of business has become more "volatile," "turbulent," and "complex" (Christopher & Holweg, 2011; McKinsey, 2021; World Economic Forum, 2013) and that firms that depend on global supply chain networks continually face changing circumstances (Christopher & Holweg, 2017). In light of this "new normal," managers of global sourcing firms view better protection of their supply chains as a priority (ORN, 2011).

In order to respond to their more volatile and risky environments (or in anticipation thereof), firms increasingly rely on *location flexibility*. In this study, we take an explorative approach in order to address two research questions. First, in order to mitigate risk and pursue opportunities in an increasingly volatile and uncertain environment, how do sourcing firms achieve location flexibility in their global supply chains? Second, how can location flexibility help firms sustain or obtain a competitive advantage in their global supply chains?

We define location flexibility in global supply chains as the firm's ability to operate from alternative locations in order to ensure a stable supply of services, raw materials, or intermediate products for their domestic or global operations, thereby meeting low-cost and high-quality expectations despite changing and uncertain external environmental conditions. Location flexibility involves the ability to temporarily or permanently move operations to other locations in order to reduce the impact of location-specific risks and to benefit from emerging location-related opportunities.

Supply chain flexibility includes not only location flexibility but also manufacturing, supplier, and governance flexibility; see Fig. 1.

Hence, while location flexibility shares some features with the three other forms of flexibility, it also complements them. Manufacturing flexibility is the ability of individual production sites to quickly adjust the capacity/volume of existing production lines or swiftly shift to new lines in response to suddenly changing supply or demand conditions (D'souza & Williams, 2000; Jain et al., 2013; Vokurka & O'Leary-Kelly, 2000). Supplier flexibility is a central issue in the strategy and management literature, especially in the debate on strategic networks (e.g., Ring &

Fig. 1 Scope of the study
(authors' own figure)

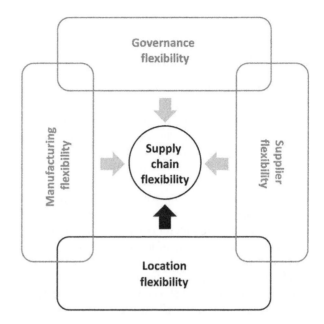

van de Ven, 1992) and project networks (e.g., Starkey et al., 2000), and in the supply chain literature (e.g., Wagner & Bode, 2006; Yu et al., 2009). Supplier flexibility is the ability to switch among providers if particular providers fail to deliver or if new providers with superior capabilities emerge. Governance flexibility is the ability to change delivery models (e.g., from in-house to outsourced activities) and thereby keep switching costs low if other models prove more effective (e.g., Atkinson, 1984; Eisenhardt et al., 2010; Volberda, 1996). By comparison, location flexibility has not attracted much attention. As we illustrate in Fig. 1, there is a certain overlap between location flexibility on the one hand and manufacturing and supplier flexibility on the other hand. To the extent that manufacturing sites and suppliers are replicable in different locations (countries and regions), this provides location flexibility. We will elaborate this in later sections.

We focus on location flexibility in global supply chains and apply the resource-based perspective (Barney, 1991; Hitt et al., 2016) to highlight three modes to accomplish location flexibility: (i) the use of tasks and processes that are standardized across firms and countries, (ii) the use of firm-specific resources that are replicated across countries, and (iii) the use of unique and rare resources that are mobile across countries. We propose that a firm's location flexibility is shaped by these three modes and that they can offer insights useful for a resource-based theory of location flexibility. A basic tenet of our study is that without location flexibility, firms engaged in global sourcing will struggle to sustain their competitive positions in a volatile and uncertain environment. Moreover, consistent with the resource-based perspective (Barney, 1991; Hitt et al., 2016), we also suggest that each of the three modes entails an efficiency-imitability tradeoff. We elaborate on the role this tradeoff plays and the mechanisms that firms put in place to manage it (Adler et al., 1999).

Our chapter offers four contributions: First, we incorporate the spatial dimension. Our literature review (see the next section) suggests that location flexibility is somewhat overlooked as a source of global supply chain agility and resilience and that it can serve as a mechanism for sustaining competitive advantage in global supply chains. Second, we outline how location flexibility can be achieved in global supply chains. More specifically, we describe the three basic modes alluded to above. In this regard, we respond to calls for closer integration of international business and strategic management theories with operations management research (Hitt, 2011; Hitt et al., 2016). Third, we formulate assumptions about an essential managerial dilemma in the pursuit of location flexibility in firms' global supply chains, namely, that between cost efficiency and deployment of firm-specific resources that are difficult for competitors to imitate. Fourth, we submit propositions as to how a combined use of location-flexibility modes can sustain firms' competitive advantage in their global sourcing.

Given this background, the chapter proceeds as follows: First, we review the extant research on global supply chain flexibility. We then introduce location flexibility and its three basic modes, after which we zoom in on one particular tradeoff that challenges firms' use of the modes—the tradeoff between cost efficiency and imitability—and we outline assumptions regarding this tradeoff. Subsequently, we discuss how location flexibility can help global sourcing firms sustain their competitive positions in a volatile and uncertain environment. We propose that firms are compelled to search for balanced combinations of the modes in order to sustain their competitive advantage in global sourcing. Finally, we summarize our contributions and suggest avenues for future research.

2　Prior Flexibility Research: Insights and Limitations

The operations management literature emphasizes the importance of flexibility in dealing with supply chain disruptions, delays, supply chain agility, and supplier performance (e.g., Braunscheidel & Suresh, 2009; Chiang et al., 2012; Gligor et al., 2015; Manuj & Mentzer, 2008; Prater et al., 2001). Operations management research has highlighted flexible manufacturing and supply chain agility as sources of competitive advantage (Camison & Lopez, 2010; Gligor et al., 2015), while it has paid little attention to the spatial dimension. The operations management literature somewhat abstracts from the geographical dimension of sourcing (one exception is Mair (1994)). However, operation flexibility and routing flexibility (Parker & Wirth, 1999) imply elements of location flexibility. The operations management literature reflects ideas of the "flexible firm," as it focuses on the role of redundant structures in supplier networks. More specifically, prior research emphasizes the use of multiple suppliers rather than single sourcing in order to increase sourcing flexibility and reduce the risks of a supply failure (e.g., Sánchez & Pérez, 2005; Stecke & Kumar, 2009; Xanthopoulos et al., 2012). Hence, some studies suggest that the presence of multiple suppliers improves performance in volatile environments (e.g., Wagner & Bode, 2006) because the use of multiple suppliers "can be an effective tool in dealing with unexpected supply breakdowns" (Yu et al., 2009: 789).

Research on flexibility has a long tradition in other literature streams outside the operations management field. The international business literature links flexibility to location factors. For example, researchers have examined the relationship between geographical diversification and the performance of multinational enterprises (MNEs) (Aaker & Mascarenhas, 1984; Allen & Pantzalis, 1996). Geographical diversification may stabilize performance not only by reducing volatility in sales and ensuring more stability in supplies but also through better exploitation of global opportunities in general (e.g., Kim & Mathur, 2008). Hence, studies on operational flexibility suggest that the scalability of production and sales (Swafford et al., 2006) helps firms manage changing location conditions, such as changing cost differentials between countries due to tax differentials (Kogut, 1985), investment incentives (Kogut, 1985), volatile exchange rates (Kogut & Kulatilaka, 1994; Rangan, 1998), or labor costs (Belderbos & Zou, 2007; Fisch & Zschoche, 2012). By the same token, several studies suggest that international network structures that provide operational flexibility improve overall MNE performance (Fisch & Zschoche, 2011; Huchzermeier & Cohen, 1996; Tang & Tikoo, 1999). However, the literature on diversification and scalability strategies remains silent about the conditions under which resources can be flexibly allocated and shifted across locations in the first place. Moreover, the conditions under which different locations allow for the ramping up of comparable scalable operations are unclear.

In the management and organization literature, the flexibility concept is typically associated with an organization's adaptive capability in the face of rapidly changing competitive environments (Eisenhardt et al., 2010; Volberda, 1996). The notion of flexibility is rooted in early discussions of organizational responses to dynamic, unpredictable, and often risky environments. For example, Burns and Stalker (1961) propose that "organic structures" are most suitable for effectively dealing with dynamic environments. Similar notions can be found in the literature on new organizational forms, according to which regular hierarchical forms are inferior to "adhocracies" (Mintzberg & McHugh, 1985), "network organizations" (Miles & Snow, 1986), and "latent organizations" (Starkey et al., 2000) when dealing with environmental contingencies. Most of these views share the notion that adaptable structures and processes along with available, "on-demand" resource pools are needed to respond to frequent changes in environmental opportunities and risks.

Based on this principle, the notion of the "flexible firm" has been developed by several scholars. In Atkinson's model of the flexible firm (1984), a distinction is made between the core and the periphery. The core is constituted by the full-time workforce, while the periphery is composed of both highly qualified experts who are hired on a contract basis and pools of redundant, less-skilled labor hired on demand. Similar notions apply to the model of project networks in project-based industries (see, e.g., Starkey et al., 2000; Windeler & Sydow, 2001) where firms rely on external labor pools and supplier networks in order to flexibly adapt to emerging project opportunities and unanticipated, project-specific challenges.

In the strategic management literature, flexible structures and processes have been linked to sustained competitive advantage. For example, several contributions have focused on incorporating dynamic capabilities and demand-side factors into theories of sustained competitive advantage (e.g., Hitt et al., 2016; Priem & Butler, 2001; Priem & Swink, 2012;Teece et al., 1997 ; Winter, 2003). In addition, strategy scholars have investigated the construct of strategic flexibility in different domains, such as product innovation (Zhou & Wu, 2010), product modularity and organizational design (e.g., Sanchez & Mahoney, 1996), foreign operation modes (Petersen et al., 2000), and in relation to financial performance (e.g., Ebben & Johnson, 2005). In strategy research, the literature on dynamic capabilities deserves mention, as flexibility is one of its central assumptions. This stream of literature, which seeks to add dynamism to resource-based theory (Allred et al., 2011; Barney, 1991; Hitt et al., 2016), investigates how the acquisition, development, and deployment of resources influence firms' sustained competitive advantage (Teece et al., 1997; Winter, 2003).

In sum, the various streams of literature, including research on operations management, offer insights into the flexible firm but tend to neglect the geographical dimension of flexibility. Across research domains, firms' flexibility has largely been treated as a matter of building adaptable and agile structures in the form of multiple supplier networks, agile manufacturing systems, external labor pools, and modular product architectures. Little attention has been paid to contingencies in the actual process of shifting resources and processes across locations in response to increasingly volatile and unpredictable environments.

3   Three Modes of Location Flexibility in Global Supply Chains

At their core, global sourcing practices concern the cost-efficient (re-)allocation of tasks and resources across national and regional borders (e.g., Kedia & Mukherjee, 2009). As we argue above, the long-term capacity of firms to engage in efficient allocation relates to the flexibility with which they can manage or anticipate location-specific risks and benefit from emerging location-related opportunities by temporarily or permanently moving operations to different locations. As our focus is on sourcing rather than market-expansion activities, we emphasize the role played by the properties of tasks and resources in supporting (or constraining) location flexibility rather than, for example, product or market features, which may also affect firms' abilities to move operations across locations, especially when such moves are motivated by market opportunities and constraints. Also, unlike prior sourcing-related research, which has emphasized agile manufacturing or flexibility in switching governance modes and/or suppliers, we focus on the ability to switch locations.

In particular, we propose the three modes of location flexibility, which we have derived from the resource-based perspective. By *modes*, we mean factors that influence the capacity of firms to increase their location flexibility. As such, firms

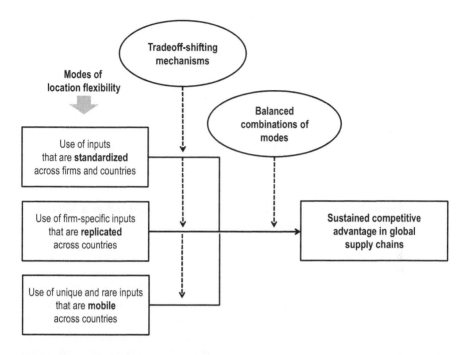

Fig. 2 Analytical model of the study (authors' own figure)

can use these modes to increase their location flexibility and, thereby, sustain their competitive advantage in global supply chains. The central elements in the three modes—tasks and firm resources—are theoretically related, as the firm's resources create the foundation for task execution. This implies that the firm's resources are translated into task execution and that the firm's ability (or inability) to translate resources into task execution influences its competitive advantage (Ray et al., 2004). From the perspective of resource-based theory (Barney, 1991; Hitt et al., 2016), therefore, we posit that the higher the degree of location flexibility mastered by the firm in its global sourcing practice, the greater the positive influence of location flexibility on the firm's competitive advantage (Fig. 2).

As illustrated in Fig. 1, we argue that the three modes have a direct influence on location flexibility as a strategy for sustaining competitive advantage in global sourcing (i.e., the outcome variable in the model). Location flexibility may also be moderated by two other factors: tradeoff-shifting mechanisms and the firm's ability to combine the three modes in a balanced way. We denote tradeoff-shifting mechanisms as organizational mechanisms that enable the ambidextrous firm to improve the use of one mode without deteriorating the other (Adler et al., 1999; O'Reilly & Tushman, 2008). On the other hand, combining modes in a balanced way entails the optimization of outcomes by introducing modes in accordance with their marginal utility for the firm.

As mentioned above, the three modes are derived from the resource-based perspective, which primarily looks inward. We recognize that various exogenous factors may influence the desirability and relevance of location flexibility. All else equal, the greater the firm's dependency on factors embedded in the local environment or the greater its reliance on critical resources residing in partner firms, the less leeway the firm has to use these modes (Andersson et al., 2002; Gulati & Sytch, 2007; Hitt et al., 2016). However, in this study, our focus is on endogenous rather than exogenous factors.

In the following, we account for the basic tenets of the three location-flexibility modes.

3.1   Provision and Use of Inputs That Are Standardized Across Firms and Countries

To a great extent, location flexibility depends on the standardization of processes related to the execution of a chain of interrelated tasks. Standardization has been a pervasive trend across industries (e.g., Brunsson et al., 2012, p. 616), where a standard can be defined as "a rule for common and voluntary use, decided by one or several people or organizations." In global supply chains, such rules typically relate to process activity and flow standards, process performance standards, and process management standards. They facilitate hand-offs, ease comparative measures of performance, and make information less "sticky," such that it is easier to communicate across distances (Kumar et al., 2009; von Hippel, 1994). In other words, standardization often runs parallel to an increasing codification of knowledge, including the specification of tasks and the processes needed to accomplish these tasks, which eases the transfer of tasks and related knowledge across locations (e.g., Cowan & Foray, 1997). Standardization reduces the need for costly coordination and makes the global distribution of tasks and processes more feasible (e.g., Apte & Mason, 1995).

The low coordination costs associated with standardization is a property shared with modularization (e.g., Baldwin, 2008; Baldwin & Clark, 2000; Frandsen, 2017). However, the two constructs differ in other respects—modularization usually implies uniformity in smaller production units ("modules"), and this uniformity is often firm specific. In contrast, standardization typically applies to industries and, thus, transcends firm boundaries. As we will discuss later, an important implication of this difference is that modularization can serve as a source of competitive advantage (Ethiraj et al., 2008), but standardization (as an industry-defined construct) can only do so for a short while, if at all. As an example of the firm specificity of modularization, the major automotive manufacturers have modular systems, called scalable product architecture or "platforms," that are proprietary to the individual corporation (e.g., Ford, Toyota, Volkswagen Group) or, in rare cases, used jointly in strategic alliances (e.g., Hyundai-Kia). However, no single platform is available to all incumbent firms. In contrast, the automotive manufacturers are developing various industry-wide standards, such as the ISO/TS 16949 that covers quality management system requirements for the design, development, production, installation, and service of automotive-related products.

To illustrate how task standardization and the subsequent process standardization affect location flexibility, we can examine capability maturity model index (CMMI) standards. CMMI standards are frameworks for defining and measuring processes and practices in general and software-development processes in particular. They can be used by both clients and service providers. The standards were defined by Carnegie Mellon University and were first introduced in 2002. The adoption of CMMI standards at different "maturity" levels (from 1 to 5) has been important in the evolution of the global service outsourcing industry (Athreye, 2005; Ethiraj et al., 2005; Niosi & Tschang, 2009), and they have been adopted by providers in particular locations as they attempt to attract projects from global clients (see also Manning et al., 2010). CMMI adoption across service locations (e.g., India, Latin America, and Eastern Europe) allows client and provider firms to move operations to those locations. For example, recent studies indicate that clients frequently relocate particular software-development processes from initial offshore locations (e.g., India) to emerging hotspots, like Ukraine, to utilize emerging talent pools, to exploit temporary labor-cost advantages associated with second-tier locations, or in response to various operational challenges in existing locations (e.g., Manning, 2014).

Two facets of standardization are important in this regard. On the one hand, an increasing number of service providers have adopted CMMI models *across* locations, which simplifies the interface with clients and reduces switching costs in relation to both suppliers and locations. Relatedly, an increasing number of software developers and service staff are trained in CMMI processes across locations, which simplifies recruitment. On the other hand, given the resources at hand, client firms are increasingly standardizing their task requests in line with established models, such as CMMI. This eases the ramp-up of new facilities or operations in new locations. In manufacturing, a number of standards (e.g., quality control) have eased transfers of tasks and processes to new locations in a similar way. The abovementioned standard, ISO/TS 16949, exemplifies an interpretation agreed upon by major automotive manufacturers in the United States and Europe.

We argue that standardization not only facilitates the choice of alternative governance models or alternative suppliers (Baldwin, 2008; Tanriverdi et al., 2007) but also eases the flexible sourcing of tasks and processes from various locations over time. Importantly, the standardization of tasks and processes across firms on the global level has to be understood as a continuous inter-organizational learning process (Ethiraj et al., 2005). Therefore, certain pioneer MNEs may take a pivotal role in establishing standards in certain locations. Motorola played such a role in training local suppliers in CMMI adoption in India and Latin America (Manning et al., 2010; Patibandla & Petersen, 2002). Notably, however, this strategy is not without risks from the firm's perspective. Other competing standards may emerge and eventually become dominant in the industry. In that case, the lead firm assumes pioneering costs but without a return on its investment.

3.2   Provision and Use of Firm-Specific Inputs That Are Replicated Across Countries

Another modality that independently affects location flexibility is a firm's ability to replicate resources across borders, including those that are highly firm specific. The notion of replication relates to the potential *availability* of more or less firm-specific resources (e.g., human, physical, or technological) needed to carry out particular tasks across multiple locations. The ability to ensure the availability of firm resources across locations helps the firm avoid a situation in which it becomes too dependent on the specific resource composition present at one of its sites (Jensen & Petersen, 2013). The case of ECCO—a shoe manufacturer targeting the high-end market segment with eight factories located across the world—exemplifies how a value-chain disruption may prompt a company to change its global sourcing strategy. When some of the worst monsoon rains in decades hit Thailand in October 2011, the impact was severe. In the city of Ayutthaya, north of Bangkok, ECCO experienced a sudden disruption in the production process, as local dikes failed and its buildings were flooded with 2 meters of water. ECCO was able to shift part of its value-chain activities to its unit in Portugal where similar machinery was available and where local staff were able to scale up production at short notice. This specific machinery was necessary for ECCO's injection-sole technology, which is used in the manufacturing of shoes. In other words, through the replication of firm resources, ECCO managed to mitigate some of the damage. Notably, however, this was sheer luck, as ECCO had not planned to maintain a replication of resources at another factory. The incident in Thailand eventually led to a strategic change in the firm's location of value-chain activities (ECCO, 2012).

This raises a key question: Under which conditions is production substitutability possible and how? Only if the resources needed to perform tasks are readily available can switching locations become a feasible option. Importantly, resource availability stems from external factor endowments (e.g., labor pools, external expertise) that are explored and exploited through the firm's (or its partner firms') internal operations. Nevertheless, "external resource availability" at a particular location can be more or less in tune with the firm's needs. We argue that the alignment of external resource conditions with the firm's needs for resources is critical in order for firms to move operations across locations in response to location-specific risks.

The cross-border replication of resources requires a combination of firm-specific capabilities and external resource conditions. Internally, firms need to be able to establish (replicate) capabilities and relationships in new locations according to their needs. This includes political management capabilities (Oliver & Holzinger, 2008) that may help align local stakeholders with their needs. However, this typically only works if locations are willing to accommodate firms' needs by, for instance, letting firms "modify" the local environment in line with their operations. In fact, in some locations, such as Bangalore, India, universities have adopted a sponsorship model in which incoming clients have the opportunity to establish customized courses, internship programs, and other (firm-specific) recruitment channels. Similarly, many suppliers across locations invite clients to specify their needs and establish joint client-supplier teams to train staff and monitor performance (Luo et al., 2012). Furthermore, suppliers may offer their client firms location flexibility by setting up parallel production sites in different parts of the world. As an example, India-based Bharat Forge (https://www.bharatforge.com), a world-leading supplier in forgings for the automobile industry, is pursuing a "dual-source supply model" whereby it can supply any component to a client from two distinct locations. Plants in Europe and the United States reduce supply chain risks to the major automobile manufacturers (Buckley et al., 2018, p. 38).

3.3   Provision and Use of Unique and Rare Inputs That Are Mobile Across Countries

The cross-border mobility of resources is a third location-flexibility mode in global supply chains. Here, an interesting case of mobility concerns human resources. Over time, the mobility of human resources has increased globally, as evidenced by growth in multi-cultural diaspora communities, especially those involving core economic clusters, such as Silicon Valley and Bangalore (e.g., Bresnahan et al., 2001). Resource mobility is pertinent when the resources needed for a task are only available in one or a few locations and replication is not an option. In other words, the resources are characterized by their uniqueness and rarity on a global scale. Human resource mobility is particularly important in the early and explorative phases of business processes, when new process and product innovations are introduced and knowledge is confined to a few people in the firm. Examples are scientists mastering highly specialized laboratory services or IT personnel providing extremely specialized special effects for movies. The relocation of these rare human resources does not occur in response to risks or cost considerations, such as the political persecution of individuals or wage inflation. Instead, relocation is used to maintain a high degree of causal ambiguity among outsiders (Dierickx & Cool, 1989; Lippman & Rumelt, 1982) and, thereby, protect resources that are critical (Pfeffer & Salancik, 1978; Wernerfelt, 1989) for the continued operations of the corporation as a whole. In comparison, the importance of human resource mobility may diminish at a later stage when business processes become more routinized and embedded in the wider organizational structures and practices.

We consider the importance of resource mobility for enabling firms to operate from multiple, alternative locations, especially when there are practical limits to the use of standardized or replicable tasks and resources. To some extent, resource mobility compensates for the inability to use the two other modes. The global sourcing strategy of GN Audio, a Danish firm producing audio equipment for professional and consumer use under the brand name Jabra©, shows that it is possible to exercise flexibility to switch between locations when required (annual reports and personal communication with GN Audio management). GN Audio outsources its manufacturing to a range of electronics suppliers, who are mainly located in the urban area close to Hong Kong (Dongguan and Shenzhen). If one of GN Audio's suppliers develops its own tool for the production process, GN Audio may opt to buy that tool from the supplier. This enables GN Audio to relocate the tool to an alternative production site and to an alternative supplier.

4   Assumptions About the Efficiency-Imitability Tradeoff

We now turn our attention to some key competitive implications and tradeoffs associated with the modes. In particular, we focus on the managerial tension between cost efficiency and imitability in relation to location flexibility. Prior research suggests that flexibility is a capacity "in tension," as it increases a firm's adaptability at the cost of stability and predictability (e.g., highly flexible firms may underutilize economies of stable routines, structures, and processes; Schreyoegg & Sydow, 2010; Eisenhardt et al., 2010). Some researchers have argued that flexibility and stability are irreconcilable operational objectives in organizations (e.g., Thompson, 1967). More recently, authors have suggested that it is possible to attain both objectives at the same time (Adler et al., 1999). These authors have discussed the circumstances under which the firm may be "ambidextrous," such that it manages to explore new resources, processes, and structural configurations while simultaneously exploiting existing processes and capabilities (e.g., Eisenhardt et al., 2010; Simsek, 2009).

We contribute to this discussion but shift the focus toward another important but less understood tension—the tension between cost efficiency and imitability when establishing flexible global operational structures. By "cost efficiency," we mean the ability to keep operational costs in check through low factor costs, economies of scale and scope, and other means. By "imitability," we refer to the idea that in order to generate and maintain a competitive advantage (Barney, 1991), firms must deploy firm-specific resources and capabilities that are characterized by a high degree of inimitability.

We argue that in the context of location flexibility, these two partly contradictory considerations are particularly important. We are not the first to examine this efficiency-imitability tradeoff. In a computational experiment, Ethiraj et al. (2008) analyzed the tradeoff between performance gains through innovation achieved in modular architectures that reduce design complexity and the erosion of these gains due to imitation by competitors. In other words, modularization enhances firms' innovation aptitude but makes it easier for other firms to emulate the innovations. Although the beneficial outcome in Ethiraj et al.'s (2008) study is innovation rather than cost efficiency, innovation is driven by an instrument (i.e., modularization) that shares some properties with standardization. Modularization reduces design complexity as well as coordination costs. Hence, the cost-efficiency aspect is to some degree addressed in Ethiraj et al.'s (2008) study.

4.1   The Efficiency-Imitability Tradeoff When Using Standardized Inputs

We introduced the use of standardized tasks and processes as a potentially important mode of location flexibility. When tasks and processes are standardized beyond the boundaries of the firm and across country borders, the sourcing firm can access the resources and capabilities needed to accomplish those tasks through the market, which decreases its dependency on firm-specific resources and operations across locations. Therefore, this is an effective way to reduce relocation and switching costs. Standardization not only facilitates location flexibility but also helps the sourcing firm create efficiency gains and reduce operational risks (e.g., single location dependency, value-chain disruption, holdup risks from outsourcing partners) in global sourcing. However, while the standardization of non-critical tasks (e.g., payroll administration) may aid both flexibility and efficiency without much risk, this is not true for more critical tasks, such as those related to product development. The standardization of these tasks, including the simplification of interfaces with other processes (Baldwin, 2008), may increase location flexibility but at the risk of knowledge leakage and imitation by competitors.

Thus, the role of standardization is ambiguous. On the one hand, task and process standardization is a source and even a driver of location flexibility and contributes to the firm's competitiveness through potential cost-efficiency gains. This relates, in particular, to the execution of transactional tasks, such as back-office service activities. On the other hand, such practices are generally available to and applied by sourcing firms. As such, standardization can, at best, provide the sourcing firm with a situation of competitive parity with other incumbent firms. Even though task standardization is an effective facilitator of location flexibility and a driver of cost efficiency, the associated competitive advantage is ephemeral—other firms can easily emulate this source of cost efficiency. Hence, we present the following assumption:

Assumption 1 *Location flexibility in global supply chains achieved through the use of tasks and processes that are standardized across firms and countries is associated with low costs as well as high imitability.*

4.2   The Efficiency-Imitability Tradeoff When Using Replicated Resources

Another source of location flexibility is the presence of similar and predominantly firm-specific resources (human, physical, technological) in more than one location. Such resources may be available within the boundaries of the firm or reside with external partner firms. We focus on the availability of resources across locations, especially in situations where task and process standardization is low or absent, such as in the hiring of functionally flexible engineers in multiple locations that are able to take on tasks from other locations. Another example is machinery that is set up in multiple locations with the capacity to duplicate the production process and, hence, buffer the risk of production disruptions in any one location.

Similar to task standardization, resource replication across locations may increase a firm's location flexibility. However, its implications for the efficiency-imitability tradeoff differ from those of task standardization. With regard to cost-efficiency implications, making similar resources available in multiple locations reduces a firm's dependency on those resources in any one location. This, in turn, lowers a firm's vulnerability to value-chain disruptions, which may be caused by various factors, including natural disasters (e.g., the Toyota and ECCO examples described earlier) or the turnover of strategically critical staff. The establishment of redundant resources in multiple locations facilitates the temporary or permanent relocation of processes among locations in case of such disruptions and, thereby, helps reduce potential costs arising from the disruptions (e.g., client-litigation costs). However, the establishment of such redundancies may involve not only considerable upfront costs (e.g., costs of acquiring talent, technology, and other equipment) and costs associated with transferring knowledge, but also running costs (e.g., owing to a need to keep a redundant pool of staff available to handle additional tasks if needed). Several case studies indicate that globally dispersed firms are willing to accept such costs to mitigate the risk of operational disruptions (e.g., Manning, 2014). Notably, the magnitude of such costs depends on the firm's ability to operate efficiently and effectively across multiple international locations. In any case, these often "invisible" costs should not be ignored, as they may be significant and influence firm performance (e.g., Stringfellow et al., 2008).

Despite the added costs of establishing and running replicated operations, firms' perception of such costs may change in the wake of the COVID-19 pandemic. Replication of operations across locations is a strategy for safeguarding against and mitigating risks of value-chain disruption—a risk that became the reality for many firms as the spread of the pandemic affected firms' international supply chains and operations with resulting delays, bottlenecks, and disruptions (e.g., Gereffi, 2020; World Economic Forum, 2020). Shortly after the outbreak of the pandemic, these disruptions spurred a debate about possible firm responses to overcome the challenges. Such responses could include a contraction of global supply chains to regional supply chains combined with a replication of operations across multiple locations and (in the case of offshore outsourcing) multiple suppliers (McKinsey, 2020; UNCTAD, 2020; World Economic Forum, 2020). However, as Verbeke (2020) points out, the international supply chain of a firm did not appear overnight. Rather, its configuration has evolved gradually over a long period, and it exists because it rests on a business case that benefits the firm. According to Verbeke (2020), it is therefore not likely to change fundamentally. Here, a strategy with replication of resources across locations presents itself as a way to maintain the international supply chain but at the same time ensure safeguarding against disruptions. In this context, the added cost of replication may seem as an acceptable price to pay.

Moreover, unlike task and process standardization, the replication of resources across locations does not necessarily make firms vulnerable to knowledge leakages or to imitation by competitors as long as resources in the global supply chain are configured to achieve an inimitable advantage (Allred et al., 2011). The ways in which resources are utilized may be highly firm specific and deeply embedded in the firm's processes and culture, thereby supporting a high degree of interfirm causal ambiguity (King, 2007; Reed & DeFillippi, 1990), which serves as a barrier to competitor imitation. We therefore formulate the following assumption:

Assumption 2 *Location flexibility in global supply chains achieved through the use of firm-specific resources that are replicated across countries is associated with low imitability as well as high costs.*

4.3 The Efficiency-Imitability Tradeoff When Using Mobile Resources

We argued above that resource mobility between locations increases a firm's location flexibility. However, while explicit knowledge (e.g., process specifications) can be easily shared, tacit knowledge is difficult to disseminate across locations. In this regard, we focus on the mobility of *human* resources (Khadria, 2004; OECD, 2001). More specifically, we consider a situation in which the sourcing firm operates with a high degree of human resource mobility, while the availability of resources across multiple locations is limited, and task/process standardization within the firm and in the industry is low or absent. Such a situation may be evident for various types of activities, such as activities that are part of the explorative stage of an R&D process. In this case, research staff from the firm's central R&D unit would need to travel to foreign subsidiaries or visit external partners to tap into local specialized knowledge. This implies that the travelling members of the head office's staff simultaneously act as boundary spanners and system integrators. Another example would be a sourcing firm with poorly developed knowledge-transfer capabilities or a high degree of tacit knowledge. If the firm operates in a market for customized solutions, the importance of the mobility of human resources and experiential knowledge is amplified.

The costs involved in making unique and rare resources mobile across locations are high. In fact, many firms do not account for these costs, such as the costs of moving and accommodating expatriates, when setting up new locations (e.g., Peréz & Pla-Barber, 2005). Scale advantages are difficult to achieve, and the costs related to human resource mobility remain stable with little possibility of cost reductions through increased efficiency. In addition, firms may depend on the idiosyncratic knowledge embedded in individuals in order to ramp up new locations, which makes location flexibility a costly and risky endeavor when tasks and processes are not standardized and resources not replicable across locations.

However, a reliance on idiosyncratic knowledge embedded in mobile individuals who have an incentive to pursue a career in the respective firm may ensure and protect tacit knowledge flows. Competitors will find it difficult, if not impossible, to copy the ramping up of new locations by the respective firm. Therefore, increasing location flexibility through resource mobility makes firms adaptable to changes in location conditions while protecting them from knowledge leakages. We therefore assume the following:

Assumption 3 *Location flexibility in global sourcing achieved through the use of non-replicable (i.e., unique and rare) resources that are mobile across countries is associated with low imitability as well as high costs.*

In general terms of costs and imitability, the two modes—resource replication and use of mobile resources—are similar. However, this does not imply that they are mutually substitutable. If resources are unique and rare, they do not easily lend themselves to replication. On the other hand, if resources are replicable, situation-specific cost structures may determine whether mobility or replicability should be the preferred mode.

5   Location Flexibility to Sustain Competitive Advantage: Implications for Managers and Some Propositions

Our analysis of location flexibility has thus far been predominantly descriptive. Therefore, we now redirect our analysis toward a more management-oriented, prescriptive approach to sustaining competitive advantage. First, we summarize our analysis from the previous sections in a general proposition:

Proposition 1 *In a volatile global environment, firms must achieve location flexibility in order to sustain a competitive advantage in their global supply chains.*

Based on this general proposition, in the following, we discuss how global sourcing firms may shift the efficiency-imitability tradeoff in a positive direction by making either standardized inputs less imitable or firm-specific inputs less costly.

5.1   Use of Standardized Tasks and Processes to Sustain Competitive Advantage

When industry standards exist, they serve as facilitators for all firms and increase the degree of location flexibility among lead firms and follower firms (i.e., firms that do not possess agenda- and standard-setting power in an industry; see, e.g., Gereffi et al., 2005). However, for follower firms, the increase in location flexibility tends to be accompanied by adaptation costs, which must be borne in order to internalize and comply with industry standards that apply across countries. For example, a multinational shoemaker that is a lead firm in its industry is better positioned to lobby for new ILO environmental standards for leather production (e.g., tanning of rawhides). Those new international standards would impose adaptation costs on (some) competitors and their suppliers. For follower firms, there is consequently a tradeoff between the benefits of increasing location flexibility by adopting the standards and related adaptation costs. While standardization thus enables location flexibility, it does not move the firm into a superior competitive situation but instead ensures competitive parity relative to incumbent firms. Given this background, we derive the following proposition:

Proposition 2 *Location flexibility based on standardized tasks and resources that are cost efficient is a necessary but not sufficient condition for sustaining competitive advantage in a firm's global supply chain.*

5.2   Use of Replicated and Mobile Resources to Sustain Competitive Advantage

Upfront costs, coordination costs, as well as potential costs of switching production from one location to another are major managerial considerations when replicating firm-specific resources across locations. In this context, the case of the German automotive supplier MoTeC and its resource-replication strategy is interesting (see Manning et al., 2012). MoTeC's strategy includes entering second-tier locations as a first mover, which allows it to customize the local supply of engineering talent to accommodate its needs while keeping training costs relatively low. In other words, the company's local economic power as a foreign lead firm allows it to partly externalize firm-specific training to the local university. Moreover, by duplicating this strategy across multiple locations, the firm has managed to replicate firm-specific resources at multiple locations at a relatively low cost. This implies that follower firms will face considerable adaptation costs when rolling out similar strategies, as they are less likely to customize local talent supplies for their own needs unless they adjust their demand to already established local capabilities.

Location flexibility based on resource replication may be challenged by high switching costs or the costs of holding production capacity idle. Therefore, firms may be concerned with increasing capacity and soaring switching costs. The switching of production from location A to location B typically implies the downsizing of production resources in country A, at least temporarily, in order to reduce "idle" production capacity. In practice, this usually means laying off employees in location A, which not only creates an ethical problem but also is often difficult for firms complying with local labor regulations (e.g., protection against layoffs and severance pay requirements; Ackers & Wilkinson, 2003). For this reason, we suggest that increasing location flexibility through the replication of (human) resources while adjusting production capacity is a practice firms are likely to apply when labor market regulations are "liberal" in that they allow for seamless hiring and firing. In contrast, adjusting production capacity in support of location flexibility can become costly in countries like Spain, France, and Germany, where employees enjoy high levels of protection.

These differences and the tendency of firms to relocate to "liberal" locations create not only an ethical dilemma but also important challenges for local economies trying to sustainably generate employment through "attractive" location factors. In addition, we expect large firms to perceive this tradeoff mechanism as a risk factor in relation to their corporate social responsibility policies of being "good citizens," as it may evoke an adverse image of these firms as "footloose" MNEs.

Similar to resource replication, resource *mobility* is intrinsically associated with relatively high costs. To mitigate this problem, many firms have adopted global HR policies with various components that individually and in combination promote employee mobility without excessively high costs. The expatriation of employees in connection with long-term assignments is often associated with high failure rates because the employees and their families do not thrive in the foreign environment. Therefore, several sourcing firms have developed policies that facilitate the expatriation and repatriation of individual employees and their families. For example, studies show that firms may initiate "re-culturalization" (Wang & Yeh, 2005) or "transnationalization" processes (Papastergiadis, 2000) that aim to give the employees and their families a global mindset or, at least, help them better adapt to foreign environments.

Furthermore, studies suggest that long-term assignments are often supplemented with short stays abroad as part of more systemized international rotation schedules (Manning et al., 2013; Welch, 2003). Firms are moving toward global HR policies that include performance policies and career-development measures across different MNE units. One related method to increase employee mobility is tax-liability packages that safeguard employees against double taxation and complex income tax filing procedures. For instance, firms from the European Union can form a "European firm" in which the employees are taxable by only one European country even though they hold job assignments in several countries during the year. In this way, the employees can work across borders without ending up in complicated and delicate tax situations.

Tradeoff-shifting mechanisms in relation to both the mobility and replication of resources are primarily directed toward cost efficiency. However, as these two location-flexibility modes are not perfectly immune to imitation by competitors, tradeoff-shifting mechanisms that aim to increase inimitability may also be relevant. In the context of resource replication, there may be knowledge-spillover and leakage problems. In terms of the mobility of unique human resources, the degree of inimitability may depend on the retention of key staff members. Interfirm mobility (i.e., competitors' capacity to attract key staff members) may erode the inimitability of human capital. Consequently, some firms may develop measures to reduce interfirm mobility by either introducing competition clauses (although these may conflict with labor-market legislation in many countries) or establishing strong ties with key employees (see Demirbag et al., 2012). Retention policies may include a wide range of HRM instruments, such as career-development schemes, attractive work environments, stock options and other financial rewards, outcome-based compensation, and various benefit packages.

In the global sourcing of science and engineering in particular, staff retention is a major challenge, as it affects the financial position of the organization (Lewin et al., 2009). High attrition rates incur significant recruitment and training costs and make it difficult to maintain quality standards. Notably, employee turnover rates in major offshoring destinations may be quite high in these areas.

Hence, we present our third proposition in relation to replicated and mobile firm-specific resources:

P3 *Location flexibility based on the replication and mobility of firm-specific resources that are difficult for competitors to imitate is a necessary but not sufficient condition for sustaining competitive advantage in a firm's global supply chain.*

5.3 Combined Use of the Three Modes to Sustain Competitive Advantage in Global Sourcing

Aside from tradeoff-shifting mechanisms, some firms have started to develop capabilities that allow them to combine the three location-flexibility modes and, thereby, increase their overall adaptive capacity. One important facilitating factor is the distinction between critical and non-critical tasks and resources (Ellram et al., 2013; Pfeffer & Salancik, 1978; Wernerfelt, 1989). When critical resources (e.g., certain machinery) or managerial or product-development skills that relate to a firm's competitiveness are involved, firms are more likely to promote resource mobility or replication than task or process standardization in order to increase location flexibility (e.g., Manning et al., 2013). Conversely, in support of location flexibility, firms may choose to adopt standard solutions for non-critical tasks and processes, such as payroll administration, IT infrastructure, and tech support. For most firms, inimitability is not crucial in relation to these non-core resources, while cost efficiency is.

Hence, one important "combinative capability" (Kogut & Zander, 1992) is to mix the different modes in a balanced way. This involves finding a combination that maximizes the cost-efficiency and inimitability properties of location flexibility. The GN Audio example mentioned earlier demonstrates not only how sourcing firms can make critical resources mobile but also how they can combine different types of components in their global sourcing activities. GN Audio distinguishes between three component types in its sourcing. *Standard* components are off-the-shelf standard components with multiple suppliers. These components made up only 11.5 percent of GN Audio's total sourcing costs in 2015. *Custom* components are modified to comply with GN Audio's specifications and are only available form a few suppliers. In terms of value, these components represented the bulk of GN Audio's sourcing (64.2 percent of total sourcing costs in 2015). *Unique* components are often intellectual property and covered by a number of patents. Usually, only one supplier is available. These components made up 24.3 percent of total sourcing costs in 2015.

The GN Audio example illustrates how location-flexibility modes hinge on the type of components that are sourced. In relation to GN Audio's custom and unique components, we see elements of replication and mobility. Furthermore, GN Audio is attempting to increase the relatively low proportion of standard components by encouraging more competition among suppliers in the industry. Importantly, the GN Audio example points to the importance of finding the right mode *balance*. This balance is important in supply-chain competition, as firms need to identify and understand how the deployment of strategic and non-strategic resources determines their performance (Ellram et al., 2013). We translate these observations of diminishing returns to scale in the use of (costly) firm-specific resources into a principle for combining the three location-flexibility modes in a balanced way.

In summary, the principle of a balanced combination of the three location-flexibility modes prescribes the extensive use of standardized tasks and processes and sparse use of replicated or mobile firm-specific, critical resources. This leads to our fourth proposition:

P4 *Location flexibility that combines standardized, replicated, and mobile resources constitutes a necessary and sufficient condition for sustaining competitive advantage in a firm's global supply chain.*

---

6 Conclusion and Further Research Avenues

6.1 Conclusions and Contributions

In order to fill a gap at the intersection of international business and operations management research, we have taken a resource-based perspective (e.g., Hitt et al., 2016) to discuss location flexibility as a somewhat overlooked but important type of flexibility in today's increasingly volatile and uncertain environment for global sourcing firms. In relation to our first research question about how sourcing firms achieve location flexibility, we discussed the standardization of tasks and processes as well as the replication and mobility of resources across locations. For our second research question on how location flexibility can help firms sustain their competitive advantage, we elaborated on the efficiency-imitability tradeoff as a central managerial dilemma faced by global sourcing firms. We discussed several ways in which firms manage this tension when trying to increase their global supply chain agility across locations. We proposed that the balanced use of the three modes in combination is likely to be the most efficient and effective mechanism for helping firms sustain their competitive advantage in global sourcing. This is echoing the point made by Christopher and Holweg (2011) that flexible options on average will pay off and "(. . .) that firms that are considering flexibility in their supply chain design will be much better equipped to deal with (. . .) turbulence. We need to move away from the 'control' mindset that seeks to eradicate variability, towards building structures that can cope with turbulence, and embrace volatility as an opportunity" (Christopher & Holweg, 2011: 80).

In sum, our study opens up for new interesting research directions concerning location flexibility in global supply chains.

6.2   Avenues for Future Research

Our analysis complements prior research on manufacturing, supplier, and governance flexibility (Argyres & Liebeskind, 2002; Atkinson, 1984; Mayer, 2006; Theyel & Hofmann, 2021; Volberda, 1996; Yu et al., 2009). We argue that these types of flexibility become increasingly intertwined with location flexibility through the distribution and integration of operations across globally dispersed locations. We propose a combined and balanced use of the three location-flexibility modes as a way to sustain competitive advantages in global sourcing. Such an approach could enhance our understanding of how firms with globally dispersed operations can develop the capacity to reconfigure the spatial dimensions of their global supply chains in response to or in anticipation of volatile and uncertain environments while keeping reconfiguration costs low. Second, and consistent with the resource-based perspective, we have focused our study on firm-specific modes of location flexibility. However, as mentioned earlier, exogenous factors related to locations in which the sourcing firm operates also influence the firm's location flexibility. Therefore, we encourage future research that explores this aspect. In this regard, resource dependence theory (e.g., Hillman et al., 2009) may serve as a useful theoretical lens for investigating the influence of locally embedded resources on location flexibility. With regard to dependence on locally embedded suppliers and networks, and the resulting influence on the location flexibility of global sourcing, theories considering network perspectives (e.g., Johanson & Vahlne, 2009; Vahlne & Johanson, 2020), global value-chain governance (Gereffi et al., 2005; Pananond et al., 2020), and interfirm relations and relational resources (e.g., Dyer et al., 2018; Dyer & Singh, 1998; Kedia & Lahiri, 2007) may all offer fruitful theoretical perspectives.

References

Aaker, D. A., & Mascarenhas, B. (1984). The need for strategic flexibility. *Journal of Business Strategy, 5*(2), 74–82.

Ackers, P., & Wilkinson, A. (2003). *Understanding work and employment: Industrial relations in transition*. Oxford University Press.

Adler, P., Goldoftas, B., & Levine, D. I. (1999). Flexibility versus efficiency? A case study of model changeovers in the Toyota production system. *Organization Science, 10*(1), 43–68.

Allen, L., & Pantzalis, C. (1996). Valuation of the operating flexibility of multinational operations. *Journal of International Business Studies, 27*, 633–653.

Allred, C. R., Fawcett, S. E., Wallin, C., & Magnan, G. M. (2011). A dynamic collaboration capability as a source of competitive advantage. *Decision Sciences, 42*(1), 129–161.

Andersson, U., Forsgren, M., & Holm, U. (2002). The strategic impact of external networks - subsidiary performance and competence development in the multinational corporation. *Strategic Management Journal, 23*(11), 979–996.

Apte, U. M., & Mason, R. O. (1995). Global disaggregation of information-intensive services. *Management Science, 41*(7), 1250–1262.

Argyres, N. S., & Liebeskind, J. P. (2002). Governance inseparability and the evolution of US biotechnology industry. *Journal of Economic Behavior & Organization, 47*(2), 197–219.

Athreye, S. S. (2005). The Indian software industry and its evolving service capability. *Industrial and Corporate Change, 14*(3), 393–418.

Atkinson, J. (1984). Manpower strategies for flexible organizations. *Personnel Management, 16-* (August), 28–31.

Baldwin, C. Y. (2008). Where do transactions come from? Modularity, transactions, and the boundaries of firms. *Industrial and Corporate Change, 17*(1), 155–195.

Baldwin, C. Y., & Clark, K. B. (2000). *Design rules: The power of modularity.* MIT Press.

Barney, J. (1991). Firm resources and sustained competitive advantage. *Journal of Management, 17*(1), 99–120.

Belderbos, R., & Zou, J. (2007). On the growth of foreign affiliates: Multinational plant networks, joint ventures, and flexibility. *Journal of International Business Studies, 38*, 1095–1112.

Braunscheidel, M. J., & Suresh, N. C. (2009). The organizational antecedents of a firm's supply chain agility for risk mitigation and response. *Journal of Operations Management, 27*(2), 119–140.

Bresnahan, T., Gambardella, A., & Saxenian, A. (2001). 'Old economy' inputs for 'new economy' outcomes: Cluster formation in the new Silicon Valleys. *Industrial and Corporate Change, 10*(4), 835–860.

Brunsson, N., Rasche, A., & Seidl, D. (2012). The dynamics of standardization: Three perspectives on standards in organization studies. *Organization Studies, 33*(5–6), 613–632.

Buckley, P. J., Enderwick, P., & Cross, A. R. (2018). *International business.* Oxford University Press.

Burns, T., & Stalker, G. M. (1961). *The management of innovation.* Oxford University Press.

Camison, C., & Lopez, A. V. (2010). An examination of the relationship between manufacturing flexibility and firm performance. *International Journal of Operations & Production Management, 30*(8), 853–878.

Chiang, C.-Y., Kocabasoglu-Hillmer, C., & Suresh, N. (2012). An empirical investigation of the impact of strategic sourcing and flexibility on firm's supply chain agility. *International Journal of Operations & Production Management, 32*(1), 49–78.

Christopher, M., & Holweg, M. (2011). "Supply chain 2.0": Managing supply chains in the era of turbulence. *International Journal of Physical Distribution & Logistics Management, 41*(1), 63–82.

Christopher, M., & Holweg, M. (2017). Supply chain 2.0 revisited: A framework for managing volatility-induced risk in the supply chain. *International Journal of Physical Distribution & Logistics Management, 47*(1), 2–17.

Cowan, R., & Foray, D. (1997). The economics of codification and the diffusion of knowledge. *Industrial & Corporate Change, 6*(3), 595–622.

D'souza, D., & Williams, F. (2000). Toward a taxonomy of manufacturing flexibility dimensions. *Journal of Operations Management, 18*(5), 577–593.

Demirbag, M., Mellahi, K., Sahadev, S., & Elliston, J. (2012). Employee service abandonment in offshore operations: A case study of a US multinational in India. *Journal of World Business, 47*(2), 178–185.

Dierickx, I., & Cool, K. (1989). Asset stock accumulation and sustainability of competitive advantage. *Management Science, 35*(12), 1504–1511.

Doh, J. P., Bunyaratavej, K., & Hahn, E. D. (2009). Separable but not equal: The location determinants of discrete services offshoring activities. *Journal of International Business Studies, 40*, 926–943.

Dyer, J. H., & Singh, H. (1998). The relational view: Cooperative strategy and sources of interorganizational competitive advantage. *Academy of Management Review, 23*(4), 660–679.

Dyer, J. H., Singh, H., & Hesterly, W. (2018). The relational view revisited: A dynamic perspective on value creation and value capture. *Strategic Management Journal, 39*(3), 3140–3162.

Ebben, J. J., & Johnson, A. C. (2005). Efficiency, flexibility, or both? Evidence linking strategy to performance in small firms. *Strategic Management Journal, 26*(13), 1229–1259.

ECCO. (2012). Annual report for 2011.

Eisenhardt, K. M., Furr, N. R., & Bingham, C. B. (2010). Microfoundations of performance: Balancing efficiency and flexibility in dynamic environments. *Organization Science, 21*(6), 1263–1273.

Ellram, L. M., Tate, W. L., & Feitzinger, E. G. (2013). Factor-market rivalry and competition for supply chain resources. *Journal of Supply Chain Management, 49*(1), 29–46.

Ethiraj, S. K., Kale, P., Krishnan, M. S., & Singh, J. V. (2005). Where do capabilities come from and how do they matter? A study in the software services industry. *Strategic Management Journal, 26*(1), 25–45.

Ethiraj, S. K., Levinthal, D., & Roy, R. R. (2008). The dual role of modularity: Innovation and imitation. *Management Science, 54*(5), 939–955.

Fisch, J. H., & Zschoche, M. (2011). Do firms benefit from multinationality through production shifting? *Journal of International Management, 17*(2), 143–149.

Fisch, J. H., & Zschoche, M. (2012). The role of operational flexibility in the expansion of international production networks. *Strategic Management Journal, 33*(13), 1540–1556.

Frandsen, T. (2017). Evolution of modularity literature: A 25-year bibliometric analysis. *International Journal of Operations & Production Management, 37*(6), 703–747.

Gereffi, G. (2020). What does the COVID-19 pandemic teach us about global value chains? The case of medical supplies. *Journal of International Business Policy, 3*(3), 287–301.

Gereffi, G., Humphrey, S., & Sturgeon, T. (2005). The governance of global value chains. *Review of International Political Economy, 12*(1), 78–104.

Gligor, D. M., Esmark, C. L., & Holcomb, M. C. (2015). Performance outcomes of supply chain agility: When should you be agile? *Journal of Operations Management, 33–34*, 71–82.

Gulati, R., & Sytch, M. (2007). Dependence asymmetry and joint dependence in interorganizational relationships: Effects of embeddedness on a manufacturer's performance in procurement relationships. *Administrative Science Quarterly, 52*(1), 32–69.

Hahn, E. D., Doh, J. P., & Bunyaratavej, K. (2009). The evolution of risk in information systems offshoring: The impact of home country risk, firm learning, and competitive dynamics. *MIS Quarterly, 33*(3), 597–616.

Hillman, A. J., Withers, M. C., & Collins, B. J. (2009). Resource dependence theory: A review. *Journal of Management, 35*(6), 1404–1427.

Hitt, M. A. (2011). Relevance of strategic management theory and research for supply chain management. *Journal of Supply Chain Management, 47*(1), 9–13.

Hitt, M. A., Xu, K., & Carnes, C. M. (2016). Resource based theory in operations management research. *Journal of Operations Management, 41*, 77–94.

Huchzermeier, A., & Cohen, M. A. (1996). Valuing operational flexibility under exchange rate risk. *Operations Research, 44*(1), 100–113.

Jain, A., Jain, P. K., Chan, F. T. S., & Singh, S. (2013). A review on manufacturing flexibility. *International Journal of Production Research, 51*(19), 5946–5970.

Jensen, P. D. Ø., & Petersen, B. (2013). Global sourcing of services: Risk, process, and collaborative architecture. *Global Strategy Journal, 3*(1), 67–87.

Johanson, J., & Vahlne, J. (2009). The Uppsala internationalization process model revisited: From liability of foreignness to liability of outsidership. *Journal of International Business Studies, 40*, 1411–1431.

Kedia, B. L., & Lahiri, S. (2007). International outsourcing of services: A partnership model. *Journal of International Management, 13*(1), 22–37.

Kedia, B. L., & Mukherjee, D. (2009). Understanding offshoring: A research framework based disintegration, location and externalization advantages. *Journal of World Business, 44*(3), 250–261.

Khadria, B. (2004). Human resources in science and technology in India and the international mobility of highly skilled Indians. In *OECD science, technology and industry working papers, 2004/07*. OECD Publishing.

Kim, Y. S., & Mathur, I. (2008). The impact of geographic diversification on firm performance. *International Review of Financial Analysis, 17*(4), 747–766.

King, A. W. (2007). Disentangling interfirm and intrafirm causal ambiguity: A conceptual model of causal ambiguity and sustainable competitive advantage. *Academy of Management Review, 32*(1), 156–178.

Knemeyer, A. M., Zinn, W., & Eroglu, C. (2009). Proactive planning for catastrophic events in supply chains. *Journal of Operations Management, 27*(2), 141–513.

Kogut, B. (1985). Designing global strategies: Profiting from operational flexibility. *Sloan Management Review, 26*(4), 15–28.

Kogut, B., & Kulatilaka, N. (1994). Operating flexibility, global manufacturing, and the option value of a multinational network. *Management Science, 40*(1), 123–139.

Kogut, B., & Zander, U. (1992). Knowledge of the firm, combinative capabilities, and the replication of technology. *Organization Science, 3*(3), 383–397.

Kumar, K., van Fenema, P. C., & von Glinow, M. A. (2009). Offshoring and global distribution of work: Implications for task interdependence theory and practice. *Journal of International Business Studies, 40*, 642–667.

Lewin, A. Y., Massini, S., & Peeters, C. (2009). Why are companies offshoring innovation? The emerging global race for talent. *Journal of International Business Studies, 40*, 901–925.

Lippman, S. A., & Rumelt, R. P. (1982). Uncertain imitability: An analysis of interfirm differences in efficiency under competition. *The Bell Journal of Economics, 13*(2), 418–438.

Luo, Y., Wang, S., Zheng, Q., & Jayaraman, V. (2012). Task attributes and process integration in business process offshoring: A perspective of service providers from India and China. *Journal of International Business Studies, 43*, 498–524.

Mair, A. (1994). Honda's global flexifactory network. *International Journal of Operations & Production Management, 14*(3), 6–23.

Manning, S. (2014). Mitigate, tolerate or relocate? Offshoring challenges, strategic imperatives and resource constraints. *Journal of World Business, 49*(4), 522–535.

Manning, S., Hutzschenreuter, T., & Strathmann, A. (2013). Emerging capability or continuous challenge? Relocating knowledge work and managing process interfaces. *Industrial and Corporate Change, 22*(5), 1159–1193.

Manning, S., Ricart, J. E., Rique, M. S. R., & Lewin, A. Y. (2010). From blind spots to hotspots: How knowledge services clusters develop and attract foreign investment. *Journal of International Management, 16*(4), 369–382.

Manning, S., Sydow, J., & Windeler, A. (2012). Securing access to lower-cost talent globally: The dynamics of active embedding and field structuration. *Regional Studies, 46*(9), 1201–1218.

Manuj, I., & Mentzer, J. T. (2008). Global supply chain risk management strategies. *International Journal of Physical Distribution & Logistics Management, 38*(3), 192–223.

Mayer, K. J. (2006). Spillovers and governance: An analysis of knowledge and reputational spillovers in information technology. *Academy of Management Journal, 49*(1), 69–84.

McKinsey. (2020). *Risk, resilience, and rebalancing in global value chains*. McKinsey Global Institute. August 2020.

McKinsey. (2021). *The resilience imperative: Succeeding in uncertain times*. McKinsey Global Institute. May 2021.

Miles, R. E., & Snow, C. C. (1986). Organizations: New concepts for new forms. *California Management Review, 18*(3), 62–73.

Mintzberg, H., & McHugh, A. (1985). Strategy formation in an adhocracy. *Administrative Science Quarterly, 30*(2), 160–197.

Niosi, J., & Tschang, F. T. (2009). The strategies of Chinese and Indian software multinationals: Implications for internationalization theory. *Industrial and Corporate Change, 18*(2), 269–294.

O'Reilly, C., & Tushman, M. L. (2008). Ambidexterity as a dynamic capability: Resolving the innovator's dilemma. *Research in Organizational Behavior, 28*, 185–206.

OECD. (2001). *International mobility of the highly skilled. OECD Proceedings*. OECD Publications.

Oliver, C., & Holzinger, I. (2008). The effectiveness of strategic political management: A dynamic capabilities framework. *Academy of Management Review, 33*(2), 496–520.

ORN. (2011). *Organizational flexibility: The strategic differentiator of global sourcing effectiveness*. ORN annual corporate client report. Durham, NC.

Pananond, P., Gereffi, G., & Pedersen, T. (2020). An integrative typology of global strategy and global value chains: The management and organization of cross-border activities. *Global Strategy Journal, 10*(3), 421–443.

Papastergiadis, N. (2000). *The turbulence of migration: Globalization, deterritorialization, and hybridity*. Polity Press and Blackwell.

Parker, R. P., & Wirth, A. (1999). Manufacturing flexibility: Measures and relationships. *European Journal of Operational Research, 118*(3), 429–449.

Patibandla, M., & Petersen, B. (2002). Role of transnational corporations in the evolution of a high-tech industry: The case of India's software industry. *World Development, 30*(9), 1561–1577.

Peréz, J. B., & Pla-Barber, J. (2005). When are international managers a cost effective solution? The rationale of transaction cost economics applied to staffing decisions in MNCs. *Journal of Business Research, 58*(10), 1320–1329.

Petersen, B., Welch, D. E., & Welch, L. S. (2000). Creating meaningful switching options in international operations. *Long Range Planning, 33*(5), 690–707.

Pfeffer, J., & Salancik, G. R. (1978). *The external control of organizations: A resource dependence perspective*. Harper and Row.

Porter, M. E. (1986). Competition in global industries: A conceptual framework. In M. E. Porter (Ed.), *Competition in global industries* (pp. 15–60). Harvard Business School Press.

Prater, E., Biehl, M., & Smith, M. A. (2001). International supply chain agility – Tradeoffs between flexibility and uncertainty. *International Journal of Operations and Production Management, 21*(5/6), 823–839.

Priem, R. L., & Butler, J. E. (2001). Is the resource-based view a useful perspective for strategic management research? *Academy of Management Review, 26*(1), 22–46.

Priem, R. L., & Swink, M. (2012). A demand-side perspective on supply chain management. *Journal of Supply Chain Management, 48*(2), 7–13.

Rangan, S. (1998). Do multinationals operate flexibly? Theory and evidence. *Journal of International Business Studies, 29*, 217–237.

Ray, G., Barney, J. B., & Muhanna, W. A. (2004). Capabilities, business processes, and competitive advantage: Choosing the dependent variable in empirical tests of the resource-based view. *Strategic Management Journal, 25*(1), 23–37.

Reed, R., & DeFillippi, R. J. (1990). Causal ambiguity, barriers to imitation, and sustainable competitive advantage. *Academy of Management Review, 15*(1), 88–102.

Ring, P. S., & van de Ven, A. H. (1992). Structuring cooperative relationships between organizations. *Strategic Management Journal, 13*(7), 483–498.

Sanchez, R., & Mahoney, J. T. (1996). Modularity, flexibility, and knowledge management in product and organization design. *Strategic Management Journal, 17*(S2), 63–76.

Sánchez, A. M., & Pérez, M. P. (2005). Supply chain flexibility and firm performance: A conceptual model and empirical study in the automotive industry. *International Journal of Operations & Production Management, 25*(7), 681–700.

Schreyoegg, G., & Sydow, J. (2010). Organizing for fluidity? Dilemmas of new organizational forms. *Organization Science, 21*(6), 1251–1262.

Simsek, Z. (2009). Organizational ambidexterity: Towards a multilevel understanding. *Journal of Management Studies, 46*(4), 597–624.

Starkey, K., Barnatt, C., & Tempest, S. (2000). Beyond networks and hierarchies: Latent organizations in the U.K. television industry. *Organization Science, 11*(3), 299–305.

Stecke, K. E., & Kumar, S. (2009). Sources of supply chain disruptions, factors that breed vulnerability, and mitigating strategies. *Journal of Marketing Channels, 16*(3), 193–226.

Stringfellow, A., Teagarden, M., & Nie, W. (2008). Invisible costs in offshoring services work. *Journal of Operations Management, 26*(2), 164–179.

Swafford, P. M., Ghosh, S., & Murthy, N. (2006). The antecedents of supply chain agility of a firm: Scale development and model testing. *Journal of Operations Management, 24*(2), 170–188.

Tang, C. Y., & Tikoo, S. (1999). Operational flexibility and market valuation of earnings. *Strategic Management Journal, 20*(8), 749–761.

Tanriverdi, H., Konana, P., & Ge, L. (2007). The choice of sourcing mechanisms for business processes. *Information Systems Research, 18*(3), 280–299.

Teece, D. J., Pisano, G., & Shuen, A. (1997). Dynamic capabilities and strategic management. *Strategic Management Journal, 18*(7), 509–533.

Theyel, G., & Hofmann, K. H. (2021). Manufacturing location decisions and organizational agility. *Multinational Business Review, 29*(2), 166–188.

Thompson, J. D. (1967). *Organizations in action.* McGraw-Hill.

UNCTAD. (2020). *World investment report 2020: International production beyond the pandemic.* United Nations Conference on Trade and Development.

Vahlne, J. E., & Johanson, J. (2020). The Uppsala model: Networks and micro-foundations. *Journal of International Business Studies, 51*, 4–10.

Verbeke, A. (2020). Will the COVID-19 pandemic really change the governance of global value chains? *British Journal of Management, 31*(3), 444–446.

Vokurka, R. J., & O'Leary-Kelly, S. W. (2000). A review of empirical research on manufacturing flexibility. *Journal of Operations Management, 18*(4), 485–501.

Volberda, H. W. (1996). Towards the flexible form: How to remain vital in hypercompetitive environments. *Organization Science, 7*(4), 359–374.

von Hippel, E. (1994). "Sticky information" and the locus of problem solving: Implications for innovation. *Management Science, 40*(4), 429–439.

Wagner, S. M., & Bode, C. (2006). An empirical investigation into supply chain vulnerability. *Journal of Purchasing and Supply Management, 12*(6), 301–312.

Wang, G., & Yeh, E. Y. (2005). Globalization and hybridization in cultural products: The cases of Mulan and crouching Tiger, hidden dragon. *International Journal of Cultural Studies, 8*(2), 175–193.

Welch, D. E. (2003). Globalisation of staff movements: Beyond cultural adjustment. *Management International Review, 43*(2), 149–169.

Wernerfelt, B. (1989). From critical resources to corporate strategy. *Journal of General Management, 14*(3), 4–12.

Windeler, A., & Sydow, J. (2001). Project networks and changing industry practices – Collaborative content production in the German television industry. *Organization Studies, 22*(6), 1035–1060.

Winter, S. G. (2003). Understanding dynamic capabilities. *Strategic Management Journal, 24*(10), 991–995.

World Economic Forum. (2013). *Building resilience in supply chains – An initiative of the risk response network in collaboration with Accenture.* World Economic Forum.

World Economic Forum. (2020). *How to rebound stronger from Covid-19 – Resilience in manufacturing and supply systems.* World Economic Forum.

Xanthopoulos, A., Vlachos, D., & Iakovou, E. (2012). Optimal newsvendor policies for dual-sourcing supply chains: A disruption risk management framework. *Computers & Operations Research, 39*(2), 350–357.

Yu, H., Zeng, A. Z., & Zhao, L. (2009). Single or dual sourcing: Decision-making in the presence of supply chain disruption risks. *Omega, 37*(4), 788–800.

Zhou, K. Z., & Wu, F. (2010). Technological capability, strategic flexibility, and product innovation. *Strategic Management Journal, 31*(5), 547–561.

Peter D. Ørberg Jensen is Associate Professor of Strategy and International Management at Copenhagen Business School, Denmark. His research specializes in global sourcing of advanced and high-value activities and internationalization of service firms and activities. From 1992 to 2005, he worked in business consulting and for the United Nations Development Programme.

Stephan Manning is a Professor of Strategy and Innovation at the University of Sussex Business School. His research focuses on responses to global societal challenges, social innovation and entrepreneurship, global value chains, and films as vehicles for social change. His research has been published widely. For more information, visit www.stephanmanning.com.

Bent Petersen is professor in International Business at the Copenhagen Business School, Department of International Economics, Government and Business. He has co-authored 3 books, 10 book chapters, and around 50 articles in journals such as JIBS, JWB, and GSJ. His current research interests are in GVCs, dynamics of foreign operation modes, and strategic contracting.

Emerging Non-market Risk in International Business

Chang Hoon Oh and Jennifer Oetzel

1 Introduction

While globalization has opened new markets to multinational enterprises (MNEs), it has also potentially exposed them to novel sources and higher levels of risk. There is growing evidence that the cost and prevalence of risk are increasing and that the management of risk is becoming more complex for businesses, governments, and communities (Alexander, 2006; Theisen, 2008). Over the course of any given year, various types of external, catastrophic non-market events are likely to occur worldwide. These events will, at least temporarily, change the business environment at local, national, regional, or global levels.

Recently, for example, the Covid-19 pandemic has affected daily life of virtually all human beings on earth. According to the Brookings Institution (2021), the unemployment rate of large metropolitan areas in the United States has declined by more than three percent over a year from November 2019 to November 2020. Hurricane Katrina decimated the city of New Orleans, Louisiana, and the Gulf Coast of Mississippi (Vigdor, 2008). Other examples of catastrophic non-market events include the 2004 tsunami that devastated large parts of Indonesia, the 2008 Sichuan earthquake in China, the 2011 tsunami and nuclear disaster in Japan, the 1984 Bhopal chemical disaster in India, the 1986 Chernobyl nuclear disaster in Ukraine (formerly the Soviet Union), and terrorist attacks in various parts of the world, including in the Palestinian Territories, the United States, Northern Ireland, Spain, England, Iraq, and Afghanistan.

C. H. Oh (✉)
William & Judy Docking Professor of Strategy, University of Kansas School of Business, Lawrence, KS, USA
e-mail: changhoon_oh@ku.edu

J. Oetzel
American University, Kogod School of Business, Washington, DC, USA
e-mail: oetzelj@american.edu

© Springer Nature Switzerland AG 2022
H. Merchant (ed.), *The New Frontiers of International Business*, Contributions to Management Science, https://doi.org/10.1007/978-3-031-06003-8_13

The loss of life is, of course, the most tragic and troubling aspect of such catastrophic non-market events. However, these events can also increase transaction costs, lower firm profits, threaten business survival, discourage business entrants into new markets, and cause business exit from existing ones. The ramification can be felt over a number of years and can disrupt economic life at both the micro and macro levels. For example, even 16 years after Hurricane Katrina, the rebuilding of New Orleans is still a work in progress. While communities are trying to return to pre-hurricane conditions, certain areas may never fully recover (Santos, 2019). While the city had about 90% of the pre-storm population in 2019, low-income communities enjoyed very little of the post-Katrina recovery and growth in the region (Santos, 2019).

While catastrophic non-market events can devastate businesses, their impact conceivably may vary across countries and firms, depending on various attributes. However, until recently, only a few business scholars have raised the importance of this topic (Greening & Johnson, 1996; Mascarenhas, 1982; Miller, 1992; Quarantelli, 1988), and the issue has generally received little attention in the fields of international business (IB) and business strategy. Traditionally, IB heavily focuses on political/institutional risks and economic/financial crises (Chung et al., 2010; Henisz et al., 2010; Lee & Makhija, 2009; Tallman, 1988). This is likely due to the influence of institutional theory and resource-based view in these fields. These theories/views explain that managers can handle these types of risk based on the quality of governments, politics, and firm capabilities.[1]

The political/institutional risk and economic/financial risk literatures show that these types of risk generally increase transaction costs, thereby reducing investment, production, and income. In particular, several studies examine the effect of political risk (e.g., Delios & Henisz, 2003; Tallman, 1988) and institutional transitions (e.g., Hoskisson et al., 2000; Peng, 2003) on IB transactions and MNE strategy. This stream of literature extends to internal and external political conflicts and violence and their effects on MNE ownership choice and location decision (e.g., Albino-Pimentel et al., 2021; Dai et al., 2017; Oh & Oetzel, 2017). In contrast, it is only in the past decade that other types of risks such as natural disasters, technological disasters, and social conflicts have received some, but not enough, attention (e.g., Buckley et al., 2020; Jiménez et al., 2021; McKnight & Linnenluecke, 2016, 2019; Oetzel & Miklian, 2017; Oetzel & Oh, 2021; Oh & Oetzel, 2011; Pek et al., 2018; Ramos & Ashby, 2017; Rao & Greve, 2018).

Recently, the Covid-19 pandemic has triggered much interest in pandemics and other health-related disruptions from IB scholars, but it seems that scholars narrowly focus on the Covid-19 pandemic (e.g., Muzio & Doh, 2021) and do not explore other types of important risk events and their implications for international strategic

---

[1] There are a series of studies on natural disasters and philanthropic donations after the Sichuan earthquake in China and on the identification of entrepreneurial opportunity in the 2020 Haiti earthquake. However, those studies mainly investigate social responsibility of domestic and foreign firms in disaster aftermaths and thus have little relevance to risk management and preparation in international strategic management.

management. Many studies about the Covid-19 pandemic are done from the view of political risks and economic risks without careful understanding about the characteristics of pandemics and natural disasters. Yet, we have little knowledge about the cause of the Covid-19 virus and its impact on individuals, businesses, and society. While it is important to pursue research on important phenomena or issues of society, researchers should also have a proper understanding of issues related to social and natural phenomena. If not, the research outcomes do not have any academic or practical value.

Therefore, scholars should understand the characteristics of catastrophic non-market risks and their similarity with and differences from other types of well-researched risks and uncertainties. Catastrophic non-market risk differs from market-based or other types of non-market types in at least two ways. First, catastrophic non-market risks are much more unpredictable due to the complexity of underlying and triggering causes. Second, whereas economic, financial, and political risks are typically a country-specific state of affairs, catastrophic non-market risk can suddenly strike and may involve either a narrow location or a broader region. These differences can shape the business environments of MNEs. Understanding how such non-market risks affect MNEs and their environments offers new research opportunities for scholars.

The existing literature provides four types of catastrophic non-market risk events for businesses: natural disasters, technological disasters, political conflicts, and social conflicts (see Dai et al., 2017; Oh, 2017; Oh & Oetzel, 2011; Perrow, 2007; Ruggie, 2007; Zanini, 2009). In this chapter, we will refer to these as NTPS risks and will further define and focus on these risks in the context of MNEs.

The purpose of this chapter is to explore each type of NTPS risk and their characteristics and to provide a better understanding about their complexity. We then examine factors that determine MNE awareness of, preparedness for, and response to NTPS risks. We conclude with recommendations for future research topics that will contribute to both academic research and managerial practices in risk management, specifically for MNEs.

2   Types and Characteristics of Non-market Risk Events

Over the past three decades, risk and uncertainty—and how these affect firm decisions and performance—have been an important area of inquiry in management research, drawing the attention of researchers from across the spectrum of management/business disciplines (see Bloom & Milkovich, 1998; Madsen, 2009; March & Shapira, 1987; McNamara & Bromiley, 1999; Shapira, 1995; Sheffi, 2015; Singh, 1986; Teece et al., 2016; Vaaler, 2008). Knight (1921) differentiates risk from uncertainty. According to Knight (1921), risk is a situation where we can accurately estimate the odds and uncertainty in a situation where we cannot accurately estimate the odds because we do not have all the information. The Knightian distinction between risk and uncertainty on risk management implies that uncertainty is not estimable or avoidable and so people might not be able to prevent or overcome

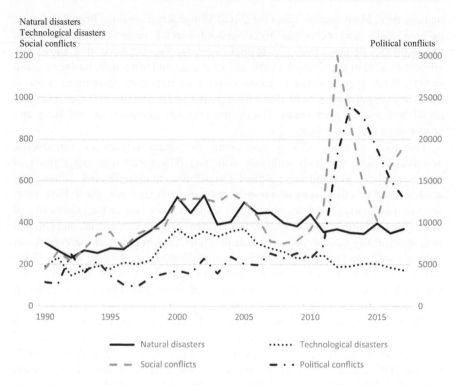

Fig. 1 Number of events by type. Note: For natural disasters, technological disasters, and political conflicts, the data account for events all over the world. For social conflicts, the data only include non-governmental events in Latin America and Africa. Source: Authors' own figure based on EM-DAT (2020), Georeferenced Event Dataset by Sundberg and Melander (2013), and Social Conflict Analysis Database by Salehyan et al. (2012)

uncertainty. Thus, the Knightian distinction has likely influenced scholars to focus on seemingly predictable uncertainty including economic, financial, political, and institutional risks rather than unpredictable and uncertain NTPS risks (O'Malley, 2004).[2] However, NTPS risks are a major threat to the economy and society. Figure 1 shows the number of NTPS risks between 1990 and 2017.

Few studies in this area seek to integrate different types of risks and examine managerial risk management. For example, Boddewyn (1988), Fitzpatrick (1983), Mascarenhas (1982), Miller (1992), and Quarantelli (1988) outline strategies for responding to risk, and Baird and Thomas (1985) propose new approaches for identifying the relationship between specific risks—such as environmental, industry, organizational, strategic problems, and risks associated with decision-making—and

---

[2]Likewise, Courtney et al. (1997) classify uncertainty into four levels based on predictability and knowableness. They note that level 4 uncertainty is a true ambiguity and so it is impossible to predict level 4 uncertainty. In fact, they noted that "[a] t level 4, it is critical to avoid the urge to throw up your hands and act purely on gut instinct."

risk-taking behavior of firms. However, much of this work was published at least three decades ago, and not many of these studies thoroughly address risk in the context of MNEs. To date, it is not easy to find research that provides a systematic discussion about the different types of risks and their impacts on businesses. As MNEs extend their geographic and organizational boundaries, they have increasing exposure to new types of risks that have been traditionally under researched in various management and business disciplines.[3]

As noted above, researchers in IB and related disciplines tend to focus on seemingly predictable and manageable risks such as political and institutional risks (e.g., Delios & Henisz, 2003; Fitzpatrick, 1983; Henisz et al., 2010; John & Lawton, 2018; Tallman, 1988), economic and financial risks (e.g., Chung et al., 2010; Click, 2005; Lee & Makhija, 2009; Rugman & Oh, 2011; Tran, 2020), or organizational risks (e.g., Gong, 2003; Habib, 1987; Joshi et al., 2002; Le Nguyen et al., 2016). Recently, a few studies have addressed the risks of natural and technological disasters (Oetzel & Oh, 2021; Oh & Oetzel, 2011; Oh & Reuveny, 2010; Pek et al., 2018), violent conflicts (Dai et al., 2017; Oetzel & Getz, 2012; Oh & Oetzel, 2017), and social conflicts such as ethnic conflicts (Oetzel & Oh, 2019), conflicts between companies and communities (Andrews et al., 2017; Calvano, 2008; Dorobantu & Odziemkowska, 2017), and organized violent crime (Ramos & Ashby, 2017). There is also some recognition that risks are, at times, inter-related. For example, some researchers suggest that natural disasters may exacerbate political risks (Barnett & Adger, 2007; Oh & Reuveny, 2010; Olson, 2005) and that political risks may exacerbate economic risks (Helm & Boffey, 2012). Yet, research on these emerging and significant non-market risks and their impacts (e.g., ethnic/ religious disputes, social movements/collective actions, demographic changes, and crime/vandalism) are at the early stage in IB and related disciplines. An integrative and more comprehensive conceptual and theoretical framework for NTPS risks, including their complexity and levels of uncertainty, is needed to better to understand and mitigate risk.

2.1   Types of Non-market Risk Based on Causes

Natural Disasters The first of the NTPS risks is posed by natural disasters (earthquakes, storms, floods, wildfires, volcanic eruptions, insect infestations, epidemics, etc.) and is shown directly and indirectly to discourage international

---

[3] According to the BBC, *Time* magazine, and *USA Today*, NTPS risk events represent the most intensively covered events since 2000 and certainly have impacted the operations of MNEs worldwide. These include the events of 9/11 (2001); the Chechen rebels attacks in Moscow (2002); the Iraq War (2003 and 2004); the Indian Ocean earthquake and tsunami and Hurricane Katrina (2005); the death of Saddam Hussein (2006); the US mortgage crisis (2007); the US presidential election (2008); economic crises (2009); Haiti earthquake (2010); the Arab Spring uprisings (2011); Crimean crisis (2014); election of Donald Trump (2016); Hurricane Harvey (2017); Northern California wildfires (2018); Hong Kong protests (2019); and Covid-19 (2020).

trade, foreign investment, and economic growth (Escaleras & Register, 2011; Oh & Reuveny, 2010; Raddatz, 2007), as well as the foreign investment decision of MNEs (Buckley et al., 2020; Jiménez et al., 2021; Oetzel & Oh, 2014; Oh & Oetzel, 2011). The United States is frequently hit by devastating hurricanes and wildfires, and South East Asia is often hit by cyclones, earthquakes, and tsunamis. Sub-Saharan Africa is often hit by droughts and famines, while floods and mudslides frequently occur in South and Central America. In Europe, storms and river overflows often cause large floods. Perhaps the most shocking example is the Covid-19 pandemic and 2011 Japanese tsunami and earthquakes. The average economic loss from natural disasters has risen from about $12 billion/annum in the 1970s to $83 billion per year in the 2000s (United Nations, 2008).

Research shows that as the likelihood of natural disasters increases, so too does the cost to the global economy, reportedly at least $1.271 trillion between 2010 and 2019 alone (EM-DAT, 2020). The costs posted by natural disasters are extensive enough that they are recognized in federal tax policy for both individuals and businesses in US tax legislation. Legislation was originally enacted in response to the terrorist attacks on September 11, 2001, in New York City, New York, and they have now been extended to federally declared natural disasters in the United States. Since 2001, any individuals or businesses affected by federally recognized natural disasters are eligible for tax relief. Such tax policies for the damages from natural disasters have also existed in other countries such as Australia, Canada, Japan, and South Korea, even before the outbreak of the 2019 novel coronavirus.

Technological Disasters Although technological developments have led to dramatic improvements in labor productivity and economic development in recent decades, technological disasters (resulting from the breakdown of technological systems or accidents associated with the processing, storage, and transportation of hazardous materials) may cause massive loss of life and property or endanger the wider social environment (England, 1988; Evan & Manion, 2002). Take, for example, the 2008 outbreak of listeriosis in Canada from ready-to-eat meat products made by Maple Leaf Foods, one of the largest food and beverage producers in North America, which resulted in 15 deaths. This event represented not only a public health crisis but also a managerial catastrophe for Maple Leaf Foods, forcing it to recall more than 220 products from the United States, Japan, Hong Kong, China, Europe, and Canada, at an immediate financial loss of $20 million (Powell, 2008). Following the recall, Maple Leaf Foods' market shares plunged by 21%. Flavelle (2008) estimates that the cost of regaining consumer confidence could exceed $20 million.

Other recent prominent examples of technological disasters include accidents such as the explosion of British Petroleum's Deepwater Horizon oil rig in 2010, which killed 11 people and became the largest offshore oil spill in the history of the United States; the Qinghe Special Steel Corporation disaster in China in 2007, which killed 32 workers (Zio & Aven, 2013); and the Samarco mine's dam collapse in Brazil in 2015 that killed more than 25 people and led to an over 5% decline in BHP Billiton's stock price (Kiernan & Hoyle, 2015; Phillips, 2015). The latter half of the twentieth century saw a dramatic increase in incidences of technological disasters and damages by these disasters (EM-DAT, 2020). These disasters not only have major impacts on communities and the natural environment but can also have major impacts on firms.

Political Conflicts Political conflicts (as opposed to coup d'états, civil strife, threats to the peaceful transfer of power, expropriation of assets, policy instability, or other forms of political turmoil) may directly affect the profitability and survival of firms (Root, 1972). The 9/11 attacks represent an example of this type of risk. While terrorism generally destroys only a small fraction of a country's capital, it might have a larger adverse economic impact. Frederick W. Smith, Chairman, President, and CEO of the FedEx Corporation, alludes to the far-reaching impacts on businesses: "The security challenges in the post-9/11 era require new thinking and new approaches that go far beyond traditional physical security models. Companies need to embed security in all aspects of their business processes and operations" (Business Roundtable, 2008). Until Hurricane Katrina, the 9/11 economic loss was the most expensive insured loss in the United States (Romilly, 2007). The 9/11 attacks also reduced tourism spending by $50 billion in the United States and led to the loss of 559,000 jobs (Blake & Sinclair, 2003).

There is empirical evidence that inward FDI flows into the United States declined precipitously after 9/11. Data from Vale Columbia Center at Columbia University (Kornecki, 2013) show that inward foreign direct investment flows dropped substantially after September 11, 2001. In 2000, total inward FDI flows from around the world amounted to $314 billion; in 2001, $159.5 billion; in 2002, $74.5 billion; and in 2003, $53.1 billion. It was not until 2006 that flows surpassed 2001 levels. Although the aggregate data do not enable us to determine which firms put their investments on hold, moved them to another country, or cancelled them altogether or, for that matter, to pinpoint the degree to which 9/11 contributed to the decline in investment, it does show an important trend after the violent attack. Media outlets, such as *The Telegraph* (September 8, 2011) and BBC (September 5, 2011), often reported that the starting point of the recent US and European financial crises could be the 9/11 terrorist attacks. More recently, civil wars and uprisings in the Middle East have increased uncertainty about the security of contracts. MNEs, such as BP, Royal Dutch Shell, and BASF, have responded by either cutting production or repatriating staff (Peel, 2011).

Social Conflicts Social conflicts constellate when an empowered segment of civil society takes up a social issue and applies pressure on a company (Kytle & Ruggie, 2005), forcing an organization to change its policies. Research shows that social movements and collective actions affect shareholders' valuation of companies that create negative externalities for society and the natural environment (Oh et al., 2021). This, for instance, was the case at the 2002 Barcelona AIDS conference, where AIDS activists protested against Coca-Cola, not because the organization had an intrinsic connection to AIDS, but because it was a prominent global brand with one of the largest distribution networks on the African continent. To mitigate the risk, Coca-Cola agreed to provide treatment to the staff of its independently owned African bottlers and corporate employees (Ruggie, 2007).

A lack of understanding of local culture(s) and miscommunications with stakeholders triggers social conflicts and, at times, precipitates extreme actions, such as suicides, homicides, spontaneous strikes, bullying, and sabotage, thus constituting a non-market risk for specific industries or companies (Denenberg & Braverman, 2001). For example, an industry-wide 16-day oil strike in the Norwegian North Sea triggered a 2% increase in the price of oil. The strike occurred simply because an American oilfield company, Baker Hughes, did not correctly understand the local workforce in Norway (Malkenses, 2012).

2.2 Impact of NTPS Risks

Studies show that risk—depending on (1) context (i.e., the country) (Davis & Seitz, 1982; Kasperson & Pijawka, 1985; Oh & Oetzel, 2011; Oh & Reuveny, 2010); (2) the actor (i.e., the MNE) (Chung et al., 2010; Oetzel & Oh, 2014; Oh & Oetzel, 2017, 2021); and (3) types of risk (Buckley et al., 2020; Oh & Oetzel, 2011) – can produce different casualties, losses, and economic impacts. The above examples in the previous section illustrate just some of the ways in which NTPS risks negatively impact the economy and society as well as the activities and performance of MNEs. Theoretically, NTPS risks can reduce international transactions by increasing transaction costs within and between companies (Oh, 2017). First, NTPS risks are likely to damage physical assets of companies and their suppliers and victimize their employees. Firms cannot maintain pre-disaster-level production in a short time and require time and resources to recover to a normal operation process (Albala-Bertrand, 1993; Tavares, 2004). In addition, NTPS risks can lower employees' motivation to engage in production and consumption (Oh & Reuveny, 2010). It is also likely that as a result of these uncertainties, firms will face higher financial capital costs due to higher interest rates, lower creditability, and discouraged financial investors. Finally, unstable and unexpected changes in regulations and foreign policies, as we have experienced from the Covid-19 pandemic, generate additional transaction costs for MNEs.

However, such a risk can also affect economies and businesses in positive ways (Awokuse & Gempesay, 2005; Deryugina et al., 2018; Oetzel & Oh, 2015; Vigdor, 2008). Researchers find that rebuilding in areas affected by risk events leads to increased government capital expenditure which, in turn, attracts foreign MNEs and investments, as well as technology and expertise, boosting overall productivity. Local employers may increase wages and provide more economic opportunities to attract and retain workers (Deryugina et al., 2018). MNEs may decide to enter local markets depressed by an NTPS risk (Awokuse & Gempesay, 2005), motivated by the opportunity to make money by increasing market share (Kobrin, 1979; Oh, 2017), and the government of a country hit by an NTPS risk may choose public policies aimed at increasing the national IB transactions in order to attract funds, technology, and expertise that could be used to rebuild affected areas (Vigdor,

2008). Thus, risk events can also be seen as opportunities for creative destruction, where new investments replace outdated infrastructure (Schumpeter, 1942).

2.3   Characteristics of NTPS Risks

There are a few distinct characteristics of NTPS. First, a unique feature of NTPS risks is their geographic scope. Risks from financial/economic crises and political instability directly affect firms and other actors within the boundaries of sovereignty, typically national boundaries. In contrast, the direct impacts of NTPS risks typically do not have clear geographic boundaries. Some events can only affect firms and other actors within an affected area. The affected area can be as large as Earth in the case of Covid-19 or as small as a mining site in the case of company-community conflict or technology failure.

When the affected area is large, many sovereignties try to manage and control the damage by using their own policies and regulations, like we have seen in different countries or municipalities in treating Covid-19. When the affected area is very small, some sovereignties may have limited response to the risk. However, the severity or damage of a risk event is not necessarily correlated with the size of affected area. For example, several producers in industrial complexes in Thailand had to shut down their operations due to floods in 2011. The floods damaged the production of hard drives, increased their prices, and disrupted global supply chains in the computer industry for a couple of years (Sanders, 2018).

The second unique feature is the potential of recurrence. Some countries or locations are more susceptible to a specific type of risk. For examples, natural resource-rich countries likely experience social and political conflicts more than other countries. Typhoons likely affect South East Asian countries every year. The potential of recurrence has two seemingly contradictory implications. First, using the information from past occurrences and intensity, managers may have a better prediction about future events. Thus, firms and other organizations can make more accurate preparations for and responses to future events. Second, because of frequent experience with low-impact risks, managers may become over-confident about managing future events. Such confidence lowers the level and likelihood of preparation.

3   Determinants of MNE Awareness, Preparedness, and Response

MNEs change their strategy and structure based on NTPS risks. NTPS risks also affect MNEs' performance and sustainability. The relationship between NTPS risks and MNE strategy, structure, performance, and sustainability may depend on the risk management process, awareness, preparedness, and response: see Fig. 2. The risk management process is determined by various factors such as the characteristics of the risk, the location of MNE operations, and the organizational capability/structure

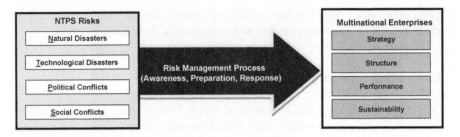

Fig. 2 NTPS risks and MNEs. Source: Authors' own figure

of the MNE involved. The existing literature examines factors such as the level of uncertainty, severity of risk, institutional quality, firm experience, firm capability, and firm's geographic network.

First, the level of uncertainty depends on the type of risk involved: for example, individuals rate natural disasters as relatively low risk, regardless of their probability or severity, while minor technological disasters, such as industrial accidents, or political conflicts (e.g., acts of terrorism)—even if they result in little damage or loss of life—tend to evoke a dramatic response and are likely to be socially amplified by the media (Kasperson et al., 1988). This implication is in line with the notion that individuals tend to overestimate the risks associated with dramatic and sensational events, while they tend to underestimate the risks associated with unspectacular but deadlier events (Oh & Oetzel, 2011; Slovic et al., 2000). In addition, the level of uncertainty would be high for events that have multiple causes (Andrews et al., 2017; Oh & Oetzel, 2021). The complexity in causes makes it difficult to predict, prepare for, and respond to the uncertainty.

Second, generally speaking, the severity of the risk determines the level of damage. The level of uncertainty of a risk would not necessarily be correlated with its severity. For example, while it is almost certain that several storms will hit the coast of Florida every year, and organizations and individuals will likely prepare for those storms, the severity of a storm differs by each storm. Thus, if an organization is well aware of and prepared for storms, its damage might be lower than other organizations in the same location who did not prepare for it. However, the preparation would not always provide reward. Even an organization that is well prepared for storms would get much damage when a severe storm moves right through the location of the organization, while other organizations are not affected if they locate miles away from the path of storm. Therefore, there are very complex causality and endogeneity issues among the severity of risk, risk awareness, risk preparedness, and risk response.

Third, in regard to the location of MNE operations, the capacity of governments in managing these risks are well documented in the institutional perspective in IB. The institutional perspective, in general, implies that strong and effective governments in a host country may lower the cost of doing business, including contracting and monitoring costs, and thus attract MNE investments into the host country (North, 1990). Governments often determine a society's ex post disaster and conflict response. Oh and Oetzel (2011) note that "governments that are prepared for disasters and have the capacity to respond to them are better able to minimize the economic and human costs of a catastrophe as well as the time it takes to recover (p. 662)." While strong and effective governments will provide better business environments to MNEs under the threat of NTPS risks (Andrews et al., 2018), the government-driven preparation may also adversely provide the wrong idea to managers that disaster preparation and response are the roles of governments and their agencies rather than those of firms and private sectors. Thus, MNEs may not be fully aware of the importance of risk management.

Fourth, whether an organization has a capacity to prepare for NTPS risks is critical. The monitoring and assessment of available information and past experience enable an MNE to predict the likelihood of risk and its probable outcome. Except for social conflicts, previous studies (Oetzel & Oh, 2014; Oh & Oetzel, 2017) provide theoretical and empirical underpinnings suggesting that the MNE's level of experience at the location level or MNE level not only help but also at times hurt its risk awareness and responses when MNEs gain false confidence from the experience with low-intensity risks. There is a general consensus that experience is valuable when it is location-specific experience (Oh & Oetzel, 2017) as well as when organizations gain experience from recent, frequent, and high-impact uncertainties (Oetzel & Oh, 2014; Oh et al., 2021). Research also provides other important types of capabilities for managing risk such as philanthropic, technological, and safety management capabilities (Pek et al., 2018).

Fifth, firms' geographic networks will help MNEs to be aware of and prepare for NTPS risks. As firms need information related to uncertainties, locations, and actors, managers should be able to gather information across organizations. This will lower the bounded rationality of managers and enable them to make effective decisions under uncertainties (Oh & Oetzel, 2021; Sobel & Leeson, 2007). To gather location-specific information efficiently, firms may need to decentralize their information gathering and decision-making processes (Oh et al., 2020). For instance, firms will likely gain trusted information from their own affiliates in a location compared to their competitors or other organizations (Oh et al., 2020). Firms also need to consider making strong trusting relationships with other sectors such as multilateral organizations, governments, non-profit organizations, civil society organizations, and industry organizations at both firm level and subsidiary level (Oh & Oetzel, 2021).

These factors will determine the level of predicted damage, which in turn also determines how an organization prepares, responds, and behaves when facing risk (Oetzel & Oh, 2021; Singh, 1986). Based on these factors, the MNE can enact a number of alternative strategies (e.g., avoidance, adaptation, mitigation, transfer to third parties, and transform to opportunities). Thus, unexpected damage from a risk (equaling *realized* minus *predicted* damage) will be exacerbated when there are misfits between the level of damages, organizational preparedness to the risk, and organizational response. These misfits often exist either because the NTPS risk is highly unpredictable, unidentifiable, and unknowable or because the MNE does not have the capability to analyze adequately and respond to the risk (Quarantelli, 1988).

4   Future Research Agendas and Conclusion

While researchers have developed excellent theoretical and empirical foundations for researching NTPS risks in IB and strategic management, the topic is still very new to the discipline. In this section, we will provide some future research agendas to improve our understanding about NTPS risks and MNE risk awareness, preparedness, and response.

One factor that has been ignored in previous studies is managers' visions and insights. Because these NTPS risks are very uncertain and unpredictable, relying on statistical prediction for risk preparation has its own limitations. Some managers may have a strong vision and insights for their business continuity and sustainability, which make them aware of the importance of NTPS risks and the need to prepare for them. On the other hand, other managers likely value their daily operations and do not have excess resources to prepare for uncertain challenges. Future research could answer why and how some managers gain visions and insights for business continuity when others do not, all else being equal.

Second, focusing more on research in IB, current studies emphasize the location and ownership choice of MNEs with respect to NTPS risks. Findings from these studies provide important implications about when MNEs avoid or manage NTPS risks, but the findings do not provide other alternative strategies like risk transfer, risk mitigation, and risk preparation. Due to their greater geographic exposure, MNEs may need to integrate various types of risk management strategies and programs at the level of headquarters and at the level of subsidiary (Oh & Oetzel, 2021). It would be important to analyze when and how MNEs adopt different types of risk management strategies based on their geographic exposure, location characteristics, and firm characteristics.

Third, industry differences can also be very important. Industry may play an important role as firms in natural resources and labor-intensive industries are more familiar with challenging host country environments. MNEs in these industries may prepare more (or less) for NTPS risks than those in other industries. For example, according to PWC (2021), top 40 mining companies outperformed – their total capitalization rose more than 60% – in the Covid-19 pandemic. Because of challenges they have had with various stakeholders and natural environments, these companies have invested in sustainable technologies and stakeholder relationships (Shapiro et al., 2018). With increased commodity prices, these mining companies have been resilient during the pandemic (PWC, 2021), which is very different from the difficulties and economic losses that other industry sectors have experienced.

Fourth, some disasters/conflict events can have a devastating impact on human life and the economy, as well as the business environment. If humans are unable or unwilling to provide relief resulting in a total breakdown in social order, history tells us that it is possible for large-scale chaos to ensue. In Darfur, Sudan, for instance, droughts played a large role in fomenting ethnic violence since 2003 (Straus, 2005). Many observers, including the United Nations, have labeled this event in Sudan the first climate change conflict (Sova, 2017). In another example, the delays in relief efforts after the Bhola cyclone in 1970 triggered the secession of East Pakistan and the India-Pakistan war (Oh & Reuveny, 2010). We have experienced chaos and inhumanity in some countries in the Covid-19 pandemic combined with political extremism. Thus, it is likely that a disaster or conflict will generate a bigger societal catastrophe combined with other types of market and non-market risk and uncertainty. Future research should examine how various types of risk interact with each other and challenge businesses. Research also investigates how MNEs can participate in reducing such complex risks and improve socioeconomic sustainability.

Fifth, while on balance it would be beneficial for MNEs to collaborate with other organizations to prepare for and response to NTPS risk due to their unique characteristics and resources (Oh & Oetzel, 2021), some MNEs may be able to manage by themselves. In fact, because some capable MNEs are better able to prepare for NTPS risk, at times, NTPS risks in a host country can provide unique opportunities for those MNEs. In such cases, MNEs will not be likely to share their knowledge, or to collaborate with others, since they can take advantage of their own preparedness skills and potentially gain a competitive advantage in the process. However, it is yet unclear whether even some large MNEs can prepare for NTPS risks alone or whether such preparation is effective when NTPS risks are catastrophic. In addition, it is an ethical conundrum whether capable firms should take advantage of business opportunities arising from social catastrophes and chaos. During a crisis, MNEs also need to consider their role in society and help individuals, organizations, and the broader community to recover and become more sustainable.

5   Conclusion

Experts expect that non-market risks including NTPS risks will likely continue, if not increase, in various severities and frequencies in many parts of the world. The potential challenges facing MNEs in dealing with NTPS risks are likely to grow more complex as the scope, incidence, and magnitude of risks increase. Facing this growing complexity, managerial decisions involving IB are expected to benefit from the understanding of characteristics of NTPS risks, which in turn improve managers' awareness, preparedness, and response to NTPS risks.

References

Albala-Bertrand, J. M. (1993). Natural disaster situations and growth: A macroeconomic model for sudden disaster impacts. *World Development, 21*(9), 1417–1434.
Albino-Pimentel, J., Oetzel, J., Oh, C. H., & Poggioli, N. (2021). Positive institutional changes through peace: The relative effects of peace agreements and non-market capabilities on FDI. *Journal of International Business Studies, 52*, 1256–1278.
Alexander, D. E. (2006). Globalization of disaster: Trends, problems and dilemmas. *Journal of International Affairs, 59*(2), 1–22.

Andrews, T., Elizalde, B., Le Billon, P., Oh, C. H., Reyes, D., & Thompson, I. (2017). *The rise in conflict associated with mining operations: What lies beneath?* Canadian International Resources and Development Institute.

Andrews, T., Gamu, J., Le Billon, P., Oh, C. H., Reyes, D., & Shin, J. (2018). *The role of host governments in enabling or preventing conflict associated with mining.* Canadian International Resources and Development Institute and United Nations Development Programme.

Awokuse, T. O., & Gempesay, C. M., II. (2005). Foreign political instability and U.S. agricultural exports: Evidence from panel data. *Economics Bulletin, 6*(15), 1–12.

Baird, I. S., & Thomas, H. (1985). Toward a contingency model of strategic risk taking. *Academy of Management Review, 10*(2), 230–243.

Barnett, J., & Adger, W. N. (2007). Climate change, human security and violent conflict. *Political Geography, 26*, 639–655.

Blake, A., & Sinclair, M. T. (2003). Tourism crisis management: US response to September 11. *Annals of Tourism Research, 30*(4), 813–832.

Bloom, M., & Milkovich, G. T. (1998). Relationships among risk, incentive pay, and organizational performance. *Academy of Management Journal, 41*(3), 283–297.

Boddewyn, J. J. (1988). Political aspects of MNE theory. *Journal of International Business Studies, 19*(3), 341–363.

Buckley, P. J., Chen, L., Clegg, L. J., & Voss, H. (2020). The role of endogenous and exogenous risk in FDI entry choices. *Journal of World Business, 55*(1), 101040.

Business Roundtable. (2008). *Business Roundtable releases strategic CEO-level guidance to combat terrorism and protect the nation's assets.* Accessed July 12, 2021, from http://www.businessroundtable.org

Calvano, L. (2008). Multinational corporations and local communities: A critical analysis of conflict. *Journal of Business Ethics, 82*(4), 793–805.

Chung, C. C., Lee, S.-H., Beamish, P. W., & Isobe, T. (2010). Subsidiary expansion/contraction during times of economic crisis. *Journal of International Business Studies, 41*(3), 500–516.

Click, R. W. (2005). Financial and political risks in US direct foreign investment. *Journal of International Business Studies, 36*, 559–575.

Courtney, H., Kirkland, J., & Viguerie, P. (1997). Strategy under uncertainty. *Harvard Business Review, 75*(6), 67–79.

Dai, L., Eden, L., & Beamish, P. W. (2017). Caught in the crossfire: Dimensions of vulnerability and foreign multinationals' exit from war-afflicted countries. *Strategic Management Journal, 38*(7), 1478–1498.

Davis, M., & Seitz, S. T. (1982). Disasters and governments. *Journal of Conflict Resolution, 26*(3), 547–568.

Delios, A., & Henisz, W. J. (2003). Political hazards, experience, and sequential entry strategies: The international expansion of Japanese firms. *Strategic Management Journal, 24*, 1153–1164.

Denenberg, R. V., & Braverman, M. (2001). *The violence-prone workplace: A new approach to dealing with hostile, threatening, and uncivil behavior.* Cornell University Press.

Deryugina, T., Kawano, L., & Levitt, S. (2018). The economic impact of hurricane Katrina on its victims: Evidence from individual tax returns. *American Economic Journal: Applied Economics, 10*(2), 202–233.

Dorobantu, S., & Odziemkowska, K. (2017). Valuing stakeholder governance: Property rights, community mobilization, and firm value. *Strategic Management Journal, 38*(13), 2682–2703.

EM-DAT. (2020). The emergency events database – Universite catholoque de Louvain (UCL) – CRED, D. Guha-Sapir. Brussels, Belgium. www.emdat.be.

England, R. W. (1988). Disaster-prone technologies, environmental risks, and profit maximization. *Kyklos, 41*(3), 379–395.

Escaleras, M., & Register, C. A. (2011). Natural disasters and foreign direct investment. *Land Economics, 87*(2), 346–363.

Evan, W. M., & Manion, M. (2002). *Minding the machines: Preventing technological disasters.* Prentice Hall.

Fitzpatrick, M. (1983). The definition and assessment of political risk in international business: A review of the literature. *Academy of Management Review, 8*(2), 249–254.

Flavelle, D. (2008). *Maple Leaf's recall costs could top $20M.* Toronto Star. August 25.

Gong, Y. (2003). Subsidiary staffing in multinational enterprises: Agency, resources, and performance. *Academy of Management Journal, 46*(6), 728–739.

Greening, D. W., & Johnson, R. A. (1996). Do managers and strategies matter? A study in crisis. *Journal of Management Studies, 33*(1), 25–51.

Habib, G. M. (1987). Measures of manifest conflict in international joint ventures. *Academy of Management Journal, 30*(4), 808–816.

Helm, T. & Boffey, D. (2012). Scottish independence carries huge economic risk, says Alistair Darling. *The Guardian.* January 14.

Henisz, W. J., Mansfield, E. D., & Von Glinow, M. A. (2010). Conflict, security, and political risk: International business in challenging times. *Journal of International Business Studies, 41,* 759–764.

Hoskisson, R. E., Eden, L., Lau, C. M., & Wright, M. (2000). Strategy in emerging economies. *Academy of Management Journal, 43*(3), 249–267.

Jiménez, A., Bayraktar, S., Lee, J. Y., & Choi, S.-J. (2021). The multi-faceted impact of host country risk on the success of private participation in infrastructure projects. *Multinational Business Review.* https://doi.org/10.1108/MBR-10-2020-0195. forthcoming.

John, A., & Lawton, T. C. (2018). International political risk management: Perspectives, approaches and emerging agendas. *International Journal of Management Reviews, 20*(4), 847–879.

Joshi, A., Labianca, G., & Caligiuri, P. (2002). Getting along long distance: Understanding conflict in a multinational team through network analysis. *Journal of World Business, 37*(4), 277–284.

Kasperson, R. E., & Pijawka, K. D. (1985). Societal response to hazards and major hazard events: Comparing natural and technological hazards. *Public Administration Review, 45,* 7–18.

Kasperson, R. E., Renn, O., Slovic, P., Brown, H. S., Emel, J., Goble, R., Kasperson, J. X., & Ratick, S. (1988). The social amplification of risk: A conceptual framework. *Risk Analysis, 8*(2), 177–187.

Kiernan, P. & Hoyle, R. (2015, November 30). Brazil files civil suit against Samarco, Vale, BHP over dam disaster. *The Wall Street Journal.*

Kobrin, S. J. (1979). Political risk: A review and reconsideration. *Journal of International Business Studies, 10*(1), 67–80.

Kornecki, L. (2013). Inward FDI in the United States and its policy context. In K. P. Sauvant (Ed.), *Columbia FDI profiles.* Vale Columbia Center, Columbia University.

Kytle, B. & Ruggie, J.G. (2005). *Corporate social responsibility as risk management.* A working paper of the corporate social responsibility initiative. Harvard University CSRI No. 10.

Le Nguyen, H., Larimo, J., & Ali, T. (2016). How do ownership control position and national culture influence conflict resolution strategies in international joint ventures? *International Business Review, 25*(2), 559–568.

Lee, S.-H., & Makhija, M. (2009). Flexibility in internationalization: It is valuable during an economic crisis? *Strategic Management Journal, 30*(5), 537–555.

Madsen, P. M. (2009). These lives will not be lost in vain: Organizational learning from disaster in U.S. coal mining. *Organization Science, 20*(5), 861–875.

Malkenses, K. (2012, June 11). Norway oil workers strike, forcing rig shutdown. *The Wall Street Journal.*

March, J. G., & Shapira, Z. (1987). Managerial perspectives on risk and risk taking. *Management Science, 33*(11), 1404–1418.

Mascarenhas, B. (1982). Coping with uncertainty in international business. *Journal of International Business Studies, 13*(2), 87–98.

McKnight, B., & Linnenluecke, M. K. (2016). How firm responses to natural disasters strengthen community resilience: A stakeholder-based perspective. *Organization & Environment, 29*(3), 290–307.

McKnight, B., & Linnenluecke, M. K. (2019). Patterns of firm responses to different types of natural disasters. *Business & Society, 58*(4), 813–840.

McNamara, G., & Bromiley, P. (1999). Risk and return in organizational decision making. *Academy of Management Journal, 42*(3), 330–340.

Miller, K. D. (1992). A framework for integrated risk management in international business. *Journal of International Business Studies, 23*(2), 311–331.

Muzio, D., & Doh, J. (2021). COVID-19 and the future of management studies. Insights from leading scholars. *Journal of Management Studies, 58*(5), 1371–1377.

North, D. C. (1990). *Institutions, institutional change, and economic performance.* Cambridge University Press.

O'Malley, P. (2004). *Risk, uncertainty and government.* The Glass House.

Oetzel, J., & Getz, K. (2012). When and how might firms respond to violent conflict? *Journal of International Business Studies, 43*, 166–186.

Oetzel, J., & Miklian, J. (2017). Multinational enterprises, risk management, and the business and economics of peace. *Multinational Business Review, 25*(4), 270–286.

Oetzel, J. M., & Oh, C. H. (2014). Learning to carry the cat by the tail: Firm experience, disasters, and multinational subsidiary entry and expansion. *Organization Science, 25*(3), 732–756.

Oetzel, J., & Oh, C. H. (2015). Managing non-market risk: Is it possible to manage the seemingly unmanageable? In T. C. Lawton & T. Rajwani (Eds.), *The Routledge companion to non-market strategy* (pp. 285–300). Routledge.

Oetzel, J., & Oh, C. H. (2019). Melting pot or tribe? Country-level ethnic diversity and its effect on subsidiaries. *Journal of International Business Policy, 2*(1), 37–61.

Oetzel, J., & Oh, C. H. (2021). A storm is brewing: Antecedents of disaster preparation in risk prone locations. *Strategic Management Journal, 42*(8), 1545–1570.

Oh, C. H. (2017). How do natural and man-made disasters affect international trade? A country-level and industry-level analysis. *Journal of Risk Research, 20*(2), 195–217.

Oh, C. H., & Oetzel, J. (2011). Multinationals' response to major disasters: How does subsidiary investment vary based on the type of risk and the quality of country governance? *Strategic Management Journal, 32*(6), 658–681.

Oh, C. H., & Oetzel, J. (2017). Once bitten twice shy? Experience managing violent conflict risk and MNC subsidiary-level investment and expansion. *Strategic Management Journal, 38*(3), 714–731.

Oh, C. H., & Oetzel, J. (2021). *Multinational enterprises and natural disasters: Challenges and opportunities for IB research.* Working Paper.

Oh, C. H., Oetzel, J., Rivera, J., & Lien, D. (2020). Natural disasters and MNC sub-national investments in China. *Multinational Business Review, 28*(2), 245–274.

Oh, C. H., & Reuveny, R. (2010). Climate natural disasters, political risk, and international trade. *Global Environmental Change, 20*(2), 243–254.

Oh, C. H., Shin, J., & Oetzel, J. (2021). How does experience change firms' foreign investment decisions to non-market events? *Journal of International Management, 27*(1), 100802.

Olson, R.S. (2005). *A critical juncture analysis, 1964–2003.* The Office of U.S. Foreign Disaster Assistance of the United States Agency for International Development. Retrieved from http://www.usaid.gov/our_work/humanitarian_assistance/disaster_assistance/publications/

Peel, M. (2011, February 21). Oil groups draws up plans for swift Libya exit. *Financial Times.*

Pek, S., Oh, C. H., & Rivera, J. (2018). MNC foreign investment and industrial disasters: The moderating role of technological, safety management, and philanthropic capabilities. *Strategic Management Journal, 39*(2), 502–526.

Peng, M. W. (2003). Institutional transitions and strategic choices. *Academy of Management Review, 28*(2), 275–296.

Perrow, C. (2007). *The next catastrophe: Reducing our vulnerabilities to natural, industrial, and terrorist disasters.* Princeton University Press.

Phillips, D. (2015, November 25). Brazil's mining tragedy: Was it a preventable disaster? *The Guardian.*

Powell, B. (2008, August 24). Maple leaf expands recall to 220 products. Toronto Star.

PWC. (2021, June 2021). *Mine 2021: Great expectations, seizing tomorrow.* https://www.pwc.com/gx/en/energy-utilities-mining/assets/mine-2021/pwc-mine-2021.pdf

Quarantelli, E.L. 1988. Disaster crisis management: A summary of research findings. Journal of Management Studies, 25 (4): 373–385.

Raddatz, C. (2007). Are external shocks responsible for the instability of output in low-income countries? *Journal of Development Economics, 84*(1), 155–187.

Ramos, M. A., & Ashby, N. J. (2017). The halo effect: Violent crime and foreign direct investment. *Multinational Business Review, 25*(4), 287–306.

Rao, H., & Greve, H. R. (2018). Disasters and community resilience: Spanish flu and the formation of retail cooperatives in Norway. *Academy of Management Journal, 61*(1), 5–25.

Romilly, P. (2007). Business and climate change risk: A regional time series analysis. *Journal of International Business Studies, 38*, 474–480.

Root, F. R. (1972). Analyzing political risks in international business. In A. Kappor & P. A. Grub (Eds.), *The multinational enterprise in transition* (pp. 354–365). Darwin Press.

Ruggie, J. G. (2007). Global markets and global governance: The prospects for convergence. In S. Bernstein & L. W. Pauly (Eds.), *Global liberalism and political order: Toward a new grand compromise?* (pp. 23–50). State University of New York Press.

Rugman, A. M., & Oh, C. H. (2011). Regional multinational enterprise and the international financial crisis. In E. Hutson & R. Sinkovics (Eds.), *Firm-level internationalization, regionalism and globalization* (pp. 64–78). Palgrave Macmillan.

Salehyan, I., Hendrix, C. S., Hamner, J., Case, C., Linebarger, C., Stull, E., & Williams, J. (2012). Social conflict in Africa: A new database. *International Interactions, 38*(4), 503–511.

Sanders, J. (2018, July 17). Why HDD factor closure means you may need to migrate to solid state. *Tech Republic.*

Santos, N. (2019, April 26). Fourteen years later, New Orleans is still trying to recover from Hurricane Katrina. Environmental and Energy Study Institute. https://www.eesi.org/articles/view/fourteen-years-later-new-orleans-is-still-trying-to-recover-from-hurricane-katrina

Schumpeter, J. (1942). *Capitalism, socialism, and democracy.* Harper & Bros.

Shapira, Z. (1995). *Risk taking: A managerial perspective.* Russell Sage Foundation.

Shapiro, D., Hobdari, B., & Oh, C. H. (2018). Natural resources, multinational enterprises, and sustainable development. *Journal of World Business, 53*(1), 1–14.

Sheffi, Y. (2015). *The power of resilience: How the best companies manage the unexpected.* The MIT Press.

Singh, J. A. (1986). Performance, slack, and risk taking in organizational decision making. *Academy of Management Journal, 29*(3), 562–585.

Slovic, P., Fischhoff, B., & Lichtenstein, S. (2000). Rating the risks. In P. Slovic (Ed.), *The perception of risk* (pp. 104–120). Earthscan Publications.

Sobel, R. S., & Leeson, P. T. (2007). The use of knowledge in natural-disaster relief management. *The Independent Review, 11*(4), 519–532.

Sova, C. (2017). *The first climate change conflict.* United Nations World Food Program USA. https://www.wfpusa.org/articles/the-first-climate-change-conflict/.

Straus, S. (2005). Darfur and the genocide debate. *Foreign Affairs, 84*(1), 123–133.

Sundberg, R., & Melander, E. (2013). Introducing the UCDP georeferenced event dataset. *Journal of Peace Research, 50*(4), 523–532.

Tallman, S. B. (1988). Home country political risk and foreign direct investment in the United States. *Journal of International Business Studies, 19*(2), 219–234.

Tavares, J. (2004). The open society assesses its enemies: Shocks, disasters and terrorist attacks. *Journal of Monetary Economics, 51*, 1039–1070.

Teece, D., Peteraf, M., & Leih, S. (2016). Dynamic capabilities and organizational agility: Risk, uncertainty, and strategy in the innovation economy. *California Management Review, 58*(4), 13–35.

The Brookings Institution. (2021). https://www.brookings.edu/research/explaining-the-economic-impact-of-covid-19-core-industries-and-the-hispanic-workforce/

Theisen, O. M. (2008). Blood and soil? Resources scarcity and internal armed conflict revisited. *Journal of Peace Research, 45*(8), 801–818.

Tran, Q. T. (2020). Uncertainty avoidance culture, cash holdings and financial crisis. *Multinational Business Review, 28*(4), 549–566.

United Nations. (2008). *World economic and social survey 2008: Overcoming economic insecurity.* Department of Economic and Social Affairs, United Nation.

Vaaler, P. (2008). How do MNCs vote in developing country elections? *Academy of Management Journal, 51*(1), 21–43.

Vigdor, J. (2008). The economic aftermath of Hurricane Katrina. *Journal of Economic Perspective, 22*(4), 135–154.

Zanini, M. (2009). Power curves: What natural and economic disasters have in common. *The McKinsey Quarterly, 1*, 10–15.

Zio, E., & Aven, T. (2013). Industrial disasters: Extreme events, extremely rare. Some reflections on the treatment of uncertainties in the assessment of the associated risks. *Process Safety and Environmental Protection, 91*(1/2), 31–45.

Chang Hoon Oh is Docking Professor of Strategy at University of Kansas. He is Co-Editor-in-Chief for Multinational Business Review. He has published more than 60 articles in business, economics, and political science journals. His research centers on business strategy in challenging environments, business continuity and sustainability, and globalization versus regionalization. His research has been supported by the Social Sciences and Humanities Research Council of Canada (SSHRC), Canadian International Resources and Development Institute (CIRDI) and the National Research Foundation of Korea (NRF). He has collaborated with World Wildlife Fund of Nature (WWF), United Nations Development Programme (UNDP), and EY-Hanyoung, Korea.

Jennifer Oetzel is the Kogod IB Professor in the Kogod School of Business at American University. She received her Ph.D. degree in Business Strategy from the University of North Carolina at Chapel Hill. Her research broadly focuses on the competitive implications of social, economic, and environmental sustainability challenges. She studies how multinational enterprises (MNEs) can reduce business risk at its source rather than trying to avoid or react to risks as they occur. By adopting strategies aimed at peacebuilding, managers may not only reduce investment risk but also contribute to stability and prosperity in the communities where they operate and gain a competitive advantage by doing so. Prof. Oetzel's research has been published in the Journal of International Business Studies (JIBS), the Journal of International Business Policy (JIBP), the Strategic Management Journal (SMJ), and Organization Science, among other outlets.

The Future of Multinational Enterprises: An Optimist's View

Julian Birkinshaw

The purpose of this short article is to offer some thoughts on the role of multinational enterprises (MNEs) in the global economy—looking backward to see what has changed and looking forward to see what might be coming over the next decade or so. These thoughts are not deeply researched, rather they are based on casual empiricism and reflection: a point of view on the business world as I see it. Hopefully they are also a little contrarian as well. A reflective piece like this is a good opportunity to challenge some of the conventional orthodoxies that dominate our literature.

I should note at the outset that I am focusing on large established MNEs, with revenues in the tens of billions of dollars, activities in dozens of countries, and operating on a for-profit basis. I am also talking predominantly about MNEs from developed markets, though emerging market MNEs from China, India, and other places will also get a mention. These are the "big beasts" of the corporate world that the academic literature has mostly addressed, and they will be my focus here.

1 A Fast-Changing Business World?

It is remarkable how many academic papers and business articles start out with the observation that we live in a fast-changing world or that the level of uncertainty in business has never been higher. As a rhetorical device to justify studying a particular phenomenon, it makes sense. But is it really true?

It goes without saying that the business world is ever-changing. Each generation likes to believe that it is facing a unique set of circumstances that are more challenging than those that came before. However, we tend to notice the things

J. Birkinshaw (✉)
Strategy and Entrepreneurship, Institute of Entrepreneurship and Private Capital, London Business School, Regent's Park, London, UK
e-mail: jbirkinshaw@london.edu

© Springer Nature Switzerland AG 2022   299
H. Merchant (ed.), *The New Frontiers of International Business*, Contributions to Management Science, https://doi.org/10.1007/978-3-031-06003-8_14

that are new and different and ignore the things that are relatively stable. So we talk a lot about the exponential growth in processing power and connectivity, for example, but we don't notice that the way we clothe ourselves (buttons, zips, shoelaces) hasn't changed significantly for a century or more.

It may not be possible to come to a definitive view on how fast-moving the business world really is. There are plenty of books and articles making the case for accelerating change, for example, Ismail et al. (2014), D'aveni (2010), Schwab (2017), and Brynjolfsson and McAfee (2014). But there are also thoughtful counterpoints: McNamara et al. (2003) finding no objective evidence of increasing levels of competition, Ghemawat (2011) showing how Globalization 3.0 is in many ways *less* global than what came before, and Eccles et al. (1992) exposing the games executives play with language when making the case for accelerating change.

So agreeing to write a piece on the future role of MNEs gave me a choice. I could have written about all the things changing in the world—the energy transition, the digital revolution, global warming, and the deglobalization of world trade—but then I realized in looking through the table of contents that plenty of other chapters would cover those issues better than I could. So instead, I took the other approach. I decided to write about what's *not* changing, that is, the enduring presence and stability of large MNEs despite everything else that's going on.

My argument, in a nutshell, is that the size and diversity of MNEs, coupled with their embeddedness in the institutions of capitalism, make them very resilient to changing external circumstances. While their resilience sometimes creates problems, it is more generally a force for good—as a moderating influence over some of the more volatile features of the global economy. It's an optimistic view, I acknowledge, but there is no harm in a bit of optimism in the challenging times we are living through.

2 Changes in the Fortune 500 and Global 500

Let's start with some data. I analyzed the change in makeup of the Fortune 500 and Global 500 from 1995 to 2020. The Fortune 500 is the largest US companies ranked by revenues. The Global 500 is the equivalent list for the world. I chose 1995 as the starting point because that is when the Internet revolution really took off.

Looking at the Fortune 500 first (Fig. 1), only 17 of the current list did not exist (in any form) before 1995. I won't name them all here, but it is the companies you would expect—Google, Facebook, Amazon, Netflix, Uber, and so on. But the point is there are only 17 of them. The other 483 consists of 198 "stalwarts" who have been in the list since 1995, 54 spinouts from large companies, and 232 "risers" who were around for many years before 1995 and grew to become members of the top-500 club.

The Global 500 analysis (Fig. 2) exhibits a similar pattern, with only 12 entirely new firms, 164 stalwarts, and 324 that were either spinouts or risers. But what's interesting about that list is the changes in the home countries of the companies on

1995 Fortune 500 2020 Fortune 500

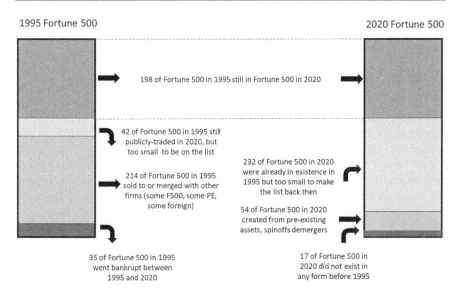

Fig. 1 Change in makeup of Fortune 500, 1995 to 2020. Source: figure compiled by author

1995 Global 500 2020 Global 500

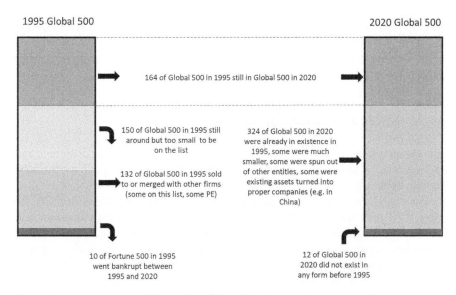

Fig. 2 Change in makeup of Global 500, 1995 to 2020. Source: figure compiled by author

it. In 1995 were 148 US firms, 147 Japanese, and 3 Chinese, but by 2020 there were only 121 US firms, 52 Japanese, and 119 Chinese.

I realize this analysis might be criticized for "sampling on the dependent variable" so I also did the equivalent analysis from the other direction, i.e., taking the original 500 lists from 1995 and examining what happened to them over the ensuing

25 years. It's a similar story, with a very small number of bankruptcies and fairly larger numbers of "fallers" and acquisitions.

3   What to Make of this Data? Some Observations

First, there is remarkably little change. Fewer than 4% of the top 500 firms were formed in the Internet era. There is so much talk about the Googles, Amazons, and Tencents of the world that we sometimes forget about the parts of the economy that are not being disrupted. It turns out that most of the big changes have occurred in just two parts of the economy—the technology media and telecoms (TMT) sector, and the retail sector. Other sectors, such as consumer products, industrial products, engineering, energy, financial services, and healthcare, have seen virtually no changes.

Second, the Fortune lists are based on revenues not on market capitalization. This helps to explain why we don't see more Internet-era companies on the list. It also reminds us that the capital market version of the economy is only loosely linked to the real economy. I would argue that this revenue-based ranking is a much better proxy for how the economy actually works than one based on market sentiment.

Third, the only notable thing about the Global 500 list is the changes by country. In 1995 Japan had 147 companies on the list because its economy was strong, and the Yen was highly valued. By 2020 Japan had stagnated, and China was the emerging superpower, with many of its formerly state-run assets now being managed as for-profit companies.

4   MNEs as Bastions of Stability

The simple takeaway from this analysis is that despite all the talk of disruption and change, there is also a lot of inertia and stability in the global economy. And the reasons behind this are not exactly surprising.

First, MNEs are hugely resilient *because* they are large and diversified. For the most part, they have strong balance sheets to help them weather shocks and downturns. They are diversified in both business activities and countries of operations, which gives them a hedge against problems in one particular region or area of activity. Many of them also operate in industries with high barriers to entry—sometimes based on scale economies, sometimes on long-term customer relationships, and sometimes based on regulatory protection. It takes a lot to kill these companies off.

Second, MNEs are better at reinventing themselves from within than anyone gives them credit for. We all know the stories of Kodak, Blockbuster, and Sears, but they are exceptions. Most MNEs are highly aware of the risks of disruption and are proactive in addressing those risks. Internal reinvention takes many forms—it includes acquiring promising start-ups, creating new operating units in fast-growth areas, behind-the-scenes cost cutting and reengineering, and portfolio-level redeployments of investment. Nokia is a fascinating case in point here: you can think of it as a failure if you take a short-term view of what happened in 2007–2010, but with a long-term perspective its actually highly resilient—it has been around for a hundred years, and it has bounced back from the smart-phone debacle to become once again a world leader (in 5G networks), with 100,000 employees.

Third, and contributing to the first two points, MNEs are better managed than smaller or single-country companies. This has been shown empirically by Nick Bloom and his associates (Bloom et al., 2012; Bloom & Van Reenen, 2007), when looking at the quality of management across multiple industries and countries. It is also entirely consistent with expectations and experience. In most cases, MNEs put huge amounts of money into training and development, they use rigorous management control systems to monitor performance across their worldwide operations, and they proactively use best-practice sharing and knowledge management systems.

These three points are unlikely to brook any argument, and indeed there is a good amount of empirical evidence to support them. But let me now offer some slightly more controversial arguments about the role MNEs play in the global economy as bastions of stability.

First, the leaders of MNEs are very conscious of their reputations and will go to great lengths to show to the world that they are "doing the right thing." These leaders understand that legitimacy is important, both in terms of their license to operate vis-à-vis national governments and in terms of how customers, employees, and other stakeholders perceive them. MNEs are often highly vocal in supporting societal trends, such as the Black Lives Matter movement, the sustainability agenda, diversity and inclusion more generally, and stakeholder-based governance systems.

Second, MNEs are constrained by the institutions that support them. This includes the capital markets (i.e., the rights of stockholders and bondholders), reporting requirements, employment and competition laws, tax systems, intellectual property rights, and a host of sector-specific regulations. These regulations and norms are sufficiently powerful and multifaceted that even if an MNE wanted to operate in a less-than-legitimate way, it might not be able to.

Not every reader will agree with these last two points. Indeed many observers (though probably not the type of people to read this article) will argue that MNEs are the "bad guys"—they exploit low-power workers, they pillage the earth's natural resources, they avoid paying taxes, they deny global warming, they launder money, and so on. Of course, there are examples of all these things happening, and we can point to high-profile protests (Greenpeace vs Shell, Occupy Wall Street, etc.) and legal verdicts (Apple, Google, HSBC, Rio Tinto, etc.) to underline that MNEs sometimes get it wrong. But in my experience, the leaders of MNEs are happy – even eager – to address these problems as they come to light. For me, it is a sign of strength in the global economy that activists and social movements bring injustices and problems into public view and that the leaders of MNEs listen and respond. A recent case in point is the G7-led plan to create a global minimum 15% corporate tax rate. While some countries, such as Ireland, have pushed back against this plan, MNEs seem entirely comfortable with it—indeed many of them have welcomed it as a way of creating greater clarity.

Another concern often raised is that MNEs from developed western economies may be trying to do the right thing, but emerging market MNEs from China, India, Russia, or the Middle East don't have the same scruples, or they lack the same constraints on their occasionally illicit behavior. There is some truth to this, but I would also observe that most of these emerging market MNEs aspire to a seat at the top table. This means, for example, adopting globally agreed accounting standards, listing on western stock exchanges and complying with all the rules that such a listing requires, hiring executives from western competitors, and sending senior executives to top western business schools to learn the latest best practices. I have personally worked with MNE executives from China, India, Brazil, Turkey, Ukraine, Mexico, Sri Lanka, and Saudi Arabia in recent years, and in all cases their intention is to become more like their western counterparts, essentially as a means of building their legitimacy.

Finally, there is a different but equally valid worry that MNEs can succumb to a herd mentality. By following the norms set by others, they increase their legitimacy in the short term, but they risk getting things badly wrong (as a collective) in the medium term. The global financial crisis is the obvious example of this—MNEs, regulators, ratings agencies, and others all following each other's lead and resulting in a systemic failure of huge proportions.

5 The Yin and Yang of Progress

How should we make sense of the role of MNEs in the global economy? I would argue that they aren't good or evil—they are large institutions operating across multiple sovereign jurisdictions, full of people trying to do their best for a sometimes-conflicting set of stakeholders, and within a complex set of institutions that constrain their actions in multifaceted ways.

I like to think of MNEs as bulwarks against the more volatile features of the global economic system as a whole. By volatile features I mean both exogenous shocks such as COVID and also specific agents of change such as entrepreneurial start-ups, venture capital funds, activist investors, and global movements such as BLM and Occupy. Progress occurs in a yin-yang like fashion—with MNEs and host country governments on the "yin" side of the equation and the entrepreneurs and social movements on the "yang" side.

So looking to the future, what does this mean for today's large MNEs?

First, there will be some creative destruction. There will be occasional failures (a la Kodak), there will be further consolidation especially in mature industries, and there will be a lot of internal reallocation of resources, with diversified MNEs shifting into the growing parts of the economy, as they have always done.

Second, there will be a lot of internal reinvention within these MNEs. Huge amounts of investment in information technology, automation of processes through AI, cost cutting, delayering and simplification, outsourcing of activities, and so on. This happens all the time, and thanks to continuing advance in digital technology, it is likely to accelerate further. But it is mostly below-the-radar activity.

Third, the increasing importance of Asia to the global economy will of course lead to more Asia-based MNEs. While it is tempting to see them as operating by a different rule book because of their heritage, my expectation is that they will increasingly adopt the strategies and practices of developed-world MNEs, for all the reasons I have already discussed. The forces for isomorphism are strong.

Finally, and this is more of a wish than a prediction, I see MNEs taking an increasingly active role as amplifiers of important societal trends. Writing this in mid-2021, the big challenges facing the world economy are (in order) recovering from and living with COVID, getting to grips with global warming, and promoting diversity and inclusion. Governments of course play a central role in addressing these society-wide challenges, but the large MNEs are arguably more influential in terms of the number of people and families they support. There are many good examples of MNEs taking on leadership roles around these contemporary challenges, and I am optimistic that this trend will continue.

References

Bloom, N., Genakos, C., Sadun, R., & Van Reenen, J. (2012). Management practices across firms and countries. *Academy of Management Perspectives, 26*(1), 12–33.

Bloom, N., & Van Reenen, J. (2007). Measuring and explaining management practices across firms and countries. *The Quarterly Journal of Economics, 122*(4), 1351–1408.

Brynjolfsson, E., & McAfee, A. (2014). *The second machine age: Work, progress, and prosperity in a time of brilliant technologies*. WW Norton & Co.

D'aveni, R. A. (2010). *Hypercompetition*. Simon and Schuster.

Eccles, R. G., Nohria, N., & Berkley, J. D. (1992). *Beyond the hype: Rediscovering the essence of management*. Beard Books.

Ghemawat, P. (2011). *World 3.0: Global prosperity and how to achieve it*. Harvard Business Press.

Ismail, S., Malone, M. S., & Van Geest, Y. (2014). *Exponential organizations: Why new organizations are ten times better, faster, and cheaper than yours (and what to do about it)*. Diversion Books.

McNamara, G., Vaaler, P. M., & Devers, C. (2003). Same as it ever was: the search for evidence of increasing hypercompetition. *Strategic Management Journal, 24*(3), 261–278. Company.

Schwab, K. (2017). The fourth industrial revolution. *Currency*.

Julian Birkinshaw is Professor of Strategy and Entrepreneurship, and a Fellow of the British as well as the American Academy of Management. He is a recognized thought leader on the impact of digital technology on the strategy and organization of established companies. Professor Birkinshaw is frequently ranked as one of the "Thinkers 50" top thought leaders in the field of Management.

International Business' Broader Societal Role

Reviews of "Gifford Lecture Society" for

Multinational Enterprises and the Circular Economy

Gabriel R. G. Benito and Corina Fehlner

1   Introduction

The circular economy (CE) is an important route towards a more sustainable development. CE focuses on preserving product and material value, preventing waste, and keeping products and resources within the system by cycling them. CE represents a distinct logic to the prevailing linear economic reasoning that has proved inadequate in providing ecologically sustainable economies. Although the concept is promising, adoption of CE has been limited so far with the global recycling rate of total material use estimated to be only around 10% (de Wit et al., 2020a). Scaling up CE is challenging. Large-scale adoption of CE will require multipronged efforts across current systems for production, logistics, and consumption, modifying them to become circular. In some cases, moving to a CE may require a complete dismantling of an existing business system and setting up an entirely new one instead.

A business system is principally composed of firms and moving towards a CE involves reshaping the value-creating processes that take place within and between them. However, firms and the roles they play in a business system differ a lot. Many have very focused roles, concentrating on one particular activity in a given location. Some firms may perform a few activities or operate in several locations but typically within a limited domain and without taking a coordinating role in the system. A few firms take on orchestrating roles across the whole system of value activities, and they often own and manage units in various locations. The latter, commonly termed a multinational enterprise (MNE), are key actors that make decisions with system-wide ramifications, including the crucial why, when, and how of transitioning towards CE, especially in value systems that comprise multiple locations (countries).

G. R. G. Benito (✉) · C. Fehlner
Department of Strategy and Entrepreneurship, BI Norwegian Business School, Oslo, Norway

© Springer Nature Switzerland AG 2022

H. Merchant (ed.), *The New Frontiers of International Business*, Contributions to
Management Science, https://doi.org/10.1007/978-3-031-06003-8_15

In this chapter, we probe into the role of MNEs in circular business systems: a topic that has received very little attention in the international business literature (Rygh et al., 2022). After a sketch of the components of business systems (see, e.g., Asmussen et al., 2009)—activities, locations, and governance structures (or operation modes)—we provide a brief description of the logic of circular business systems and how it differs from noncircular (i.e., linear) systems (McDonough & Braungart, 2002; Murray et al., 2017; Stahel, 1981). Key actors in a business system are typically firms, and in this chapter our emphasis is on MNEs, although stakeholders (e.g., regulators) and other agencies such as nongovernmental organizations may also be involved (Folke et al., 2019). On that foundation, we move on to discussing how MNEs act towards implementing (or transitioning to) CE, taking into account corporate as well as contextual considerations. With a focus on the international business ramifications of CE, we distinguish between three key designs for circularity, depending on their spatial scope: local, regional, or global. We close the chapter by providing some ideas for further research.

2   The Building Blocks of Business Systems

Brought down to its basic elements, a business system is generally composed of a set of interdependent value *activities* (a)—such as the extraction of resources, production, logistics, sales, and a range of administrative support functions—that are carried out in a set of *locations* (L), ranging from one single location in the case of systems in which all activities are collocated to highly spatially dispersed systems where activities are done in a variety of different locations. Whenever locations include more than one country, the system is per definition international (Welch et al., 2018). Value activities are connected to each other, often in a sequence where the output of an activity becomes the input to another, thereby making up a so-called value chain (Porter, 1985). Figure 1 displays a very simple system consisting of five activities $\{a_1, \ldots, a_5\}$ spread out on three locations $\{L_1, L_2, L_3\}$, where the dotted crossbars denote country borders.

Value chains are applicable to a variety of industries, especially manufacturing industries. However, the value chain is just one of several distinct templates for activity arrangements. In service industries, production sequences are less discrete, and activities are connected to each other in iterative and cyclical ways.

A key point is that the ways various value activities can be organized involve different types of interdependencies (Thompson, 1967). On one end of the scale, activities may be very loosely connected, such as when they can be done independently of each other, with the only coordination needed being at the last stage (s) where they combine to deliver the final product. This is what is labeled pooled interdependence. At the other end of the scale are activities that involve continuous interaction and joint efforts and which hence need persistent coordination to be carried out effectively. This is what is labeled reciprocal interdependence. In between these opposites lies sequential interdependence, where activities are coordinated to ensure proper sequencing, inasmuch as an activity cannot begin before it

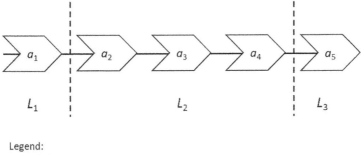

Legend:
a_i = activity i
L_j = location j

Fig. 1 A very simple international linear business system. Source: Authors' own figure

receives inputs from a preceding activity. For simplicity of exposition, the system depicted in Fig. 1 implies a sequential interdependence, but the following applies generally regardless of type of interdependency.

Performing an activity requires deciding how to organize it. In principle, three distinct main categories of governance (G) are feasible (Williamson, 1985, 1991) as follows: (i) a firm can perform the activity itself; i.e., doing it "in-house"; (ii) a firm can source (or supply) on the market, making a transaction one by one depending on the best offer available; or (iii) the firm may enter an agreement with another firm specifying the terms for having the activity done and supplied (sourced) over some duration. The first option is the integrated solution, which gives a focal firm full discretion on how it is managed and coordinated with other activities done by the firm. Consequently, the firm also assumes responsibility for the activity and must commit resources to perform it. The second option is the market solution, which entails a flexible—"no strings attached"—arrangement where the firm can shop around for the best offer available at any point but also exposes the firm to the risk of not being supplied at the terms (e.g., price, quantities, specifications, and timing) it wishes. The third option is the contract—or "hybrid"—solution, which straddles coordination benefits (terms of the contract) with some degree of flexibility (limits committed resources) but denies the firm full discretion on managing the activities and their interfaces. In Fig. 2, the activities encircled by full lines represent those done in-house, whereas those involving a contractual partner are encircled with a dotted line. Absence of a line indicates a market interface between two successive activities. Since the activities occur in more several countries, the depicted system is international (Welch et al., 2018).

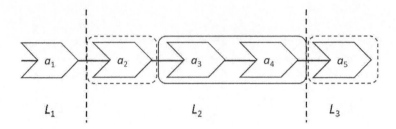

Legend:
a_i = activity i
L_j = location j
Full encirclement = in-house
Dotted encirclement = contract
No encirclement = market

Fig. 2 The economic organization of an international linear business system. Source: Authors' own figure

---

3   Differences Between Circular and Linear Systems

Linear systems are typically sequential, although they do not have to be. Linear systems, such as value chains, may also build on pooled and reciprocal interdependencies, either for the whole system or for parts of it; for example, some activities may be done in a way that implies joint effort and requires considerable interaction (Stabell & Fjeldstad, 1998), yet the activities themselves may be linked sequentially with other activities in a value chain. In other cases, certain activities can be done in parallel and then link to subsequent activities in the chain. However, the hallmark of a linear system, such as that depicted in Fig. 1, is that it does not include any reverse loop between value chain activities or at the end of product usage cycle.

It is important to recognize that circularity occurs at various levels. Specifically, circularity may occur at the activity level and at the system level. At the activity level, this is especially a matter of reusing material associated with doing certain activities or a set of activities (or several activities performed as a joint set and that together constitute a certain part of the value system). A linear system cannot per se be circular—unless, of course, a feedback loop is added to it, thereby fundamentally transforming it. However, a simple step towards achieving some circularity could be to introduce activity-related circular loops.

At the system level, circularity is a matter of the design and type of system, especially whether or not the system is linear. Denoting, as previously, activities and locations as a and L, respectively, while the system schematically presented in Fig. 3 is equivalent to that of Fig. 1 in terms of activities and locations—i.e., a_1 is done in L_1, a_2, a_3, and a_4 in L_2, and a_5 in L_3—its configuration is structurally different due to the link between activities a_5 and $a_{1.}$, which ensures that residue material after

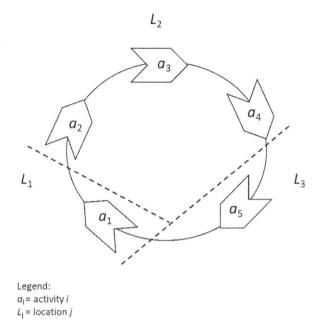

Fig. 3 An international circular business system. Source: Authors' own figure

Legend:
a_i = activity i
L_j = location j

use/consumption is recycled, either by entering the loop of the same system again or by entering another apposite system.

Circularity may go beyond just recycling material at the end of a product's life. A more extensive notion of the CE incorporates three principles. First, traditional recycling closes the resource loop between post-usage and inbound logistics for production. Second, narrowing resource flows fundamentally increases resource efficiency by reducing the absolute amount of resources per product and the total number of products needed to cover consumers' needs. Third, slowing resource flows and material erosion implies prolonging products' life for as long as possible (Bocken et al., 2016). These three principles can create a more material-efficient economy, but they carry implications throughout the product life and for most value activities (a), location choices (L), and operation mode (or governance) decisions (G).

In a CE, initial product and process design works with alternative, recycled materials and incorporates product longevity as a central design parameter. The products are made upgradable and engineered based on a modular technique to ease repairability and refurbishment, thereby extending the product lifetime. The business model design in a CE focuses on providing access to sharing concepts instead of individual ownership, which reduces the absolute amount of products in the market. Reusing the same product or a repaired or refurbished version of it introduces the tightest cycle that can create value in a CE. Remanufacturing components and reusing them in new products are a longer reverse process, yet more powerful than material recycling (Ellen MacArthur Foundation, 2013). A system-wide adaptation of CE practices can be advanced if traditionally separate industries cooperate in exchanging their materials or by-products, known as "industrial symbiosis" (Chertow, 2000). In such a symbiotic process, one firm's waste becomes a secondary resource for another. The previously mentioned CE principles aim to boost effectiveness in resource savings that limit natural resource depletion and CO_2 emissions. It may also help economies grow due to macro-economic cost savings in material and energy, for instance, up to 630 billion USD in the EU manufacturing sector annually (Ellen MacArthur Foundation, 2013; Tuladhar et al., 2016).

However, circular systems are prone to entail a higher degree of complexity and require more careful coordination than linear systems. Hence, CE may carry a higher cost of organizing. The additional loops within and between firm activities increase interdependencies and uncertainty levels that may raise the cost of transacting. For example, feeding secondary material back into the system creates additional transportation costs and indirect transaction costs between material collectors, inbound logistics, procurement, and product developers whose collaboration must be adjusted, coordinated, and made reliable.

Shifting the focus from one linear product life to loops that slow down and close resource flows involves achieving cooperation between more further actors operating in previously unrelated industries and value chain sections, which in turn likely increase transaction and governance costs. Some of these costs occur due to the need for establishing—or setting up—the cooperation, which involves importantly the ex ante costs of searching, screening, and assessing information, generating contacts with viable parties, and of negotiating between them. In addition, there are various, typically more recurrent, ex post costs of ensuring that the needed coordination is achieved (Benito & Tomassen, 2010).

4 MNEs and Approaches to Circularity

Per definition, multinational enterprises operate across national borders, by owning and controlling units that conduct value activities in at least two different locations (Buckley & Casson, 1976). MNEs are key actors in designing and managing business systems that span several countries and sometimes even have a global reach (Bartlett & Ghoshal, 1989; Buckley, 2018; Ghemawat, 2007). In many industries MNEs take a dominating role, which they typically attain by owning superior revenue-generating brands, by controlling activities with high value-creating potential such as sales and marketing, and by performing innovation activities such as research and product development that ensure sustained competitiveness for companies (Mudambi, 2008). In contrast, MNEs often leave the activities in their business systems that have lower projected value-creating potential—such as sourcing of generic inputs, standardized manufacturing and assembly tasks, and transportation—to outside suppliers and service providers. Control over such activities is retained, not by owning—which is deemed unnecessary for several reasons, including offering more flexibility and lower governance costs than the in-house alternatives—but by contractual means (Benito et al., 2019; Buckley, 2018; Forsgren & Holm, 2021; Strange & Humphrey, 2019).

As the pivotal actors in international (i.e., multilocation) business systems, MNEs have considerable discretion in designing a system, specifying its roles and selecting those that perform them, and overseeing its operations as a whole (Kano, 2018). Consequently, MNEs take a leading role in determining the circularity of a business system. However, striving for economic efficiency and profitability on their own part, due to the higher organizational costs of CE, it seems at present practically axiomatic that MNEs are inclined to adopt linear business systems. In most instances, the potential efficiencies due to material savings, etc. may not be perceived as sufficiently high to outweigh the increased uncertainty and complexity of adopting CE solutions.

However, CE solutions may become more advantageous as crucial resources get scarcer, resulting in pricier and more fragile supply. Still, although material and energy costs may be lower in CE, many companies may not be aware of their actual cost-reducing potential. Policy-makers could also play a part through regulations (sanctions as well as incentives) that tilt in favor of adopting CE solutions and doing so earlier than what could otherwise be expected. At the same time, science and technology, such as data sharing infrastructure, advance and ease CE implementation, while many consumers and voters expect decision-makers to adequately respond to the climate and resource-use emergencies.

As powerful lead firms orchestrating international value chains, MNEs increasingly face pressures to implement sustainable and value-maximizing practices, such as the CE (Zhan, 2021). In what different ways do MNEs act or react to circularity opportunities?

Some lead firms may choose to advance their CE transition at a greater speed and effort than their competitors and use that as a brand differentiator. One such example is Patagonia, which has announced it aims to be carbon-neutral by 2025. To achieve that goal, it needs to convince its value chain partners to use 100% renewable and recycled materials (Patagonia, 2020a). Processed waste comes from diverse supply chain members, such as mills and factories, and consumers. Patagonia thereby inverts its relationship with suppliers by recycling worn clothes and selling them back to the suppliers as secondary material at lower rates than virgin resources, or directly to customers, for a second time, as used clothes (Patagonia, 2020b; Rattalino, 2018). Of course, early-moving firms also become exposed to "liabilities of newness" as their actions will be based on trial and error rather than templates or "recipes," as well as face the challenges of taking on structural and knowledge investments that later become available for (free-riding) followers.

Other MNEs may take a somewhat reactive approach being urged by governments to engage in collaborative CE initiatives. For example, in governmentally managed Chinese industrial parks such as the Suzhou Industrial Park, international and domestic MNEs cooperate locally to implement the CE. They act under the guidance of governmental regulators striving for an environmentally friendly industry and self-reliance based on national plans and concrete strategies (Zhang et al., 2009).

4.1   Corporate and Contextual Influences on CE Strategies

The scope of MNEs may facilitate or impede the degree of their CE advancement. Scope relates to the vertical scope of firms, i.e., decisions on activity integration, as well as to their horizontal scope, i.e., product diversification choices (Collis & Montgomery, 2005). Vertical scope is about the governance choices MNEs make, which influence their CE-related behavior inasmuch as hierarchical integration of CE-relevant activities, instead of sourcing them in the market, will make the firm more directly engaged in CE. On the one hand, hierarchical integration allows controlling collaboration efforts along the value chain and might ease the effective establishment of reverse chains for repair or recycling—albeit possibly increased governance costs, as noted above. On the other hand, sourcing recycled material on the market might be an efficient and easily implementable advancement towards CE. For example, permanent materials such as aluminum are particularly appropriate for an early transformation towards circularity; their metallurgical characteristics are well-specified and standardized, and a recycling infrastructure already exists in many countries. As a result, metals currently represent the category with the highest circularity rates in Europe (Eurostat, 2020). Because handling these resources generates little uncertainty and shortages are relatively rare, they are often prone to be handled by spot market governance and efficiently so.

The horizontal scope, or diversification strategy, of MNEs may also be a determining factor of the extent of companies' circularity. The number of distinct businesses a corporation chooses to operate and the relatedness of these businesses may influence the design and ability to implement the CE. The degree of diversification ranges from a single or very dominant business to a large number of businesses; the similarities between products, technologies, and resources involved in the various businesses represent their relatedness (Hitt et al., 2015; Rumelt, 1974). The higher the relatedness between businesses, the less costly sharing and implementing learning becomes—a core benefit of diversification. Once knowledge on how to achieve waste elimination is developed, the relatedness of business activities allows sharing these insights and applying them to similar products and production processes, thereby advancing circularity for an MNE. Also, high levels of related diversification can be advantageous since efficiency advantages can be augmented by scaling them. However, an opposite view is that a diversified conglomerate (i.e., one made up of highly unrelated businesses) might be advantageous to achieve the CE as it can benefit from the symbiosis between unrelated businesses to circulate material. The possibilities to reuse and recycle materials are extended beyond the focal industry and offer options to close the loop outside of it. Their ability to implement CE is supported by potential synergies among unrelated business units that may offer various synergetic advantages. Exploiting industry differences and the reusability of materials across product categories might ease the advancement towards CE.

In addition to scope, MNEs also differ regarding scale, i.e., the product volume produced or assembled per a given time period. Unlike Patagonia, which leads a tightly coordinated network of suppliers, many MNEs do not control an entire value system. MNEs can be small, specialized firms that simply are present in more than one location. This includes, for example, component or service suppliers that operate in multiple locations within a global value chain. Such companies would participate in the CE as per the guidance of their business partners, especially the lead firm of the global value chain, and its discretion to pursue a CE-oriented approach would be limited. Also, obtaining knowledge on how to improve the efficiency of production process—a key to reduce resource needs—would be difficult for most such companies on their own, which makes them dependent on exchanges with other companies. Likewise, synergies in recycling processes are limited inside one single company, unless the scale is large. Developing links to network partners is therefore key to achieve similar degrees of circularity.

A company's small scale also influences its position in the value chain. Not only do large-scale firms enjoy substantial negotiation power with their business partners (Porter, 1980); they also have more possibilities to create the material feedback loops necessary for circularity. The relatively larger gains from CE for firms with higher product output quantities should help them recognize CE as a relevant lever. In particular, economies of scale enable firms to distribute the initial investment costs— in production as well as governance—across more units, thereby making the transition a more realistic and attractive opportunity.

Based on the above, it becomes clear that the reasons why MNEs move towards CE solutions to a different extent and at different pace is to a considerable degree a result of their own strategic choices. However, besides the decisions made by their owners and managers, industry and institutional contexts also influence MNEs' CE advancement.

First, industry-level factors are at play. At the industry level, the largest CO_2 emitters globally are the manufacturing industries, construction of buildings and infrastructure, and transportation (IEA, 2021). However, MNEs in these sectors are also among the most prone to adapt their value chain activities and business models, with CE transformation increasingly being a viable solution. The bulk of research on the CE investigates the manufacturing industries, while the service economy remains under-researched (Kirchherr & Van Santen, 2019). This is despite services accounting for the greater and increasing part of the GDP in many economies and product-service systems increasingly being conceptualized as key to advance the CE, for instance, through sharing economy solutions. Still, even though the literature suggests that the sharing economy likely contributes to more efficient resource usage, this is not necessarily the case for all industries and business models (Ciulli & Kolk, 2019).

Second, regulations and policies shape the advancement of CE development. On the positive side, they may facilitate transitioning from the predominant linear economic systems to a CE. Importantly, they can convey trust and continuity in transforming the economic system and guide related investment decisions (Ranta & Saari, 2019). Sanctions in the form of CO_2 taxes and import-export duties may discourage further investments into resource depletion and the linear "take-make-waste" economy. Alternatively, CE opportunities might be highlighted by incentivizing certain sustainable activities. Europe and China are considered leaders of legislative obligations influencing MNE's CE decisions. The EU Circular Economy Action Plan focuses on a new industrial strategy that decouples economic growth from resource use (European Commission, 2020). Legislators point out that the CE offers potentials for EU manufacturing firms to increase profitability as they spend on average 40% on materials—a cost component with considerable reduction potential in the CE. In the Action Plan, the Commission suggests initiatives and legislations to regulate product design, empower buyers, and regulate production processes for selected industries to advance the CE. In China, a comprehensive CE strategy was already introduced with the 11th Five-Year-Plan in 2005, and a concrete "CE Promotion Law of the PRC" was adopted in 2008 (Mathews & Tan, 2016). After the recent China-US trade war, the political ideology in China shifted towards an internal, self-sufficient focus that supports the CE. The recent 2020 Five-Year-Plan reiterates the CE's importance not only for environmental reasons but particularly for self-reliant economic development and supply chain security objectives. A supplement plan provides specific directives for regional governments to implement CE initiatives tailored to local conditions with the aim to serve concrete national targets for 2025. Correspondingly, a disproportionate majority of authors publishing research on the CE is based in China, which furthers the foundation for the country's advancement in CE (Geissdoerfer et al., 2017). The policies and regulations in an MNE's core location, either the country where its decision-making headquarters are located or its key markets, may spur strategic decisions towards designing and implementing CE-related activities. On the negative side, policies, and regulations—or lack thereof—could impede or delay transitioning to a CE. Political concerns based on protectionist (or nationalistic) perspectives could hinder MNEs in pursuing efficient CE solutions for the global value chains that they lead and instead engage in creating local (national) circular business models. For example, local food production is often proclaimed as an ecologically sustainable approach to nutrition generation as it circumvents transnational transportation. However, not all locations are equally well suited to maximize calorie output per farmed land unit, and one may ask whether the same amount of resources could not be used more productively in transnational settings.

Beyond formal institutions such as laws, regulations, and policies, the informal institutional context may also play a role in how MNEs relate to CE (North, 1990). The social norms of a young generation regard the transition towards a sustainable economy as inevitable (cf. Fridays for Future and Extinction Rebellion activism). Voters express their desire for sustainable practices in surging election results for the "Green" parties in the European context, which can again formally institutionalize regulations for sustainable CE practices. In contrast to the civil society pressuring for a more sustainable economy, social inertia, or outright resistance due to vested interests in, inter alia, technology, organizational, or locational choices, may constitute a barrier to make effective changes towards CE. Consumerism largely encourages sales of new products that serve to communicate one's social status and personality. For example, a new car is an important status symbol in many countries, such as China. While a used car or choosing access to a shared fleet over ownership—both CE solutions—may be beneficial from a financial or practical perspective, its market acceptance requires a shift in the cultural denotation of the product. In China, car ownership loses its meaning as a status symbol while alternative, more sustainable mobility services gain momentum (Tsang et al., 2018). Collectivist societies such as many European countries and China seem to transition to the CE more successfully than individualistic societies such as the USA or Australia. For example, the Netherlands is the global leader in terms of a CE with a circularity of 25% (de Wit et al., 2020b). Collectivist societies value a collective well-being over immediate personal benefits—a characteristic that could facilitate investment-intensive CE transitions.

4.2   The Geographical Scope of CE

Transitioning to CE evokes questions on the geographical setup of MNEs and potential differences between international corporate strategies. The geographical dimensions of business systems are important, as locations differ and some are for various reasons better suited or prepared for accommodating CE solutions than others. Reasons include principally (i) existing infrastructure, regulations, and CE competence and awareness, which are results of political and economic decisions (investments and commitments) made in the past; (ii) informal institutional characteristics of locations, especially cultural markers such as trust among business actors and between a population and its political institutions, and willingness to forsake profits in the short term to invest in a sustainable economic setup; as well as (iii) traditional geographical dimensions such as size and density of populations, degree of urbanization, and distance, which affect scale and scope decisions and costs and hence have implications for the viability and design of CE solutions.

Location choices can be activity-specific and can either include linkages crossing national boundaries or remain concentrated in locally limited settings. From an economic perspective, location choices traditionally reflect advantages in production costs, transportation costs, and tariffs (Casson et al., 2016). As per Williamson (1996), the geographical co-location of business partners sometimes reveals a choice of "site specificity," a distinct type of asset specificity, resulting from decisions to reduce transportation and inventory costs. Such co-location may also express considerations about access to assets such as resources, knowledge, and network connections. Spatial economics generally focus on optimizing plant locations taking into account consumer markets. In CEs, not only the initial production and consumption activities are to be considered but also circular loops to enable repair or post-usage returns to the manufacturer.

MNEs follow different international corporate strategies and choose structures accordingly. According to Bartlett and Ghoshal (1989); see also Westney & Zaheer, 2009), MNEs' internationalization can take the form of international, global, multi-domestic, or transnational strategies, depending on companies' analysis of integration and responsiveness considerations.

MNEs' internationalization strategies directly relate to the locational aspects of CE, with two juxtaposed situations defining the range of options. On the one end, resource circulation could be organized entirely in one location. This would be a CE solution emphasizing geographic, political, and cultural proximity. Essentially, the decision to implement CE would be taken on a country-by-country basis, and its design would reflect the specificities of each location. Conceivably, local firms may often have the upper hand vis-à-vis MNEs in designing and implementing CE in such circumstances, especially if locations have many idiosyncratic features. However, MNEs frequently have specific advantages that are not location-bound and can therefore be applied across the locations in which the MNE operates and as such provide a scale advantage for the MNE versus local competitors (Grøgaard & Verbeke, 2012). Superior general-purpose technologies and competence in logistics are examples of such advantages, which can be applied in multiple locations simultaneously across the MNE, effectively providing a public good that is internalized by the company. So, while each CE would be in a single location, there would be gains from being designed and managed by MNEs operating in multiple locations. On the other end, the CE could have a global reach, having been set up by an MNE spanning its entire global network. A global CE setup could maximize resource (re-)usage by tapping into a larger number of opportunities for synergies than what would be possible for a more locally constrained CE (Chertow, 2000). However, the uncertainties arising from operating in multiple locations and the higher costs related to coordinating a more spread-out system are likely to challenge the implementation of global CE solutions. Between the single-location and the global solutions are various intermediate forms with some, but not necessarily all CE-related activities taking place in different locations (see Fig. 3).

Presumably, the local solutions would seem to align particularly well with international and multi-domestic MNE strategies, whereas global solutions being more suitable for global MNE strategies and with transnational strategies involving both. However, distinct CE principles—such as narrowing, closing, and slowing— have an impact on localization strategies. While setting up reverse supply chains to recycle resources back to the original manufacturing site may prove (initially) unfeasible for most markets, the establishment of circular loops closer to the local end-consumer should be easier to implement across the global network if this has been built into the product design. These could include reusage activities, customers sharing products with local peers (such as in access-based services), and locally present facilitators that can perform repairing activities. However, we envisage that other factors than MNEs' strategies are likely to weigh in as well and possibly in decisive ways. For example, the costs involved in setting up and coordinating global CE solutions may simply make them an unattractive alternative beyond the drawing board.

Regional solutions represent a compromise between the local and the global, offering some of the benefits of both without incurring some of the associated costs (Asmussen, 2012). For example, regionalization may deliver scale effects similar to those of global reach but at the same time provide some of the positive proximity and fungibility effects of local focus. Likewise, regionalization may also help alleviate some of the costs, for example, in terms of complexity, distance, and liability of foreignness associated with global solutions, as well as reducing suboptimal resource use resulting from (overly) local solutions (Verbeke & Asmussen, 2016). Hence, the regional level represents an important middle-ground in terms of the locational scope of MNEs CE involvement. Given a need to establish sufficient commitment to coordinate circularity beyond national borders, regional integration arrangements such as the European Union (EU); the Agreement between the United States of America, the United Mexican States, and Canada (USMCA); the Regional Comprehensive Economic Partnership between 15 Asia-Pacific nations (RCEP); and Mercosur may indeed prove instrumental in scaling up CE solutions beyond local (i.e., national or sub-national) efforts.

Globalization has advanced noticeably in the past decades, and value creation has become more dispersed across the globe, in the form of global value chains (Hernández & Pedersen, 2017; Kano, 2018), although not necessarily in terms of value appropriation, which has remained concentrated (Mudambi, 2008). However, globalization rates are stagnating (Gygli et al., 2019; OECD, 2020) and MNEs increasingly consider reconfiguring their production networks and value chains to improve efficiency in changing circumstances, inter alia by de-internationalizing, which has been defined as actions "that reduce a company's engagement in or exposure to current cross-border activities" (Benito & Welch, 1997, p. 9). While international business research has previously mainly engaged with market entry and expansion, the globalization of business activity may face a reverse trend with an increased focus on nationalism and sustainability, including the circular economy, potentially leading to increased activity within countries, but less between them (Herczeg et al., 2018; UNCTAD, 2020). Yet, the effect of reshoring on environmental sustainability remains underexplored (Gupta et al., 2021).

As noted earlier, transaction and governance costs in a CE are likely to be relatively higher for most value chain activities than in the linear economy. However, geographically bounded and institutionally homogeneous CE initiatives could curb rising transaction costs. Minimizing distances between actors might, consequently, be an efficient approach to implement the CE. As the burdens of coordination and communication increase with distance (Casson et al., 2016), piloting a new economic setup in locally bounded environments will save coordination and information costs. Also, information gathering could be eased, and information asymmetry, often a challenge in unfamiliar host countries (Wu & Salomon, 2017), can be avoided, promoting the assessing and monitoring of reverse supply chains. Being an outsider in a network abroad is a root of uncertainty (Johanson & Vahlne, 2009), while trust and knowledgeable relationships support new business endeavors. Geographical boundedness and institutional homogeneity potentially help curb opportunistic behavior, ease expectation management, limit complexity, and scale down bureaucratic contracting efforts—all reasons for high transaction and governance costs. MNEs can potentially expect efficiency advantages once committing to a local CE transition. This may explain why most pilot CE systems are established at locally constrained levels such as (sub-national) regional developments (e.g., the German IN4climate.NRW initiative), industrial parks (e.g., the Chinese Suzhou Industrial Park), or smart cities. Such locally bounded and collaborative economic setups represent a counterpoint to global value chains with largely independent actors.

Nevertheless, any MNE needs to consider other location cost parameters (e.g., resources, labor, production costs) as well. Increased localization to lower CE transaction and governance costs comes with a trade-off to low production costs in globally dispersed chains, a core benefit of the global factory (Buckley, 2018). By de-globalizing economic activity, firms naturally reduce the scale of their business, which can also negatively affect transaction cost efficiency. CE limits resource availability compared to the global market suggesting small-number circumstances that provoke higher costs of transacting (Williamson, 1975). Yet, this circumstance leads to a higher frequency of exchange between the local parties, which may justify the contractual costs (Williamson, 1985). Relying on new secondary resources in the production process, especially if adapted to local synergy partners, can result in the firm being geographically bounded and less flexible in using global alternatives in uncertain circumstances. Thus, limited resource availability in regionally bounded and contractually limiting CEs may also raise transaction and governance costs asking for a differentiated analysis of CE location choices.

5   Concluding Remarks

Moving towards a more sustainable future requires dealing with a broad palette of issues (Folke et al., 2019), as laid out in the United Nations Sustainable Development Goals (SDG) (van Zanten & van Tulder, 2018), and discussed in more detail in other chapters in this Handbook. Here, we focus on the specific issue of circularity. Attaining more circularity in the economy to reduce waste and depletion of resources is part of the solution and key for achieving several SDGs, in particular SDGs 8 (work and economic growth), 9 (industry, innovation, and infrastructure), 11 (sustainable cities and communities), 12 (responsible consumption and production), and 13 (climate action), and we believe 17 (partnerships for the goals) will be instrumental towards their achievement.

In this chapter, we have discussed the key role of MNEs as dominant actors in the economic arena to make the transition to CE (Zhan, 2021); Table 1 provides an overview. We have demonstrated the applicability of established strategic and international business conceptualizations to explain how MNEs' decisions regarding activity, location, and governance setup can facilitate or impede CE development. Corporate and contextual influences play significant roles in shaping MNEs' approach to CE. However, further research is needed about how MNEs can help implement the transition towards CE, which we believe international business scholarship should contribute to. Most extant research describing the relationship between firms and the CE is qualitative and lacks a clear theoretical foundation (Lahti et al., 2018).

While we provide a first attempt to apply strategic and international business theory to circularity as part of a more sustainable future economy, extending our conceptualizations is needed for a more profound understanding. For example, theories of economic organization such as transaction cost and internalization theories serve as suitable tools to advance knowledge on how value activities are

Table 1 Factors that facilitate and impede MNEs' CE adoption

		CE facilitators	CE impediments
Corporate factors	*Activities (governance)*	Integration provides control for collaboration (e.g., for reverse chains) Existing markets (e.g., for permanent material transactions)	Costly integration (higher complexity) and inefficient (weaker internal incentives) Feeble markets (e.g., uncertain material quality and availability)
	Products (diversification)	High degree (large number of businesses) and economies of scale Unrelated (industrial symbiosis) Related (knowledge sharing)	Low degree (single, small-scale, specialized, independent firm; dependent on market)
	Markets (location)	Geographical proximity in CE system (local, regional, multi-domestic)	Overly locally restricted or exaggerated global aspirations
Contextual factors	*Industry*	Pressure on manufacturing industry, buildings, and transportation	Sectors not currently in the focus of linear waste accumulation
	Formal institutions	Support system (incentives, penalties) at national, regional (e.g., EU), or global levels (e.g., UN) Homogeneity	Lack of support at national, regional, or global levels Heterogeneity
	Informal institutions	Sustainability norms and customs Collectivist society (institutionalized change) Trust, pragmatism	Social inertia Individualistic society (activism) Conflict-orientation, competition

Source: Compiled by authors

organized and how their related costs and benefits differ between linear and circular solutions. With a better understanding of efficiency differences, MNEs, as well as other firms, will be able to improve their strategic decisions.

Since the CE literature is currently dominated by case studies, it would benefit from more general explanations of the mechanisms underlying the implementation of CE solutions. In addition to theoretical advancement, empirical studies based on large-scale samples would be useful to systematically examine the relationships involved. As a counterweight to the prevalence of process studies, a fruitful path for future research is to uncover the effects of MNEs' strategies—especially in terms of product and geographic diversification—on circularity (Hofstetter et al., 2021). Since the potential for circularity and the readiness for CE transition currently differs substantially across industries and countries (e.g., in terms of their formal and informal institutions), it is also pertinent to examine the influence of such factors on MNEs' CE decisions.

References

Asmussen, C. G. (2012). Foundations of regional versus global strategies. In A. Verbeke & H. Merchant (Eds.), *Handbook of research on international strategic management* (pp. 271–290). Edward Elgar Publishing.

Asmussen, C. G., Benito, G. R. G., & Petersen, B. (2009). Organizing foreign market activities: From entry mode choice to configuration decisions. *International Business Review, 18*(2), 145–155.

Bartlett, C. A., & Ghoshal, S. (1989). *Managing across borders: The transnational solution.* Harvard Business School Press.

Benito, G. R. G., Petersen, B., & Welch, L. S. (2019). The global value chain and internalization theory. *Journal of International Business Studies, 50*(8), 1414–1423.

Benito, G. R. G., & Tomassen, S. (2010). Governance costs in headquarters-subsidiary relationships. In U. Andersson & U. Holm (Eds.), *Managing the contemporary multinational: The role of headquarters* (pp. 138–159). Edward Elgar Publishing.

Benito, G. R. G., & Welch, L. S. (1997). De-internationalization. *Management International Review, 37*(SI 2), 7–25.

Bocken, N. M. P., De Pauw, I., Bakker, C., & Van Der Grinten, B. (2016). Product design and business model strategies for a circular economy. *Journal of Industrial and Production Engineering, 33*(5), 308–320.

Buckley, P. J. (2018). *The global factory - networked multinational enterprises in the modern global economy.* Edward Elgar Publishing.

Buckley, P. J., & Casson, M. (1976). *The future of the multinational enterprise.* Macmillan.

Casson, M., Porter, L., & Wadeson, N. (2016). Internalisation theory: An unfinished agenda. *International Business Review, 25*(6), 1223–1234.

Chertow, M. R. (2000). Industrial symbiosis: Literature and taxonomy. *Annual Review of Energy and the Environment, 25*(1), 313–337.

Ciulli, F., & Kolk, A. (2019). Incumbents and business model innovation for the sharing economy: Implications for sustainability. *Journal of Cleaner Production, 214*, 995–1010.

Collis, D. J., & Montgomery, C. A. (2005). *Corporate strategy: A resource-based approach.* McGraw-Hill.

de Wit, M., Haigh, L., & von Daniels, C. (2020b). *The circularity gap report: The Netherlands.* Accessed August 19, 2021, from https://www.circularity-gap.world/netherlands

de Wit, M., Hoogzaad, J., & von Daniels, C. (2020a). *The circularity gap report 2020.* Accessed August 10, 2021, from https://www.circularity-gap.world/global

Ellen MacArthur Foundation. (2013). *Towards the circular economy Vol. 1: An economic and business rationale for an accelerated transition.* Ellen MacArthur Foundation.

European Commission. (2020). *A new circular economy action plan. For a cleaner and more competitive Europe.* Accessed May 11, 2020, from https://eur-lex.europa.eu/resource.html?uri=cellar:9903b325-6388-11ea-b735-01aa75ed71a1.0017.02/DOC_1&format=PDF

Eurostat. (2020). *EU circular material use rate.* European Commission. Accessed August 18, 2021, from https://ec.europa.eu/eurostat/web/products-eurostat-news/-/DDN-20200312-1

Folke, C., Österblom, H., Jouffray, J. B., Lambin, E. F., Neil Adger, W., Scheffer, M., Crona, B. I., Nyström, M., Levin, S. A., Carpenter, S. R., Anderies, J. M., Chapin, S., III, Crépin, A.-S., Dauriach, A., Galaz, V., Gordon, L. J., Kautsky, N., Walker, B. H., Watson, J. R., Wilen, J., & de Zeeuw, A. (2019). Transnational corporations and the challenge of biosphere stewardship. *Nature Ecology & Evolution, 3*, 1396–1403.

Forsgren, M., & Holm, U. (2021). Controlling without owning – Owning without controlling: A critical note on two extensions of internalization theory. *Journal of International Business Studies.* https://doi.org/10.1057/s41267-021-00416-3

Geissdoerfer, M., Savaget, P., Bocken, N. M. P., & Hultink, E. J. (2017). The circular economy – A new sustainability paradigm? *Journal of Cleaner Production, 143*, 757–768.

Ghemawat, P. (2007). *Redefining global strategy.* Harvard Business School Press.

Grøgaard, B., & Verbeke, A. (2012). Twenty key hypotheses that make internalization theory the general theory of international strategic management. In A. Verbeke & H. Merchant (Eds.), *Handbook of research on international strategic management* (pp. 7–30). Edward Elgar Publishing.

Gupta, S., Wang, Y., & Czinkota, M. (2021). Special issue call for papers: Reshoring and sustainable development goals. *British Journal of Management*.

Gygli, S., Haelg, F., Potrafke, N., & Sturm, J.-E. (2019). The KOF globalisation index – Revisited. *Review of International Organizations, 14*(3), 543–574.

Herczeg, G., Akkerman, R., & Hauschild, M. Z. (2018). Supply chain collaboration in industrial symbiosis networks. *Journal of Cleaner Production, 171*, 1058–1067.

Hernández, V., & Pedersen, T. (2017). Global value chain configuration: A review and research agenda. *Business Research Quarterly, 20*(2), 137–150.

Hitt, M. A., Hoskisson, R. E., & Ireland, D. R. (2015). *Strategic management: Competitiveness & globalization* (11th ed.). Cengage Learning.

Hofstetter, J. S., De Marchi, V., Sarkis, J., Govindan, K., Klassen, R., Ometto, A. R., Spraul, K. S., Bocken, N., Ashton, W. S., Sharma, S., Jaeger-Erben, M., Jensen, C., Dewick, P., Schröder, P., Sinkovics, N., Ibrahim, S. E., Fiske, L., Goerzen, A., & Vazquez-Brust, D. (2021). From sustainable global value chains to circular economy – Different silos, different perspectives, but many opportunities to build bridges. *Circular Economy and Sustainability, 1*(1), 1–27.

IEA. (2021). *Greenhouse gas emissions from energy: Overview*. IEA, Paris. Accessed August 30, 2021, from https://www.iea.org/reports/greenhouse-gas-emissions-from-energy-overview

Johanson, J., & Vahlne, J.-E. (2009). The Uppsala internationalisation process model revisited: From liability of foreignness to liability of outsidership. *Journal of International Business Studies, 40*(9), 1411–1431.

Kano, L. (2018). Global value chain governance: A relational perspective. *Journal of International Business Studies, 49*(6), 684–705.

Kirchherr, J., & Van Santen, R. (2019). Research on the circular economy: A critique of the field. *Resources, Conservation and Recycling, 151*, 104480.

Lahti, T., Wincent, J., & Parida, V. (2018). A definition and theoretical review of the circular economy, value creation, and sustainable business models: Where are we now and where should research move in the future? *Sustainability, 10*(8), 2799.

Mathews, J. A., & Tan, H. (2016). Circular economy: Lessons from China. *Nature, 531*(7595), 440–442.

McDonough, W., & Braungart, M. (2002). *Cradle to cradle: Remaking the way we make things*. North Point Press.

Mudambi, R. (2008). Location, control and innovation in knowledge-intensive industries. *Journal of Economic Geography, 8*(5), 699–725.

Murray, A., Skene, K., & Haynes, K. (2017). The circular economy: An interdisciplinary exploration of the concept and application in a global context. *Journal of Business Ethics, 140*(3), 369–380.

North, D. C. (1990). *Institutions, institutional change and economic performance*. Cambridge University Press.

OECD. (2020). *FDI flows (indicator)*. https://doi.org/10.1787/99f6e393-en

Patagonia. (2020a). *Our footprint*. Accessed November 9, 2020, from https://www.patagonia.com/our-footprint/

Patagonia. (2020b). *Worn wear*. Accessed November 9, 2020, from https://wornwear.patagonia.com/

Porter, M. E. (1980). *Competitive strategy: Techniques for analyzing industries and competitors*. Free Press.

Porter, M. E. (1985). *Competitive advantage: Creating and sustaining superior performance*. Free Press.

Ranta, V., & Saari, U. (2019). Circular economy: Enabling the transition towards sustainable consumption and production. In W. Leal Filho, A. M. Azul, L. Brandli, P. G. Özuyar, &

T. Wall (Eds.), *Responsible consumption and production (the encyclopedia of the UN sustainable development goals)*. Springer.

Rattalino, F. (2018). Circular advantage anyone? Sustainability-driven innovation and circularity at Patagonia, Inc. *Thunderbird International Business Review, 60*(5), 747–755.

Rumelt, R. P. (1974). *Strategy, structure, and economic performance*. Harvard University.

Rygh, A., Chiarapini, E., & Segovia, M. V. (2022). How can international business research contribute towards the sustainable development goals? *Critical Perspectives on International Business, 18*(4), 457-487.

Stabell, C., & Fjeldstad, Ø. D. (1998). Configuring value for competitive advantage: On chains, shops, and networks. *Strategic Management Journal, 19*(5), 413–437.

Stahel, W. R. (1981). The product-life factor. In S. Grinton Orr (Ed.), *An inquiry into the nature of sustainable societies: The role of the private sector* (pp. 72–104). HARC.

Strange, R., & Humphrey, J. (2019). What lies between market and hierarchy? Insights from internalization theory and global value chain theory. *Journal of International Business Studies, 50*(8), 1401–1413.

Thompson, J. D. (1967). *Organizations in action*. McGraw Hill.

Tsang, R., Boutot, P.-H., & Cai, D. (2018). *China's mobility industry picks up speed*. Bain & Company.

Tuladhar, S., Yuan, M., & Montgomery, W. D. (2016). *An economic analysis of the circular economy* [Presented at the 19th Annual Conference on Global Economic Analysis, Washington, DC, USA].

UNCTAD. (2020). *International production beyond the pandemic* (World Investment Report, Issue 2020). https://unctad.org/system/files/official-document/wir2020_overview_en.pdf

van Zanten, J. A., & van Tulder, R. (2018). Multinational enterprises and the sustainable development goals: An institutional approach to corporate engagement. *Journal of International Business Policy, 1*(3–4), 208–233.

Verbeke, A., & Asmussen, C. G. (2016). Global, local, or regional? The locus of MNE strategies. *Journal of Management Studies, 53*(6), 1051–1075.

Welch, L. S., Benito, G. R. G., & Petersen, B. (2018). *Foreign operation methods: Theory, analysis, strategy* (2nd ed.). Edward Elgar.

Westney, D. E., & Zaheer, S. (2009). The multinational enterprise as an organisation. In A. M. Rugman (Ed.), *The Oxford handbook of international business* (2nd ed., pp. 241–336). Oxford University Press.

Williamson, O. E. (1975). *Markets and hierarchies: Analysis and antitrust implications*. Free Press.

Williamson, O. E. (1985). *The economic institutions of capitalism*. Free Press.

Williamson, O. E. (1991). Comparative economic organization: The analysis of discrete structural alternatives. *Administrative Science Quarterly, 36*(2), 269–296.

Williamson, O. E. (1996). *The mechanisms of governance*. Oxford University Press.

Wu, Z., & Salomon, R. (2017). Deconstructing the liability of foreignness: Regulatory enforcement actions against foreign banks. *Journal of International Business Studies, 48*(7), 837–861.

Zhan, J. X. (2021). GVC transformation and a new investment landscape in the 2020s: Driving forces, directions, and a forward-looking research and policy agenda. *Journal of International Business Policy, 4*(2), 206–220.

Zhang, H. Y., Hara, K., Yabar, H., Yamaguchi, Y., Uwasu, M., & Morioka, T. (2009). Comparative analysis of socio-economic and environmental performances for Chinese EIPs: Case studies in Baotou, Suzhou, and Shanghai. *Sustainability Science, 4*(2), 263–279.

Gabriel R. G. Benito is Professor, Department of Strategy and Entrepreneurship, BI Norwegian Business School. He earned his doctorate from NHH Norwegian School of Economics. His research agenda focuses on corporate governance, the strategies of multinational enterprises, and the economic organization of international business.

Corina Fehlner is a doctoral candidate in Strategy, Entrepreneurship, and Innovation at BI Norwegian Business School. She holds a Master of Science degree in Strategic Management Innsbruck University, Austria, and has managerial experience from the automotive industry. Her research interests are sustainability and business.

MNEs and United Nations' Sustainable Development Goals

Pervez N. Ghauri and Fang Lee Cooke

1 Introduction

United Nations' Millennium Declaration emphasized the collective responsibility to uphold the principles of human dignity, equality, and equity at the global level. In the Millennium Summit of 2000, the world leaders agreed on eight sets of Millennium Development Goals (MDG). At the same time, the Millennium Project Committee put forward 15 global challenges to be addressed. These included reduce poverty, improve healthcare, promote human rights, enhance education, strive for gender equality, ensure environmental sustainability, clean water, and develop global partnerships (Millennium Project, 2006, 2021). Encouraged by the results thus far, such as on poverty reduction (World Bank, 2013), at the Sustainable Development Summit of 2015, a new document, "Transforming our World: The 2030 agenda for Sustainable Development" was agreed upon and released. This document presented the revised agenda for MDGs, extending them to 17 and giving them a new name, "Sustainable Development Goals" (SDGs) with 169 accompanying targets (United Nations, 2015).

It was realized that reducing the poverty level to 50% by 2015, which was already achieved in 2013 was considered a big achievement (World Bank, 2013). The biggest contribution came from China, and if we took away the China effect, the progress was less impressive (Ghauri et al., 2018). There were several important sectors such as health and sanitation, energy supply, and improvements in infrastructure that had not made much progress since the inception of the MDGs in 2000. New promises and commitments were made to achieve the renamed SDGs by 2030. It was

P. N. Ghauri (✉)
International Business, University of Birmingham, Birmingham, UK
e-mail: p.ghauri@bham.ac.uk

F. L. Cooke
Human Resource Management, Monash University, Melbourne, Australia
e-mail: Fang.Cooke@monash.edu

© Springer Nature Switzerland AG 2022
H. Merchant (ed.), *The New Frontiers of International Business*, Contributions to Management Science, https://doi.org/10.1007/978-3-031-06003-8_16

also emphasized that these SDGs are interconnected, so that to reach the target for one goal, progress must be made in reaching the targets for other goals. For example, poverty alleviation can only be achieved if more employment opportunities and working conditions are created, education levels are increased, and there are improvements in health and sanitation (Ghauri et al., 2018; Michailova et al., 2020). Similarly, the resources and technological capabilities of the governments in many of the developing and emerging economies are not conducive to achieving any of these goals on their own. The role of MNEs is therefore imperative for the achievement of the SDGs (Kolk et al., 2017).

In this chapter, we argue that without MNEs' participation and commitment and collaborations between MNEs and international and local policy makers, it is impossible to make real progress toward achieving the SDGs. Several earlier studies have called for such collaborations for achieving an inclusive society (Boddewyn & Doh, 2011; Hadjikhani et al., 2012). In recent years, more and more studies have highlighted positive and negative externalities created by MNE activities in developing and emerging economies (Comyns, 2019; Ghauri & Wang, 2018). We outline how MNEs can contribute to each of the SDGs by adding value or mitigating harm through their activities directly related to their business as well as indirectly through their engagement with the community and society more broadly in the developing world.

2   The Role of MNES

Several studies have investigated the role of MNEs in technology transfer and linkage effects in developing countries (Firth & Ghauri, 2010; Giroud & Scott-Kennel, 2009). We can also find several studies that have been studying the role of MNEs in developing countries for different development issues, for example, sustainable energy, climate change (Kolk, 2016), decreasing inequalities (Newburry et al., 2014), and promoting public-private partnership (Hadjikhani et al., 2012; Ritvala et al., 2014). As we can see most of these studies were performed prior to the announcement of SDGs, these deal with one or two issues related to development and technology transfer. In that period, connecting these issues was not envisioned by researchers in IB.

Most of the IB research in the past encircled the idea how MNEs can create a competitive advantage using their resources and capabilities in the most efficient way (Buckley & Ghauri, 2004, 2015; Kano & Verbeke, 2019). This means that incorporating the SDGs and externalities of MNE activities abroad and how these can influence the competitive advantage of MNEs has largely been ignored. More recently it has been proposed that positive externalities can help MNEs build a stronger competitive advantage, while negative externalities can damage their competitive advantage (Montiel et al., 2021). This means that to theorize the role of MNEs in achieving the SDGs and achieving competitive advantage through the SDGs, IB researchers need to think differently. This also means that MNEs need to think about creating positive externalities and minimize negative externalities if they want to be competitive in global markets. This is a major departure from the earlier perspective where the main task of firms, including MNEs, was profit maximization (Debaere, 2018; Friedman, 1962). We support the argument that this would lead to a different decision-making process where MNEs will be forced to work together with local governments and international organizations and place their CSR at a higher priority (e.g., Forcadell & Aracil, 2019; Kolk, 2016).

We therefore believe that MNEs can play a significant role in achieving the SDGs. In other words, we contend that without MNEs' participation, the mission of achieving the SDGs will be seriously undermined. Zooming in on the SDGs, we illustrate below what MNEs could do and how they might go about it in each of the SDGs and ultimately contribute to achieving all of them (see also Montiel et al., 2021).

2.1   17 SDGs and the Role of MNEs

Goal 1: No poverty—End poverty in all its forms everywhere. Generating good-quality employment, not least measured by wage level, working conditions, and skill development opportunities, is critical to address this goal. MNEs can contribute to this through responsible sourcing of their products in poor countries and marginalized communities and by setting up and operating subsidiaries directly in or nearby these locales. This will contribute to decent work and human capital development to eradicate poverty. MNEs can also address the corruption problem through enhancing financial inclusion, particularly in countries with a relatively high level of corruption (Forcadell & Aracil, 2019, see also Goal 16).

Goal 2: Zero hunger—End hunger, achieve food security and improved nutrition, and promote sustainable agriculture. Wars, poor farming conditions, and the lack of manpower and human capital have been some of the main reasons for food insecurity in poor communities and war-torn territories. MNEs can assist in deploying technology and artificial intelligence to develop smart agriculture in poor regions through collaborations with international organizations and local governments to facilitate sustainable agriculture.

Goal 3: Good health and well-being—Ensure healthy lives and promote well-being for all at all ages. Good health and well-being are achieved, among other things, through preventative actions and making medical supplies accessible and affordable to the poor communities. MNEs can contribute to this goal by promoting good occupational health and safety standards at the workplace and raise the workforce's knowledge about health and well-being. In developing countries, many of which have a collectivist culture and a paternalist style in which the company treats its employees and their family members as part of the extended family, MNE subsidiaries may adopt employee involvement schemes by involving the employees and their family members to identify health and safety hazards at home and the workplace and suggest solutions. Town hall meetings, billboards, and community outreach programs can also be used to promote employees' and communities' understanding of health and safety issues as part of the CSR schemes (e.g., Cooke, 2018).

Medicine security is another important aspect of achieving this goal (Beran et al., 2019). The COVID-19 pandemic has accentuated the continuing, if not widening, inequality in access to medicine and other medical supplies between the developed and the developing world. What role have MNEs played in exacerbating or mitigating this gulf of inequality?

Goal 4: Quality education—Ensure inclusive and equitable education and promote lifelong learning opportunities for all. Good-quality education is the most important means for children and adults to acquire the human capital essential for their access to gainful employment. MNEs can be incentivized to participate in vocational education and training in developing countries to enhance their capabilities in ICT and other relevant technologies that will assist the labor force to develop skills for the digital future of work and lifelong learning. For instance, using Etisalat Telecommunication as a case study, Bello and Othman's (2020, p. 96) study revealed that this MNE "has made a significant contribution towards the development of the education sector in Nigeria."

Goal 5: Gender equality—Achieve gender equality and empower all women and girls. Gender inequality forms a significant part of inequality in many aspects of life (e.g., education, employment, access to healthcare) and is a major source of poverty. MNEs can contribute to this goal by promoting education for girls and women, providing skill training and employment opportunities to them, adopting work-life-balance policy to accommodate their family responsibilities, and other diversity and inclusion policies and practices in their subsidiaries. It is also an area where MNEs can work closely with international agencies, local stakeholders, and host country governments to make an impact (Terpstra-Tong, 2017).

Goal 6: Clean water and sanitation—Ensure available and sustainable water resources and sanitation resources for all. MNEs need to monitor and improve their environmental performance by reducing water pollution and providing clean water facilities in remote areas in developing countries. In some of the countries, there are no toilets or proper toilets in the rural area. Some small privately funded foreign firms also have very poor sanitary facilities for their workers in African countries (e.g., Akorsu & Cooke, 2011). MNEs can therefore contribute hugely to this matter by providing better and clean sanitation in their factories in developing countries and villages nearby. Some of the industries that are big users of water, such as leather and textile producers, beverages producers, and companies involved in some agricultural products, need to find more efficient ways to save water and to replenish the water they use with clean drinkable water. For example, BP is aiming to restock more freshwater than it consumes by 2035 (BP, 2021).

Goal 7: Affordable and clean energy—Ensure access to affordable, reliable, sustainable, and clean energy for all. Affordable and clean energy underpins the success in mitigating the negative effect of climate change (see also Goal 13). However, renewable and green energy, for example, green hydrogen is expensive to produce. One major barrier for poor countries to combat climate change is their lack of affordability to renewable energy or indeed any energy for some. MNEs can play an important role in the transition from fossil fuels to green and sustainable energy sources through developing green energy projects in developing countries, taking advantage of natural resources such as wind and solar availability. Indeed, a small but growing number of multilateral agreements have been signed involving MNEs and governments to develop green hydrogen plants in Africa. For example, a partnership was established between Italian energy company Eni and local companies in Algeria and Egypt to explore the possibility of producing green and blue hydrogen in North African countries (Matalucci, 2021); and a green hydrogen production agreement was signed between Belgian DEME Group and the Egyptian Electricity Holding Company (Egypt Oil & Gas Newspaper, Sunday, 7th March 2021). It remains to be seen how effective these plans can be rolled out.

Goal 8: Decent work and economic growth—Promote sustained, inclusive, and sustainable economic growth, full employment, and decent work for all. Providing resources, opportunities for participation, and empowerment through inclusive business models is essential to achieving this goal, and the SDGs' overall aims of poverty reduction, ecosystem conservation, and improved food security (Vabi-Vamuloh et al., 2019). What are the drivers for Western MNEs to adopt inclusive business models? For example, according to Vabi-Vamuloh et al. (2019), contract farming, a common MNE strategy in the global food sector, can play a significant role in achieving SDGs. However, such a role is contingent upon the ability and willingness of small farmers to participate in the global food chain. MNEs in the global food sector can consider what mechanisms they can adopt to enable gainful participation from small farmers. In particular, MNEs and supermarket giants can consider extending contract farming to small farms in the developing world and poor communities to create decent work and economic growth in these regions.

An important issue to note here is the tendency of MNEs to outsource their production and service provision to low-income countries to exploit the abundance of cheap labor and low labor standards (Garcia-Sanchez et al., 2020). As Nobel Laureate Stiglitz (2002) cogently argued, global capitalism with its associated proliferation and expansion of MNEs in developing countries has so far aggravated income and spatial inequalities and reinforced the dependency of the poor on the rich and of the less developed on the developed countries. In the global value chain, the regulation of employment for decent work has taken place unevenly across different parts of the world, contingent upon the negotiation between the corporation and the state in transnational space, allowing for "commodification and exploitation of international labour" (Morris et al., 2021, p. 3), as evidenced in the 2013 Rana Plaza disaster in Bangladesh (Hoskins, 2015).

Goal 9: Industry, innovation, and infrastructure—Build resilient infrastructure, promote inclusive and sustainable industrialization, and foster innovation. Innovations to develop products and provide services that are accessible and affordable to the mass population especially in the rural areas in developing countries are critical to lifting people out of poverty and improving their quality of life. MNEs can adapt their innovation strategy (e.g., decentralized R&D and scalable design) to foster innovation capacity in developing countries particularly in marginalized communities. Young digital MNEs are well-positioned to play a role in accelerating this goal (Denoncourt, 2020). In addition, MNEs can embrace the three elements essential to achieving this goal more strategically: engaging in innovations to solve problems simply and inexpensively, developing "'business model innovation' to bring the technological solution to market and reach new users," and "creating a new value chain or business system, which draws the innovator together with other participating companies and stakeholders to organize coherent economic models" (Denoncourt, 2020, p. 199).

Goal 10: Reduce inequality—Reduce inequality within and among countries. This goal is closely linked with Goal 8 in terms of what MNEs can do. MNEs can influence global talent mobility (e.g., brain drain) by creating skilled jobs to keep the skilled workers in poor regions to stay where they are to help the local development. This will contribute to reducing inter- and intra-regional inequality. MNEs can play a major role in creating qualified jobs in all the markets they go to. Several MNEs choose only to serve customers in cities and ignore rural markets, that is why they are blamed for serving only the elite populations in developing and emerging markets. It is therefore important that MNEs serve the whole market also people at the base of the pyramid (BOP). For this purpose, they will need to develop products that are suitable/affordable to these customers and use distributors and sales force from these rural areas. This will lead to a more inclusive society.

Goal 11: Sustainable cities and communities—Make cities and human settlements inclusive, safe, resilient, and sustainable. Resilience is an important dimension of SDG 11 (and a few other SDGs too explicitly and implicitly). Acuti et al. (2020, p. 99) explored the gaps "between theoretical considerations about the role of companies in fostering urban resilience and the practices they implement and disclose" by analyzing "138 sustainability reports from organizations operating in Italy and Japan to identify how the SDGs, in particular those targets concerning environmental and social resilience, are implemented in their activities and communicated in their nonfinancial reports." The authors concluded that the resilience components of cities will be given more space and articulation in reports and that highly technical and complex details are unlikely to be included in the reports to maintain their readability for a wide range of stakeholders (Acuti et al., 2020). Acuti et al. (2020, p. 99) went on to suggest that because "greater attention to disclosure on the impacts of companies on resilience is a starting point for action towards achieving the SDGs," future research can adopt new approaches to examining issues related to urban resilience and communicate the findings in a stakeholder-friendly way to improve the efficacy of urban resilience reporting.

Since many MNEs have their regional headquarters and subsidiaries in urban areas, there are many activities that MNEs can engage in to improve the resilience where they operate and communicate them to the stakeholders effectively. As examples, here are a few questions relevant for research and practice: in what ways, and to what extent, are premium cities attractive sites for undocumented labor with exploitative employment terms and conditions, particularly in ethnic and migrant businesses and communities (e.g., Cooke et al., 2021a, 2021b)? What may be the tension among sustainability, affordability, and inclusiveness, and how can MNEs navigate through these competing demands by working with the local governments and contribute to achieving this goal?

Goal 12: Responsible consumption and production—Ensure sustainable consumption and production patterns. MNEs can contribute to developing the circular economy through their R&D capability, enhancing efficiency in the global value chain, packaging, and marketing campaigns. Leading MNEs have introduced recycling practices to reuse materials. For example, Nike is promoting a zero-waste policy by designing waste out of its products from the start, increasing production efficiency, and using alternative packaging (Nike Website, n.d.). Unilever has introduced refillable detergent and other toiletries bottles and reduced the number of brands in this category to almost half (Cavusgil et al., 2021).

Goal 13: Climate action—Take urgent action to combat climate change and its impacts. There has been limited research on the role of MNEs in climate change and energy transition (Kolk et al., 2017) even though the energy transition policy adopted by an increasing number of governments would have strong implications MNEs, for example, in regulating their energy use behavior and in incentivizing them to develop new products and production methods to reduce carbon emission (Ghauri et al., 2021). MNEs can influence the climate policy of nation states and their institutional systems. They can also participate in climate initiatives promoted by international organizations in developing countries. Moreover, MNEs can promote the adoption of renewable energy in their value chain and lead the energy transition and adopt sustainable/green human resource management practices to encourage the workforce to adopt green behavior (Chams & García-Blandón, 2019; Ren et al., 2018). It is important to note that economic and cultural factors in developing countries may affect the level of acceptance of climate initiatives promoted by international organizations and MNEs.

Goal 14: Life below water—Conserve and sustainably use the oceans, seas, and marine resources for sustainable development. MNEs can play a role through their R&D, innovation technology, and packaging to achieve pollution and protection of marine ecosystem throughout the globe. In the past few years, several scientists and television documentaries have consistently pointed out that our oceans are polluted with plastic. All the plastic packaging materials that are thrown in the seas and are not degradable are being swollen by fish and other marine lives. This has led to the fact that most fish we eat contain tiny plastic particles and doctors are recommending not to east fish too often. Packaging material is the biggest culprit in polluting our rivers and oceans. The second biggest are chemicals that are thrown directly into the seas from manufacturing. There are now stringent regulations about this in the developed world but MNEs and/or their suppliers are not always following these rules. This can be easily avoided if MNEs follow the same rules and principles all over the world.

Goal 15: Life on land—Protect, restore, and promote sustainable use of terrestrial ecosystems. MNEs can influence farming and agriculture both in developed and developing countries by deploying digital technology to improve terrestrial ecosystems on a global scale. This must be done by protecting animals, especially endangered species, birds, and agriculture. MNEs that are using wood in their products must look at sustainable forestry and check their suppliers, for example, through responsible sourcing. Destroying forest without a sustainable plan not only destroys the forest but also the life, animals, and birds, that live in the forest and destroys the ecosystem. It influences the weather systems and leads to more cyclones and floods.

Goal 16: Peace and justice strong institutions—Promote peaceful and inclusive societies for sustainable development. MNEs can contribute to this goal by facilitating institutional development and promoting equality and justice through their diversity and inclusion policy and practice in their host countries. For instance, the SDGs aim to alleviate poverty (SDG Goal 1), enhance health and well-being (SDG Goal 3), improve education (SDG Goal 4), and ensure access to clean water and sanitation (SDG Goal 6) (Sartor & Beamish, 2020, p. 725). However, extant research evidence indicates that corruption, which SDG Goal 16 targets, adversely impacts the achievement of these goals due to the uneven distributions of opportunities between those who hold power and those marginalized who are particularly in need of education and healthcare that has not been accessible to them, for example (Sartor & Beamish, 2020). Corruption is interpreted differently across cultural/societal settings, takes different forms, and involves both public and private institutions/organizations (Sartor & Beamish, 2020). We cannot presume that Western MNEs are the victims of corruption in host countries in the developing world; rather, they might be tempted to engage with the corrupt behavior when disincentives to do so are perceived not to be strong (Cooke et al., 2021a, 2021b). MNEs may consider the structure of their subsidiaries (e.g., joint ventures or wholly owned) to mitigate the investment environment (Luo, 2006; Sartor & Beamish, 2020) on the one hand and work proactively and positively with host country institutions to combat corruption and improve the institutional environment as part of their CSR (Rodriguez et al., 2006) on the other.

Goal 17: Partnerships for these Goals—Strengthen the means of implementation and revitalize the Global Partnership for Sustainable Development. It is unrealistic, as policy makers have recognized, to leave the task of achieving SDGs to private hands and MNEs, who have different goals than the well-being of the society and face institutional constraints. Several governments and supranational organizations have thus taken some actions. For example, the European Union (EU), where policy makers have been more proactive, has pressured MNEs to address their climate change, value chain, and sustainable packaging including recycling mechanisms responsibilities (Ghauri et al., 2018). As a result, positive outcomes have emerged. Due to all these initiatives, the overall impact on society has been quite positive. Moreover, companies have realized that the competitiveness of the MNEs involved had improved (Ghauri et al., 2014; Patnaik, 2020). A combination of regulatory pressures and MNE actions has brought positive results (Hsueh, 2019). Other policy initiatives, such as Net Zero 2030, are having a significant impact in certain industry sectors. For instance, in the automotive industry, all major car manufacturers are now switching their production to electric vehicles almost over-night (Yeganeh, 2019). In fact, some scholars and industry experts are raising alarms that when more than 80% of the energy generation is dependent on fossil fuels, transitioning to electric vehicles, with zero emissions, would have any positive impact or not, as most of the electricity that is needed to charge these vehicles is still produced from fossil fuels (BP, 2021; Ghauri et al., 2021).

Clearly, to achieve SDGs, collaborations between the state, society, and MNEs and involvement of local actors and grassroots are essential (Arnold, 2018). Through the example of three case study MNEs, Forcadell and Aracil (2019, p. 101) illustrate, from a CSR aimed at institutional necessities (CSRIN) perspective, how MNEs "can co-evolve their CSR strategies" with the host country institutional system more proactively than responding to external pressure passively through adaptation and accommodation. Forcadell and Aracil (2019, p. 100) observed that MNEs "tend to join efforts with local governments or other firms and small entrepreneurs" in their CSRIN actions. These included, for example, bank funding MNEs' clean investment and telecom infrastructure building through the public-private partnership program. Stakeholder alliances like these promote institutional changes by meeting different institutional necessities and contribute to SDGs (Forcadell & Aracil, 2019).

2.2   Bigger than the Sum: Interconnections and Mutually Reinforcing Effects of SDGs

So far, we have exemplified how MNEs can play a role in achieving each of the 17 SDGs. However, as we alluded to, achieving one SDG depends on that of the others, and the impact of achieving each one of them is larger than the sum because SDGs are interconnected and efforts in achieving one SDG will contribute to the achievement of the others directly and indirectly. For example, innovation (see also SDG Goal 9), in particular, frugal innovation, can help provide solutions to problems confronting the lives of those in poor communities by using limited resources (e.g., Brem & Wolfram, 2014; Rosca et al., 2016). In a review of 50 frugal innovation cases targeting low incomes or Bottom of Pyramid (BOP) markets, Arnold (2018) found that inclusive approaches are key to frugal innovations, which have been mainly provided by the private sector, particularly by small- and medium-sized enterprises and nongovernmental organizations. Arnold (2018, p. 265) went on to argue that inefficient institutions in BOP markets can serve as drivers for MNEs "to develop new and inclusive businesses to create values and to enforce the SDGs more directly and at a higher level than have been found the case. Similarly, SDGs 6, 7, 13, and 15 are interconnected and MNEs can contribute to achieving these goals by 'reducing the overuse of natural resources" and fostering positive change (Montiel et al., 2021).

3   Looking to the Future in a Realistic Way

The COVID-19 Pandemic has exposed our weaknesses in many dimensions, including the unpreparedness for governments to combat the global crisis, policy (mis-) orientation, and poor implementation of policies. The inequalities in the world are in

Table 1 Value of investment projects in SDG sectors (a), by region (Millions of US dollars)

Region	2010–2014 average	2015–2019 average	Pre-COVID-19 trend (b) (%)	COVID-19 impact (c) (%)
Developed economies	79,036	86,739	10	21
Developing and emerging economies	124,571	151,779	22	−33
Africa	21,099	32,943	56	−39
Developing Asia	59,873	75,452	26	−23
Latin America and the Caribbean	34,395	31,967	−7	−40
Transition economies	8344	11,226	35	−28

Source: Based on UNCTAD, 2021a and on Financial Times, FDI Markets (www.fdimarkets.com).
(a) Which are partially or fully owned by foreign public or private entities. (b) Changes in the five +year averages from the period of 2010–2014 to the period of 2015–2019. (c) Changes from 2019 to 2020

fact increasing and not decreasing. The optimism of the last two decades where emerging economies were considered the focal points for sources of growth for the world (Cavusgil et al., 2021) has now vanished. The share of developing and emerging economies toward global growth has fallen by 60% (UNCTAD, 2021b).

In 2019, achieving SDGs by 2030 was considered to be on track, as there were plenty of new investments coming from international organizations and public and private sectors into the SDG-related sectors. This has been disrupted due to the pandemic; the SDG-related new investments have fallen, particularly investments in infrastructure and climate change-related projects (UNCTAD, 2021a). Infrastructure projects financed by the private sector and international organizations have fallen by 60%, and food and agricultural projects are down by around 50% (UNCTAD, 2021a).

The investment level in the developed world relevant for SDGs has, however, not been influenced to that extent. Table 1 shows the decline in investment in sectors that are directly relevant to SDGs in developed versus developing countries and different regions of the world. Table 1 is quite revealing as it shows the investments prior to SDGs, the progress immediately after its announcement (2015–2019), and the impact of COVID-19.

The decline is more pronounced in the developing and emerging economies and even more so for least developed countries in Africa and Latin America. The situation is opposite to the developed world, where many large infrastructure projects have been announced by governments to stimulate the recovery after the pandemic. Most of these projects are in sectors that are directly related to the SDGs. This means that developing economies are more exposed to post-pandemic depressions as these countries are not able to finance large publicly financed projects and remedies. These countries were already struggling with foreign debts and have drowned further in debts due to COVID-related lockdowns and their impact on economies. There is an increase in poverty and inequalities in most of these countries due to job losses, illness in families, and depressing prospects in most sectors (UN-DESA, 2020).

MNEs are thus in an unprecedented position to play a role in developing countries and to finance SDG-related projects that will in the long run help them improve their competitive advantage as well as their "do good" image in international markets. Several MNEs are thus financing infrastructure projects in emerging economies. Some examples are Enel (Italy), Engie and EDF (France), KEPCO (South Korea), and Iberdrola (Spain); all these companies are investing in sustainable alternative energy sources. Unilever has been one of the first companies that have taken several actions toward the achievement of SDGs. It was the first company to introduce paper-based laundry detergent bottles and created refillable bottles for several other products, recyclable toothpaste tubes, and eco-friendly toothbrushes to contribute positively against climate change and environmental protection. Unilever has declared that it will achieve zero emission from its operations by 2030 (Cavusgil et al., 2021; Unilever, 2021).

BP has integrated the achievement of SDGs in its mission for each of its focal areas, people, and the planet. It is aiming to reduce emissions to achieve net zero by 2050. It has committed to creating a safe and secure workplace for workers all over the world. It is working with other MNEs such as Microsoft to create efficient energy systems to reduce pollution (BP, 2021). MNEs can play a significant role not only by collaborating with governments and international organizations but also by working with other companies to create synergetic impacts.

It is, however, important to point out that policy makers and managers from MNEs are often creating new discourses to hide their inefficiencies and to show that they are taking actions on important matters for people and society. When transplanting to the business, the rhetoric may or may not have any meaning or different managers might give different meanings to these terms for cognitive or performative reasons. Fancy terms are often used in corporate communications to fill a vacuum or to impress their stakeholders that they are doing something good to establish their credibility that they are keeping up with the new realities. IB research therefore needs to look deeper into these issues to separate rhetoric from reality and the impacts of corporate actions on various stakeholders, particularly in developing countries. For instance, van den Broek (2020, p. 1) analyzed available online SDG-related communications, including financial and nonfinancial reports, of 29 large French MNEs for 2016–2017 and found that these firms were able to develop a variety of narratives to interpret their past actions, project their images, articulate corporate aspirations, and outline strategies related to CSR and SDGs. Van den Broek's (2020) study shows how MNEs use narratives in sequential steps (e.g., past, present, and future) to "build a new corporate identity." It will be fruitful to research further the extent to which these firms have been able to use these narratives to help them distill clearer visions, strategies, and implementation plans regarding their CSR and SDGs. Such research endeavor requires an interdisciplinary lens based on sociology, political science, economic geography, and so on. This will enable us to discover new realities, identify problems to be addressed, and explore how they can be tackled and lessons to be learned, with implications for policy makers and MNEs so that they can create positive externalities for society in general.

Equally, we should not assume that MNEs are superheroes. Instead, they are learning by doing and learning by failing as they embrace CSR and the SDG agenda. For example, Kumi et al. (2020, p. 1) examined CSR initiatives undertaken "in the mining and telecommunications sectors in Ghana in their bid to operationalize the SDGs" and found that, while there is potential for the private sector to contribute to the achievement of several SDGs, "the short-term nature of interventions, the lack of coordination between private sector actors and meaningful community participation, stand to limit this potential." Nevertheless, progress has been made in different parts of the world. Derqui's (2020, p. 1) longitudinal study (2013–2019) of the evolution of MNEs' CSR strategy in Spain suggests that "a paradigm shift is taking hold"; in other words, "sustainability is not an altruistic option for managers anymore, it is now considered a source of revenue." MNEs may also pick and choose those SDGs that are less costly and yield more results quickly. For example, van Zanten and van Tulder's (2018, p. 208) study of 81 European and North American Financial Times Global 500 companies indicates that "MNEs engage more with SDG targets that are actionable within their (value chain) operations than those outside of it, and more with SDG targets that 'avoid harm' than those that 'do good'". More research can be conducted in the future to capture how MNEs' SDG attitudes, strategy, and practice are evolving and maturing and what may be the key driving forces for the transformation in this area.

4   Conclusion

SDGs are essentially a global vision for a better world developed by the UN to eradicate poverty and inequality. Encouraged by the achievements of millennium goals of poverty reduction in 2015, these SDGs were put forward with a hope to achieve most of these goals by 2030. However, social and economic problems that SDGs seek to address are often historically and politically entrenched. Achieving SDGs, therefore, requires stakeholders' joint efforts to think of ways to mitigate political, economic, and social exclusion by creating and providing resources, participation opportunities, and venues of income generation to improve the quality of life of millions of those trapped in poverty and are facing inequality. MNEs can play an important role to mitigate harm and create value for society and communities where they operate directly and indirectly through inclusive financing and subcontracting, capital investment, technology transfer, frugal innovation, employment creation, education promotion, skill training, health and safety intervention, and more. As we have discussed above, many of these goals can be tackled by MNEs directly, while for others they can play an indirect role and/or work with other stakeholders to play a positive role. We have also provided several examples of companies such as Unilever and BP, showing that many of these goals can be achieved. Building on the emerging body of publications in this field, the research community can also engage in research in this area more deeply to identify challenges, opportunities, constraints, and good practices. That would provide us with useful lessons that can be learned and can provide recommendations for policy decisions and management practices. However, as with CSR, many companies have realized that they need to show that they are actively working to reduce inequalities and injustice in society and are using the "right" slogans in their marketing material, the so-called green washing. It is, therefore, our responsibility as researchers to investigate how much of this is really happening and how much of this is green-washing, to separate the rhetoric from the reality. As for achieving the SDGs, we believe that the COVID-19 pandemic has left a deep scar and it is improbable that all these goals can be achieved by 2030. As soon as we are back to normality, these SDGs need to be revisited, and the UN and other international organizations need to rethink how the world can get back on track to reduce inequality and injustice, particularly in developing and emerging markets.

References

Acuti, D., Bellucci, M., & Manetti, G. (2020). Company disclosures concerning the resilience of cities from the sustainable development goals (SDGs) perspective. *Cities, 99*, 102608.

Akorsu, A., & Cooke, F. L. (2011). Labour standard application among Chinese and Indian firms in Ghana: Typical or atypical? *The International Journal of Human Resource Management, 22*(13), 2730–2748.

Arnold, M. G. (2018). Sustainability value creation in frugal contexts to foster sustainable development goals. *Business Strategy & Development, 1*(4), 265–275.

Bello, I., & Othman, M. F. (2020). Multinational corporations and sustainable development goals: Examining Etisalat telecommunication intervention in Nigeria's basic education. *International Journal of Educational Management, 34*(1), 96–110.

Beran, D., Mirza, Z., & Dong, J. (2019). Access to insulin: Applying the concept of security of supply to medicines. *Bulletin of the World Health Organization, 97*(5), 358–364.

Boddewyn, J., & Doh, J. (2011). Global strategy and the collaboration of MNEs, NGOs and governments for the provisioning of collective goods in emerging markets. *Global Strategy Journal, 1*(3–4), 345–361.

BP Sustainability Report. (2021). http://bp.com/en/global/corporate/sustainability.html. visited on 26/07/2021.

Brem, A., & Wolfram, P. (2014). Research and development from the bottom up-introduction of terminologies for new product development in emerging markets. *Journal of Technology Management for Growing Economies, 3*(1), 1–22.

Buckley, P., & Ghauri, P. (2004). Globalization, economic geography and the strategy of multinational enterprise. *Journal of International Business Studies, 35*(2), 81–98.

Buckley, P., & Ghauri, P. (Eds.). (2015). *International business strategy: Theory and practice.* Routledge.

Cavusgil, S. T., Ghauri, P., & Liu, L.-A. (2021). *Doing Business in Emerging Markets* (3rd ed.). Sage.

Chams, N., & García-Blandón, J. (2019). On the importance of sustainable human resource management for the adoption of sustainable development goals. *Resources, Conservation and Recycling, 141*, 109–122.

Comyns, B. (2019). Climate change reporting and multinational companies: Insights from institutional theory and international business. *Accounting Forum, 42*, 65–77.

Cooke, F. L. (2018). Concepts, contexts and mindsets: Putting human resource management research in perspectives. *Human Resource Management Journal, 28*(1), 1–13.

Cooke, F. L., Wang, J. T., & Wood, G. (2021a). A vulnerable victim or a tacit participant? Extending the field of multinationals and corruption research. *International Business Review*, 101890. https://doi.org/10.1016/j.ibusrev.2021.101890

Cooke, F. L., Wood, G., & Saunders, S. (2021b). Migrants working for migrants: Dependence and discourse in Chinese-owned small commercial businesses in South Africa. *The International Journal of Human Resource Management*. https://doi.org/10.1080/09585192.2021.1949625

Debaere, P. M. (2018). *The profit-maximizing firm as multinational corporation*. Darden Case No. UVA-G-0623, Available at SSRN: https://ssrn.com/abstract=1583773.

Denoncourt, J. (2020). Companies and UN 2030 sustainable development goal 9 industry, innovation and infrastructure. *Journal of Corporate Law Studies, 20*(1), 199–235.

Derqui, B. (2020). Towards sustainable development: Evolution of corporate sustainability in multinational firms. *Corporate Social Responsibility and Environmental Management*, 1–12. https://doi.org/10.1002/csr.1995

Egypt Oil & Gas Newspaper (Sunday, 7th March 2021). *Agreement with Belgian DEME for studies of green hydrogen production*. Accessed 9 September, 2021, from https://egyptoil-gas.com/news/agreement-with-belgian-deme-for-studies-of-green-hydrogen-production/

Firth, R., & Ghauri, P. (2010). Multinational enterprise acquisitions in emerging markets: Linkage effects on local firms. *European Journal of International Management, 4*, 135–162.

Forcadell, F. J., & Aracil, E. (2019). Can multinational companies foster institutional change and sustainable development in emerging countries? A case study. *Business Strategy & Development, 2*(2), 91–105.

Friedman, M. (1962). *Capitalism and freedom*. The University of Chicago Press.

Garcia-Sanchez, I. M., Rodriguez-Ariza, L., Aibar-Guzman, B., & Aibar-Guzman, C. (2020). Do institutional investors drive corporate transparency regarding business contribution to the sustainable development goals? *Business Strategy and the Environment, 29*(5), 2019–2036.

Ghauri, P., Fu, X., & Vaatanen, J. (Eds.). (2018). *Multinational enterprises and sustainable development*. Bingley.

Ghauri, P., Strange, R., & Cooke, F. L. (2021). Research in international business: The new realities. *International Business Review, 30*(2), 101794.

Ghauri, P., Tasavori, M., & Zaefarian, R. (2014). Internationalization of service firms through corporate social entrepreneurship and networking. *International Marketing Review, 31*(6), 576–600.

Ghauri, P., & Wang, F. (2018). The impact of multinational enterprises on sustainable development and poverty reduction. In P. Ghauri, X. Fu, & J. Vaatanen (Eds.), *Multinational enterprises and sustainable development*. Bingley.

Giroud, A., & Scott-Kennel, J. (2009). MNE linkages in international business: A framework for analysis. *International Business Review, 18*, 555–566.

Hadjikhani, A., Elg, U., & Ghauri, P. (Eds.). (2012). *Business, society and politics (international business and management)* (Vol. 28). Emerald Group Publishing Limited.

Hoskins, T. (2015, April, 10). Rana Plaza: Are fashion brands responsible for those they don't directly employ?. *The Guardian*. Available at www.theguardian.com/sustainable-business/sustainablefashion-blog/2015/apr/10/rana-plaza-are-fashion-brands-responsible-for-those-they-dontdirectly-employ.

Hsueh, I. (2019). Opening up the firm: What explains participation and effort in voluntary carbon disclosure by global businesses? An analysis of internal firm factors and dynamics. *Business Strategy and the Environment, 28*, 1302–1322.

Kano, L., & Verbeke, A. (2019). Theories of the multinational firm: A microfoundation perspective. *Global Strategy Journal, 9*(1), 117–147.

Kolk, A. (2016). The social responsibility of international business: From ethics and the environment to CSR and sustainable development. *Journal of World Business, 51*(1), 23–34.

Kolk, A., Kourula, A., & Pisani, N. (2017). Multinational enterprises and the sustainable development goals: What do we know and how to proceed? *Transnational Corporations, 24*(3), 9–32.

Kumi, E., Yeboah, T., & Kumi, Y. A. (2020). Private sector participation in advancing the Sustainable Development Goals (SDGs) in Ghana: Experiences from the mining and telecommunications sectors. *Extractive Industries and Society, 7*, 181–190. https://doi.org/10.1016/j.exis.2019.12.008

Luo, Y. (2006). Political behavior, social responsibility, and perceived corruption: A structuration perspective. *Journal of International Business Studies, 37*(6), 747–766.

Matalucci, S. (2021). *The Hydrogen Stream: Italy's Eni lays out plans in Algeria and Egypt, UAE joins race with help from Japan.* Accessed September 9, 2021, from https://www.pv-magazine.com/2021/07/09/the-hydrogen-stream-hydrogen-arrives-in-long-island-eni-lays-out-plans-in-algeria-and-egypt-uae-joins-race/

Michailova, S., Stringer, C., & Mezias, J. (2020). Letter from the editors: Special issue in investigating modern slavery: How IB scholarship can contribute. *AIB Insights*, 1–2.

Millennium Project. (2006). *Millennium development goals.* Online: http://www.unmillenniumproject.or/goals/.

Millennium Project. (2021). http://www.millennium-project.org/challenges-history/

Montiel, I., Cuervo-Cazurra, A., Park, J., Antolin-Lopez, R., & Husted, B. (2021). Implementing the United Nations' sustainable development goals in international business. *Journal of International Business Studies, 52*(5), 999–1030.

Morris, J., Jenkins, J., & Donaghey, J. (2021). Uneven development, uneven response: The relentless search for meaningful regulation of GVCs. *British Journal of Industrial Relations, 59*(1), 3–34.

Newburry, W., Gardberg, N., & Sanchez, J. (2014). Employer attractiveness in Latin America: The association among foreignness, internationalization and talent recruitment. *Journal of International Management, 20*(3), 327–344.

Nike. (n.d.) *Waste*, Accessed September 9, 2021, from https://purpose.nike.com/waste

Patnaik, S. (2020). Emissions permit allocation and strategic firm behaviour: Evidence from the oil sector in the European Union emissions trading scheme. *Business Strategy and Environment, 29*, 976–995.

Ren, S., Tang, G., & Jackson, S. E. (2018). Green human resource management research in emergence: A review and future directions. *Asia Pacific Journal of Management, 35*(3), 769–803.

Ritvala, T., Salmi, A., & Andersson, P. (2014). MNCs and local cross-sector partnerships: The case of a smarter Baltic Sea. *International Business Review, 23*(5), 942–951.

Rodriguez, P., Siegel, D. S., Hillman, A., & Eden, L. (2006). Three lenses on the multinational enterprise: Politics, corruption, and corporate social responsibility. *Journal of International Business Studies, 37*(6), 733–746.

Rosca, E., Arnold, M., & Bendul, J. (2016). Business models for sustainable innovation—An empirical analysis of frugal products and services. *Journal of Cleaner Production, 126*, 133–145.

Sartor, M. A., & Beamish, P. W. (2020). Private sector corruption, public sector corruption and the organizational structure of foreign subsidiaries. *Journal of Business Ethics, 167*(4), 725–744.

Stiglitz, J. (2002). *Globalization and its discontent.* Penguin Books.

Terpstra-Tong, J. L. Y. (2017). MNE subsidiaries' adoption of gender equality and women empowerment goal: A conceptual framework. *Transnational Corporations, 24*(3), 89–102.

UNCTAD. (2021a). *UNCTAD's SDG investments: Trend monitor, April 2020.* UNCTAD.

UNCTAD. (2021b). *World investment report 2021, June 2020.* UNCTAD.

UN-DESA. (2020). *Impact of Covid 19 on SDG Progress: A statistical perspective.* United Nations.

Unilever. (2021). http://unilever.com/new/new-and-features.html. visited on 26/07/2021.

United Nations. (2015). *Transforming our world: The 2030 agenda for sustainable development.* https://sustainabledevelopment.un.org/post2015/transformingourworld/publication.

Vabi-Vamuloh, V., Panwar, R., Hagerman, S. M., Gaston, C., & Kozak, R. A. (2019). Achieving sustainable development goals in the global food sector: A systematic literature review to examine small farmers engagement in contract farming. *Business Strategy & Development, 2*(4), 276–289.

van den Broek, O. (2020). Narrative fidelity: Making the UN sustainable development goals fit. *Corporate Communications*, 1–20. https://doi.org/10.1108/CCIJ-01-2020-0032

van Zanten, J. A., & van Tulder, R. (2018). Multinational enterprises and the sustainable development goals: An institutional approach to corporate engagement. *Journal of International Business Policy, 1*(3–4), 208–233.

World Bank. (2013). *Poverty overview*. Washington DC. http://www.worldbank.org/en/topic/poverty/overview/

Yeganeh, H. (2019). A critical examination of the social impacts of large multinational corporations in the age of globalization. *Critical Perspective on International Business, 16*(1), 193–208.

Pervez N. Ghauri completed his PhD at Uppsala University. Currently, Pervez is Professor of International Business at the University of Birmingham (UK). Pervez was the founding Editor of International Business Review (IBR) and is Consulting Editor for the Journal of International Business Studies (JIBS). Pervez is a Fellow of the European International Business Academy (EIBA) and the Academy of International Business (AIB), where he was also Vice President between 2008 and 2010. Pervez has published more than 30 books and more than 100 academic journal articles. Pervez has been consulting with several companies such as BP, Ericsson, and Airbus Industries.

Fang Lee Cooke is Distinguished Professor at Monash Business School, Monash University, Australia. Her research interests are in the area of strategic HRM, knowledge management and innovation, international HRM, diversity and inclusion management, migrant studies, digitalization and implications for employment and HRM; climate change, energy transition, and the future of work; Sustainable Development Goals; and the role of multinational firms. Fang Lee Cooke's recent research projects examine some of the tensions, challenges, and implications associated with these topics for various key stakeholders such as the state, employers' associations, trade unions, workers, and labor NGOs.

The Cultural Mosaic of Corporate Social Responsibility: MNEs' Role in Attaining Sustainable Development Goals

Rekha Rao-Nicholson and Ru-Shiun Liou

1 Introduction

The extant literature has explored in detail the drivers, motivations, and processes of multinational enterprises' (MNEs) Corporate Social Responsibility (CSR) activities (van Tulder & Kolk, 2001). "Simply meeting government CSR regulations is no longer viewed as a differentiating factor; MNEs must exceed mandated levels of social and environmental activities to build a reputation and positively affect their financial performance (Miller et al., 2020)" (Eden & Wagstaff, 2021). The CSR activities adopted by the MNEs range from community relations (Attig & Brockman, 2017; Park et al., 2015), environmental issues (Ambec & Lanoie, 2008), and employee and workplace management (Bolton et al., 2011; van Tulder & Kolk, 2001). Furthermore, these CSR activities that are directed to address multiple stakeholders' concerns help MNEs reduce uncertainty in the host country context as well as strengthen their host country legitimacy (Amos, 2008; Eweje, 2006; Reimann et al., 2012). Nevertheless, there have been some questions on whom these CSR really benefit, whether it is the MNEs or the host countries that they invest in. This is especially pertinent since MNEs have been noted to be doing CSR activities in one area while engaging in practices damaging to the local communities (Hennchen, 2015).

At the level of the supranational institutions, United Nations 70th General Assembly ratified Sustainable Development Goals (SDGs) in 2015 which was supported by 193 member nations (Griggs et al., 2013; Waage et al., 2015). These SDGs aim to *eliminate* rather than *reduce* poverty and set a more ambitious agenda

R. Rao-Nicholson (✉)
Essex Business School, University of Essex, Colchester, UK
e-mail: rekha.raonicholson@essex.ac.uk

R.-S. Liou
Sykes College of Business, The University of Tampa, Tampa, FL, USA
e-mail: rliou@ut.edu

© Springer Nature Switzerland AG 2022
H. Merchant (ed.), *The New Frontiers of International Business*, Contributions to Management Science, https://doi.org/10.1007/978-3-031-06003-8_17

for health, education, and gender equality in all countries regardless of the country's economic status or its development (UN General Assembly, 2015). Some of the recent studies have explored how MNEs can contribute to SDGs (Liou & Rao-Nicholson, 2021; Montiel et al., 2021). Montiel et al. (2021) propose that MNEs can engage effectively with SDGs in their value chain activities while improving returns to their investment. Liou and Rao-Nicholson (2021) present a conceptual model taking into consideration the economic differences between the home and host countries. Although there is some notional engagement with country-level differences between the home and host nations, their work does not explicitly consider the culture within the country and its influence on MNEs' SDG-related CSR activities. Similarly, Montiel et al. (2021) do not consider the local cultural context. Thus, in order to link their CSR activities to SDGs, MNEs might have to engage in what Maon et al. (2017:418) call "Discretionary, community-oriented, non-embedded approach to CSR."

In this study, we will explore theoretically the MNEs' cross-border CSR activities, how these contribute to SDGs, especially in the cultural context of the host country. Following the literature review, we present a conceptual framework that first highlights the industry effect on selecting relevant SDGs; second, draws on the work of Albareda et al. (2007), which can help ascertain the societal expectations of CSR in the host country; and, third, suggests how cultural dimensions in the host country influence MNEs' global CSR strategy. We conclude by summarizing our research contribution and identifying future avenues for research.

2 Literature Review

2.1 MNEs' Corporate Social Responsibility Strategies

The one stream of CSR literature focuses primarily on the firm perspective and has detailed how, in most cases, CSR activities are motivated by economic gains and are performance-driven (Burke & Logsdon, 1996; Husted & Allen, 2009; Maignan & Ralston, 2002; Swanson, 1995). On the one hand, Campbell (2007) notes the close association between the businesses' social responsibility and the presence of rules, regulations, the level of enforcement, and pressures from civil society. When a firm feels the pressures to comply with societal expectations, the firm adopts a reactive approach to CSR. On the other hand, authors have noted the closer embedding of CSR within the firm in terms of the development of corporate policies and processes which are focused on communities' interests and are value-driven (Maon et al., 2017). In the context of cross-border investments and trade, MNEs might be motivated to engage in CSR to build a good reputation in the host country (Chapple & Moon, 2005).

In fact, some MNEs might adopt a standardized approach to CSR in their international operations and deploy a global CSR strategy (Eden & Wagstaff, 2021), while others might attempt to be more responsive and adopt a localized approach (Muller, 2006). In the case of countries with lower CSR standards, there is a danger that a responsive approach might lead to fewer CSR activities by the MNEs. Yet, studies have noted that despite this challenge, MNEs have consistently strived to achieve higher CSR standards in countries with lower CSR levels (Muller, 2006; Muller & Kolk, 2010). On the other hand, studies have noted that CSR activities might be "diluted" due to host market characteristics (Jamali, 2010). In this context, the culture of the host country might emerge as one of the key factors influencing the CSR activities of the MNEs. Polonsky and Jevons (2009) identify local social issues as one of the indicators impacting the MNEs' CSR strategies.

2.2   Societal Expectations of Corporate Social Responsibility in Different Cultures

Given the wide variance of MNEs' strategies in leading CSR activities, the national differences are pertinent to CSR activities conducted by the MNEs. For example, Maon et al. (2017) argue the same in the context of Europe and note that even within European Union, countries continue to display different cultural identities, economic and political beliefs, and labor market approaches. These contextual differences will have implications for the degree to which an MNE pursues specific CSR activities in the host countries. Albareda et al. (2007) discuss the four typologies of governmental CSR action in the former EU-15, namely, a partnership-oriented model in Nordic countries (i.e., Denmark, Finland, Sweden) and the Netherlands; a sustainability and citizenship model in Austria, Belgium, France, Germany, and Luxembourg; an Agora model in Mediterranean countries, including Greece, Italy, Portugal, and Spain; and a business in the community, an explicit model of CSR in the United Kingdom and Ireland.

While the typology highlights the different levels of government involvement in the CSR strategies, these four typologies are greatly influenced by the contextual differences, including cultural norms and values, in these countries. For example, the good neighbor philosophy and cultural values drive the "sustainability and citizenship model" in Austria, Belgium, France, Germany, and Luxembourg (Albareda et al., 2007). In this case, the cultural values of these countries support the idea that companies can work for the benefit of society and can act as agents of social change. In these countries, the welfare state, as well as values of personal freedom and social justice, drives the CSR activities observed in the companies. On the other hand, countries like Greece, Italy, Portugal, and Spain have a limited tradition of corporate CSR activities, and much of the business landscape is dominated by small and medium firms. At the same time, these countries have been traditionally used to collective decision-making and consensus to drive action. Thus, these countries will have a different perception of CSR activities and how they can bring about social change in their context.

Ioannou and Serafeim (2012) study the impact of national business systems, including (1) the political systems, (2) the financial system, (3) the education and labor system, and (4) the cultural system (Whitley, 1999) on corporations' performance in CSR activities. Among others, the cultural system was shown to be even more crucial than the influence of the financial systems. Also, they find that firms in countries with leftist political ideology score lower on corporate social performance. Local culture, measured by cultural dimensions of power distance and individualism, also has an influence on the firm's corporate social performance. Further, Maon et al. (2017) observe that Nordic companies build their business activities around societal issues. These firms encourage the wider participation of their various stakeholders and actively involve stakeholders in their CSR activities. On the other hand, they observe the firms in Eastern Europe which do not actively engage with their stakeholders or show only limited interest in the CSR activities (Csafor, 2008; Koleva et al., 2010) and deploy CSR activities in a rather less integrated CSR model. These firms achieve their CSR objectives via philanthropic initiatives (Maon et al., 2017).

Similarly, studies have shown that firms in countries like China have actively engaged with some aspect of CSR, especially those pertaining to the environment (Huang et al., 2017) and employment (Chan, 2009), but these firms are still reluctant to engage with CSR activities related to democracy (Zhao, 1998). By contrasting European and the US firms, Aaronson and Reeves (2002) suggested that US-based firms generally have a less accepting attitude of CSR practices due to a lack of emphasis of public policies in the United States. Ringov and Zollo (2007) adopt Hofstede's definition of national culture and observe that power distance and masculinity have a negative effect on the CSR, whereas there is an impact of individualism and uncertainty avoidance on CSR activities.

The majority of the aforementioned studies did not consider the cross-border nature of the investment, rather focused on only the domicile of the firms. Although CSR activities might engage with SDGs in the host country context, there is no requirement that all firms will adapt their CSR activities to the local SDGs. Montiel et al. (2021) attempt to link MNEs' cross-border activities and investments with SDGs. They note that MNEs' activities can increase positive externalities with regard to wealth, knowledge, and health, and it can reduce negative externalities in terms of the overuse of nature-related resources, harm to social cohesion, and overconsumption. Furthermore, they suggest that these CSR activities need to be embedded in the MNEs' extended supply chain. Overall, they propose that these activities will effectively target the SDGs while generating positive externalities for the MNEs' subsidiaries. Despite some resounding suggestions for MNEs' cross-border investment, Montiel et al. (2021) do not consider the host country's culture. Thus, there is limited understanding of how and if MNEs effectively engage with the SDGs in the varying host country cultural contexts. In the next section, we will explore the links between SDGs, national culture, and MNEs' socially responsible activities.

2.3   Sustainable Development Goals and National Cultures

Some of the earliest discussions on SDGs included the notion of cultural differences and their salience for outcomes (Vlassis, 2015; Wiktor-Mach, 2020; Zheng et al.,

2021). Nevertheless, the final version of SDGs failed to consider the impact of national culture on SDG implementation and success (Adger et al., 2013; Zheng et al., 2021). On the other hand, organizations like United Nations Educational, Scientific, and Cultural Organization (UNESCO) have noted the importance of culture to SDGs (Zheng et al., 2021). These studies have suggested that a lack of understanding of the local cultural context is not only detrimental to the success of these SDG-related actions but can also undermine the gains made via other mechanisms. For example, though typically, developmental activities by MNEs might involve building schools without considering the cultural barriers for local children from attending these schools. Barsoum and Refaat (2015) examine CSR activities in Egypt and identify three themes in the CSR discourse in the local context. The primary theme is related to the difference in the perception of CSR between the West and Egypt, and in the local cultural context, CSR is discredited as something vulgar and where the underlying idea is to take more than what is given. Another key theme relates to the idea that, culturally, CSR is seen as "bad" development. The lack of understanding of the local cultural values can, thus, understate challenges to achieving the SDG targets in these contexts.

Some of the studies have strongly recommended that certain aspects of culture can profoundly limit the impact of SDG-related targets like corruption and subjective well-being (Davis & Ruhe, 2003; Zheng et al., 2021). For example, cultures that have higher power distance can limit the effectiveness of certain SDGs that encourage gender parity and social inclusion (SDG 10) or corruption (SDG 16). Davis and Ruhe (2003) observe that power distance and uncertainty avoidance are closely linked to perceived corruption in the country. Similarly, Boateng et al. (2021) find that national culture, measured by the cultural dimensions of power distance, uncertainty avoidance, has a much higher impact on levels of corruption within a country than even the corporate governance adopted by the firms.

Zheng et al. (2021) observe that the cultural perspective of SDG implementation is crucial to achieving success in SDG targets. Their study used a panel data analysis and correlated the well-known cultural indices with country-level scores of SDGs and notes that the national culture is linked to the achievement of all 17 SDGs and explains 26% of the variations in the achievement of the SDGs. They further highlight the fact that these links are divergent across cultures. For instance, a country with a more individualistic culture tends to have better performance in subjective well-being, gender equality, high-tech development, income equality, etc. but worse performance in electricity accessibility.

Further, Adger et al. (2013) examine the response of societies to the climate change challenge and observe the striking role of culture in the societies' responses to the climate change risks and social strategies. As societies share the vision and values around the natural environment, they selectively and exclusively create their own narratives on how to engage with these challenges. Some cultures might be progressively engaging with these issues, while other cultures might be regressing from their climate commitments and adopting stances that discourage adaptations. In sum, effectively addressing climate change issues requires certain adaptations of human activities and the key to success lies in how the adaptions are impacting the cultural identity of the given community.

3 MNE's Role in Implementing Localized CSR and Contributing to SDGs

From our literature review, it can be seen that much of the discussion on MNEs' CSR activities supporting SDGs are in the nascent stage, and most of these studies do not explicitly consider the role of cultural differences in these activities and linkages between the MNEs' CSR activities and SDGs. Hence, in the rest of this section, we will endeavor to build a conceptual model that takes into account the cultural dimension of MNEs' SDG-related CSR activities. We take a contingency perspective of strategy formulation and implementation to identify key contingencies for MNEs to partake in the SDGs in the host country. As shown in Fig. 1, we identify three categories of contingencies, including (1) industry competitive dynamic, (2) host country CSR expectations, and (3) cultural adaptations of subsidiary management.

3.1 Industry Competitive Dynamic

Each country has different levels of attainment of the United Nation's list of 17 SDGs (Zheng et al., 2021). The MNEs may play a significant role in improving SDGs in the given country if the attention and resources are directed toward needed SDGs in the host country. For instance, many MNEs were found to be recruiting female managers in South Korea and contribute to SDG 5 gender equality (Nobel, 2010). These MNEs may not have the same CSR strategy in their home country to

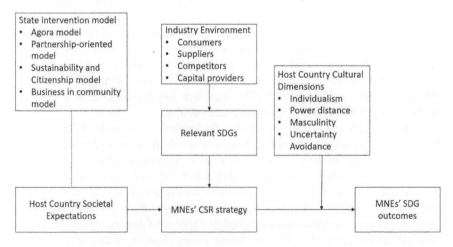

Fig. 1 MNE's role in implementing SDGs in the host country. Source: figure compiled by authors

promote gender equality in the senior management, as in the case of Japanese MNEs. The industry dynamic in South Korea provides a compelling business case for MNEs to hire talented female managers who are in abundant supply since they are not traditionally hired for the high-level positions among South Korean firms. Female managers become a source of competitive advantages for the MNEs because these managers have innate knowledge about the increasingly large size of target consumers, women, who are making most of the household purchasing decisions in recent years (Nobel, 2010).

In addition to employees and consumers, capital providers are influential in making MNEs shift their strategic resources allocations and support SDGs in a given host country. Particularly, many stock exchanges require listed firms to report their CSR activities tracking SDGs, which are bases for investors to evaluate companies' impacts on the environment and society (Pineiro et al., 2018). Montiel et al. (2021) highlight the fact that MNEs' external investments geared toward SDGs can generate positive competitiveness externalities on host country subsidiaries. The key mechanisms to achieve this positive competitiveness externality emerges from the MNEs' investments in knowledge capabilities which can improve labor productivity, income, value added, and competitiveness within a supply chain and MNEs' investment in building human capital. This increased industrial competitiveness in the host country can encourage other domestic and foreign companies to increase their investment in knowledge capabilities, thereby creating a mutually beneficial business system in the host country that caters to the local SDG gaps. Similarly, investments in human capital building can encourage local competitiveness with the generation of entrepreneurial capacity and capability, leading to further positive knowledge spillovers. Typically, these external investments activities target SDGs like local education (SDG 4) and innovativeness (SDG 9), both of which can improve the host country's industrial competitiveness. Montiel et al. (2021) note the example of BBVA, a Spanish financial services company that engages in the training and development of host country nationals. In Chile, BBVA has led the training of micro-entrepreneurs.

3.2   Host Country CSR Expectations

To analyze the degree to which MNEs are under the societal expectations to partake in local SDGs, we consider the MNEs' perspective and discuss the host country's societal expectations of CSR strategies. Built upon the Albareda et al. (2007) empirical study of Europe-15 countries, we extend the CSR models and conceptualize the societal stakeholders' expectations of CSR strategies along the continuum between a strong state model and a free-market model. In some emerging economies, the government plays a crucial role not only to direct economic development but also to explicitly mandate corporations' cooperation to support SDGs. For instance, since 2013, India has introduced a mandatory CSR contribution for all firms with a net worth above 5 billion rupees (Sharma, 2013).

In a society with a strong government-initiated mandate, MNEs do not have discretion in not complying with the host country governmental rules, which also shape the societal expectations of how MNEs would contribute to the economic prosperity and the social and environmental issues in the host country. On the other end of the spectrum, the free-market economies have diverse levels of corporations' participation in the governmental agenda in contributing to SDGs. For instance, Albareda et al. (2007) suggest that in the Mediterranean countries, including Greece, Italy, Portugal, and Spain, the societies fall in line with the Agora model and do not traditionally have a strong set of norms for CSR, so the government will take a more active role in engaging corporations to contribute to SDGs. By contrast, in the Business in Community model, the firms which embrace CSR do not only comply with the governmental rule but to proactively engage stakeholders in their CSR strategies so they may develop competitive advantages and sustain their bottom-line performance. Given the various societal expectations in the host countries, MNEs will need to be able to assess the partnership orientation of the given society and address the prevailing CSR expectations. In the host country where the government has an active agenda in implementing SDGs, MNEs' global strategy will need to be adjusted accordingly and comply with the public policy.

Likewise, civil society also plays an important role to hold MNEs responsible for engaging with SDGs. To compete well in a given host country, it is no longer enough to provide quality products and services. Particularly, in the sustainability and citizenship model, the MNEs will be expected to take their place as citizens in civil society, whereas in a partnership-oriented model, MNEs will be expected to engage multiple stakeholders and form public-private partnerships across sectors. For example, HP Inc., headquartered in Palo Alto, California, has worldwide subsidiaries in 70 countries. The company has published environmental and social impact reports since 2001. To maximize impacts, HP carefully assessed the business model and selected human rights (SDG5, 8, 10), Climate Action (SDG12, 13, 15), and Digital Equity (SDG3, 4, 8) as major areas of reporting the company's sustainability practices (HP Sustainable Impact Report, 2020). Further, various local impacts are reported according to the host country's societal expectations of CSR strategies. In Japan, one HP employee volunteered in partnership with Disability Impact Network; in Tunisia, HP. Life courses are offered in partnership with the Tunisian government, the US agency of international development (USAID), Italian Cooperation, and United Nations Industrial Development Organization (UNIDO).

3.3   Subsidiary Management of MNEs' CSR Strategy in a Focal Subsidiary

According to the traditional discussion of corporate international strategy, an MNE would need to adapt its practices not only to the external environment but also to the subsidiary management practices (Mudambi, 2011). Similarly, to successfully adapt the MNE's global CSR strategy in the host cultural context, we posit that the adaptations to the localized SDGs implementation require an understanding of a host cultural context of subsidiary management. In this regard, we use Hofstede's four dimensions of national culture—power distance, individuality, masculinity, and uncertainty avoidance (Hofstede, 1980). Although this cultural lens has faced few criticisms over the years, we observe that for our study, these national cultural dimensions are adequate to explore the limitations and challenges in the national context that can impede or facilitate the implementation of SDGs.

First, power distance measures how much less powerful members in a society accept the unequal power distribution, whereas individualism indicates how much a society values personal goals and achievements over a group's goals and achievements (Hofstede, 1980). In countries with high power distance and high collectivism, subsidiary management is likely to embrace MNE's global CSR strategy to facilitate a centralized and collective decision-making process in managing the business practices in the host country. However, the host country societal stakeholders' expectations may not be considered in implementing SDG-related CSR activities in a focal subsidiary. As discussed in Hennchen (2015), Royal Dutch Shell oil company in Nigeria serves as a good example of how a centralized governance mechanism in a country with high power distance and low individuality may put the MNE's CSR strategy out of touch with the local reality. Once a front-running company in the CSR area, Shell was accused of supporting the Nigerian military as it attached villages in the late 1990s. On the other hand, in countries where power distance is low and individuality is high, the subsidiary management will be more likely to proactively engaged in the implementation of the SDGs in the host market.

Second, the cultural characteristic of femininity represents a societal value of caring for others while masculine society values dominance, assertiveness, and competition (Hofstede, 1980). In cases of countries with higher masculinity, subsidiary management may be more proactive in seeking a competitive advantage by enacting its own unique strategy aside from the MNEs' global strategy of SDG implementation. Unilever's activities in India are a good example of this type of MNE approach to SDG-related actions. According to Hofstede's masculinity scores, India ranks higher on this score and can be considered as a masculine society with greater emphasis on power and success. In this context, Unilever targeted women directly with their activities and included them in their projects. Over time, this not only improved the financial access and education of these women, many in marginalized communities, but it also improved the economic output of these women who became entrepreneurs in their own right (Neath & Sharma, 2008). Thus, these targeted activities can greatly achieve SDG goals in such high masculinity societies where the global SDG approach might not always meet the local expectations.

Third, uncertainty avoidance refers to a society's tolerance for uncertainty and ambiguity (Hofstede, 1980). In a culture with high uncertainty avoidance, subsidiary management may be more accepting for the MNE's global CSR strategy as it reduces uncertainty. For instance, Uzhegova et al. (2019) explore, among other factors, the role of uncertainty avoidance on internationalizing Finnish and Russian small and medium businesses. In the Russian context, where businesses are still forming, trust plays a great role in reducing uncertainty and improving business interactions. In such a context, an established global CSR strategy can be considered a valuable resource by the MNEs to engage with the local Russian market while meeting some of the local SDG goals. The aforementioned cultural dimensions and associated challenges of implementing MNEs' global CSR strategy are summarized in Table 1.

4   Conclusions

Various studies have argued that this lack of reflection on cultural differences and culturally motivated local challenges will reduce the effectiveness of implementing SDGs (Zheng et al., 2021). This creates an interesting foundation for us to explore the contingencies for MNEs to implement SDG-related activities in host countries. In most cases, MNEs will need to work closely with the local stakeholders like the government, NGOs, and public to effectively develop, implement, and diffuse their SDG-related activities. In our conceptual framework, we identify major conditions that constrain or facilitate the MNEs' CSR strategies to contribute to SDGs in the host countries. By examining these conditions, we contribute to the discussion of how MNEs take an active role to improve sustainable competitive advantage by contributing to SDGs in the host countries.

The commonly used host-home country framework in international business research offers great insights into the formulation and implementation of an MNE's CSR strategy. Given various societal expectations of CSR strategies, host country stakeholders may not be always receptive to an MNE's global CSR strategy. The MNE business executives will need to carefully assess the relationship among business, government, and civil society so they can formulate the optimal host country-specific CSR strategy to contribute to the attainment of SDGs in the host country. The MNEs that are originated from a country with a drastically societal view on CSR from the host country's view will need to adapt their global CSR strategy substantially. For instance, most western MNEs operating in China will need to comply with the government-directed approach in setting their CSR agenda and carefully selecting the target SDGs in China. Additionally, while implementing a CSR strategy in the host country, MNE business executives will need to be cognizant of the cultural dimensions of the host country and adapt their managerial approach accordingly.

4.1   Limitations and Future Avenues for Research

Our theoretical framework outlines three important contingencies of how MNEs' global CSR strategies may facilitate or inhibit the host country's SDG agenda. Given the increasing uncertainty in the global business environment, MNEs' proactive stand in tackling SDGs is likely to result in a sustainable competitive advantage for managing environmental uncertainty (Sun et al., 2021). It will be a fruitful research

Table 1 National culture, subsidiary management, and SDG implementation challenges

Dimensional scores of national culture	Power distance	Individualism	Masculinity	Uncertainty avoidance
High	The subsidiary management will open to accept the MNE's global CSR strategy. However, the host country societal stakeholders' expectations may not be considered in implementing SDGs-related CSR activities	The countries with higher individualism values will proactively adopt host country SDG targets, and subsidiary management will be proactive in SDG implementation. There will be wider diffusion of SDGs in the country	The subsidiary management in countries with higher masculinity values might be reluctant to share the powers vested in their position so uptake of MNE's global CSR strategy will be lower in such countries	In countries with higher uncertainty avoidance values, subsidiary management may be more accepting of the MNE's global CSR strategy as it reduces uncertainty
Low	The subsidiary management will be proactively engaged in the implementation of the SDGs. There will be wider legitimacy from the power structures for the adaptation of the MNE's CSR strategy	Some countries with lower individualism will adopt the key position of MNE's CSR strategy in country and thus, lack the attention to the host country SDGs Whereas, in some other countries with high in-group collectivism, the subsidiary management might be against the MNE's global CSR strategy and focus on host country SDGs	The subsidiary management in countries with higher masculinity values will be proactively engaged in the implementation of the SDGs. There will be wider legitimacy from the power structures for the adoption of the SDGs	In the case of countries with lower uncertainty avoidance values, subsidiary management is more likely to adopt a novel approach and proactively address SDGs in the host country

Source: Table compiled by authors

avenue for researchers to study MNEs' strategic CSR activities that align with host country SDGs and resulting in triple bottom-line performance. Additionally, a more nuanced approach to examine the micro-foundations, such as subsidiary identity (Liou & Rao-Nicholson, 2021), of MNEs executives' decision-making will garner insights into how cultural characteristics of the host culture plays a role in influencing the SDG implementation in the host country.

Similarly, our conceptualization is not without limitations as we do not consider other potential contingencies that might drive or influence the SDG-related activities and uptake in the host countries. For example, the legitimacy of the MNEs' activities can improve the uptake of the host country's SDG activities. Similarly, the limited legitimacy of the MNEs can impede wider adoption of the CSR activities and restrict SDG targets. Also, home country actors can impede or improve MNEs' SDG-related activities in the host country. These home country actors can also create channels for engaging with other stakeholders in the host country. The future conceptual models as well as empirical works can explore the links between the home and host country actors and stakeholders in the diffusion of the SDG-related activities.

Further, the international business field has traditionally discussed proactively engaging the host country government as one major strategy to mitigate political risk (Ramamurti, 2001; Vernon, 1971). Ramamurti (2001) further proposes a two-tier bargaining model for MNEs to first bargain with the host country government and then bargain through multilateral institutions like World Bank and WTO. The framework presented in the current study has great implications for MNEs to leverage the supernational institution, the United Nations, and bargain with the host country government for favorable investment treatment. It is also in the host country's best interest to involve MNEs in public policy discussions for attaining SDGs. Future studies on MNE's adaptation of global CSR strategy according to host country SDG agenda will further offer insights into the MNE's role as an agent for change in attaining a sustainable future across the globe.

References

Aaronson, S., & Reeves, J. (2002). *The European response to public demands for global corporate responsibility*. National Policy Association.

Adger, W. N., Barnett, J., Brown, K., Marshall, N., & O'Brien, K. (2013). Cultural dimensions of climate change impacts and adaptation. *Nature Climate Change, 3*(2), 112–117.

Albareda, L., Lozano, J., & Ysa, T. (2007). Public policies on corporate social responsibility: The role of governments in Europe. *Journal of Business Ethics, 74*(4), 391–407.

Ambec, S., & Lanoie, P. (2008). Does it pay to be green? A systematic overview. *Academy of Management Perspectives, 22*(4), 45–62.

Amos, G. J. (2008). Corporate social responsibility in the mining industry: An exploration of host-communities' perceptions and expectations in a developing-country. *Corporate Governance, 18*(6), 1177–1195.

Attig, N., & Brockman, P. (2017). The local roots of corporate social responsibility. *Journal of Business Ethics, 142*, 479–496.

Barsoum, G., & Refaat, S. (2015). "We don't want school bags": Discourses on corporate social responsibility in Egypt and the challenges of a new practice in a complex setting. *International Journal of Sociology and Social Policy, 35*(5/6), 390–402.

Boateng, A., Wang, Y., Ntim, C., & Glaister, K. W. (2021). National culture, corporate governance and corruption: A cross-country analysis. *International Journal of Finance & Economics, 26*(3), 3852–3874.

Bolton, S. C., Kim, R. C., & O'Gorman, K. D. (2011). Corporate social responsibility as a dynamic internal organizational process: A case study. *Journal of Business Ethics, 101*, 61–74.

Burke, L., & Logsdon, J. M. (1996). How corporate social responsibility pays off. *Long Range Planning, 29*(4), 495–502.

Campbell, J. L. (2007). Why would corporations behave in socially responsible ways? An institutional theory of corporate social responsibility. *Academy of Management Review, 32*(3), 946–967.

Chan, A. (2009). Challenges and possibilities for democratic grassroots union elections in China: A case study of two factory-level elections and their aftermath. *Labor Studies Journal, 34*(3), 293–317.

Chapple, W., & Moon, J. (2005). Corporate social responsibility (CSR) in Asia: A seven-country study of CSR web site reporting. *Business & Society, 44*(4), 415–441.

Csafor, H. (2008). Corporate social responsibility in central and Eastern Europe. In M. Carmona, J. Szlavik, & E. Zam (Eds.), *Perdiodica Oeconomica—Regional Development and Competitiveness* (pp. 115–126). University of Paris-Sorbonne IV and Eszterházy Károly College.

Davis, J. H., & Ruhe, J. A. (2003). Perceptions of country corruption: Antecedents and outcomes. *Journal of Business Ethics, 43*(4), 275–288.

Eden, L., & Wagstaff, M. F. (2021). Evidence-based policymaking and the wicked problem of SDG 5 gender equality. *Journal of International Business Policy, 4*, 28–57. https://doi.org/10.1057/s42214-020-00054-w

Eweje, G. (2006). The role of MNEs in community development initiatives in developing countries. *Business and Society, 45*(2), 93–129.

Griggs, D., Stafford-Smith, M., Gaffney, O., Rockström, J., Öhman, M. C., Shyamsundar, P., Steffen, W., Glaser, G., Kanie, N., & Noble, I. (2013). Policy: Sustainable development goals for people and planet. *Nature, 495*(7441), 305.

H.P. Sustainable Impact Report. (2020). *2020 Executive Summary*. Retrieved from https://www8.hp.com/h20195/v2/getpdf.aspx/c05179523.pdf

Hennchen, E. (2015). Royal Dutch shell in Nigeria: Where do responsibilities end? *Journal of Business Ethics, 129*(1), 1–25.

Hofstede, G. (1980). Culture and organizations. *International Studies of Management & Organization, 10*(4), 15–41.

Huang, H., Wu, D., & Gaya, J. (2017). Chinese shareholders' reaction to the disclosure of environmental violations: A CSR perspective. *International Journal of Corporate Social Responsibility, 2*(1), 1–16.

Husted, B. W., & Allen, D. B. (2009). Strategic corporate social responsibility and value creation: A study of multinational enterprises in Mexico. *Management International Review, 49*(6), 781–799.

Ioannou, I., & Serafeim, G. (2012). What drives corporate social performance? The role of nation-level institutions. *Journal of International Business Studies, 43*(9), 834–864.

Jamali, D. (2010). The CSR of MNC subsidiaries in developing countries: Global, local, substantive or diluted? *Journal of Business Ethics, 93*(2), 181–200.

Koleva, P., Rodet-Kroichvili, N., David, P., & Marasova, J. (2010). Is corporate social responsibility the privilege of developed market economies? Some evidence from central and Eastern Europe. *International Journal of Human Resource Management, 21*(2), 274–293.

Liou, R. S., & Rao-Nicholson, R. (2021). Multinational enterprises and sustainable development goals: A foreign subsidiary perspective on tackling wicked problems. *Journal of International Business Policy, 4*(1), 136–151.

Maignan, I., & Ralston, D. A. (2002). Corporate social responsibility in Europe and the U.S.: Insights from businesses' self-presentations. *Journal of International Business Studies, 33*(3), 497–514.

Maon, F., Swaen, V., & Lindgreen, A. (2017). One vision, different paths: An investigation of corporate social responsibility initiatives in Europe. *Journal of Business Ethics, 143*, 405–422.

Miller, S. R., Eden, L., & Li, D. (2020). CSR reputation and firm performance: A dynamic approach. *Journal of Business Ethics, 16*(3), 619–636.

Montiel, I., Cuervo-Cazurra, A., Park, J., Antolín-López, R., & Husted, B. W. (2021). Implementing the United Nations' sustainable development goals in international business. *Journal of International Business Studies, 52*, 1–32.

Mudambi, R. (2011). Hierarchy, coordination, and innovation in the multinational enterprise. *Global Strategy Journal, 1*(3–4), 317–323.

Muller, A. (2006). Global versus local CSR strategies. *European Management Journal, 24*(2–3), 189–198.

Muller, A., & Kolk, A. (2010). Extrinsic and intrinsic drivers of corporate social performance: Evidence from foreign and domestic firms in Mexico. *Journal of Management Studies, 47*(1), 1–26.

Neath, G., & Sharma, V. (2008). The Shakti revolution: How the world's largest home-to-home operation is changing lives and stimulating economic activity in rural India. *Development Outreach, 10*(2), 13–16.

Nobel, C. (2010). *It pays to hire women in countries that Won't.* Harvard Business School. Retrieved from https://hbswk.hbs.edu/item/it-pays-to-hire-women-in-countries-that-wont

Park, Y. R., Song, S., Choe, S., & Baik, Y. (2015). Corporate social responsibility in international business: Illustrations from Korean and Japanese electronics MNEs in Indonesia. *Journal of Business Ethics., 129*, 747–761.

Pineiro, A., Dithrich, H. & Dhar, A. (2018). *Financing the sustainable development goals: Impact investing in action.* Global Impact Investing Network. Retrieved from https://thegiin.org/research/publication/financing-sdgs

Polonsky, M. J., & Jevons, C. P. (2009). Global branding and strategic CSR: An overview of three types of complexity. *International Marketing Review, 26*(3), 327–347.

Ramamurti, R. (2001). The obsolescing 'bargaining model'? MNC-host developing country relations revisited. *Journal of International Business Studies, 32*(1), 23–39.

Reimann, F., Ehrgott, M., Kaufmann, L., & Carter, C. R. (2012). Local stakeholders and local legitimacy: MNEs' social strategies in emerging economies. *Journal of International Management, 18*(1), 1–17.

Ringov, D., & Zollo, M. (2007). The impact of national culture on corporate social performance. *Corporate Governance, 7*(4), 476–485.

Sharma, S. (2013). Corporate social responsibility in India - the emerging discourse & concerns. *Indian Journal of Industrial Relations, 48*(4), 582–596. Retrieved August 18, 2021, from http://www.jstor.org/stable/23509816

Sun, P., Doh, J. P., Rajwani, T., & Siegel, D. (2021). Navigating cross-border institutional complexity: A review and assessment of multinational nonmarket strategy research. *Journal of International Business Studies, 52*, 1–36.

Swanson, D. L. (1995). Addressing a theoretical problem by reorienting the corporate social performance model. *Academy of Management Review, 20*(1), 43–64.

U.N. General Assembly. (2015). *Transforming our world: The 2030 agenda for sustainable development.* Accessed April 21, 2021, from www.un.org/ga/search/view_doc.asp?symbol=A/RES/70/1&Lang=E

Uzhegova, M., Torkkeli, L., & Ivanova-Gongne, M. (2019). The role of culture in responsible business practice: An exploration of Finnish and Russian SMEs. In *The changing strategies of international business* (pp. 177–197). Palgrave Macmillan.

van Tulder, R., & Kolk, A. (2001). Multinationality and corporate ethics: Codes of conduct in the sporting goods industry. *Journal of International Business Studies, 32*(2), 267–283.

Vernon, R. (1971). *Sovereignty at bay.* Basic Books.

Vlassis, A. (2015). Culture in the post-2015 development agenda: The anatomy of an international mobilization. *Third World Quarterly, 36*(9), 1649–1662.

Waage, J., Yap, C., Bell, S., Levy, C., Mace, G., Pegram, T., Unterhalter, E., Dasandi, N., Hudson, D., Kock, R., & Mayhew, S. (2015). Governing the U.N. sustainable development goals:

Interactions, infrastructures, and institutions. *The Lancet Globalization and Health, 3*(5), e251–e252.

Whitley, R. (1999). *Divergent capitalisms: The social structuring and change of business systems.* Oxford University Press.

Wiktor-Mach, D. (2020). What role for culture in the age of sustainable development? UNESCO's advocacy in the 2030 agenda negotiations. *International Journal of Cultural Policy, 26*(3), 312–327.

Zhao, Y. (1998). *Media, market, and democracy in China: Between the party line and the bottom line* (Vol. 151). University of Illinois Press.

Zheng, X., Wang, R., Hoekstra, A. Y., Krol, M. S., Zhang, Y., Guo, K., Sanwal, M., Sun, Z., Zhu, J., Zhang, J., & Lounsbury, A. (2021). Consideration of culture is vital if we are to achieve the sustainable development goals. *One Earth, 4*(2), 307–319.

Rekha Rao-Nicholson is a Professor of Management at the University of Essex. Her research interests are strategies of emerging economies' firms, innovation, and development. She has published in Research Policy, Journal of World Business, Human Resource Management, International Journal of Human Resource Management, and International Business Review, among others.

Ru-Shiun Liou is an Associate Professor in Management at the University of Tampa. Her research interests include international business, global sustainability, and cross-cultural management. Her research has been published in the Journal of Management Studies, Journal of Business Research, Journal of World Business, and International Business Review, among others.

Institutionalization of MNEs' Sustainability Reporting: Progressing Toward the United National Sustainable Development Goals

Hussain Gulzar Rammal

1   Introduction

The notion of sustainability in business practices has evolved over the last few decades (Linnenluecke & Griffiths, 2013). Historically, corporate social responsibility (CSR) was used to address organizational responsibilities toward employees' well-being and contributions to society (Carroll, 1979). In contemporary usage, *sustainability* captures activities that emphasize economic, social, and environmental issues and efforts to create equitable and fair working conditions devoid of discrimination (Husted, 2005; WCED, 1987).

Previously, CSR and sustainability-related activities were undertaken voluntarily and considered beyond the legal obligations that organizations had to fulfill. However, there has been a sense of urgency in dealing with sustainability-related issues (Bansal & Knox-Hayes, 2013). For example, the Intergovernmental Panel on Climate Change (IPCC) report published in 2021 warns that within a decade, global warming could push temperatures up significantly (IPCC, 2021). These developments have led to greater public awareness about the carbon footprint of human commercial activities. In addition, concerns about the planet's future have prompted organizations to disclose their operations' environmental and social impact.

Governments are taking initiatives to meet their commitments to reduce carbon emissions and improve their population's economic and social well-being at the national level. Business organizations are expected to comply with the relevant policies implemented by the institutions in these countries. This poses a challenge for multinational enterprises (MNEs) as the lack of global standards means that international firms must adapt their practices and report according to each territory's requirements. Furthermore, the poor implementation of the regulation in many

H. G. Rammal (✉)
Adelaide Business School, The University of Adelaide, Adelaide, Australia
e-mail: hussain.rammal@adelaide.edu.au

© Springer Nature Switzerland AG 2022
H. Merchant (ed.), *The New Frontiers of International Business*, Contributions to
Management Science, https://doi.org/10.1007/978-3-031-06003-8_18

developing economies has resulted in MNEs being accused of poor business practices, including unsafe working conditions and the use of child labor that have affected their global reputation and sales. This chapter highlights these issues and discusses how firms report their sustainability activities to communicate with various stakeholders worldwide directly.

2   Sustainability and the UN SDGs

The issue of CSR came to prominence in 1970 when Milton Friedman argued that the social responsibility of a business is to maximize the return for its stockholders. In discussing his stockholder theory (also known as the Friedman doctrine), Friedman opposed the idea of organizations taking on the responsibility of concerning themselves with the greater good of society (Friedman, 1970). This was in response to an initiative that General Motors had taken by setting up a committee that would study the company's performance in areas such as safety and pollution. Friedman contended that it is the responsibility of governments to address issues of public interest. Unless these initiatives were mandatory or part of the "rules of the game," organizations should not be undertaking them. If managers feel a personal desire to address these concerns, they should do so in their capacity as private citizens and not on behalf of the organization. For Friedman, the stockholder theory was a natural extension of his views on capital and opportunities for individual to maximize their benefits (Friedman, 1962).

In contemporary CSR literature, such a view is considered a straw man. While some critics may question the motivation of the firms in undertaking such activities, there is a consensus that organizations have a social responsibility and need to play a role in ensuring that their operations are sustainable (Hahn et al., 2017; Tregidga et al., 2018). Therefore, regardless of whether the term environmental management, CSR, or corporate sustainability is used, it is understood that sustainability incorporates the economic, environmental, and social perspectives (Burritt et al., 2020), and organizations must improve their performance along each of these dimensions (Shapiro et al., 2018).

At the institutional level, the United Nations (UN) is leading a significant effort to address sustainability issues under their Sustainable Development Goals (UNSDGs). In 2015, the UN member states adopted the 2030 Agenda for Sustainable Development, emphasizing 17 goals (United Nations, 2022). These goals cover several issues ranging from poverty reduction, addressing inequalities, general health and well-being, right to education, safe working conditions, and securing a sustainable future for the planet. Table 1 lists the 17 UNSGDs.

The COVID-19 pandemic has confirmed the significant inequalities between countries and their population, especially regarding access to vaccines for people living in developed versus developing economies. The impact of the pandemic on increasing inequalities and poverty, challenges of migration, and access to finance are issues that the UNSDGs are attempting to address. To achieve the stated objectives of the 2030 Agenda, various stakeholders need to take ownership of the

Table 1 United Nations sustainable development goals

1. No Poverty	2. Zero Hunger	3. Good Health and Well-Being	4. Quality Education	5. Gender Equality
6. Clean Water and Sanitation	7. Affordable and Clean Energy	8. Decent Work and Economic Growth	9. Industry, Innovation and Infrastructure	10. Reduced Inequalities
11. Sustainable Cities and Communities	12. Responsible Consumption and Production	13. Climate Action	14. Life Below Water	15. Life on Land
	16. Peace, Justice and Strong Institutions		17. Partnerships for the Goals	

Source: United Nations (2022)

implementation of the SDGs. MNEs' global networks make them an important player in promoting sustainability (Liou & Rao-Nicholson, 2021; Rygh et al., 2021). Some of the world's largest MNES have cash-flows and assets that exceed the gross domestic product of developed countries (Amba-Rao, 1993). Hence, they have the power to implement these goals in their operations and influence the relevant institutions and related policies in the countries where they operate.

However, MNEs face a myriad of challenges and criticism regarding CSR and sustainability practices (Kolk, 2010a, 2010b). Due to their sheer size and global recognition, they are also targets of greater scrutiny about their operations from a social justice perspective. One of the accusations leveled against MNEs is that they outsource and move their operations to countries that have fewer regulations regarding environmental standards, workers' safety, or working conditions, such as minimum wage rates. Hence, they are seen to be exploiting workers in poorer countries, and their actions lead to a "race to the bottom" (Burritt et al., 2020).

In their defense, MNEs argue that they comply with local standards and regulations set up by the institutions in the countries they operate. The United Nations Declaration of Human Rights states that equal work deserves equal pay and workers' rights need to be protected. However, there are no globally accepted standards for minimum wages or working conditions that can be followed. Instead, organizations either set standards that they follow worldwide or follow the rules and regulations of the host country. In either case, the monitoring and implementations of the CSR and sustainability practices are carried out by local staff and institutions.

Despite this defense, the choice of countries for the internationalization of manufacturing raises the most questions. Critics argue that MNEs choose to relocate manufacturing to countries that maximize their returns even though they are aware of poor working conditions and standards. Hence, the choice of markets is neither based on the notion of the home and host countries sharing low psychic or institutional distances but rather the cost of manufacturing that drives these decisions (Ambos & Håkanson, 2014; Brewer, 2007; Dow & Karunaratna, 2006; Evans et al., 2008; Hutzschenreuter et al., 2014, 2016; Johanson & Vahlne, 2009; Ojala, 2015; Sousa & Bradley, 2005; Tihanyi et al., 2005). Therefore, these managerial decisions seem to follow the Friedman doctrine of maximizing the stockholders' return as long as the actions are within the rules of the game. This makes the MNEs' claims of being socially responsible and emphasizing sustainability questionable. One way to address these concerns is for MNEs to communicate directly with the stakeholders (Freeman, 1984) by reporting their sustainability activities (Ike et al., 2021).

3   Sustainability Reporting and MNEs

The speed at which information technology systems have improved and adopted by the general population worldwide has been unprecedented. News and information about publicly listed organizations in much of the world remain largely free and easily accessible via electronic modes, replacing mediums like locally printed newspapers. Greater use of technology means that people, as the key stakeholder, are better informed of organizational activities than before, enabling them to judge the sustainability credentials of the firms. However, there is the risk that unchecked news stories or fake news about organizations may cloud the readers' judgment and influence their decisions as consumers of the firms' products.

Organizations can address this concern by directly communicating information about their sustainability activities to consumers and other key stakeholders. While reporting the firms' financial information is mandated, sustainability reporting remains voluntary in many countries. Despite this, we have witnessed a growth in reporting sustainability activities covering social and environmental information in the last few decades (Diouf & Boiral, 2017). This growing interest in sustainability reporting is a response to the demands by stakeholders for more transparency and accountability of how organizations undertake their business activities (Tagesson et al., 2013). Specifically, there has been growing stakeholder activism to ensure that organizations' activities are undertaken sustainably, and this information is transmitted through the organizational reports (Doh & Guay, 2006).

These developments have also prompted institutions, like the European Union (EU), to require organizations to produce nonfinancial and diversity information, which includes disclosures about environmental matters, social and employee aspects, respect for human rights, anti-corruption and bribery issues, and diversity in their board of directors (European Commission, 2016). In addition, in the United Kingdom, under the Equality Act of 2010 (Legislation.Gov.Uk, 2022), firms are required to report their gender pay gap information. For MNEs, these developments mean that in addition to producing consolidated financial statements, they also have to prepare specific reports and disclose their activities under the formal and informal institutional requirements and expectations in the territories where they operate (Lee et al., 2021).

Analyzing this issue from an institutional theory perspective, we can argue that the trend in reporting sustainability activities is set to continue. This growth can be explained by the isomorphism occurring at various levels (DiMaggio & Powell, 1983). For example, contemporary professional management training emphasizes decision-making that considers socio-economic and environmental impacts and reports the outcomes. This *normative isomorphism* can be observed at the micro/managerial level and emphasizes sustainability considerations as part of all business decisions.

At the meso level, we expect organizations to attempt to match other firms' sustainability reporting practices to demonstrate their credentials and ensure that they do not concede any competitive advantage. This *mimetic isomorphism* acts as a trigger for wider reporting of sustainability activities across industries. Finally, at the macro/country/institutional level, we are witnessing a renewed push by nations taking action to meet their sustainability goals. The Paris Agreement is one such example of a legally binding treaty addressing global warming challenges. Achieving the environmental targets requires social and economic transformation. The *coercive isomorphism* at this level has resulted in the introduction of laws and regulations that aim to ensure that the targets set by the countries can be achieved.

MNEs can be proactive and voluntarily report their sustainability practices to communicate with stakeholders or be reactive and report the practices in countries where the laws require them. A reactive approach is more likely to be met with cynicism from the wider community, especially since many developing countries are yet to mandate sustainability reporting. However, as we discuss later, MNEs have been some of the biggest contributors in developing and implementing reporting initiatives and systems such as triple bottom-line reporting. There are also sustainability reporting templates that MNEs can use to report their activities. One such option is using the Global Reporting Initiative (GRI) standards (Farneti & Rammal, 2013)

The GRI standards are seen to provide best practices for reporting organizational impact on the economy, the environment, and people (Milne & Gray, 2013). The GRI has a range of standards that can demonstrate impact (GRI, 2021). The Universal Standards apply to all organizations and emphasize transparency in organizational operations. In addition, these standards have a forward-looking approach that aims to help organizations be well-positioned to respond to emerging institutional mandated regulatory disclosure requirements, including the EU Corporate Sustainability Reporting Directive and the planned International Financial Reporting Standards (IFRS) initiatives to report enterprise value standards.

A more recent initiative is the GRI's Sector Standards reporting, which aims to develop standards for 40 sectors with the highest impact. Approved in 2019, the first sector standards were released in 2021 and covered the oil and gas standards. In using these standards, organizations can register and disseminate their reports through GRI's website and make them publicly available (GRI, 2021). The available reports include those produced by commercial organizations and an increasing number by public sector organizations facing similar calls for transparency from stakeholders, including the taxpayers (Farneti & Siboni, 2011).

The next section provides examples of MNEs highlighting the significance of stakeholder engagement in CSR and sustainability practices and its reporting.

4 Ethics, CSR, and MNEs

The International Business (IB) literature is littered with examples of MNEs being accused of unethical behavior. Before discussing some of these examples, it is important to clarify what is deemed ethical or unethical and differentiate between ethics and social responsibility. Although used interchangeably in many studies, ethics and social responsibility have different legal implications. Ethical decisions comply with laws and regulations (such as paying the minimum wage rate), and unethical decisions are those that do not. While people may make a moral judgment about a decision made by an organization, it has no legal standing in deciding whether it is ethical or unethical. In contrast, CSR activities are voluntary and do not have a legal requirement. This again confirms the view that while the Friedman doctrine is a straw man, it is still very much relevant to the way contemporary business activities are undertaken.

To illustrate the issues covered in the chapter, we discuss three well-known examples of MNEs' operation in developing countries: Shell in Nigeria, the Rana Plaza incident in Bangladesh, and the accusations of child labor leveled against Nike. Although the legal obligations and responsibilities of the MNEs in these cases can be questioned, there is no doubt over their CSR obligations. With the help of these examples, we demonstrate how MNEs have learned from their mistakes and how various reporting initiatives are used to communicate their CSR activities and their commitment to sustainability in business operations.

4.1 Shell in Nigeria

The Royal Dutch/Shell company has a long history in Nigeria, dating back to 1936 when the first Shell company in Nigeria was founded. In the 1990s, Shell expanded exploration and other activities in Nigeria (Shell, 2021). At the time, the country was being ruled by the military head of Nigeria, General Sani Abacha. Shell dealt directly with government officials, but their operations affected the local population. One of the groups affected was the Ogoni people, an ethnic minority in Nigeria whose homeland, the Ogoniland, is situated near the Niger Delta and was an area targeted by Shell for oil exploration. The Ogoni people protested Shell's operations due to the environmental degradation of the Niger delta and its impact on the local ecosystem and agriculture in the Ogoniland. The protests were led by Ken Saro-Wiwa, an environmental activist, who criticized both Shell for the environmental damage and the Nigerian government for failing to enforce environmental regulations.

The military government arrested Ken and his supporters on charges of inciting violence against other Ogoni chiefs who were murdered. After a generally compromised trial, Ken and eight of his colleagues were sentenced to death. There was worldwide condemnation of the ruling, and many activists asked Shell to play their part in seeking a pardon for Ken and his supporters. Although Shell claims to have made appeals to the military rulers, many observers questioned the sincerity of these efforts. Nevertheless, the sentence was carried out, and the nine accused were executed on 10 November 1995. In 1996, Ken's family started legal proceedings against Shell in the United States. In 2009, before the trial commenced, an out-of-court settlement was reached (Mouawad, 2009).

Shell faced worldwide criticism and consumer boycott. The company realized its biggest mistake in Nigeria was not engaging with the local population and relevant stakeholders. Learning from the experience, Shell took several steps to address its sustainability practices. The company launched its environmental and social reporting with "The Shell Report 1998," which marked the beginning for Shell to measure its operations against a "triple bottom line" of financial, social, and environmental factors. The company also restructured its operations in Nigeria, and from 2004 the top management positions have been occupied by local managers who understand the country's sociocultural, political, and institutional environment. These initiatives have improved Shell's standing in the community in Nigeria, and the social reporting initiative has enhanced the engagement with consumers and other stakeholders worldwide.

4.2   The Rana Plaza Accident in Bangladesh

Bangladesh is one of the world's leading manufacturers of ready-made garments (RMG), and the sector is a major source of the country's foreign income earning and employment. Due to the low-cost benefits that manufacturing in the country provides, many international brands outsource their apparel production to factories in Bangladesh. However, there have been concerns about working conditions such as the safety of the workers and gender inequality in Bangladeshi factories, with men positioned in leadership roles. In contrast, women employees work mostly on the factory floor.

These concerns about the working conditions in the Bangladesh RMG sector came to the forefront after the Rana Plaza incident in 2013, where over 1100 people died after the building, in which five garment factories were operating, collapsed (ILO, 2021). These factories manufactured for global brands, including Benetton, Prada, Gucci, Primark, and Walmart. The accident itself was a result of structural faults in the building. However, further investigations highlighted several issues that led to the building's collapse. This included extra floors being built, which was not approved in the original plan, using the premises as a factory when it was planned and designed for shops and residential use. The lack of safety checks relating to working conditions and building safety were also contributors to the tragedy. However, as with incidents involving well-known brands, the MNEs were blamed for failing to ensure safe working conditions even though they did not own the factories and legally were not liable for the accident.

The MNEs decided that it would be inappropriate to cancel the manufacturing agreements in Bangladesh as this would result in increased unemployment as factories would close. Instead, they worked with trade unions to agree to standards for working conditions that would be implemented in the factories and monitored by independent inspectors. As a result, in 2013 the *Accord on Fire and Building Safety in Bangladesh*, a legally binding agreement, was signed, covering more than 1600 factories that manufacture for more than 190 brands and employ over two million workers (Bangladesh Accord, 2021). Under the agreement, factories are inspected to ensure safety standards, identify areas for improvement, and implement safety remediation work to rectify any minor issues. The inspectors would temporarily evacuate the premises for major structural issues until the problems were fixed. These inspections have resulted in major improvements in the factories, with 84% of the factories fixing their electrical wiring and 97% of factories removing lockable or collapsible gates, which would make it easier for workers to escape the building in case of emergency. The evidence would suggest that the accord has successfully averted another accident in the RMG sector in Bangladesh, and the reporting mechanism ensures transparency about the processes followed.

4.3 Nike's Use of Child Labor

Nike is one of the most recognized global brands. The company's business model is based on keeping the research, development, and marketing functions in-house and outsourcing the manufacturing. Nike's decision to move the manufacturing to factories located in developing countries was criticized by workers' unions in the United States. In addition to their members' job losses, the unions claimed that child labor and low safety standards were widespread in manufacturing in many developing countries. Thus, Nike could potentially have their products manufactured unethically by outsourcing production to these countries.

In response, Nike claimed that the individual contracts with each factory clearly stated that child labor was prohibited and audits of the factories would be undertaken periodically to ensure compliance. In 1996, a Life Magazine article exposed the working conditions in one of the factories in Pakistan that manufactured Nike's shoes (Schanberg, 1996). The article included a photo showing a 12-year-old boy stitching leather panels on a soccer ball with the Nike swoosh visible. The article exposed Nike's claims of manufacturing without child labor. The article also claimed that the boy was paid 6 cents an hour to stitch the soccer balls, which Nike's critics pointed out as evidence that the company's products were being manufactured in sweatshops.

Nike pleaded ignorance and claimed that such issues were not found in any factory audits. Additionally, the factory also manufactured goods for companies other than Nike, and the local authorities should act against the factory for breaching the laws. However, as we have seen in the previous examples, such defense doesn't sway the wider community, which argues that with their large asset base and high profits, MNEs should be proactively working toward identifying and rectifying such issues rather than denying their responsibility.

Nike took immediate and long-term measures to address the issue of child labor in manufacturing. In the short run, Nike moved the children from undertaking labor-intensive tasks like stitching leather panels and moved them into other areas. The company also provided free education for all the children working at the factory. In the long run, Nike set standards for the factories contracted to manufacture for the company. A robust audit mechanism has been put in place. Factories are warned if their performance starts to wane. Failure to remedy their performance can result in the factory's contract being terminated. Nike uses the GRI standards and makes its reports available freely. The reports also reference the UNSGDs and the United Nations Global Compact (UNGC) Principles. The company acknowledges their mistakes in the past in labor conditions and explains how they have rectified them as part of their global supply chain systems. So confident are Nike of their monitoring system that they publish the details of their factories in the reports and website.

The Nike incident, and similar ones involving other sports manufacturers like Reebok, resulted in a fundamental change in the manufacturing of sports goods, especially soccer balls. The stitching of soccer balls was eliminated from the process. The 2006 FIFA World Cup in Germany saw the introduction of balls using various technologies such as thermal bonding of panels.

5 Conclusion

This chapter covers the evolution of responsible management in MNEs and the various reporting initiatives. We have witnessed a move from a narrower CSR focus to a more defined sustainability emphasis that captures the economic, social, and environmental concerns. The enhanced emphasis on sustainability in MNEs has been triggered by two developments: the rapid growth of information technology and the adverse environmental effects of human activities.

The information technology revolution means that MNEs' operations are no longer viewed within the domestic or regional institutional context. While compliance with local regulations is necessary, stakeholders can access organizational information globally. Hence, the reporting of sustainability activity (Schaltegger & Burritt, 2010) needs to detail the impact of the MNEs' activities at the domestic, regional, and global levels. In addition, the second trigger of climate change has brought about a sense of urgency to how the world deals with environmental issues and the role that MNEs can play.

The three examples that we covered demonstrate why MNEs need to look beyond their legal obligations and consider their CSR and sustainability activities. While meeting legal responsibilities ensures that MNEs are operating within the rules of the game, the heightened stakeholder activism that we are witnessing today means that firms need to consider their obligations to society. We see from these examples that the MNEs involved changed their operations and reported their sustainability activities to engage directly with all stakeholders. However, it should be noted that these changes were a reactive response from the MNEs rather than a proactive one. Had these incidents not taken place and the institutional efforts to set standards for sustainability not been on the agenda, the MNEs may not have made these changes. Future sustainability practices and reporting changes should grow organically, and MNEs should proactively take actions to support these activities.

To achieve this, MNEs need to constantly scan the environment to preempt potential labor and supply chain challenges. A recent example of this is the COVID-19 pandemic. While the world became aware of the virus' spread and the potential challenges to the global mobility of workers and goods, a practical solution was not forthcoming. As a result, even a few years since the pandemic began, unemployment is at a record high in many countries, school education has been disrupted, and MNEs' supply chains face delays, leaving many store shelves bare.

Despite the growing awareness among the populations globally of sustainability and the impact of business and other activities, there is still much to do to improve practice. Having improved the reporting of sustainability activities, the next step for MNEs is to move from having transparency about operations toward achieving the sustainable development goals. This requires consensus on standards and expectations that consider the social, economic, and environmental concerns of developed and developing countries and can be applied globally without exception. The role of global institutions is critical in achieving this. Like the UN, a global umbrella body could be a feasible option to bring together national governments, leading MNEs, institutions, and other stakeholders together to develop such standards.

These global standards bodies would also need to form independent sustainability audit options (Liu et al., 2020) to ensure that MNEs comply with the agreed standards and don't merely make claims or window-dress their activities. This issue is evident in the current reporting system, where MNEs work on fairness, justice, and equality. Yet, reports from Transparency International show that public sector corruption remains a major concern in many developing economies. For example, reporting gender imbalance in organizations in the United Kingdom and other parts shows that year-on-year firms acknowledge the imbalance but do not highlight any practical steps to rectify the problem. Unless it can be demonstrated that certain actions are being taken, MNEs will be merely identifying the problem without being part of the solution.

Based on the observations made in the chapter, we provide an agenda for future research. The rise of emerging market MNEs (EMMNEs) makes for an interesting context (Golgeci et al., 2021). It is assumed that the institutional environment in emerging markets is still in its infancy (Doh et al., 2015). Hence, the minimum sustainability standards followed by EMMNEs in their home markets are lower than those applied in developed economies. Future research can address this issue by exploring how EMMNEs adjust to the differences in the institutional environment? Does it affect their operations in the host markets? How do they report the differences in their sustainability activities across countries?

Other areas of study include exploring how the harmonization of reporting sustainability practices can be achieved. This would ensure global consistency in reporting practices and facilitate comparing MNEs' sustainability performance by stakeholders.

In concluding this chapter, we observe that our examples suggest that the legal system governing business practices follows the Friedman doctrine. However, in practice, even if MNEs prioritize the stockholders' return, it makes economic sense to be engaged with promoting sustainability practices. This is because the modern consumer considers a range of information before purchasing from an organization. This includes the sustainability credentials of the organization, information about the production methods, the well-being of the workers and working conditions, and so on. Hence, MNEs that fail to proactively engage and be sustainable in their operations will lose their customer base to their more engaged competitors.

References

Amba-Rao, S. C. (1993). Multinational corporate social responsibility, ethics, interactions and third world governments: An agenda for the 1990s. *Journal of Business Ethics, 12*(7), 553–572.

Ambos, B., & Håkanson, L. (2014). The concept of distance in international management research. *Journal of International Management, 20*(1), 1–7.

Bangladesh Accord. (2021). *Accord on fire and building safety in Bangladesh.* Accessed May 16, 2021, from https://bangladeshaccord.org/

Bansal, P., & Knox-Hayes, J. (2013). The time and space of materiality in organizations and the natural environment. *Organization & Environment, 26*, 61–82.

Brewer, P. A. (2007). Operationalizing psychic distance: A revised approach. *Journal of International Marketing, 15*(1), 44–66.

Burritt, R. L., Christ, K. L., Rammal, H. G., & Schaltegger, S. (2020). Multinational enterprise strategies for addressing sustainability: The need for consolidation. *Journal of Business Ethics, 164*(2), 389–410.

Carroll, A. B. (1979). A three-dimensional conceptual model of corporate social performance. *Academy of Management Review, 4*, 497–505.

DiMaggio, P. J., & Powell, W. W. (1983). The iron cage revisited: Institutional isomorphism and collective rationality in organizational fields. *American Sociological Review, 48*(2), 147–160.

Diouf, D., & Boiral, O. (2017). The quality of sustainability reports and impression management. *Accounting, Auditing & Accountability Journal, 30*(3), 643–667.

Doh, J. P., & Guay, T. R. (2006). Corporate social responsibility, public policy, and NGO activism in Europe and the United States: An institutional-stakeholder perspective. *Journal of Management Studies, 43*(1), 47–73.

Doh, J. P., Littell, B., & Quigley, N. R. (2015). CSR and sustainability in emerging markets: Societal, institutional, and organizational influences. *Organizational Dynamics, 44*(2), 112–120.

Dow, D., & Karunaratna, A. (2006). Developing a multidimensional instrument to measure psychic distance stimuli. *Journal of International Business Studies, 37*(5), 578–602.

European Commission. (2016). *Non-financial reporting.* Accessed February 13, 2016, from http://ec.europa.eu/finance/company-reporting/non-financial_reporting/index_en.htm

Evans, J., Mavondo, F. T., & Bridson, K. (2008). Psychic distance: Antecedents, retail strategy implications, and performance outcomes. *Journal of International Marketing, 16*(2), 32–63.

Farneti, F. & Rammal, H. G. (2013). Sustainability reporting in the Italian public sector: Motives and influences. *The Seventh Asia Pacific Interdisciplinary Research in Accounting Conference,* Kobe, 26–28 July. Accessed November 28, 2021, from www.apira2013.org/proceedings/pdfs/K137.pdf

Farneti, F., & Siboni, B. (2011). An analysis of the Italian governmental guidelines and of the local governments' practices for social reports. *Sustainability Accounting, Management and Policy Journal, 2*(1), 101–125.

Freeman, R. E. (1984). *Strategic management: A stakeholder approach.* Pitman.

Friedman, M. (1962). *Capitalism and freedom.* University of Chicago Press.

Friedman, M. (1970). A Friedman doctrine – The social responsibility of business to increase its profits. *New York Times.*

Golgeci, I., Makhmadshoev, D., & Demirbag, M. (2021). Global value chains and the environmental sustainability of emerging market firms: A systematic review of literature and research agenda. *International Business Review, 30*(5), 101857.

GRI. (2021). *Global reporting initiative.* Accessed December 20, 2021, from http://database.globalreporting.org/

Hahn, T., Figge, F., Aragon-Correa, J., & Sharma, S. (2017). Advancing research on corporate sustainability: Off to pastures new or back to the roots? *Business & Society, 56*(2), 155–185.

Husted, B. W. (2005). Culture and ecology: A cross-national study of the determinants of environmental sustainability. *Management International Review, 45*(3), 349–371.

Hutzschenreuter, T., Kleindienst, I., & Lange, S. (2014). Added psychic distance stimuli and MNE performance: Performance effects of added cultural, governance, geographic, and economic distance in MNEs' international expansion. *Journal of International Management, 20*(1), 38–54.

Hutzschenreuter, T., Kleindienst, I., & Lange, S. (2016). The concept of distance in international business research: A review and research agenda. *International Journal of Management Reviews, 18*(2), 160–179.

Ike, M., Donovan, J. D., Topple, C., & Masli, E. K. (2021). Corporate sustainability reporting in Japanese multinational enterprises: A threat to local legitimacy or an opportunity lost for corporate sustainability practices? *Multinational Business Review.* https://doi.org/10.1108/MBR-06-2020-0129. ahead-of-print.

ILO. (2021). *The Rana Plaza Accident and its aftermath.* Accessed August 31, 2021, from https://www.ilo.org/global/topics/geip/WCMS_614394/lang%2D%2Den/index.htm

IPCC. (2021). *Climate change 2021: The physical science basis. Contribution of working group I to the sixth assessment report of the intergovernmental panel on climate change* [Masson-Delmotte, V., P. Zhai, A. Pirani, S.L. Connors, C. Péan, S. Berger, N. Caud, Y. Chen, L. Goldfarb, M.I. Gomis, M. Huang, K. Leitzell, E. Lonnoy, J.B.R. Matthews, T.K. Maycock, T. Waterfield, O. Yelekçi, R. Yu, and B. Zhou (eds.)]. Cambridge University Press. In Press.

Johanson, J., & Vahlne, J.-E. (2009). The Uppsala internationalization process model revisited: From liability of foreignness to liability of outsidership. *Journal of International Business Studies, 40*, 1411–1431.

Kolk, A. (2010a). Social and sustainability dimensions of regionalization and (semi)globalization. *Multinational Business Review, 18*(1), 51–72.

Kolk, A. (2010b). Trajectories of sustainability reporting by MNCs. *Journal of World Business, 45*(4), 367–374.

Lee, J. Y., Choi, J., Xiao, S., Lew, Y. K., & Park, B. I. (2021). How do the institutions matter for MNE subsidiaries' CSR in host countries? Evidence from Chinese overseas subsidiaries. *BRQ Business Research Quarterly*, ahead-of-print. https://doi.org/10.1177/23409444211044732

Legislation.Gov.UK (2022). *Equality act 2010.* Accessed January 3, 2022, from https://www.legislation.gov.uk/ukpga/2010/15/contents

Linnenluecke, M. K., & Griffiths, A. (2013). Firms and sustainability: Mapping the intellectual origins and structure of the corporate sustainability field. *Global Environmental Change, 23*(1), 382–391.

Liou, R.-S., & Rao-Nicholson, R. (2021). Multinational enterprises and sustainable development goals: A foreign subsidiary perspective on tackling wicked problems. *Journal of International Business Policy, 4*(1), 136–151.

Liu, S. Y. H., Napier, E., Runfola, A., & Cavusgil, S. T. (2020). MNE-NGO partnerships for sustainability and social responsibility in the global fast-fashion industry: A loose-coupling perspective. *International Business Review, 29*(5), 101736.

Milne, M. J., & Gray, R. (2013). W(h)ither ecology? The triple bottom line, the global reporting initiative, and corporate sustainability reporting. *Journal of Business Ethics, 118*(1), 13–29.

Mouawad, J. (2009, June 8). Shell to pay $15.5 million to settle Nigerian case. *The New York Times.* https://www.nytimes.com/2009/06/09/business/global/09shell.html.

Ojala, A. (2015). Geographic, cultural and psychic distance to foreign markets in the context of small and new ventures. *International Business Review, 24*(5), 825–835.

Rygh, A., Chiarapini, E., & Segovia, M. V. (2021). How can international business research contribute towards the sustainable development goals? *Critical Perspectives on International Business*, ahead-of-print. https://doi.org/10.1108/cpoib-08-2020-0123

Schaltegger, S., & Burritt, R. L. (2010). Sustainability accounting for companies: Catchphrase or decision support for business leaders? *Journal of World Business, 45*(4), 375–384.

Schanberg, S. (1996, June). Six cents an hour. *Life Magazine*: 38–45.

Shapiro, D., Hobdari, B., & Oh, C. H. (2018). Natural resources, multinational enterprises and sustainable development. *Journal of World Business, 53*(1), 1–14.

Shell. (2021). *The history of Shell in Nigeria*. Accessed July 31, 2021, from https://www.shell.com.ng/about-us/shell-nigeria-history.html

Sousa, C. M. P., & Bradley, F. (2005). Global markets: Does psychic distance matter? *Journal of Strategic Marketing, 13*(1), 43–59.

Tagesson, T., Klugman, M., & Ekström, M. L. (2013). What explains the extent and content of social disclosures in Swedish municipalities' annual reports. *Journal of Management & Governance, 17*(2), 217–235.

Tihanyi, L., Griffith, D. A., & Russell, C. J. (2005). The effect of cultural distance on entry mode choice, international diversification, and MNE performance: A meta-analysis. *Journal of International Business Studies, 36*, 270–283.

Tregidga, H., Milne, M. J., & Kearins, K. (2018). Ramping up resistance: Corporate sustainable development and academic research. *Business & Society, 57*(2), 292–334.

United Nations. (2022). *The United Nations Sustainable Development Goals*. Accessed January 3, 2022, from https://sdgs.un.org/goals

WCED. (1987). *Our common future: Report of the World Commission on Environment and Development*. Oxford University Press.

Hussain Gulzar Rammal is Professor of International Business at The University of Adelaide. Hussain is co-editor-in-chief of the Review of International Business and Strategy journal, founding editor of the Emerging Issues in International Business and Global Strategy book series, and the Real Impact Editor (Oceania) for the Journal of Knowledge Management.

Foreign Direct Investment and Human Development

Irina Orbes Cervantes, Hang Dang, and Alex Eapen

Scholars in the area of international business have long been interested in the impact of foreign direct investment (FDI) on host countries (e.g., Caves, 1974). An important body of research on this topic examines whether the presence of FDI in a host country leads to knowledge and productivity spillovers to local firms. Interestingly, while some studies in this "FDI spillover" stream of research have found positive effects of inward FDI on the productivity of domestic firms (e.g., Blomström, 1986; Javorcik, 2004; Kokko et al., 1996), others have documented negative effects (Aitken & Harrison, 1999; Chen et al., 2011; Haddad & Harrison, 1993; Lee & Wie, 2015). This body of research has grown substantially over the past decades, both through more nuanced analyses of moderating conditions (e.g., Du et al., 2014; Eapen, 2012; Jude, 2016; Papaioannou & Dimelis, 2019) and meta-analyses that summarize the overall spillover effect of inward FDI on host-country firms (Bruno & Cipollina, 2018; Gorg & Strobl, 2001; Luo et al., 2019; Meyer, 2004; Meyer & Sinani, 2009).

Despite the extensive literature on FDI effects, however, studies in this stream of work collectively describe only a narrow sliver of the effect inward FDI exerts on host countries. Their focus is almost solely on the economic consequences—specifically, productivity benefits (or costs)—for domestic firms. Broader effects of FDI on human development have received comparatively less attention (Kolk, 2016). Human development comprises the education, health, and income opportunities available to people in a country (United Nations Development Program [UNDP], 2015b). It is fundamental to human well-being and constitutes the bedrock of freedom and opportunity for any human population (Streeten, 1999; UNDP, 2015b). Further, over 689 million poor people today live in inadequate and extremely poor human development conditions (World Bank, 2020). Despite the undeniable importance of human development for host-country populations, it is

I. O. Cervantes · H. Dang · A. Eapen (✉)
Research School of Management, Australian National University, Canberra, Australia
e-mail: irina.orbes@anu.edu.au; hang.dang@anu.edu.au; alex.eapen@anu.edu.au

© Springer Nature Switzerland AG 2022
H. Merchant (ed.), *The New Frontiers of International Business*, Contributions to Management Science, https://doi.org/10.1007/978-3-031-06003-8_19

reasonable to say that the international business literature has largely bypassed the issue of how FDI impacts human development in host countries.

Fortunately, some work in the development economics literature has attended to this issue. These studies have generally found a positive association between FDI and human development (Arcelus et al., 2005; Lehnert et al., 2013; Reiter & Steensma, 2010; Sharma & Gani, 2004; Stiglitz, 2006). There are, however, also findings suggestive of negative consequences, for example, on wages in the host country (Chen et al., 2011; Lee & Wie, 2015; Pan-Long, 1995). In general, however, studies in this stream have tended to be one-sided—they highlight either benefits or costs of FDI, giving short shrift to the "net (positive and negative) effect" of FDI on human development.

Taken together, in order to better understand the effect of FDI on host countries, two areas of further progress deserve good attention. First, FDI spillover research ought to go beyond its focus on how FDI affects domestic firms' productivity; the broader effect of FDI on human development in host countries is too important to ignore. Second, a more balanced approach to the effect of FDI on human development—one that simultaneously considers both positive and negative effects—is necessary. Such a conceptualization will help nudge current theoretical frameworks on the human development impact of FDI to a closer reflection of reality.

Our goal in this chapter is to contribute in both these ways. We explore the effect of inward FDI on human development while integrating its positive and negative effects. *First*, we suggest that while FDI can indeed enhance human development in a host country, it can also exert a negative effect by worsening income inequality (Basu & Guariglia, 2007; Chen et al., 2011; Chintrakarn et al., 2012; Choi, 2006; Herzer et al., 2014; Johansson & Liu, 2020; Lee & Wie, 2015; Pan-Long, 1995) and economic insecurity (Bachmann et al., 2014; Dill & Jirjahn, 2016; Scheve & Slaughter, 2004). These, in turn, lead to unequal access to capabilities that underpin human development (Coelli, 2011; Melamed & Samman, 2013). *Second*, given the opposing positive and negative effects of FDI on human development, we propose that the net effect of FDI is likely curvilinear. Inward FDI, as just suggested, can be a positive force for human development; but any such benefit will likely also taper off at higher levels of FDI. Further, alongside these diminishing marginal benefits, FDI increases income inequality and economic insecurity in the host country. This negative effect, eventually, will outweigh the positive benefits of FDI. The resulting pattern of the relationship between FDI and human development, we hence suggest, will be inverted U-shaped. This formulation encompasses the full range of effects that FDI exerts on human development. *Third*, we examine how ambient institutional settings in the host country play a role in conditioning the effect of FDI on human development. This section of our chapter proposes institutional environment as an important contingency factor in the relationship between FDI and human development.

To test our hypotheses, we collected data from multiple sources on FDI, human development, and other macroeconomic variables and merged them together. Our resulting dataset, as we describe in more detail later, is at the country-year level and consists of 139 countries over the period 2000–2014.[1] Employing fixed-effects panel data methods, we find that inward FDI does have an inverted U-shaped relationship with human development in a host country. This result is robust to more precise methods of testing inverted U-shaped relationships (cf. Haans et al., 2016) and to alternative measurement and model specifications. Furthermore, consistent with our core narrative, we also find evidence that the inverted U-shaped effect of FDI on human development is more pronounced in countries with weak institutions. Taken together, these multiple lines of evidence lend credibility to our core argument for how FDI impacts human development.

This chapter makes three core contributions to knowledge. *First*, as mentioned before, the FDI spillover literature in international business has primarily focused on the productivity impact of inward FDI on domestic firms. Our study broadens this focus to encompass the consequences of FDI for social well-being (indicated by human development) in the host country. *Second*, our research adds to development economics scholars' analysis of human development. We simultaneously consider the benefits and costs of FDI for human development and provide a framework that integrates both positive and negative effects into a *curvilinear* relationship between the two. We also examine the conditioning effect of ambient institutional settings in the host country. Our *third* contribution is an empirical one. Teasing out the effect of FDI on human development is fraught with identification challenges. While we cannot claim to have eliminated all such challenges, we take the approach of seeking out multiple sources of confirmation for our core thesis. We use current best practice methods for testing curvilinear relationships, test additional hypotheses (on the impact of host-country institutions) that should also be true given our core storyline, and test the sensitivity of our results to measurement and model specifications. Empirically, therefore, we rest our findings not on a single analysis but on multiple lines of confirmation. This multipronged search for evidence helps progress empirical identification of the innately complex effect of FDI on human development.[2]

---

[1] The mechanisms we propose and test are on the relationship between FDI and HDI. As such, what matters more for our core argument is not so much the recency of the dataset than whether we have sufficient cross-country variation in both variables to allow us to correctly estimate the relationship. Furthermore, given the mechanisms underlying the relationship between FDI and HDI are time period-insensitive, they should extrapolate very well to more recent time periods as well.

[2] As we do acknowledge again at the end of this chapter, empirically identifying the causal effect of FDI on human development from secondary data is extremely challenging. While we pursue multiple tests of our core argument in our dataset (and find confirmation), we acknowledge that our empirical approach is not foolproof. Notwithstanding this caveat, our conceptual arguments and multiple lines of empirical confirmation point in the same direction. Collectively, this confers reasonable plausibility to our findings.

1   Past Literature

1.1   FDI Spillovers and Host-Country Productivity

The literature on FDI spillovers has mainly focused on knowledge spillovers from foreign to domestic firms in a host country and on subsequent productivity improvements for the latter (De Mello, 1999; Eapen, 2013; Gorg & Strobl, 2001; Javorcik, 2004; Meyer & Sinani, 2009). The key premise in this literature is that foreign firms in a host country are sources of useful knowledge and conduits for the transfer of this knowledge to domestic firms (Buckley et al., 2002; Jindra et al., 2009; Jude, 2016; Liu, 2008). The presence of collocated foreign firms gives local firms the opportunity to learn by interacting with and observing the advanced technologies of foreign firms. This, in turn, could allow domestic firms to upgrade their technology, upskill their employees, and acquire new knowledge (Buckley et al., 2002; Kemeny, 2010; Perri & Peruffo, 2016). A recent review of knowledge spillover has developed an analytical framework that integrates both micro- and macro-level antecedents of spillovers. This review analyzed three different constructs—magnitude, speed, and scope—and highlights the importance of internal and external networks as well as role of social and political context in activating the flow of knowledge (Perri & Peruffo, 2016).

FDI spillovers are not limited only to flows of technical knowledge. There have been studies on spillovers on managerial knowledge from foreign to domestic firms, inclusive of both tacit and explicit elements of management practices of foreign MNEs (Fu, 2012). FDI spillovers also emanate from foreign MNEs' research and development (R&D) and export-focused activities in the host country (Hejazi & Safarian, 1999; Jefferson et al., 2006; Wei & Liu, 2006). Spillover studies have also emphasized how FDI can amplify host-country competition which, in turn, can help improve domestic firm efficiency, innovation, and productivity (Marcin, 2008). A substantial number of studies have conceptually and empirically explored these themes and analyzed how FDI inflows into a host country lead to improvements in efficiency, innovation, and productivity for domestic firms (Caves, 1974; Eapen, 2012; Fu, 2012; Javorcik, 2004; Jefferson et al., 2006; Liu et al., 2000; Marcin, 2008). Furthermore, studies have also investigated contingency factors such as host countries' institutions and technical absorptive capacity to explain variations observed across firms and contexts in spillover effects (Du et al., 2014; Sánchez-Sellero et al., 2014; Wang et al., 2013).

Another group of studies has highlighted the importance of carefully treating the heterogeneity in FDI that could arise from its motivation, nature, tenure, and origin (Aitken & Harrison, 1999; De Mello, 1999; Zhang et al., 2014). For example, Driffield and Love (2007) have observed that FDI motivation predicted its various effects on host countries' domestic productivity. One way to classify FDI motivation is into technology "exploiting" and "sourcing." Technology-exploiting FDI includes the class of foreign firms that possess an "ownership" advantage—usually, superior technology or capital stock quality—and exploit this ownership advantage in the host country (Driffield & Love, 2007). Technology-sourcing FDI refers to the class of foreign firms that bring in limited technology to the host country but, instead, is motivated by the need to acquire knowledge from the host country. Driffield and Love's (2007) results suggest that technology-exploiting FDI has positive spillovers on the host country's productivity, while technology-sourcing FDI leads to no productivity spillovers. Similarly, Ha and Giroud (2015) address whether competence-creating or competence-exploiting activities by foreign MNEs influence FDI spillovers on host country's firms and find that competence-creating activities of MNEs generate positive technology spillovers. Exploring further types of heterogeneity in FDI, Zhang et al. (2010) examine the diversity of FDI country origins on domestic firms' productivity and find that diversity can facilitate FDI spillovers by increasing the variety of technology and management practices that foreign firms introduce into the host country.

Several meta-analytic studies have served to synthesize findings in this literature. Gorg and Strobl (2001), through a large meta-analysis, conclude that there is a positive relationship between FDI and productivity spillovers (Gorg & Strobl, 2001). Meyer and Sinani (2009) apply competitive dynamics theory in their meta-analysis and observe a curvilinear relationship between FDI spillovers and the host country's development level in terms of income, institutional framework, and human capital. Although studies in this stream of work have become increasingly sophisticated, it remains true that scholars have primarily studied FDI's effect on domestic firms and left its broader social consequences comparatively unexplored.

1.2   FDI and Host-Country Socioeconomic Development

A related set of studies have also examined the effects of foreign firms on macro-economic features of host countries. These features have included its economic development (Borensztein et al., 1998; Cipollina et al., 2012; Yamin & Sinkovics, 2009), human capital, human rights, and child labor (Buller & McEvoy, 1999; Kolk & Van Tulder, 2004; Neumayer & de Soysa, 2005; Wettstein et al., 2019). Some studies in this stream have also examined whether FDI enhances human development (Arcelus et al., 2005; Lehnert et al., 2013; Oetzel & Doh, 2009; Reiter & Steensma, 2010; Sharma & Gani, 2004). The general conclusion from this collection of studies is that FDI is positively correlated with human development.

This is true even in more nuanced analyses that consider interaction effects between FDI inflows and host-country FDI policy. Sharma and Gani (2004) have found a positive correlation between FDI and human development for middle- and low-income countries. Other studies have attempted to better understand this relationship by examining mediation and moderation effects. Lehnert et al. (2013) conclude that the positive relationship between FDI and human development is mediated by the quality of national governance. Similarly, Reiter and Steensma (2010) have found this relationship to be moderated by FDI policy and strongest when FDI policy restricts foreign investors from entering certain economic sectors. This study has also observed this relationship to be moderated by host-country corruption and strongest when corruption is low. Similarly, Stiglitz (2006) has documented a positive relationship between FDI and human development, with the strength of that relationship depending on the government's capability to regulate the right balance between itself and the markets.

However, there is also evidence for negative consequences of FDI inflows into a country. Within the FDI spillover literature, for example, Aitken and Harrison (1999) find that foreign firms negatively affect domestic firms' productivity. They point to increased competition and crowding out as responsible mechanisms. Further, scholars in development economics have raised concerns over wage inequality (Aitken et al., 1996; Aitken & Harrison, 1999; Feenstra & Hanson, 1997; Figini & Gorg, 2011; Wu & Hsu, 2012) and economic insecurity effects (Bachmann et al., 2014; Dill & Jirjahn, 2016; Scheve & Slaughter, 2004) of FDI. They argue that higher levels of FDI can raise wages for skilled workers, but not for low-skilled workers (Figini & Gorg, 2011; Herzer et al., 2014), and worsen labor market volatility and insecurity (Scheve & Slaughter, 2004).

1.3   The Role of Human Development

While the economic effects of globalization and foreign capital have received ample attention from scholars, their effects on people have been, relatively speaking, overlooked (Streeten, 1999). That is not to say that there has been complete disregard for the issue. Some recent studies have indeed examined the relationship between different predictors of human development. For example, Sharma and Gani (2004) have studied the influence of FDI on socioeconomic progress (which includes human development) and concluded that a positive correlation exists between FDI and human development. In addition, this study also found that FDI has a higher positive effect on human development in middle-income countries (Sharma & Gani, 2004).

There have also been studies that examine the relationship between human development and economic growth. Naturally, economic growth provides resources that facilitate sustained human development improvement (Ranis et al., 2000). Accordingly, studies have found a strong positive relationship between economic growth and human development. In particular, Ranis et al. (2000) highlight the importance of government expenditure on health and education, which in turn boosts human development. Studies have also identified a reverse link between human development and economic growth, whereby increased human development increases national income (Ranis et al., 2000). So, all considered, there is a mutual reinforcing upward spiral exists between economic growth and human development—high levels of economic growth lead to high levels of human development (Ranis et al., 2000) and vice versa. Similarly, Anand and Sen (2000) have observed a positive relationship between economic sustainability and human development.

Nevertheless, FDI effects are not always positive. Studies have increasingly demonstrated that FDI has negative effects (Haddad & Harrison, 1993); for example, Aitken and Harrison (1999) have found that foreign firms negatively affect domestic firms' productivity and suggested that increasing competition in the domestic market causes a crowding-out effect for domestic firms (Aitken & Harrison, 1999). Further, economic scholars have progressively raised concerns over growing inequality. While FDI may offer benefits to the economy in which they locate, it is unclear whether the majority of individuals will benefit to the same extent (Figini & Gorg, 2011). FDI has been found to have a strong positive relationship with wage inequality (Aitken et al., 1996; Aitken & Harrison, 1999; Feenstra & Hanson, 1997; Figini & Gorg, 2011). These studies have examined FDI and its association with higher wages for skilled workers, concluding that FDI affects the income and employments prospects of less skilled workers (Figini & Gorg, 2011; Herzer et al., 2014). This generates a rising demand for skilled workers, causing their wages to rise and thus causing income and wage inequality to deteriorate (Aitken et al., 1996). In addition, the extent to which FDI causes inequality may depend on FDI motivation and the host country's capabilities to absorb the effects. FDI focused on high technology may flow more toward economies with high educational levels, further contributing to the development of human capital in these economies (Basu & Guariglia, 2007; Blomström et al., 2003). Conversely, economies with low levels of initial human capital may attract asset-exploiting FDI, which plays a smaller role in the future development of these economies (Blomström et al., 2003).

The positive and negative potential effects of inward FDI, thus, have certainly featured in past work. But their treatment has largely been fragmented with positive and negative effects emphasized in different pockets of the literature. Moreover, the net effect (both positive and negative) of FDI on human development has not received much attention. Given these gaps, there is value in a conceptual framework that simultaneously models both the positive and negative consequences of FDI for human development. This is what our research aims to do.

2   FDI and Human Development

2.1   Benefits of FDI for Human Development

Inward foreign direct investment can potentially support human development in a host country through three mechanisms: (i) greater employment and income, (ii) greater revenue received by the government, and (iii) foreign firms' technology diffusion. Such growth drivers collectively contribute to the host country's greater national economic competitiveness and human development (Borensztein et al., 1998; Ranis et al., 2000).

FDI increases demand for employees, often expanding labor force participation in the host country (Feenstra & Hanson, 1997). This increased demand, in turn, results in higher income for workers. Although income is potentially spent on a range of different things, it also trickles down to factors associated with human development (e.g., education and health (Ranis et al., 2000)). Indeed, higher income has been positively related to more years spent at school and a higher average education threshold (Brückner & Gradstein, 2013). Higher income also enables members of the host country's population to invest in their own and their family's education. This also enables individuals to undertake higher level skilled employment or to launch their own companies (Spender, 2013). Higher income is also associated with health improvements (Bloom & Canning, 2000), as individuals tend to spend a larger share of their income on healthcare and improving their living standards. As a result, human development improves (Acemoglu et al., 2013).

A second potential effect of FDI is increased government tax revenues. This could allow governments to increase investment and public spending in the host country (Basu et al., 2003) and allocate resources to activities that contribute to human development. These could include investments in the host country's social infrastructure to improve education, health, subsistence, and support for the unemployed (Ranis et al., 2000).

The third channel through which inward FDI can improve human development in a host country is technology diffusion. MNEs, with a broader network of subsidiaries spanning the globe, often possess firm-specific advantages in a variety of business areas such as strategy, innovation, technology, or management practices. These valuable practices can spill over to domestic firms and, as a result, enhance their efficiency and technology (Blomström & Kokko, 1998; Eapen & Krishnan, 2019; Jindra et al., 2009; Kemeny, 2010; Liu, 2008). This technology diffusion, in turn, can be an important conduit of economic development and growth (Borensztein et al., 1998), translate into better healthcare and education access (Blomström et al., 2003; Borensztein et al., 1998; Walz, 1997), and, eventually, result in improvements in human development (Ranis et al., 2000).

The positive effects of FDI on human development, however, are unlikely to monotonically increase. Early gains in human development are comparatively easier to attain than later ones. That is, getting some quick runs on the board when current human development standards are low is relatively easier. Some improvements in basic education, health, and economic infrastructure will usually suffice. However, as human development standards of a population improve, achieving even further improvements becomes relatively harder. As an example, providing basic education and healthcare facilities when they do not already exist is comparatively easier than providing higher-end versions of such facilities (e.g., specialist healthcare and world-class education) that improve on what already exists. By this token, even if FDI exerts a positive effect on human development in a host country (as we describe above), the magnitude of this effect is likely greater at low levels of preexisting human development in a host country. Improvements are still possible at high levels of preexisting human development, but the same quantum of improvement will likely come only from much greater FDI inflows. The marginal improvement in human development from FDI, therefore, is likely nonlinear; it tapers off with additional inward FDI into a host country.

2.2   Costs of FDI for Human Development

While FDI brings benefits to the host country, evidence also suggests that these benefits are not always evenly distributed within the country; some individuals benefit considerably more than others from such opportunities (Acosta et al., 2011; Figini & Gorg, 2011). In addition, FDI can create labor market volatility that results in economic insecurity in workers (Scheve & Slaughter, 2004). Although foreign firms may require workers of all types, excessive demand for those with advanced technical or managerial capabilities may mean that these workers are paid dispro-portionately more (Johansson & Liu, 2020). For example, highly skilled and educated professionals (who may be in short supply) are more likely to reap the most benefit. This, in turn, widens the skilled-unskilled income gap and deepens income inequality (Chen et al., 2011; Gopinath & Chen, 2003; Herzer et al., 2014; Lee & Wie, 2015; Wu & Hsu, 2012).

In parallel, FDI also raises economic insecurity among workers (Bachmann et al., 2014;Dill & Jirjahn, 2016 ; Scheve & Slaughter, 2004). Given the fact that foreign-owned firms can shift production to other locations and substitute their labor consumption in response to wage fluctuations, their presence is usually correlated with higher labor demand elasticities (Andrews et al., 2012; Fabbri et al., 2003) and increased labor market volatility. This volatility manifests itself in higher turnover rate among multinational firms (Fabbri et al., 2003) and a substitution of irregular jobs in place of regular ones (Kim & Lee, 2015). As a net result of high elasticities of labor demand, high turnover, and fewer regular jobs in multinational firms, workers in these firms experience a higher degree of economic insecurity (Dill & Jirjahn, 2016; Scheve & Slaughter, 2004).

Both income inequality and economic insecurity are consequential for human development. For example, high-income earners gain better access to healthcare, while those at the lower end of the income distribution are constrained in their access (Subramanian & Kawachi, 2004; Wilkinson & Pickett, 2006). Educational attainment is also negatively affected (Mayer, 2000; Organization for Economic Cooperation and Development, 2014; Stewart & Samman, 2014). The gap between low- and high-income earners results in a variation between their children's educa-tion levels, with low-income individuals facing limited capacity to invest in educa-tion (Haveman & Smeeding, 2006; Ostry et al., 2014). Additionally, income inequality escalates the cost of high-quality education—it elevates the cost of attending college far more for low-income students than for high-income students (Haveman & Smeeding, 2006). And most disconcerting, income inequality has a contagion effect in that it is transferred to subsequent generations (Melamed & Samman, 2013). It has particularly negative consequences for poorer children's educational outcomes and college graduation rates (Haveman & Smeeding, 2006).

Economic insecurity has similar negative effects on human development. Eco-nomically insecure workers experience a significant increase in stress levels, anxiety, and minor psychiatric disorders (Ferrie et al., 2002; Rugulies et al., 2008). As a result, economic insecurity has been found to be related to poor well-being and life satisfaction (Silla et al., 2009). There is also a negative relationship between economic insecurity and education. Parental job losses during children's high school have a significant detrimental effect on their subsequent enrollments in university and community college (Coelli, 2011). Job losses result in poorer mental health, lower adolescent academic performance, and falling class attendance, especially among students from low-income families (Ananat et al., 2017).

It is reasonable also to expect that the human development costs of FDI increase at an accelerating rate. At higher levels of inward FDI, competition intensifies among (the now many) foreign firms in the host country for high-skilled workers. Income is driven even higher for those few people, further worsening income inequality between low- and high-skilled workers in the host country. Heightened competition for labor between foreign firms also accelerates the economic insecurity effect, with more jobs now being at risk of substitution or relocation by foreign firms. The negative human development consequences we outlined above are therefore amplified by a greater multiple when there are high levels of FDI in the country. In sum, the human development cost of inward FDI increases but an increasing rate, with the level of FDI in the host country.

2.3   The "Net" Effect of FDI on Human Development

It is clear from the above discussion that inward FDI can exert both positive and negative forces on human development in a host country. However, while the positive effects increase at a decreasing rate with inward FDI, the negative effects are likely to increase at an increasing rate. Taking together latent effects of this nature, it is likely that the net effect of FDI on human development will be curvilinear (Haans et al., 2016). At low levels of inward FDI, the marginal benefit from an increase in FDI for human development overshadows its marginal cost. The net effect of FDI on human development will thus be positive. But as inward FDI increase into the country, not only do the positive effects of FDI taper off, but its negative consequences also rapidly increase. Eventually, at higher levels of FDI, the marginal human development benefit from an increment in FDI will trail behind its marginal cost. And with every additional influx of FDI generating greater marginal costs than benefits, the relationship between FDI and human development will likely turn negative.

Taken together, the overall effect of FDI on human development will not be uniform but vary with existing levels of inward FDI already in the host country. At low levels of inward FDI, the net effect of FDI on human development will be positive, and at high levels of inward FDI, it will be negative. Figure 1 visually depicts the essence of this argument.

Hypothesis 1 (H1) There will be an inverted U-shaped relationship between inward FDI in a host country and its level of human development.

Hypothesis 1 embodies the core proposition in this chapter. However, as part of our empirical identification strategy, we develop additional hypotheses that also derive from this core argument. Our intuition is that empirical support for multiple hypotheses that are derivative of the same core thesis offers confidence in the above curvilinear link between FDI and human development.

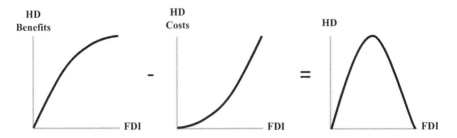

Fig. 1 Graphical representation of H1 on the effect of FDI on human development (HD). Source: figure created by authors

3   FDI, Host-Country Institutions, and Human Development

If FDI exerts a curvilinear effect on human development in a host country, what ambient institutional conditions might strengthen or weaken this effect? We suggest that the curvilinear relationship we propose between FDI and human development will flex with the quality of institutions in the host country. Any inverted U effect will be flatter when the latent benefits and costs accumulate slowly and steeper when the latent forces accumulate at a faster rate (Haans et al., 2016). The rate at which benefits and costs of FDI for human development increase, we argue below, varies with the quality of institutions in the host country. As such, the curvilinear effect we propose (in Hypothesis 1) will steepen for host countries with weak institutions but flatten for those with strong institutions.

Institutions effectively define accepted business practices (i.e., the "rules of the game") in commerce and industry (Mair et al., 2012). Institutions are crucial to shaping and supporting the markets in which domestic and foreign firms interact (Campbell & Lindberg, 1990; De Soto, 2000; Greif, 2006; Sen, 1999). At the organizational level, institutions create and manage the existing rules that determine MNEs' actions and strategies in the host country (DiMaggio & Powell, 1983). At an aggregate level, institutions play an important role in economic growth and the norms and accepted business practices that determine economic development (Webb et al., 2009). Therefore, it is important to understand and analyze how institutions channel FDI and, in turn, the expectations of MNEs and the business practices they implement (Banerjee & Duflo, 2011). Yet there is considerable variation across different economies regarding the extent to which institutions might be present and strong or absent and weak. Strong institutions connote an environment in which domestic players are already established and have secure regulations for businesses in the private sector and the transparent public sector. In this environment, new players become a part of an existing system and, as they are thus less likely to shape these markets, are more likely to comply with existing business rules and transparent regulations. Conversely, weak or absent institutions create an environment in which economies experience lack of knowledge and opportunities and relatively uncontrolled market systems (Crow, 2001; Mair et al., 2012; Rodrik, 2008), as a result of

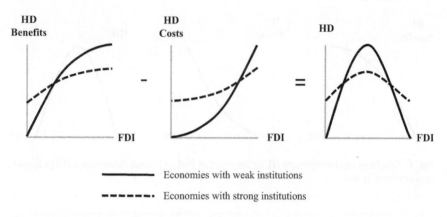

Fig. 2 Graphical representation of H2 and H3 on the moderated effects of FDI on human development (HD). Source: figure created by authors

their limited clarity or transparency of expected business practices and regulations. Thus, new entrants have far greater latitude to be active participants that serve as agents of change (Kwok & Tadesse, 2006).

When public and private sector institutions are well developed in a host country, there is relatively less room for the human development benefits of FDI to make a difference. Governments in these countries have already made progress on education and healthcare and typically display good governance. Given this progress that strong institutions have already brought about, the human development benefits of FDI will likely be at the margins. In low-quality host-country institutional settings, on the contrary, there is ample room for FDI to play a prominent role (e.g., D'Amelio et al., 2016). Given the vacuum in institutional mechanisms that uplift human development, the human development benefits of FDI assume prominence. (As an analogy, turning on a lamp makes a negligible difference in a room that has good ambient lighting but significantly brightens up a room with poor lighting. The lamp in the analogy denotes FDI and ambient lighting the host country's institutions). The human development benefit from a given increment in inward FDI, hence, will be weaker in host countries with strong private and public institutions and more pronounced in those with weak institutions. We represent this in Fig. 2 with a benefit curve that is steeper for countries with weak institutions and flatter for those with strong institutions.

The same is true when it comes to the cost side of FDI for human development. We contend that strong host-country institutions play a buffering role and shield the local population from negative consequences. More precisely, strong local institutions help soften the inequality and insecurity-driven effects of FDI on human development. The income gap between skilled and unskilled workers and economic insecurity can be remedied with government benefits allocated to those in need. In contrast, in countries with weak local institutions, there is likely only limited buffer that institutions can offer to the economically marginalized. (To continue with the earlier lamp analogy, turning on a lamp can also have a negative "blinding effect" on peoples' eyes. This blinding effect will be stronger if ambient lighting is poor and buffered against when ambient lighting is good). The human development cost from a given increase in FDI in a host country (just as in the case of its benefits) will hence be more pronounced when ambient institutions are weak and softer when host-country institutions are strong. This is represented in Fig. 2 as a steeper cost curve for countries with weak institutions and a flatter curve for those with strong institutions.

In our empirical exercise, we consider both private and public forms of institutions. We use the term "business sophistication" to represent the quality of institutions, practices, and business environment in the private sector. This includes a country's overall business networks and the quality of individual firms' operations and strategies (World Economic Forum, 2015). And for public sector institutions, we use "transparency" as a proxy for public sector institutions and regulations. Transparency refers to the extent to which government employees are held accountable for administrative decisions and their use of funds and resources (World Bank, 2016). We treat economies with low levels of business sophistication and transparency to have weak local (private and public) institutions. In contrast, economies with high business sophistication and high transparency possess strong local institutions.

In summary, if our core argument in Hypothesis 1 is true, then we should also expect—based on our arguments in this section—the human development benefits and costs of FDI to be more pronounced (i.e., steeper) for countries with weak public and private institutions. This translates to a steeper inverted U effect for these countries. Figure 2 represents this prediction. Given our proxies for private and public institutions (business sophistication and transparency, respectively), we propose:

Hypothesis 2 (H2) The inverted U-shaped relationship between FDI and human development will be steeper for countries with low business sophistication and flatter in countries with high business sophistication.

Hypothesis 3 (H3) The inverted U-shaped relationship between FDI and human development will be steeper in countries with a low transparency and flatter in countries with a high transparency.

4   Data and Methodology

4.1   Data and Sample

Our empirical approach aims to explore the extent to which cross-country variations in human development can be attributed to differences in foreign direct investment across countries. Since the measure for our dependent variable—human development—is available only at the country-year level, we are forced to situate our empirical work at the "country-year" level of analysis. We constructed a database comprising variables from various sources. Measures of human development (the dependent variable) and its components (education index, health index, and income per capita) came from the UNDP (2015a), measures of foreign investment (the independent variable) came from the United Nations Conference on Trade and Development [UNCTAD] (2016), and measures of institutional quality (business sophistication and transparency index) came from the World Economic Forum (2016) and the World Bank's World Development Indicators (World Bank, 2016). Finally, we also collected data on control variables from the International Monetary Fund (2016). We merged data from these different sources and arrived at an unbalanced country-year panel that includes 139 countries over 15 years (2000–2014).

4.2   Measures

Dependent Variable We used a country's score on the UNDP Human Development Index (HDI) as our indicator of its level of human development. This index incorporates three important aspects of human well-being: a long and healthy life, knowledge, and a decent standard of living (UNDP, 2015b). A long and healthy life is captured by life expectancy at birth, the ability to acquire knowledge is measured by mean years of schooling and expected years of schooling, and the ability to achieve a decent standard of living is represented using by gross national income (GNI) per capita. HDI is an unweighted average of these three dimensions (UNDP, 2015b) and, thereby, reflects *both* economic and social dimensions of human development.

Independent Variables Our key independent variable, FDI, was measured using FDI stock in a host country at its book value (historical cost). This measure represents the dollar value of inward investments at the time it was made. We used a cumulative measure of FDI inflows (which allows us to explore the cumulative, long-term, effect of FDI). As part of our robustness tests, we also used variants of this measure: FDI inflows, inward FDI stock as a percentage of GDP (inward FDI stock/GDP), and FDI inflows distinguished by source countries of origin.

We used country scores on the "business sophistication" and "transparency" indices published by the World Economic Forum to represent the quality of private and public institutions in a host country (World Economic Forum, 2016). Business sophistication represents two linked elements: the quality of a country's overall business networks and the quality of individual firms' operations and strategies (World Economic Forum, 2015). The quality of business networks and supporting industries reflects the quantity and quality of local suppliers in a country and the extent of their interaction. The measure represents sophisticated and modern business processes across the country's business sectors (World Economic Forum, 2015). The index takes the form of a 6-point scale, with 1 representing low business sophistication and 6 denoting high sophistication.

The World Bank's Transparency index incorporates ratings on three dimensions of public sector governance. The first is executives' accountability to overseeing institutions and public sector employees' accountability and performance. The second is civil society's access to information about public affairs. And the third is the extent to which the state is captured by narrow vested interests. The index takes the form of a 6-point scale, with 1 representing low transparency and 6 denoting high transparency. The transparency index is part of the Country Policy and Institutional Assessment database of the World Bank (2016).[3]

Control Variables Foreign aid is considered an important source of foreign funding for human development and economic growth (Bourguignon & Platteau, 2017; Gomanee et al., 2005; Kosack & Tobin, 2006). The UNDP (2015b) has pointed out that foreign donors significantly contribute to achieving greater human development. Hence, we included this as a control variable in our models. The data we used represent the net bilateral aid flows from Development Assistance Committee (DAC) donors. In other words, these amounts are the net disbursements of official development assistance or official aid from DAC members. Net disbursements are gross payments of grants and loans minus repayments of principal on earlier loans. This data came from the World Bank's World Development Indicators (World Bank, 2016).

Some countries have increasingly relaxed trade barriers and allowed more inward FDI as part of their growing interconnectivity with the global market. Trade openness could affect human development via two different paths. First, countries begin exporting more, boosting economic growth and income. Second, trading allows countries to gain knowledge, expertise, and technology (Cooray et al., 2014). We controlled for trade openness with a measure of each country's total imports plus total exports (Figini & Gorg, 2011). This data came from the World Development Indicators (World Bank, 2016) and was included in our models as a percentage of GDP (in order to take into account country size).

Government savings have also been considered a determinant of human development; countries with higher savings tend to have better human and economic performance (Caceres & Caceres, 2015). In particular, the importance of savings has been demonstrated in a comparison made by Dayal-Ghulati and Thimann (1997) between South East Asia and Latin America, revealing that regions with greater savings improved their development. In our study, we hence controlled for gross national savings (as a percentage of GDP). We sourced this data from the International Monetary Database (International Monetary Fund, 2016).

Gross national expenditure is the amount of money the government and the population expend in the host country. Governments' spending on social infrastructure (e.g., hospitals, schools) facilitates better systems for, and access to, basic human needs, thus improving human development. Second, increased expenditure from the population means that people have more opportunities to earn and spend on

---

[3] The data files from the World Economic Forum and The World Bank contain missing values on both "business sophistication" and "transparency" variables. In our examination, there is a systematic pattern in the missing observations whereby values on both business sophistication and transparency variables are missing predominantly for high-income countries. We discuss the possible implications of this in our "robustness checks" section later in the paper.

education to develop their capabilities (Kottaridi & Stengos, 2010). The data represent the sum of household final consumption expenditure, general government final consumption expenditure, and gross capital formation. This construct was measured in US dollars, and the data were extracted from the World Development Indicators (World Bank, 2016).

Finally, GDP has been shown to lead to better human development (Ranis et al., 2000). The variable we use represents GDP at purchasers' prices and is the sum of gross value added by all resident producers in the economy plus any product taxes less any subsidies not included in the products' value. It was calculated without making deductions for depreciation of fabricated assets or for depletion and degradation of natural resources. The data were sourced from the World Development Indicators and expressed in US dollars. Dollar figures for GDP were converted from domestic currencies using 2005 official exchange rates (World Bank, 2016).

4.3   Methodology

To test our hypotheses, we used ordinary least squares (OLS) estimation with fixed effects. We tested for the relative benefit of fixed versus random effects using the Hausman test and, based on this, chose to employ a fixed-effects model. The advantage of using fixed effects is that it accounts for time-invariant unobserved heterogeneity across countries. After all, countries may not only differ in terms of their systematic societal characteristics but also feature varying growth paths because of prolonged differences in technological progress (Binder & Georgiadis, 2010). Generally, in panel data analysis, the fixed-effects model assumes that each country differs in its intercept term (Ranjan & Agrawal, 2011). We also used a lagged structure across the model to allow for a better test of the causal relationship. Our main set of analyses is based on estimations of the following equation:

$$HDI_{it} = \beta_0 + \beta_1 \text{Inward FDI}_{it-1} + \beta_2 (\text{Inward FDI}_{it-1})^2 + \text{Controls}_{it-1} + \alpha_i + u_{it-1}.$$

In the above, subscripts i and t are country and year identifiers, α_i denotes country fixed effects, and u_{it-1} is the country-year specific error term. Based on H1, we expect the coefficient of inward FDI (β_1) to be positive and significant and the coefficient of inward FDI squared (β_2) to be negative and significant. These would indicate an inverted U-shaped relationship between inward FDI and human development. To test H2, we estimate an equation of the form:

$$HDI_{it} = \beta_0 + \beta_1 \text{Inward FDI}_{it-1} + \beta_2 (\text{Inward FDI}_{it-1})^2 + \beta_3 \text{Bus.Sophistication}_{it-1}$$
$$+ \beta_4 \text{Inward FDI}_{it-1}{}^* \text{Bus.Sophistication}_{it-1}$$
$$+ \beta_5 (\text{Inward FDI}_{it-1})^{2*} \text{Bus.Sophistication}_{it-1} + \text{Controls}_{it-1} + \alpha_i + u_{it-1}.$$

Given H2 predicts that the inverted U-shaped effect of FDI on human development will be flatter at high levels of business sophistication in the host country, we expect β_5 in the above equation to be positive. This is because Haans et al. (2016: 1187) suggest that "...testing for flattening or steepening is equivalent to testing whether [the coefficient of the interaction term between the moderator and the quadratic term of the main variable] is significant. A flattening occurs for inverted U-shaped relationships when [this coefficient] is positive... Conversely, a steepening occurs for inverted U-shaped relationships when [this coefficient] is negative." Similarly, to test H3, we estimated the following equation and take a positive β_8 as confirmation for our prediction in H3.

$$HDI_{it} = \beta_0 + \beta_1 Inward\ FDI_{it-1} + \beta_2 \left(Inward\ FDI_{it-1}\right)^2 + \beta_6 Transparency_{it-1}$$
$$+ \beta_7\ Inward\ FDI_{it-1}{}^* Transparency_{it-1}$$
$$+ \beta_8 \left(Inward\ FDI_{it-1}\right)^{2^*} Transparency_{it-1} + Controls_{it-1} + \alpha_i + u_{it-1}$$

After estimating the above equations, we also followed the three-step procedure recommended by Haans et al. (2016) to accurately test inverted U-shaped relationships. Haans et al. (2016) present three criteria that need to be met for a precise test of a U-shaped relationship. First, the coefficient for inward FDI (β_1) needs to be positive and significant, while the coefficient of its squared term (β_2) is negative and significant. Second, the slope of our estimated inverted U-shaped curve needs to be sufficiently steep at both low and high values of FDI. We tested for this by taking two points at low and high ends of our FDI variable (FDI_L and FDI_H) and examining the slope of the estimated curve at both these points. We calculated the slope of the curve at the lowest point of FDI (i.e., at FDI_L) using the expression $Slope_{FDIL} = \beta_1 + 2\beta_2 FDI_L$ and, that at the highest value of FDI (i.e., at FDI_H) using $Slope_{FDIH} = \beta_1 + 2\beta_2 FDI_H$. Finally we calculated the turning point using the following equation $-\beta_1/2\beta_2$. As we report below, all three criteria for a more precise verification of an inverted U-shaped effect were satisfied in our analyses.

Furthermore, in robustness tests, we accounted for possible path dependency in human development. We employed dynamic panel data estimation using general methods of moments (GMM). Dynamic panel data GMM models extend the OLS fixed-effects model by including lagged values of the dependent variable.

5 Results

5.1 Main Results

Table 1 reports summary statistics and correlations for the variables we use in our analyses. The correlations between some variables are high, indicating that multicollinearity might be a problem. Examining variance inflation factors confirmed that the variables GDP and government expenditure are collinear. While we still include these variables in our main analyses, we also ran additional analyses that excluded the collinear variable government expenditure. The results provided support for an inverted U-shaped relationship between inward FDI and human

Table 1 Descriptive statistics and correlations

	Mean	Standard deviation	(1) Human development	(2) Inward FDI stock	(3) Business soph.	(4) Transparency	(5) Foreign aid	(6) Trade openness	(7) Gov. savings	(8) Gov. expenditure	(9) GDP
(1) *Human development*	0.54	0.10	1.00	–	–	–	–	–	–	–	–
(2) *Inward FDI stock*	1.33	3.40	0.14	1.00	–	–	–	–	–	–	–
(3) *Business sophistication*	3.49	0.39	0.11	0.57	1.00	–	–	–	–	–	–
(4) *Transparency*	2.90	0.51	0.10	0.21	0.09	1.00	–	–	–	–	–
(5) *Foreign aid*	0.08	0.09	−0.14	0.35	0.29	0.07	1.00	–	–	–	–
(6) *Trade openness*	77.94	34.93	0.39	−0.07	−0.18	0.03	−0.18	1.00	–	–	–
(7) *Government savings*	20.04	11.31	0.32	0.30	0.17	0.35	0.13	0.18	1.00	–	–
(8) *Government expenditure*	6.75	23.33	0.08	0.94	0.56	0.22	0.26	−0.18	0.25	1.00	–
(9) *Gross Domestic Product (GDP)*	6.44	22.12	0.08	0.94	0.57	0.21	0.27	−0.18	0.26	0.99	1.00

Notes: Examining variance inflation factors suggested potential multicollinearity due to the inclusion of the variables government expenditure and GDP. As a precaution, thus, we ran all our analyses with and without government expenditure and our empirical results remained the same
Source: Table compiled by authors

development; so our core findings are robust to the inclusion (or exclusion) of this potentially problematic variable.

Table 2 reports our main results on the effect of inward FDI stock on human development. Model 1 includes only control variables, while model 2 includes FDI and its squared term to test our hypothesis of an inverted U-shaped effect. Models 3 and 4 include variables to test interaction effects, i.e., how the main inverted U-shaped FDI effect varies with the quality of host country institutions. As reported in model 2, we find a main effect of FDI that is positive and significant and a squared effect that is negative and significant. This offers preliminary confirmation for Hypothesis 1.

As mentioned above, we also conducted the three-step procedure suggested by Haans et al. (2016) to test the inverted U-shaped relationship between FDI and human development. First, as we have seen in model 2 in Table 2, the main effects of inward FDI stock and inward FDI stock squared coefficients are statistically significant and of the expected sign. Second, as we report in Table 3 (model 1), slope of our estimated inverted U-shaped curve is positive and significant at low levels of FDI ($\beta = 0.005$, $p < 0.001$). Also, the slope is negative and significant at high levels of FDI ($\beta = -0.004$, $p < 0.001$). This satisfies the second criterion in Haans et al.'s test. Third, the turning point of the inverted U-shaped curve is located well within the range of our FDI variable. Taken together, these results provide further evidence in support of an inverted U-shaped relationship between FDI and human development.

Our results also indicate that countries with low business sophistication exhibit a steeper inverted U-shaped curve between FDI and human development, while those with high business sophistication exhibit a flatter curve (Hypothesis 2). The coefficient of the interaction term between inward FDI stock squared and business sophistication in model 3 of Table 2 is positive and significant. As per Haans et al.'s (2016) directive, this suggests a flattening of the inverted U-shaped curve when business sophistication in the host country is high. These results suggest support for Hypothesis 2.

We also find in model 4 of Table 2 that the coefficient of the interaction term between inward FDI stock squared and transparency is positive and significant. Using Haans et al.'s interpretation, this suggests that countries with low transparency exhibit a steeper inverted U-shaped relationship between FDI and human development. Conversely, countries with high transparency displayed a flatter relationship. This finding renders support for Hypothesis 3.

5.2 Additional Analyses

We conducted several additional tests to assess the robustness of our results to different measurement and model specifications. As the contribution of our work is centered on the inverted U-shaped effect of FDI on HDI, we focused our robustness tests on validating this aspect of our analysis.

The Human Development Index comprises of a country's scores on three different dimensions—education, health, and income. We first examined whether our

Table 2 Fixed-effects analysis: main and moderated effects of FDI on human development

Variables	Model 1	Model 2	Model 3	Model 4
Main effects				
Inward FDI stock		0.005***	0.019***	0.109***
		(0.000)	(0.003)	(0.018)
Inward FDI stock squared		−0.000***	−0.000**	−0.011***
		(0.000)	(0.000)	(0.003)
Institution effects				
Business sophistication			0.024***	
			(0.004)	
Inward FDI stock x bus sophistication			−0.004***	
			(0.001)	
Inward FDI stock sq x bus sophistication			0.000**	
			(0.000)	
Transparency				0.012**
				(0.004)
Inward FDI stock x transparency				−0.028***
				(0.006)
Inward FDI stock sq x transparency				0.003***
				(0.001)
Controls				
Foreign aid	0.126***	0.066***	0.019*	0.022
	(0.027)	(0.015)	(0.009)	(0.013)
Trade openness	0.001***	0.000**	0.000	0.000
	(0.000)	(0.000)	(0.000)	(0.000)
Government savings	0.001***	0.001***	−0.000**	0.000
	(0.000)	(0.000)	(0.000)	(0.000)
Government expenditure	0.005***	0.000	0.000	−0.001
	(0.001)	(0.001)	(0.001)	(0.002)
GDP	−0.003***	−0.000	0.000	0.004
	(0.001)	(0.001)	(0.001)	(0.002)
Constant	0.513***	0.574***	0.532***	0.453***
	(0.007)	(0.005)	(0.015)	(0.014)
Observations	1040	916	512	351
Country no.	131	130	82	60
Fixed effects	Incl.	Incl.	Incl.	Incl.

Notes: (a) $*p < 0.05$, $**p < 0.01$, $***p < 0.001$. Standard errors in parentheses. (b) All independent and control variables were included with a 1-year lag. (c) The sample is an unbalanced panel data that includes up to 139 countries over a period of 14 years which explains the different number of observations in each model. (d) We ran variance inflation factors and confirmed potential collinearity between GDP and government expenditure. Therefore, we ran additional analyses that excluded the variable government expenditure. Our core findings are robust to the inclusion (or exclusion) of this potentially problematic variable
Source: Table compiled by authors

Table 3 Testing for the existence of an inverted U-shaped relationship (Haans et al., 2016)

	Model 1	Model 2	Model 3
Slope:			
Inward FDI stock			
Slope at lowest point	0.005***	0.019***	0.109***
	(11.58)	(5.99)	(5.944)
Slope at the highest point	−0.004***	−0.021*	−0.378***
	(−7.131)	(−2.145)	(−3.298)
Data range			
Inward FDI stock			
Extremum point	48.354	39.253	5.076
95% confidence interval	[43.261–54.195]	[29.752–73.977]	[3.591–8.599]
Lowest point	0.000	0.000	0.000
Highest point	83.288	83.288	22.655
Appropriate inverted U test:	7.13***	2.15*	3.3***

Notes: (a) *p < 0.05, **p < 0.01, ***p < 0.001. (b) Model (1) in this table is based on estimated coefficients for inward FDI stock and its squared term from model 2 in Table 2. Models (2) and (3) in this table are based on estimated coefficients for the two variables from models 3 and 4, respectively, in Table 2. (c) t-values are in parentheses
Source: Table compiled by authors

hypothesized inverted U-shaped effect holds even if we look at the effect of FDI on each of these individual components. The results are in Table 4. The coefficients for FDI and its squared term in models 1, 2, and 3 confirm an inverted-U effect (as in our main set of results) even when we look at components of the HDI index and not the aggregated index itself.

Second, we tested the sensitivity of our results to alternative measures of FDI. Our main results are based on a stock measure of FDI. In this set of robustness tests, we replaced this measure with FDI inflows and FDI stock as a percentage of GDP (FDI stock/GDP). Further, since we treated FDI from all sources are equal in our main analyses, we also explored whether the source of origin of FDI would make a difference in our hypothesized effects. In particular, we distinguished between FDI from developed and developing economies. The results are presented in Table 5. We find that the inverted U-shaped effect is confirmed irrespective of the way we measure inward FDI. As models 1 and 2 show, the main effects of FDI inflows and FDI stock/GDP are positive and statistically significant ($\beta = 0.026, p < 0.001$; $\beta = 0.002, p < 0.001$), while the effects of FDI inflows squared and FDI stock/GDP squared are negative and statistically significant ($\beta = -0.003, p < 0.001$; $\beta = -0.000, p < 0.001$). Equally, as models 3 and 4 show, the inverted-U effect persists for both FDI from developed and developing countries, albeit with a stronger effect in the case of the former. The results of these robustness tests are largely immune to whether or not we also include business sophistication or transparency in our models.

Third, since there could be path dependencies by which HDI in a given year is partly dependent on its values in the previous year, we sought to account for this in

Table 4 Robustness test—nonlinear effects of FDI on dimensions of human development

	Model 1	Model 2	Model 3
	Education index	Health index	GNI per capita
Main effects			
Inward FDI stock	0.010***	0.004***	368.147***
	(0.001)	(0.001)	(26.684)
Inward FDI stock sq	−0.000***	−0.000***	−3.348***
	(0.000)	(0.000)	(0.289)
Controls			
Foreign aid	0.294***	0.059**	579.7
	(0.055)	(0.019)	(874.932)
Trade openness	0.001***	0.000**	−15.436***
	(0.000)	(0.000)	(3.107)
Government savings	0.001**	0.000*	43.175***
	(0.000)	(0.000)	(7.188)
Government expenditure	−0.002	0.000	−51.695
	(0.002)	(0.001)	(39.336)
GDP	0.002	0.000	57.757
	(0.002)	(0.001)	(34.299)
Constant	0.456***	0.681***	7797.103***
	(0.011)	(0.006)	(277.764)
Observations	623	913	939
Country no.	115	137	137
Fixed effects	Incl.	Incl.	Incl.

Notes: (a) * $p < 0.05$, ** $p < 0.01$, *** $p < 0.001$. (b) All independent and control variables were included with a 1-year lag
Source: Table compiled by authors

our analyses. Including a lagged value of HDI in our models, however, necessitates the use of dynamic panel data models. We used GMM system with lagged independent variables—with up to 3-year lags—as instruments (Arellano & Bond, 1991). We also included year dummies as a regressor. The results are presented in Table 6. We find that the inverted U-shaped effect is confirmed as model 1 shows the main effect of inward FDI stock is positively and statistically significant ($\beta = 0.001$, $p < 0.05$), while the effect of inward FDI stock squared is negative and statistically significant ($\beta = -0.000$, $p < 0.05$).

When applying GMM models, there are two post-estimation tests that determine the validity of a model. These tests are (i) the Hansen test to determine whether the instruments are correctly specified and (ii) the Arellano-Bond to test for no second-order correlation [AR(2)]. As reported in Table 6, the values we obtain for both these post-estimation tests imply no concerns about the validity of our instruments or serial correlation.

Finally, we closely examined the drop in sample size in models 3 and 4 in Table 2 where we include interaction terms with business sophistication and transparency.

Table 5 Robustness test—nonlinear effects of FDI (measured as inflows, inward FDI stock/GDP, inward FDI stock from developed and developing economies, respectively) on human development

	Model 1	Model 2	Model 3	Model 4
Main effects				
FDI inflows	0.026***			
	(0.004)			
FDI inflows squared	−0.003***			
	(0.000)			
Inward FDI stock/GDP		0.002***		
		(0.000)		
Inward FDI stock /GDP squared		−0.000***		
		(0.000)		
Inward FDI stock from developed economies			0.006***	
			(0.001)	
Inward FDI stock sq from developed economies			−0.000***	
			(0.000)	
Inward FDI stock by developing economies				0.002*
				(0.001)
Inward FDI stock sq by developing economies				−0.000***
				(0.000)
Controls				
Foreign aid	0.069***	0.063***	0.031**	0.104***
	(0.016)	(0.015)	(0.011)	(0.022)
Trade openness	0.000*	0.000**	0.000	0.000
	(0.000)	(0.000)	(0.000)	(0.000)
Government savings	0.000**	0.001***	−0.000	−0.000
	(0.000)	(0.000)	(0.000)	(0.000)
Government expenditure	−0.000	0.002***	0.001*	0.002***
	(0.001)	(0.001)	(0.001)	(0.000)
GDP	0.001	−0.001**	−0.001	−0.000
	(0.001)	(0.001)	(0.000)	(0.000)
Constant	0.577***	0.544***	0.614***	0.606***
	(0.005)	(0.006)	(0.006)	(0.006)
Observations	904	915	570	584
Country no.	128	129	119	120
Fixed effects	Incl.	Incl.	Incl.	Incl.

Notes: (a) $*p < 0.05$, $**p < 0.01$, $***p < 0.001$. (b) All independent and control variables were included with a 1-year lag

Source: Table compiled by authors

Table 6 Robustness test—generalized method of moments (GMM) of non-linear main effects of FDI on human development		Model 1
	Dependent variable	
	Human development $_{t-1}$	0.867***
		(0.048)
	Independent variables	
	Inward FDI stock	0.001*
		(0.001)
	Inward FDI stock sq	−0.000*
		(0.000)
	Controls	
	Foreign aid	0.016
		(0.019)
	Trade openness	0.000
		(0.000)
	Government savings	−0.000
		(0.000)
	Government expenditure	0.000
		(0.000)
	GDP	−0.000
		(0.000)
	Constant	0.088**
		(0.011)
	Observations	613
	Country no.	93
	Number of instruments	35
	Arellano-Bond test for second-order serial correlation AR(2)	
	Z	−0.03
	Pr > z	0.973
	Hansen test of overidentifying restrictions	
	Chi2	31.83
	Prob > chi2	0.131

Notes: (a) *$p < 0.05$, **$p < 0.01$, ***$p < 0.001$. Standard errors in parentheses. (b) Model (1) in this table refers to the dynamic panel model on the inverted U-shaped relationship between Inward FDI stock and human development. (c) The instruments that have been included in this dynamic model are all the independent variables and controls lagged 1 to 3. (d) We used GMM system. We control for year effects as dynamic data models requires their inclusion
Source: Table compiled by authors

The reason sample size drops in those models, as we alluded to earlier, is due to missing values on our "business sophistication" and "transparency" variables. As the first step in our investigation into this, we confirmed that values that were missing our sample were also missing in the source data. In other words, the missing observations were not due to any data transformations we employed in our analyses but, rather, missing at source in the files we obtained from the World Economic

Forum (2016) and World Bank (2016). As our next step, we examined whether there is any systematic pattern in our missing data. Unfortunately, there is. Values on both business sophistication and transparency variables are missing predominantly for high-income countries. Armed with this information, and as the third step in our investigation, we considered the potential effect of this on our results. There is surely a restricted range of values for business sophistication and transparency that we use in our analyses. High-income countries are also likely to have high values on business sophistication and transparency. As such, our analyses in models 3 and 4 are based on a limited range of values for both moderator variables. Does this bias our findings? We suggest that the limited range of values available for our analyses only renders our moderator tests conservative. If our moderator hypotheses are correct, they will easily show through in a dataset with the full range of values for our moderator variables. Not having the full range of values sets the bar high for us to find any support for our moderator hypotheses. The pattern in our missing data works against us finding support for our moderator hypotheses. We interpret this to mean that (while it would have been ideal to have a dataset with no missing values) the drop in sample size in models 3 and 4 is likely a benign problem. The drop arose due to values on our moderator variables being missing in the official source files (and not just in our sample) and biases our analyses against us finding support for our moderator hypotheses. Our tests for hypotheses 2 and 3 are, therefore, more conservative than usual.

6   Discussion

This research in this chapter was motivated by the need to better understand how FDI affects human development. This matters as human development reflects the well-being and breadth of choices and opportunities available to the population in a country. As noted earlier, prior research has primarily studied FDI's effect on economic growth, domestic productivity, and knowledge spillovers. While these studies have been crucial to understand the economic effects of FDI on host countries, our work extends scholarly analysis to its social effects as well. Moreover, to our knowledge, our work is novel in terms of integrating the potential positive and negative effects of FDI on human development into a curvilinear conceptualization.

Our discussion and empirical observations in this chapter present important findings. First, our theory and empirics suggest that FDI has an inverted U-shaped relationship with human development. At modest levels of FDI, it assists with human development. Yet, as the level of FDI increases in a host country, not only do the benefits for human development taper off, but negative effects also prominently manifest themselves. Thus, FDI might improve human development through positive impacts on the host country's economic growth and income; but, eventually, that improvement might not be reflected in individuals' lives and development since FDI also increases income inequality.

A second key finding to emerge from our discussion and empirical tests is that the positive and negative effects of FDI for human development depend on the quality of private and public institutions in the host country. We exploited the variation across countries in their institutional quality to examine how private and public institutions affect the relationship between FDI and human development. Our results show that countries with weak institutions experience a steeper inverted U-shaped curve between FDI and human development. In other words, these economies are more likely to experience the benefits that enhance human development, as well as the higher human development costs that come with too much FDI. Conversely, countries with high-quality institutions have a flatter inverted U-shaped curve. They experience moderate benefits and costs from FDI for human development. Existing good governance and mature institutions in these countries not only renders the positive effects of FDI redundant but also buffers against its negative consequences.

6.1   Reverse Causality: Does FDI Follow HDI Instead?

A legitimate concern to consider is that our results, contrary to our assertions, merely reflect the phenomenon of FDI seeking out host locations on the basis of human development. In other words, rather than FDI influencing human development in a host country, our results could instead be the result of human development attracting or dissuading FDI investments in the host country. While this reverse causality appears to be a plausible alternative explanation, there are two reasons that strengthen our confidence in our argument.

First, if human development is indeed influencing the level of FDI in a host country, it is likely that inward FDI will be relatively high in contexts of both high and low human development. Countries with high human development, by virtue of their high disposable incomes of consumers, will attract "market-seeking" FDI. Countries with low human development too, by virtue of low wages and low-cost production bases, will attract "resource-seeking" inward FDI. The net effect of FDI chasing human development locations, hence, will likely be a U-shaped—and not inverted U-shaped—relationship between the two. Market-seeing FDI will be disproportionately attracted to high human development locations and resource-seeking FDI to low human development locations. Our theory instead proposes an inverted U-shaped relationship between inward FDI and human development. Our prediction, therefore, is incompatible with a logic based on the reverse influence of human development on inward FDI. If our arguments too had led to a U-shaped hypothesis, then the reverse causal logic would have been a viable alternative explanation.

Second, our argument in this paper that inward FDI influences human development yielded both a main effect hypothesis and two interaction effect hypotheses. Our empirical results are consistent with these. If reverse causality logic is to be a viable alternative explanation, it should explain not only our main effect finding but also our interaction effects. Our main effect result (of an inverted U), as we explain above, is not consistent with the argument that human development determines the levels of inward FDI in a country (which would be a U-shaped effect). But additionally, there are two other interaction effect predictions in our work that are also consistent with our argument that FDI has an effect on human development. If the reverse argument that FDI flows to locations with certain levels of human development is true, logically, that effect should be amplified by the host country's business sophistication and transparency. Market-seeking and resource-seeking FDI should find it easier to enter desirable locations when local business conditions are sophisticated and government interactions are transparent. Yet, we find the opposite. We find empirically that business sophistication and transparency weaken our (inverted U-shaped) relationship between FDI and human development.

In sum, the threat of reverse causality being a viable alternative explanation for our results is weak. The predictions that emerge from a reverse causality story are not only contrary to the predictions from our narrative (that the direction of causality is from FDI to human development) but are also inconsistent with the results we find.

6.2   Policy Implications

Our findings in this chapter carry important implications for policymakers. Our key result is that FDI will be likely to boost human development in host countries yet also weaken their economies via associated costs such as inequality and economic insecurity. As such, the first core implication of our work for policymakers is that they need be cautious in their approach to FDI (Luo et al., 2019). At the very least, it is important to be alert to monitoring the resulting benefits and costs for human development that arise from welcoming FDI into the country. Hoping for a magic bullet—i.e., for FDI to continually deliver positive gains—is likely wishful thinking.

Second and relatedly, policymakers may need to pay particular attention to those sections of the population that are likely to be negatively affected by FDI. On the basis of our arguments around the economic inequality and insecurity effects of FDI, these sections are likely to be unskilled or casual workers. These groups disproportionately bear the burden of the economic costs of FDI. Accordingly, policymakers should endeavor to provide social safety nets, labor retraining, and reskilling in order to reduce FDI costs to human development.

Third, our study also emphasizes the critical importance of the ambient institutional context. In economies with weak institutions, MNEs are likely to contribute toward human development. At the same time, however, these economies are also most exposed to the income inequality consequences that come with higher levels of FDI. The key lesson from this for policymakers is that effort should be expended on local institution-building in parallel to increasing inflows of FDI. In other words, there is a need for strong local institutions to buffer a host country's populace from the potential human development costs of "too much" FDI.

Fourth, our findings also provide suggestions for policymakers on how to manage FDI inflows in a way that maximizes its benefits to human development. A call to unconditionally accelerate inward FDI into the host country may not always be the best approach; the related human development cost of FDI needs to be borne in mind. A moderate amount of FDI (i.e., around the inflection point of the inverted

U-shaped curve) is likely where maximum human development benefits can be realized. Additional inward FDI will most likely result in human development reductions, unless local institutions can be strengthened to buffer against these reductions. Part of these institutional development initiatives could include policymakers redistributing the social benefits of FDI to those vulnerable to inequality and job insecurity and creating more equal opportunities for those in need by leveraging government taxation of FDI. Taken together, our results also speak to ongoing debates around the gains and pains from globalization. When both the benefits and costs of FDI on a host economy are simultaneously considered, the prescription would be that globalization can be beneficial to an extent. To prolong these benefits in a host economy, ambient institutions need to be strong enough to shield vulnerable sections of the population from being economically displaced.

7   Limitations and Future Research

As with any empirical study, ours too has limitations. The limitations of this study arise primarily from the data used in our analysis. First, since the Human Development Index is available only at the country level, we restricted our analysis to the country-year level. Finer levels of analyses (e.g., the region, or city level) were not feasible. Second, we have not fully distinguished between the different types of inward FDI into a country. The differing nature of FDI may have an effect on human development. For instance, asset-seeking and asset-exploiting types of FDI may generate demand for different pools of skilled and unskilled labor. This, in turn, may interfere with the mechanisms we have proposed. Studies that are able to distinguish the effects of different types of FDI (e.g., based on entry modes, whether FDI is largely asset or technology-seeking or asset or technology-exploiting, etc.) might provide a more nuanced understanding of the human development effects of FDI.

In addition, while we argue above that the restricted range of values in our data on "business sophistication" and "transparency" variables only render our hypotheses tests to be more stringent than usual, it would be useful for future research to explore other possible proxies for institutional quality in the host country. Corroborative evidence to ours that uses alternative measures (that do not suffer from missing data like ours) will be useful.

Finally, we acknowledge that empirically identifying the effect of FDI on human development is a challenging task. Nonetheless, we have presented in this paper a collection of material to investigate the relationship—i.e., our conceptual reasoning for an inverted U-shaped effect (that is amplified by weak institutions), our empirical evidence that corroborates these predictions, and the resilience of our results to a variety of alternative measurement and model specifications. These collectively suggest that there are human development benefits and costs from inward FDI in a host country that likely have the "net effect" that is inverted U-shape.

References

Acemoglu, D., Finkelstein, A., & Notowidigdo, M. J. (2013). Income and health spending: Evidence from oil price shocks. *Review of Economics and Statistics, 95*(4), 1079–1095.

Acosta, P., Kim, N., Melzer, I., Mendoza, R. U., & Thelen, N. (2011). Business and human development in the base of the pyramid: Exploring challenges and opportunities with market heat maps. *Journal of World Business, 46*(1), 50–60.

Aitken, B. J., & Harrison, A. E. (1999). Do domestic firms benefit from direct foreign investment? Evidence from Venezuela. *American Economic Review, 89*(3), 605–618.

Aitken, B., Harrison, A., & Lipsey, R. E. (1996). Wages and foreign ownership: A comparative study of Mexico, Venezuela, and the United States. *Journal of International Economics, 40*(3–4), 345–371.

Ananat, E. O., Gassman-Pines, A., Francis, D. V., & Gibson-Davis, C. M. (2017). Linking job loss, inequality, mental health, and education. *Science, 356*(6343), 1127–1128.

Anand, S., & Sen, A. (2000). Human development and economic sustainability. *World Development, 28*(12), 2029–2049.

Andrews, M., Bellmann, L., Schank, T., & Upward, R. (2012). Foreign-owned plants and job security. *Review of World Economics, 148*(1), 89–117.

Arcelus, F. J., Sharma, B., & Srinivasan, G. (2005). Foreign capital flows and the efficiency of the HDI dimensions. *Global Economy Journal, 5*(2), 1–12.

Arellano, M., & Bond, S. (1991). Some tests of specification for panel data: Monte Carlo evidence and an application to employment equations. *The Review of Economic Studies, 58*(2), 277–297.

Bachmann, R., Baumgarten, D., & Stiebale, J. (2014). Foreign direct investment, heterogeneous workers and employment security: Evidence from Germany. *Canadian Journal of Economics, 47*(3), 720–757.

Banerjee, A. V., & Duflo, E. (2011). *Poor economics: A radical rethinking of the way to fight global poverty*. Public Affairs.

Basu, P., Chakraborty, C., & Reagle, D. (2003). Liberalization, FDI, and growth in developing countries: A panel cointegration approach. *Economic Inquiry, 41*(3), 510–516.

Basu, P., & Guariglia, A. (2007). Foreign direct investment, inequality, and growth. *Journal of Macroeconomics, 29*(4), 824–839.

Binder, M., & Georgiadis, G. (2010). *Determinants of human development: Insights from state-dependent panel models* (UNDP-HDTO Occasional Papers No. 2010/24).

Blomström, M. (1986). Foreign investment and productive efficiency: The case of Mexico. *The Journal of Industrial Economics, 35*(1), 97–110.

Blomström, M., & Kokko, A. (1998). Multinational corporations and spillovers. *Journal of Economic Surveys, 12*(3), 247–277.

Blomström, M., Kokko, A., & Mucchielli, J.-L. (2003). The economics of foreign direct investment incentives. In R. Lipsey & H. Herrmann (Eds.), *Foreign direct investment in the real and financial sector of industrial countries* (pp. 37–60). Springer.

Bloom, D. E., & Canning, D. (2000). The health and wealth of nations. *Science, 287*(5456), 1207–1209.

Borensztein, E., De Gregorio, J., & Lee, J.-W. (1998). How does foreign direct investment affect economic growth? *Journal of International Economics, 45*(1), 115–135.

Bourguignon, F., & Platteau, J. P. (2017). Does aid availability affect effectiveness in reducing poverty? A review article. *World Development, 90*, 6–16.

Brückner, M., & Gradstein, M. (2013). *Income and schooling*. Discussion Paper No. 9365. Centre for Economic Policy Research.

Bruno, R. L., & Cipollina, M. (2018). A meta-analysis of the indirect impact of foreign direct investment in old and new EU member states: Understanding productivity spillovers. *The World Economy, 41*(5), 1342–1377.

Buckley, P. J., Clegg, J., Wang, C., & Cross, A. R. (2002). FDI, regional differences and economic growth: Panel data evidence from China. *Transnational Corporations, 11*(1), 1–28.

Buller, P. F., & McEvoy, G. M. (1999). Creating and sustaining ethical capability in the multi-national corporation. *Journal of World Business, 34*(4), 326–343.

Caceres, L. R., & Caceres, S. A. (2015). Financing investment in sub-Saharan Africa: Savings, human development, or institutions? *The Journal of Developing Areas, 49*(4), 1–23.

Campbell, J. L., & Lindberg, L. N. (1990). Property rights and the organization of economic activity by the state. *American Sociological Review, 55*(5), 634–647.

Caves, R. E. (1974). Multinational firms, competition, and productivity in host-country markets. *Economica, 41*(162), 176–193.

Chen, Z., Ge, Y., & Lai, H. (2011). Foreign direct investment and wage inequality: Evidence from China. *World Development, 39*(8), 1322–1332.

Chintrakarn, P., Herzer, D., & Nunnenkamp, P. (2012). FDI and income inequality: Evidence from a panel of US states. *Economic Inquiry, 50*(3), 788–801.

Choi, C. (2006). Does foreign direct investment affect domestic income inequality? *Applied Economics Letters, 13*(12), 811–814.

Cipollina, M., Giovannetti, G., Pietrovito, F., & Pozzolo, A. F. (2012). FDI and growth: What cross-country industry data say. *The World Economy, 35*(11), 1599–1629.

Coelli, M. B. (2011). Parental job loss and the education enrollment of youth. *Labour Economics, 18*(1), 25–35.

Cooray, A., Mallick, S., & Dutta, N. (2014). Gender-specific human capital, openness and growth: Exploring the linkages for South Asia. *Review of Development Economics, 18*(1), 107–122.

Crow, B. (2001). *Markets, class and social change: Trading networks and poverty in rural South Asia.* Springer.

D'Amelio, M., Garrone, P., & Piscitello, L. (2016). Can multinational enterprises light up developing countries? Evidences from the access to electricity in sub-Saharan Africa. *World Development, 88*, 12–32.

Dayal-Ghulati, A., & Thimann, C. (1997). *Saving in Southeast Asia and Latin America compared: Searching for policy lessons* (IMF Working Paper WP/97/110).

De Mello, L. R. (1999). Foreign direct investment-led growth: Evidence from time series and panel data. *Oxford Economic Papers, 51*(1), 133–151.

De Soto, H. (2000). *The mystery of capital: Why capitalism triumphs in the west and fails everywhere else.* Basic Civitas Books.

Dill, V., & Jirjahn, U. (2016). Foreign owners and perceived job insecurity: Evidence from linked employer-employee data. *International Journal of Manpower, 37*(8), 1286–1303.

DiMaggio, P., & Powell, W. W. (1983). The iron cage revisited: Collective rationality and institutional isomorphism in organizational fields. *American Sociological Review, 48*(2), 147–160.

Driffield, N., & Love, J. H. (2007). Linking FDI motivation and host economy productivity effects: Conceptual and empirical analysis. *Journal of International Business Studies, 38*(3), 460–473.

Du, L., Harrison, A., & Jefferson, G. (2014). FDI spillovers and industrial policy: The role of tariffs and tax holidays. *World Development, 64*, 366–383.

Eapen, A. (2012). Social structure and technology spillovers from foreign to domestic firms. *Journal of International Business Studies, 43*(3), 244–263.

Eapen, A. (2013). FDI spillover effects in incomplete datasets. *Journal of International Business Studies, 44*(7), 719–744.

Eapen, A., & Krishnan, R. (2019). Transferring tacit know-how: Do opportunism-safeguards matter for firm boundary decisions? *Organization Science, 30*(4), 715–734.

Fabbri, F., Haskel, J. E., & Slaughter, M. J. (2003). Does nationality of ownership matter for labor demands? *Journal of the European Economic Association, 1*(2–3), 698–707.

Feenstra, R. C., & Hanson, G. H. (1997). Foreign direct investment and relative wages: Evidence from Mexico's maquiladoras. *Journal of International Economics, 42*(3), 371–393.

Ferrie, J. E., Shipley, M. J., Stansfeld, S. A., & Marmot, M. G. (2002). Effects of chronic job insecurity and change in job security on self reported health, minor psychiatric morbidity, physiological measures, and health related behaviours in British civil servants: The Whitehall II study. *Journal of Epidemiology and Community Health, 56*(6), 450–454.

Figini, P., & Gorg, H. (2011). Does foreign direct investment affect wage inequality? An empirical investigation. *The World Economy, 34*(9), 1455–1475.

Fu, X. (2012). Foreign direct investment and managerial knowledge spillovers through the diffusion of management practices. *Journal of Management Studies, 49*(5), 970–999.

Gomanee, K., Girma, S., & Morrissey, O. (2005). Aid, public spending and human welfare: Evidence from quantile regressions. *Journal of International Development, 17*(3), 299–309.

Gopinath, M., & Chen, W. (2003). Foreign direct investment and wages: A cross-country analysis. *Journal of International Trade & Economic Development, 12*(3), 285–309.

Gorg, H., & Strobl, E. (2001). Multinational companies and productivity spillovers: A meta-analysis. *The Economic Journal, 111*(475), 723–739.

Greif, A. (2006). Family structure, institutions, and growth: The origins and implications of Western corporations. *The American Economic Review, 96*(2), 308–312.

Ha, Y. J., & Giroud, A. (2015). Competence-creating subsidiaries and FDI technology spillovers. *International Business Review, 24*(4), 605–614.

Haans, R. F., Pieters, C., & He, Z. L. (2016). Thinking about U: Theorizing and testing U-and inverted U-shaped relationships in strategy research. *Strategic Management Journal, 37*(7), 1177–1195.

Haddad, M., & Harrison, A. (1993). Are there positive spillovers from direct foreign investment? Evidence from panel data for Morocco. *Journal of Development Economics, 42*(1), 51–74.

Haveman, R., & Smeeding, T. (2006). The role of higher education in social mobility. *The Future of Children, 16*(2), 125–150.

Hejazi, W., & Safarian, A. E. (1999). Trade, foreign direct investment, and R&D spillovers. *Journal of International Business Studies, 30*(3), 491–511.

Herzer, D., Hühne, P., & Nunnenkamp, P. (2014). FDI and income inequality—Evidence from Latin American economies. *Review of Development Economics, 18*(4), 778–793.

International Monetary Fund. (2016). *World economic outlook.* https://www.imf.org/en/Data

Javorcik, B. S. (2004). Does foreign direct investment increase the productivity of domestic firms? In search of spillovers through backward linkages. *The American Economic Review, 94*(3), 605–627.

Jefferson, G. H., Bai, H., Guan, X., & Yu, X. (2006). R&D performance in Chinese industry. *Economics of Innovation and New Technology, 15*(4–5), 345–366.

Jindra, B., Giroud, A., & Scott-Kennel, J. (2009). Subsidiary roles, vertical linkages and economic development: Lessons from transition economies. *Journal of World Business, 44*(2), 167–179.

Johansson, A. C., & Liu, D. (2020). Foreign direct investment and inequality: Evidence from China's policy change. *The World Economy, 43*(6), 1647–1664.

Jude, C. (2016). Technology spillovers from FDI. Evidence on the intensity of different spillover channels. *The World Economy, 39*(12), 1947–1973.

Kemeny, T. (2010). Does foreign direct investment drive technological upgrading? *World Development, 38*(11), 1543–1554.

Kim, H.-H., & Lee, H. (2015). Different types of liberalization and jobs in South Korean firms. *East Asian Economic Review, 19*(1), 71–97.

Kokko, A., Tansini, R., & Zejan, M. C. (1996). Local technological capability and productivity spillovers from FDI in the Uruguayan manufacturing sector. *The Journal of Development Studies, 32*(4), 602–611.

Kolk, A. (2016). The social responsibility of international business: From ethics and the environment to CSR and sustainable development. *Journal of World Business, 51*(1), 23–34.

Kolk, A., & Van Tulder, R. (2004). Ethics in international business: Multinational approaches to child labor. *Journal of World Business, 39*(1), 49–60.

Kosack, S., & Tobin, J. (2006). Funding self-sustaining development: The role of aid, FDI and government in economic success. *International Organization, 60*(01), 205–243.

Kottaridi, C., & Stengos, T. (2010). Foreign direct investment, human capital and non-linearities in economic growth. *Journal of Macroeconomics, 32*(3), 858–871.

Kwok, C. C., & Tadesse, S. (2006). The MNC as an agent of change for host-country institutions: FDI and corruption. *Journal of International Business Studies, 37*(6), 767–785.

Lee, J.-W., & Wie, D. (2015). Technological change, skill demand, and wage inequality: Evidence from Indonesia. *World Development, 67*, 238–250.

Lehnert, K., Benmamoun, M., & Zhao, H. (2013). FDI inflow and human development: Analysis of FDI's impact on host countries' social welfare and infrastructure. *Thunderbird International Business Review, 55*(3), 285–298.

Liu, Z. (2008). Foreign direct investment and technology spillovers: Theory and evidence. *Journal of Development Economics, 85*(1), 176–193.

Liu, X., Siler, P., Wang, C., & Wei, Y. (2000). Productivity spillovers from foreign direct investment: Evidence from UK industry level panel data. *Journal of International Business Studies, 31*(3), 407–425.

Luo, Y., Zhang, H., & Bu, J. (2019). Developed country MNEs investing in developing economies: Progress and prospect. *Journal of International Business Studies, 50*(4), 633–667.

Mair, J., Martí, I., & Ventresca, M. J. (2012). Building inclusive markets in rural Bangladesh: How intermediaries work institutional voids. *Academy of Management Journal, 55*(4), 819–850.

Marcin, K. (2008). How does FDI inflow affect productivity of domestic firms? The role of horizontal and vertical spillovers, absorptive capacity and competition. *The Journal of International Trade & Economic Development, 17*(1), 155–173.

Mayer, S. E. 2000. Income inequality, economic segregation and children's educational attainment. : Irving B. Harris Graduate School of Public Policy Studies, University of Chicago.

Melamed, C., & Samman, E. (2013). *Equity, inequality and human development in a post-2015 framework*. UNDP, Human Development Report Office.

Meyer, K. E. (2004). Perspectives on multinational enterprises in emerging economies. *Journal of International Business Studies, 35*(4), 259–276.

Meyer, K. E., & Sinani, E. (2009). When and where does foreign direct investment generate positive spillovers? A meta-analysis. *Journal of International Business Studies, 40*(7), 1075–1094.

Neumayer, E., & de Soysa, I. (2005). Trade openness, foreign direct investment and child labor. *World Development, 33*(1), 43–63.

Oetzel, J., & Doh, J. P. (2009). MNEs and development: A review and reconceptualization. *Journal of World Business, 44*(2), 108–120.

Organization for Economic Cooperation and Development (OECD). (2014). *Focus on inequality and growth—December 2014*. http://www.oecd.org/social/inequality-and-poverty.htm

Ostry, M. J. D., Berg, M. A., & Tsangarides, M. C. G. (2014). *Redistribution, inequality, and growth* (International Monetary Fund Staff Discussion Note SDN/14/02).

Pan-Long, T. (1995). Foreign direct investment and income inequality: Further evidence. *World Development, 23*(3), 469–483.

Papaioannou, S. K., & Dimelis, S. P. (2019). Does FDI increase productivity? The role of regulation in upstream industries. *The World Economy, 42*(4), 1012–1031.

Perri, A., & Peruffo, E. (2016). Knowledge spillovers from FDI: A critical review from the international business perspective. *International Journal of Management Reviews, 18*(1), 3–27.

Ranis, G., Stewart, F., & Ramirez, A. (2000). Economic growth and human development. *World Development, 28*(2), 197–219.

Ranjan, V., & Agrawal, G. (2011). FDI inflow determinants in BRIC countries: A panel data analysis. *International Business Research, 4*(4), 255–263.

Reiter, S. L., & Steensma, H. K. (2010). Human development and foreign direct investment in developing countries: The influence of FDI policy and corruption. *World Development, 38*(12), 1678–1691.

Rodrik, D. (2008). *One economics, many recipes: Globalization, institutions, and economic growth*. Princeton University Press.

Rugulies, R., Aust, B., Burr, H., & Bültmann, U. (2008). Job insecurity, chances on the labour market and decline in self-rated health in a representative sample of the Danish workforce. *Journal of Epidemiology and Community Health, 62*(3), 245–250.

Sánchez-Sellero, P., Rosell-Martínez, J., & García-Vázquez, J. M. (2014). Absorptive capacity from foreign direct investment in Spanish manufacturing firms. *International Business Review, 23*, 429–439.

Scheve, K., & Slaughter, M. J. (2004). Economic insecurity and the globalization of production. *American Journal of Political Science, 48*(4), 662–674.

Sen, A. (1999). *Development as freedom.* Oxford Paperbacks.

Sharma, B., & Gani, A. (2004). The effects of foreign direct investment on human development. *Global Economy Journal, 4*(2), 1–17.

Silla, I., de Cuyper, N., Gracia, F. J., Peiró, J. M., & de Witte, H. (2009). Job insecurity and well-being: Moderation by employability. *Journal of Happiness Studies, 10*(6), 739–751.

Spender, D. (2013). *The education papers* (Vol. 1). Routledge.

Stewart, F., & Samman, E. (2014). Inequality and development: An overview. In *International development: Ideas, experience, and prospects* (pp. 98–115). Oxford University Press.

Stiglitz, J. E. (2006). *Stability with growth: Macroeconomics, liberalization and development.* Oxford University Press.

Streeten, P. (1999). Components of a future development strategy: The importance of human development. *Finance and Development, 36*(4), 30–33.

Subramanian, S., & Kawachi, I. (2004). Income inequality and health: What have we learned so far? *Epidemiologic Reviews, 26*(1), 78–91.

United Nations Conference on Trade and Development (UNCTAD). (2016). *UNCTAD.* http://unctadstat.unctad.org/wds/ReportFolders/reportFolders.aspx?sCS_ChosenLang=en

United Nations Development Programme (UNDP). (2015a). *Human development data.* http://hdr.undp.org/en/data

United Nations Development Programme (UNDP). (2015b). *Human development report 2015.* http://hdr.undp.org/sites/default/files/2015_human_development_report.pdf

Walz, U. (1997). Innovation, foreign direct investment and growth. *Economica, 64*(253), 63–79.

Wang, D. T., Gu, F. F., Tse, D. K., & Yim, C. K. (2013). When does FDI matter? The roles of local institutions and ethnic origins of FDI. *International Business Review, 22*, 450–465.

Webb, J. W., Tihanyi, L., Ireland, R. D., & Sirmon, D. G. (2009). You say illegal, I say legitimate: Entrepreneurship in the informal economy. *Academy of Management Review, 34*(3), 492–510.

Wei, Y., & Liu, X. (2006). Productivity spillovers from R&D, exports and FDI in China's manufacturing sector. *Journal of International Business Studies, 37*(4), 544–557.

Wettstein, F., Giuliani, E., Santangelo, G. D., & Stahl, G. K. (2019). International business and human rights: A research agenda. *Journal of World Business, 54*(1), 54–65.

Wilkinson, R. G., & Pickett, K. E. (2006). Income inequality and population health: A review and explanation of the evidence. *Social Science & Medicine, 62*(7), 1768–1784.

World Bank. (2016). *World development indicators.* http://data.worldbank.org/data-catalog/world-development-indicators

World Bank. (2020). *Poverty and shared prosperity 2020: Reversals of fortune.* The World Bank. https://openknowledge.worldbank.org/bitstream/handle/10986/34496/9781464816024.pdf

World Economic Forum. (2015). *The global competitiveness report 2015–2016.* http://www3.weforum.org/docs/gcr/2015-2016/Global_Competitiveness_Report_2015-2016.pdf

World Economic Forum. (2016). *Global competiveness data.* http://reports.weforum.org/global-competitiveness-index/competitiveness-rankings/

Wu, J. Y., & Hsu, C. C. (2012). Foreign direct investment and income inequality: Does the relationship vary with absorptive capacity? *Economic Modelling, 29*(6), 2183–2189.

Yamin, M., & Sinkovics, R. R. (2009). Infrastructure or foreign direct investment? An examination of the implications of MNE strategy for economic development. *Journal of World Business, 44*(2), 144–157.

Zhang, Y., Li, Y., & Li, H. (2014). FDI spillovers over time in an emerging market: The roles of entry tenure and barriers to imitation. *Academy of Management Journal, 57*(3), 698–722.

Zhang, Y., Li, H., Li, Y., & Zhou, L. A. (2010). FDI spillovers in an emerging market: The role of foreign firms' country origin diversity and domestic firms' absorptive capacity. *Strategic Management Journal, 31*(9), 969–989.

Irina Orbes Cervantes is a PhD Candidate at the Australian National University. Her current research focuses on executive leadership, strategic change, and corporate governance. Her other interests are FDI spillover effects and knowledge transfer. Her work has received a best paper award at the Academy of Management—International Management Division.

Hang Dang is a final-year PhD candidate in Business and Economics at the Australian National University. Her research is interdisciplinary in nature and draws upon theory of the firm, environmental economics, and international business. She also works as an Environmental Economist consultant for the World Bank in Vietnam.

Alex Eapen is Associate Professor of Strategic Management at the Australian National University. His research interests include knowledge transfers and governance structures in strategic alliances and FDI spillover effects of foreign multinational enterprises in a host country. His research has appeared in journals such as Organization Science, Journal of International Business Studies, and Economic Modelling.

History and Future of Migration in International Business: From River to Tidal Flows

Aminat Muibi and Stacey R. Fitzsimmons

Migrants are individuals who move across international borders, such as refugees, economic immigrants, temporary foreign workers, and expatriates (IOM, 2020). They are an increasingly prevalent portion of the global workforce. Worldwide, the stock of international migrants increased steadily from 173 million in 2000 to an estimated 281 million in 2020 (United Nations, 2020), representing an increasing share of the global population, from 2.8 to 3.6% (IOM, 2020). The growing size of migrant populations matter for IB research, as international organizations are more likely than domestic organizations to engage migrants within their supply chains, markets, workforces, or as venture capital investors (Hajro et al., 2021). For example, migrants influence innovation (Laursen et al., 2020), entrepreneurship (Sinkovics & Reuber, 2021), and facilitate global flows of both knowledge and capital (Choudhury & Kim, 2019).

We argue that migrants ought to be central to both the research and practice of international business (IB), as IB is fundamentally interested in firms' cross-border activities. Migrants at all skill levels play a significant role in their home and home countries' economies, facilitate cross-border activities ranging from entrepreneurial (Sinkovics & Reuber, 2021) to subsidiary location choice and survival (Hernandez, 2014), and are said to contribute an estimated 9.4% of the global GDP (McKinsey Global Institute, 2016). The contributions of low-skilled migrants, who are overrepresented in frontline service positions, have become salient in the past 2 years due to the COVID-19 pandemic (Hajro et al., 2021).

Despite the centrality of migration to IB, recent reviews indicate that migration research is more commonly the domain of other disciplines, such as economics, psychology, sociology, and political science (Adamson & Tsourapas, 2020; Schewel, 2020). For example, foundational research from psychology commonly uses a developmental lens to find that immigrant youth who maintain links to both

A. Muibi · S. R. Fitzsimmons (✉)
Peter B. Gustavson School of Business, University of Victoria, Victoria, BC, Canada
e-mail: aminatmuibi@uvic.ca; sfitzsim@uvic.ca

© Springer Nature Switzerland AG 2022   409
H. Merchant (ed.), *The New Frontiers of International Business*, Contributions to
Management Science, https://doi.org/10.1007/978-3-031-06003-8_20

cultures improve psychological well-being, especially compared to those who do not maintain strong links to either one (Berry et al., 2006). Heavily cited economics research found that immigration has economic benefits (Coppel et al., 2001) and lowers poverty rates globally, though it also lowers host country wages in the short run (Borjas, 2003). Research from sociology found that migration can harm welfare programs by reducing public support for them (Brady & Finnigan, 2014). These disciplines shed light respectively on migration policy and psychological and economic outcomes. Yet they are not commonly leveraged to advise international managers or migrant employees about the best ways to leverage migrants' experiences at work or how to take migration flows into consideration when developing MNE strategy.

We argue that IB's limited contributions to migration research so far may be partly due to a limited metaphor for understanding migration, which we attempt to update with a richer metaphor in this chapter. IB's historical approach to migration was like studying river, which includes the two characteristics of being relatively small flows of water with a unidirectional flow. Akin to the unidirectional flow of rivers, IB's foundational migration-related research was about expatriates' acculturation while away from home (Mendenhall & Oddou, 1985). This was an important foundation, as expatriation was largely ignored by fields outside of IB. Distinct from other forms of migration, research on expatriation tends to focus on how organizations support international migrants (Andersen, 2019). Yet this foundation has unnecessarily limited subsequent IB research on migration, beyond expatriation. The "small river" of mobility within MNEs ignores the much bigger flows of migrants and refugees, limiting IB's relevance in recommending practical solutions to current challenges related to immigrant employment. Instead, we argue that the future of migration research is studying how IB is affected by migration at large, including refugees, low-skilled migrants, and those with and without documentation.

Although the metaphor of unidirectional river flows has generated lively research conversations, such as those within the *Journal of Global Mobility*, it may also limit fuller, more multidirectional theorizing about migrant flows in the future. McNulty and Brewster (2020) go so far as to argue that research on relatively elite expatriates has been so productive to date that further research on them, to the detriment of research on the much larger group of other migrants, has "limited additional value" (p.334). Before proposing a solution in the form of a more inclusive metaphor, we first address contentious definitional issues around who is considered a migrant. Despite the working definition we offered at the beginning of this chapter from the International Organization for Migration, debate remains in the research literature around the boundary conditions between a series of interrelated constructs.

1   Who Is a Migrant?

The term migrant is politically charged and fluid, with different stakeholders using definitions that align with their goals or purpose. For instance, popular media often conflates it with asylum seekers (Baker et al., 2008). Cerdin and Selmer's (2014) article remains a popular source for differentiating migrants from self-initiated expatriates. They encode status and value judgments in their four criteria for distinguishing these groups: relative to self-initiated expatriates, they claim that migrants are more likely to originate from less developed countries, migrate involuntarily (e.g., refugees), are referred to with negative connotations, and are less likely to return. Two other foundational articles offered a decision tree (Andresen et al., 2014) and a Venn diagram (McNulty & Brewster, 2017) to distinguish among different types of internationally mobile employees, such as migrants, self-initiated expatriates, and assigned expatriates. Both continue to be popular sources for defining and distinguishing these groups. We agree with their inclusion criteria of geographic relocation across a national border, paired with a change in primary residence. Yet we take issue with both articles' subsequent distinction of migrants from self-initiated expatriates, such that migrants are those who either work without legal documentation, or who do not work, while self-initiated expatriates work legally in the destination country (Andresen et al., 2014; McNulty & Brewster, 2017; Shao & Ariss, 2020).

There is little theoretical rationale for this distinction. Research about work outcomes following migration are essential to understanding different levels of career success, such as tracking careers among skilled female migrants (Van den Bergh & Du Plessis, 2012). However, defining migrants by their career outcomes embeds an outcome into the definition itself. Further, our impression of the literature is that the intent behind distinguishing migrants from self-initiated expatriates is often to categorize based on status without naming it as such. Finally, it introduces unnecessary complications, such as categorizing an individual as a migrant until they secure employment, at which time they may be recategorized as a self-initiated expatriate. McNulty and Brewster (2017) explain that these categories are fungible, with individuals frequently moving between categorizations. Yet, we go further to conclude that these categorizations may not be as meaningful as they seem.

Instead, we recommend adopting an inclusive approach to the term migrant, as defined by the International Organization for Migration (IOM) at the beginning of this chapter. IB research about expatriates (Takeuchi, 2010; Vaiman et al., 2021), self-initiated expatriates (Howe-Walsh & Schyns, 2010), highly skilled migrants (Hajro et al., 2019), refugees (Lee et al., 2020), and undocumented workers (Chand & Tung, 2019) would thus all fall under the umbrella term of migrant employees. Our rationale for including such a wide range of employee migration under the same umbrella term is that it allows researchers to be more purposeful about studying relevant mechanisms related to each project, rather than using definitions that embed theoretical mechanisms like status and power into the group's boundary conditions. For example, we argue it is preferable to study migrants as a large group but explicitly distinguish based on status, power, or agency, if those constructs are relevant to the research question (McNulty & Brewster, 2020). In effect, this approach could result in similar groupings as in current research, with the added benefit of making the theoretical constructs explicit. A good illustration is a study that explicitly modeled status changes among Chinese movie actors who migrated to work in Hong Kong's film industry (Shipilov et al., 2020). Instead of making hidden status assumptions about the sample of actors by defining them as self-initiated expatriates, they measured status changes before and after migration.

One further note on terminology. Migrants' countries of birth are commonly referred to as their countries of origin (COO) and their current countries called countries of residence (COR). This is in contrast to the expatriation literature, which assumes individuals stay temporarily in their host countries, and therefore refers to countries of origin as "home" countries. We adopt the COO/COR terminology, as it makes no assumption about return flows or determining which country is the migrant's "home." It is therefore more consistent with our inclusive definition of migrants. Finally, the term immigrant refers to migrants from the destination country's perspective. We will primarily use the term migrant but substitute immigrant when describing a claim from the perspective of migrants' current countries of residence.

This chapter comes at an auspicious time as public discussions regarding migrants often skew toward negative portrayals and protectionism. For example, Brexit was predicated on concerns about immigrant flows into the UK, Turkey, and other Mediterranean countries are concerned about the size of incoming refugee flows, and there are global concerns about how to handle the possibility of future forced migration as a result of rising ocean levels (Reade et al., 2019). Thus, the world is simultaneously experiencing increasing numbers of migrants, along with increasing backlash against them. Both trends are relevant for international organizations, as they attempt to balance both sides. That is, many international organizations encourage new immigration by facilitating employment-based visas, while also appeasing domestic politicians and citizens who view immigration suspiciously. We agree with Ozkazanc-Pan (2019: 477), who argues that "Migration has become a lightning rod for conversations about the value of diversity and inclusion in liberal democracies."

2   Current Theoretical Approach to Migration in IB

Expatriates will continue to be an important part of future IB research, in part because company-sponsored expatriation is the only form of migration that exists solely within MNEs (Vaiman et al., 2021). The focus on expatriates hacks back to the type of migrant visible in MNEs which are unavoidable actors when discussing the impact of IB on a global scale. The move toward including the broader migrant population within IB is of how we study migrants is fueled by gaps in knowledge and recent inclusion of categories such as migrant entrepreneurs (cite) and migrant farm workers (cite). Due to the growing migrant population, IB's historical focus on expatriates over other migrants is shifting, as highlighted by two special issues dedicated to migration in IB (Barnard et al., 2019; Hajro et al., 2021). Both special issue introductions exhort IB researchers to draw a more inclusive boundary around who matters for IB migration research. For example, as we discuss in more detail ahead, both admit that IB has emphasized migrants' influence on MNE strategic decisions such as FDI flows and subsidiary placements (Chung & Enderwick, 2001;

Chung & Tung, 2013). This focus unnecessarily limits research to migrants within top management teams or diaspora communities as relevant for entrepreneurial or MNE subsidiary location decisions.

A productive legacy of IB's foundational expatriation research is that the field has some authority when explaining integration and acculturation challenges experienced by migrants (Stahl & Tung, 2015). It less commonly addresses local employees' reactions to immigrants, such as their potential stress responses to societal changes as a result of immigration (Lau & Shaffer, 2021). Indeed, domestic employees—those who did not migrate—are necessary for any explanation of migrant employees' contributions (Caprar, 2011). When domestic employees feel like they are under threat from immigrant employees, migrants' contributions are constrained (Lau & Shaffer, 2021). It is possible that IB's reluctance to study the backlash against migrants is due partly to its limited range of migrants considered. As described in our earlier clarification around who is a migrant and elaborated by McNulty and Brewster (2019), IB focuses far more attention on high-status, highly skilled migrants than on low-status, low-skilled migrants. The former are rarely the focus of public backlash.

3 Tidal Flows: A New Metaphor

Our chapter attempts to synthesize migration research in IB by arguing that it is time to reconceptualize migration from river flows to tidal flows. Tidal flows more accurately represent migration with respect to both directionality and scale (see Table 1). In terms of directionality, most people assume the tide flows back and forth with the moon's pull, compared to rivers that always flow in one direction. Even more accurately, the tide flows in multiple directions at once, such as rising on shores to both the East and South while ebbing on shores to the North and West. In the same way, migration in IB needs to move from an assumption of unidirectional flows from home to host countries, to multidirectional flows, such as migrating through intermediary countries and returning to home countries. This has already started, such as with research on repatriation (Burmeister et al., 2018), Chinese "sea turtle" returnees (Han et al., 2019; Zhang et al., 2018), and other bidirectional flows (Caligiuri & Bonache, 2016). Ahead, we propose taking this research a step further into multidirectional flows. Migrants sometimes take an indirect path to their final destination country, accumulating social network connections, knowledge, and cultural capital along the way.

Table 1 Defining characteristics of each metaphor

	River flows	Tidal flows
Directionality	Unidirectional	Multidirectional
Scale	Relatively small flows	Relatively large flows

*Table compiled by authors

In terms of scale, IB has historically focused on the small river of expatriates, relative to the vast ocean of migrants. More recent research has started to consider a broader range of migrants but still tends to focus on the most highly skilled, highest-status migrants. Among all 250 million individuals classified as international workers, only a few millions are company-sponsored expatriates (IOM, 2020; OECD, 2017). We argue that the future of migration research is studying how IB is affected by this broader group of migrants, including refugees, low-skilled migrants, and those with and without documentation. This larger conceptualization merits a broader theoretical base, such as considerations around status and power conveyed by migrants' countries of origin. A new metaphor could spur new directions for migration research in IB to address future challenges, such as responding to societal backlash around employing migrants, treating migrant employees equitably across countries, designing effective human resource practices for a wider range of migrants, and advocating for or responding to regulatory changes related to work visas.

In the rest of this chapter, we illustrate how the new metaphor generates new research questions by applying our proposed metaphor shift to four foundational theoretical concepts common within migration research: flows of social ties, flows of capital, flows of innovation, and flows of knowledge. Within each of these areas, we review and critique the current state of research as a basis for proposing future directions. But first, we explain how we reviewed the literature as a basis for drawing our conclusions.

4   How We Reviewed the Literature

We followed a three-step process to evaluate the literature on how IB addresses migration (Gaur & Kumar, 2018). First, we created a list of relevant search terms "immigrant," "migrant," "immigration," "diaspora," "expatriate," "migration," and "ethnic communities." Second, we followed Meyer et al. (2020) to define articles within IB. That is, we assumed everything published in these seven IB journals was within the IB domain: Asia Pacific Journal of Management (APJM), International Business Review (IBR), Journal of International Business Studies (JIBS), Journal of International Management (JIM), Journal of World Business (JWB), Management International Review (MIR), and Management and Organization Review (MOR). We then reviewed titles and abstracts to include IB-related articles in the same set of strategy and management journals used by Meyer and colleagues (2020). Strategy journals included the Global Strategy Journal (GSJ) and Strategic Management Journal (SMJ), while management journals included the Academy of Management Journal (AMJ), Academy of Management Review (AMR), Administrative Science Quarterly (ASQ), Journal of Management (JoM), Management Science (MS), Organization Science (OS), and Organization Studies (OSt). Across all 16 journals, we included articles in our corpus for review as long as they were both IB-focused and related to long-term migration consistent with our inclusive definition. That is, research on short-term international travel (expatriate research) was outside the

Articles Reviewed from Selected Journals

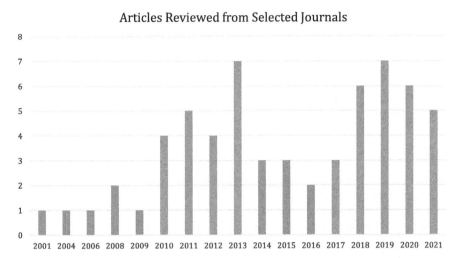

Fig. 1 Histogram of articles reviewed by year published. *Authors' own figure

scope of this review. While this sample is not comprehensive, it allowed us to draw a reasonable picture of migration-related research within IB.

This process yielded 62 articles, with significant contributions from journals such as JWB (12), JIBS (7), JIM (7), and IBR (8). Our database contains 57 empirical articles, 3 review articles, and 2 conceptual articles. We also categorized the articles across the various journals by number of articles published per give a visual representation of the amount of research being conducted on immigration in IB. (See Fig. 1 for more details.) Of the empirical papers, 82% were quantitative papers, with 32% of those using survey data and 51% using archival data. The share of primary data in our sample was far higher than that within IB more broadly, which has been progressively decreasing over time as it becomes easier to access archival data (Cerar et al., 2021). Within our sample, studies using archival data commonly used government data or that from world governing bodies to examine immigrant flows and their impact on exports, new ventures, and internationalization strategies. Out of the 18% that were qualitative studies, case studies involving interviews were the most common approach.

Finally, we catalogued theories and findings from each paper to identify trends. We coded the papers for research domains and primary theories, in order to highlight popular theoretical concepts, assumptions, and potential blind spots within IB research that explains migration-related effects.

5 Findings

We selected four flows that illustrate how IB approaches migrant scholarship. Each of these flows is commonly studied in IB but occur at different levels and using different theories from the others. Our description and critique of this exemplary set of flows forms the basis for our proposed new "tidal flows" direction for future research, as illustrated in Table 2. Consistent with our proposed metaphor shift, we propose new research that widens the scope of who is studied in IB migration research and examines flows as multidirectional.

5.1   Flows of Social Ties

Social network research encompasses concepts like social ties, personal connections, relational networks, and network of relationships. Historically, migration literature within IB has explored how immigrants influence their firms' internationalization strategies through social networks in their countries of origin (Chung, 2004; Chung & Tung, 2013; Tung & Chung, 2010). The strategic value of social networks occurs through mechanisms such as knowledge exchange, advising on cross-border activities, referral trust, and interpersonal relationship linkages (Zhou et al., 2007). A good example is Rana and Elo's (2017) work on immigrants as distinct social actors who facilitate the creation of international joint ventures in their COO.

Migrants' social networks benefit firms by allowing firms to bypass traditional barriers to internationalization (Coviello & Martin, 1999). Immigrants' social networks act as webs of personal connections and relationships for the purpose of securing favors (Zhou et al., 2007) and reducing the likelihood of contractual breaches. Useche et al. (2020) took a detailed approach by examining how migrant inventors in MNEs that actively engage in R&D influence cross-border mergers and acquisitions through network connections in their COO. They argued migrant inventors belong to three social groups (worldwide migrant population, highly skilled migrant population, and a professional group of scientists and engineers), and they can use these three social networks to provide knowledge that will directly influence long-term investments with strategic objectives (Useche et al., 2020). This was a departure from prior studies on immigrants' effect on FDI strategies, in that it explicitly examined the boundary conditions under which a positive relationship exists. Using Useche et al. (2020) as an illustrative example, it's possible to see how migrant inventors are a privileged subset of highly skilled migrants, whose positions give them some degree of influence over their firms' strategic choices. Prior studies have also examined what happens when immigrants are the direct decision-makers of FDI objectives for firms (Chung, 2004). Migrant employees in strategic positions do indeed make more globally oriented strategic choices than nonmigrants (Szymanski et al., 2019). Yet the majority of migrant employees are in positions that have no influence on strategic decision-making.

Looking beyond the traditional MNE structure, scholars have also advanced the resource-based view by theorizing that immigrants in founding teams possess a special resource bundle (human and social capital) which is difficult to substitute (Barney, 2001) and helps the new venture develop an international orientation (Drechsler et al., 2019). The reasoning behind this is that immigrant membership in founding teams helps to attract international attention through the use of their social capital. Thus, the combination of an international strategic orientation and

Table 2 Illustrating a shift from river to tidal flows

Type of flow	River flows Illustrative research questions	Selected common theories and exemplary papers	Benefits and limitations of prior research	Tidal flows Proposed future research questions
Social ties	How do migrants use their networks to facilitate activities between their COO and COR? What is the strategic value of migrants' COO networks?	Social network theory (Chung, 2004; Chung & Tung, 2013; Tung & Chung, 2010) Resource-based view (Drechsler et al., 2019). Social embeddedness perspective (Morgan et al., 2021; Riddle & Brinkerhoff, 2011)	When migrants are in strategic or high-level positions that involve cross-border activities, their social network ties across countries benefits firm-level activities like innovation and internationalization strategies Yet, it is not yet known whether or how migrants outside of those positions draw on social networks to influence firm activities	How do migrants working in nonstrategic positions (e.g., anywhere within the global supply chain) use social network connections within their work? How do social identity threats or identity groupings influence migrants' social network interactions? How do refugee employees use social network resources during the integration process or to influence firm activities?
Capital—remittances	Until the launch of JIBP, remittances research was primarily done outside of IB journals. For more, see Barnard et al. (2019); Hajro et al. (2021)	TCE (Vaaler, 2011) Social knowledge perspective (Piteli et al., 2021) Institutional theory (Martinez et al., 2015)	Remittances are important drivers of new venture creation Yet, earlier research assumed remittances were primarily altruistic, to support friends and family with living expenses, and therefore were outside the purview of IB research	Do remittances influence competition for established international organizations? Do remittances affect workforce skill levels (do they diminish or enhance skill levels)? How do egoistic versus altruistic remittances differentially influence international entrepreneurial ventures?
Capital—trade	How does the "immigrant effect" influence trade between COR and COO?	Immigrant effect (Chung & Enderwick, 2001)	Migrants can act as conduits for increased trade between their COO and COR or through entrepreneurial activities in COR But, unidirectional in terms of how immigrant managers influence trade Also, overly restrictive in terms of whose social networks matter; namely, high-skilled migrants in strategically proximal positions	How does international trade influence the flow of low-skilled migrants? How can contextualized knowledge from low-skilled migrant employees be used to create new trade opportunities?

(continued)

Table 2 (continued)

Type of flow	River flows Illustrative research questions	Selected common theories and exemplary papers	Benefits and limitations of prior research	Tidal flows Proposed future research questions
Knowledge	How do migrants facilitate knowledge flows between their COO and COR? What boundary conditions restrict these knowledge flows?	Knowledge transfer process (Liu et al., 2015) Immigrant adaptation (Lin & Yang, 2017)	Migrants' knowledge can influence their firms' activities, including innovation. It can ultimately improve cross-border performance between their two countries Most prior research examined knowledge flows only between the COO and COR. But knowledge flows may also include knowledge beyond the COO-COR, especially for transit migrants Also, migrants' knowledge of the COO can become obsolescent over time Finally, prior research has just started to examine contextual influences such as anti-immigrant sentiment on knowledge flows	Do transit migration patterns facilitate different knowledge flows than traditional patterns? For example, are knowledge flows better, worse, more expansive, or shallower, when migrants transition through intermediary countries? How does time since migration—extending to include the children or even grandchildren of migrants—change knowledge flows? How does the inclusiveness of the new environment (city, region, or country) influence knowledge flows? For example, to what degree does the welcoming nature of a city to immigrants influence the direction and scale of knowledge flows?
Innovation	How do migrants encourage innovation within their firms?	Multicultural social networks (Chua, 2018) Social identity theory (Cheng et al., 2008) Identity integration (Vora et al., 2019) Cultural brokerage (Jang, 2017)	There is a clear relationship between migration and innovation across levels, meaning individuals who cross borders reap innovation benefits, as do firms and teams that employ them But disparate streams of research on the same topic, from different theoretical perspectives (e.g., multicultural creativity and migrant innovation) are difficult to combine. Findings in one stream are not examined in others	To what degree are innovativeness outcomes dependent on the cultural relevance of the creative task? What are the boundary conditions under which migrant influence on innovation could dissipate?

*Table compiled by authors

impact of international attention is said to positively influence new venture's internationalization efforts.

Using a social embeddedness perspective, immigrant owners' social connections across borders are at least one of the factors influencing SMEs' financial performance (Morgan et al., 2021). The premise is that immigrant-owned SME outcomes are influenced by the degree to which the immigrant owner is simultaneously integrated in their country-of-origin social network and the institutional and proximate distance between the countries of origin and residence. The social embeddedness framework has primarily been applied to immigrant firm survival in the early stages of internationalization. While other scholars have not been explicit in their use of this framework, the concurrent benefits of an immigrant's access to COO and COR advantages in an MNE leads us to numerous studies that have identified immigrants as a special resource used as part of a firm's internationalization strategy (Chung, 2004; Riddle & Brinkerhoff, 2011).

Conclusions and future research directions about the flow of social ties. By now, it is known that when migrants are employed in strategic or entrepreneurial positions, they can use their social connections to influence firm strategies, international investments, and internationalization strategies. Yet, most migrant employees are not in these positions. We encourage future researchers to widen the scope on the positions of migrant employees whose network matters. For example, examine whether—or how—migrants located in nonstrategic positions draw on social networks influential their firms' practices. Those employed anywhere in the international supply chain seem likely to draw on social network ties in the course of their work.

Some immigrant managers in Germany from either Eastern Europe or India helped their colleagues in their COO due to shared identities and perceived status, while others actively hindered colleagues in their COO due to identity threats related to perceived lower status (Kane & Levina, 2017). We encourage more research about how identities influence the way migrants interact with social network connections. At the other extreme from immigrants employed in strategic decision-making positions in MNEs are refugee employees, who must often take any work available. It is already known that refugees' social ties strongly influence their integration into their new COR (Lee et al., 2020). It is unknown whether refugees' employed in nonstrategic positions can also use their social ties to influence their firms' activities, such as by advertising jobs within social circles. Overall, we would like to see more research about the role of social ties for migrants outside of strategic decision-making positions.

5.2   Flows of Capital

Capital flows attributed to migrants generally refer to either remittances or trade. We address remittances first, followed by trade.

Remittances are money or its equivalent sent from migrants to their home countries. They can be individual-to-individual or household-to-household transactions from host to home countries and are therefore an integral part of the migrant experience (Vaaler, 2011). Worldwide, remittances were estimated at 707 billion in 2019 with forecasts expected to reach 768 billion in 2021 (World Bank, 2019). This estimate pales in comparison to the true number and size of remittances when taking unreported flows of funds into account, such as those through informal and nonfinancial institutions. These include remittances sent through informal third parties, individuals acting as courier services, people who take physical cash over borders, and transfers disguised as bill payments (Brown, 2006). Since remittances themselves are so difficult to track, researchers' ability to assess migrants' influence on remittances is also limited.

Research has long assumed remittances are either driven by egoism or altruism (Lucas & Stark, 1985). The egoistic motive signals entrepreneurial considerations and investment through a network of potential business partners in a migrant's country of origin, while altruism refers to remittances meant to support friends or family members (Piteli et al., 2021). IB scholars were slow to view remittance beyond a household expense lens, largely ignoring the egoistic motive and therefore assuming remittances were not a topic of concern for IB research (Barnard et al., 2019; Hajro et al., 2021). IB research is starting to investigate remittance as a source of capital in the COO (Vaaler, 2011) and new business startups which ultimately leads to internationalization of the broader economy (Martinez et al., 2015).

Following the launch of the *Journal of International Business Policy*, we expect to see more studies on remittances in the future. For example, developing countries are able to influence remittance inflows through organizations designed to engage diasporas and enhance their feelings of identity and attachment to the COO (Cummings & Gamlen, 2019). Inward FDI increased the inflow of remittances received in that country (Piteli et al., 2021). Piteli and colleagues explain the effect using the egoistic narrative, by arguing that inward FDI encourages local entrepreneurs to create new small business ventures that support, complement, or compete with the MNE's activities. Those local entrepreneurs often rely on migrant friends and family for financial support through egoistic remittance investments.

Sudden events such as COVID-19 were expected to dramatically reduce remittance flows, particularly to low- and middle-income countries. Recent reports show there were only minor contractions from 2019 to 2020, with a 1.6% drop from $548 billion in 2019 to $540 billion in 2020 (World Bank, 2021). This is in line with past research which has highlighted the counter cyclical nature of remittances with economic recessions in host countries having little effect on the size or payment of these transfers (Brown, 2006). The pandemic acted as a situational context which affected all countries. Future research could examine how it changed the ratio of altruistic or egoistic remittances and how that affected new business ventures or the availability of capital in COOs.

Trade. While remittances account for a significant portion of many countries' GDP (Hosny, 2020), it is just one conduit through which migrants influence the flow of money across borders. Migrants can also influence venture capital investments in their COO by virtue of residing in their COR (Leblang, 2010), accessing, and selling goods from their COO to diaspora networks in the COR (Lin & Yang, 2017), facilitating trade between the COO and COR (Gould, 1994), and influencing resource commitments of MNEs in their COR (Chung & Enderwick, 2001; Chung & Tung, 2013). There is also a stream of research on the *immigrant effect*, referring to immigrant managers who create competitive advantages through characteristics that are rare, valuable, and unique (Chung et al., 2012).

By focusing almost exclusively on entrepreneurial founders or top managers, much of this research implicitly assumes formal education and highly ranked skills are the best—or only—conduits through which valuable information is translated into trade between COO and COR. Low-skilled migrants' influence on MNE decisions is a relatively unexplored area. Most research on low-skilled migrants has focused on their short-term effects on average income per capita and adoption of more labor-intensive opportunities in COR (Orefice, 2010). While this is a legitimate inquiry, there is an assumption that skill levels directly correlate with impact on a range of outcomes. Drawing on either the knowledge-based view, or social network theory, it is possible that low-skilled migrants employed in supply chain positions offer insider knowledge or social ties that translate into new trade opportunities (Grant & Phene, 2021).

Gould's (1994) work was one of the first to investigate how migrants connect their COO and COR by facilitating trade. Using panel data from 47 US trading partners, he showed that migrants influence bilateral trade by preferring home country products and by lowering MNE transaction and information costs by bringing foreign market information and contacts. Countering the tendency to focus primarily on high-skilled migrants, Lin and Yang (2017) found that low-skilled migrants were more likely to increase bilateral trade than high-skilled migrants. Their explanation is that lower-skilled migrants create new trade opportunities through entrepreneurial aspirations. These two studies indicate that further research might reveal other ways low-skilled migrants contribute to trade.

Conclusions and future research questions about the flow of capital. Recent work has started to highlight the importance of remittances for new venture creation (Vaaler, 2011) and understand how migrants can act as conduits for increased trade between their COO and COR or through entrepreneurial activities in COR. While this stream of research on trade is relatively well established, there are still opportunities that have not been explored in depth that will benefit scholarship on immigrants in IB.

IB research on migrant-driven capital flows has identified such a strong relationship between immigrant managers and trade that it has given this relationship a name, the immigrant effect. Yet this relationship is almost exclusively studied in terms of high-skilled immigrant managers influencing trade with the COO. An exception is a study of capital flows in the opposite direction. Shukla and Cantwell (2018) found that migrants from developing countries attract FDI into their COR from their COO by increasing institutional affinity. Remittance research was largely absent in IB until the past few years.

Our suggestion for transitioning both trade and remittances research involves studying multidirectional capital flows influenced by a more inclusive group of migrants. For example, expatriate doctors in Tanzania reduced out-migration among some Tanzanian doctors by building local capacity, though the more important factor seems to have been Tanzanian doctors' sense of purpose in their work (Emmanuel et al., 2019). We would like to see more exploration of how international trade influences migration by changing push and pull factors. It's possible that inflows of international trade could encourage more outbound migration by enabling it through connections and infrastructure, or alternatively it could instead encourage potential migrants to stay home through favorable work opportunities. The relationship between trade and migration can be developed further by examining how contextualized knowledge from low-skilled migrant employees is used to create new trade opportunities. This would include first analyzing the specific knowledge low-skilled migrants possess. For instance, their knowledge could help firms serve customers at the base of the pyramid (Kolk et al., 2014).

We also suggest comparing remittances made for egoistic versus altruistic reasons, to see how each stream changes business activities. Following from Piteli and colleagues' (Piteli et al., 2021) findings that remittances increase following FDI, we propose research that investigates whether remittances influence competition for international organizations in migrants' COO and how it affects skill levels of the labor (does it diminish skill levels, indicating overreliance on handouts, or enhance skill levels, indicating investment in skill development).

5.3   Flows of Knowledge

We elaborate two of the most common ways migrants can influence flows of knowledge. First, they can use their knowledge of the COO to facilitate cross-border activities like investment and subsidiary activities. To date, most research that seeks to link international migration with economic consequences like FDI and MNE resource commitment in host countries has largely assumed that this is a result of the knowledge advantage a migrant brings to a specific firm. Many scholars use the term *immigrant effect* to refer to the knowledge-driven contribution of a firm's immigrant managers to strategic activities in the immigrant employee's COO or a proximate country (Chung et al., 2012; Chung & Enderwick, 2001).

Second, migrants can add value to global value chain activities through tacit or explicit knowledge that acts as a conduit of information and trust between their COO and COR (Chand & Tung, 2019). At a micro-behavioral level, this may be enacted when immigrants bridge cultural gaps between people across countries, facilitating knowledge flows (Backmann et al., 2020). This differs from the first pathway in part because of its bidirectionality. For instance, a study of highly skilled Chinese migrants living in the UK found that they facilitated knowledge flow between their two countries by identifying key contacts in each country, helping peers establish a relationship, and subsequently drawing on cultural and language skills to send and receive knowledge (Liu et al., 2015).

Research has examined boundary conditions around both routes to knowledge flow. For example, migrants' knowledge of the COO becomes less valuable over time, as their experiences living in the COO recede further into the past (Kunczer et al., 2019). Competitive and institutional environments evolve and change, but migrants' memories are not updated frequently once they move away from the COO. Our overview of the literature shows that IB research rarely acknowledges the obsolescence of immigrant knowledge due to changing policies in immigrants' COO or strong network ties becoming weak due to compounded distance. We encourage IB researchers to explore the potentially nonlinear relationship between migrants' knowledge flows and time from migration.

Another boundary condition is that firms are less likely to absorb migrants' knowledge of the COO when the COR exhibits high levels of anti-immigrant sentiment (Kunczer et al., 2019). Anti-immigrant sentiment occurs when nonmigrants (aka locals) feel threatened. This can feel comparably stressful to going through an acculturation process but with the added pressure that locals can feel like acculturation is imposed upon them, rather than choosing it for themselves (Lau & Shaffer, 2021). Locals may also feel threatened if they fear dropping wages. By and large, local wages may drop with an influx of immigrants with complementary skills to those of local employees (Ruhs, 2013). However, wage drops are usually negligible and may reverse when the influx of immigrants is stabilized (Ruhs, 2013).

One of our concerns with knowledge-based theorizing about migrants in IB is that as the world continues to open up and more people migrate, it can become surprisingly difficult to identify an individual's COO and COR (Czaika & de Haas, 2014). Past research relied heavily on an individual's country of birth and current country of residence to determine who qualifies as a migrant. The unspoken assumption is that migrants move between two countries such that a migrant's only two options are to either settle in the (new) country of residence or return to the country of origin. Instead, some migrants take a more circuitous route to their final destinations, sometimes spending many years in intermediary countries. This pattern is now called *transit migration* by human geographers, though it was referred to as the *new migration* in the 1990s (Collyer et al., 2012; King, 2012). For instance, some students who study for a degree in a foreign country are in transit, on their way to a third country for their first jobs. Over time the term has evolved to refer primarily to illegal migration patterns, such as refugees who land in a first safe country, and then migrate onward sometime later (Collyer et al., 2012).

Conclusions and future research about the flow of knowledge. Research on knowledge flows to date has benefited IB by showing how migrants' knowledge can influence their firms' activities and ultimately improve cross-border performance between their two countries (Choudhury & Kim, 2019). Research has also started to examine the boundary conditions for bidirectional flows among immigrant inventors (Miguelez & Temgoua, 2020). Future research will need to take into account how transit migration might affect the quantity, range, and quality of knowledge resources migrants bring into their organizations. For example, do the ties to the COO dematerialize the longer an immigrant spends in intervening countries, or are they maintained and supplemented with new ties in the transit country? Knowledge possessed by migrants at the time of the first move inevitably degrades over time and especially the longer migrants reside in intervening countries. COO environmental conditions change and familiarity with potential customers or suppliers may weaken, calling into question the immigrant effect (IE) on resource commitment or entry market modes. Instead, we exhort future researchers to model these effects over time, especially for transit migrants who pass through intermediary countries. Finally, research has already started to examine how anti-immigrant sentiment is a contextual antecedent that influences migrant knowledge flows. Further research could examine whether this is most usefully measured at the city, region, or country level and what role MNEs and other international organizations have in reducing backlash against immigrant employees.

5.4   Flows of Innovation

There is evidence for a positive relationship between migration and innovation for individuals, teams, firms, and societies. Indeed, innovation and creativity are among the most common outcomes assessed with respect to migration in IB.

Migration and individual creativity. At the individual level, researchers more commonly predict creativity than innovation. Mere exposure to multiple cultures increases individuals' creativity, and creativity increases even more when exposure is more extensive (Leung et al., 2008). International mobility in all forms increases creativity, from international travel to permanent migration (Choudhury, 2021). Social networks, identity integration, and knowledge combination have all been used to explain this relationship.

Multicultural social networks enhance creativity through access to culturally embedded ideas, but this domain-specific relationship only held when the creative task was somehow relevant to societal cultures (Chua, 2018). That is, the cultural diversity in participants' social networks increased creativity when participants were trying to sell a new drink to an imaginary global audience, or propose a new global news service, but not when selling a drink to an imaginary local audience or proposing a new local newspaper. Explanations that draw on social identity theory and identity integration also found that creativity benefits of multiculturalism were often limited to creative outputs that had some relevance for culture (Cheng et al., 2008). For example, participants with high levels of identity integration—meaning they saw their social identities as compatible—created more creative fusion recipes when offered multicultural ingredients but did not create more creative recipes when offered only American ingredients (Cheng et al., 2008). Research on migrant inventors commonly explains creativity benefits through the combination of information from different cultural sources (Choudhury & Kim, 2019; Sinkovics & Reuber, 2021). Therefore, creativity benefits of migration may be limited to the cross-cultural domain.

Migration and team innovation. As already described, it is possible for innovation to emerge from transferring knowledge from migrants' COOs to their CORs. More importantly, research has revealed the combinatory process through which COO knowledge transforms into creative outcomes. For example, multicultural individuals who straddle two or more cultures engage in *cultural brokerage*, where they facilitate others' interactions across cultures (Jang, 2017; Vora et al., 2019). In an experiment, teams of Indians and Americans were asked to propose ideas for an Indian-American wedding (Jang, 2017). When an Indian-American was placed on a team, they built innovation by combining information from both cultures together, such as a western wedding song remixed Bollywood style. In comparison, when someone from Canada or South Korea were placed on the teams, they built innovation by eliciting information from each side, such as asking about wedding music, food, or rituals. Migrants' innovativeness through combining information was also found in a study of migrant inventors (Choudhury & Kim, 2019). When migrant inventors were placed within teams composed of other migrants, they collectively recombined their knowledge to create something new. Therefore, at the team level, innovation emerges when migrants combine their own knowledge with knowledge from others.

Migration and firm-level innovation. The relationship between migrant employees and firm-level innovation depends on a series of boundary conditions and moderators. The value of migrants' COO knowledge as a source for innovation depends on the degree to which individuals are embedded in their ethnic communities (Almeida et al., 2015). Socially embedded migrants accessed information from ethnic networks more easily than migrants who were less embedded, and this information drove innovation. A multi-year comparative ethnographic study of two French MNEs found that they did not increase innovation as a result of merely employing multicultural (migrant) employees (Hong & Minbaeva, 2021). Instead, firms benefited through increased innovation when they set up firm processes that enabled multicultural employees' knowledge, skills, and abilities to emerge. Examples include differentiating the HR architecture for multicultural employees, such that they primarily worked in the same departments together or creating a more flexible language policy that caters to multicultural employees. Therefore, the mere presence of migrant employees is unlikely to be enough to drive innovation. Instead, firms need to strategically manage migrant employees to set up the conditions that allow them to innovate.

Migration and societal-level innovation. Research at the societal level examines how migration policies and diaspora management influence societal innovation. For example, a study of the number of STEM migrants in a country found that they increase international knowledge diffusion, as represented by patent citations (Miguelez & Temgoua, 2020). Somewhat mitigating the common brain drain critique, migrants in this study benefited their COO the most when they originated from low-/middle-income countries, and the COR was a high-income country. A study of diaspora management found that returnees often became entrepreneurs, inadvertently boosting innovation in the COO (Lin, 2010).

Conclusions and future research directions about the flow of innovation. Research about migration and innovation has revealed clear relationships across levels, meaning individuals who cross borders reap innovation benefits, as do firms and teams that employ them. Research about the migrant-innovation relationship appears in isolated pockets that each examine very similar mechanisms but use different theoretical lenses. For example, research on multicultural individuals' creativity (Vora et al., 2019) generally describes similar effects as research on migrant inventors or migrant entrepreneurs (Sinkovics & Reuber, 2021). This is problematic when effects in one pocket don't appear in another. For example, the creativity outcomes were constrained to culture-relevant tasks when assessed at the micro level. The same is not assessed for migrant inventors or entrepreneurs. Future research would do well to incorporate findings from cross-cultural management which emphasize the relationship between creativity, as a precursor to innovation, and multicultural identity (e.g., Vora et al., 2019). Unsettled questions remain about the boundary conditions within which multicultural individuals are more creative, such as exploring which types of positions or roles benefit from migrants' creativity, or the extent to which any anti-immigrant sentiment in the COR affects migrants' creativity and innovation (see Sédès et al., 2022, for an example of identity shifts among migrants post-Brexit).

6 Conclusion: A New Metaphor Reveals What We Missed and How to Make Waves in the Future

Throughout this chapter, we have argued for a more inclusive definition of the term migrant, explained and critiqued four flows that emerge from migration, and made recommendations for the future. Across all flows, we make a few common recommendations. First, we recommend studying a wider, more inclusive range of migrants, especially moving beyond high-skilled migrants to also examine low-skilled migrants or refugees. This is especially pertinent to our metaphor of tidal flows, as there is so much attention on ocean-going refugees who travel by boat (Lee et al., 2020). For instance, unpredictable wave patterns in the ocean could illustrate the unpredictable identity work and sensemaking processes highly skilled refugees engage in together with inputs from newcomer support organizations, as the refugees construct new pathways for life and employment in the COR (Nardon et al., 2020).

Second, we recommend examining flows in multiple directions rather than the same directional flows as were studied in the past. Historically, IB research has been most interested in migrants as a strategic resource for the firm's international activities. We wonder about two oppositional flows: How do migrants draw on the resources of international organizations to support their own objectives? And how do international organizations influence migration flows in the first place? Illustrating both questions, it is possible for MNEs to benefit from treating underrepresented minorities better than they are treated domestically. MNEs that recruit women or lower-class employees in Latin America (Newburry et al., 2014) and women in South Korea (Siegel et al., 2019) have been rewarded with higher performance, in part driven by low turnover and high loyalty among talented employees who would have been overlooked by local employers. Migrants are often paid less than nonmigrants, and this effect is exacerbated by the intersectional effects of race, gender, or language (Fitzsimmons et al., 2020). International organizations engaging in HR practices that value overlooked local talent may suppress out-migration, while practices that value overlooked migrant groups may allow individuals to exploit MNEs resources (like higher pay) in pursuit of their own individual goals.

Finally, we want to conclude with a recommendation that did not emerge in the rest of our analysis. Compared to research about migration outside of the international business field, we have an impression that our field's research is unusually transactional. Individuals are almost exclusively seen in terms of their potential resources that may be exploited to facilitate international firm activities. It would be akin to looking at a beautiful river and seeing only the energy production possibilities of building a dam.

As a field, changing our migration metaphor from river to tidal flows can—and perhaps should—change the way we think about migration. The ocean is a complex, fluctuating environment that is the world's most biodiverse environment. Similarly, international organizations employ people in a complex, fluctuating business environment that includes a wide diversity of individuals who flow from shore to shore. We see the tide shifting in IB research, toward research that is broader, more encompassing of all migrants' experiences, and therefore also more pragmatic for international organizations.

References

Adamson, F. B., & Tsourapas, G. (2020). The migration state in the global south: Nationalizing, developmental, and neoliberal models of migration management. *International Migration Review, 54*(3), 853–882.

Almeida, P., Phene, A., & Li, S. (2015). The influence of ethnic community knowledge on Indian inventor innovativeness. *Organization Science, 26*(1), 198–217.

Andersen, N. (2019). Mapping the expatriate literature: A bibliometric review of the field from 1998 to 2017 and identification of current research fronts. *The International Journal of Human Resource Management, 22*, 1–38.

Andresen, M., Bergdolt, F., Margenfeld, J., & Dickmann, M. (2014). Addressing international mobility confusion–developing definitions and differentiations for self-initiated and assigned expatriates as well as migrants. *The International Journal of Human Resource Management, 25* (16), 2295–2318.

Backmann, J., Kanitz, R., Tian, A. W., Hoffmann, P., & Hoegl, M. (2020). Cultural gap bridging in multinational teams. *Journal of International Business Studies, 51*(8), 1283–1311.

Baker, P., Gabrielatos, C., Khosravinik, M., Krzyżanowski, M., McEnery, T., & Wodak, R. (2008). A useful methodological synergy? Combining critical discourse analysis and corpus linguistics to examine discourses of refugees and asylum seekers in the UK press. *Discourse & Society, 19*(3), 273–306.

Barnard, H., Deeds, D., Mudambi, R., & Vaaler, P. M. (2019). Migrants, migration policies, and international business research: Current trends and new directions. *Journal of International Business Policy, 2*(4), 275–288.

Barney, J. B. (2001). Resource-based theories of competitive advantage: A ten-year retrospective on the resource based view. *Journal of Management, 27*(6), 643–650.

Berry, J. W., Phinney, J. S., Sam, D. L., & Vedder, P. (2006). Immigrant youth: Acculturation, identity, and adaptation. *Applied Psychology, 55*(3), 303–332.

Borjas, G. J. (2003). The labor demand curve is downward sloping: Reexamining the impact of immigration on the labor market. *The Quarterly Journal of Economics, 118*(4), 1335–1374.

Brady, D., & Finnigan, R. (2014). Does immigration undermine public support for social policy? *American Sociological Review, 79*(1), 17–42.

Brown, S. S. (2006). Can remittances spur development? A critical survey. *International Studies Review, 8*(1), 55–76. https://doi.org/10.1111/j.1468-2486.2006.00553.x

Burmeister, A., Lazarova, M. B., & Deller, J. (2018). Repatriate knowledge transfer: Antecedents and boundary conditions of a dyadic process. *Journal of World Business, 53*(6), 806–816.

Caligiuri, P., & Bonache, J. (2016). Evolving and enduring challenges in global mobility. *Journal of World Business, 51*(1), 127–141.

Caprar, D. V. (2011). Foreign locals: A cautionary tale on the culture of MNC local employees. *Journal of International Business Studies, 42*(5), 608–628.

Cerar, J., Nell, P. C., & Reiche, B. S. (2021). The declining share of primary data and the neglect of the individual level in international business research. *Journal of International Business Studies, 52*, 1–10.

Cerdin, J. L., & Selmer, J. (2014). Who is a self-initiated expatriate? Towards conceptual clarity of a common notion. *The International Journal of Human Resource Management, 25*(9), 1281–1301.

Chand, M., & Tung, R. L. (2019). Skilled immigration to fill talent gaps: A comparison of the immigration policies of the United States, Canada, and Australia. *Journal of International Business Policy, 2*(4), 333–355.

Cheng, C. Y., Sanchez-Burks, J., & Lee, F. (2008). Connecting the dots within: Creative performance and identity integration. *Psychological Science, 19*(11), 1178–1184.

Choudhury, P. (2021). Geographic mobility, immobility, and geographic flexibility: A review and agenda for research on the changing geography of work. *Academy of Management Annals, 16*(1), 258–296. https://doi.org/10.5465/annals.2020.0242

Choudhury, P., & Kim, D. Y. (2019). The ethnic migrant inventor effect: Codification and recombination of knowledge across borders. *Strategic Management Journal, 40*(2), 203–229.

Chua, R. Y. (2018). Innovating at cultural crossroads: How multicultural social networks promote idea flow and creativity. *Journal of Management, 44*(3), 1119–1146.

Chung, H. F. (2004). An empirical investigation of immigrant effects: The experience of firms operating in the emerging markets. *International Business Review, 13*(6), 705–728.

Chung, H. F., & Enderwick, P. (2001). An investigation of market entry strategy selection: Exporting vs foreign direct investment modes—A home-host country scenario. *Asia Pacific Journal of Management, 18*(4), 443–460.

Chung, H. F., Rose, E., & Huang, P. H. (2012). Linking international adaptation strategy, immigrant effect, and performance: The case of home–host and cross-market scenario. *International Business Review, 21*(1), 40–58.

Chung, H. F., & Tung, R. L. (2013). Immigrant social networks and foreign entry: Australia and New Zealand firms in the European Union and greater China. *International Business Review, 22*(1), 18–31.

Collyer, M., Düvell, F., & De Haas, H. (2012). Critical approaches to transit migration. *Population, Space and Place, 18*(4), 407–414.

Coppel, J., Dumont, J. & Visco, I. (2001). *Trends in immigration and economic consequences* (OECD Economics Department Working Papers, No. 284). https://doi.org/10.1787/553515678780.

Coviello, N. E., & Martin, K. A. M. (1999). Internationalization of service SMEs: An integrated perspective from the engineering consulting sector. *Journal of International Marketing, 7*(4), 42–66.

Cummings, M. E., & Gamlen, A. (2019). Diaspora engagement institutions and venture investment activity in developing countries. *Journal of International Business Policy, 2*(4), 289–313.

Czaika, M., & De Haas, H. (2014). The globalization of migration: Has the world become more migratory? *International Migration Review, 48*(2), 283–323.

Drechsler, J., Bachmann, J. T., & Engelen, A. (2019). The effect of immigrants in the founding team on the international attention of new ventures. *Journal of International Entrepreneurship, 17*(3), 305–333.

Emmanuel, N. D., Elo, M., & Piekkari, R. (2019). Human stickiness as a counterforce to brain drain: Purpose-driven behaviour among Tanzanian medical doctors and implications for policy. *Journal of International Business Policy, 2*(4), 314–332.

Fitzsimmons, S. R., Baggs, J., & Brannen, M. Y. (2020). Intersectional arithmetic: How gender, race and mother tongue combine to impact immigrants' work outcomes. *Journal of World Business, 55*(1), 101013.

Gaur, A., & Kumar, M. (2018). A systematic approach to conducting review studies: An assessment of content analysis in 25 years of IB research. *Journal of World Business, 53*(2), 280–289.

Gould, D. M. (1994). Immigrant links to the home country: Empirical implications for U.S. bilateral trade flows. *The Review of Economics and Statistics, 76*(2), 302–316. https://doi.org/10.2307/2109884

Grant, R., & Phene, A. (2021). The knowledge based view and global strategy: Past impact and future potential. *Global Strategy Journal, 12*(1), 3–30. https://doi.org/10.2139/ssrn.3840708

Hajro, A., Caprar, D. V., Zikic, J., & Stahl, G. K. (2021). Global migrants: Understanding the implications for international business and management. *Journal of World Business, 56*(2), 101192.

Hajro, A., Stahl, G. K., Clegg, C. C., & Lazarova, M. B. (2019). Acculturation, coping, and integration success of international skilled migrants: An integrative review and multilevel framework. *Human Resource Management Journal, 29*(3), 328–352.

Han, Q., Jennings, J. E., Liu, R., & Jennings, P. D. (2019). Going home and helping out? Returnees as propagators of CSR in an emerging economy. *Journal of International Business Studies, 50*(6), 857–872.

Hernandez, E. (2014). Finding a home away from home: Effects of immigrants on firms' foreign location choice and performance. *Administrative Science Quarterly, 59*(1), 73–108.

Hong, H.-J., & Minbaeva, D. (2021). Multiculturals as strategic human capital resources in multinational enterprises. *Journal of International Business Studies, 53*(1), 95–125. https://doi.org/10.1057/s41267-021-00463-w

Hosny, A. (2020). Remittance concentration and volatility: Evidence from 72 developing countries. *International Economic Journal, 34*(4), 553–570.

Howe-Walsh, L., & Schyns, B. (2010). Self-initiated expatriation: Implications for HRM. *The International Journal of Human Resource Management, 21*(2), 260–273.

IOM. (2020). *World migration report 2020*. Geneva: United Nations. Accessed May 15, 2021, from https://www.un.org/sites/un2.un.org/files/wmr_2020.pdf

Jang, S. (2017). Cultural brokerage and creative performance in multicultural teams. *Organization Science, 28*(6), 993–1009.

Kane, A. A., & Levina, N. (2017). 'Am I still one of them?': Bicultural immigrant managers navigating social identity threats when spanning global boundaries. *Journal of Management Studies, 54*(4), 540–577.

King, R. (2012). Geography and migration studies: Retrospect and prospect. *Population, Space and Place, 18*(2), 134–153.

Kolk, A., Rivera-Santos, M., & Rufín, C. (2014). Reviewing a decade of research on the "base/bottom of the pyramid"(BOP) concept. *Business & Society, 53*(3), 338–377.

Kunczer, V., Lindner, T., & Puck, J. (2019). Benefiting from immigration: The value of immigrants' country knowledge for firm internationalization. *Journal of International Business Policy, 2*(4), 356–375.

Lau, V. P., & Shaffer, M. A. (2021). A typological theory of domestic employees' acculturation stress and adaptation in the context of globalization. *Academy of Management Review.* https://doi.org/10.5465/amr.2019.0408

Laursen, K., Leten, B., Nguyen, N. H., & Vancauteren, M. (2020). Mounting corporate innovation performance: The effects of high-skilled migrant hires and integration capacity. *Research Policy, 49*(9), 104034.

Leblang, D. (2010). Familiarity breeds investment: Diaspora networks and international investment. *American Political Science Review, 104*(3), 584–600.

Lee, E. S., Szkudlarek, B., Nguyen, D. C., & Nardon, L. (2020). Unveiling the canvas ceiling: A multidisciplinary literature review of refugee employment and workforce integration. *International Journal of Management Reviews, 22*(2), 193–216.

Leung, A. K. Y., Maddux, W. W., Galinsky, A. D., & Chiu, C. Y. (2008). Multicultural experience enhances creativity: The when and how. *American Psychologist, 63*(3), 169.

Lin, X. (2010). The diaspora solution to innovation capacity development: Immigrant entrepreneurs in the contemporary world. *Thunderbird International Business Review, 52*(2), 123–136.

Lin, X., & Yang, X. (2017). From human capital externality to entrepreneurial aspiration: Revisiting the migration-trade linkage. *Journal of World Business, 52*(3), 360–371.

Liu, X., Gao, L., Lu, J., & Wei, Y. (2015). The role of highly skilled migrants in the process of inter-firm knowledge transfer across borders. *Journal of World Business, 50*(1), 56–68.

Lucas, R. E., & Stark, O. (1985). Motivations to remit: Evidence from Botswana. *Journal of Political Economy, 93*(5), 901–918.

Martinez, C., Cummings, M. E., & Vaaler, P. M. (2015). Economic informality and the venture funding impact of migrant remittances to developing countries. *Journal of Business Venturing, 30*(4), 526.

McKinsey Global Institute. (2016). *People on the move: Global migration's impact and opportunity*. Report available from www.mckinsey.com

McNulty, Y., & Brewster, C. (2017). The concept of business expatriates. In *Research handbook of expatriates*. Edward Elgar Publishing.

McNulty, Y., & Brewster, C. (2019). *Working internationally: Expatriation, migration and other global work*. Edward Elgar Publishing.

McNulty, Y., & Brewster, C. (2020). From 'elites' to 'everyone': Re-framing international mobility scholarship to be all-encompassing. *International Studies of Management & Organization, 50*(4), 334–356.

Mendenhall, M., & Oddou, G. (1985). The dimensions of expatriate acculturation: A review. *Academy of Management Review, 10*(1), 39–47.

Meyer, K. E., Li, C., & Schotter, A. P. (2020). Managing the MNE subsidiary: Advancing a multilevel and dynamic research agenda. *Journal of International Business Studies, 51*(4), 538–576.

Miguelez, E., & Temgoua, C. N. (2020). Inventor migration and knowledge flows: A two-way communication channel? *Research Policy, 49*(9), 103914.

Morgan, H. M., Sui, S., & Malhotra, S. (2021). No place like home: The effect of exporting to the country of origin on the financial performance of immigrant-owned SMEs. *Journal of International Business Studies, 52*(3), 504–524.

Nardon, L., Zhang, H., Szkudlarek, B., & Gulanowski, D. (2020). *Identity work in refugee workforce integration: The role of newcomer support organizations* (p. 0018726720949630). Human Relations.

Newburry, W., Gardberg, N. A., & Sanchez, J. I. (2014). Employer attractiveness in Latin America: The association among foreignness, internationalization and talent recruitment. *Journal of International Management, 20*(3), 327–344.

OECD. (2017). *G20 global displacement and migration trends report*. OECD.

Orefice, G. (2010). Skilled migration and economic performances: Evidence from OECD countries. *Swiss Journal of Economics and Statistics, 146*(4), 781–820.

Ozkazanc-Pan, B. (2019). "Superdiversity": A new paradigm for inclusion in a transnational world. *Equality, Diversity and Inclusion: An International Journal, 38*(4), 477–490.

Piteli, E. E., Kafouros, M., & Pitelis, C. N. (2021). Follow the people and the money: Effects of inward FDI on migrant remittances and the contingent role of new firm creation and institutional infrastructure in emerging economies. *Journal of World Business, 56*(2), 101178.

Rana, M. B., & Elo, M. (2017). Transnational diaspora and civil society actors driving MNE internationalisation: The case of Grameenphone in Bangladesh. *Journal of International Management, 23*(1), 87–106.

Reade, C., McKenna, M., & Oetzel, J. (2019). Unmanaged migration and the role of MNEs in reducing push factors and promoting peace: A strategic HRM perspective. *Journal of International Business Policy, 2*(4), 377–396.

Riddle, L., & Brinkerhoff, J. (2011). Diaspora entrepreneurs as institutional change agents: The case of Thamel.com. *International Business Review, 20*(6), 670–680.

Ruhs, M. (2013). *The price of rights* (pp. 187–200). Princeton University Press.

Schewel, K. (2020). Understanding immobility: Moving beyond the mobility bias in migration studies. *International Migration Review, 54*(2), 328–355.

Sédès, C. J., Miedtank, T., & Oliver, D. (2022). Suddenly I felt like a migrant: Identity and mobility threats facing European self-initiated expatriates in the UK under Brexit. *Academy of Management Discoveries.* https://doi.org/10.5465/amd.2020.0162

Shao, J. J., & Ariss, A. A. (2020). Knowledge transfer between self-initiated expatriates and their organizations: Research propositions for managing SIEs. *International Business Review, 29*(1), 101634. https://doi.org/10.1016/j.ibusrev.2019.101634

Shipilov, A. V., Li, S. X., & Li, W. (2020). Can you do Kung Fu and also act? New entrants' status attainment in the creative industries. *Journal of World Business, 55*(3), 101043.

Shukla, P., & Cantwell, J. (2018). Migrants and multinational firms: The role of institutional affinity and connectedness in FDI. *Journal of World Business, 53*(6), 835–849.

Siegel, J., Pyun, L., & Cheon, B. Y. (2019). Multinational firms, labor market discrimination, and the capture of outsider's advantage by exploiting the social divide. *Administrative Science Quarterly, 64*(2), 370–397.

Sinkovics, N., & Reuber, A. R. (2021). Beyond disciplinary silos: A systematic analysis of the migrant entrepreneurship literature. *Journal of World Business, 56*(4), 101223.

Stahl, G. K., & Tung, R. L. (2015). Towards a more balanced treatment of culture in international business studies: The need for positive cross-cultural scholarship. *Journal of International Business Studies, 46*(4), 391–414.

Szymanski, M., Fitzsimmons, S. R., & Danis, W. M. (2019). Multicultural managers and competitive advantage: Evidence from elite football teams. *International Business Review, 28*(2), 305–315.

Takeuchi, R. (2010). A critical review of expatriate adjustment research through a multiple stakeholder view: Progress, emerging trends, and prospects. *Journal of Management, 36*(4), 1040–1064.

Tung, R. L., & Chung, H. F. (2010). Diaspora and trade facilitation: The case of ethnic Chinese in Australia. *Asia Pacific Journal of Management, 27*(3), 371–392.

United Nations Department of Economic and Social Affairs, Population Division. (2020). *International Migrant Stock 2020.* https://www.un.org/development/desa/pd/content/international-migrant-stock

Useche, D., Miguelez, E., & Lissoni, F. (2020). Highly skilled and well connected: Migrant inventors in cross-border M&As. *Journal of International Business Studies, 51*(5), 737–763.

Vaaler, P. M. (2011). Immigrant remittances and the venture investment environment of developing countries. *Journal of International Business Studies, 42*(9), 1121–1149.

Vaiman, V., McNulty, Y., & Haslberger, A. (2021). Herding cats: Expatriate talent acquisition and development. In I. Tarique (Ed.), *The Routledge companion to talent management* (pp. 359–371). Routledge.

Van den Bergh, R., & Du Plessis, Y. (2012). Highly skilled migrant women: A career development framework. *Journal of Management Development, 31*(2), 142–158.

Vora, D., Martin, L., Fitzsimmons, S. R., Pekerti, A. A., Lakshman, C., & Raheem, S. (2019). Multiculturalism within individuals: A review, critique, and agenda for future research. *Journal of International Business Studies, 50*(4), 499–524.

World Bank. (2019). *Data release: Remittances to low- and middle-income countries on track to reach $551 billion in 2019 and $597 billion by 2021.* Accessed July 3, 2021, from https://blogs. worldbank.org/peoplemove/data-release-remittances-low-and-middle-income-countries-track-reach-551-billion-2019

World Bank. (2021). *Migration and development brief 34.* Washington DC: World Bank. Accessed September 18, 2021, from https://www.knomad.org/sites/default/files/2021-05/Migration%20 and%20Development%20Brief%2034_1.pdf

Zhang, L. E., Harzing, A., & Fan, S. X. (2018). *Managing expatriates in China: A language and identity perspective.* Palgrave Macmillan.

Zhou, L., Wu, W. P., & Luo, X. (2007). Internationalization and the performance of born-global-SMEs: The mediating role of social networks. *Journal of International Business Studies, 38*(4), 673–690.

**Aminat Muibi** is a PhD candidate at University of Victoria's Peter B. Gustavson School of Business. Her research focuses on how stigma occurs across a variety of contexts—including among immigrants—and how stigma-driven evaluations change over time.

**Stacey R. Fitzsimmons** is an Associate Professor of International Management at University of Victoria's Peter B. Gustavson School of Business (Canada). Her research examines how multicultural, immigrant, and refugee employees contribute to global teams and organizations. She received the AOM's International Human Resources Scholarly Research award and WAIB's emerging scholar award.

IEDC and CEEMAN: A Historical Response to the Societal Role of Business Schools

Danica Purg and Arnold Walravens

1 Introduction

"If you think education is expensive, try ignorance" is a well-known adage. Less known, but not less true, is our statement "If you think social responsibility is expensive, you take the consequences of irresponsibility." When I (Danica Purg) was asked by a visionary president of the Chamber of Commerce of Slovenia, Mr. Marko Bulc, to establish a "modern" management school in 1985 in the then "self-management socialist Yugoslavia," I had some personal doubts about accepting this invitation. I asked some people I respected and trusted to give me advice. What convinced me the most was that some of them told me this: "If you want to do something important and relevant in your life for your country, then accept this challenge." In other words, this is a unique opportunity to implement the idea of "social responsibility."

The big idea behind this initiative was the need for professionalization of business leadership and management. Only a few years later, it became very evident how important this initiative was, not only for Slovenia but also for the entire Central and Eastern Europe (CEE). When the political landscape changed drastically at the beginning of the 1990s and the mainly centralized economic models used until then were abolished and replaced by market-oriented ones, it became evident that business leaders and managers were not prepared for this new reality. A rough estimate showed also that there was a shortage of about 2500 professors of management and that most business leaders and managers in the region needed to be reeducated.

The stories of IEDC-Bled School of Management, the first "modern" management school in the region, and of CEEMAN, established as an association of management schools in the CEE region, are stories of pioneers, change, and

D. Purg (✉) · A. Walravens
IEDC Bled School of Management, Bled, Slovenia
e-mail: danica.purg@iedc.si

© Springer Nature Switzerland AG 2022
H. Merchant (ed.), *The New Frontiers of International Business*, Contributions to Management Science, https://doi.org/10.1007/978-3-031-06003-8_21

"innocent naivety": the belief that "modern" management knowledge and skills would naturally offer something "positive" for society.

Already in the 1990s we saw how individuals enriched themselves by succeeding in taking over former state companies through suspicious transactions. Existing business schools in the region did not publically criticize these actions, often because they did not even understand what happened. But particularly the financial crisis of the first decennium of the new century was a hard lesson also for business schools (Giacalone & Wargo, 2009).

2   IEDC: Education and Research with Impact

Was there a blueprint in 1985 for the transformation of a training center for "leading workers in the economy," that is, managers chosen by workers' councils in their companies, (Mirvis et al., 2011) and other organizations in a "modern," or more correctly, "Western-style" business school? No, there was no blueprint. There was only a vision and a rough sketch of a mission and its implementation. There was only this very original and surprising idea that also in a (self-management) socialist environment, combining political centralization with local and regional economic decentralization, "modern" management education would serve society through offering professional knowledge and skills to business leaders and managers.

We chose the name "International Executive Development Center." We did not use the word "management," as it was not well regarded in those times of self-management. The shorter name of the school was IEDC, Center Brdo.[1] Only in 2000, when the school moved to Bled, did we start to use the name IEDC-Bled School of Management.

The establishment of IEDC was a fully socially oriented activity, which can be concluded from the fact that in the "business" plan of the school, there was no precise underlying financial analysis and no word about being financially profitable. Although at the beginning of the century, the school got a shareholder structure in order to finance the building of new premises, none of the shareholders has ever objected to this not-for-profit policy.

Since its inception, IEDC has tried to place itself in the middle of society. This can be seen from the important issues in the "Book of the Year" of the school published between 1988 and 2010 (see Tables 1 and 2; Mirvis et al., 2011: 156–157).

The same can be said about the "Books of the Year" published after 2010. Important keywords in that period were "crisis," "globalization," "digitalization," and "AI" (also "beyond AI), as well as the impact on the role of leadership. These "Books of the Year" are all based on conferences where business leaders and politicians gather, generally in an international setting. Since the beginning, IEDC has also been trying to integrate itself as much as possible in the world it was primarily established for by introducing real consulting projects in its MBA and

---

[1] Brdo, Slovenia was the first location of IEDC, from 1986 to 2000.

Table 1 The main themes in the books of the year 1988–2010 (Mirvis et al., 2011: 156)

First mentioned	Theme	Later mentioned
1988	Change	(1992, 2001)
	↓	
	Leadership	(1997, 1998, 2001, 2004, 2006)
1989	Innovation	(1991, 2002, 2008)
	Competition	(1994, 1999, 2001)
	↓	
1990	Strategy	(1995)
	↓	
1993	Globalisation	(1999, 2004)
	Values and ethical standards	(2002, 2003)
	↓	
1997	Customers	(2008, 2009)
	↓	
2004	Trust	(2006)
	↓	
2008	Risk and risk management Crisis	(2009, 2010)
	↓	
2010	Redefining capitalism	

general management program. The slogan of IEDC, "What you learn today, you can use tomorrow," represents this philosophy.

Was this always well received? Generally, yes. There was no public criticism, not event, when the school started to introduce ethics, already in 1989.[2] At the beginning of the 1990s, participants from the new countries in CEE were surprised by the high ethical business standards that were promoted through the Corporate Governance and Ethics[3] program because of the big difference from the reality that they then lived in.

Shortly after the establishment of UN Global Compact in 2000, IEDC took responsibility for the promotion and coordination of this initiative in Slovenia. Global Compact and its principles represented precisely what the school stood for. A surprising number of companies signed on and agreed to report annually on their policies and activities related to the principles of the program. It is not surprising that IEDC was among the first 100 signatories to the UN Principles of Responsible Management Education (PRME) in 2007. In 2008, the school introduced sustainability as a mandatory subject in the main programs. The education and research in this field gained momentum when Coca-Cola agreed to finance a Chair of Sustainable Development. The result was a big number of conferences devoted to this topic and many scientific and professional publications, as, for example,

---

[2]The first lecture on ethics was delivered by a bishop, who had a great theoretical contribution on the daily dilemmas of business people.

[3]This program was launched in 1993.

Table 2 Important issues in the "Books of the year" 1988–2010 (Mirvis et al., 2011: 157)

1988	1989	1990	1991	1992	1993	1994	1995
• Change	• Technical innovation	• Long term strategy	• Stupidity to transfer ideas and concepts of USA, West Europe, Japan, Asia to CEE countries		• European values and human rights	• Dramatic change	• Strategic alliances
• Transferability of leadership concepts and methods	• Growing competition				• Globalisation	• Innovative production	
						• Urgency to be and stay competitive	

1996	1997	1998	1999	2000	2001	2002	2003
• Book on 10 years of IEDC	• Manage yourself and then the company, set an example	• Maintaining personal value	• Slovenia has potential to compete in global race	• Getting a leading position in your branch	• Increasing speed of changes	• Global world and role of EU	• Joining international and new paradigms
	• Ask customers what are the strengths of the company		• New value proposition on intangible assets, harnessing knowledge that is difficult to copy		• Innovative imperatives of leadership	• Size of countries not important, policies are	• Core values of Europe: respect for differences
					• Companies in CEE are normal companies	• Plea for building common world of values	
					• Global world needs global solutions	• A world of high ethical standards	

2004	2005	2006	2007	2008	2009	2010
• Competitive advantage created by human dimensions: leadership and corporate value	• (Reprint of the book of 1997)	• What is in fact leadership	• How to avoid the set-up-to fail-syndrome	• Innovation is a management issue	• Response to changing customer needs	• The crisis is not something completely new
• Bright and dark sides of leadership		• "Trust" as a main element of leadership and business success		• Everything begins with the customer	• The crisis (leadership beyond the crisis)	• Redefining capitalism
• The failure factor of leadership				• Risk and risk management		
• Life balance						

"Sharing Vocabularies: Exploring the Language of Values-Driven Business" (Painter et al., 2018).

IEDC became the first PRME Champion in CEE in 2016. In the meantime, the School built a great network, also beyond CEE. The Coca-Cola Chair had a very international orientation. The result of the theoretical and practically developed ground for partnerships was the establishment of the World Institute for Sustainability and Ethics in Rising Economies (WISE), in 2018. IEDC shared this initiative with:

- Center for Advanced Sustainability Management (CASM) at CBS International Business School, Germany
- National Institute for Innovation Management at Zhejiang University, China
- University of Stellenbosch Business School, South Africa

The Central and Eastern European Management Development Association (CEEMAN), established in 1993, played an important role in the development of partnerships, particularly among business schools in rising economies (Mirvis & Walravens, 2013).

3   CEEMAN, the Management Development Association in Central and Eastern Europe

In early 1990s, CEE suffered from a crisis of moral standards after the fall of the Soviet Union and that initiated the establishment of CEEMAN. Not everybody saw only short-term opportunities for business and becoming rich. Deans of management schools in Croatia, Estonia, Hungary, Poland, Romania, and Russia joined the initiative of IEDC to unite forces for the acceleration of leadership and management development in CEE. While the political leaders and citizens of many ex-Soviet countries saw more differences than similarities, these pioneers of leadership and management development found a common vision and mission in the interests of their societies. They decided to take their fate and future in their own hands, observing that for educators and consultants from outside the region, it was too difficult to understand the specific history and situation of the countries in CEE. Outsiders often underestimated the rich cultural and educational policies and programs in the region. Because of the lack of understanding of the ambition in the region and the intellectual capacity of its professors and researchers, Western institutions did not send their best people to support the region. Following the slogan of the initiator of CEEMAN: "Give us the best from the West and leave the rest," educational institutions in CEE formulated their own connections for cooperation and support. Some excellent educators and consultants from outside the region understood this reaction and found a common basis for speeding up the development of business schools' leaders and professors. In this way, they helped build the infrastructure for successful leadership and management development, institutions, and programs. CEEMAN was established in 1993 after IEDC failed to find understanding at the European Foundation for Management Development, where the school in vain tried to get support for its efforts "to draw more attention to CEE, to organize conferences in CEE, and to include students of management in European competitions" (Mirvis & Walravens, 2013: 14). Nobel prizes have been given for less important societal accomplishments than bringing representatives of CEE countries together in those times of chaos and enmity.

The first annual conference in 1993 brought together 65 participants from 25 countries. That number rose to 163 participants from 36 countries at the conference in Turkey in 2007. Every annual conference had a social, political, and economic content, giving special attention to the problems of the organizing country. It is understandable that at first a lot of attention was given to questions such as improving business school structure and management, availability, recruiting, and development of educators and business school cooperation. However, very soon CEEMAN looked outward, understanding that management development had to be based on the needs of society. Therefore, the focus was on topics such as managing in transition and entrepreneurship and the impact on management development of internationalization, globalization, and European integration. In the last years, the focus has shifted onto the impact of technology, digitalization, and AI.

In the last 10 years, an increasing number of CEEMAN members have originated from countries outside CEE and particularly from schools in the so-called rising economies. As in most other associations, the focus has been on delivering an excellent education, research, and service to participants and companies. This drive for excellency was also promoted by accreditation and rating agencies, taking the old schools, such as Harvard and Stanford, as models of high quality. The financial crisis of 2008, seen by many as a leadership crisis, made it clear that excellence alone is not a guarantee for the prevention of such a disaster for society, and it could happen again. It was in a way a kind of taught "excellence" that caused the crisis. CEEMAN reacted by introducing its own accreditation scheme, International Quality Accreditation (IQA), including the issue of the impact of business schools on society. Twenty out of the first 100 signatories to PRME were business schools from CEE. In 2016, the PRME CEE Chapter was established, which shows that many CEEMAN members had already integrated this societal responsibility in their missions.

CEEMAN declared that business school education and research has to be not only excellent but also relevant for business and society. In September 2018, CEEMAN published "The Manifesto" (Abell et al., 2018) entitled "Changing the Course of Management Development: Combing Excellence with Relevance". The Manifesto says that "relevance requires that teaching and research that an institution undertakes has practical utility and impact in the real world that current and future executives will inhabit" /.../ "With respect to markets served, no matter how local, the presumption must be made that executives have nevertheless to keep their eyes on two balls, namely, the nature of their own local problems and the global best practices that may have relevance to their local situation in the present or future." / .../ "Society's needs and purposes are increasingly one of these, and preparing students and executives to deal with the social, environmental, ethical, and sustainability issues with which business is now challenged must figure centrally in any assessment of relevance." All members of CEEMAN signed the Manifesto.

4   Conclusions and Recommendations

Just as there was no blueprint in 1985 for the establishment of a management school in self-management socialist Yugoslavia, today there is no blueprint for the fulfill-ment of business schools' societal obligations. The situation differs from continent to continent, from country to country, and from region to region. Therefore, UN initiatives, such as Global Compact and PRME, are working with principles that are clear targets but are on the other hand leaving room for regional and local interpretation. Societal obligations based on principles help to escape living by the issues of the day.

4.1   What Lessons Can We Learn from the IEDC-CEEMAN Case?

First of all, societal obligations or social responsibility have to be a part of the mindset of everybody in a business school and particularly of the leading people. Is this something to take for granted or easy to realize? We believe it will take special efforts. Business schools have always been mainly focused on the left side of the brain and on serving shareholders, a single category of people. It is quite a change to focus on stakeholders and on society at large. This implicates a more holistic approach, and management and leadership development focused on the right side of the brain to boost creativity, in order to be able to find sustainable solutions in complex situations and relations. Of course, if business schools operate in a "for profit" environment, it will be probably more difficult to adjust their mission. The only consolation or advantage in this case is that the school will learn more of the dilemmas all businesses have or will be willing to confront them.

In the past, societal obligations were often seen as a side activity of a school, and sometimes they still are. As all elements of social responsibility, promoting business ethics and sustainability were at first treated as particular, stand-alone issues. Later it was understood that it was necessary to integrate them in all education and research. The principles of PRME have to become a way of life.

Societal obligation is a big notion, but in its application, it starts small, first of all in the local and regional environment of the school. Of course, obligations to society at large need to be respected also in these activities. This means that a school has to be aware of the typical problems in its environment and try to find solutions to them.

IEDC felt that it was its obligation to bring CEE business schools together in order to join forces for accelerating excellent and relevant management develop-ment. Recently, it took a new initiative through CEEMAN to create an association of management development institutions in rising economies. Associations from Africa, Latin America, China, India, Russia, and CEE have already joined this alliance, realizing how much they could assist each other in finding solutions to common problems.

It is important for business schools to join such networks. This offers a unique experience to realize that also in the field of social responsibility, there are many common problems and dilemmas but also many ways to fulfill societal obligations.

To be able to adjust the mission and activities in the abovementioned direction, it is first of all necessary to convince the important parties in business schools that this is the right way. The next step is to join PRME and sign the CEEMAN Manifesto.

The history of IEDC covers a period of 35 years. That of CEEMAN is 28 years old. We hope that the IEDC-CEEMAN experience can help accelerate processes in business schools so that they fulfill their societal obligations.

References

Abell, D. F., Purg, D., Braček Lalić, A., & Kleyn, N. (2018). *Manifesto: Changing the course of management development: Combining excellence with relevance.* CEEMAN.

Giacalone, R. A., & Wargo, D. T. (2009). The roots of the global financial crisis are in our business schools. *Journal of Business Ethics Education, 6,* 147–168.

Mirvis, P. H., Purg, D., Walravens, A., Filipović, N., Zhexembayeva, N., Rant, M., Sutherland, I., ... Čehovin, E. (2011). *The vision and the voices of IEDC - Bled School of Management: 25 years learning history.* IEDC - Bled School of Management.

Mirvis, P. H., & Walravens, A. (2013). *CEEMAN - 20 years of creating history.* CEEMAN.

Painter, M., Russon, J.-A., Karakilic, E., & Purg, D. (2018). *Sharing vocabularies: Exploring the language of values-driven business.* IEDC-Bled School of Management.

Danica Purg is President of IEDC-Bled School of Management, Slovenia, President of CEEMAN, the International Association for Management Development in Dynamic Societies, and of Alliance of Management Development Associations in Rising Economies. She is professor of leadership at IEDC and a frequent speaker at many international conferences on management and leadership development.

Arnold Walravens is Chair of the Postgraduate Studies and Quality Commission at IEDC-Bled School of Management, Slovenia. He teaches Corporate Governance and Arts and Leadership in Executive MBA and General Management Program at IEDC. His academic research focuses on participation and human resources, corporate governance, arts and leadership, executive development, and artificial intelligence.